BOOKLIST'S Guide To The

YEAR'S
BEST
BOOKS

———

Definitive Reviews of Over 1,000
Fiction and Nonfiction Titles
in All Fields

———

Edited by Bill Ott,
American Library Association

Triumph Books, Inc.
CHICAGO

©1992 American Library Association

Library of Congress Catalog Card Number: 92-050110

International Standard Book Number: 1-880141-08-6 (paper)
                                        1-880141-07-8 (cloth)

Triumph Books, Inc.
644 South Clark Street Suite 2000
Chicago, IL 60605

Exclusively distributed to the library trade by Gale Research, Inc.

Printed in the United States of America

CONTENTS

INTRODUCTION

The search for a good book continues. This literary Easter egg hunt grows more difficult every year, not because the number of eggs diminishes, but because there are so many brightly colored rotten eggs trying to pass themselves off as the real thing. The problem, for most readers, is that they don't have time to crack thousands of eggs in search of a few good ones. At BOOKLIST magazine, a book review journal published by the American Library Association, we do the egg cracking for you. Nearly 50,000 books come through our office every year, and we diligently crack all of them. The rotten ones we gingerly move to the side, leaving some 7,000 to be reviewed in the magazine. This total includes children's books, reference books, and many specialized titles designed to fill particular subject needs in libraries. That 7,000 has been whittled down to around 1,000 for inclusion in this book. The titles were selected with the book-loving adult reader in mind, the kind of person who reads not just to find out how to do something but to be entertained and enlightened—and to feel the sublime rhythm of well-crafted words rolling off the page. Whether our mythical general readers use libraries or bookstores to hunt their Easter eggs, we think *BOOKLIST's Guide to the Year's Best Books* will simplify the search and improve their chances for success. After all, books aren't really like Easter eggs. It's the thrill of the chase that inspires egg hunters, not the eggs themselves. With books, it's the book we want, not the chase.

We hope that this guide will serve multiple uses. The general reader may purchase it as an aid to buying gifts as well as selecting books for personal reading; the library user may consult it on his or her own in the library or be directed to it by a reader's advisory librarian; the collection development librarian may use it as a way of assessing collection building over a given year. To reflect these multiple uses, we've elected to change the guide's title. Our premier edition, which appeared last year, was called *The Book Buyer's Advisor*, and while advising book buyers is certainly one of the things we think this book does, it isn't the only thing. Thus, we've decided to focus our title on what we *do* rather than who we do it for. Finally, *BOOKLIST's Guide to the Year's Best Books* should find its audience wherever book people congregate.

The reviews included here are organized first under nonfiction and fiction and then by broad subject categories, which appear alphabetically. Ideally, of course, the volume is designed to encourage browsing: find a subject area that interests you, and start flipping pages. For those searching for a specific book, however, the author and title indexes should ensure easy access. A note about biographies: the most difficult organizational decision an editor faces is deciding when to consider a book "Biography" and when to group it with the subject most related to the life being studied. For the purposes of this book, all lives of sports figures have been classified under "Sports & Recreation," all lives of musicians appear under "Music," and, in general, other biographical and autobiographical works are considered "Biography."

All reviews are prefaced by the following bibliographical information: author, or editor, which appears in boldface; title, which appears in italics; and publisher, price, ISBN (International Standard Book Number), and number of pages. The word *index* appears following the page numbers when a book is indexed.

The editor's choices of the best books within each subject category are indicated by a check mark (✔) appearing to the left of the author's or editor's name.

In the introduction to last year's edition, we observed that there are more good books published in one year than anyone has time to read. That statement is every bit as true this year as it was last. Those who criticize the condition of the publishing industry like to focus on the obsession with bottom lines, but for the average reader the bottom line isn't measured in profit and loss, it's measured in the answer to the ubiquitous question, "Read anything good lately?" *BOOKLIST's Guide to the Year's Best Books* is our response to that question. The answer is a resounding, "Yes!"

Bill Ott
Editor & Publisher, BOOKLIST

NONFICTION

Art

✔**Barron, Stephanie.**
"Degenerate Art": The Fate of the Avant-Garde in Nazi Germany.
Abrams, $75 (0-8109-3653-4). 424p. index.

This reconstruction of the infamous Nazi exhibition of officially proscribed or degenerate art in 1937 is revealing for the issues of aesthetic taste and artistic censorship it raises and explores. The curators of the current exhibition have reassembled much of the surviving artwork that the German government found so objectionable and in certain instances have reinstalled the pieces in settings identical to their original display. This combination of art and politics is potent and revealing, both in the historical events the book covers and in the questions the exhibitions of 1937 and 1991 will raise for current viewers. Certainly, the Nazi opposition to modern art was not consistently enforced, as some officially approved artists eventually were placed on the forbidden list; even stranger, artists whose beliefs were sympathetic to the Nazi cause but who worked in unacceptable styles also found their work condemned. Moreover, the Nazis often used the techniques of modernism to attack the modern movement itself. The contributing scholars help to clarify the Nazi approach to art as a moral prop and also examine the Nazi attitude toward literature and film as well. The catalog proper covers the artists and their works, with reproductions and brief discussions of the individual artists' careers and styles, including details of their lives after many had left Germany in the 1930s. A volume that gives the viewer something to look at and something to think about, all accomplished with startling contemporary relevance. Chronology; bibliography. —*John Brosnahan*

Berger, John.
Keeping a Rendezvous.
Pantheon, $21 (0-679-40632-8). 230p.

About a quarter of these essays are on topics ranging from the author's mother to philosophy (specifically, the nature of time) to farmers shoveling manure to Berger's love of dogs to Atlantic isles. They will be cherished by lovers of the traditional essay. All the other essays are about art, which they do not criticize so much as evoke. Berger's seasoned sensibility—romantic, compassionate, noble and ennobling—turns here to the nature of film; Velazquez's Aesop (and Spanish painting and the Spanish countryside); the magical "palace surpassing all imagination" built by the untutored French

Art

postman, Ferdinand Cheval; the relation between the paintings of Jackson Pollock and those of his wife, Lee Krasner; the photographs of Marketa Luskacova; the painter Renoir's abhorrence of self-exposure. Berger is never argumentative; he is emotional but never sacrifices analytic acuity. He's at ease with his learning. He has no single theory to illustrate or defend. He can be political or psychoanalytic or historical or spiritual, but only when the occasion calls for it. He is always finding the concepts, the language suited to the particularities of the subject at hand. (*Keeping a Rendezvous* has been published simultaneously with the first collected edition of Berger's trilogy, *Into Their Labors* [Pantheon, $30 (0-679-40629-8)], which BOOKLIST has called "one of the great works of fiction in this century.") —*Roland Wulbert*

Capa, Robert.
Children of War, Children of Peace.
Little, Brown/Bulfinch Press, $50 (0-8212-1789-5). 184p.

Robert Capa (1913–54) photographed war within its deadly grip, finally losing his life in the process. His famous war photographs have burned their way into our consciousness, symbols of war's horrors and heroics and the stunned silence of its aftermath. But Capa's real subject was people, with children a central theme and preoccupation. This volume collects and publishes Capa's photographs of children for the first time, opening a new window onto the photographer's sensitivity for the human condition. Edited by Capa's brother, Cornell, a photojournalist, and biographer Richard Whelan, this is a labor of love. The pictures, chosen from thousands of negatives, were taken all over Europe and in the Soviet Union, Israel, China, Japan, Indochina, and the U.S. Most of them exhibit evidence of war, casting the utter tenderness and vulnerability of the children in high relief. Each photograph glows with the unconcealed emotions of children's faces and gestures, but "his pictures are never cute—they always have an edge." These are beautiful and compassionate works of art that "uncover the secrets of a loving, lonely heart." —*Donna Seaman*

Cohen, David, ed.
The Circle of Life: Rituals from the Human Family Album.
HarperCollins, $39.95 (0-06-250152-6). 248p. index.

A dazzling collection of photographs that reaffirms the magic universality of Edward Steichen's *Family of Man* (1955). This volume of 200 powerful color and black-and-white photographs is the result of an inspiration of David Cohen, cocreator of the popular "Day in the Life" series of photo books. Cohen organized a group of international photographers and scholars to search for and record rituals that mark rites of passage. Cultures from every continent have developed celebrations for each stage of life from birth to initiation and puberty, marriage and adulthood, death and remembrance. The ceremonies captured in these expressive photographs display a great variety of appearance and atmosphere, but, at the same time, share a striking similarity of emotional depth and sense of tradition. As we turn the pages of this vibrant "human family album," we see people of every color, religion, and landscape, all dramatizing the universal need to celebrate the sacred and mysterious cycle of life. Descriptive detail is furnished by insightful commentary and brief essays by Gabriel Garcia Marqauez and Peter Matthiessen. —*Donna Seaman*

Eldredge, Charles C.
Georgia O'Keeffe.
Abrams, $39.95 (0-8109-3657-7). 160p.

Georgia O'Keeffe continues to reign as the high priestess of American art. Numerous recent biographies have sprouted in the rich loam of her seemingly romantic, certainly enigmatic, and now legendary life, but this fascination with persona threatens to "overwhelm and obscure the art." This handsome volume with its superb reproductions, many never previously published, and Eldredge's sensitive text concentrates on O'Keeffe's paintings by exploring her resonant themes and striking imagery. Eldredge traces the sources and impact of O'Keeffe's rich and evocative visual vocabulary by looking at her work in groups: first the early, startlingly original abstractions and then the series on organic objects such as fruits and leaves, flowers, and bones. Place is a primary force, from the strong, clean lines of her cityscapes to the coziness of Lake George to the grand desert of New Mexico. Even the most modest of American art collections needs a book of O'Keeffe's paintings; this one is highly recommended. —*Donna Seaman*

Fane, Diane and others.
Objects of Myth and Memory: American Indian Art at the Brooklyn Museum.
Univ. of Washington, $60 (0-295-97023-5). 320p. index.

The Brooklyn Museum's seminal collection of American Indian art is the achievement of a passionate, diligent, and competitive collector, Stewart Culin. During this century's first decade, Culin amassed more than 9,000 objects from field trips in the Southwest, California, the Northwest coast, and Oklahoma. His forays and finds in each region are discussed in separate essays, while other chapters cover Culin's methods and attitudes, particularly his zeal to preserve what seemed to be a dying culture. He collected items from every aspect of life, from the mundane to the sacred, from games to weapons. Some 300 objects are shown, each with a detailed description and source information. Noted for "his flair for the visual," Culin certainly did acquire stunning and powerful artifacts. This striking volume is enriched by the inclusion of history and anecdotes about both the creators of these objects of beauty and significance and their eager purchasers. Connoisseurs will find much to exclaim over, as will novices. —*Donna Seaman*

✔Friedlander, Lee.
Nudes.
Pantheon, $50 (0-679-40484-8). 84p.

He's done it again. The photographer who reinvented self-portrayal (see *Self Portrait* [Haywire Press, 1970]), Friedlander has now reinvented the nude photograph. Emphasize the word *photograph* because these frank and

Art

surprising nudes are, above all, photographic. Revealed in the harsh light of the photoflash are the very real skin, shapes, and body hair (*lots* of pubic hair—this book couldn't have been published 50 years ago) of very real young women. The awkwardness of poses and settings and the distortions of bodies seen through the wide-angle lens share equally in producing pictures that are shocking and disturbing in their candor, that make no effort to disguise the powerful passion of the photographer's "male gaze." Feminists and others may find much to protest in these pictures' emphatic objectification of the young, prone, female body, and yet—as with all Friedlander's work—there is about these images a direct honesty that prevails and, in the end, enriches. The works of Edward Weston and Bill Brandt, acknowledged great photographers of the nude, suddenly seem polite overtures—with Friedlander the curtain has opened. Although it may be controversial, this book is highly recommended for art and photography collections. —*Gretchen Garner*

Fulton, Marianne.
Mary Ellen Mark: 25 Years.
Little, Brown/Bulfinch Press, $60 (0-8212-1837-9). 200p.

The pictures, although they are presented a mite haphazardly, definitely make the book in this selection from a fine documentary photographer's career. Best known for *Streetwise*, the complement to her husband Martin Bell's film about homeless teenagers, Mark has made poor and institutionalized youngsters the subjects of most of the photographic projects so strikingly sampled by this album. Subjects also include lepers, blind children, and youthful acrobats in the traveling circuses of India. When she chooses adult subjects (other than her movie publicity assignments, which are usually chosen for her), she chooses again from among severely socially constrained groups—mental patients, the dying who come to Mother Teresa's Missions of Charity, the desperately poor. She strives to put an emotional—but not sentimental—charge into each black-and-white image. She succeeds powerfully, economically yet artfully inspiring awe, often fear, and often compassion. In contrast to Mark's accomplished photography, Fulton's essay on her life, working practices, and working conditions as a photo-essayist when the form's magazine markets are dwindling is, although informative, awkward. —*Ray Olson*

Gottner-Abendroth, Heide.
The Dancing Goddess: Principles of a Matriarchal Aesthetic.
Beacon, paper, $15.95 (0-8070-6753-9). 249p.

Imagine art, created by nonprofessionals, that could not be bought or sold and that might, in fact, never result in a finished object. How could it, then, be art? According to current conceptions, it couldn't: with no art object, it cannot enter the marketplace of dealers and investors; no reputations could be made, no reproductions sold. But, according to this radical German theorist, this description fits "matriarchal" art, art based in women's realities. She does not call it "feminist," although artists like Judy Chicago, whom she discusses, would be comfortable with that label. Instead, she hearkens back to theories of a primeval matriarchy in which women controlled culture. Such a woman-centered world, she contends, would find such art suitable. We might call these works "happenings" or "rituals"; they would be seasonally based festivals in which entire communities participate joyously or mournfully. There would be no separation between "life" and "art," between what Gottner-Abendroth calls "hard reality" and "beautiful semblance." Her soaring, unifying vision should have broad appeal. —*Pat Monaghan*

Gruen, John.
The Artist Observed: 28 Interviews with Contemporary Artists.
Chicago Review Press/A Cappella Books, $19.95 (1-55652-103-0). 324p.

Gruen has written extensively about art and music, contributing regularly to the *New York Times*, *ArtNews*, and *Dance Magazine*, among others. This is his second collection of interviews, the first was *People Who Dance*. This compilation again displays Gruen's adeptness at winnowing out key statements about the artist's inner life from the often uneven harvest of an interview. Biographical detail, a narrative approach embracing the artists' appearance and presence, and descriptions of their work give each piece an informative three-dimensionality. Gruen conducted these interviews over a period of about 15 years, speaking with artists such as Francis Bacon (in spite of a warning about his being "unbearable"), Lucian Freud, Agnes Martin, Richard Diebenkorn, Lucas Samaras, Jack Youngerman, Bridget Riley, Saul Steinberg, and Rufino Tamayo. This volume is dedicated to Keith Haring, the subject of a recent Gruen biography. —*Donna Seaman*

Heide, Robert and Gilman, John.
Popular Art Deco: Depression Era Style and Design.
Abbeville, $35 (1-55859-030-7). 228p.

The term *popular art deco*, or *dime store deco*, embraces the countless mass-consumer objects manufactured in the geometrically sleek, optimistically futuristic style first seen by American designers in Paris at a 1925 exposition. Perfect unions of art and industry, these everyday objects offered the promise of a better future during the Depression era. The authors track deco's origins, its burst on the American scene, and its influence on the design of everything from ashtrays to radios, graphics to furniture, and, moving into the grand scale, skyscrapers to trains. Lively commentary accompanies excellent illustrations. Both a broader and, in terms of individual objects, more detailed treatment than *Art Deco Interiors*, this appropriately well designed volume will delight fans of Bakelite jewelry, Fiesta-ware, and other hot collectibles featuring this perennially popular style. —*Donna Seaman*

Mexico: Splendors of Thirty Centuries.
Little, Brown/Bulfinch Press, $75 (0-8212-1797-6). 712p.

A monumental survey of 3,000 years of Mexican art. Nobel Prize winner Octavio Paz introduces this definitive work with a learned and insightful overview of Mexico's complex history. Identifying art as "one of the most ancient and simple manifestations of the will for life," Paz perceives a unique

Art

and sustained sensibility in Mexican art throughout the region's dramatic cultural changes. Each contributor to the four main sections—pre-Columbian, viceregal, nineteenth century, and twentieth century—follows Paz's lead linking history to aesthetics. The path is circular, from the solidity and silent power of Olmec sculptures, to early hybrids of indigenous and European styles, to the voluptuous glitz of Spain's colonial brand of Christianity in fine and decorative arts, and, finally, back to images of the land and its first people, so expressively depicted in pre-Columbian carvings. From Mayan temples to the murals of Diego Rivera, Mexican art is suffused with grandeur and vigor, well documented in this splendid volume, which will entrance both the scholar and the neophyte. —*Donna Seaman*

Porter, Eliot and Auerbach, Ellen.
Mexican Celebrations.
Univ. of New Mexico, $35 (0-8263-1209-8). 115p.
Porter, Eliot.
Monuments of Egypt.
Univ. of New Mexico, $40 (0-8263-1232-2). 160p.

More Eliot Porter books keep appearing, in a flow not diminished in the least by the master photographer's death last year. The Porter files seem to be inexhaustible. These volumes feature photographs made in the 1950s (*Mexican Celebrations*) and the 1970s (*Monuments of Egypt*). As in Porter's other recent books, their exquisite color photographs are coupled with scholarly texts, making them much more than picture books. Wilma Stern contributes a short history of ancient Egypt to *Monuments*, while in *Celebrations*, Donna Pierce and Marsha C. Bol write on the traditions of the Christian calendar in rural Mexico—a valuable record of observances and churches that have already changed immensely since the photographs were made. Along with stately and detailed views of altars and church interiors, the Mexican book is full of snapshots of celebrants—pictures made with a small camera and very un-Porteresque in their sometimes blurry aspect. To be sure, this book was a collaboration with photographer Ellen Auerbach (who also collaborated with Porter on *Mexican Churches* [Univ. of New Mexico, 1987]), and the pictures date from the 1950s when color film was about 20 times less sensitive than it is today; still, they don't sit well in the light of Porter's famous lapidary style. On the other hand, that style can be seen in all its perfection in *Monuments of Egypt* exquisitely sharp, perfectly composed views of the wall paintings, reliefs, and monumental sculpture of ancient Egypt, this is classic Porter at its best. —*Gretchen Garner*

✔**Scully, Vincent.**
Architecture: The Natural and the Man-Made.
St. Martin's, $40 (0-312-06292-3). 512p. index.

Renowned, eloquent, and inspired art historian Vincent Scully gathers the work of 45 years of research and teaching into one magnificent volume. His central concern is "the relationship of man-made structures to the natural world." With the lucidity of a philosopher, the eye of an artist, and the imagination of a poet, Scully tours key examples of Western architecture, investigating how each edifice reflects or is in contrast to its environment. He delves into the meaning of the structure, its symbolism and intended effect on those who encounter it. Beginning with Manhattan's towers, Scully moves fluidly to Mayan temples, on to Egypt, and then to the Greek temple, "an image of victory," which permanently changed the art of building. As he circles back to the present, he lingers longest on the technology and experience of Gothic cathedrals, explicating their iconography of faith, power, and immortality. French Classic gardens such as Versailles and Vaux-le-Vicomte are analyzed for the first time in terms of their political symbolism and connection to the art of fortification. Lavishly illustrated, this is a masterful evocation of humanity's grandest creative achievements. —*Donna Seaman*

Solomon, Andrew.
The Irony Tower: Soviet Artists in a Time of Glasnost.
Knopf, $25 (0-394-58513-5). 304p. index.

Gossipy, intelligent, and great fun to read, this mostly anecdotal insider look at the Soviet artistic milieu manages at the same time to be a highly insightful and sophisticated piece of criticism. It is sure to interest anyone who really cares about the formerly "nonconformist" or "unofficial" artists who, with glasnost, have suddenly attracted worldwide attention. Most of the emphasis, as at Sotheby's watershed auction of contemporary Soviet art in 1988, is on the Moscow artists (whom Solomon is on intimate terms with). The remarkably different situation of the less conceptual Leningrad painters is always referred to, however, as a counterpoint. Solomon gives a lively account of how international recognition flustered the artists themselves more, perhaps, than it did the Soviet authorities. Accustomed as they were to placing very little importance on their artwork as product—instead, encoding secrets for an audience well versed in reading between the lines— the artists' purpose was undermined and lost by having to explain themselves to a Western audience. Solomon chronicles the artists' individual adaptations to their new life with humor and concern. —*Anne Schmitt*

Varnedoe, Kirk and Gopnick, Adam.
High & Low: Modern Art and Popular Culture.
Abrams, $60 (0-8109-6002-8). 464p.

While this exhibition examining the influence of popular culture on high art has received mixed notices—too much familiar material and too unfocused a viewpoint, say the critics—the catalog fares much better in laying out and developing the author's argument. Within the constraints that time and their own tastes impose, Varnedoe and Gopnick engage in a dense if occasionally witty dialogue with their selected artists, illustrating the influence that printed words, graffiti, caricature, comics, and advertising have had on modern artists. Painting and sculpture are the prime media for this translation and interpretation of popular culture, with the barrier between public communication and private art both dissolved and demolished. The sequence of color illustrations enhances both the authors' theory and the visual appeal of their study. —*John Brosnahan*

Yoe, Craig and Morra-Yoe, Janet.
The Art of Mickey Mouse.
Hyperion, $35 (1-56282-994-7). 128p.

Nearly 100 artists pay homage to a pop-culture icon by contributing their renditions of the famous mouse to this attractive volume, which treats its subject with both the seriousness and the whimsy that he deserves. The participants include fine artists (Andy Warhol, Keith Haring), commercial illustrators (Milton Glaser, Patrick McDonnell), children's book illustrators (Maurice Sendak, William Steig), comics artists (Charles Schulz, Jack Kirby), and one ringer—Michael Jackson, whose well-known fondness for the mouse led the editors to ask him to take part. As John Updike points out in his lengthy introduction tracing Mickey's development, most of the artists instinctively reverted to his early, "classic" form: bare chest, red shorts, and simplified eyes. The two most noteworthy things about the project are the genuine affection all the artists—even normally subversive underground cartoonists like R. Crumb and Gary Panter—show toward their subject and the fact that the Disney studio, known in the past for jealous overprotection of its leading star's image, would not only allow such tampering with that image but would be the one to publish it, as one of the first titles from its new Hyperion imprint. —*Gordon Flagg*

Biography

✔**Abbott, Shirley.**
The Bookmaker's Daughter: A Memory Unbound.
Ticknor & Fields, $19.95 (0-89919-518-0). 290p.

Abbott, author of the widely acclaimed *Womenfolks: Growing Up Down South,* has written an enveloping and magical memoir about her unusual father and her challenging childhood in Hot Springs, Arkansas. Alfred ("Hat") Abbott the bookmaker did indeed love books, but he didn't work as a bookbinder as his young fiancée first thought. No, the books Hat made were betting tallies. Each day, dressed like a "gentleman bandit," he handled the money at the politically protected Southern Club, where bets were run on all the major horse races. Life was a cash-and-carry situation—when he had it they spent it, and when the political climate changed they suffered. Shirley rode these reversals of fortune on a raft of books, encouraged to read by her father who, unlike most southerners in the 1940s and 1950s, wanted his daughter to know about the world and think for herself. Her mother, enthralled to the hard, thankless toil of housework, just wanted her to be normal. As Shirley matured, she realized that nothing about women's lives appealed to her—they seemed to do little but drudge and weep—but when she tried to live according to what she learned from her father and the world of books, he reacted with anger and incomprehension. Abbott's conflicted life embraces the extremes of a fairy tale, and she writes about Hot Springs with tenderness, amusement, sorrow, and wonder. In scrutinizing and articulating her past, Abbott illuminates the infrastructure of southern culture and gender roles, the value of literature, the purpose of work, and the rarity of love, enriching us with her generosity of insight and spirit. —*Donna Seaman*

Abinader, Elmaz.
Children of the Roojme: A Family's Journey.
Norton, $24.95 (0-393-02952-2). 352p.

A terrace of stone (the *roojme* of the title) between the homes of three brothers in a small Lebanese village forms the foundation for Abinader's memoir of her family and their homeland. The author's parents immigrated to the U.S. and settled in Pennsylvania, and the chasm between these two locales forms a valley that traps both the memories of life in Lebanon and the struggles experienced in the new country where the author was born. But the stories told here take the reader mostly back to Lebanon, in accounts both of the family's existence there and of her parents' visits back to their childhood home. Abinader poetically evokes this landscape with a great deal of feeling for the history of Lebanon and her people in the early part of the twentieth century, in a sense outlining a pattern of affliction that would presage current conditions. —*John Brosnahan*

✓Ackroyd, Peter.
Dickens: Life & Times.
HarperCollins, $35 (0-06-016602-9). 195p.

"Charles Dickens was the last of the great eighteenth-century novelists and the first of the great symbolic novelists, and in the crushing equilibrium between these two forces dwells the real strength of his art." And in that sentence dwells the real strength of Ackroyd's massive yet never less than compelling biography: its fluid eloquence, its startling insight, its tantalizing complexity. There have been many lives of the Victorian era's most revered writer, of course, and this one follows by only two years Fred Kaplan's well-received *Dickens*. So what does Ackroyd give us we can't find elsewhere? First of all, there is the stunningly detailed vision of Dickens' world—the London of the early nineteenth century, a city of unrivaled vigor but also one "in which the odour of the dead emanated from metropolitan graveyards, where open sewers and cesspools spread their miasma into the foggy air." Next, there is the marvelous intertwining of life and work, the way Ackroyd makes us see how, finally, Dickens' reality became "a reflection of his own fiction." For the melodramatic among us (and aren't all Dickens fans susceptible to melodrama?), there is a new interpretation of the dissolution of Dickens' marriage and his relationship with actress Ellen Ternan. (Unlike Kaplan and others, Ackroyd argues that Ternan was not Dickens' mistress, but instead the last in a series of idealized virgin princesses whom the novelist worshiped with an all-consuming if dissembled passion.) But most of all, Ackroyd's biography, in its wealth of vivid detail and in the headlong, excited rumble and roll of its smoothly flowing sentences, gives us a sense of Dickens' energy, of his "unmistakable urge to encompass everything, to comprehend everything, to control everything." We don't think that way anymore, and our novelists certainly don't write that way. Seeing Dickens through Ackroyd's eyes makes us wish ours was a less attenuated age. —*Bill Ott*

Adams, Richard.
The Day Gone By: An Autobiography.
Knopf, $25 (0-679-40117-2). 398p.

The English author of the best-selling *Watership Down* was born in 1920 a physician's son and grew up in a large comfortable house in the country amid nature in its fullest blossom. His memoir of childhood, adolescence, and early manhood embodies a sterlingly rendered fondness for times past shorn of nostalgia. With lovely descriptions of scenery and gentle anecdotes about people and events, Adams recollects his public school days, his stint at Oxford, and off to the army in World War II, when his idyllic existence came to a decided halt. Compelling in its pastoralism, this glance backward will greatly appeal not simply to lovers of Adams' popular fiction but also to readers who appreciate the fine art of autobiography. —*Brad Hooper*

Alexander, Paul.
This Rough Magic: A Biography of Sylvia Plath.
Viking, $24.95 (0-670-81812-7). 448p. index.
Hayman, Ronald.
The Death and Life of Sylvia Plath.
Birch Lane, $19.95 (1-55972-068-9). 256p. index.
Middlebrook, Diane Wood.
Anne Sexton.
Houghton, $24.95 (0-395-35362-9). 462p. index.

Sylvia Plath and Anne Sexton first met in Robert Lowell's poetry class in 1959, little knowing then that, sisters in suicide, their names would be forever linked in death. These three biographies provide an interesting contrast in terms of how scholars were provided access to material on a famous author's life and work.

When Plath died, her husband, poet Ted Hughes, became executor of her estate. He has since exercised rigid control over all her published and unpublished writings, allowing biographers permission to quote only after they agree to submit their work for his approval. Neither Alexander nor Hayman complied with his terms. As a result, both books depend heavily on paraphrased material, making them less lively than they might otherwise have been. Alexander's biography, nevertheless, is richly detailed, particularly in terms of Plath's early life, her schooling at Smith, and the publication history of her work. Alexander analyzes Plath's life and work in the context of the social climate of the 1950s, an atmosphere that, to his mind, contributed to her unhappiness and sense of failure.

Hayman's book is more a psychological autopsy than a full-fledged biography. The emphasis here, as the title indicates, is on Plath's death and the events that lead her to take her own life—events, as portrayed by Hayman, that reflect unfavorably on Ted Hughes and his sister, Olwyn. The final chapter, "Posthumous Life," provides a valuable overview of biographical research on Plath with details of the biographers' relationships with the Hughes family. Both Alexander's and Hayman's works should serve as useful correctives to Anne Stevenson's *Bitter Fame*, a biography heavily sanitized by Ted and Olwyn Hughes.

Linda Gray Sexton, on the other hand, provided Diane Wood Middlebrook with full, unhampered access to all of Anne Sexton's papers, including medical records and over 300 audiotapes of Sexton's psychotherapy sessions with Dr. Martin Orne. Dr. Orne, who treated Sexton from 1956 through 1964, cooperated fully with Middlebrook, calling into question the role of doctor-patient confidentiality. Middlebrook insists that the therapy tapes significantly changed her view of Sexton. Although she places a strong emphasis on psychoanalysis, she is careful to avoid writing a case study. She allows the facts of Sexton's life to speak eloquently for themselves, supplemented by readings drawn from her poems. Sexton's difficult relationships with parents, husband, and children as well as her friendships with fellow poets including W. D. Snodgrass, James Wright, and Maxine Kumin are fully explored. Middlebrook concludes that Sexton was a woman who battled with her demons throughout her life and who, in spite of (not because of) her madness, became a gifted poet and teacher. Despite the controversy Middlebrook's biography has engendered— it is the first literary story to draw on "confidential" psychiatric records—it will probably remain the standard work on Sexton for many years to come. —*Bill Gargan*

✔Ambrose, Stephen E.
Nixon: Volume Three: Ruin and Recovery, 1973-1990.
Simon & Schuster, $27.50 (0-671-69188-0). 594p. index.

There may never be too many words written about the latter twentieth century's most frustrating and fascinating political figure, and acclaimed historian/biographer Ambrose concludes his multivolume profile of Richard Nixon with perhaps the best installment of all. Here we see Nixon the kingly winner of the 1972 presidential election, Nixon the masterful foreign policy doyen, Nixon the insular, distrustful executive, Nixon the beleaguered unindicted co-conspirator of Watergate, Nixon the media hater, Nixon the tough defender of executive privilege, Nixon the devoted family man, Nixon the arrogant, Nixon the resigned, and finally, Nixon the ailing, who flees to San Clemente only to resurface but a few years later in New York as dogged elder statesman, respected international traveler, and esteemed purveyor of well-regarded political thought. In the main, Ambrose focuses, quite rightly, on Watergate, though those of us who lived through that period will find it almost as incredible to read about as it was to experience. All those unforgettable names are here—Jaworski, Sirica, Dean, Ehrlichman, Haldeman, Colson, Liddy, etc.—with Ambrose holding the depressing events together with solid research and excellent writing. In addition, Ambrose's further evaluations of the "new" Nixon are honest, balanced, and fair, as are his assessments of the

Biography

man's place in history (which may yet be deemed considerable). Love him or hate him, you just can't ignore him, and Ambrose deftly and deeply appraises just why that is. —*Martin Brady*

✔**Angier, Carole.**
Jean Rhys: Life and Work.
Little, Brown, $35 (0-316-04263-3). 776p. index.

The first thorough, authorized biography of writer Jean Rhys (1890–1979), best known for her masterpiece, *Wide Sargasso Sea.* Angier's exhaustive analysis of Jean's rocky life and dark fiction is a true labor of love, and her deep affinity for her subject's incomparable prose is immediately obvious in the opening description of Jean's homeland, the wild, lush, and conflictful island of Dominica. Angier carefully lays the foundation for understanding Jean's frustratingly perverse personality: the irreversible fact that although her father spoiled her, she and her mother could not love each other. Jean forever after felt divided, angry, and lonely and sought the protection of older men. She is abruptly uprooted, sent to school in London, and quickly ditches her studies for the cheap escapades of a chorus girl. Beautiful, fragile, and helpless, she is rescued for a time by a wealthy man named Lancelot, but their melodramatic breakup precipitates the first of many periods of poverty and heavy drinking. Jean is incompetent, passive, violent, and obsessed but finds some relief in writing in her diaries, a habit that gets her introduced to Ford Madox Ford. They conduct a messy affair, but he recognizes her as "a natural, completely original writer," teaches her about fiction, and gets her published. The remainder of Jean's long, traumatic life is spent in mutually maddening marriages and a constant "battle between strength and weakness, honesty and self-deception . . . between a great writer and a drunkard." Angier's meticulous analyses of Jean's novels link them not only to events in her life but to literature at its most arresting. A resounding achievement. —*Donna Seaman*

Barker-Benfield, G. J. and Clinton, Catherine.
Portraits of American Women: From Settlement to the Present.
St. Martin's, $35 (0-312-05789-8). 642p.
Keil, Sally Van Wagenen.
Those Wonderful Women in Their Flying Machines: The Unknown Heroines of World War II.
Four Directions Press, $24.95 (0-9627659-0-2). 418p. index.

Two eye-opening accounts of the lives of outstanding American women and their impact on society.

Portraits of American Women contains profiles of 25 influential women from diverse backgrounds throughout American history. Eight sections cover major periods from colonial days to the present, and each is introduced by an overview of the main events and characteristics of the era. The authors have injected color and femininity into the formerly traditional focus on white men, creating a more rounded, accurate, inclusive, and personal picture of our past, taking into account the effect European mores had on the gender roles of native Americans and African Americans. Some names will be familiar, such as Anne Hutchinson, Jane Addams, Georgia O'Keeffe, and Betty Friedan, but many will be new, offering rare windows on the lives of native American women, slaves and the free daughters of slaves, wives of presidents, writers, and activists against racism, sexism and unfair labor practices. Consistently well written and revelatory.

Not many people are aware of the fact that the U.S. Air Force had more than 1,000 women pilots flying everything from P-51 Mustangs to B-29 Superfortresses during World War II. *Those Wonderful Women in Their Flying Machines* tells the story of the courageous, dynamic, and trailblazing WASPs (Women's Airforce Service Pilots) in colorful, anecdotal detail. Originally published in 1979, this unexpected, exciting, and frustrating tale—WASPs weren't accorded veteran status until 1977—has been revised and expanded at a time when America is seeing greater numbers of women in the armed forces than ever before, raising numerous issues. If the first edition isn't part of your collection, we strongly recommend the revision. *—Donna Seaman*

Bernier, Rosamond.
Matisse, Picasso, Miró as I Knew Them.
Knopf, $50 (0-394-58670-0). 288p. index.

Picasso and Matisse are in for a lot of scrutiny these days. Francoise Gilot has written her memoirs, *Matisse and Picasso*, and John Richardson has undertaken a four-volume biography of Picasso, *A Life of Picasso, Volume I: 1881–1906*. Now Rosamond Bernier, a sought-after lecturer and journalist, has committed her memories of these two giants, plus a third, Miro, to paper. Bernier lived in France in the 1940s through the 1960s writing about art for *Vogue* and founding and editing *L'Oeil*, an art magazine. Her recollections of visits and conversations with these diverse and intense artists and articulated understanding and appreciation for their work are expressed with clarity, economy, and animation. We see Matisse in his last years, working diligently from his bed, drawing on the walls with a stick of charcoal tied to the end of a fishing pole. A browned and mischievous Picasso, "The Presence," holds court on the beach, and Miro points out favorite details of Gaudi's Barcelona buildings. Bernier reveals the private aspects of each artist's attitudes, work habits, images, and fascinations, recharging our experience of their unforgettable work. Richly illustrated. *—Donna Seaman*

Bok, Sissela.
Alva Myrdal: A Daughter's Memoir.
Addison-Wesley, $22.95 (0-201-57086-6). 400p. index.

Bok, a professor of philosophy at Brandeis University, has written a captivating, searching biography of her accomplished mother, noted Swedish feminist Alva Myrdal (1902–86), one of the founders of the Swedish welfare state, an ambassador to India, and winner of the Nobel Peace Prize. The author shows most poignantly how Myrdal was a woman ahead of her time—every bit the contemporary woman, torn between her duty as a wife and mother and her career aspirations. Although Bok offers a very personal

Biography

look at her mother, she maintains her distance and objectivity by puzzling through contradictions and ferreting out facts and sources that reveal previously hidden facets of her mother's life. This journey of discovery is a worthwhile one for readers as well, for on it we come to know a feisty, fascinating, and inspiring woman who helped shatter traditional stereotypes of womanhood and achieved international prominence. Sadly, it is also a very human story about the losses suffered on the road to personal freedom, including an embittered son and grave public misunderstandings. A colorfully written, moving account. Part of the Radcliffe Biography series in women's studies. Contains excerpts from Myrdal's books and previously unpublished letters. —*Mary Banas*

Bowlby, John.
Charles Darwin: A Biography.
Norton, $24.95 (0-393-02940-9). 544p.

Charles Darwin and his theories have remained controversial for more than a century after his death. One debate that has occupied scholars is the source of Darwin's chronic ill health. Bowlby, psychologist and expert on the emotional development of children, zooms in on this issue, using it as a key to Darwin's astonishingly prolific life. He asserts that Darwin suffered from hyperventilation syndrome, a condition traceable to the death of his mother when he was eight: the family repressed their grief and never spoke of her, leaving Charles bereaved and unconsoled, and, in later life, a ceaseless workaholic and victim of debilitating, stress-related illnesses. Bowlby maintains this psychological focus throughout his exhaustively detailed, often subtle, and always sensitive account of Darwin's life and phenomenal achievements. By venturing beneath the surface of Darwin's relationships with family, friends, and colleagues, Bowlby illuminates the personality behind the genius. —*Donna Seaman*

✔**Boyd, Brian.**
Vladimir Nabokov: The American Years.
Princeton, $35 (0-691-06797-X). 735p. index.

Boyd completes his splendid biography of the Russian American novelist and poet with a narrative that covers 1940–77. As in the first volume, not only is Nabokov's life discussed, but there are extensive analyses of all his works. And what beauts they are: *Speak, Memory; Lolita; Pnin; Pale Fire; Ada;* and *Look at the Harlequins!* to name the best. There is even a fascinating chapter on Nabokov's controversial (but quite extraordinarily faithful) translation of Pushkin's *Eugene Onegin.* Boyd's project, of course, is to revive an interest in the novelist too often dismissed as mere brilliant exterior, a man Boyd believes to be thoughtful, profound, and often noble. And what fool would ever argue that these 1,200 or so pages over two volumes do not make the case? On the other hand, it is possible that Nabokov will always remain an acquired taste. Read the chapter on *Pale Fire*—Nabokov's masterpiece—and you will find your resistance (if it's there) melting; but will you ever be eager to embrace

the man who hides behind the dazzling mirrors of his over-finished, shockingly perfect art? Boyd was eager, of course, and so will others be after reading this quite magnificent study beautifully sculpted and intellectually profound.
—*Stuart Whitwell*

Bramly, Serge.
Leonardo: Discovering the Life of Leonardo da Vinci.
HarperCollins, $35 (0-06-016065-9). 496p. index.

Rose, June.
Modigliani: The Pure Bohemian.
St. Martin's, $22.95 (0-312-06416-0). 264p. index.

Two devoted biographers reexamine the lives of artists, determined to lift the veils of legend.

A best-seller in France, Bramly's book sheds light on the more personal aspects of Leonardo, a perennially fascinating and enigmatic figure. Reputed to be a splendidly handsome, well-made man, Leonardo was shrouded in myth while still alive. Known for centuries after his death as only a painter, albeit a remarkable one, his astonishing notebooks finally came to light, revealing the tremendous range of his scientific interests and "unique, fertile universal genius." Bramly combed these often cryptic notebooks, deciphering Leonardo's left-handed and backwards script, searching for glimpses into his thoughts and emotions. Abandoning the prissy reticence of previous biographers, Bramly discusses Leonardo's illegitimate birth and homosexuality with sensitivity, sophistication, and relevance. As he follows da Vinci's often frustrating career and ever-widening sphere of inquiries, inventions, and discoveries, he also patches together overlooked clues about his private life, causing us to marvel anew at Leonardo's fertile and versatile mind while acquiring a sharper image of Leonardo the man. A richly detailed, expansive, and thoroughly enjoyable portrait.

Other than being painters, Italian, and devastatingly handsome, Leonardo and Amedeo Modigliani have nothing in common, but the serendipity of book reviewing can lead to some odd connections. Unlike Leonardo, Modigliani was raised dotingly by his resourceful mother, who nurtured his artistic ambition. He soon left Italy for Paris, plunging headlong into the notoriously bohemian society of Montparnasse. Modigliani left scant autobiographical materials as he wrote little, reserving his energies for sculpting, painting, and carousing, but Rose does an admirable job of divining his personality and tracking his growth as an artist. Adored by women, Modigliani always had his pick of free models and doggedly pursued his own style, staying on the periphery of the various art movements. His work received little recognition during his brief life, and he was always broke, but he still "had a glamour about him, a sense of intensity, that excited envy and admiration." Rose insists that the canonized image of Modigliani as the drunk, drug-addicted womanizer has been exaggerated, fueled by his early death and the tragic suicide of his common-law wife. A tender and respectful biography of the painter whose portraits have become icons of modern art. —*Donna Seaman*

Biography

Breitman, Richard.
The Architect of Genocide: Himmler and the Final Solution.
Knopf, $23 (0-394-56841-9). 352p. index.

Breitman, professor of history at American University, has written a probing biography of Heinrich Himmler, the head of the SS and chief planner of the Holocaust. The text is based on voluminous war-crimes interrogations (taken from the National Archives), conducted between 1945 and 1949, of surviving Nazis, government officials and military men, victims of persecution, members of the German resistance, and witnesses of Nazi crimes. Breitman also gained access to even-more-detailed interrogations, witness testimony, and expert analysis in later West German war-crimes proceedings as well as in confidential American diplomatic and intelligence reports. Breitman focuses on Himmler's role in the decision making of the final solution, on how Himmler and the SS gained control of Nazi Germany's Jewish policy, and on other related World War II activities. Himmler killed himself (with cyanide) in May 1945 in a British interrogation camp. His prime role in the destruction of the Jews is documented here in detail for the first time in what is an exceptional piece of work. —*George Cohen*

✓**Breslin, Jimmy.**
Damon Runyon.
Ticknor & Fields, $24.95 (0-89919-984-4). 369p.

Breslin is a New Yorker, Pulitzer Prize–winning journalist, columnist, novelist, and tough guy. It's no wonder he was drawn to Damon Runyon—they've so much in common. Breslin paints Runyon's life on a mural-sized canvas, cramming in as much detail as the surface can hold. Blustering and feverish, with inside dope on everything and everyone, a brash sense of drama, and keen cynicism, Breslin's book raises the curtain on Runyon's poor, loveless childhood in Manhattan, Kansas, where he discovered writing, newspapers, and cigarettes at the ripe age of 11, setting the course for his entire life. He worked and partied his way across country to the real Manhattan, where his love of larceny flourished and his peculiar and irresistible blend of swagger and talent made him an immediate darling of newspaperman William Hearst. Runyon covered all the major news and sports stories of his times in his distinctive style, which, ultimately, created the myth and coined the phrases of the Roaring Twenties. Breslin follows Runyon from one outrageous escapade to another, pausing to dash off quick sketches of mobsters, politicians, boxers—all the guys and dolls—and their flamboyant scams. The author homes in on the impeccably tailored Runyon while he gambles, hangs out, cheats on his wife, and writes with great concentration and dedication, completely neglecting his family. Behind all the razzle-dazzle, fame, and success, however, sits a man who kept his emotions bottled-up tight until his lonely death. A commanding and dynamic portrait of a legendary writer and his world by his indisputably worthy heir apparent. —*Donna Seaman*

Bugul, Ken.
The Abandoned Baobab: The Autobiography of a Senegalese Woman.
Lawrence Hill, $18.95 (1-55652-113-8). 168p. paper, $9.95 (1-55652-114-6).

This is a beautiful, tragic book. As a young woman, the author (who writes under a pseudonym because of the book's sensational revelations) traveled on university scholarship from her African home to Brussels, where she expected to find the ancestral homeland promised by her French teachers in Africa. Homeland it may have been, but not for a colonial black woman of exquisite sensibility. Treated as an exotic, sensual animal, she began to act the part, dropping out of school to become the mistress of artists, then a dancer, and eventually a prostitute. In harrowing prose, she tells the story of her painful embrace of European expectations. "Always the same thing, always the same old song. We, Black women, we're all alike . . . white man and Black woman, life, a jumble of history and meta-history." We should be grateful that Ken Bugul found her way back at last to Africa and that she created this searing document as testimony of her suffering. —*Pat Monaghan*

Burgess, Anthony.
You've Had Your Time: The Second Part of the Confessions.
Grove Weidenfeld, $21.95 (0-8021-1405-9). 416p.

Picking up where he left off in *Little Wilson and Big God*, the brilliant Burgess gives us the rest of his life story, starting in 1959. Facing death, after a doctor's diagnosis of a fatal brain tumor, Burgess the erstwhile writer becomes Burgess the machine, cranking out novels and all manner of high and low journalism in order to pay his bills and leave his wife a legacy. But Burgess lives—and stays living—and the writerly career is launched, sometimes to acclaim, more often to critical lamentations. Then Burgess becomes an opinionated media personality, a status confirmed on the international scale with the appearance of Stanley Kubrick's movie of the author's *Clockwork Orange*. After first-wife Lynne dies horribly of cirrhosis of the liver (with Burgess the repentant boozing buddy), the author jet-sets from London to New York to Toronto, plays college gigs as guest lecturer all over the States, co-writes the musical *Cyrano*, composes pieces for the orchestra, expatriates from England to Malta to Monaco to Lugano, and finally wins over the critics for good with *Earthly Powers*. When Burgess is talking of people and ideas, he's priceless—from the preponderance of *dogmerd* on the streets of Manhattan to the failures of Pope John XXIII ("If he had been so saintly, why was Catholicism falling to pieces?"), from Ford Madox Ford ("the greatest British novelist of the century") to Barbara Cartland ("one of the most dangerous women in the world"), from Michael Korda to Norman Mailer ("Burgess, you're last book was shit"). One is less taken with the writer's complaints about his dyspepsia and neuralgia and his recitation of lines of verse and song lyrics. Still, the reader is glad, in the end, that AB has found happiness with a second wife and acceptance of his literary output. Finally, it's the freely, sometimes outrageously, stated opinions, the sexy badinage, and the endlessly witty world view that entertains. —*Martin Brady*

Biography

Califano, Joseph A.

The Triumph and Tragedy of Lyndon Johnson: The White House Years.
Simon & Schuster, $25 (0-671-66489-1). 360p. index.

No question about it, LBJ was a control freak as president, and Califano's look back to his three and one-half years as a White House aide might as well be his own emancipation from the grip of the larger-than-life Texan. The anecdotal preponderance in this memoir tilts toward numerous episodes of the famous Johnson "treatment": vulgar cajolery characterized by threats and pleas and pees. Califano's introduction to it in 1965 was an invitation to inspect a bare presidential buttock for boils, and thereafter he served as hatchet man or shock absorber for the recipients of LBJ's energetic ire or praise. Substantively, Califano carried the congressional water on Great Society legislation, which years later he administered as Carter's welfare secretary. Thus very little about the premier ruination of Johnson's reputation—the Vietnam War—is accounted for here, with the significant exception of the jawboning efforts to conceal its true fiscal dimensions. Ergo the "credibility gap" and like ethical lapses, which Califano, to his credit, admits: "Johnson and Fortas [a corrupt crony] . . . believed they were exempt from many of the traditional rules." So working for the prince of the Perdanales was—What? Exhilarating, infuriating, exasperating, exhausting, inspiring? Califano's experience runs the emotional gamut, and after the passage of 20 years, he is probably glad it's over. —*Gilbert Taylor*

Campbell, James.

Talking at the Gates: A Life of James Baldwin.
Viking, $21.95 (0-670-82913-7). 297p. index.

Campbell was a friend of Baldwin during the last decade of the writer's life. This biography offers a moving record of its subject's personality and work. In particular, Campbell reveals much about writings that were unpublished or unfinished at Baldwin's death, including biographies, plays, and a slave novel. In the main, this portrait covers mostly familiar incidents from Baldwin's early years as a writer and recounts the by-now-familiar charges that Baldwin confronted as a black, a homosexual, an exile, and a writer. Campbell's study acknowledges the complexities in each of these areas, and without his text dissolving into a pure apology highlights some of Baldwin's own ambivalence and insecurity. Campbell also gives short critical readings of Baldwin's works and quotes from correspondence to give a fuller picture of the man's talent and achievement. —*John Brosnahan*

Cannon, Lou.

President Reagan: The Role of a Lifetime.
Simon & Schuster, $24.95 (0-671-54294-X). 910p.

"The deficit," Reagan once quipped, "is big enough to take care of itself." While such cracks perhaps confirmed to skeptical reporters like Haynes Johnson that the president was "sleepwalking through America" (the title of his recent book), to more sympathetic members of the press corps like Lou Cannon, it is an example of Reagan's sunny optimism, his stubborn confidence that somehow every story (or movie) would always have a happy ending. The farcical deficit drama is not yet over, but with the curtain lowered on Reagan's unique political career, the reviewers are scrambling to critique the leading man's performance. Rather than hoot from the peanut gallery, Cannon embraces the theatrical metaphor to explain Reagan's incumbency, whose script was based on "The Speech," as Reagan's conservative creed had become known since he began delivering it in the early 1960s: cut government spending, cut income tax rates, and add to the military's prestige and resources. Delivering it on cue, and adept at embellishing it with a ready stock of jokes and anecdotes, he left the details of implementation to a retinue whose constant infighting was a notorious constant of the Reagan presidency. They made more news than the boss, and hence take up a large part of this hefty account. Cannon, an authority-by-acclamation on Reagan due to 25 years of covering the man, interviewed scores of significant stage managers, such as Michael Deaver, Peggy Noonan, and David Gergen, as well as the stars themselves, Ronnie and his astrology-minded consort, Nancy. Though the work stalls on a tedious chapter about the Iran-Contra Affair (which hysterically copies the name of Koestler's anti-Stalinist novel *Darkness at Noon*), overall it is a resounding success, as close as one can humanly come to knowing Reagan without being Reagan himself. —*Gilbert Taylor*

Caputo, Philip.
Means of Escape: Memoirs of the Disasters of War.
HarperCollins, $25 (0-06-018312-8). 400p. index.

The Pulitzer Prize–winning Caputo notes a "spiritual kinship between the terrorist and the journalist: Both are incapable of coping with normality." While it is the journalist's duty to cover the terrorist, it is the terrorist's role to make news. However, Caputo blurs the line between covering and making news. In this follow-up to his well-received *Rumor of War*, Caputo tells us that, rather than wait in the St. George Hotel in Beirut for the news to reach him, he hired a driver and sought out an eyewitness dispatch on the fighting between the Lebanese Army and the Palestinian guerrillas, pretty soon finding himself a hostage (quite a scoop). Caputo also felt an affinity with the Bedouin, who rode camels instead of commercial airlines. The itch to travel captured Caputo's fancy at an early age, embodied by the symbolic hobo, dubbed Oneway, he saw on a freight car as a child, who continued to lure him to one exotic land after another in the guise of a recruitment officer for the U.S. Marines and, later, his editor at the *Chicago Tribune*. As a foreign correspondent, Caputo jumped at the opportunity to cover the Yom Kippur War in 1973, the fall of Saigon in 1975, and the Afghan resistance to the Soviet Union in 1979. Caputo seems to desert his family at every opportunity. The means of escape of the title refers to his flight from home and hearth (i.e., normality) and his addiction to living dangerously. Ultimately burning out, Caputo now contents himself with writing novels (*Indian Country*) and learning how to "find peace in a room." —*Benjamin Segedin*

Biography

✓**Cary, Lorene.**
Black Ice.
Knopf, $19.95 (0-394-57465-6). 256p.

Black ice is "a clear, glittering ice.... The surface acts like a prism to break winter sun into a brilliant spectrum of browns." Cary's triumphant autobiography is, indeed, black ice, freeze-framing the past for in-depth examination, refracting assumptions into truths. In 1971, Cary was halfway through high school in a Philadelphia suburb when she was told that St. Paul's, a New Hampshire boarding school and longtime bastion of upper-class white males, had gone coed and was interested in enrolling young black women. In a narrative glistening with emotional nuance and crystal integrity, Cary replays her complex and demanding experiences at St. Paul's. Adolescence is always a time of displacement and confusion, but for Cary the usual traumas were compounded by her role as a token black. She felt tremendous pressure to succeed in this rarefied arena and struggled with harsh self-analysis that found achievements suspect, difficulties deserved—the inherited mind-sets of being a woman and black in the U.S. In the end, Cary taught herself how to glide above these old fears and prejudices, and now, generously and eloquently, tells her resplendent story to mark the path. —_Donna Seaman_

Chang, Jung.
Wild Swans: Three Daughters of China.
Simon & Schuster, $25 (0-671-68546-5). 502p.

Chinese American literature, including the work of Amy Tan, Maxine Hong Kingston, and newcomers Gish Jen and David Wong Louie, has struck a universal and resounding chord, stirring the imagination and eliciting empathy and recognition. The massacre at Tiananmen Square has also aroused a new wave of brooding curiosity about China and its enigmas and, in response, a spate of memoirs and politically minded novels. Jung Chang, who has lived in London since 1978, adds her vibrant voice to the chorus with a riveting family history. Writing with tremendous clarity and restraint, Chang relates the trauma-filled life stories of her maternal grandmother, mother, and herself. The three generations span the end of Old China's repression and the rise and fall of Mao's insane and inhuman reign. Chang's beautiful and cultured grandmother was subjected to the grotesqueness of bound feet, the indignity of concubinage, and the terrors of the Japanese occupation of Manchuria. Her well-educated, brave, and willful daughter welcomed the revolution, believing that it would better the lot of women; instead, she endured brutal regimens of forced self-criticism, torture, hard labor, rotten health care, frequent detention, and a complete lack of privacy or family life. Chang recounts the atrocities of the Communists coolly and devastatingly, patiently explaining Mao's crude and diabolically effective exploitation of ignorance, envy, and aggression and the toll it took on her and her extended family. An intense, reflective, and probing testimony that combines the magnetism of fiction with the undeniable power of truth. —_Donna Seaman_

Cheever, John.
The Journals of John Cheever.
Knopf, $25 (0-394-52728). 384p.

From the early 1940s till his death in 1982, this emiment American novelist and short-story writer confided much of his private thinking in the pages of a journal, which, as the years progressed, grew to several volumes. It was his wish, so his editor and family aver, that these diaries be published posthumously; and in extract form (representing approximately one-twentieth of the complete version) they now appear. Day-to-day activities mix with ruminations on himself (primarily the bruises his ego and libido take in his ever-aggressive search for stimulation in the company of both men and women), commentary on how well he is getting along with this family member or that, and reflections on the status of his writing. These journals are enlightening to a degree but discomfitting at the same time: Cheever nevers seems comfortable with himself, and what he says about the people who share his life seems more narrow and crabby than honest and understanding. Some artists' diaries open out into life-affirming documents full of honesty, freshness, and wisdom—and thus transcend, in the nature of their appeal, any narrow range of readership. Sadly, Cheever's testimony—indicative primarily of personal pettiness—will hold the attention only of his most devoted readers, who will enjoy the comments on his writing and view the rest with melancholy. Still, this is a necessary purchase for literature collections. —*Brad Hooper*

Clark, Tom.
Charles Olson: The Allegory of a Poet's Life.
Norton, $27.95 (0-393-02958-1). 480p. index.

Clark has written a thorough and readable biography of Olson, author of The Maximus Poems and the father of projective verse. Olson's interest in Melville, his academic career at Wesleyan and Harvard, his service in the War Information Office under Alan Cranston, and his tenure as rector and poetry teacher at Black Mountain College are covered in detail. Clark sees Olson as a complex, often difficult personality struggling against his own insecurity and trying to come to terms with unresolved Oedipal conflicts that colored both his relationships with women and his stormy friendships with mentor figures like Edward Dahlberg and Ezra Pound. While Clark recognizes the darker side of Olson's genius, he is sympathetic to the poet who sacrificed so much for the sake of his art. Highly recommended. —*William Gargan*

Cohen, Roger and Gatti, Claudio.
In the Eye of the Storm: The Life of General H. Norman Schwarzkopf.
Farrar, $19.95 (0-374-17708-2). 342p. index.

This may be the first biography of General Norman Schwarzkopf of enduring value. The two journalist-authors have used not only published sources but extensive interviews, and the text benefits from a post–Gulf War perspective. The story Cohen and Gatti tell is comparatively familiar: of Schwarzkopf's dedication to the army, of the professionalism of the officer corps, and of the general's concern for saving the lives of his men. But these topics are discussed in more detail, and the general's remarkable family (especially his father) are brought more to the fore. Highly recommended for current affairs and biography collections. —*Roland Green*

Conquest, Robert.
Stalin: Breaker of Nations.
Viking, $25 (0-670-84089-0). 334p. index.

Stalin's true self and regime have been, until glasnost, shrouded in Communist officialese. With new extensive research, Hoover Institute fellow and prolific author Conquest reveals a terrifying portrait of a Russian despot not far removed from the Mongol monsters. An unhappy, impoverished childhood, a lust for power, and an amoral drive marked Josif Dzhugashvili, and his double dealings during the early days of communism and subsequent denials of Lenin and Trotsky make for fascinating, albeit horrifying, reading. Still cloaked in much conjecture and conflicting data, Stalin's times seemed to be filled with larger-than-life falsehoods to justify achieving a true collective state—a goal marked by purges, anti-Semitism, treachery, exile, and wholesale murders. Conquest's instructive prose, though academically oriented, manages to conquer readers' attention. In sum, we simply nod in agreement with a perestroika-era comment: "The servile terror of Stalin lives in the bones and veins of people who never knew him." —*Barbara Jacobs*

Cott, Jonathan.
Wandering Ghost: The Odyssey of Lafcadio Hearn.
Knopf, $24.95 (0-394-57152-5). 430p.

Cott, seen frequently in the pages of *Rolling Stone* and author of *The Search for Omm Sety*, resurrects a lively and unique personality and collection of nineteenth-century writings in this penetrating biography. Born in 1850 on a Greek island to a young, illiterate native and an Irishman who soon deserted her, Lafcadio Hearn had a dramatic, Dickensian childhood. Shipped to America without a penny to his name, Hearn managed to get himself off the streets into the offices of a Cincinnati newspaper, where he soon became famous for his articles about "the macabre and the morbid," the forbidden and the strange. He identified with American blacks, wrote about their lives, and was fired for marrying a "woman of color." He took to wandering, soaking up the ambience of New Orleans and Martinique and, finally, settling in Japan. Cott generously shares the stage with Hearn, quoting extensively from his published works and letters. Hearn's cross-cultural quest for a meaningful life is a remarkable tale, well told by both the subject himself and his biographer. —*Donna Seaman*

Cronyn, Hume.
A Terrible Liar: A Memoir.
Morrow, $23 (0-688-10080-5). 448p. index.

One of the most distinguished American actors, half of arguably the century's most distinguished theatrical couple (he and Jessica Tandy are second only, perhaps, to Lynn Fontanne and Alfred Lunt), Cronyn has led a blessed life. At least, and despite the inevitable first-night closings and accidents, that's the impression one gathers from this memoir that he cuts off at 1966, just as the most successful, fully mature phase of his career was beginning. Of course, as he reminds in his title, memory is a terrible liar. Lies or not, his anecdotes of working with most of the great names in American theater from the 1930s on and with such great filmmakers as Hitchcock and Joseph L. Mankiewicz on that writer-director's famous, ill-starred behemoth, *Cleopatra*, will give stage and film mavens plenty of warm fuzzies. They don't ever shape up into an autobiography, a life *story*—only professional writers seem to give literary form to their recollections—but then, that's why Cronyn calls his book a memoir. —*Ray Olson*

Dallck, Robert.
Lone Star Rising: Lyndon Johnson & His Times, 1908–1960.
Oxford, $30 (0-19-505435-0). 784p. index.

Dallek delivers the first volume of his thoughtful biography of Lyndon Baines Johnson, chronicling LBJ's formative years, his impressive congressional tenure, and his nomination as vice-president in 1960. The author combines painstaking historical research with acute sociological insight, producing a fascinating and balanced account of the life and times of one of the most influential legislators of the twentieth century. While Dallek duly documents LBJ's universally acknowledged shortcomings and crudities, he also recognizes the late president's extraordinary political perception and social impact. What emerges is a complex portrait of a shrewd opportunist who promoted both himself and his increasingly progressive vision of the New South. This penetrating scholarly analysis of an often misunderstood and underrated statesman is a worthwhile acquisition for all public library collections. —*Margaret Flanagan*

✔**De Mille, Agnes.**
Martha: The Life and Work of Martha Graham.
Random, $30 (0-394-55643-7). 477p. index.
✔**Graham, Martha.**
Blood Memory.
Doubleday, $25 (0-385-26503-4). 288p.

Martha Graham (1894–1991) made the spiritual physical and changed the art of dance for all time. Her long, full, and devoted life is the stuff of legend, superbly told in these two complementary volumes.

Biography

Graham couldn't have had a more perfect biographer than De Mille, a dancer and fine choreographer, and so an expert on Graham's work, but also a best-selling author and Graham's friend for more than 60 years. Her vivid descriptions of Graham's inspirations, techniques, and the evolution of her evocative language of gesture and motion crackle with invaluable insight. A brazen, rebellious, and passionate girl, Graham knew she was a dancer the moment she saw Ruth St. Denis perform. She instantly perceived that dance was, or could be, a sacred act, "a religious celebration . . . a deep revelation of life." De Mille traces Graham's uphill path to greatness, chronicling the long, arduous hours of practice, the austere discipline of her teaching methods, her poverty, and uncompromising dedication to her visions. She was astonishingly prolific, courageous, and strong, but there is always a toll for such relentless creativity, and Graham paid hers in full, suffering a traumatic private life. De Mille is frank about Graham's sexuality, doomed marriage, fierce rages, and loneliness. Fighting age tooth and nail, Graham continued to perform her daunting solos well into her seventies, precipitating a period of ill health. She made a triumphant recovery, went back to work, and achieved international, nearly superstar-level recognition. An astute and knowledgeable biography of one grande dame by another.

Graham's self-portrait, written during the last year of her life, is as controlled and proud as her performances. She lingers on key events in her childhood, particularly the influence of her father, and, in a manner both regal and confiding, free-associates, gliding from anecdote to strikingly poetic statements about her work. She writes about the inherent truth of the body and the importance of breath, about myth and "blood memory," the source of art. Characterizing herself as a "devotee of sex," she discusses the eroticism of her work, but glosses over her love life while dropping more names than a gossip columnist. Graham is blunt, evasive, sly, and mystical; witty, poetic, and tough, and ready for more, even at age 96. A remarkable final work from a singular artist. Photos from Graham's private collection round out the volume. —*Donna Seaman*

Doolittle, James H.
I Could Never Be So Lucky Again.
Bantam, $22.50 (0-553-07807-0). 592p. index.

The famous eponym of the raid against Japan in April 1942, Doolittle, age 94 and still counting, has at long last written his autobiography. That he has survived this long is a minor miracle, given an impish nature that led him into numerous plane crashes during the barnstorming days of aviation. He would fly under bridges, through hangers, and once buzzed a fellow soldier a bit too closely, conking him on the head with the landing gear but somehow not injuring the guy. Just one of hundreds of sprily recalled incidents starting with frontier life in Alaska, a short professional boxing career, his flying "firsts," the 30 seconds over Tokyo (naturally the fount of his fame), his direction of the strategic bombing of Germany, and his postwar career in industry, this man's life is entwined with the development of flight. These memoirs, a window on his feisty and honest personality, must be mustered into the ranks of all popular aviation collections. —*Gilbert Taylor*

Duberman, Martin.
Cures: A Gay Man's Odyssey.
Dutton, $19.95 (0-525-24955-9). 304p.

When in his history of the great experimental college, *Black Mountain* (Doubleday, 1972), Duberman announced that he, like a few of the school's prominent figures, was homosexual, it caused quite a fuss. It also betokened, his autobiography imparts, his final cure from the bane of homosexuality, a cure accomplished not by the psychotherapy he endured, but by coming out. It took him more than 20 years to get to that public announcement, from the time when a fortune-teller proffered him the first cure at age 18 ("join our gypsy family so that I can be constantly by your side") through a distinguished career as a scholar, teacher, and playwright. Personally, alongside his professional triumphs he was suffering, entirely consensually, through psychiatric indignities that seem scarcely credible these days. Fortunately, he also allowed himself gay friends and gay love, and he could not stifle the inquisitiveness and skepticism that had led him to black civil rights and antiwar activism. At last, those qualities got him into gay activism. Although the fact that Duberman's a professor may turn off some, his testimony is both affecting and a gay liberation document of the first water. —*Ray Olson*

Eisler, Benita.
O'Keeffe and Stieglitz: An American Romance.
Doubleday, $29.50 (0-385-26122-5). 560p. index.

A dual biography of painter Georgia O'Keeffe and photographer Alfred Stieglitz, offering a close-up of their relationship, in and out of love, over three decades. Both personal and professional associations occupy Eisler's text, which illustrates how the two fell in love and later married, how Stieglitz helped build O'Keeffe's reputation, and how the complex chemistry of their passion for each other and for others bubbled, subsided, and sparked again over the years. Eisler is particularly inclined to emphasize the psychosexual implications of her subjects' behavior, and her interpretation lends both a spark of erotic ardor and controversy to the group portrait of the artistic life in the early half of the twentieth century. Although other studies of both O'Keeffe and Stieglitz offer better records of their separate and united careers and more expert judgments on their work, this volume focuses effectively on the unorthodox impulses and patterns that flowed through both of their lives before they met and after they married. —*John Brosnahan*

Ellerbee, Linda.
Move On: Adventures in the Real World.
Putnam, $21.95 (0-399-13623-1). 269p.

TV journalist Ellerbee's first book, *And So It Goes*, leapt onto the *New York Times* best-seller list and stayed there, delighting readers with its wry humor

Biography

and candid assessment of network television. Her second book takes stock of the many changes experienced in her adventurous life. Ellerbee tells stories of her Texas childhood, her family, friends, and colleagues. She writes about jobs, dogs, rock 'n' roll, marriage, motherhood, and alcoholism, from Houston, Tennessee, and a Texas border town to an Alaskan commune, Chicago, and New York. She married four times between the ages of 20 and 30, had a son and a daughter, and worked as a housewife before becoming a journalist. In recent years, Ellerbee has established her own production company, worked for CNN, written a syndicated newspaper column, seen her children grow up and leave home, and served time at the Betty Ford Center. Television, Hollywood, and journalism get their fair share of wickedly funny and right-on tongue-lashings here, while feminism gets an equally hilarious boost. A witty, intelligent, and warm memoir. —*Donna Seaman*

Epstein, Edward Z. and Morella, Joe.
Mia: The Life of Mia Farrow.
Delacorte, $19 (0-385-30446-3). 272p.

Epstein and Morella have collaborated on more than a dozen movie-star bios including books about Jane Wyman, Rita Hayworth, Loretta Young, Paul Newman, and Joanne Woodward, and they approach their latest subject with efficiency and respect. Several chapters are devoted to Farrow's parents, the actress Maureen O'Sullivan, and the director and religious scholar John Farrow, both fascinating individuals in their own right. Mia, an angelic child with an "old soul," is introduced as a self-possessed, beautiful, and seemingly vulnerable young lady whose delicate appearance concealed tremendous strength of character and a penchant for doing the unexpected: for example, falling in love with Frank Sinatra when she was 19 and he was 50; chopping off her famous long, blond hair while still on the cast of *Peyton Place*; making *Rosemary's Baby*; being friends with Salvador Dali; traveling around India alone; giving birth to twins fathered by Andre Previn while he was still married; gradually adopting five Korean and Vietnamese children; and having Woody Allen's son at 41 while they continue to live in their separate homes. The authors present the facts as best they can, offer tentative interpretations of Mia's behavior, and comment on how rapacious the paparazzi have been. However, they remain on the outside, knowledgeable observers not privy to Mia Farrow's heart and mind, which is, one assumes, the way she wants it. A thoroughly engaging portrait, in spite of its limitations, of an intriguing and unusual woman. —*Donna Seaman*

Fang, Lizhi.
Bringing Down the Great Wall: Writings on Science, Culture and Democracy in China.
Knopf, $19.95 (0-394-58842-8). 326p.

Fang Lizhi is China's most famous dissident. An astrophysicist, Fang (called China's Sakharov) believes that the "search for truth is among our most basic human rights." This conviction has led Fang to speak out fearlessly and consistently against the "injustice and irrationality in Chinese society," first as a student and then as a "rehabilitated" but nevertheless progressive university vice-president who championed democracy and was blamed (wrongly) for the student demonstrations that led to the massacre of Tiananmen Square. This selection of Fang's essays and speeches from the last 11 years covers a wide range of topics from cosmology to the contrast between China and the modernized world, as well as his bold public statements on governmental actions. Fang's essays and speeches are succinct and logical, injecting a melody of sanity, honesty, intelligence, and reason into the cacophony of rhetoric surrounding China's policies. A primary addition to the annals of China and the fall of communism. —*Donna Seaman*

Fiffer, Sharon Sloan.
Imagining America: Paul Thai's Journey from the Killing Fields of Cambodia to Freedom in the U.S.A.
Paragon House, $19.95 (1-55778-326-8). 224p.

In 1981, equipped with little more than faith, Cambodian refugee Paul Thai, his parents, and seven siblings stepped off an airplane in Dallas, Texas, to remake their lives. By then, 17-year-old Paul had coped with war and the callous disregard for human life. Early in her book, Fiffer argues that immigrants and refugees are quintessential Americans, and, in Paul Thai's life, the values Americans cherish—hard work, serving others, freedom—are revered and followed. How Paul perceived his experiences, and what he does now as the first Asian-born member of the Dallas police force, is told with charm and a good bit of insight. History, urban studies, and social science have seldom been combined so effectively. —*Virginia Dwyer*

Fleming, G. H.
James Abbott McNeill Whistler: A Life.
St. Martin's, $24.95 (0-312-05995-7). 416p. index.

Fleming, author of books about Rossetti and various Victorian subjects, has fun with Whistler's (1834–1903) contentious life, eccentric personality, and innovative art. He follows young Jimmy to Russia when his engineer father was hired as an adviser by the czar, and then back and forth between England and America for his schooling, which included several years at West Point. Whistler began drawing at an early age and was chastised for not "finishing" his paintings, a harbinger of criticism to come. Whistler soon left America for good, reveling in the bohemian life of an artist in Paris and London. He "saw beauty in what others found ugly" and revitalized portrait and landscape painting, meeting with both success and ridicule. He also earned a reputation for combativeness, first with his fists, then with lawsuits and venomous letters. Fleming shares some of Whistler's brilliant bon mots in his accounts of the infamous libel case against John Ruskin and the rivalry with Oscar Wilde. Free of the "prudery" of Whistler's earlier biographers, Fleming candidly discusses the artist's love life, his indifference to his illegitimate children, and the emotional forces behind his often extreme behavior, creating a whole and vital profile. —*Donna Seaman*

Fussell, Samuel Wilson.
Muscle: Confessions of an Unlikely Bodybuilder.
Poseidon, $18.95 (0-671-70195-9). 252p.

How—and why—does a six-foot-four, 170-pound weakling, a graduate of Oxford University, remake his body and his spirit in the image of Arnold Schwarzenegger? Fussell recounts his own experience as an unlikely bodybuilder and the four years he spent molding his muscles into competition shape in this lively account of his own quest and of the hermetic world of the other men and women who pursue the image of the body beautiful. Interestingly enough, it's both the physical and the mental qualities of his hero that the author strives to match. His fear while walking the mean streets of New York City forced him to remake himself as a form of physical and psychic protection. And working out hour after hour, day after day in gyms in New York and California, Fussell reached his awesome goal. But his story has its downside as well; the obsession and the dedication that other bodybuilders demonstrate don't dwell so comfortably in Fussell's soul. The author is all too aware of the problems that steroids, outlandish diets, and dogged training routines can create, and his own decision to become a bodybuilding dropout makes the potential for disaster all too clear. But Fussell's portrait of himself and of other bodybuilders examines, with a good deal of sympathy, understanding, and humor, what drives these people to train and to compete. —*John Brosnahan*

Gaines, Steven.
Simply Halston: The Untold Story.
Putnam, $22.95 (0-399-13612-6). 320p. index.

During the 1970s and early 1980s, the word *fashion* was synonymous with designer Halston. His stunning success all went bad, due to a combination of arrogance and drugs. Seemingly on the road to recovery, he was stricken with AIDS and died in 1990. Though it's easy to blame Halston for a lot of his business problems, Gaines writes so perceptively about the man, most readers will pity rather than censure him. The extensively researched text includes 200 interviews with business acquaintances and friends, Jacqueline Onassis among them. (Liza Minnelli and other close pals are not included. They had a falling out with Gaines when he wrote a roman à clef, *The Club*, that featured Liza, Halston, etc.) Even without the cooperation of some of the biggies in Halston's life, the book is filled with wry, witty anecdotes and plenty of business machinations. But, as he did with his real life cronies, it is Halston himself, vividly portrayed by his biographer, who steals the show. —*Ilene Cooper*

Geyer, Georgie Anne.
Guerrilla Prince: The Untold Story of Fidel Castro.
Little, Brown, $22.95 (0-316-30893-5). 407p. index.

Written with assurance, syndicated columnist Geyer's acutely incisive biography of Fidel Castro unfolds one rich layer of information and interpretation after the other. Based on interviews with 500 individuals, including one-on-one discussions with Castro himself, Geyer's "intensely psychological" treatment is indeed unclumsily that. Admitting Castro is enigmatic, she nonetheless succeeds in getting at much of the truth—from the effects of his illegitimacy, to his relations with women (including a wife and mistresses), to his "gangster years" at college, to motives behind adopting Communist sentiments. Concluding that Castro is a "destroyer," Geyer projects for U.S. readers an understanding of the man that is perhaps even clearer than that held by the people who surround him. Her biography sits well beside the recent *Cuba: A Journey*, in which Argentine journalist Jacobo Timerman toured the shabby landscape of Castro's realm. —*Brad Hooper*

Gilbert, Martin.
Churchill: A Life.
Holt, $35 (0-8050-0615-X). 1,088p. index.

Pearson, John.
The Private Lives of Winston Churchill.
Simon & Schuster, $27.50 (0-671-63153-5). 432p. index.

Two new books on Sir Winston Churchill take different approaches to the life of this great twentieth-century British statesman.

In the condensation of his authorized eight-volume biography, Gilbert navigates through Churchill's momentous life by nailing chronology to the mast and never deviating from it. Each birthday, for example, is duly recorded in the phrase "On November 30 Winston Churchill turned X years old. . . . " Repeated 90 times, this formula furnishes one one-thousandth of this dense, detailed, workmanlike bookend; the remaining length uncoils naturally. Commencing with young Winston's luxurious but emotionally threadbare upbringing during the zenith of Queen Victoria's empire, surveying the wars he traveled to in Cuba, India, the Sudan, and South Africa, where he was determined to achieve fame or die in the attempt, and tracing his subsequently legendary parliamentary career that began in 1901, this work reads like a daily log that summarizes the man's words and acts. Churchill's sepulchral cadence in written and spoken verbiage as well as his incandescent imagination both literary and administrative were acknowledged by his contemporaries, but lapses in judgment occasionally derailed him politically, as in Britain's Dardanelles disaster of 1915 or his lone support of Edward VIII in 1936. This author phlegmatically avoids verdicts on these and other controversies as he reports just the facts. Even if this work reads like a dry, objective index to the man whose obstinate indomitability in 1940 perhaps changed the course of history, so much the better ought it earn permanence of place in the public library.

Biography

Switching gears from Gilbert's index of the public man to Pearson's narrative of his domestic life, the second book examines the formative influences that propelled Churchill to the top of the political heap. His bloodlines converged in an appallingly negligent set of parents, American beauty Jennie Jerome and British aristocrat and stymied politician Lord Randolph Churchill. They lived at Blenheim, a gloomy country mansion built in the early 1700s by Winston's ancestor and military hero, the first duke of Marlborough. The two men must have captivated the young boy, since both figured later as his biographical subjects. Winston was especially driven to outdo and prove wrong his father, who amid fits of syphilitic insanity prophesied failure for his wastrel son. Pearson also theorizes that a family proclivity to mental depression accounted for Churchill's ceaseless energy, which functioned as a counterweight. If depression is hereditary, it was passed on to three of his four children. Whatever the strength of Pearson's case, domestic bliss was elusive, and people who subscribe to *People* will have ample fat to chew over in a rendering that is quite sympathetic to the great man—and less so to his relatives. —*Gilbert Taylor*

✔Gold, Arthur and Fizdale, Robert.
The Divine Sarah: A Life of Sarah Bernhardt.
Knopf, $30 (0-394-52879-4). 383p.

A captivating, colorfully written biography of French dramatic actress Sarah Bernhardt. The authors have exhaustively researched Bernhardt's private life, turning up some new information about the personal sorrows and tragedies that fueled her public ambitions and launched her onto a rocky career path that nonetheless won her lasting international acclaim. While Gold and Fizdale draw on much anecdotal material due to the paucity of published information about Bernhardt's private life, the results are anything but gossipy. Instead, the authors have turned out a polished, seamlessly crafted work that tastefully blends Hollywood-style tidbits about Bernhardt's salacious background (her mother and aunt were prostitutes) with poignant revelations about her behind-the-scenes struggles to master her craft and, more difficult still, display her art onstage. At times, this biography is off-putting in its dropping of once famous but now obscure names and in its casual references to the dimly remembered French popular culture of the late 1800s. But so well written is this novel-like biography that even those unfamiliar with Bernhardt or her body of work will find the book an irresistibly good read. By the authors of *Misia: The Life of Misia Sert.* —*Mary Banas*

Golden, Eve.
Platinum Girl: The Life and Legends of Jean Harlow.
Abbeville, $27.50 (1-55859-214-8). 224p. index.

Born Harlean Carpenter in 1911 in Kansas City, Missouri, she died only 26 years later as Jean Harlow, the reigning sex goddess of American movies. It would be easy enough to dismiss the life and career of Jean Harlow as the tragic if predictable story of a vamp, but Golden digs deeper. Her Jean Harlow is a loving and loved, sensitive, happy young woman at variance with her screen image of sexpot. After two years of bit parts, Harlow broke into the big time in 1930 with *Hell's Angels*. She wanted more serious roles, but by the time of her premature death in 1937 of kidney disease, she had carved out a niche as a great comedian. Harlow, Golden makes clear, had more to offer than platinum hair and a full figure. While establishing Harlow's credentials as an actress, Golden also handles her private life with care, reporting the facts, including the suicide of the actress' second husband, but refusing to treat them salaciously. Far from the typical star bio, this book is as unartificially buoyant as Harlow herself. —*Brad Hooper*

✔Good, Kenneth and Chanoff, David.
Into the Heart: One Man's Pursuit of Love and Knowledge among the Yanomama.
Simon & Schuster, $21.95 (0-671-72874-1). 349p.

An irresistible love story that transcends culture, language, time, and place. The Yanomama live simply in the relatively unexploited Venezuelan rain forest. Kenneth Good, an aspiring anthropologist and doctoral candidate, arrives to do field work for his study of protein intake. His first months are stressful. The climate is debilitating, he can't speak the language, and he feels like the clown of the Amazon as the Yanomama watch his every move with glee. But soon a warm rapport is established, and Good discovers that he's very happy there and even falls in love with and marries, Yanomama-style, a young girl named Yarima. But this is no tropical idyll. A series of unimaginable conflicts and hardships conspire to separate the lovers, but their strength and love prevail, and Good brings Yarima out of the jungle into the blare of civilization. Now it's her turn to face an unknown, radically different world. The story is so dramatic, Good's insights and observations so sharp and revelatory, you have to keep reminding yourself that this isn't brilliant fiction but rather a tale of unforgettable truths. Not to be missed. —*Donna Seaman*

✔Graham, Martha.
Blood Memory.
Doubleday, $25 (0-385-26503-4). 288p.

See p.23.

Grobel, Lawrence.
Conversations with Brando.
Hyperion, $19.95 (1-56282-990-4). 224p.

"I just don't believe in washing my dirty underwear for all to see, and I'm not interested in the confessions of movie stars." But having said that, it's clear that Marlon Brando is one man whose dirty underwear attracts a lot of attention. This fascinating volume reprints Brando's January 1979 interview in *Playboy*, wherein the great actor eventually—after interviewer Grobel painstakingly nurtures his sometimes obstinate subject into a state of openness—delivers freely on topics such as the plight of the American Indian, the CIA, TV, comedy, children's rights, moviemaking, and a host of other issues.

As interesting as the interview itself is the "before and after" material Grobel provides, which details the circumstances leading up to Grobel's trip to Brando's South Seas island, provides the necessary facts about Brando's life and career, and catches the reader up on Brando's most recent activities, not the least of which was his uncharacteristically public role as father of the accused in Christian Brando's celebrated murder trial. Whether he's denigrating acting as an art form—"There are no artists. We are businessmen. We're merchants. There is no art. Picasso was the last one I would call an artist"—quoting Shakespeare liberally and knowledgeably, praising acting teacher Stella Adler, or taking the American government to task for its hypocrisies, Brando remains one of the century's truly remarkable and intriguing characters. A must purchase for libraries. —*Martin Brady*

✔Gruen, John.
Keith Haring: The Authorized Biography.
Prentice Hall Press, $35 (0-13-516113-4). 352p. index.

Few artists hit it big when they're young. Keith Haring did, although par for the course for American artists, he was far more critically acclaimed in Europe, Japan, Australia, Brazil—anywhere but in his chosen home, New York. Not that he wasn't popular there. His energetic drawings of radiant babies, animals, aliens, dancers, copulating couples (of both sexual persuasions), and such conceits as Andy Mouse, a composite of two of his artistic mentors—Andy Warhol and Mickey Mouse—drew upon the techniques and brio of a quintessentially popular art form, the increasingly colorful and accomplished graffiti that kid artists as young as 13 were scrawling and spray-painting on subway cars during the late 1970s and early 1980s. Dropping out of art school because he'd realized his own style, he broke through to citywide recognition by taking to the subways himself, decorating blank spaces among the underground hoardings. He befriended many even younger graffiti artists, and he aggressively marketed his work through such endeavors as the Pop Shop. He became a celebrity and the friend of celebrities. He jetted about the globe to execute huge public commissions both alone and with schoolchildren, with whom his rapport was uncanny. And at 32, he died, a victim of AIDS, which he'd arrived in Manhattan's gay scene at precisely the moment to fatefully intercept. Before he died, he started talking to Gruen and getting his friends and family to talk to Gruen. The results are this book, which takes the form of an oral history utterly without connective prose between the various speakers' testimonies and which is as fascinating as any artist's biography has ever been, as instantaneously classic as Haring's imagery. —*Ray Olson*

Grumbach, Doris.
Coming into the End Zone: A Memoir.
Norton, $19.95 (0-393-03009-1). 256p.

Old age was rapidly becoming an unacceptable state of being for novelist and critic Grumbach on her seventieth birthday, so she began this memoir, "hoping to find in the recording process a positive value to living so long." She complains regally about the toll age takes on the body and the idiocies, pretensions, and dangers of modern life. Gruff honesty is wittily countered with defiant misanthropy as Grumbach bluntly and eloquently identifies things she "actively dislikes" such as "most new books," noise, junk mail, and people. She mourns the loss of a distressing number of younger friends to AIDS, admits to increasing fear for her safety in her violence-prone Washington, D.C., neighborhood, and muses on her past. But her life is active, including trips to Paris and the Mayan ruins in Yucatan, and plenty of reading and writing. Rather than settling into a careful routine, Grumbach embarks on a new adventure: she moves to Maine. By the end of the book, she is "no longer burdened by the weight of her years" and we, too, are uplifted. Grumbach's most recent novel was *The Magician's Girl. —Donna Seaman*

Guthke, Karl S.
B. Traven: The Life behind the Legends.
Lawrence Hill, $24.95 (1-55652-132-4); paper, $14.95 (1-55652-131-6). 496p. index.

Did B. Traven, author of *The Death Ship* and *The Treasure of the Sierra Madre*, among others, and, reportedly, Albert Einstein's favorite writer, keep his identity secret all those years out of fear, or out of some eccentric instinct for publicity? Guthke takes on the enigma of Traven's pseudonymous life with painstaking research and a healthy tolerance for mystery. With full access to the Traven estate, the archives of his German publisher, and the gracious conversation of Traven's widow, Guthke has written the first true biography of a man of many names and incarnations. Traven's first documented persona was that of Marut, a German actor turned revolutionary. Arrested and charged with treason, Marut escaped and eventually landed in Mexico in the early 1920s. He took to the jungle like a long-lost child to home, working as a day laborer and writing under the most trying conditions. His publisher ended up with a best-selling author who categorically refused to be photographed or interviewed, frequently disappeared, and carried on a taunting campaign of "obfuscation and revelation." By combining literary analysis with anecdote and sleuthing with psychological insight, Guthke has fashioned an intriguing portrait of a man who lived a life of mystification, dread, determination, and achievement. *—Donna Seaman*

Hamilton, Charles V.
Adam Clayton Powell, Jr.: The Political Biography of an American Dilemma.
Atheneum, $24.95 (0-689-12062-1). 448p. index.

Baptist preacher, civil rights activist, congressman representing Harlem for 26 years, egocentric bon vivant with a moral blind side the size of a barn, Adam Clayton Powell, Jr., had one of the more electrifying and controversial public careers of mid-twentieth-century American politics. That era's central problem, the yawning chasm between professed ideals of equality and the reality of racial discrimination, carried Powell to initial prominence in 1930s New York. Until the gap began to be closed by the southern-based mass civil

Biography

rights movement, the loudest voice was that of the emotive orator with the ready biblical phrase who held up the dilemma at every possible opportunity. His predominately black constituency was inspired by his feistiness, returning him repeatedly to Congress until a concatenation of malfeasances—tax evasion, a libel judgment he flouted, and payroll padding—forced the House of Representatives to expel him in 1967. Hamilton's biography delivers as advertised: the story of how Powell acquired and wielded power in the wards along 125th Street and in the corridors of Capitol Hill earns this work a place in even the smallest collections on the civil rights struggle. —*Gilbert Taylor*

Harvey, Andrew.
Hidden Journey: A Spiritual Awakening.
Holt, $22.50 (0-8050-1454-3). 256p.

Since Harvey first charted his personal road to enlightenment via Tibetan Buddhism in *The Road to Ladakh*, he has progressed further into the spiritual realm. Now he tells how he returned to his native India with despair and skepticism, but "got religion" and emerged a true believer. This account is less a travel book and more a guide to the inner Harvey: the writer's extravagant dreams expressing the mystic identity that captivates him and becomes his divine goal. A young Indian woman eventually becomes Harvey's master, and whenever doubt begins to trouble the writer, he unhesitatingly rushes across the country or around the world in search of her wisdom. Some readers may not emerge as "blissed out" as Harvey seems to have become, but the result certainly won't be the fault of the writer's mesmerizing style or the artless sincerity of his quest. —*John Brosnahan*

Hayman, Ronald.
The Death and Life of Sylvia Plath.
Birch Lane, $19.95 (1-55972-068-9). 256p. index.
See p.10.

Hearst, William Randolph and Casserly, Jack.
The Hearsts: Father and Son.
Roberts Rinehart, $29.95 (1-879373-04-1). 450p. index.
Robinson, Judith.
The Hearsts: An American Dynasty.
Univ. of Delaware, $49.50 (0-87413-383-1). 441p. index.

Apparently, it's time to dispel the mist of myth and rumor that obscures the life story of America's most famous publisher, William Randolph Hearst (1863–1951), and his unusual family.

Hearst, Jr., one of Hearst's five sons and the only one to follow him into the newspaper business with passion and commitment, has decided, at age 83, to break his family's silence and share the facts about Hearst, Sr., and their unusual lives. He's frank about the fairy-tale opulence of his childhood, but, through numerous anecdotes and examples, drives home the point that Hearst, Sr., believed in work and achievement and kept after his sons to do more than just live off his money. Hearst, Jr., and coauthor Casserly examine

Hearst, Sr.'s notorious brand of journalism, extraordinary communications empire, contentious politics, devotion to art, obsession with San Simeon, and complex love life in a detailed, straightforward, and earnest manner that strives for perspective, accuracy, and insight into "Pop's" supercharged personality. Two men emerge from this captivating memoir: the flamboyant and brilliant Hearst, Sr., and his son, a ground-breaking journalist in his own right.

Judith Robinson expands the circle to include George and Phoebe Apperson Hearst, William Randolph Hearst's parents. The name Hearst first became synonymous with money when George made his fortune from gold and silver mines. George and Phoebe (22 years younger than her husband) married at the height of the Civil War and headed to California where George became a U.S. senator and Phoebe, the primary focus of this fluid and discerning family history, became involved in educational and social causes. William was their only child, creating a triangle of love and conflict between three powerful, strong-minded people. When George died, he left his entire fortune to his wife, who became "one of the richest and most influential women in the world." In between fretting over William's independence and pumping money into his bold ventures, Phoebe, a woman of great dignity and generosity, oversaw numerous philanthropic projects, including the establishment of kindergartens and the PTA, archaeological explorations, the restoration of Mount Vernon, and various scholarships and educational programs for women. A fresh, thorough look at an exceptional American matriarch and her memorable family. —*Donna Seaman*

Hepburn, Katharine.
Me: Stories of My Life.
Knopf, $25 (0-394-0-679-40051-6). 420p.

Katharine Hepburn has said many times that she would never write her autobiography. Despite appearances, she's kept her word. This long-awaited book is pithy, pleasing, and sounds just like its author—lots of cropped sentences, dashes, Hepburnian phrasing. But it's not a full-dress autobiography; as the subtitle proclaims, this is a collection of stories, and, in many ways, they are a lot like the author's acting: lots of style, not much substance. Why did she love Spencer Tracy? Because it pleased her; she seems to have enjoyed thinking about someone other than herself. But as to their life together—that is, the details that made up a 27-year relationship—those memories Kate'll take with her. Still, fans will not be disappointed. Beginning with her early years surrounded by a strong but, by some standards, eccentric family, moving through the ups and many downs of her early career, spotlighting her most famous movies, and concluding with her relationship with Tracy, Hepburn delivers all kinds of wry moments and, of course, a most interesting cast of characters. A clever book, and, like Hepburn herself, definitely out of the ordinary: "I expected I would remember most of the pictures and the people who were in them. Well, the fact is, I don't—I'm trying to, but I can't." Illustrated with 165 wonderful black-and-white photographs. —*Ilene Cooper*

Herbst, Josephine.
The Starched Blue Sky of Spain: And Other Memoirs.
HarperCollins, $19.95 (0-06-016512-X). 224p.

Novelist Herbst grew up in Sioux City, Iowa, dreaming of bohemian freedom, travel, and witty and passionate conversation with literary luminaries. She worked her way through college, lived her dream in Greenwich Village and Paris' Left Bank, and wrote it all up in these four analytic memoirs. Readers interested in literary and political history will skim the first, a childhood memoir, to get what they're after in the second's account of life in the Village and in a Connecticut colony of not-yet-acclaimed artists. Although Herbst intimates unflattering complexities, she is charitable to her friends and competitors, euphoric about the life she lived. She seems not to exaggerate: yes, we conclude wistfully, the bohemian life was pretty much what it was cracked up to be. The remaining essays, respectively on McCarthyism and a writers' conference in Russia and on the writers in the Hotel Florida during the Spanish civil war, are illuminating, morally and politically ambivalent, and, in their own way, page-turners. Diane Johnson's model introduction, more absorbed in its subject than in erudition, is engagingly old-fashioned in its concerns with wisdom and character. —*Roland Wulbert*

✔**Heyerdahl, Thor and Ralling, Christopher.**
Kon-Tiki Man: An Illustrated Biography of Thor Heyerdahl.
Chronicle, $35 (0-8118-0026-1); paper, $19.95 (0-8118-0069-5). 336p. index.

The first image the name Thor Heyerdahl brings to mind is that of *Kon-Tiki*, the balsa raft Heyerdahl built and sailed across the Pacific from Peru to Polynesia. But that seminal voyage was only one of Heyerdahl's many revelatory expeditions. This generously illustrated book combines biography with autobiography to tell the dynamic tale of Heyerdahl's life from his childhood fantasies about a Pacific paradise to his latest archaeological endeavor in northwest Peru. Ralling, who accompanied Heyerdahl on one of his journeys, provides the background and the links between events while Heyerdahl's firsthand accounts capture the spirit and excitement of his adventures and discoveries. His quest for knowledge about ancient civilizations and their travels began when he encountered evidence of a seafaring culture that inhabited islands in the Pacific prior to the Polynesians. Never content with theory, Heyerdahl tested his hypothesis by constructing and sailing *Kon-Tiki* and several reed boats based on ancient drawings. He proved not only that ocean travel was possible long before Columbus, but, based on common images found in the ancient stonework of places as diverse and scattered as Easter Island, Peru, and the Maldives, it seems to have been utilized on a global scale for trade and migration. A compelling and provocative account of the work and vision of a man who has changed our perception of the past, —*Donna Seaman*

Hirschfeld, Al.
Hirschfeld: Art and Recollections from Eight Decades.
Scribner, $50 (0-684-19365-5). 304p.

There's darned little biography here, and there certainly isn't any hoity-toity commentary. What there is, and what makes this tome so appealing, is some 200 drawings by the century's greatest caricaturist of performers. Hirschfeld is famous for his long, swooping outlines that seem the perfect artistic fit to dancers and actors in motion, and for his custom of inserting his daughter Nina's name in the zigzags he uses for details, such as hair, creases in clothing and skin, background foliage. (He appends to his signature the number of times "Nina" appears in the drawing—"Hirschfeld 5," "Hirschfeld 3," etc.—making neat puzzles of already entrancing artwork.) The collection starts with his first published drawing and ends with one from 65 years later—i.e., this year. In between are his affectionate cartoon portraits of virtually every really big stage, movie, TV, and concert star, with several nonperformer public figures, playwrights, and theater composers thrown in for good measure. A must for cartoon and theater collections. —*Ray Olson*

✓Holroyd, Michael.
Bernard Shaw: Volume III, 1918–1950: The Lure of Fantasy.
Random, $30 (0-394-57554-7). 544p. index.

Holroyd's vast biography of the man-who-wouldn't-shut-up ends only because Shaw had the bad manners to die in 1951 (at the age of 95). Certainly, both for the biographer and his subject, ending seems somehow inappropriate: Shaw's life reads like a picaresque, and Holroyd doesn't do him the disservice of trying to shape it. Still, all this vastness is vastly interesting, and like many great figures Shaw is often easier to read about than to read. (Who, really, can read the preface to, say, *Heartbreak House*—one of the relatively minor verbosities—without suffering indigestion?) What we find in this volume is the author of the "fantastic" plays of his maturity (beginning with the above-mentioned and including *Saint Joan*), the man irritated by the honors the world wanted to bestow on him, the author of unconsciously fantastic political programs, and the surprisingly genial and playful individual who couldn't understand the concept of cornering on his motorcycle and was generous with everyone who asked him for money. Naturally, a lot went on in the world between 1918 and 1950, and so the backdrop itself seems fantastic. But of course, from another perspective it is all very true; this outstanding document may not appeal to the widest of audiences, but it belongs, nonetheless, in every public library. —*Stuart Whitwell*

Houghton, Norris.
Entrances & Exits: A Life in and out of the Theatre.
Limelight Editions, $29.95 (0-87910-144-X). 432p.

A charming, witty, stylized memoir spanning 80 years of passionate devotion to theatrical life and public service. Houghton's strong ancestral roots in dramaturgy and evangelism account not only for his fascinating choice of career but also for the irresistible enthusiasm with which he draws readers into his world. And what a world it is, studded with luminous names and events rarely brought together in one book, let alone one lifetime: Margaret Sullavan, Adlai Stevenson, Henry Fonda, Jean-Paul Sartre, Konstantin Stanislavski, Laurence Olivier, Yukio Mishima, and the Queen Mother, among many other of the author's illustrious friends and acquaintances. Houghton never fails to delight readers with his often digressive but always information-packed anecdotes about his variegated career as a set designer, director, producer, cofounder of the Phoenix Theatre off Broadway, author, college educator and administrator, and diplomat (he attended the Yalta Conference and served on various governmental commissions). A candid and joyous celebration of a life well lived and a welcome relief from the scandal-filled autobiographies so common among Houghton's contemporaries and associates. —*Mary Banas*

Ishikawa, Yoshimi.
Strawberry Road: A Japanese Immigrant Discovers America.
Kodansha, $18.95 (4-7700-1551-8). 263p.

Ishikawa came to America in 1965 to join his brother on a strawberry farm 80 miles southeast of L.A. Full of grand ideas about America's wealth and greatness, he found reality to be much shabbier, complicated, and circumscribed. He's surprised by the muddle of "Japlish" and the immigrants' clinging to Japanese culture and the hard life his brother leads. Yoshimi labors in the fields in the searing heat, suffers prejudice and embarrassment in high school, and observes California's dependence on illegal Mexican farm workers. Ishikawa's style is straight-shooting as he offers his personal and often original analyses of the plight of Japanese Americans, the competitiveness and rites-of-passage attitude between old and new immigrants, and the problems of mixed Japanese and American marriages. He provides an unusual and articulate perspective on America and Japan in the 1960s. Acute social commentary alternates with memories of the awkwardness of sexual awakening and funny anecdotes including one about meeting Henry Miller. A best-seller in Japan, this story has been made into a film set for international release. —*Donna Seaman*

Kahn, E. J.
Supermarketer to the World.
Warner, $24.95 (0-446-51495-0). 336p. index.

Soybean crusader Dwayne Andreas, CEO of Archer Daniels Midland, is profiled here in a not-fully-authorized biography by longtime *New Yorker* contributor Kahn. In this age of consumer affairs and investigative reporting, there's a mindset that such a flattering (though not obsequiously so) portrait hides flaws. Yet it's difficult to find fault in the epitome of the American Dream: a practical businessman who built the world's largest soybean processor in downstate Illinois and a humanitarian who unflaggingly crusades to save the world from hunger and the environment from the world. Andreas, who socializes with senators, presidents, and other high-powered notables, is equally at ease with Mother Teresa and Pope John Paul II. The Andreas tales—convincing Pepsi and Coke to buy high-fructose corn syrup, proselytizing for the vegeburger, promoting the use of ethanol—not only make entertaining reading but also provide a real sense of what business should be. —*Barbara Jacobs*

✓**Kanigel, Robert.**
The Man Who Knew Infinity: A Life of the Indian Genius, Ramanujan.
Scribner, $24.95 (0-684-19259-4). 448p. index.

Indian mathematician S. Ramanujan Iyengar lived a life so improbable in its decisive events and so abstruse in its governing obsessions that few biographers would even attempt to unlock its enigmas. Kanigel deserves high praise for a work of arduous research and rare insight. Ramanujan's life unfolds on two levels: first, in his personal relationships with family, friends, and other mathematicians in Victorian India, then in Edwardian England; second, in his intellectual exploration of formulas and numbers, an exploration stunning in its raw originality and daunting even to specialists today. Though Kanigel sacrifices rigor and details in describing Ramanujan's professional achievements, he largely succeeds in conveying their significance. Kanigel displays even greater talent in recounting Ramanujan's unlikely friendship with the great British mathematician G. H. Hardy, his sponsor and patron at Cambridge. The collaboration of these two minds, both brilliant yet utterly different in outlook, makes a compelling tale. —*Bryce Christensen*

Keil, Sally Van Wagenen.
Those Wonderful Women in Their Flying Machines: The Unknown Heroines of World War II.
Four Directions Press, $24.95 (0-9627659-0-2). 418p. index.

See p.12.

Kelly, Mary Pat.
Scorsese: A Journey.
Thunder's Mouth, $21.95 (0-938410-79-2). 336p. index.

"My whole life has been movies and religion. That's it. Nothing else," says Martin Scorsese, director of such acclaimed films as *Taxi Driver* and *Raging Bull*. Those two paramount concerns also surface continually in this oral history of the director, based on interviews with some 70 motion picture figures—ranging from actors Robert De Niro and Paul Newman to various scriptwriters, cameramen, and producers who have worked on Scorsese's films—and family members. Their reminiscences cover Scorsese's life from his boyhood in New York's Little Italy (the mob "wiseguys" that surrounded him then show up in 1973's *Mean Streets* and 1990's *GoodFellas*) and his early efforts at New York University's film school, through the filming of his remake of *Cape Fear*. The interviews—particularly extensive remarks from Scorsese himself—provide valuable insight into both Scorsese's technique and working methods and his struggles to produce personal works within Hollywood's studio system (a particularly fascinating section details his decade-long effort to adapt Niklos

Kazantzakis' *Last Temptation of Christ* and the controversy that surrounded the film's release). Although Kelly (who was studying to become a nun when she began her acquaintance with Scorsese in 1966) provides commentary at the beginning of each chapter and occasional connecting passages, there's not enough background for the book to quite work as a biography or a critical guide to Scorsese's output; but the interviews make this valuable source material for anyone studying the director's career an well as a fascinating read for those who simply admire his work. —*Gordon Flagg*

Kennedy, Shirley.
Pucci: A Renaissance in Fashion.
Abbeville, $75 (1-55859-057-9). 214p. index.

The appearance of this biography reflects the current resurgence of interest in fashion's master of kaleidoscopic prints, Emilio Pucci. Kennedy begins with Pucci's Italian/Russian aristocratic background—he is formally the Marchese Emilio Pucci di Barsento—which traces to early thirteenth-century Florence. However, Pucci's life as a sort of medieval doge remained unencumbered by his ivory tower heredity. His fashion notoriety began in 1947 when he was photographed wearing ski clothes of his own design. That same year, after the photo appeared in a 1948 *Harper's Bazaar*, Pucci began designing women's ski wear for Lord & Taylor. His first shop opened in Capri in 1949, and by 1950 Pucci established his couture house. His designs, such as the "capsula" bodysuit, helped women liberate their bodies, as did his introduction of "Emilioform," his trademark fabric used from swim wear to evening dresses. Licensing also entered the line, as Pucci prints decorated pottery, linens, and cars. Although Pucci's popularity waned in the 1970s, the late 1980s brought reemergence as women's clothes became even more uninhibited and once again demanded his signature—electrically colored prints and "elasticized" fabrics. An excellent mix of biography and fashion history. Photos are in color and black and white. —*Janet Lawrence*

King, James.
William Blake—His Life.
St. Martin's, $24.95 (0-312-05292-8). 271p. index.

A new biography of William Blake that aims not only to update his life with new research but also to integrate pertinent literary and artistic discussion. King pinpoints the darker aspects of Blake's personality in describing the demons within and the opposition from without that the poet and artist faced throughout his life. Blake's mystical bent is also examined, as is the complex symbology that resulted in his searing words and images. A series of conflicts over fame, sex, and religion are also effectively studied, but perhaps most persuasive are the connections that King draws between Blake's experiences and his works, which are illuminated in inexorable relation and counterpoint. King's study is well illustrated with many of Blake's designs and with the works of contemporaries who influenced, and were influenced by, the artist. —*John Brosnahan*

Lacey, Robert.
Little Man: Meyer Lansky and the Gangster Life.
Little, Brown, $24.95 (0-316-51168-4). 527p. index.

Something about the perverted, American-dream romanticism of gun-toting, amoral hoodlums and "wiseguys" captures the popular imagination, and America's love affair with the gangster continues to grow, revitalized annually by the myth-making machinery of Hollywood (e.g., *Mobsters* and Warren Beatty's *Bugsy*). In encountering the choice between the fantastic myths and the more banal reality, most would rather believe the myths. Take the case of Meyer Lansky, friend and colleague of Lucky Luciano and Bugsy Siegel. Immortalized as the character Hyman Roth in Mario Puzo's *Godfather*, in reality, Lansky never came close to the embodiment of evil depicted by the press and the federal government. The government's cases against him rested on flimsy or illegally obtained evidence, so Lansky spent very little of his life behind bars. When he died in 1983, no "hidden empire" materialized, leaving his heirs with little. In fact, according to Lacey, Lansky's life was "shadowy, passive, essentially bloodless." Born in Poland around 1902, Lansky came to New York when he was nine. At an early age, he was intrigued by the neighborhood crap games, and soon determined how to profit from them. He graduated to bootlegging during Prohibition, and later made his biggest killing in the casino trade, losing most of his stake when Castro ousted Batista in Cuba in 1959. (Lansky was no killer, but associated with many.) Lacey details Lansky's rather pathetic family life as well as his failed efforts to gain citizenship in Israel. In life, Lansky was modest, extremely meticulous, and, by Mob standards, honest; Lacey's well-documented, thorough, almost sympathetic account will correct many of the misperceptions about an enduringly fascinating bad guy. —*Benjamin Segedin*

Lamar, Jake.
Bourgeois Blues: An American Memoir.
Summit, $20 (0-671-69191-0). 170p.

Lamar's blues are a new verse in an old tune—America's racial conundrum. Born in 1961, he grew up in a black middle-class home, attended private schools, graduated from Harvard, and immediately landed a job as a staff writer for *Time*. Smooth sailing? Not quite. Lamar's tale is anchored in the contrast between his life and that of his extremely conflicted and powerful father. Jake Lamar, Sr., grew up poor but brilliant in segregated Georgia, won a college scholarship, and moved to New York, where he both prospered and weathered economic disaster. His ambition for his son was downright tyrannical, and his belligerence and cruelty toward his wife terrified their children. As Lamar, Jr., sorts out his feelings for his father, he traces his experience with racism in forms at first subtle, and then more overt in the conscienceless 1980s. He muses on interracial relationships and offers a revealing look at the right-wing machinations of *Time*. Important testimony in this era of eroding civil rights, and the first of, we hope, many books from a promising new writer. —*Donna Seaman*

✔**Larsen, Stephen and Larsen, Robin.**
A Fire in the Mind: The Life of Joseph Campbell.
Doubleday, $25 (0-385-26635-9). 656p. index.

Joseph Campbell (1904–87), a courtly scholar of mythology and art, would seem an unlikely celebrity, but his stupendous knowledge about the creation of myths to describe the experiences of life, combined with an unflagging drive to teach, ensured his fame. His books, including *The Hero with a Thousand Faces* and *The Power of Myth*, expand our definition of the spiritual. So vast was Campbell's knowledge and so sure and seemingly effortless his fluency, the simple fact of his humanity was often obscured. This marvelous and vivid biography delivers Joseph Campbell the man as well as the philosopher. The Larsens artfully quote from previously private autobiographical materials and extensive conversations with Campbell's wife of almost 50 years, the dancer and producer Jean Erdman. In addition, they trace the evolution of Campbell's involvement with myth from a boyhood obsession with American Indians. Detailed accounts of his education, travels, and mentors introduce us to a handsome athlete-scholar who adored and respected women (a reciprocal relationship) and taught himself to learn languages and absorb and decode erudite texts at a fantastic rate. Knowing that readers will be curious about whether Campbell's knowledge translated into genuine wisdom about living and what truth lies behind allegations of his anti-Semitism, the Larsens examine his personality from many perspectives, recognizing and analyzing Campbell's ivory-tower syndrome, conservative outlook and scorn for politics, unresolved conflicts with the Judeo-Christian tradition, and emphasis on the individual. Campbell was a strongly opinionated, brilliant, driven, generous, and radiant man who, according to Bill Moyers, did nothing less than give us "the vocabulary for a new effort to define what it means to be spiritual today." A penetrating, moving, and suitably complex portrait. —*Donna Seaman*

✔**Lax, Eric.**
Woody Allen.
Knopf, $24 (0-394-58349-3). 384p.

We think we know all about Woody Allen: he's the hilarious, bumbling, fearful little guy—unlucky in love, often absurd, and always endearing. We watch his films and assume that they're autobiographical. We're wrong. Eric Lax, longtime friend and confidant, takes us behind Allen's cinematic persona to reveal the man and consummate artist. Born Allan Konigsberg, he endured his parents' relentless arguments, got lousy grades, practiced magic tricks for hours, loved baseball and Manhattan, and spent as many hours as possible at the movies. His flare for comedy was obvious by age 16, when he worked after school writing one-liners for newspaper columns. Writing has always been at the heart of Allen's creativity. He wrote for radio and TV until he overcame his stage fright and starting doing stand-up, and, so far, has 20 films to his credit, having also mastered acting and directing. Lax illuminates each stage of Allen's astonishing career with tremendous insight into the art and business of comedy, writing, and filmmaking, highlighting Allen's unflagging discipline, drive, and inventiveness. Fluidly blending anecdote, analysis, background information, and excerpts from scripts, letters, and conversations with Allen and people close to him, Lax has put together a magnetic, often surprising, and vital portrait of a funny, brilliant, complex, enigmatic, and uncompromising man. —*Donna Seaman*

Leider, Emily Wortis.
California's Daughter: Gertrude Atherton and Her Times.
Stanford, $24.95 (0-8047-1820-2). 379p. index.

In this colorful, first-ever biography of Gertrude Atherton, Leider skillfully captures the flair, bravado, and driving ambition of the early twentieth century's most popular female novelist, who, in her time, was better known and read than Sinclair Lewis (Atherton's scandalous 1923 novel *Black Oxen* beat out Lewis' *Babbit* on the best-seller list). Among her friends and acquaintances were such famous writers as Gertrude Stein, Ambrose Bierce, Oscar Wilde, Rebecca West, and George Meredith, whose talents won them lasting fame and immortality, while Atherton—a vain and tireless self-promoter—sank into obscurity despite having written more than 50 books. Why, then, resurrect her name? According to Leider, Atherton and her assertive fictional heroines embodied the "values and fantasies" held by most women of her time. Atherton was, despite her acknowledged narcissism, snobbishness, competitiveness, and cruelty, a sophisticated "new woman" before her time (not to mention a descendant of Benjamin Franklin). While more notable female contemporaries of Atherton are arguably more deserving of a biography, few lived as fascinating a life as Atherton or illuminate so well the interests and proclivities of the average woman of that time. A sharply written biography with an eye to the social and literary history of a threshold era in feminism. —*Mary Banas*

Leo, Richard.
Edges of the Earth: A Family's Alaskan Odyssey.
Holt, $19.95 (0-8050-1575-2). 303p.

For the U.S., it is not so much space as Alaska that is the final frontier, and this book is one man's story of his trials and tribulations in living with, off, and on Alaskan land. But don't think it is about the "glories of nature" and encounters with cute, fuzzy, anthropomorphic critters. Abandoning a comfortable New York existence, Leo was, upon his arrival in wintry Alaska, confronted with frozen smog that hung in the air, and subsequent travels afforded him such strange sights as oil revenue–rich Eskimos watching Cubs baseball via their satellite dish. As much as anything, this is a story of how the isolation of the wilderness can destroy some relationships while nurturing others. A sense of loss permeates the book, due, in part, to the deaths of Leo's father and of his friend, Alexander, as well as the departure of the woman who bore Leo's son, but chiefly to the disappearance of the wilderness under the tracks of snowmobiles and ATVs. Yet there is also joy as Leo and his son learn to live with the plants and animals that are their neighbors. Anyone with idyllic

Biography

ideas of heading north to live in our forty-ninth state should read Leo before departing. Nature, he tells us, is both cruel and beautiful, and only cynics and fools believe it is one or the other. —*Jon Kartman*

Leonard, Hugh.
Out after Dark.
Andre Deutsch, $24.95 (0-233-98474-7). 192p.

Leonard is the most generous of writers as he reminisces on his boyhood in Dalkey, a town outside of Dublin. In this current work, a companion of sorts to his previous book *Home before Night*, Ireland once again is almost palpably re-created by a resonant and elegant use of language all too rare today. Although it may, at times, raise a wealth of emotions, the narrative never manipulates. Instead, with a gently if unflinchingly direct gaze, the author recounts bittersweet memories, as when the fact of his illegitimacy served to complicate his young life. Various threads are woven together: a complex relationship with his mother and father, the naïveté and frustration of early sexual experiences, and an enduring aspiration to become a writer (along with the long-standing desire to quit his job as a government clerk). Leonard's abiding regard for those he writes about combines with captivating humor to make this volume a must for all literary collections. —*Alice Joyce*

✔Lewis, R. W. B.
The Jameses: A Family Narrative.
Farrar, $35 (0-374-17861-5). 596p. index.

Critic and biographer Leon Edel has been "at" eminent American novelist Henry James for years, and undoubtedly no treatment will surpass for comprehensiveness Edel's magisterial biography of the master, published in five parts between 1953 and 1972. But, that said, it is a *broader* context of the spawning and raising of Henry James that is supplied by Lewis' collective biography of three generations of the distinctive James clan, from which sprang not only Henry the novelist but also his brother William the philosopher-psychiatrist and several other interesting, though not as well known, individuals. Lewis, author of the brilliant (and prize winning) *Edith Wharton: A Biography* (1975), follows the fortunes of the James family from the 1789 advent of William James (grandfather of the famous writer and his scholar brother) onto these shores from County Cavan in Ireland, to the death of Henry the novelist in 1916. Sprouts of success soon germinated once the family turned American, and it is the task of defining the nature of "Jamesian" success that Lewis has set for himself—i.e., the set of experiences and body of ideas that, instilled in family members from one generation to another, drove the individuals to accomplish or at least be colorful. This magnificent book has the magical and infinitely compelling ability to be at once workman-like and lyrically beautiful. —*Brad Hooper*

Lewis, Tom.
Empire of the Air: The Men Who Made Radio.
HarperCollins, $25 (0-06-018215-6). 416p.

Three men "of genius, vision, determination, and fascinating complexity" created radio and the industry of radio broadcasting. Lee De Forest, who tried to crown himself the "Father of Radio," invented the vacuum tube. Edwin Howard Armstrong invented devices for amplifying and transmitting signals and eventually created the FM system. And David Sarnoff of RCA turned the "first modern mass medium" into a corporate industry of immense proportions. Lewis energetically delves into the family history, intense personalities, and motivations of each of these men, maintaining a captivating balance between the private and public aspects of each man's life. He follows the paths that brought the three together, resulting, first, in a grueling and acrimonious patent battle between De Forest and Armstrong. Sarnoff, the embodiment of the classic immigrant success story, started out as Armstrong's ally, but eventually put corporate needs first and forced Armstrong into yet another debilitating round of lawsuits, driving the brilliant and honest inventor to suicide. Behind these dramatic confrontations lies the story of the rise of radio from the early wireless communications to the golden age of radio in the 1930s and 1940s. Lewis' ability to combine telling detail with broad strokes enlivens every facet of this story of man and machine. Published in conjunction with a PBS documentary. —*Donna Seaman*

Lindwer, Willy.
Anne Frank: The Last Seven Months.
Pantheon, $22 (0-679-40145-8). 202p.

The title's misleading: very little of this is about Anne Frank, and, except for the title, there's no milking of her romantic legend. An introduction summarizes the facts of her story, there are some photos of her as a child; but most of the book is made up of the oral histories of six Dutch Jewish women who went through experiences similar to Anne's in the last terrible months of the camps. They survived to bear witness, and Dutch filmmaker Lindwer made a prizewinning documentary based on these interviews. Some glimpsed Anne in the camps or on the transports to Auschwitz. Her former best friend met a "broken" Anne at the barbed-wire fence in Bergen-Belsen. One woman told Otto Frank after the war how she saw his daughters, Anne and Margot, die of starvation and typhus. But the book's focus is on each survivor's personal experience. Their accounts don't have the intellectual rigor of the great Holocaust writer Primo Levi, but, like him, they tell without sensationalism of the worst that people can do to each other. There are stories here that make you gasp for breath, like the woman who escaped from the crammed cubicle next to the gas chambers, ran out stark naked under the arm of the guard when the door was opened to throw in the next victim. There are those who stole each other's shoes and those who shared every piece of bread. And there's the woman who sang for Anne Frank and others in the hospital barracks. Always, of course, there are the piles of bodies, the ovens.

Readers may be drawn by the sentiment of the title, but they won't be able to forget the stark truth told here. —*Hazel Rochman*

Lobas, Vladimir.
Taxi from Hell: Confessions of a Russian Hack.
Soho, $20.95 (0-939149-58-3). 304p.

Lobas, a Russian émigré living in New York City, writes and broadcasts a weekly editorial on Radio Liberty but has to find a second job. He is able to get a taxi license with what is essentially a Soviet learner's permit and finds himself at the wheel of a yellow cab having never driven a car before. Yes, he's one of *those* cabbies—the type you have to direct to your destination. Now we get the view from the other side of the partition, and it is an eyeful. Aptly comparing his recitation of experiences to looking through a kaleidoscope, Lobas describes the hustles and shenanigans of cabbies and his experiences with lunatic passengers in colorful, indelible details. His naïveté and zeal lead to some painfully funny and sometimes dangerous situations, but he gets the hang of it, becoming savvy and cynical. Lobas' unusual and compelling memoir not only provides an insider's view of the cutthroat cabbie scene, but also chronicles an émigré's changing perspective on America, a process and viewpoint that tell us a lot about ourselves. —*Donna Seaman*

Lottman, Herbert.
Colette: A Life.
Little, Brown, $24.95 (0-316-53361-0). 336p. index.

French writers are Lottman's specialty. He's written biographies of Flaubert and Camus and now tackles the robust, frequently exhibitionist and controversial Colette (1873–1954). Born into a feud- and poverty-prone rural family, Colette was saucy and adventurous. Her life took an unexpected turn when she married Willy. Critic, man-about-town, and philanderer, Willy ran a Parisian "novel factory," signing the works of others, particularly those written by his cowed, young wife. Together they produced the infamous Claudine series, creating a naughty cultural icon. After their divorce, Colette took to the stage, shocking and delighting audiences with her skimpy attire and lesbian relationships. Writing ceaselessly both as a journalist and as a novelist, Colette experienced both world wars, two more marriages, the birth of a daughter, and a liaison with her stepson. Lottman re-creates the literary climate of Colette's time and substantiates or discredits oft-repeated myths about this energetic, enigmatic, tough, and creative woman. —*Donna Seaman*

Lovell, James Blair.
Anastasia: The Lost Princess.
Regnery Gateway, $24.95 (0-89526-536-2). 492p. index.

Anastasia, the youngest daughter of Czar Nicholas II, is the one that is said to have survived. Although there were several women who claimed to be the grand duchess, one, commonly remembered as Anna Anderson, seemed to have the most valid claim. It was on her life that the movie *Anastasia* was loosely built. Lovell is sure that Anna Anderson was the real Anastasia, and he seems to have the facts to back it up. Relying on previously unpublished material and on his own friendship with Anna Anderson, Lovell not only makes his case, but also demolishes many of the arguments that have been brought forth to prove Anderson was not who she said she was. Surprisingly, though, it is not the Anastasia information that is the most provocative. Lovell also follows the path of a woman who claims to be the fifth daughter of the czar and who says she was given up for adoption at birth because the royal family thought they would be vilified for producing yet another daughter. Though the fifth-daughter theory seems preposterous on the surface (and Lovell admits he cannot prove the woman's identity), this new strain in the Romanov mystery is a tempting one. Lovell is not the smoothest of writers, and though it is by necessity that he injects himself into his story, that device is, at times, disconcerting. His material, however, carries the day. Death, intrigue, secrets, a woman with a haunted past—it doesn't come much juicier than that. —*Ilene Cooper*

MacDonald, Peter and Schwarz, Ted.
The Last Warrior: Peter MacDonald and the Navajo Nation.
Knightsbridge, $21.95 (1-56129-093-9). 416p.

"Dealing with diversity" is a catchphrase in education, business, even law enforcement; this autobiography of the longtime chairman of the Navajo nation (currently in prison appealing tribal-court convictions for bribery, conspiracy, and ethics and election-law violations) suggests just how poorly the U.S. has handled diversity, even in the late-twentieth century, in its dealings with native Americans. A World War II veteran and engineer who headed Hughes Aircraft's Polaris missile project, MacDonald returned to Arizona in 1963, set up the Navajo war-on-poverty programs, was elected the tribe's chairman for three consecutive terms, and was returned to office in 1986. Detractors see MacDonald as the most corrupt Navajo chairman ever; defenders note that different cultures embody different ethical standards and that many of his accusers violated the tribe's ethics more egregiously than the chairman infringed on "white man's rules." Until a definitive history of U.S.-Navajo relations over the past quarter-century is written, this autobiography provides an important corrective to the sanitized official version of the complex cultural, sociological, political, and economic issues at the heart of MacDonald's story. —*Mary Carroll*

✔MacFarlane, David.
Come From Away: Memory, War, and the Search for a Family's Past.
Poseidon, $20 (0-671-74705-3). 224p.

In great loops and sweeps of prose, David MacFarlane captures us in this strange and profound work. It is simultaneously a study of the history and economics of Newfoundland; a musing on the intangibles of heritage; a celebration of northern beauties; a history of a commercial company; and the most sensuously detailed (and therefore most excruciating) narrative of war to appear in decades. Masterfully, MacFarlane lanyards these strains together into a dense prose coil: we move from the unquenchable fires of Newfoundland to an uncle lighting a match, to the lost writings of that uncle—gone to flames in Canada—and back to the uncle's death by unfriendly fire. Newspaper articles, family stories, official history, rumors, and imagination all play their part in this stunning book, one of the best nonfiction titles of the year. —*Pat Monaghan*

MacLaine, Shirley.
Dance While You Can.
Bantam, $22.50 (0-553-07607-8). 303p.

Though metaphysics is never far away in MacLaine's writings, this time out her primary topic is mother-daughter relationships, with Shirley being the meat in a family sandwich that includes her aging mother on one side and her daughter, Sachi, on the other. At 57, MacLaine feels it's time to work out family affairs, especially the hidden agenda dictating that she and her brother, Warren Beatty, were to fulfill their parents' unrealized dreams; the still-unresolved problems stemming from the fact she allowed her husband to raise Sachi in Japan, making MacLaine a part-time parent at best; and the not-so-hidden contempt she felt from her father, who thought it was his job to keep his children safe by discouraging them from taking chances. Whether she's writing about past lives or this one, the best part about MacLaine's books is her openness. She seems to hold almost nothing back, demanding that the reader stand as witness to all her varieties of angst. Remarkably, given the glamorous life MacLaine has led, most readers not only will be able to witness, but also will identify with the actress' worries, fears, and dreams. Even those who have ridiculed Shirley MacLaine for having her head in the clouds will have to admit that this time her feet are firmly on the ground. —*Ilene Cooper*

Martin, Ralph G.
Henry and Clare: An Intimate Portrait of the Luces.
Putnam, $24.95 (0-399-13652-5). 464p. index.

Henry and Clare delves into the chilly marriage of Henry Robinson Luce, the founder of the *Time-Life* magazine empire, and Clare Boothe Brokaw, a former managing editor of *Vanity Fair,* a playwright, a congresswoman, and the first female U.S. ambassador to Italy. According to Martin, the couple were extremely competitive and carried on a social rather than a love relationship (each had numerous affairs). Martin's close examination of their tumultuous marriage serves as a springboard for his in-depth probing into those relationships that did bring the couple satisfaction, namely their business interactions (tellingly, says the author, Luce's passport listed Time, Inc., as his next of kin to be notified in the event of his death). This crisp, vivid account is awash in the events of the day, evoking both the corporate culture established by Luce and the popular culture of the time. Despite his enormous wealth and power, Luce emerges a lonely man in this stunning portrait, and Clare, a brilliant, gorgeous, but disconnected woman. A masterful life study by an expert biographer, whose works include historical biographies of the Windsors, the Roosevelts, and the Kennedys. —*Mary Banas*

Martin, Robert Bernard.
Gerard Manley Hopkins: A Very Private Life.
Putnam, $29.95 (0-399-13610-X). 480p. index.

Another superb literary biography by the author of *Tennyson: The Unquiet Heart* and *With Friends Possessed: A Life of Edward Fitzgerald.* Martin gained access to previously restricted papers and skillfully reveals little-known aspects of poet Hopkins' (1844–89) cloistered life. Hopkins was a gifted student drawn to poetry and the religious life at an early age. As Martin discusses his subject's traumatic conversion from Anglicanism to Catholicism, and then to a Jesuit order, he frankly discusses his repressed sexuality. Fastidious, pious, frail, and "faintly effeminate," Hopkins used the rigors of institutionalized celibacy to combat his attraction to men. He channeled his sensuality into his poetry, which links powerfully erotic imagery with spirituality. This profound conflict exacerbated Hopkins' habitual swings from depression to hyperactivity and affected his health—but also led him to write his revolutionary poems. His poetry was almost incomprehensible in its time, but when it finally reached the public, some years after his death, the world had caught up to his passionate vision. Now we can catch up on our understanding of the man behind the words. An important acquisition for literature collections. —*Donna Seaman*

Martin, William.
A Prophet with Honor: The Billy Graham Story.
Morrow, $25 (0-688-06890-1). 717p. index.

More than a biography of Billy Graham, this book outlines the history of evangelical Christianity and highlights Graham's contribution to it. Martin, himself an evangelist, theologian, and sociology professor who writes about preachers, here presents his scholarly account of U.S. history from an evangelical point of view: Graham is a presence in the lives of Nixon, Johnson, Carter, Martin Luther King, Jr., and in the politics of Vietnam and Watergate. The author succeeds at explaining just how far Graham's influence reaches— the sheer numbers who have heard him speak are staggering. Beginning in the early 1940s, Graham preached in the southeast U.S., then throughout the country and in the British Isles for the International Youth for Christ ministry. Then, when William Randolph Hearst picked up Graham in his newspapers, the preacher became a celebrity—accorded play in all the major media—living up to his reputation as a "soul-winner." Martin echoes the praise of millions who respect Graham for his organizational efforts in spreading the word internationally (even behind the Iron Curtain and in Southeast Asia); for keeping his Billy Graham Evangelistic Association free of financial scandal; for his acceptance of other churches; for his strict adherence to biblical authenticity; and for his devotion to evangelism and an inner circle of lifelong friends. There is a definite audience for this book in public libraries. —*Kathryn LaBarbera*

Biography

Biography

Mashinini, Emma.
Strikes Have Followed Me All My Life: A South African Autobiography.
Routledge, $39.95 (0-415-90414-5); paper, $13.95 (0-415-90415-3). 142p.

Held for six months in 1981 in solitary confinement without trial, apartheid fighter and labor leader Emma ("Tiny") Mashinini found that she couldn't remember her youngest daughter's name. (It's taken years for her to tell anyone about that.) The chapters about her interrogation and imprisonment are the most compelling parts of this book, but Mashinini also writes with quiet passion about her life as a black South African, a woman, and a worker, and about her gradual politicization. Far from sloganizing, she's honest about the changes in herself: how she learned to throw out the skin lighteners, to resist the role of subservient housewife, and to stand up to the white bosses who humiliated her. At the heart of this account is Mashinini's struggle as a trade union leader and feminist to win wage increases and job security for blacks at a time when political activity was viciously suppressed. A fine introduction by Gay Seidman places this autobiography within the context of daily life under apartheid. *—Hazel Rochman*

Mason, Francis.
I Remember Balanchine: Recollections of the Ballet Master by Those Who Knew Him.
Doubleday, $25 (0-385-26610-3). 640p. index.
Perlmutter, Donna.
Shadowplay: Antony Tudor's Life in Dance.
Viking, $24.95 (0-670-83937-X). 366p. index.

The lives, careers, and dances of two choreographers—who, in their individual manners, changed the course of ballet history in the twentieth century—are remembered in two new books.

Mason has collected a composite memoir of Balanchine from his dancers, friends, family, artistic associates, and fellow choreographers. They each recall the impression that Balanchine made on their professional lives and often on their more private moments as well. Teacher, taskmaster, inspiration, and colleague, Balanchine is here recollected with fondness and love. Mason himself pens the opening biographical sketch and laments the fact that he could not include some of the more affecting remembrances that no doubt will surface in other Balanchine volumes.

While Balanchine specialized in plotless neoclassic ballets, Antony Tudor pioneered the dramatic narrative based in human psychology. *Los Angeles Times* dance critic Perlmutter perceives in Tudor's compositions the psychic impulses that made Tudor's private life so troubled and turbulent. Tudor's relationship with dancer Hugh Laing becomes the chart on which Perlmutter maps out a fascinating speculation on just how much of himself Tudor put into his dances and how his choreography reflected his ambivalence about his attraction to women and to men on both the artistic and erotic levels. Along with this psychosexual narrative, the author also provides a revealing account of Tudor's work in both England and the U.S., showing just how manipulative Tudor could be off stage and on. Although Perlmutter sometimes gets the details wrong, her overall impression is conveyed with sureness and conviction. —*John Brosnahan*

McCauley, Michael.
Jim Thompson: Sleep with the Devil.
Mysterious; dist. by Ballantine, $19.95 (0-89296-392-1). 304p. index.

Jim Thompson's life was nearly as bleak as his novels—and anyone who's read *The Killer inside Me* knows just how bleak that is. Dead-end jobs, unpublished manuscripts, pulp novels that didn't sell; critical acclaim when it no longer helped; ill treatment from Hollywood; debilitating alcoholism—Thompson lived the life of the failed writer almost as from a script. McCauley summarizes the sad story effectively, drawing on reminiscences from family members and the author's few friends, as well as excerpts from the novels. He attempts to mix critical commentary with the biographical material, and though he relies far too heavily on overlong, almost chapter-by-chapter synopses, he manages to communicate a strong sense of Thompson's unique fictional world—a teeming cesspool populated, as the psychotic narrator of *Killer* puts it, by "all of us that started the game with a crooked cue." What emerges most forcefully here is Thompson's conviction that his cue was as crooked as his characters'. That notion may have doomed him to living a "lonely, marginal life in a near-vacuum," but it also produced a string of unforgettable novels that, at their fiercest and most painful, evoke the nightmare visions of Louis-Ferdinand Celine. —*Bill Ott*

McFeely, William S.
Frederick Douglass.
Norton, $24.95 (0-393-02823-2). 544p. index.

McFeely's biography of Frederick Douglass supplies a welcome portrait of the slave-turned-abolitionist-orator and a careful reconsideration of his ideas and writings. The chapters on Douglass' youth and adolescence in Maryland establish not only the harshness of the slave life he witnessed firsthand but also the special treatment he was granted by the Baltimore family in which he was raised. The ambivalence that this created for Douglass is examined in detail, particularly in juxtaposition with the dark picture Douglass' own biographical writings give of this period. Douglass' escape on the underground railroad and his activities in the abolitionist movement, both in the U.S. and internationally, are also recorded. In addition, McFeely offers criticism of Douglass as a man who distanced himself from his black heritage. McFeely is also the author of *Grant: A Biography* (1981). —*John Brosnahan*

Mervin, Sabrina and Prunhuber, Carol.
Women: Around the World and through the Ages.
Atomium Books, $34.95 (1-56182-016-4). 240p.

A thoroughly delectable collection of succinct, colorfully illustrated profiles of women, both historic and mythic. Beginning with creation myths and figures such as Ishtar, Gaia, and Pandora, the authors move forward in time to epic heroines like Sita and Helen of Troy, queens of early civilizations, "mothers and mistresses, madwomen and wise women, angels and demons, martyrs and betrayers, warriors and patient wives, women of shadow and light." The roll call is international, with unexpected parallels between cultures, organized into ranks of outlaws, femmes fatales, healers, fighters, writers, artists, stars, the politically powerful, "seekers of wisdom," and even fantasy figures like Sheherazade and Carmen. Each of the vivid 112 sketches places the woman in the context of her times and summarizes her life with respect, humor, and insight. The great diversity of this creative sampling is perhaps best described by name-dropping: Mata Hari, Maria Bonita, Al-Kahina, Pope Joan, Creek Mary, Margaret Sanger, Agatha Christie, Sarah Bernhardt, Billie Holiday, Tz'u-Hsi, Benazir Bhutto, Marie Curie, Simone de Beauvoir . . . A fascinating resource with wide appeal. —*Donna Seaman*

Meyers, Jeffrey.
Joseph Conrad.
Scribner, $27.50 (0-684-19230-6). 416p. index.

Meyers, author of *D. H. Lawrence* and other literary biographies, takes us once again through the adversities and adventures of Conrad's early life: the aristocratic and romantically conspiratorial father, the exile to a penal colony, the lonely teenager's emigration to England, the seaman's travels, the friendships with Henry James, John Galsworthy (another ex-sailor—they seem to have been as prevalent then as literary policemen are today), Ford Madox Ford, and Stephen Crane. Meyers is sympathetic to Conrad's romantic vision of his life despite its clashes with hard facts. We suffer with the proud author until, after 200 pages, we learn that he had to have "maids, gardeners, nurses, tutors, private schools, a London club, cars, holidays abroad and expensive hotels." The intriguing ambivalence of Conrad's life reflects the disparities between the worlds in which he lived. Meyers' account of those worlds is both scholarly and evocative, so that we learn the intriguing trivium that Vladimir Nabokov's grandfather repressed a rebellion incited by Conrad's father, but we also come to understand the political, social, and physical contexts in which the novelist lived. —*Roland Wulbert*

Middlebrook, Diane Wood.
Anne Sexton.
Houghton, $24.95 (0-395-35362-9). 462p. index.

See p.10.

Miller, Ruth.
Saul Bellow: A Biography of the Imagination.
St. Martin's, $24.95 (0-312-03927-1). 416p. index.

Miller, one of Saul Bellow's students in the 1930s and a longtime friend (at least until she wrote this biocritical study of the American writer), offers a densely argued account of just how Bellow's personal life has influenced the literary world of his novels and stories. Miller knows both the private and the public Bellow, and she uses this knowledge to draw parallels between many aspects of her subject's life and work. The impression that Miller has cut close to the bone is confirmed by Bellow's prepublication protests that resulted in a nine-month delay in the book's printing. Bellow has always possessed a rather cantankerous and defensive personal side, and Miller's use of her privileged access may have offended him. The resulting changes in the text appear to be minimal, however, with the revisions not even noting Bellow's swelling number of marriages (five at last count). Still, the portrait of Bellow that emerges here seems drawn from real life and from long experience with both the man and his writing. Appendixes and sources. —*John Brosnahan*

Morgan, Janet.
Edwina Mountbatten: A Life of Her Own.
Scribner, $19.95 (0-684-19346-9). 480p. index.

Edwina Mountbatten (1901–60) was the wife of Lord Louis Mountbatten, who was an auxiliary member of the British royal family, the last viceroy of India before its independence and its split into Hindu and Muslim republics, and an admiral in the Royal Navy. Copious research and a smooth writing style make it possible for author Morgan to weave the facts of Lady Mountbatten's life into a compelling biography of a woman who was more than simply the spouse of a dashing war hero. Edwina, Morgan makes clear, was a beautiful and unconventional heiress—her grandfather was the chief financial adviser to King Edward VII and bequeathed her a fortune—when she married "Dickie" Mountbatten. The marriage was unsuccessful on various levels, but the couple eventually arrived at a truce: they would be great friends greatly respectful of each other. As Morgan depicts it, Edwina changed with World War II, when she took a decided serious turn and became involved in relief work, an interest that remained with her even after war's end. A compelling portrait of a woman of remarkable depth and dimension. —*Brad Hooper*

Morrison, John.
Boris Yeltsin: From Bolshevik to Democrat.
Dutton, $20 (0-525-93431-6). 303p.

Do not let this title deceive: This is not a biography. That is to say, it is not a cradle-to-crutch-style tour of the life of "Yeltsin, the Man." Rather, *Boris Yeltsin* is a study of the recent political struggle to democratize the Communist oligarchy in the Soviet Union (including the August 1991 unsuccessful coup d'état, in response to which this book was rushed to press) and the resistance to and leadership of this struggle within the vast Russian republic. Boris Yeltsin—one-time Communist Party member, now elected president of the Russian republic—demands the focus of this study as the most dynamic reformer in recent history. However, journalist Morrison is not an insider, and though he reconstructs Yeltsin's political rise with a definite favorable bias and a lively style, it is not with any in-depth personal view. Neither does he give any substantive sense of the feelings of the Russian masses who have been Yeltsin's vehicle to power. Yet, as a system narrative—touching briefly on the characters involved (names: Gorbachev, Ligachev, Ryzhkov, Sakharov) and critical events—*Boris Yeltsin* is clearly written and will easily engage the politically minded, even those with limited knowledge of the USSR. —*Angus Trimnell*

Morris, Michael.
Madam Valentino: The Lives of Natacha Rambova.
Abbeville, $29.95 (1-55859-136-2). 256p. index.

A scintillating, fact-filled biography of Natacha Rambova, the dancer-turned-theatrical-designer who was largely responsible for creating Rudolph Valentino's Latin-lover image and subsequent success as a film icon. Morris dispels the many myths surrounding Rambova's (the former Mrs. Valentino) much-glamorized life, especially those fictions portrayed in such popular movies as *The Private Life of Rudolph Valentino* (1975), starring Franco Nero and Yvette Mimieux, and *Valentino* (1977), starring Rudolf Nureyev and Michelle Phillips. Even readers unfamiliar with Rambova will be enthralled by the complexities of this astounding woman's life as vibrantly depicted here. Born Winifred Shaughnessy (1896) in Utah, Natacha transformed her life many times over. First she became a dancer, then a costume designer for Cecil B. deMille, later a set designer, a playwright, an actress, and a Spanish civil war participant, and finally a spiritualist and an Egyptologist who counted Carl Jung among her admirers. But the focal point of the book is Natacha's storied relationship with Valentino, for which she is best remembered. Contains 150 vintage photos, movie stills, and designs by Rambova herself. —*Mary Banas*

Mura, David.
Turning Japanese: Memoirs of a Sansei.
Atlantic Monthly Press, $19.95 (0-87113-431-4). 384p.

Poet Mura, a sansei, or third-generation Japanese American, grew up knowing little about his heritage and feeling even less curiosity. Then he was awarded an artist exchange fellowship and went to Japan for a year. Living in Tokyo and traveling in Japan are revelatory experiences. He struggles self-consciously with the language, feeling that because he looks like a native he should intuitively know how to speak and act like one, yet he also feels the "joy of being part of the visual majority for the first time." His engrossing memoir includes piquant descriptions of Japanese life: the stylish crowds, bright streets, and cramped interiors, as well as perceptions into Japanese etiquette and attitude. His discoveries also lead him to reflect on his childhood, issues of assimilation and racism, his relationship with his white wife, and the dark, raging side of sexuality. An eloquent account of a catharsis that illuminates both personal and societal aspects. —*Donna Seaman*

Murphy, Kenneth.
André Malraux: Man's Fate, Man's Hope.
Grove Weidenfeld, $30 (0-8021-1033-9). 752p. index.

La condition humaine, a phrase that has penetrated almost every language, leapt from Malraux's pen in 1933 and installed his name as a synonym for the literary man of action. A novelist first, he engaged on the Communist end of France's enervating prewar political divisiveness, fought with the antifascist hodgepodge that lost Spain's civil war, and in an astonishing metamorphosis given his leftist pedigree, sided with Charles de Gaulle and his mystical vision of French destiny. Sartre and his existentialist clique never forgave him, but Malraux, as Murphy explains, always claimed it was he, not the Left, who remained consistent. This critical biographer is completely immersed in his subject, respectful of Malraux's firm place in the literary firmament, yet pointedly blunt in condemning personal deficiencies, i.e., his tolerance of the "necessary murder" inherent in the clash of ideologies that consumed his youth. A sensitive and authoritative portrait that will certainly attract students of French history and followers of the Malrauvian way of life. —*Gilbert Taylor*

Nelson, Nancy.
Evenings with Cary Grant: Recollections in His Own Words and by Those Who Knew Him Best.
Morrow, $23 (0-688-10610-2). 384p.

Here's a book that's as charming and likable as its subject—and that's saying a lot. Nelson's relationship with Grant began late in the actor's life. As vice-president of a speakers' bureau, she was the one who talked him into doing a lecture series. Billed as "A Conversation with Cary Grant," these evenings of patter and questions and answers were a big hit throughout the country and occupied most of Grant's time in the months before he died. Drawing on transcripts of some of the conversations, as well as extensive interviews with the likes of Katharine Hepburn, Elizabeth Taylor, and Jimmy Stewart, Nelson evokes the image of a man every bit as delightful as the image audiences saw on the screen—current unfavorable biographies notwithstanding. Nelson even allows Grant to address some of the charges that these books have made: "They all repeat the rumors that I'm a tightwad and a homosexual. Now, I don't feel that either of these is an insult, but it's all nonsense." Whatever the truth of Grant's personal life, fans will remember the moments of pure pleasure he brought them, and this book is surely a fitting celebration of those. —*Ilene Cooper*

✔Nolan, Alan T.
Lee Considered: General Robert E. Lee.
Univ. of North Carolina, $22.95 (0-8078-1956-5). 219p. index.

They won't like it south of the Mason-Dixon Line. Not when an Indianapolis lawyer takes on a severe reassessment of the character and career of "Marse Robert." With all the accuracy of an Alabama sharpshooter, Nolan takes aim at what he calls the Lee orthodoxy and blows away 125 years of largely unchallenged historical notions. Lee, says Nolan, was no closet abolitionist and, in fact, considered the master-slave relationship to be the "correct" one. Most damning is Nolan's dissection of Lee's acumen on the battlefield: yes, he was a master tactician, the author confirms, but Lee's attack grand strategy was fatally flawed, serving only to appease his own audacious nature and offensive military inclinations but doing nothing to further the ultimate Southern goal of frustrating the North into suing for peace. And why, asks

Biography

Nolan, did Lee continue to prosecute the war to the bloody end, at the cost of thousands of young lives, when his correspondence as much as 20 months beforehand indicated his belief that victory was impossible? Finally, Nolan gives us the picture of a bitter postwar Lee, failing to recognize the moral imperative epitomized by the freedman and defensive about the legitimate questions raised regarding the timing of his resignation of his U.S. Army commission and the acceptance of his commission with the Confederacy. Nolan uses sources cleverly to build his case, and he adroitly pits this new "truth" against the words of Lee's historically staunchest promoters. Civil War buffs will be debating this one for years to come. —*Martin Brady*

Orlov, Yuri.
Dangerous Thoughts.
Morrow, $21 (0-688-10471-1). 352p. index.
Shklovsky, Iosif.
Five Billion Vodka Bottles to the Moon: Tales of a Soviet Scientist.
Norton, $19.95 (0-393-02990-5). 288p. index.

An autobiography and collection of anecdotal memoirs by two Soviet scientists who survived the tragedies of their homeland.

Orlov's recap of his full and demanding life in some ways parallels parts of Andrei Sakharov's momentous two-volume work. He begins with a riveting moonlit scene—his grandmother is controlling a horse-drawn sledge with one hand and brandishing an ax at a racing pack of wolves with the other. Natural terrors are replaced by man-made horrors when the family moves to Moscow. Determined to escape their deprived routine and become a physicist, Orlov works his way through school and lands a good job, but his political conscience keeps pace with his scientific achievements and he is soon fired, expelled from the party, and stripped of credit for his publications. Orlov dispassionately recounts his years in Armenia, his marriages, his return to Moscow in the early 1970s, and the full-fledged dissident activities that landed him in prison and labor camps until his surprise release in America as part of the Daniloff exchange.

Shklovsky (1916–85) strikes a different tone. An intuitive and brilliant thinker who contributed mightily to the field of radio astronomy, he wrote these tragicomic "real-life tales" for his friends and colleagues. His autobiographical stories are fresh, vivid, and gleeful in spite of his anger and sorrow for those who suffered the wrenching and cruel absurdities of the Stalin era. Shklovsky was Jewish, outspoken, mischievous, and extremely lucky. He tells charming anecdotes peopled by the likes of Sakharov, Carl Sagan (with whom he coauthored, long distance, a book about extraterrestrial life), and a rabbi who manages to stay true to his beliefs against great odds. Sporadically granted travel privileges resulted in memorable if not downright farcical trips to Paris, Prague, and New York and a riotous expedition to Brazil in 1947 to observe a total eclipse of the sun. Each tale is driven by amazing coincidences, powerful personalities, sudden revelations, and irrepressible humor and zest for life. A unique perspective on notoriously horrendous times. —*Donna Seaman*

Pearson, John.
The Private Lives of Winston Churchill.
Simon & Schuster, $27.50 (0-671-63153-5). 432p. index.
See p.29.

Perlmutter, Donna.
Shadowplay: Antony Tudor's Life in Dance.
Viking, $24.95 (0-670-83937-X). 366p. index.
See p.50.

Pfaff, Daniel W.
Joseph Pulitzer II and the Post-Dispatch: A Newspaperman's Life.
Pennsylvania State Univ., $29.95 (0-271-00748-6). 448p. index.

Pfaff's biography of the son of Joseph Pulitzer, who founded the vast and mighty newspaper empire, is somewhat lackluster compared with Martin's buoyant book, but it's no less exhaustive. We learn in almost microscopic detail about the ins and outs of the life of the least-known Pulitzer, who, according to the author, shunned publicity. Yet it was the seemingly irresponsible, at least in the eyes of his father, Joseph II who made his father's papers, especially the *St. Louis Post-Dispatch,* rank among the nation's most distinguished. Moreover, he was a benevolent, highly ethical publisher, we learn, who practiced the kind of principled journalism one reads about only in textbooks. While Pfaff's is an interesting study on how such an obscure and untrained personage could rise to the top of his field, the author's stilted and sometimes infelicitous use of language makes the reading hard going. Mainly readers with a strong interest in newspaper history will be drawn to this volume, which is enlivened by illustrations, numerous quotes, and lengthy excerpts from letters—all of which capture the flavor of the time (early nineteenth century) and of the main players in this drama. —*Mary Banas*

Pinkwater, Daniel.
Chicago Days / Hoboken Nights.
Addison-Wesley, $17.95 (0-201-52359-0). 175p.

Like *Fish Whistles*, this new book for grown-ups by the prolific and ever-popular children's author is a collection of pieces originally aired on National Public Radio's "All Things Considered." In his preface, Pinkwater expresses surprise that this volume turned out to be a "fragmentary autobiography," but that's what makes it so very good. Episodes from his childhood introduce us to his cryptic, intimidating father, the thrills and discomforts of Chicago, and Pinkwater's first ill-fated venture into art. Endearingly free of vanity, he tells us that he "used to be a jerk, a wimp, and a weenie"; but as we laugh with him over incidents from his adolescence and peculiar but happy college years, we know that he's actually talented, funny, and smart—a real mensch. His Hoboken stories are poignant and absolutely hilarious, as fresh and unexpected as his quirky children's books. Pouncing on the kernel of absurdity hidden in every situation, Pinkwater gently reminds us of what really counts. —*Donna Seaman*

Pogrebin, Letty Cottin.
Deborah, Golda, and Me: Being Female and Jewish in America.
Crown, $22.95 (0-517-57517-5). 400p.

Pogrebin, best known as a founder of *Ms.* magazine, confronts head-on her struggles as a feminist to maintain a sense of Judaism—a religion not considered to be on the leading edge where women's issues are concerned. While Pogrebin adopts a heartfelt confessional tone, especially when discussing family secrets and her reasons for eschewing religion for 20 years, she never gets lost in a morass of feelings; instead, she views both her religion and her political stance clearly and is able to see the positive and negative in each. Though raised in a religious environment, Pogrebin turned away from Judaism when, because she was not a man, she was not allowed to say the traditional prayer for the dead following the death of her mother. The effects of this incident, combined with her burgeoning sense of feminism, made her return journey to religion a long and arduous one. She combs the Bible looking for role models and then looks further into other eras. She also turns her feminist eye on Israel, whose government restricts where women can worship at the Wailing Wall. In fact, there is almost no issue, from Christmas in America through race relations to the Palestinian question, that Pogrebin doesn't tackle, viewing each as both a feminist and a Jew. The double vision that occasionally results in this process is both enlightening and perplexing. Pogrebin works very hard to make sense of what she sees, and her thought-provoking examination serves as a road map for others embarking on similar journeys. —*Ilene Cooper*

Rappleye, Charles and Becker, Ed.
All American Mafioso: The Johnny Rosselli Story.
Doubleday, $19 (0-385-26676-6). 384p.

Johnny Rosselli's career was a kind of perverse affirmation of the American dream. He grew up desperately poor in Boston and left school early to go to work—as a hoodlum and bootlegger. Chronic respiratory ailments forced him to leave Chicago, where he'd become a favorite of Al Capone. Moving to Los Angeles, he became friend, confidant, or neighbor of movie-industry personalities as diverse as Marilyn Monroe, Harry Cohn, and Annette Funicello. Rosselli was hardworking, smart, and likable. Later, he adopted the manners and speech of a gentleman. People who knew him said he *was* a gentleman. He became the "Henry Kissinger of the mob," an ambassador and troubleshooter dispatched to Las Vegas, Havana, anywhere the mob needed his talents. He also became procurer for JFK, the CIA's Mafia point man in the plots to kill Fidel Castro, and collaborator with Bobby Baker, whose schemes almost brought down the Johnson administration. *All American Mafioso* is a grand book, and it's carefully researched—Rappleye is a journalist, Becker a private investigator who once helped prepare Rosselli's legal defense. —*Thomas Gaughan*

Ratushinskaya, Irina.
In the Beginning.
Knopf, $23 (0-394-57141-X). 320p.

Dissident poet Irina Ratushinskaya has told the ennobling story of her years in a harsh Soviet camp in the celebrated *Grey Is the Color of Hope.* Here she reaches further back, sharing memories of her childhood and the events that led inexorably to her imprisonment. Ratushinskaya grew up in Odessa, a precocious and gutsy child surrounded by adoring adults. After starting first grade in 1961, she soon realizes that school is rank with propaganda. The compulsory atheistic instruction confirms her fledgling belief in God, which in turn teaches her to think for herself, to face cruelty with dignity, and that "there is nothing more terrible than feeling ashamed of yourself in solitude." Poems begin to come to her at a very young age and keep pace with her political consciousness and commitment. Ratushinskaya's resonant memoir offers us an intimate perspective on the mind and heart of a poet of freedom in stark contrast to a brutal and insane world. Her poems are collected in *Pencil Letter.* —*Donna Seaman*

Richardson, John and McCully, Marilyn.
A Life of Picasso, Volume I: 1881–1906.
Random, $39.95 (0-394-53192-2). 521p. index.

Richardson, a modern art scholar published regularly in various journals including *The New York Review of Books*, has undertaken a monumental task: a four-volume biography of Picasso (perhaps the only modern artist with a life complex and spicy enough to fill so many pages). Picasso, Richardson's friend and neighbor, encouraged the endeavor, as curious as anyone about the mystery of his prodigious creative power. Accompanied by 675 black-and-white photographs, Richardson's carefully researched narrative patiently and insightfully traces the outlines of Picasso's first 26 years, from his precarious birth to the brink of success. He debunks well-worn myths, sticking to the facts about pivotal events in the artist's childhood that gave shape to his manipulative, magnetic, and self-dramatizing personality. Richardson analyzes Picasso's early works, spotlighting the lifelong link between sex and art and his pursuit of the new in both realms, and shadows him on his trips back and forth from his native Spain to Paris, the city of poets, opium, and whores, providing vivid portraits of his lovers and peers. Picasso has had many biographers, including ex-wives, but Richardson may well prove to be the most objective and well grounded. At any rate, he's off to a good start, guaranteeing an audience for future installments. —*Donna Seaman*

Riordan, James and Prochnicky, Jerry.
Break on Through: The Life and Death of Jim Morrison.
Morrow, $20 (0-688-08829-5). 529p.

Morrison was a navy brat who suffered the usual alienation and insecurity of a kid without roots. His family moved constantly, and his father, who eventually became a rear admiral, was absent more often than present. Morrison characterized himself as a child that "didn't get enough love." He found solace in books, writing poetry, and in "hell-raising and attention-seeking behavior," a pattern that dominated his short, incendiary life. Riordan and Prochnicky write lucidly and sensitively about Morrison's school years, tracking his influences: Nietzsche, Kafka, Blake, Baudelaire, Kerouac, even *Mad* magazine, and later Greek theater. Unlike David Dalton's terrifically frenzied prose poem, *Mr. Mojo Risin': Mr. Jim Morrison, the Last Holy Fool*, this is a studied, perceptive, and thorough consideration of the forces that fueled Morrison's complex, tormented personality and inspired his devouring creativity. The authors discuss Morrison's psychedelic vision quests and cathartic performance style in terms of classic shamanism and suggest that Morrison's trances or "possession" contributed to the severity of his alcoholism and infamous, infuriating, Dr. Jekyll/Mr. Hyde behavior. They reveal the man within the "young lion," leather-clad sex symbol as well as the bearded, overweight barfly, and within him they find the best and worst of his era. This book isn't part of the retro-craze for the 1960s, but an examination of one man's immersion into the dark and dangerous aspects of life and the poetry he flung back to us from the other side. Previously unpublished photographs are included. —*Donna Seaman*

Rollyson, Carl.
The Lives of Norman Mailer.
Paragon House, $26.95 (1-55778-193-1). 358p. index.

Rollyson, a professor of literature and art history, is the author of best-selling biographies of Marilyn Monroe, Lillian Hellman, and Martha Gellhorn. His current biography, also sure to be a hit with readers, distills information from two other current books on Norman Mailer's life (*Mailer: A Biography* by Hilary Mills and *Mailer: His Life and Times* by Peter Manso) and then goes beyond those works by including new facts and insights gleaned from archival materials, such as Mailer's manuscripts and letters, and from interviews with Mailer's mother, friends, acquaintances, and Harvard classmates, as well as colleagues Max Lerner and William Styron, among others. But what really sets this book apart is Rollyson's provocative critiques of Mailer's major novels, essays, and reportage and the author's attempt to link Mailer's art with real events in Mailer's life in order to prove his thesis that this larger-than-life and highly controversial, if not downright repugnant, contemporary writer has invented multiform identities for himself precisely to *be* controversial. In Rollyson's view, Mailer equates rebelliousness with individuality, and Rollyson makes a very good, if not airtight, case to help explain Mailer's erratic behavior and fascination with violence (Mailer exulted in stabbing his second wife, Adele). A raw, earthy account that, while very well written, grates on the reader in its apologia-like defense of its subject. —*Mary Banas*

Rose, June.
Modigliani: The Pure Bohemian.
St. Martin's, $22.95 (0-312-06416-0). 264p. index.

see p.15.

✓Roth, Philip.
Patrimony: A True Story.
Simon & Schuster, $19.95 (0-671-70375-7). 238p.

In this portrait of his father's dying, Roth celebrates the ordinary Jewish immigrant experience in all its fierce "survivorship." Diagnosed with a massive brain tumor at 86, widower Herman Roth refuses to shut up, relentlessly *hocking* (badgering and bludgeoning) everyone around him for their own good. As the son drives his father to hospitals and doctors, back and forth through the ruined old Newark immigrant neighborhoods, Roth realizes that the interminably repeated family stories are his father's "sacred text... All those *people*, all that *dying*, all their *work*." Not that survival is pretty: the sadness for the decayed inner-city neighborhood hardly extends to the people who live there now. Roth's writing is casual, anecdotal, sometimes flat, with none of the barriers of some of his recent work about the writer writing about the writer. Of course, the very lack of self-consciousness is artful: even while the writer is crying in his room unable to write, we know he's going to write about that, just as he's going to find symbols of patrimony when he cleans up his "father's shit" after a bathroom accident. Yet facts do hold archetype, the elemental is surreal—whether it's an X ray of the brain or the old man holding up the paralyzed side of his face in the hope that it will stay up. The writer's triumph is that he does give his father life; the son remembers and creates his father in his story. —*Hazel Rochman*

Rubin, Nancy.
Isabella of Castile: The First Renaissance Queen.
St. Martin's, $29.95 (0-312-05878-0). 496p. index.

We remember Queen Isabella as the sponsor of Columbus' landmark 1492 voyage across the forbidding Atlantic—a journey that enabled Spain to claim vast tracks of land to "civilize." But that's probably about all many of us can recall about this consequential figure in European history. That will change for readers of Rubin's artful, sensitive biography, which captures the woman and the era wonderfully. The Iberian peninsula in the fifteenth century was composed of a handful of kingdoms, and Isabella, as inheritor of the throne of Castile, gave birth to modern Spain by marrying the king of Aragon, Ferdinand. While showing how Ferdinand and Isabella put Spain on the international map, Rubin also portrays their less admirable sides: the two of them instituted the dreadful Inquisition, and they expelled all Jews from the land. Rubin does not defend these action but explains them in terms of the queen's determination to make her country pure in the Christian faith. A prerequisite for understanding Isabella is understanding the period, and Rubin excels at delineating both. —*Brad Hooper*

Sakharov, Andrei.
Moscow and Beyond, 1986–1989.
Knopf, $19.95 (0-394-58797-9). 158p.

In Sakharov's compelling *Memoirs*, he told the story of his life from childhood through seven years of exile in Gorky. This volume, completed just

Biography

before his death in December 1989, picks up the tale with Sakharov's triumphant return to Moscow in 1986. Relieved to be free, anxious to see family members, and still dreaming of science, Sakharov has little time to reflect on personal affairs. In great demand with the media, he plunges into a "hurly-burly life" of interviews and participation in the USSR's new political forums. In carefully considered prose, Sakharov shares his views of Gorbachev, the myriad difficulties inherent in perestroika, SDI, the Armenian-Azerbaijanian conflict, and Tiananmen Square. This belongs on the shelf with the first volume, though, sadly, it will be Sakharov's last. The world has lost an invaluable interpreter of current affairs and a truly generous, moral man of power. —*Donna Seaman*

Sapinsley, Barbara.
The Private War of Mrs. Packard.
Paragon House, $19.95 (1-55778-330-6). 256p.

Sapinsley presents the first biography of social reformer Elizabeth Packard (1816–97). Packard was intelligent, intense, and confident, but she married Theophilus Packard, a narrow-minded, coldhearted, fundamentalist Calvinist minister who could not abide her questioning of Calvinist doctrine. His incredible rigidity drove him to the extreme of having his wife and the mother of his five children committed to an Illinois insane asylum. Elizabeth survived three years of internment by improving the institution's bleak conditions and writing zealously about the need for laws to protect the rights of women and control the abuses of commitment. Upon her release, Theophilus imprisoned her at home and conspired to send her to another asylum. In a series of Hitchcock-like events, Elizabeth foiled this attempt and took her husband to court, where her sanity was "proven." She then made her private battle public, lobbying successfully for changes in commitment laws in many states. Sapinsley mines all the riches inherent in this compelling drama: the struggle between the sexes, religious intolerance, the arbitrariness of definitions of insanity, and the barbarity of the treatments for mental illness, creating a vivid and stirring portrait. —*Donna Seaman*

Schickel, Richard.
Brando: A Life in Our Times.
Atheneum, $21.95 (0-689-12108-3). 221p. index.

Time's regular film critic and biographer of other movie greats such as Cary Grant and D. W. Griffith approaches Marlon Brando's erratic, eccentric, and largely unarticulated life story with respect, insight, and empathy. Wielding consistently subtle analysis in spirited prose, Schickel deftly cuts from biographical information to pointed descriptions of Brando's personality and performances. Working from the convincing assumption that Brando has exhibited the classic behavioral traits of an adult child of alcoholics, Schickel unlocks the paradox of Brando's inconsistency: his early successes like *A Streetcar Named Desire* and *On the Waterfront* giving way to "fourteen consecutive flops" followed by a period of reclusion and a triumphant return with *The Godfather* and *Last Tango in Paris*. By examining Brando's career in relationship to trends in the movie industry and the context of his generation—those who came of age right after World War II and had to slog through the blandness and hypocrisy of the 1950s—Schickel is able to assess Brando's seminal contribution to the art of acting as well as his ambivalence toward it. The author discusses Brando's political activism and messy private life with understanding and restraint, concluding with a sensitive look at how Brando has responded publicly to his family's recent tragedy. A remarkably perceptive, searching, and illuminating look at Brando the man and the performer, as well as his loyal audience. —*Donna Seaman*

Scott, Kesho Yvonne.
The Habit of Surviving: Black Women's Strategies for Life.
Rutgers Univ., $19.95 (0-8135-1646-3). 225p.

This intriguing book explores, through four lengthy oral histories, the ways in which black women survive and succeed—and how their very success strategies may finally limit them. Scott, an essayist and sociologist, documents the "chorus line" of black women's lives, exploring the steps taught by mother to daughter, the "habits of survival and denial" that work to permit success but not revolution. There is the societal dance, in which some deeply held values (feminism, for one) must be abandoned in order to take advantage of limited employment opportunities: "keeping a job is more important than making a point." There is the black community dance, where women are expected to be nurturers and protectors, "to commit themselves to lifelong service to other people." And there is the family dance, where black women's "habits of survival have become inseparable from their roles as mothers." Finally, most complexly, there is the individual dance of identity, in which steps learned in the other arenas may inhibit as well as assist. The well-told biographies that are the centerpiece of this book illuminate these stages and offer dynamic insights into the process of transcending while honoring the past. —*Pat Monaghan*

Shklovsky, Iosif.
Five Billion Vodka Bottles to the Moon: Tales of a Soviet Scientist.
Norton, $19.95 (0-393-02990-5). index. 288p.

See p.56.

Slater, Robert.
Warrior Statesman: The Life of Moshe Dayan.
St. Martin's, $27.95 (0-312-06489-6). 480p. index.

Thanks to a Vichy French bullet in World War II that took his eye and nearly his life, Dayan donned the black patch that eventually rivaled the Star of David as the internationally recognized symbol of the Jewish state. The aggressive architect of Israel's victorious wars in 1956 and 1967, he was chastened by the bloody riposte Egypt and Syria delivered in 1973 and consequently spent the last decade of his life negotiating the tortuous path to peace. Slater's portrait, the first since Dayan died 10 years ago, displays the clarity of his martial virtues and prowess, alongside the opacity of his personal

Biography

life, which was clouded by innumerable bed partners and disinherited children. Warts and all, this biography has automatic appeal to patrons interested in the man who was the embodiment of Israel's gladiatorial image. —*Gilbert Taylor*

Smith, R. Dixon.
Ronald Colman, Gentleman of the Cinema: A Biography and Filmography.
McFarland, $35 (0-89950-581-3). 322p. index.

One of the great movie stars when movie stars were embodiments of the virtues, Ronald Colman was the quintessence of the debonaire: gentle, suave, lighthearted—and thoroughly though unostentatiously manly. He was the most polished of swashbucklers in *The Prisoner of Zenda* (1937), the most gallant of rogues in *If I Were King* (1938), the most romantic of adventurers in *Lost Horizon* (1937) and, in a lighter vein, in the insouciant *Devil to Pay* (1930). He was Sydney Carton in *A Tale of Two Cities* (1935) so memorably that there virtually can be no other. He had the most beautiful speaking voice, period. Smith, in prose that answers Colman's warmth with its own, eschews the tortuous visual explication of many film studies in favor of detailed synopses of plot and dialogue. So doing, although he may strike some cinéastes as superficial, he makes abundantly clear one of Colman's great strengths—his taste for good scripts that were by turns graceful, witty, sharp, and moving. Smith's loving account of Colman's career is worthy of a place in every thoroughgoing film studies library. —*Ray Olson*

Somerset, Anne.
Elizabeth I.
Knopf, $30 (0-394-54435-8). 652p. index.

The Tudor age remains a popular field for academicians to till, and it is of perennial fascination for popular biographers and readers as well. All those who find themselves open to one more presentation on sixteenth-century English history by scholar or otherwise will receive with gratification this life of the great Tudor queen. In her Book-of-the-Month alternate selection, Lady Somerset not only builds up considerable detail with precision and color, resulting in a rigorously accurate as well as gorgeous tapestry, but in the process offers some fresh thinking about various factors and actions of Elizabeth, queen and woman, including the influence on her sense of identity played by the execution and infamy of her mother, Anne Boleyn, and, toward the end of her reign, her refusal to name a successor. Even readers essentially unfamiliar with the dynamic personalities of the Tudor era—but eager to make amends—would do well to start their quest for knowledge with this book. —*Brad Hooper*

✔Spurling, Hilary.
Paul Scott: A Life.
Norton, $24.95 (0-393-02938-7). 464p. index.

Once again Hilary Spurling proves to be an exceptional literary biographer. *Ivy: The Life of Ivy Compton Burnett* was highly praised, and now, in this first

64

biography of Paul Scott (1920–78), Spurling reveals the tormented man behind the charming public facade. Quotes from letters and interviews and keen readings of Scott's poems, plays, and 13 novels link events in his life and aspects of his often split personality to characters and plots, particularly in the Raj Quartet and his last book and winner of the Booker Prize, *Staying On.* Spurling vividly recaptures the details and atmosphere of each phase of Scott's hectic life: his difficult, unusual childhood, the unforgettable years in India, experiences as a popular literary agent, ill health, family traumas, and his slow, exhausting rise to recognition. To many people, Paul Scott was dazzling and fun, but privately Scott (who early on repressed his homosexuality, married, and fathered two daughters) was oppressive and self-absorbed, devoting himself wholly to writing, drinking heavily, and traveling often. In sum, this skillfully constructed biography is an archetypal rendering of both sides of the artistic experience: the toll it extracts from the artist and his intimates as well as the triumphant achievements of sustained, even heroic, creative effort. —*Donna Seaman*

✓Sterling, Dorothy.
Ahead of Her Time: Abby Kelley and the Politics of Antislavery.
Norton, $22.95 (0-393-03026-1). 384p. index.

Gratitude is in order: we thank Dorothy Sterling for rescuing Abby Kelley from obscurity. Kelley (1811–87) is an American hero. Born into a large Quaker family, she was honest, disciplined, modest, fearless, and, to the chagrin of her critics, quite pretty. Kelley ate and dressed simply and believed that women had a right to be single and a responsibility to act on their convictions. She joined an antislavery society while still in her twenties and dedicated the rest of her life to the fight for human rights. Her speaking career began spontaneously when she took the stage at an antislavery rally to rebuke a violently disruptive crowd of men outraged by women lecturing in public. This was the first of many dramatic encounters. Kelley became a powerful and controversial speaker and skilled fund-raiser and organizer. She traveled all over New England and the Midwest, often alone, campaigning for the end of slavery. As Sterling tracks the path of Kelley's remarkable life, she illuminates the factious politics within the abolitionist movement and the volatile yet inevitable linkage with women's rights. A compelling and moving biography of an extraordinary woman: a loving daughter, wife, and mother and a courageous and tireless activist. —*Donna Seaman*

Sugden, John.
Sir Francis Drake.
Holt, $29.95 (0-8050-1489-6). 355p. index.

Drake's life is so closely bound to the romance of fledgling English nationalism that it is difficult to separate in the stories about him—the descent on Spanish treasure fleets, the circumnavigation of the globe, the singeing of the king of Spain's beard with the raid on Cadiz, the calm finish to a game of bowls before the defeat of the Armada in 1588—the genuine

Biography

65

Biography

history from myth. Sugden overcomes the obstacle in admirable fashion in this work of scrupulous scholarship. By the end, as Caribbean waters close over Sir Francis' lead coffin in 1596, the reader begins to understand the secret of his charisma and ambition. His piratical avarice cannot be ignored (which included involvement in the slave trade), but neither can his deep conviction that he fought and explored for faith and queen. Sugden's strong story, in which one can almost hear the ropes strain, the ship timbers creak, and the cannon fire, should find a port in most public libraries. —*Gilbert Taylor*

✔Swados, Elizabeth.
The Four of Us: The Story of a Family.
Farrar, $19.95 (0-374-15219-5). 223p.

Elizabeth Swados is a remarkable woman. A composer, director, and writer, she has won numerous awards for her spiritually rich, internationally flavored music. Here, her considerable talents are channeled into a soul-searching, cathartic, and ruthlessly honest account of her tumultuous and tragic family history. The Swados family struggled mightily with a mystifying blend of genius and madness. Elizabeth's bright, hugely ambitious father and beautiful, thwarted, suicidal mother did not get along, a situation exacerbated by their bewildering first child. Swados describes her schizophrenic brother's brilliant, erratic, and bizarre behavior, her thralldom to him, and her parents' anger, shame, despair, and denial with great care and clarity. As Swados examines her family's suffering, focusing in turn on each member, she reveals her exotic and intense methods of survival and her daring search for meaning, the forces that made her an artist. Extremely moving, tender, and life affirming. —*Donna Seaman*

Taviani, Paolo Emilio.
Columbus: The Great Adventure: His Life, His Times, His Voyages.
Crown/Orion, $20 (0-517-58474-3). 288p. index.

Taviani, a world-renowned Columbus scholar, has honed his four-volume work on the explorer down to a trim, descriptive, and dramatic account of Columbus's life, character, and achievements. He stresses Columbus' Genoese roots and early love for sea travel as well as his uncanny sense of smell and an almost mystical feel for nature and the sea. Dismissing the tired myth that Columbus was the first to realize that the earth is round, Taviani explains that Columbus' "first" was to stake his life on the belief that the other side of the globe was reachable and inhabitable, and that by sailing west you would reach the legendary East and the riches of Cathay and India. As Columbus' tale of ambition, adventure, and obstinance unfolds, his limitations and contradictions emerge. Brilliant at sea, he was a sorry politician and weak leader on land. The immensity of his discovery was clouded by his stubborn insistence on having found Asia in spite of evidence to the contrary, obsession with gold, and aggression toward the natives of the lands he claimed for Spain. While stating, repeatedly, that Columbus' encounter with America is "the greatest discovery in history," Taviani doesn't shrink from painfully specific accounts of all that went wrong once these brave travelers came ashore. —*Donna Seaman*

Tomalin, Claire.
The Invisible Woman: The Story of Nelly Ternan and Charles Dickens.
Knopf, $25 (0-394-57959-3). 320p. index.

In his monumental biography, *Dickens*, Peter Ackroyd argues that Charles Dickens' affair with actress Ellen ("Nelly") Ternan was not sexual; Claire Tomalin, in this ground-breaking look at Ternan's heretofore hidden life, not only disagrees but believes it likely that Ternan bore at least one child by Dickens. There is no ultimate proof of either position, but what is abundantly clear is that the two were utterly devoted to one another in the years between 1857, when Dickens first met the teenage Ternan, and 1870, when the novelist died. As Tomalin stresses throughout, this devotion came at a stiff price to both parties: for Ternan, who was forced to live "a life of nervous isolation" or be exposed as that Victorian nightmare, the scarlet woman, and for Dickens, who endured the emotionally and physically torturous rigors of a split life. In portraying Ternan as a kind of feminist heroine, Tomalin finds both the injustice of the Victorian attitude toward actresses ("the assumption . . . seemed to be that the exercise of any talent by a woman in public was a form of prostitution") and an ironic counterpoint to the stereotypical treatment of women in nineteenth-century fiction. Nelly emerges forcefully as "the obstinate representative of all the erring women who must have kicked against the fate decreed for them in Victorian England." Perhaps Nelly would also kick at Tomalin's reluctance to see her years with Dickens as a love story. Though we have no way of knowing what Dickens and Ternan shared in private, Tomalin seems to prefer viewing her heroine as trapped in Dickens' embraces rather than relishing them. She may be right, but why not see Nelly and Charles as passionate lovers defying an age that was afraid of passion. It's much prettier that way. —*Bill Ott*

Weisskopf, Victor.
The Joy of Insight: Passions of a Physicist.
Basic Books, $26.95 (0-465-03678-3). 400p.

A scientist who helped make the world's first atom bomb here recounts his life story. Weisskopf conveys the challenges and thrills of his profession for general readers who could never fathom its technical formulas. Though self-congratulation intrudes more than once, the narrative unfolds with clarity and humor, revealing a balanced man whose scientific pursuits have not stunted his appreciation for music and nature. A Viennese-born Jew, Weisskopf learned hard truths about politics as well as physics in prewar Europe before immigrating to the U.S. in 1937. With unsettling candor, Weisskopf recalls little ethical reflection among his colleagues when making the first doomsday weapons. As part of an effort to rectify that lapse, the author concludes by warning of the perils of modern warfare. In their mission

Biography

to broaden public understanding of science, the Alfred P. Sloan Foundation has spent its resources well in subsidizing this book. —*Bryce Christensen*

✔Wilford, John Noble.
The Mysterious History of Columbus: An Exploration of the Man, the Myth, the Legacy.
Knopf, $24 (0-679-40476-7). 336p. index.

Wilford, author of *Mars Beckons* among other acclaimed works, probes deeply into the mysteries and riddles of Columbus's life, stressing the subjectivity and changeability of historical accounts. As he analyzes the sources historians have traditionally used, including Columbus' own undependable writings, he strips away biases and assumptions to reveal a shaky framework of facts and enigmas. In spite of concerted efforts by researchers and archaeologists, we still don't know where Columbus landed on his first voyage. What we do know is that his thoughts ran to conquest and exploitation when he encountered the people of the Caribbean and that his obsession with reaching Asia blinded him to the immensity of his unintentional discovery. Wilford's investigation is broad and creative, encompassing the atrocities of the Spanish and the religious superiority used to justified them, the "unwitting germ warfare" that wiped out tens of thousands of Indians and brought syphilis to Europe, and the reasons for naming the new continent after Amerigo Vespucci. His portrait of Columbus is of a man driven by the conviction that he was "God's messenger" destined to find Earthly Paradise, an ironically medieval inspiration for the man who "ushered in the modern age." Brilliantly reasoned, researched, and expressed, Wilford's interpretation recognizes that because Columbus's voyages have been as globally significant as the separation of the continents, they will continue to "serve as a barometer" of our collective self-image. He reminds us, however, that Columbus was only human, as contradictory and imperfect as the rest of us. —*Donna Seaman*

Williams, Terry Tempest.
Refuge: An Unnatural History of Family and Place.
Pantheon, $21 (0-679-40516-X).

In this poetic memoir, Terry Tempest Williams intertwines the somber tales of her mother's death from cancer and that of the slow and destructive flooding of a wildlife sanctuary by the Great Salt Lake's waters. That both losses take time makes them more wrenchingly poignant: the burrowing owls' nest disappears, her mother enters surgery; ibises are flooded out, her mother undergoes chemotherapy. A third strand moves between the others: the family heritage, including the Mormon religion as well as a strange proclivity to cancer. And it is that strand which finally, in a resonant and dramatic concluding chapter, draws the others together: when Williams discovers that Utah nuclear tests may have caused her family's cancers, she breaks her Mormon reserve to oppose the national policies that led to these disasters. A stirring and sensitive work. —*Pat Monaghan*

✔**Worthen, John.**
D. H. Lawrence: The Early Years, 1885–1921.
Cambridge, $35 (0-521-25419-1). 626p. index.

For many general readers, Jeffrey Meyers' one-volume life of D. H. Lawrence will be preferable to this first installment in Cambridge's ambitious project to publish a definitive, three-part biography, with each part authored by a different Lawrence scholar. Meyers tells the poignant tale of Lawrence's life succinctly yet effectively, and he allows the awesome passion of the man to emerge forcibly. And yet it would be very wrong indeed to slap the label "For Scholars Only" on Worthen's infinitely more detailed but finally more impressive account of Lawrence's early life. True, Worthen is speaking to readers who have a definite interest in his subject, but, given that, the rewards are many. We see more vividly than ever before the agonizing push and pull of Lawrence's youth, torn between the spontaneity and physicality of his miner father and the fearless ambition of his more educated mother, who dreamed of a life for her son far from the mining shafts of Nottinghamshire. Worthen also does a superb job of using the works to illuminate the life; drawing extensively from newly available letters and from the many early versions of *Sons and Lovers*, he constructs a compelling picture of the young Lawrence, struggling to free his sexual self from the "dreadful and deadly self-sacrificial power of the beloved mother." Perhaps because of the very detail Worthen lavishes on this picture of the tortured, sexually roadblocked Lawrence, we feel more strongly than ever the great liberation that occurred when Frieda Weekley walked into his life, allowing him to be, for the first time, "all the selves he was: sensitive *and* outgoing, intellectual *and* ordinary, spiritual *and* sexual." As Worthen's magnificent contribution to the Cambridge biography ends, we leave Lawrence having surmounted, with the help of Frieda, the barriers that *Sons and Lovers* hero Paul Morel never could overcome. Free of his mother, yet free, too, of the coal mine, Lawrence was ready to write *The Rainbow*. English literature has never been the same.
—*Bill Ott*

Yellowtail, Thomas and Fitzgerald, Michael Oren.
Yellowtail, Crow Medicine Man and Sun Dance Chief: An Autobiography.
Univ. of Oklahoma, $21.95 (0-8061-2333-8). 272p.

Thomas Yellowtail, a spiritual leader of the Crow, is one of the last of the tribe to have been raised in the traditional way. He has told his life story and explained the Sun Dance, the "heart of the Crow Indian religion," to Fitzgerald, an adopted member of the tribe since 1972. Born in 1903, Yellowtail has witnessed and survived dramatic changes in the Crow way of life, particularly the diminishment of the sacred. As he recounts his extraordinary personal experiences and defines the Crow religion, the magnitude of the loss to his people emerges along with wonder at his enduring faith and strength of spirit. Yellowtail discusses the process and meaning of the four central rites: purification in the sweat lodge, the vision quest, daily prayer and the offering of tobacco smoke, and the arduous ceremony of the Sun Dance itself, a three-day ordeal of fasting, dancing, and singing in the lodge where temperatures top 100. He explains: "The Indian way reminds us that life requires hardship, sincerity, and prayer." A book of wisdom that contributes mightily to the study of religion and native American life. —*Donna Seaman*

Business

Auerbach, Red and Dooley, Ken.
MBA: Management by Auerbach: Management Tips from the Leader of One of America's Most Successful Organizations.
Macmillan/Wellington, $19.95 (0-02-504481-8). 256p.

The successful organization referred to in the title is the Boston Celtics, and the leader is the Celtics' legendary coach and general manager, Arnold ("Red") Auerbach. With a little help from business writer Dooley, Auerbach *could* become the celebrity management guru of the 1990s, replacing the 1980s' Lee Iacocca, who graciously penned a foreword for this book. No newcomer to management training, Auerbach is a frequent guest lecturer at Harvard Business School and in other business venues. His commonsense tips on developing and maintaining a competitive edge, the psychology of winning, and the vital roles of discipline, motivation, and communication in building a successful organization are illustrated with sports anecdotes, which should appeal to those who follow professional basketball only in May and June as well as to longtime fans who continue to view roundball as a winter sport. Often portrayed as an autocratic curmudgeon, Auerbach displays more respect for players as individuals and lays more stress on listening to employees and giving them good reasons to be loyal to their manager and the organization than most sports aficionados would expect. He tackles controversial subjects like drugs, age, and managing a multicultural workforce and offers somewhat jaundiced but pragmatic advice on press relations. —*Mary Carroll*

Auletta, Ken.
Three Blind Mice: How the TV Networks Lost Their Way.
Random, $25 (0-394-56358-1). 624p. index.

When Auletta began to investigate the corporate changes in television and how they have affected the medium, he may not have realized his research would go on for five years. It takes time to tell such a twisted and tangled story, one so chock-full of small minds and expansive personalities. When Auletta first began writing about this subject in 1985, the ownership of all three networks had changed hands. He must have had incredible access because many of the big names—Robert C. Wright at NBC, Lawrence Tisch of CBS, and Tom Murphy at Cap Cities/ABC—are among those oft-quoted. That Auletta gives the reader an incredible amount of facts and figures is not surprising. That he does so in such a readable, yes, entertaining manner is a credit to his writing skills. Readers will come away not only knowing how radically the television industry has changed in the last several years and why it happened, but they will also have a feel for those who caused the changes as well as for others who got tangled up in them. A natural for those interested in business or the television industry, this fascinating study will also appeal to anyone who likes a good soap opera. —*Ilene Cooper*

Bianco, Anthony.
Rainmaker: The Saga of Jeff Beck, Wall Street's Mad Dog.
Random, $25 (0-394-57023-5). 512p. index.

Pedersen, Laura and Model, F. Peter.
Play Money: My Brief but Brilliant Career on Wall Street.
Crown, $20 (0-517-58227-9). 288p.

Now that the Michael Milkens and the Ivan Boeskys have been thoroughly portrayed, a second wave of literature examining the Avaricious Eighties is in the offing. Less well known—but not any less colorful or ambitious—characters and players have their own stories to be told.

Jeff Beck was a mergers and acquisitions dealmaker, first at Oppenheimer & Co., then Drexel Burnham, where he handled the biggest buy-out deal in history. Bianco, for 10 years *Business Week's* Wall Street correspondent, tells the bizarre tale of Beck, who rose from nowhere by concocting a whole fabric of wild and untrue stories about personal wealth and wartime heroics and by attracting attention through histrionics and crazy stunts—one time eating a whole box of dog biscuits to make a point with his boss (hence the epithet "Mad Dog"). Bianco's thoroughly researched and well-written story paints a depressing picture of how completely greed and self-indulgence permeated Wall Street during the 1980s and how everything finally came crashing down.

Laura Pedersen dropped out of school, moved to New York, and got a job as a clerk on the trading floor of the American Stock Exchange. Within a year, while still too young to buy stock legally for herself, she was trading millions of dollars in securities and options, and within three years she'd made $1 million and become the youngest person ever to get a seat on a stock exchange. She kept a diary for five years, up through the market crash of October 1987. She describes firsthand the exhilaration, terror, chaos, rude and boisterous shenanigans, and cutthroat competition of life on Wall Street and shows its emotional and physical costs. Pedersen tells her tale of survival with a mix of cynicism, bravado, hyperbole, and humor. —*David Rouse*

Coll, Steve and Vise, David.
Eagle on the Street: Based on the Pulitzer Prize–Winning Account of the SEC's Battle with Wall Street.
Scribner, $24.95 (0-684-19314-0). 384p.

Critics have charged that the Wall Street scandals, criminal misdeeds, brokerage house failures, and general excesses of the 1980s were a legacy of Ronald Reagan's policy of deregulation. Indeed, John Shad, Reagan's Securities and Exchange Commission appointee, narrowly interpreted the SEC's role in policing Wall Street, cutting back on enforcement activities in the realm of corporate public accountability. On the other hand, he did vigorously pursue insider trading violators, in part to control the growing Frankenstein monster that Wall Street had become and to restore the trust of the small investor. It is this story that investigative financial reporters Coll and Vise retell in riveting detail, a story based on their Pulitzer Prize–winning series for the *Washington Post*. On another level, the story is fascinating because it reveals how and why government works—and doesn't work—by revealing the dynamic and complicated interplay among personalities, politics, and bureaucratic professionalism within a federal agency. —*David Rouse*

Davidson, James Dale and Rees-Mogg, William.
The Great Reckoning: How the World Will Change in the Depression of the 1990s.
Summit, $22 (0-671-66980-X). 574p. index.

Davidson and Rees-Mogg believe in the cyclical nature of political, economic, and financial events and the inevitable rise and fall of empires and nations. It is their contention that the U.S. is in a long-term decline, and they offer up this massive doomsday sampler documenting their theories with historical evidence and providing advice on how best to protect oneself financially during the coming collapse. Political conservatives, Davidson is founder and chairman of the National Taxpayers Union and Rees-Mogg is a former editor of the London *Times* and vice-chairman of the British Broadcasting Corporation. Together they put out a financial newsletter called *Strategic Investment*, which they use this book to promote. Since many of the often-less-than-specific prognostications in their similar book of four years ago, *Blood in the Streets: Investment Profits in a World Gone Mad* (Summit, 1987), fell close to the mark, the authors have decided to give it another try. Recommended for basic investment collections. —*David Rouse*

Ferrell, O. C. and Gardiner, Gareth.
In Pursuit of Ethics: Tough Choices in the World of Work.
Smith Collins Company, paper, $12.95 (0-9623414-1-X). 160p. index.

Savings-and-loan scandals, junk bond schemes, defense contractor price gouging, and other white-collar corporate crimes have brought discussion of business ethics to the fore. Ferrell, a professor of marketing and business ethics, and Gardiner, a consultant specializing in problem employees and managerial ethics, demonstrate the interrelationship between organizational and individual ethical behaviors. Organizations create a climate that fosters ethical behavior; individual actions combine to create a corporate culture. Ethical behavior begins with simple honesty in situations as basic as the sales pitch, office politics, or negotiating, but it also manifests itself organizationally during such episodes as product recalls or product mislabeling. Using numerous "real life" examples, the authors demonstrate that ethical behavior is a matter of making tough-minded choices, not of being either the nice guy or the tough guy. Their approach is spirited and practical and eschews both moralistic preaching and academic theorizing. —*David Rouse*

✔Hafner, Katie and Markoff, John.
Cyberpunk: Outlaws and Hackers on the Computer Frontier.
Simon & Schuster, $22.95 (0-671-68322-5). 336p. index.

Police raids on teenage computer users' homes and on computer game manufacturers have stirred controversy over a crackdown on computer tampering. Are computer hackers simply inquisitive, sometimes mischievous youth? Are they electronic trespassers? Are they dangerous thieves, pirates, and saboteurs? Or have they played an important role by exposing the vulnerability of various computer networks? Wife-and-husband team Hafner and Markoff, who write for *Business Week* and the *Wall Street Journal*, respectively, detail stories of three recent cases of major computer misdeeds. They portray Kevin Mitnick's penetration of Digital Equipment Corporation's top-secret computer system, West Berliner Pengo's international espionage scheme, and Robert Morris' "worm" that disabled many of the nation's computer networks. The authors present objective, well-researched reporting while telling spellbinding tales that raise issues but leave conclusions to the reader. Highly recommended for all libraries. —*David Rouse*

Jacobs, Michael T.
Short-Term America: The Causes and Cures of Our Business Myopia.
Harvard Business School Press, $24.95 (0-87584-300-X). 288p. index.

Those who charge that U.S. companies are no longer able to compete either her ~t home or in the international marketplace often cite as a reason today's corporate ~eremphasis on short-term gains and the abandonment of long-term goals. Jacobs, former director of corporate finance with the U.S. Treasury Department, concurs, deftly examining the underlying factors of this "myopia" and providing solutions. Two of the reasons he identifies are the "commoditization of corporate ownership" and the demise of "relationship banking." Corporate shareholders no longer see themselves as owners of a company. Their shares of stock are simply investment instruments. Bankers are no longer partners in the business enterprise. With these two checks no longer in place, managerial self-interest dictates corporate decision-making. Jacobs' well-reasoned, thoughtful analysis belongs in most library business collections. —*David Rouse*

Kimbro, Dennis and Hill, Napoleon.
Think and Grow Rich: A Black Choice.
Ballantine/Fawcett Columbine, $20 (0-449-90612-4). 320p. index.

Perhaps no best-selling author is less well known than motivationalist Napoleon Hill. However, his *Think and Grow Rich* and *Law of Success*, in their many, various versions, have sold millions of copies. Hill first received inspiration from Andrew Carnegie when he was assigned to profile successful and famous individuals. Carnegie was able to facilitate interviews with such luminaries as Henry Ford and Thomas Edison, and Hill went on to interview more than 500 successful individuals. He determined that a common factor in all their lives was their single-minded positive outlook. Some time after his death in 1970, it was reported that Hill had left an unfinished manuscript

Business

targeting black America with his message of self-confidence and affirmative outlook. Now Kimbro, a black writer and lecturer for the Napoleon Hill Foundation, has adapted and updated Hill's manuscript. Acknowledging such barriers as lack of opportunity, racism, and discrimination, Kimbro argues that these should not be self-defeating obstacles. In some ways, his message is no different from those of others who preach pride and self-empowerment—Jesse Jackson imploring young students to "Be Somebody!" But to suggest that success is basically a matter of choice is to invite controversy. This book should draw a great deal of attention. —*David Rouse*

Leinberger, Paul and Tucker, Bruce.
The New Individualists: The Generation after The Organization Man.
HarperCollins, $24.95 (0-06-016591-X). 464p. index.

Over the last 20 years many authors have written the obituary for the organization man, the enduring symbol of the 1950s profiled in William Whyte's 1956 classic. Recently, Amanda Bennett proclaimed *The Death of the Organization Man* (Morrow, 1990). While her analysis was largely anecdotal, Leinberger and Tucker employ the vocabulary and methodology of sociology to arrive at similar conclusions. In fact, Leinberger, a management consultant specializing in high technology and son of one of Whyte's original subjects, and Tucker, a free-lance writer, spent seven years locating and interviewing many of Whyte's original subjects and their adult children. Furthermore, Whyte supplied the authors with his original notebooks. Their conclusions coincide with Bennett's. Organizations are now systems of networks rather than hierarchical structures. The new individualist is dependent upon organizations but owes his or her allegiance to none and follows an "enterprise ethic," practicing creativity and innovation within the organization. This significant piece of sociological analysis belongs in public and academic library business and social science collections. —*David Rouse*

Lewis, Michael.
The Money Culture.
Norton, $19.95 (0-393-03037-7). 256p.

When the plain facts can no longer provoke a response, a deft, incisive lampooning jab is often effective. Lewis is author of the best-selling *Liar's Poker* (Norton, 1989), which irreverently documented the decline of Wall Street at the end of the 1980s. Here he successfully skewers the familiar cast of characters that pillaged the 1980s financial landscape. He takes on the entire money cultures of Wall Street, Europe, and Japan in this collection of send-ups and put-downs. These 30-some pieces have all appeared elsewhere, mostly in *Manhattan, Inc.*, and the *New Republic*, where Lewis sometimes wrote pseudonymously to protect his job as a bond dealer with Salomon Brothers brokerage house. (He now writes for a living.) Lewis skillfully captures the previous decade in much the same way Tom Wolfe captured the 1960s and 1970s. —*David Rouse*

Mayer, Martin.
Whatever Happened to Madison Avenue? Advertising in the '90s.
Little, Brown, $22.95 (0-316-55154-6). 304p. index.

Nearly every year, for more than 30 years, Mayer has turned out books with titles like *The Lawyers, The Bankers, The Builders,* and *The Money Bazaars.* In 1958, he profiled the advertising industry in *Madison Avenue USA.* He takes a second look in this all-new book. Even though a third of the book is devoted to the history of advertising, Mayer uses material and sources not included in his earlier work. He describes the current state of agencies, media, and market research and discusses the role of advertising in the 1990s and its contribution to society. He also considers the impact advertising and international competition have upon each other. Mayer is an advertising booster, arguing that it measurably adds value to products and services. This readable, popular account of the advertising industry will make a suitable addition to public, academic, and corporate library collections. —*David Rouse*

Miller, Theodore J.
Kiplinger's Invest Your Way to Wealth: How Ordinary People Can Accumulate Extraordinary Amounts of Money.
Kiplinger Books, $21.95 (0-938721-16-X). 400p. index.

Of the myriad investment books available, few have anything to offer the first-time investor. Most explain or promote sophisticated, speculative, or unusual strategies or theories. But this book provides the kind of sound, no-nonsense, nuts-and-bolts advice one would expect from the publisher of *Changing Times* (now called *Kiplinger's Personal Finance*) and its eponymous newsletter. Miller, an editor with Kiplinger and author of Make Your Money Grow (Kiplinger, 1988), elaborates five basic investment principles, explains savings, stocks, bonds, mutual funds, and foreign securities, and suggests sources for advice. He then describes higher risk investments such as real estate and mortgages but discounts putting money into precious metals or collectibles and identifies other questionable investments. Miller also covers investing specifically for education or retirement and advises how to choose and use a broker. Final chapters discuss taxes, interest formulas, and investment terminology. Highly recommended for basic business collections. —*David Rouse*

Morris, Kenneth and others.
American Dreams: One Hundred Years of Business Ideas and Innovations from the Wall Street Journal.
Abrams, $39.95 (0-8109-3656-9). 224p.

Based on a series that appeared in the *Wall Street Journal* (marking its centennial anniversary), this volume profiles business ideas and innovations that represent American ingenuity. The eclectic collection offers a celebration of entrepreneurship and the icons of popular culture, covering everything from pantyhose to Pampers, from Donald Duck to Drexel Burnham. Important issues, such as immigration quotas, reform of the meat-packing industry, and the notorious Tylenol poisonings, are represented also. More than 600 photographs and illustrations provide fascinating documentation for the short,

Business

fact-filled reviews. The authors, experts in the fields of business communications and design research, emphasize the importance of easy-to-read, simple, and visually appealing materials (and their book effectively demonstrates it). An index makes this an especially useful reference work. —*David Rouse*

O'Shea, James.
The Daisy Chain: How Borrowed Billions Sank a Texas S & L.
Pocket, $19.95 (0-671-73303-6). 295p.

In the stock market, a daisy chain is manipulative trading among a small group designed to give the impression of heavy volume so that others will be drawn into the activity. O'Shea describes how a few savings and loans similarly used complex deals to loan each other large sums consisting of federally insured deposits while the heads of those S & L's squandered millions in self-administered, outrageous perks. An investigative reporter who has covered the S & L crisis for the *Chicago Tribune*, O'Shea profiles Texas-based Vernon Savings and Loan and its owner, Don Dixon, who completely plundered the institution in less than eight years at a cost to the taxpayers of $1–$1.3 billion. O'Shea points his finger not just at the greedy or crooked S & L directors but also at complicit politicians and regulators who allowed this crisis to happen. This is one of the better (but more depressing) books among the growing number on the problems of the S & L industry. —*David Rouse*

Pedersen, Laura and Model, F. Peter.
Play Money: My Brief but Brilliant Career on Wall Street.
Crown, $20 (0-517-58227-9). 288p.

See p.71.

Quinn, Jane Bryant.
Making the Most of Your Money: Smart Ways to Create Wealth and Plan Your Finances in the '90s.
Simon & Schuster, $24.95 (0-671-65952-9). 902p. index.

A dozen years ago, we saw the almost simultaneous publication of two encyclopedic financial planning guides that were to be standards throughout most of the 1980s. Financial advice maven Sylvia Porter updated her 1975 *Money Book* with *New Money Book for the 1980's* (Doubleday, 1979), and financial advice newcomer Jane Bryant Quinn came out with *Everyone's Money Book* (Delacorte, 1979). Both authors continued to dispense their advice in popular syndicated magazine and newspaper columns as well as on television. Porter released several new titles during the 1980s but never really completely updated her *Money Book* before she died earlier this year. Meanwhile, Quinn, now best known for her regular financial planning column in *Newsweek*, has at last substantially revised and updated her guide. She provides comprehensive, knowledgeable, easy-to-understand coverage of virtually every aspect of personal and family finance with an increased emphasis on investments and retirement. An indispensable reference for individuals and libraries alike. —*David Rouse*

demonstrated at its Festival of American Folklife, held every summer. The Kirlins have logged many miles and countless long-distance phone calls to retrieve over 275 dishes that represent 11 loosely defined areas of the country—native American, Creole/Cajun, Hawaiian, and Puerto Rican are a few of these designations. What stands out is the knowledge of the individual contributors, along with their gentle humor about eating customs and mores. Reproducing the recipes, however, requires a home cook with enough experience to interpret the variances in serving sizes (1 to 80-plus), occasionally vague directions, and frequently measureless ingredients. Yet as a recollection of foodstuffs past, this is a treasure. —*Barbara Jacobs*

✔Rojas-Lombardi, Felipe.
The Art of South American Cooking.
HarperCollins, $25 (0-06-016425-5). 528p. index.

It is a most luscious study of history that Rojas-Lombardi provides in these varied recipes reflecting the diversity of South America. As the author writes, "[his] kitchen education was a United Nations of cultural influences." Through his passion for the food and the culture, the author has crafted a readable and informative guide to the cuisine. With clear and complete instructions, these recipes employ many valuable foods (e.g., quinoa, corn, yuca, varied seafood, and game) and offer a variety of tastes from the lightly seasoned to strong curries to sweetened desserts and entrées. Instructions to make flavored doughs, oils, and other base materials abound and are cross-referenced throughout the recipes. This will be an excellent acquisition for any librarian building an international cuisines collection. —*Angus Trimnell*

Sokolov, Raymond.
Why We Eat What We Eat.
Summit, $22 (0-671-66796-3). 244p.

In this unique volume, a former *New York Times* food critic meanders through various countries to provide an intriguing history of human gastronomy since Columbus' discovery of America. Sokolov reveals the culinary impact of the Genoan's journeys; for example, on a second trip in 1493, the noted explorer introduced horses, cattle, and other animals to Mexico and Puerto Rico. He discusses such intriguing tidbits as the reason coconut milk became an important ingredient in the Caribbean islands, the origins of a favorite Brazilian cooking oil, and the evolutions of potato chips, chocolate, chowder, and other popular foods. That modern international, cross-cultural cooking is a product of the melding of cuisines that sprang up in Columbus' wake is fascinatingly demonstrated by means of Sokolov's vast culinary knowledge. —*Sue-Ellen Beauregard*

Soviero, Donaldo.
La Vera Cucina Italiana.
Macmillan, $22.50 (0-02-612570-0). 352p. index.

Soviero runs a cooking school in Italy, and his cookbook brings culinary scholarship to a general audience. He stresses the importance of starting at

Cookery

the beginning—mastering a marinara sauce, a batter, a bread dough. He underscores the advantages of experimenting with herbs and spices to discover a personal seasoning base. Organized into chapters on antipasto, salads, pasta, sauces, rice and polenta, vegetables, fish, chicken, meat, and bread and pizza, the book provides more than 200 recipes but lacks a section on soups. A well-written essay begins the book, defining *la vera cucina* and reminiscing about great meals gone by. The author's philosophy of meal preparation—"Start with the finest and freshest natural ingredients, cook with love, knowledge, and devotion, and serve everyone as if they were the most honored guest ever to come into your home"—is an important one, and he teaches it well. This volume offers a solid education in Italian cuisine. —*Kathryn LaBarbera*

Starke, Rodman D. and Winston, Mary, eds.
The American Heart Association Cookbook.
Times Books, $25 (0-8129-1895-9). 544p. index.

The American Heart Association makes it easier than ever to follow its healthy eating guidelines in this fifth edition of the cookbook published under the association's auspices, updated from the 1984 edition. There has never been so much pressure to eliminate cholesterol and high sodium content or to substitute the healthy and flavorful foods that will prevent or slow down the development of heart disease. Consequently, recipes included here have fuller nutritional information than those in earlier editions, displaying not only the calories per serving, but also the protein, carbohydrate, cholesterol, and sodium count, as well as the possibility of saturated, polyunsaturated, or monounsaturated fat. Microwaving instructions, when appropriate, follow the traditional cooking directions. Not much has been overlooked in the quest to make healthy eating a must for everyone—included are diet plans, glossary of terms, and tips on eating in restaurants that include fast food, salad bars, and regional specialties. No more comprehensive guide to the healthy eating suited to the 1990s is available. —*Iva Freeman*

Stern, Jane and Stern, Michael.
American Gourmet: Classic Recipes, Deluxe Delights, Flamboyant Favorites, and Swank "Company" Food from the '50s and '60s.
HarperCollins, $25 (0-06-016710-6). 304p. index.

Memories flood the brain. Long-ago names pique interest. Forgotten foods spark taste sensations. What pop sociojournalists Jane and Michael Stern chronicle is how Americans jumped from meat and potatoes to the freshest of cuisines, specifically the period from 1947 to 1971—after World War II to the establishment of Alice Waters' Chez Panisse. Always entertaining, they conjure up remembrances of foodstuffs and trends past: the advent of the word *gourmet*, travel's influence upon eating habits, TV chefs, high-class restaurants, food as aphrodisiac, and home entertaining. Reading the documentation is fun and often educational; adding practicality to the frolic are the over 100 recipes, representing many fads that have survived the gourmet revolt, including beef tartare, paté, Caesar salad, fondues, even noodle doodle and cheese. —*Barbara Jacobs*

Crafts

✔**Mallalieu, Huon, ed.**
The Illustrated History of Antiques: The Essential Reference for All Antique Lovers and Collectors.
Running Press, $60 (0-89471-888-6). 640p. index.

Mallalieu, through his roster of distinguished contributors, has done his best not to intimidate or overwhelm the novice collector; instead, he offers a tantalizing glimpse at the history and social milieu of a wide variety of beautiful things. Dismissing the 100-year-old definition of antiques, he sets the criteria for inclusion as objects of the highest quality, created by the greatest artists and craftspeople (when attributable), from arms and armor to "philosophical" (i.e., natural science) instruments. Technical terms are patiently explained, and mind-numbing, elaborate details about construction are avoided. Sidebars cover specific techniques, artists, and styles, and the color photographs alone are worth more than the book's list price. In this age of ever-escalating costs, a truly valuable introduction to an increasingly popular avocation. —*Barbara Jacobs*

Film & Drama

Brownstein, Ronald.
The Power and the Glitter: The Hollywood–Washington Connection.
Pantheon, $22.95 (0-394-56938-5). 426p. index.

Long before Gary Hart's tryst with Donna Rice, or, for that matter, years prior to JFK's liaison with Marilyn Monroe, the connection between stars and politicians was newsworthy. In fact, as long as there has been a Hollywood, its affairs have been inextricably entwined with those of Washington, D.C. Louis B. Mayer, one of the first of the Hollywood moguls, actively courted Herbert Hoover, supporting his candidacy for the presidency in an effort to win personal legitimacy as an important business man and gain political favors for the new and burgeoning film industry. During the Depression and, later, during World War II, Hollywood leftists had strong influence on the outcome of guild meetings, only to be blacklisted by overzealous red baiters who effectively quashed dissent in the 1950s. JFK won the support of an adoring Sinatra and his fellow Rat Packers but was later advised to distance himself from ol' blue eyes before he could be defiled by the singer's unsavory connection to the Mob. Brownstein is thorough in his investigation, uncovering a long and significant history of the Hollywood-Washington connection,

Film & Drama

up to what is perhaps its classic embodiment: Ronald Reagan. In-depth and fascinating, Brownstein's study includes discussion of the politics of such contemporary performers as Jane Fonda, Marlon Brando, Charlton Heston, Robert Redford, and Warren Beatty, whose activism garnered attention for causes, politicians, and themselves. —*Benjamin Segedin*

✓**Brustein, Robert.**
Reimagining American Theatre.
Hill & Wang, $22.95 (0-8090-8057-5). 291p. index.

A scintillating collection of reviews and essays covering the past decade in American theater, by a distinguished theater critic for the *New Republic* and the founder and director of the Yale Repertory Theatre. Brustein gives strong voice to what a vast segment of the theatergoing public has long felt but could not articulate. He explains in particular why theater remains a hopeful and dynamic cultural force despite the disintegration of New York City as a theatrical power base and the decline of Broadway, which, he says, now backs only nonrisky commercial ventures such as blockbuster musicals. His book is handily divided into three parts. Part one contains reviews and commentary on new American works. Part two discusses revivals of classics staged mainly by institutional theaters. Part three, the book's most provocative section, airs the author's views on a range of issues affecting the very existence of the theater, including NEA funding (or lack of it), the influence of politics on the dramatic arts, and obstacles to artistic freedom. A radiant work, both intellectually illuminating and written with literary grace. —*Mary Banas*

✓**Duberman, Martin.**
Mother Earth: An Epic Drama of Emma Goldman's Life.
St. Martin's, $15.95 (0-312-05954-X). 192p.

Asked 20-odd years ago to dramatize the life of Susan B. Anthony for PBS, Duberman suggested that anarchist orator Emma Goldman (1869–1940) was a far more promising subject. But Red Emma was still too hot to be allowed the free speech she'd been jailed and eventually deported for trying to exercise. The project was nixed but, fortunately, not before Duberman finished the teleplay. He presents it here cast into three acts for presumed ease of reading. Most readers will ignore the arbitrary division, so caught up in will they be in Goldman's turbulent life. Ever a radical small-*d* democrat (one of the big-*D* variety—Woodrow Wilson—was her most successful persecutor), she championed birth control, freedom of sexual expression, economic justice, and many other ideas that authoritarians of the right, left, and center still distort and try to suppress. This thrilling play, more than any biography, more than Goldman's own *Living My Life*, is the ideal introduction to the life and causes of this great immigrant American and world outcast-citizen. —*Ray Olson*

Ebert, Roger and Siskel, Gene.
The Future of the Movies.
Andrews and McMeel, paper, $9.95 (0-8362-6216-6). 113p.

This is not a "thumbs-up" guide to Hollywood's hit makers, but a serious and well-thought-out series of interviews with arguably the three most influential filmmakers in America today. Ebert and Siskel lead Martin Scorsese (*GoodFellas*, *Raging Bull*, *Taxi Driver*), Steven Spielberg (*Jaws*, *Close Encounters of the Third Kind*, *E.T.*), and George Lucas (*Star Wars*, *American Grafitti*) in discussions about the role of video in cinema, the impact of high-density television, the protection of film archives, and the significant developments in each of their own careers. Interesting and insightful reading for those more concerned with film craft than film aesthetics. —*Benjamin Segedin*

Grover, Ron.
The Disney Touch: How a Daring Management Team Revived an Entertainment Empire.
Irwin, $22.95 (1-55623-385-X). 298p.

To most of us, Walt Disney is Mickey Mouse, Snow White, and Tinkerbell. But takeover battles, aggressive marketing tactics, copyright infringement skirmishes, cable and network television programming, the international balance of payments, and even Bette Midler, Julia Roberts, and *The Golden Girls* are the stuff of this modern-day entertainment conglomerate. Grover, *Business Week*'s L.A. bureau chief, profiles Disney since the dynamic management team headed by Hollywood mogul Michael Eisner took over in 1984. "Team Disney" is credited with multiplying the company's earnings eightfold in five years and turning it into the toast of Hollywood (and Wall Street). Grover tells this story with rigorous, absorbing detail. —*David Rouse*

Hagen, Uta.
A Challenge for the Actor.
Scribner, $22.50 (0-684-10940-0). 352p. index.

In 1938, 19-year-old Uta Hagen made her Broadway debut as Nina in the Lunt-Fontanne production of Chekhov's *The Seagull*. Over the past half-century, she has starred in acclaimed New York productions of classic and contemporary drama, from Shakespeare, Shaw, and Turgenev, to Brecht, Williams, and Albee. Hagen's greater contribution to theater arts, however, may be her role as teacher at the acting studio established by her husband, European actor Herbert Berghof, described in this book and its predecessor (*Respect for Acting*, written with Haskell Frankel). Any theater buff will love the first 50 pages, in which Hagen presents a brief and highly opinionated survey of the history of American theater and distinguishes between the realistic style of acting she prefers and naturalistic acting. The balance of the book is serious instruction for actors: explanations of techniques, detailed descriptions of 10 acting exercises, and advice on the process of reading, analyzing, and "scoring" in preparing for a particular role. —*Mary Carroll*

✔**Kael, Pauline.**
Movie Love: Complete Reviews, 1988–1991.
Dutton, $24.95 (0-525-93313-1); NAL/Plume, paper, $14.95
(0-452-26635-1). 366p. index.

Love is the right word for critic Kael's involvement with movies. Ever since the publication of her electrifying first book, *I Lost It at the Movies*, Kael has watched each and every film with "giddy high excitement" and a keen understanding of the elusive art of directing. In exuberant and inventive language, Kael dispenses praise and condemnation with equal conviction and zest. She has an unerring sense of missed potentials, cop-outs, and cowardly stereotyping. Gleefully exposing phony piety, punditry, and platitudes, Kael states her preference for raw menace, emotional integrity, simmering sexuality, and dark humor. This collection, the critic's tenth, contains 80 full-length, full-strength reviews of films ranging from *Let's Get Lost* to *Dances with Wolves*. Be sure to add this wickedly brilliant volume to your collection, since, after 24 years, Kael has chosen to "retire from regular reviewing." —*Donna Seaman*

Kilgore, Emilie S.
Contemporary Plays by Women: Outstanding Winners and Runners-Up for the Susan Smith Blackburn Prize (1978–1990).
Prentice Hall Press, $29.95 (0-13-183690-0); paper, $16.95 (0-13-183708-7). 528p.

Seven contestants for a prize awarded annually to an English-language play written by a woman constitute a rich collection that belongs in virtually every theater library. They reflect very well the variety of topical and social concerns female playwrights on both sides of the Atlantic tackle with wit, theatrical savvy, and power. Caryl Churchill's *Serious Money*, for instance, is about a rapacious career woman, while at the other end of the sociopolitical spectrum, Anne Devlin's *Ourselves Alone* concerns three women from the perpetual revolutionary stratum of Irish society. Although the other six are set contemporaneously, Wendy Kesselman's examination of domestic class antagonism, *My Sister in This House*, harks back to 1930s provincial France in an imaginative reconstruction of an actual case of double murder. Lucy Gannon's *Keeping Tom Nice* is something of an answer to the likes of the film *My Left Foot* in its portrait of a working-class British family consumed by the care of a severely disabled, *un*extraordinary son. Lynn Seifert's *Coyote Ugly* is about a lumpen American clan, thus fitting squarely into a dramatic lineage that goes back at least to Kirkland's *Tobacco Road*. Perhaps best of set goes to the book's most familiar contents, Marsha Norman's brilliant *Getting Out*, about an ex-convict coming to terms with her past, and Tina Howe's drama—familiar to many from its excellent television production in the "American Playhouse" series—of a talented, aristocratic New England family dealing with aging and its infirmities, *Painting Churches*. —*Ray Olson*

Lucas, Craig.
Prelude to a Kiss.
Dutton, $16.95 (0-525-24943-5). 93p.

A sweet little play, something of a non-nasty "Twilight Zone" episode, in which boy meets girl and they marry. But at the wedding reception, an old man who's wandered into the party fervently kisses the bride, and somehow his soul and hers exchange bodies. The new husband quickly notices the change and demands to have all of the woman he married. The parents of the bride are much slower on the uptake, however, so the geezer-in-wife's-clothing flees to them, pleading that hubby's not the man "she" married! There's a happy ending for all eventually, but not before Lucas has made us feel the weight of the marital pledge "in sickness and in health, to love and to cherish." He also engages us with bright, likable characters and charming, lightly humorous dialogue. It's easy to imagine this modern dramatic fairy tale becoming a community theater staple. —*Ray Olson*

Mamet, David.
On Directing Film.
Viking, $18.95 (0-670-83033-X). 96p.

Mamet, Pulitzer Prize–winning playwright and masterful screenplay writer, has directed only two films so far—*House of Games* and *Things Change*—but they are gems. This potent, concentrated book is the distillation of a series of lectures that Mamet conducted at Columbia University's film school. He claims that films are intimately linked to dreams, depending on juxtaposition rather than narrative. His statement that the "work of the director is the work of constructing the shot list from the script" is deceivingly simplified. His lectures reveal the workings of a powerfully focused mind, particularly in the exchanges with students. He goes by the K.I.S.S. rule ("Keep it simple, stupid"), practices restraint, and believes that the story is told in the cuts. Referring to Hitchcock, Bettelheim, Aristotle, Leadbelly, and the value of cartoons, Mamet is a blunt and rigorous teacher. For anyone interested in the making of movies or what makes this director tick. —*Donna Seaman*

McGilligan, Pat, ed.
Backstory 2: Interviews with Screenwriters of the 1940s and 1950s.
Univ. of California, $29.95 (0-525-07169-7). 395p. index.

Editor McGilligan's second helping of fascinating screenwriter interviews (the first: *Backstory*) includes conversations with writer-director Richard Brooks (*The Blackboard Jungle*, *Elmer Gantry*, *In Cold Blood*); musical comedy aces Betty Comden and Adolph Green, who also scripted *Auntie Mame*; Garson Kanin, most famous for his writing partnership with his wife, Ruth Gordon; Arthur Laurents, who wrote the "books" (as the nonlyrical parts of musicals are styled) for *West Side Story* and *Gypsy*; Ben Maddow, who was blacklisted in the 1950s; Philip Yordan, who fronted for some blacklistees, including Maddow; and seven others. As before, there's not a dull palaverer in the bunch, especially for the growing number of film students who think writers have been short-shrifted in favor of directors. Some of the remarks, however, are genuine palaver in the sense of being misleading, but which? Maddow and Yordan differ on their surreptitiously shared collaborations, and the appended bibliographic notes mark further disputed points in other subjects' statements. A solid entry in Hollywood oral history, but see also Server's *Screenwriter*. —*Ray Olson*

Health & Medicine

Baulieu, Etienne-Emile and Rosenblum, Mort.
The "Abortion Pill": RU-486, A Woman's Choice.
Simon & Schuster, $22 (0-671-73816-X). 187p. index.

More than once in this information-packed little book, Baulieu, developer of the notorious antihormone named RU-486 after the French company (Roussel-Uclaf) that owns it, laments that the drug has been styled the "abortion pill." It was and remains his intent, he says, that his discovery make surgical abortion largely unnecessary. RU-486, rightly understood, "is an unpregnancy pill," acting to prevent gestation either before or in the earliest stages of pregnancy. Greatly aided by Rosenblum's popular journalistic skills, Baulieu begins the book by describing exactly how both pregnancy and the drug's action against it work. Subsequent chapters trace the substance's politically turbulent history to date and Baulieu's very active role as its promoter despite the fact that, as a consultant rather than an employee of Roussel-Uclaf, he is not entitled to a penny from RU-486's sales. They also survey abortion and abortion-related mortality worldwide, point out RU-486's potential in fighting cancer and other maladies, and answer anti-abortionist rhetoric with reason, facts, and immense compassion for the women who die every year from unsafe and illegal abortions that RU-486 could obviate. Must reading for those sincerely and open-mindedly interested in the abortion debate. —*Ray Olson*

Bogdanich, Walt.
The Great White Lie: How America's Hospitals Betray Our Trust and Endanger Our Lives.
Simon & Schuster, $23 (0-671-68452-3). 320p. index.

Bogdanich documents his charges and uses the real names of individuals and hospitals in this sweeping indictment of U.S. institutional health care. His charges include carelessness in hospital pharmacies leading to crippling and deadly mistakes in drug dosages; temporary agencies supplying poorly qualified nurses and aides (even sending LPNs who claim to be RNs); staff being overworked to the point where their minds can't function properly; poor security arrangements that let criminals into hospital buildings to rape and murder; and more. Some hospitals, he demonstrates, not only buy patients—they also sell drugs. Hospital administrators have overcharged government and other payment programs, either pocketing the extra money or using it for nonhospital purposes. Hospital accrediting bodies are often careless or unwilling to upset their supporters and sponsors. Worried readers seeking some reassurance that all is not rotten in the nation's hospitals should remember that Bogdanich dug deeply to find his examples and that many hospitals are thoroughly honest. As his book so forcefully demonstrates, however, a substantial number do cut corners and ought to be investigated, identified, and penalized. —*William Beatty*

✔**Chopra, Deepak.**
Unconditional Life: Mastering the Forces that Shape Personal Reality.
Bantam, $21.50 (0-553-07609-4). 288p. index.

The extent of the mind's power to control the physical processes of the body is still largely misunderstood and unexplored. Nevertheless, some studies in the subject have had far-reaching implications not only for philosophy, but also for the physical and health sciences as well. Chopra, an endocrinologist born in New Delhi, India, has devoted a great deal of his professional life to studying these mind-body relationships. In this fascinating book, he celebrates the untapped resources of the human spirit and the body's powers to heal itself. In an interesting chapter entitled "Magical Thinking," the author even suggests the possibility of going beyond mere mind-body to more infinite abilities of the mind, whereby intuition and ESP become valid options. Chopra presents remarkable cases of recovery from illnesses where traditional medicine has failed but the spirit and will of the individual to live prevailed. Highly recommended. —*Jane Jurgens*

Dollinger, Malin and others.
Everyone's Guide to Cancer Therapy: How Cancer is Diagnosed, Treated, and Managed on a Day-to-Day Basis.
Andrews and McMeel, $29.95 (0-8362-2418-3). 656p. paper, $19.95 (0-8362-2417-5). index.

This massive tome, full of practical information, allows its readers to grasp the complexities of diagnosis, of deciding on appropriate therapy, and of the procedures and outcomes of surgery, radiation therapy, and chemotherapy. Additional concerns include controlling pain; maintaining proper nutrition and physical fitness; and accessing *PDQ—Physicians Data Query*—a computerized database maintained by the National Cancer Institute, to keep abreast of the most up-to-date information on cancer treatment, the location of clinical trials, and physicians treating specific cancers. The lengthy section on treatment for more than 40 specific cancers is contributed to by a host of experts. Each entry in it covers the risk factors, screening test, symptoms, diagnosis, and treatment processes for that particular cancer and concludes with a short list of questions to ask a physician about the disease. Appendixes include a comprehensive glossary, a list of anticancer drugs and their side effects, and a directory of cancer centers and support groups. Highly recommended. —*Karen Graves*

Health & Medicine

Gallo, Robert.
Virus Hunting: Cancer, AIDS, and the Human Retrovirus: A Story of Scientific Discovery.
Basic Books, $22.95 (0-465-09806-1). 315p.

For most general readers, this will be a very difficult book on account of both contents and tone. Gallo heads the National Institutes of Health Laboratory of Tumor Cell Biology, in which position he was ultimately responsible for the discoveries, first, of retroviruses that caused human disease and, then momentously, of the retrovirus that causes AIDS. Although the first chapter reports upon his development into a biomedical researcher and imparts some personal details, the others are concerned with the background, progress, processes, and the findings and implications of his work. Written without condescension to the biochemically semiliterate, they are yet, thanks to their origins as lectures, far from the arcane technicality of scientific journal articles. Laypersons well acquainted with AIDS literature will have little trouble reading the book. They'll find in it arguably the best and most meticulous accounts of, for instance, "How the AIDS Virus Works" and why HIV is the cause of AIDS. Less motivated readers may be put off by Gallo's impersonal, professional tone as much as by the complexity of the material. But have no doubt about it, this is *the* book about the science of AIDS. —*Ray Olson*

✔**Katz, Stan J. and Liu, Aimee E.**
The Codependency Conspiracy: What's Wrong with Recovery Programs, What's Right about Helping Yourself.
Warner, $18.95 (0-446-51595-7). 223p.

Katz is a clinical psychologist specializing in family systems and substance abuse. With the assistance of coauthor Liu, he presents a powerful argument against self-help groups, which, he says, do not help their members achieve recovery and can even prove damaging to one's well-being. Katz criticizes 12-step programs such as Alcoholics Anonymous for keeping their members in a state of dependency instead of encouraging them to become self-reliant, a key step to healing and becoming whole. He is, however, careful to distinguish between self-help groups that seek to perpetuate themselves and rarely solve the chronic problems they purport to address, and support groups that *do* benefit members by helping them cope with situational crises, such as cancer and the loss of a child. Katz's insights and advice are clear, reassuring, and well measured. His strategies—presented in a workbook-style format— for healing old emotional wounds are well defined and very helpful. Katz also includes practical tips rarely found in self-help books: for instance, how to recognize when you're up against a real problem and not just facing an easily resolved issue and how to tell when and if you really have recovered. A candid book that's certain to become a classic in the self-help field. —*Mary Banas*

Konek, Carol Wolfe.
Daddyboy: A Memoir.
Graywolf, $19 (1-55597-153-9). 208p.

Another story of Alzheimer's disease and its effects upon an individual and a family, this will sadden or terrify many readers, just as the disease devastates those it involves. Konek, the victim's daughter, tells the familiar story of how the disease slowly destroyed her father and how it consumed most of her mother's life. Its effects upon her and her younger brother she both tells and implies as she depicts the intensity and agony of the lives of all four family members, their false hopes and mood swings, and their inevitable despair. Some of the contrasts between life before and after Alzheimer's onset are especially affecting: her father was a naturalist, keenly interested in animals, and he ended his life in terror, "stalked by [the] wild animals" of the disease's dementia. The possibility of a genetic basis for the disease occasionally rises but always lies just beneath the narrative's surface. Casting all events in the present tense, with frequent (sometimes confusing) flashbacks and asides, Konek makes several haunting, unforgettable statements and observations. Not least among them are "Alzheimer's disease is a family disease" and "the disease is a mirror from which we turn away." —*William Beatty*

Lappé, Marc.
Chemical Deception: The Toxic Threat to Health and the Environment.
Sierra Club; dist. by Random, $25 (0-87156-603-6). 420p. index.

Lappé discusses worldwide concerns about cancer and skepticism regarding the connections he sees between personal hygiene and global environmental problems. He proposes that if we take care of our bodies, we'll be taking care of the planet and vice versa. A former public health official and currently a professor of health policy and ethics, Lappé cites examples from the eighteenth century of industrial cancers and recognizes the fact that there are so many variables in the chemical mixes that abound in today's world that no one can honestly predict what will result when they combine with other chemicals in the air or in our digestive systems. A scary topic, handled thoroughly and professionally. —*Cynthia Ogorek*

Legato, Marianne J. and Colman, Carol.
The Female Heart: The Truth about Women and Coronary Artery Disease.
Prentice Hall Press, $19.95 (0-13-321811-2). 242p. index.

One of the biggest medical myths today is that heart disease is a male problem. The facts show differently. Heart disease strikes 10 times as many women—a half-million—each year as breast cancer. Shockingly enough, there has been very little research on women's risks and the ways in which heart disease manifests itself in females. Physician and researcher Legato, aided by medical writer Colman, calls attention to these facts in her comprehensive, empathetic book. She describes how women's bodies differ from

Health & Medicine

men's, how the female heart works, and what factors—from hormones to pregnancy to stress—affect the heart. She emphasizes how frequently heart problems are ignored or misdiagnosed in women; describes in detail the symptoms, signs, and risk factors women should be taught to recognize; suggests how women can take better care of themselves; and offers practical advice on coping when problems occur. One of the first good books on a subject rapidly gaining attention. —*Mary Ellen Sullivan*

Lockie, Andrew.
The Family Guide to Homeopathy: Symptoms and Natural Solutions.
Prentice Hall Press, $24.95 (0-13-306994-X). 802p.

Homeopathy, an alternative health-care system that treats the whole individual by assisting the body's own healing energies, is popular in other countries (Queen Elizabeth is a believer), but it's still looked at askance here, especially by the medical establishment. Nevertheless, homeopathy is growing in acceptance, and this comprehensive overview certainly will give interested readers both general and specific insights about the way homeopathy can be used. The book, a British import, begins with a detailed history and explanation of homeopathic principles, emphasizing first-line preventive defenses such as nutrition, exercise, etc. It goes on to discuss remedies that homeopathic doctors use for various ailments and first-aid treatments. Lockie, a British homeopathic practitioner, divides the bulk of his text by body system and disease and offers specific treatments. Though readers are cautioned to see a doctor or homeopath if a condition worsens or remains the same, the book is really an invitation for self-treatment—among those who can obtain the remedies. (Homeopathic pharmacies are often difficult to find here, unlike in London.) Homeopathy is a complicated art, and while Lockie may oversimplify it a bit, his guide is clearly the first choice for libraries building collections on the subject. —*Ilene Cooper*

Mann, Charles C. and Plummer, Mark L.
The Aspirin Wars: Money, Medicine, and 100 Years of Rampant Competition.
Knopf, $35 (0-394-57894-5). 410p. index.

It is more than a century since acetylsalicylic acid entered the pain-relief marketplace. Mann, coauthor of *The Second Creation: Makers of the Revolution in Twentieth Century Physics*, and Plummer, an economics Ph.D. who spent five years at the Federal Trade Commission, provide an exhaustively documented chronicle of 10 decades of corporate jockeying for position, scientific fashion and folly, and marketing breakthroughs and bloopers. As most consumers know by now, aspirin is like Popeye or Gertrude Stein's rose: It simply is what it is. With chemically indistinguishable products competing for what is today a $25 billion worldwide market for analgesics, aspirin manufacturers have been forced over the years to make an art of "selling the sizzle." Their interactions with the medical profession, the scientific community, government regulators, and the consuming public make this a fascinating study that belongs in most business history collections. —*Mary Carroll*

Marion, Robert.
Learning to Play God: The Coming of Age of a Young Doctor.
Addison-Wesley, $18.95 (0-201-57720-8). 304p.

Marion, a clinical geneticist and medical teacher, writes here about his internship and residency, with his views on the difficulties of the young physician coming across clearly in both theoretical and actual terms. Along the way, Marion cites specific complaints and offers practical suggestions for improving the lot of the young doctor, among them, more humanizing courses and approaches in medical education. Readers will chuckle over the tales of Marion's diagnosis of leprosy (scornfully denied by the attending physician) and his involvement in the bureaucratic web around male child Rodriguez. They will also be saddened or enraged over other clinical and administrative stories. An enjoyable and enlightening read. —*William Beatty*

✔Rothman, David J.
Strangers at the Bedside: A History of How Law and Bioethics Transformed Medical Decision Making.
Basic Books, $24.95 (0-465-08209-2). 356p. index.

Rothman deals primarily with the 25 years since Henry Beecher's controversial article, "Ethics and Clinical Research," appeared in the *New England Journal of Medicine*. After setting the stage with an account of the Committee on Medical Research set up by the federal government in 1941, Rothman shows how the doctor-patient relationship has grown more like that of investigator and subject. This changed relationship accounts for the infamous enormities of the Tuskegee syphilis project, the Willowbrook incident, and other similar events in institutions for the retarded and hospitals for the poor. Rothman also discusses such landmark medical ethics cases as those of Karen Ann Quinlan and *Roe* v. *Wade*. He feels that the disappearances of the doctor's house call and of many community-based and religious hospitals, as well as the growth of subspecialization, have contributed to making doctor and patient truly strangers at the bedside. The patients' bill of rights and the gradually increasing number of nonmedical people involved in medical decision making are also major features of this remarkable change. This solidly written book will create widespread and vigorous discussion and controversy. —*William Beatty*

Schoenewolf, Gerald.
Jennifer and Her Selves.
Donald I. Fine, $20.95 (1-55611-303-X). 229p.

Inevitably, perhaps, popular books about multiple-personality disorder describe patients who have achieved some degree of personality integration—or at least have learned to moderate and control MPD's most destructive manifestations. Without this hopeful, life-affirming conclusion, the intimacy of these explorations of very troubled human beings' devastating pain might feel voyeuristic, even claustrophobic. Schoenewolf's narrative differs from most MPD case studies in providing a session-by-session record of the author's four-month therapeutic relationship with Jennifer, a suicidal young professional dancer disabled by her inadequately diagnosed mental illness, and in its fairly candid description of mistakes the young therapist made, due to inexperience and his own unresolved issues, in managing the intricacies of that relationship. Jennifer's story is involving, and the author's self-doubts humanize him (though he waits a disturbingly long time before seeking his former supervisor's advice about his personal involvement with Jennifer). This belongs in most health collections, but it should be balanced by current studies of the physiology of other serious mental illnesses. —*Mary Carroll*

Seager, Stephen B.
Psychward: A Year behind Locked Doors.
Putnam, $21.95 (0-399-13608-8). 288p.

When Seager, a disaffected emergency-room physician, decided to retrain as a psychiatrist, he spent one year as an intern at a crumbling inner-city mental hospital. Seager recaps his surrealistic year at what was locally referred to as "The Bin," chronicling the tragic cruelties of mental illness and reevaluating the advances and limitations of contemporary psychiatric medicine. The author's commitment to his profession and the healing process was continually challenged by a daunting combination of public indifference, bureaucratic hostility, and his own morbid fears. Seager provides a number of sympathetic profiles of both patients and personnel, infusing the often horrific narrative with compassion, respect, and humanity. A sensitive and riveting firsthand account of the overburdened and understaffed mental-health-care system. —*Margaret Flanagan*

✓Stehli, Annabel.
The Sound of a Miracle: A Child's Triumph over Autism.
Doubleday, $19.95 (0-385-41140-5). 288p.

Stehli's anguish over the death of her oldest daughter, Dotsie, from leukemia and the autism of her youngest, Georgie, is directly, heartbreakingly conveyed in this autobiography. However, it isn't only anguish that is presented; the ultimate emotion here is hope. Stehli remained optimistic that Georgie could develop into a normal child despite hearing numerous doctors and medical professionals tell her that her daughter was hopelessly retarded, that the girl's emotional void was caused by a lack of maternal affection, that Stehli should, in her ex-husband's words, "let Dotsie die and institutionalize Georgie and get on with her life." Dotsie did die, but not before she lived three years longer than anyone predicted. Georgie was not institutionalized. As a teen, she was treated by a European audiologist who discovered that the acute sensitivity of autistic children causes them to turn away from sound (the human voice, even the sound of breathing) because it is so painful. Finally being accepted in the U.S., this realization that autism can have physical causes would certainly have spared the "mom-bashing" promoted by followers of Bruno Bettelheim, once considered *the* authority on dealing with autistic children. Stehli's revelations, especially her insights into battling the medical community, are invaluable for any parent of a child with a physical or psychological disorder. Due to her tenacity, her daughter was cured and is, as the story closes, in graduate school. —*Denise Perry Donavin*

Wall, Patrick D. and Jones, Mervyn.
Defeating Pain: The War against a Silent Epidemic.
Plenum, $24.95 (0-306-43964-6). 300p. index.

Wall is a pioneer in the understanding and treatment of pain, a complaint that costs the U.S. some $50 billion a year. He and collaborator Jones use the term *silent epidemic* to refer to the dismissal of research and clinical studies on pain because the topic was assumed to be insufficiently important, an attitude that started to change only recently. Wall demonstrates both the magnitude and the importance of pain and its effects, and he destroys myths about it. He discusses the types of pain, pain's mechanisms, and the changes in behavior of its victims. A major thrust of the book is the great increase in scientific knowledge of both pain and its treatment. Physicians, patients, and their families, Wall reveals, need no longer be resigned and inactive when pain becomes a problem. Although not all incidences of pain can be controlled, the general feeling among those studying and treating pain now is one of considerable optimism. Laypersons and professionals alike will benefit from this clear and informative book. —*William Beatty*

Wolpert, Lewis.
The Triumph of the Embryo.
Oxford, $21.95 (0-19-854243-7). 203p. index.

"No one who studies development can fail to be filled with a sense of wonder and delight," Wolpert opines near the end of his informative book, and any serious reader will share his feelings. He tells of the major individuals and experiments that have increased our understanding of the cell and the embryo. He goes into forms, patterns, and differentiation of cells up and down the biological scale. He emphasizes gene activity, spatial organization, and cell movement as the three key areas to study. The chapters "Wiring the Brain" and "Regeneration" are exceptionally well done, and what is still unknown is pinpointed in each section. Wolpert not only increases the reader's knowledge but also demolishes some long-held beliefs, such as that old saw about ontogeny recapitulating phylogeny. High school students might well gain ideas for careers from this book, and adults with questions about how they—and their children—developed in embryo will find some fascinating answers. —*William Beatty*

History

History

Abramson, Howard S.
Hero in Disgrace: The Life of Arctic Explorer Frederick A. Cook.
Paragon House, $21.95 (1-55778-322-5). 288p.

Counter, S. Allen.
North Pole Legacy: Black, White & Eskimo.
Univ. of Massachusetts, $24.95 (0-87023-736-5). 220p.

The Great North Pole Controversy raged across front-page headlines in the early 1900s as Robert Peary and Frederick Cook vied for recognition as the first white man to reach the North Pole. Neither claim can be verified with certainty, and the mystery still arouses great passion and eloquence.

Abramson takes Cook's side and reveals what he sees as the nastiest, most vicious scientific fraud ever perpetuated: Peary's relentless and vicious defamation of Cook's character and achievements and insistence that he, and only he, reached the North Pole. Cook, a young doctor, joined Peary's 1891 arctic expedition and discovered his deep affinity for the people and challenges of Greenland. While Cook was kind, generous, and intelligent, Peary was cold, competitive, and cruel, maniacally determined to reach the North Pole. Abramson traces Cook's activities up to and including his arduous journey to the pole, comparing his honest endeavors with the shenanigans of Peary and his influential supporters. While Abramson's scenario for the conspiracy against Cook is persuasive and dramatic, his astonishing accounts of the hardships of arctic exploration capture the imagination and make for entrancing reading.

While Counter supports Peary's claim, his primary focus is on Matthew Henson, the man responsible in many ways for the success of Peary's expeditions, the only African American to have traveled above the Arctic Circle, and a world-class explorer formerly relegated to obscurity by white historians. Intrigued by the rumor that Henson and Peary had fathered children with Eskimo women, Counter travelled to Greenland to investigate. Sure enough, he soon meets Anaukaq, an energetic man in his eighties, dark-skinned, curly-haired, and immensely proud to be Henson's son. After being introduced to Peary's son, Kali, Counter, through great effort, manages to bring the two men and their families to America. His warm and vivid descriptions of these remarkable family reunions and the belated honors bestowed on Henson are triumphant and moving. While the truth about what actually happened on the spinning ice at the top of the world 80 years ago may never be known, at least the story of Matthew Henson has been told. —*Donna Seaman*

Allen, Oliver.
New York, New York: A History of the World's Most Exhilarating and Challenging City.
Atheneum, $27.50 (0-689-11960-7). 448p. index.

At a time when New York City is re-experiencing a surge of rumors about its impending demise, it's reassuring to read about how the city has survived past assaults on its reputation. Allen's brief history of the city, while not boosterism per se, takes less than a hard-eyed look at where New York (specifically Manhattan) has been these past 400 years and where it's headed. His basic premise is that, love it or hate it, New York City is the true birthplace of our nation; for, unlike Plymouth or Jamestown, New York has always epitomized what the rest of the nation was becoming or has aimed to become. Allen puts to good use the popular history style that was his strong suit as a writer for Time-Life Books, giving this lively account broad appeal. A native New Yorker and longtime inhabitant of that city, he also has unearthed some previously overlooked nuggets of information, missing from other histories, about the people, places, and events that shaped the city. —*Mary Banas*

Anthony, Carl Sferrazza.
First Ladies: The Saga of the Presidents' Wives and Their Power, 1961–1990.
Morrow, $29.95 (0-688-10562-9). 608p. index.

The second and concluding volume of a landmark history of America's first ladies features in-depth profiles of Jacqueline Kennedy, Lady Bird Johnson, Pat Nixon, Betty Ford, Rosalyn Carter, Nancy Reagan, and Barbara Bush. As in the preceding installment, Anthony emphasizes the unique imprint each woman impressed upon the unofficial office of the first lady, reshaping and redefining the role of the president's spouse through the years. Though the arrangement is necessarily chronological, relevant information pertaining to previous first ladies is skillfully interwoven into the absorbing narrative, creating a coherent historical framework for the evolution of the first ladyship. Exhaustively researched and meticulously presented, these sensitive and insightful portraits contain a wealth of invaluable biographical material and will appeal to a wide spectrum of readers. An absolutely essential acquisition for all public libraries. —*Margaret Flanagan*

Armstrong, Karen.
Holy War: The Crusades and Their Impact on Today's World.
Doubleday, $29.95 (0-385-24193-3). 608p. index.

The concept of a holy war and the historical impact of the Crusades are given a timely investigation in Armstrong's study. Armstrong sees a relation between the Crusades and the current situation in the Middle East. Before the Crusades were organized in Europe, Christian, Jew, and Muslim lived together in relative peace in the region that gave birth to the three faiths; after the Crusaders rescued Jerusalem, a cycle of violent wars has afflicted the area throughout history in the name of one faith or another. Armstrong proves to be stronger when illuminating the details of her thesis with striking example after striking example; her rereading of history, however, sometimes suffers as she segues from the past to the present without always making clear the necessary connections. Sifting through the past for lessons for the present can be a dicey enterprise, but the author presents her ideas with skill and sensitivity to the religious beliefs involved. —*John Brosnahan*

History

Balaban, John.
Remembering Heaven's Face.
Poseidon, $19.95 (0-671-69065-5). 288p.

Balaban, safe from service in the Vietnam War as a graduate student in linguistics, volunteered to serve anyway in the unique capacity as a conscientious objector. His "moral witness" is a vivid, still-angry critique of U.S. policy and behavior in Vietnam 20 years after he assisted civilians who were unintended, inevitable targets. His memories also chart friendships there and his deepening response to Vietnamese life, history, and culture. Arranging transport of badly wounded children to the U.S. for the Committee of Responsibility (COR), being detained by the Vietcong, and caring for the wounded during the Tet Offensive were part of his experiences. The sights, sounds, and smells of the more poetic Vietnam he investigated are evoked in lovely passages woven into the more brutal accounts. A recent return trip concludes this evolving perspective. A complex, moving work, despite its often painful content. —*Virginia Dwyer*

Barnett, Correlli.
Engage the Enemy More Closely: The Royal Navy in the Second World War.
Norton, $35 (0-393-02918-2). 750p. index.

A sprawling narrative of Britannia's struggle to preserve rule of the waves from marauding Axis submarines, airplanes, and battleships, this story faithfully serves up prominent bits of war lore. Up blows the *Hood*, down goes the *Bismarck*, hard aport heels the *Warspite*, her pugnacious admiral Cunningham at the helm, and in the van follow all the lesser vessels that found themselves in battle during the six-year-long war. Standard-issue stories, yes, but Barnett's monument carries this important bonus—an extremely cogent analysis of the vital logistical and strategic backdrop to each campaign. How could His Majesty's ships prevail over prewar neglect (which turned the Royal Navy into "a fashionable yacht club"), German technical prowess, fiascos like the Norway defeat of 1940, a precarious dominance of the Mediterranean, or the crucial war of attrition in the North Atlantic? His explanations are centuries of fighting tradition (the title copies Nelson's orders from the Battle of Trafalgar in 1805), critical U.S. aid, and perhaps most of all, code-breaking courtesy of the Ultra secret—so sensitive it was not revealed until the 1970s—which time and again enabled the Royal Navy to achieve the old military maxim: get there first with the most. That's what happened in the climactic defeat of the German U-boats in 1943, so anchors aweigh with this expertly tuned balance between microscopic detail and macroscopic perspective. —*Gilbert Taylor*

Beschloss, Michael R.
The Crisis Years: Kennedy and Khrushchev, 1960–1963.
HarperCollins, $29.95 (0-06-016454-9). 786p. index.

Beschloss picks up in his newest book where he left off in *Mayday: Eisenhower, Khrushchev and the U-2 Affair*, and he doesn't disappoint. In week-by-week detail, the author and scholar covers the professional relationship between Kennedy and Khrushchev. From their first meeting years before Kennedy was inaugurated to Jacqueline's post-funeral correspondence, this lengthy portrait of two world leaders and a crucial time in history is grounded in careful research. Beschloss draws upon Soviet sources that have only recently been made available for study as well as secret letters and interviews. The Cuban missile crisis will always stand out as an example of how easily the balance of foreign relations can be upset, and this is what Beschloss explores. The author is also aware of the innate drama resulting from the interplay between young, Harvard-educated JFK and the time-tested Khrushchev (who didn't learn to read until in his thirties), and he emphasizes it throughout this very readable work. In addition, the respect both leaders had for each other comes through in Beschloss' writing, which includes commentary on diplomatic life. For a book that should generate wide interest, Beschloss perhaps too often assumes that the reader has previous knowledge of this period in world history and has met the major players before. —*Kathryn LaBarbera*

Blew, Mary Clearman.
All but the Waltz: Essays on a Montana Family.
Viking, $19.95 (0-670-83108-5). 226p.

Short-story writer Blew's narrative skills propel these essays—part memory, part history—about ranching in Montana. She recalls the Judith River flooding. She remembers her father opposing her education before fleeing home to die mysteriously one of the many violent deaths that her family suffers phlegmatically. Skeptical of the romantic distortions of the American West, she nevertheless fondly portrays herself and her sister as young cowgirls "riding the broncs we had roped and hobbled and sacked out in the old cowboy way." She ponders 100-year-old family portraits, deciphers her great-grandfather's self-consciously literary observations about ranching and nature, pieces together her mother's childhood from stories told by her aunts, and listens to ranchers rail against the encroachments upon their way of life by wage laborers. Recurring, concatenated characters, places, and themes (e.g., memory, the reconstruction of history) give these essays a novelistic unity. The collection thereby becomes simultaneously an autobiography within a family context, a family biography from the perspective of one of its members, and a chronicle of the West. —*Roland Wulbert*

Blum, John Morton.
Years of Discord: American Politics and Society, 1961–1974.
Norton, $25 (0-393-02969-7). 608p.

As a political review of the high noon of American liberalism, its lofty goals, its earnest illusion that there was no problem, foreign or domestic, that the judicious application of force or money could not solve, Blum's articulate narrative is one of the smoothest syntheses in recent years. He posits, though, that only the foreign half of the mirage—the Vietnam debacle—melted down a cast of political mind that has yet to be reforged. At the start, it was a relatively coherent agenda prepared by influential intellectuals, cautiously espoused by Kennedy, exuberantly enacted under Johnson, and rounded out by Nixon. But it degenerated into the special-interest soup of today. For that, Blum indicts the aforesaid Asian war, which, besides disagreement over its intrinsic merits, leeched funds from the Great Society programs, and the failure of the two Democratic presidents to "propose truly redistributive taxation." Thus failure and discord stemmed from the federal government not getting enough money to spend for beneficent domestic purposes. This is a debatable proposition to say the least, but, with his chapters on the activist Supreme Court, electoral campaigns, the volatile politics of the New Left and black nationalist dissenters, and the collapse of the imperial presidency in the Watergate scandal, his partisan case is presented so lucidly, if not altogether persuasively, that it ought to be in every public library. —*Gilbert Taylor*

Bowden, Charles.
Desierto: Memories of the Future.
Norton, $18.95 (0-393-02935-2). 224p.

Bowden, a renegade and soulful journalist and deep critic of our times, patrols the desert of the Southwest, galvanized by the ruthlessness of life. Fascinated with Mexico's brutal drug culture, he stalked a notorious dealer in *Red Line*, while his latest foray into the wilds of Sonora led him to the sanctuary of a paid assassin and tiny, grubby villages perched on the edge of giant marijuana and poppy fields, where gruesome torture and murder is an expected aspect of "the life" of drugs and big money. Bowden's wanderings and ponderings also bring us into the richly imagined and sensual world of the Seri and Yaqui Indians and, in stunning contrast, the cold-blooded, phony empire of Charles Keating, Jr. As Bowden plunges into each realm, he intuits its lack of morality and the pervasive power of lust and discovers a telling parallel in the behavior of mountain lions and an old song's refrain: "I am in love with your cruelty." Bowden is a seer, writing about hard truths with incantational authority. —*Donna Seaman*

Braudel, Fernand.
The Identity of France: Volume II: People and Production.
HarperCollins, $35 (0-06-016212-0). 781p. index.

The second volume of Braudel's history of French society and civilization—a project that was concluded prematurely because of Braudel's death in 1985—takes up the narrative chronology by means of cycles that show how the country expanded and contracted from prehistoric times to the twentieth century. The regions, population, and economy of France are used to illustrate the inherent diversity of the country, in both a physical and an intellectual sense, with Braudel examining a multiplicity of causes, effects, and transformations in his usual inquisitive manner. For Braudel, the frontiers of his country represented not just physical barriers but also places where nationalism ended and international influence began and where the structure of French society would grow, wither, and renew itself. —*John Brosnahan*

Buckley, Kevin.
Panama: The Whole Story.
Simon & Schuster, $19.95 (0-671-72794-X). 270p. index.

Buckley takes the story of Panamanian politics from the 1985 assassination of opposition leader-in-exile Hugo Spadafora by military forces under the control of General Manuel Noriega down through Noriega's own downfall at the hands of an American invasion force ordered by President Bush in 1990. Buckley tends to paint his players in black and white and to brush on his descriptions with the violent colors of exposé journalese; since it's not a particularly pretty picture that's being sketched out, the vivid caricatures can be forgiven. Buckley also examines the U.S.-Panama connection on the Irangate front and the Nicaraguan revolution, the author relating how the U.S. first supported Noriega despite his crime and drug connections. There is lots of juicy detail here on who was responsible and who may have known what was really happening in Central America. —*John Brosnahan*

Burns, Michael.
Dreyfus: A Family Affair, 1789–1945.
HarperCollins, $30 (0-06-016366-6). 576p. index.

Burns places the shameful Dreyfus affair of the late 1890s into proper social, cultural, and historical perspective by tracing the evolution of the extended Dreyfus family from the French Revolution to the conclusion of World War II. The fascinating chronicle of the six generations of the Dreyfus clan profiled represents the often tortuous course of the typical French-Jewish dynasty. Though thoroughly assimilated and patriotic Francophiles, the Dreyfuses were plagued by the particularly insidious brand of anti-Semitism that penetrated all levels of European society for centuries. In addition to providing a unique preface and postscript to the exhaustively analyzed and documented Dreyfus affair, the author also offers an intimate portrait of Alfred Dreyfus in the context of his personal relationships with an array of family members. Popular history at its most gripping. —*Margaret Flanagan*

Carson, Clayborne and others.
The Eyes on the Prize Civil Rights Reader: Documents, Speeches, and Firsthand Accounts from the Black Freedom Struggle, 1954–1990.
Viking, $25 (0-670-84217-6); Penguin, paper, $14.95 (0-14-015403-5). 735p. index.

An anthology of primary material important in the historiography of this country's civil rights movement. An updated revision of the 1987 Penguin publication *Eyes on the Prize: America's Civil Rights Years,* which appeared in conjunction with the acclaimed 14-part PBS television series "Eyes on the Prize," this collection gathers such essential documents as landmark Martin Luther King, Jr., speeches; the text of the *Brown* v. *Board of Education* Supreme Court case; excerpts from significant writings of Malcolm X; and a 1980 address delivered in Atlanta by African National Congress leader Nelson Mandela. Not simply for reference use, this compilation makes provocative cover-to-cover reading and is extremely worthy of consideration by every

History

library, even by those whose holdings include the previous edition. —*Brad Hooper*

Clarke, Thurston.
Pearl Harbor Ghosts: A Journey to Hawaii Then and Now.
Morrow, $22 (0-688-04468-9). 352p. index.

A sociological exploration of Pearl Harbor that juxtaposes the Hawaii of 1941 with the Hawaii of 1991 in order to analyze the abiding mystique of the "most obsessively examined battle in military history." A series of firsthand accounts by Pearl Harbor survivors serves as a mesmerizing oral history of an undisputed twentieth-century benchmark. The interview subjects include Japanese, Japanese Americans, native Hawaiians, members of the Caucasian elite, and a variety of servicemen stationed on Oahu in 1941. Each individual recollection reinforces Clarke's fundamental theory that Pearl Harbor represents a personal, national, and global turning point that continues to exert influence upon the political, economic, and cultural destiny of the U.S. In addition, the author also offers an enlightening overview of the progressively devastating cultural and environmental devolution of the Hawaiian islands during the past five decades. A valuable acquisition, even after the fiftieth anniversary of Pearl Harbor is only a dim memory. —*Margaret Flanagan*

✔Constable, Pamela and Valenzuela, Arturo.
A Nation of Enemies: Chile under Pinochet.
Norton, $24.95 (0-393-03011-3). 416p. index.

By a foreign correspondent for the *Boston Globe* teamed with the director of the center for Latin American Studies at Georgetown University, a vigorously comprehensive but very approachable examination of the 17 years (1973–90) General Augusto Pinochet ruled Chile with an iron fist. The story of this repressive military regime in a country that, unusual for South America, had a time-honored democratic tradition, actually began in 1970 with the advent into the presidential office of Salvador Allende, the first freely elected Marxist head of state *in the world*. Dissent from the Right burgeoned into open rebellion, and in a lightning coup, Allende was displaced by Pinochet, whose intention was to recast Chilean institutions and values in his own efficient but narrow mold. Responsibly, Constable and Valenzuela track the record of Pinochet's dictatorship, and in the process, they reveal Pinochet's self-aggrandizing style of government, identifying who benefited from authoritarianism and who did not, asserting that Chile under Pinochet was a society divided nearly in two by fear and hostility. Answers to how and why an advanced nation succumbed to military rule are explained both expansively and accessibly. —*Brad Hooper*

Counter, S. Allen.
North Pole Legacy: Black, White & Eskimo.
Univ. of Massachusetts, $24.95 (0-87023-736-5). 220p.

See p.94.

Daley, Robert.
Portraits of France.
Little, Brown, $24.95 (0-316-17185-9). 496p.

Daley, an American writer who for several years worked as a correspondent in Paris, came to France for the first time in the early 1950s; his recollection of this life-altering introduction to things Gallic is the first essay in a beautifully evocative collection that celebrates France's multifarious wonders. Simultaneously exercising exquisite senses of history, culture, human nature, geography, and good storytelling, Daley goes to rich length— the essays average 25 pages—to share fascinating detail about such topics as the Verdun battlefield (where a horrible exchange between French and German troops occurred in 1916), Charles de Gaulle as paradigm of the French national character, the wine industry supporting the city of Bordeaux, Monaco's history and Princess Grace's place in it, and, naturally, the lovely face and beguiling personality of Paris. Francophilia is not a prerequisite— only an asset—to enjoying these exquisitely written pieces. —*Brad Hooper*

Darnton, Robert.
Berlin Journal: 1989–1990.
Norton, $22.95 (0-393-02970-0). 352p.

Historian Darnton spent parts of 1989 and 1990 in Germany, witnessing the end of that country's division into East and West as the Berlin Wall fell. His report on that revolution and his portraits of the people involved inevitably will provoke comparisons with the French Revolution that Darnton has written about in his other works. In a journal that is informed by the historian's skill, the author focuses more on events and aftereffects in East Germany as experienced by ordinary citizens, rather than trying to write a definitive study. Darnton talks with workers, bureaucrats, and government officials and describes what was happening and what the people understood about these momentous events. Darnton also advances some cautious judgments but, with scholarly adeptness, refuses to advance predictions of the future of the new Germany. Chronology. —*John Brosnahan*

Dershowitz, Alan M.
Chutzpah.
Little, Brown, $22.95 (0-316-18137-4). 352p.

Dershowitz—lawyer, commentator, and author—is as famous for his unwavering focus on human rights as he is for his forceful personality. His three previous books, including *Taking Liberties,* have also earned him accolades for his superb legal writing, and no one has overlooked the fact that he is a Jew. Jewishness is the theme of this electric, supplely argued, deeply moral, and outspoken analysis. Dershowitz opens brashly by stating that "American Jews need more chutzpah," i.e., "assertiveness, a willingness to demand what is due." Why do American Jews need more of it? Because many still think of themselves as second-class citizens, "guests," if you will, of the "real" Americans. As Dershowitz relates his personal history—growing up Orthodox in Brooklyn, racking up honors at Yale Law School, and discovering

History

the insidious anti-Semitism of the law profession at large and at Harvard in particular (when he became a professor there)—he exposes layers of fear, guilt, and confused thinking on the part of Jews and the hatred and bigotry perpetuated by their enemies, typified by the hate mail he receives after television appearances. Moving fluidly from the personal to the historical, Dershowitz discusses the failure of the world to punish those responsible for the Holocaust, the complete erasure of Jewish history in Poland, and the double standards used to scrutinize and threaten Israel. With humor (thanks, in part, to quotes from his mother), compassion, vision, vigor, and courage, Dershowitz offers a challenging assessment of American Jews at the close of a violent century. —*Donna Seaman*

Donnelly, Thomas and others.
Operation Just Cause: The Invasion of Panama.
Lexington, $24.95 (0-669-24975-0). 435p.

Because of the diffidence and inexperience generalist journalists often bring to reporting a military event, the nuts-and-bolts mechanics of "taking down" Noriega and his Panama Defense Force was barely a story at all. Aside from articles on the baptisms of fire for the Stealth fighter and a female MP, the choreography of the nocturnal assault and ensuing firefights was usually lost in reporting on the propriety of using force and its aftermath. Rectifying the lapse is this trio of defense correspondents, who offer a platoon-level reconstruction of what actually happened on December 20, 1989, from the American soldier's point of view. Twenty-three of them died, and for the remainder who parachuted from planes and assaulted roadblocks and buildings, squeezing off magazines on the fly, the fighting "got real personal real quick," as one soldier said. Having interviewed hundreds of participants, from four-stars to privates, these writers stitch together an account that falls between the crazy quilt of personal tales of fear and bravery and the more uniform fabric of the overall planning and successful execution of the invasion. A useful pairing with treatments of the political context, such as *Divorcing the Dictator* by Kempe or *The Commanders* by Woodward. —*Gilbert Taylor*

Easton, Robert and Easton, Jane.
Love and War: Pearl Harbor through V-J Day.
Univ. of Oklahoma, $24.95 (0-8061-2336-2). 400p. index.

Reading this unique collection of personal war correspondence between a military husband and his wife, covering the years of America's involvement in World War II, is somewhat like sneaking into the attic and guiltily poring over the most intimate details of one's parents' lives. But these detailed letters by Robert and Jane Easton also have historic value, for they bring a personal perspective to the war and, in their immediacy, show how it was fought by individuals both in the war zone and on the home front. Robert's letters are filled with a subtle irony and quick wit and contain details of army life not found elsewhere, while Jane's letters are ponderous and philosophical, worrying over the war's broad implications while detailing Jane's often pressing responsibilities as a wife, mother, and daughter trying to hold her family together. The authors have slightly edited and annotated their letters for the sake of clarity and have interspersed summaries of events throughout the book in order to place their correspondence in historical context, but the Eastons' old-fashioned, somewhat formal writing style remains intact, adding a certain quaintness to the letters. A fascinating look at the human face of war. —*Mary Banas*

✔**Edmonds, Robin.**
The Big Three: Churchill, Roosevelt, and Stalin in Peace and War.
Norton, $24.95 (0-393-02889-5). 416p.

Though the formation of the Grand Alliance had the whiff of inevitability about it, the anti-Hitler triumvirate was in actual operation a rocky, ad hoc arrangement. No formal treaty ever bound the troika. As described in this work comprehensively wired to the documentary record, each member came to be allied via a highly complex series of reactions to the Nazi threat. In brief, the USSR and Britain blundered into, rather than designed, an alliance, and the U.S. came into the grouping after Pearl Harbor almost as a response to Hitler's expectations. Edmonds, a former British diplomat, delves into the ensuing chain of events from the Olympian perspective of high strategy: the rationale for and conduct of the invasion of North Africa and Italy (it comes across as a gigantic sideshow), the wrangling over when to invade Europe, and the negotiations at the several summit conferences between the leaders (which too often fudged questions about the postwar order). The author takes a scrupulously dispassionate tack toward inter-Allied diplomacy, conveying a tone that seems to overly compensate for the ideological component of Soviet policies by simply ignoring it. Yet one could equally say that it is high time for a first-rate examination of the titanic struggle unblinkered by biases that, after victory, annealed into the cold war. This, drawing on newly available Soviet material, is it. —*Gilbert Taylor*

Goetzmann, William H.
The First Americans: Photographs from the Library of Congress.
Starwood Publishing, $30 (0-912347-96-1). 144p. index.

Historian Goetzmann alerts us immediately to the fact that the turn-of-the-century commercial photographs of native Americans in this handsome volume are not straightforward documentations of life, but rather, manipulated images loaded with the values of the photographers and their customers. These pictures, submitted to the Library of Congress for federal copyright, "embodied sentimental notions about the 'vanishing American,'" a variation on the archetypal noble savage. By the 1880s, when celluloid film became available, there were few "coherent Native American cultures" left to photograph. That fact, combined with Victorian concepts of the grand and picturesque, shaped these staged yet haunting and powerful portraits. The work of Edward Curtis is emphasized in this selection of 105 striking photographs by various photographers. Goetzmann's captions accent the irony and pathos of these pictures, which, in spite of their artificiality, still capture moments in the lives of real people experiencing the destruction of their universe. —*Donna Seaman*

Gorkin, Michael.
Days of Honey, Days of Onion: The Story of a Palestinian Family in Israel.
Beacon, $24.95 (0-8070-6902-7). 286p.

Gorkin's tactile description of the life of one Palestinian Arab family living in Israel is decidedly documentary rather than political commentary. The author, an American-born Jew, keeps a low profile and tells the story of village life in Kufr Quara in the words of Abu Ahmad, his wife, and children. In accordance with Muslim tradition, Abu Ahmad and his wife, who had been called Ali and Fadwa, became known as Abu and Umm Ahmad (father and mother of Ahmad) when their first son was born. Their recollections give fascinating glimpses into the many facets of change that have transpired in the village since the establishment of the state of Israel, including an increase in literacy and a decrease in farming. Mundane events and special ones—such as weddings, deaths, and the friendships in Abu Ahmad's life—help to illuminate the complexities of relations between the sexes as well as between Arab and Jew. In addition, Gorkin explores young people's political allegiances, including their opinion of Saddam Hussein and the invasion of Kuwait, their admiration for the Intifada, and their attitudes toward the rise of Islamic fundamentalism. An ever-timely volume featuring a wealth of cultural detail. —*Anne Schmitt*

Gottlieb, Sherry Gershon.
Hell No, We Won't Go! Evading the Draft during the Vietnam War.
Viking, $21.95 (0-670-83935-3). 244p. index.

Any competent oral history of the 1960s should have nostalgic value. Any oral history of draft evasion should raise moral and ethical issues of more than passing interest. Gottlieb's oral history of draft evasion in the 1960s works on both those counts and is also surprisingly entertaining and literate. Literate because its storytellers are mostly gifted anecdotalists. Entertaining because, given time's license to exaggerate, many have transformed memories into tall tales. The humor that some of them find in choices that were, after all, criminal infuriated patriots in the 1960s and still may today, but it *is* funny. Gary Isringhaus, for instance, took group therapy "to develop a case of passive-aggressive behavior—in other words, I was a pacifist, but if I was pushed into the army, I might kill my superiors." His performance convinced his draft board to conclude that "if you're the kind of guy who would kill his superiors, you're probably the kind of guy we want." Professionally edited, sorted by type of evader (expatriates, conscientious objectors, etc.), these memoirs' attractions as documents and as literature well may increase with time. —*Roland Wulbert*

Grant, Michael.
The Founders of the Western World: A History of Greece and Rome.
Scribner, $27.50 (0-684-19303-5). 352p. index.

In multiversities where the study of the history of performance art counts toward graduation as much as a course in Greco-Roman civilization, Grant would likely be found gnashing his teeth. Perhaps the foremost living classicist, he resists the dilution of our debt to the likes of Pericles, Socrates, Augustus, Virgil, etc., in this masterful synopsis of a millennium of history. The story and Grant's personal interpretation are succinct—the rise of Hellenistic culture and philosophies, its political collapse in the Peloponnesian War, Alexander the Great's immortal but insubstantial conquests, and everything's absorption by and propagation to the future under the auspices of the Pax Romana. Sure there were problems, like slavery for one, but when folks refer to humanity rising above the law of the jungle, it is always to these awesome steps out of the muck to which they refer. A cornerstone acquisition for any and every library. —*Gilbert Taylor*

Green, Julian.
Paris.
Marion Boyars, $19.95 (0-7145-2927-3). 160p.
Wiser, William.
The Great Good Place: American Expatriate Women in Paris.
Norton, $20.95 (0-393-02999-9). 352p.

Two heartfelt tributes to Paris' singular allure and fecund artistic climate.

Green, an American born (1900) and bred in Paris, has achieved tremendous literary success there but was unknown here until the release of *The Distant Lands*, a novel about the American South. Now another of his new works is available in this country, a bilingual edition of meditations on his beloved city. Green approaches Paris in a prose equivalent of a "long, aimless stroll," claiming that the only way to really know a city is "to waste time in it." Green doesn't waste a word in his piercing descriptions of Paris in light and rain, seen from high spots or explored slowly on foot. He practices the divination of sustained observation, perceiving and expressing the moods of the Seine, the echoes of past emotions in secret places, and the poise, charm, and, sometimes, ugliness of Parisian architecture. Green's photographs of Paris over the past 70 years (some of which are traveling in a current exhibition) make this a trilingual celebration of one artist's lifelong involvement with his muse.

Wiser is another American in love with Paris. His *Crazy Years, Paris in the Twenties* documented that fervently creative and competitively social decade. Now his study focuses on the private lives of five diverse and influential expatriate women: Mary Cassatt, Edith Wharton, Caresse Crosby, Zelda Fitzgerald, and Josephine Baker. His vibrant, frank profiles are composed of imagined scenes based on letters, memoirs, and gossip with an evolving Paris in the background. Wiser dramatizes each woman's Parisian experiences, which range from release and inspiration for the disciplined Cassatt and Wharton to adventures with drugs and sex for Crosby, a miasma of unsettled-

History

ness and discouragement for Fitzgerald, and dazzling success for Baker. These succinct and revealing portraits create an illuminating and unique cross section of American women expatriates during Paris' heyday. —*Donna Seaman*

Greene, Melissa Fay.
Praying for Sheetrock.
Addison-Wesley, $21.95 (0-201-55048-2). 338p.

This is the story of the racial integration of McIntosh County, Georgia—how one particular section of the Old South, still racially separate, moved into the decidedly more egalitarian days of the post–civil rights movement. As Greene tells it, county sheriff Tom Poppell pretty much ran things as in his own private fiefdom, but by the 1970s his kind of *caudillo* had for the most part disappeared from the South. And when a certain event transpired that clearly showed the inferior status of blacks in the eyes of the law, it turned out to be the straw that broke the camel's back: the struggle to incorporate blacks into the county's political and economic institutions had begun (the success today can be measured by increased black participation in local government). Though Greene tends to overwrite—to lend more poignancy to the details, it seems—this is nonetheless a moving piece of civil-rights history. —*Brad Hooper*

Gurevich, David.
From Lenin to Lennon: A Memoir of Russia in the Sixties.
HBJ, $19.95 (0-15-149825-3). 268p.

Born in 1951, the author was raised in the obscure Volga River city of Syzran, site of his father's posting at an air force base. After becoming a translator following graduation from Moscow's Institute for Foreign Languages, Gurevich shepherded foreign tourists around the country, and finally, fed up with the Orwellian stress of living one way and thinking another, emigrated to the West and freedom in 1975. Looking back, the stifling society he remembers had slovenly cityscapes overgrown with weeds and mud, boring Marxist indoctrination, constant anxiety about real or imagined informants, and oceans of vodka. (The eventual counterbalance to all this was rock 'n' roll, "the battering ram that the West drove into our collective psyche.") The quotidian incidents connecting these dots are delivered with great emotive effect, a combination of straightforward description and some hilariously snide incidents, as when Gurevich translated an Angela Davis letter to the Soviet Women's Committee. An appropriate selection for larger libraries, but mandatory for any whose constituents include Russian émigrés. —*Gilbert Taylor*

✔Heat-Moon, William Least.
PrairyErth (a deep map).
Houghton, $24.95 (0-395-48602-5). 624p.

Heat-Moon's *Blue Highways* was acclaimed as a masterpiece and has become a standard of the American road. His second travel book is destined to once again change the way we see and think. "PrairyErth" is an old geological term for grassland soil, the type Heat-Moon covered in his latest quest, a spiraling trek through Chase County, Kansas. This rectangle in the heart of the country includes the subtly beautiful Flint Hills of eastern Kansas and the last remaining tallgrass prairie in the country. As Heat-Moon contemplated maps of the county, he realized that the lines were like the grids used at archaeological digs and that his intense exploration was vertical as well as horizontal, reaching down into the ground and into the past, creating a "deep map" in which depth is a dimension of time, space, perspective, and emotion. He studied the deceptively plain terrain and its hidden history by walking, talking, listening, and reading, amassing an astonishing collection of anecdotes, conversations, memories, and quotes from journals and books. Heat-Moon puts them all together as though he's building a farmer's wall, discovering the right fit or connection between each story, each stone. He holds us rapt with tales of tornadoes, floods, and fire; survival, conflict, greed, and murder. We meet the prairie's natives, called the Kaw or the Kansa, and the white settlers who took over—vivid personalities from the past as well as feisty characters of the present, hanging on in small, fading towns. *PrairyErth* is a feat of sustained watchfulness, concentration, passion, and spiritual vigor, a creation drenched with the magic of dreams and clarified with the sharpness of intellect. —*Donna Seaman*

Hibbert, Christopher.
The Virgin Queen: Elizabeth I, Genius of the Golden Age.
Addison-Wesley, $25 (0-201-15626-1). 336p. index.

Expectedly in a book by this esteemed British historian, a biography of the great Tudor queen that is a joy in its perceptiveness and stylishness. Hibbert offers not a reassessment but a reemphasis of Elizabeth I's qualities. As so colorfully depicted here, her childhood and young womanhood went unsmoothly, a manifestation of the vagaries of her status in the realm: as daughter of the executed Anne Boleyn, later as Protestant sister to the very Catholic Queen Mary I. Coming into her own as sovereign, Elizabeth struggled not without difficulty but indeed with talent in negotiating a successful path down the rocky road of Renaissance kingship. Gloriana fascinated people in her own time; and such a fine rendition of her quirks and accomplishments as Hibbert's—without burying his head in the sand with regard to the less polished of her actions as monarch, of course—keeps her fascination alive for modern readers. —*Brad Hooper*

Himmelfarb, Gertrude.
Poverty and Compassion: The Moral Imagination of the Late Victorians.
Knopf, $30 (0-679-40119-9). 496p. index.

Palliating poverty has never lacked proposed solutions, and Himmelfarb's repute as a cogent elucidator of the question doesn't diminish in this volume. Examining a compact space and time—London in the 1880s—she explicates the stew of ideas and sentiments that animated those stereotypically stodgy Victorians. These came out in reform-minded articles, books, and tracts that

History

defined the poor statistically, often coupled with some waif's heartrending story of abject degradation. The most admirable wave amid this veritable flood, in her view, was a massive study called *Life and Labour of the People in London*, written and financed by Charles Booth, who forsook his business empire for the purpose. Common to the Victorians was the zeitgeist notion that England's unprecedented wealth made a diminution of poverty possible—but whether it was to be done under the auspices of the state or through private philanthropy divided them (as it does us). Another incisive work by Himmelfarb, guru-by-acclamation of nineteenth-century English society. —*Gilbert Taylor*

Hourani, Albert.
A History of the Arab Peoples.
Harvard, $24.95 (0-674-39565-4). 532p. index.

This timely study covers much of the same territory as Lapidus' *History of Islamic Societies*, although Hourani restricts his account to the Arabic-speaking Islamic world. The author begins his narrative with a brief consideration of the evolution of the Arab people before Muhammad's time and then relates the development of both the religious and the temporal empires across the Middle East, northern Africa, and parts of Europe. Hourani takes into account both Muslim traditions and current scholarly research to show how Islam eventually became the dominant religion among the Arab people, and to discuss the emergence of the several important Muslim sects. Along with these religious matters, the book covers social and cultural developments and provides a political history of ruling dynasties in many Arab countries over the centuries. Of course, much interest will center on the coverage of the role of Islamic fundamentalism and current issues in the Middle East, including the Palestinian question. Here Hourani gives a number of insights into conditions within the various Arab countries, their relationships within the Arab world, and their growing role on an international level. —*John Brosnahan*

Idinopulos, Thomas A.
Jerusalem Blessed, Jerusalem Cursed: Jews, Christians, and Muslims in the Holy City from David's Time to Our Own.
Ivan R. Dee, $30 (0-929587-66-9). 368p.

Jews, Muslims, and Christians have lived in Jerusalem for more than 3,000 years, fearing and distrusting each other, spawning what Idinopulos calls the Jerusalem problem. This is a book about ancient religious traditions and about the centuries of warfare "that have permanently scarred Jerusalem, making her face both forbidding and fascinating." As one would expect, he divides this history of the world's holiest city into the meaning of Jerusalem in Jewish history, the history of Christian conflict in Jerusalem, and Jerusalem's holiness in Islamic tradition. The book is a prodigious and imposing work, as timely as it is provocative. Six maps and 22 photographs and drawings are included. —*George Cohen*

Ione, Carole.
Pride of Family: Four Generations of American Women of Color.
Summit, $19.95 (0-671-54453-5). 224p.

Ione, a writer and a psychotherapist, vibrantly and in telling detail describes what it was like to grow up in a household composed almost exclusively of accomplished black women at a time when few women of any color made successful lives for themselves. Her inspiration for this book was the diary of her great-grandmother, an ambitious, Reconstruction-era feminist, abolitionist, and writer who, by her own example, encouraged her daughters to pursue independent careers. Much of this biography focuses on Ione's colorful childhood memories of her spirited grandmother, a chorus-line dancer during the roaring 1920s and an unabashed gambler; her great-aunt, an elegant but prim and proper medical doctor and social reformer who was always at odds with her chorine sister's flamboyant life-style; and the author's oft-absent mother, a journalist and murder-mystery writer. The men in the family were equally prominent and accomplished and included a sociologist, a Reconstruction-era judge, an actor, and a lumber merchant–publisher. However, they are notably absent from Ione's account and, in fact, provided an incentive for her to write this biography as a way of discovering for herself a sense of family. Of special interest are the author's depictions of intraracial (black-on-black) prejudice. —*Mary Banas*

Johnson, Haynes.
Sleepwalking through History: America in the Reagan Years.
Norton, $24.95 (0-393-02937-9). 500p.

Under Ronald Reagan, it may have been morning again in America, but the country is just now waking up to a dreadful national nightmare. So opines Haynes Johnson in his review of the Reagan administration's accomplishments, which now seem more akin to the aftershocks of a social and political earthquake. The Pulitzer Prize–winning reporter for the *Washington Post* has harsh words for the former chief executive, but the author's judgments don't diverge that much from the already published accounts of Reagan's friends, colleagues, associates, and family members. What is highlighted here is the context of the Reagan revolution—why it succeeded in the first place and what its success portends for the future. As much an indictment of the current state of American civilization as a condemnation of Reagan, Johnson's study fingers all the usual suspects—Donald Trump, Jim Bakker, New York's nouveau society—in its examination of the consequences of Reaganomics. —*John Brosnahan*

✔**Johnson, Paul.**
The Birth of the Modern: World Society, 1815–1830.
HarperCollins, $35 (0-06-016574-X). 1,095p. index.

Johnson isolates what he terms a significant 15-year period in which the foundations of modern society and civilization took shape and took hold around the world. Between 1815 and 1830, the ideas of political reform and the technology of the industrial awakening that emerged in the late

History

eighteenth century would evolve into a structure whose full effect would not be felt until the twentieth century. To tell his story, historian Johnson relies on an orthodox chronicle-narrative that not only covers the great events and personalities of the time but also delves into the more mundane facts of everyday existence. The result is a multidimensional and cross-cultural study that is enlivened at every step by Johnson's flowing style and his observations of every aspect of human activity. —*John Brosnahan*

Johnson, Ronald.
Out of the North.
Plover Press, $16.95 (0-917635-10-8); paper, $8.95 (0-917635-11-6). 140p.

A robust and hugely entertaining memoir of life in Alaska in the 1940s and 1950s. Johnson, a Minnesotan, worked all sorts of construction jobs all over Alaska, including building docks and an airport, blacktopping roads, and running heavy equipment in steam power plants. He got to know a memorable assortment of independent, eccentric, and tough individuals—"construction stiffs, badasses, and whores"—and relates their rambunctious escapades with rough-and-ready charm, dry humor, and genuine, if somewhat bemused, respect. Johnson doesn't write about Alaska's pristine wilderness, ancient Eskimo culture, or proud, law-abiding citizens; no, his world is the land of hard, dangerous jobs, serious drinking, barroom brawls, strippers, pimps, sneak thieves, and guys "who couldn't stand prosperity." He vividly re-creates the spirit of that time and place and tells a helluva good story. —*Donna Seaman*

Kahn, Annette.
Why My Father Died: A Daughter Confronts Her Family's Past at the Trial of Klaus Barbie.
Summit, $19.95 (0-671-65883-2). 240p.

On August 17, 1944, the author's father, Robert Kahn, and 49 other French Jews were shot by the Germans after digging out unexploded bombs at the Bron airfield. The SS wanted the airport ready for their escape from advancing Allied troops. The author saw her father for the last time when she was two-and-a-half years old and her brother was three-and-a-half. Robert Kahn, a member of the French Resistance, had been arrested by Klaus Barbie, the so-called Butcher of Lyon, in late 1943, was rescued by the Resistance, and was eventually recaptured by Barbie's militia. From prison, he managed to put his children in a safe hideaway for the remainder of the war, but his non-Jewish wife would not leave Lyon without her husband. On August 11, 1944, she was sent to Auschwitz. She survived but did not speak of her suffering for more than 40 years. In this book, Kahn's mother breaks her long silence to tell the story of the Resistance, her husband's role in it (recruiting opponents of the collaborationist Vichy government), and her imprisonment in Auschwitz. Interspersed with this memoir is Annette Kahn's coverage of Klaus Barbie's trial, which she was assigned to cover for the French magazine *Le Point*. It is a significant book, offering both an exceptional look into the French Resistance movement and a firsthand account of Auschwitz, as well as a probing report on the Barbie trial from a journalist whose father died a victim of Barbie. —*George Cohen*

Kammen, Michael.
Mystic Chords of Memory: The Transformation of Tradition in American Culture.
Knopf, $40 (0-394-57769-8). 864p. index.

When and how does a young country lay claim to its past? To answer this question, Kammen identifies some of the fundamental tensions in the American character: tradition versus progress, regionalism versus nationalism, democracy versus professionalism, private initiative versus public responsibility. A distinguished historian, Kammen shows that the needs of the present have governed (often distorted) what Americans remember of their past. In many cases, different groups of Americans have celebrated divergent versions of the past. Yet as the pace of modern culture has quickened, cravings for ties to the past have grown more insistent. Kammen critically surveys the contemporary "tradition industry"—museums, reenactments, restorations, genealogy, scholarship, drama—that caters to this appetite. Upon uncovering instances of chauvinism and commercialism, the author typically responds with wit, occasionally with wrath. The scope of the book reflects not only long research but also broad sympathies. Not all readers will agree that the federal government must serve as custodian of the collective memory, but Kammen's work powerfully illustrates the need to remember and the temptation to forget. —*Bryce Christensen*

✓Katz, D. Mark.
Witness to an Era: The Life and Photographs of Alexander Gardner: The Civil War, Lincoln, and the West.
Viking, $60 (0-670-82820-3). 305p. index.

When most people think of early American photography, they think of Mathew B. Brady, who was, without question, a pioneer in the field but whose name reached far and wide more as a result of his resourceful entrepreneurship than of his artfulness. Perhaps the foremost photographic *craftsman* of Brady's era, then, was Alexander Gardner, a stiff-upper-lip sort of immigrant Scotsman who, before opening his own studio, honed his abilities working for Brady, and, in fact, is personally responsible for many of the famous Civil War photographs that are often credited to his mentor. This album of Gardner's work is nothing less than sensational, featuring the notorious photos of Antietam and Gettysburg dead, of Civil War–era military and political leaders (the section on Lincoln invites the viewer to stare in extended awe), of the places and people involved in the conspiracy to assassinate the president (the execution pictures are chilling), of the hanging of Henry Wirz, commandant of Andersonville prison (also chilling), and of folks and venues Gardner saw on his travels westward. Katz's text offers the biographical facts of Gardner's interesting life as well as thoroughgoing historical background on his photojournalistic successes. As a photo book or a volume of history, this fascinating volume really delivers the goods. —*Martin Brady*

History

✔Klinkenborg, Verlyn.
The Last Fine Time.
Knopf, $19.95 (0-394-57195-9). 256p.

While pioneers of the essay's recent resurgence—Chatwin, Angell, Hoagland, and the rest—undergo textbook apotheosis, talented younger writers arise to join in the form's renaissance. Witness Verlyn Klinkenborg, already a master of the essay about everyday life. Like Balzac and Durrell, he puts a place at the center of his book. It's a workingman's tavern in the east side of Buffalo that affords him the opportunity to write a family biography of its owners and to recount and analyze Polish immigration, working-class life, social and cultural mobility, popular culture, and really awful weather. Setting is everything here, and fortunately, *diligent* and *thorough* understate the magnitude of Klinkenborg's research. The amount of detail astonishes (some readers will find it excessive). Comparisons to McPhee are in order, but Klinkenborg is far more literary and experimental in organization and, at this point in his work, lacks McPhee's common touch. Categorizing the book is a problem: it may appeal to readers of literature, urban studies, human geography, ethnic and community sociology, and of course, to everyone in upstate New York. —*Roland Wulbert*

Kluge, P. F.
The Edge of Paradise: America in Micronesia.
Random, $21.95 (0-394-58178-4). 256p. index.

In 1966, doctorate in hand, the author joined the Peace Corps and was sent to Micronesia, where he met, befriended, and eventually worked for Lazarus Salii. In the mid-1960s, Salii was a concerned, idealistic politician seeking to make the Treaty Territory of Pacific Islands independent and not a "mini-America"—a much-debated choice between "coconuts and Coca-Cola." As the years passed, and as Kluge pursued his writing career in the States, including articles about Micronesia and occasional impassioned speeches for Salii, things changed. Corruption, vice, and the dubious comforts of cold beer and television, all funded by American dollars, turned the enchanted islands into the Federal States of Micronesia—a polluted "U.S. territory in disguise"—and Salii into the disillusioned, ineffectual president of Palau. Kluge documents his return to Micronesia, with regrets—especially after Salii's suicide in 1988—and memories enough to make the islands' former pristine beauty palpable, even while he reproaches the U.S., and himself, for actions taken and not taken. A thoughtful journey through time and circumstances, and an evocative portrayal of a paradise lost. —*Eloise Kinney*

Krauss, Clifford.
Inside Central America: Its People, Politics, and History.
Summit, $19.95 (0-671-66400-X). 309p.

What's going on in Central America—more confusingly, what's *behind* events there—is a continual puzzlement to most U.S. citizens outside of academe or the State Department. Veteran foreign correspondent Krauss endeavors to steer a course between traditional U.S. liberal and conservative viewpoints as he helps general readers sort through the pageant of "militarism, polarization, corruption, poverty, and dependency" that unfortunately has been the hallmark of Central American history. From Guatemala in the north, where civil war and repression of the Indian population show no signs of abatement, to Panama in the south, lacking a real sense of nationhood, the author profiles each of the Central American countries within the context of their history and especially their history of relations with the U.S., in the process delineating similarities in their national evolution but also highlighting the differences that have left them each a society with a distinct set of issues. This educational book is not a source of answers but one of understanding of the problems the region faces. —*Brad Hooper*

✓Lemann, Nicholas.
The Promised Land: The Great Black Migration and How It Changed America.
Knopf, $24.95 (0-394-56004-3). 320p.

Using the well-traveled route from Clarksdale, Mississippi, to Chicago, Illinois, Lemann describes the progress of blacks from the rural South to the promise of a new life in the urban North in the middle decades of the twentieth century. The author focuses on the experiences of individuals in his study, but he also expresses larger matters of more social, historical, and economic concern as he shows how the dreams of escaping from poverty and racism soon soured as hardship and prejudice reasserted themselves at the immigrants' new destination. The book's chapters on the conditions in Chicago in the post–World War II years potently illustrate the challenges these people faced as they became mired in political battles, institutional neglect, and the welfare spiral. The efforts to address—or often to confine—these problems are also analyzed as the writer describes why the war on poverty did not succeed and why the civil rights movement yielded only partial victories in trying to win improvements. While Lemann's interviews establish the human drama of this process, his assessment of the consequences of this great movement both for African Americans and for the entire country raises substantial questions of justice and equality that cut to the heart of the social situation of the impoverished and oppressed today. —*John Brosnahan*

✓Levenson, Jay A., ed.
Circa 1492: Art in the Age of Exploration.
Yale/National Gallery of Art, $59.95 (0-300-05167-0). 512p.

A magnificent feat of scholarship, aesthetics, and book production, this volume celebrates the "remarkable circumstance that the years around 1492 were a period of artistic excellence in so many different parts of the globe." Indeed, artists were making discoveries just as spectacular and world-altering as their seafaring contemporaries. This volume gamely surveys the art of four continents with 30 well-illustrated essays and 569 catalog items, each discussed in detail and displayed in color reproductions. Three main sections divide paintings, sculptures, prints and drawings, maps, scientific instru-

History

ments, and works of decorative art into geographical categories. "Europe and the Mediterranean World" includes stunning examples of West African and Islamic art as well as the work of such seminal figures as Dürer and Michelangelo. "Toward Cathay" covers the elegant art of Japan, China, and Korea, along with a few examples of India's sensual creations, all dating from 1450 to 1550. "The Americas" features art of the Aztec, the Inca, the astonishing gold work of Colombia, and rarely seen objects of the Tainos, the first people Columbus encountered in 1492, that fateful and now symbolic year. Perhaps the grandest book inspired by the Columbus quincentenary, this is a resonant celebration of humanity's creativity and diversity. —*Donna Seaman*

Litvinoff, Barnet.
Fourteen Ninety Two: The Decline of Medievalism and the Rise of the Modern Age.
Scribner, $22.95 (0-684-19210-1). 256p. index.

A free-wheeling cruiser around the life of Columbus and the dynastic struggles of his era, Litvinoff enlists the omniscience of historical hindsight to craft a snappy story that, at times, is insightful and amusing yet is also shot through with cynicism regarding the Christian cast of the times. Considering what followed the benchmark year of 1492, such as the subjugation of the Indians in the New World and the eruption of religious wars in the Old, perhaps skepticism about the motives of explorers and rulers and popes is justified. In any event, this author chalks them up as self-interested and venal people in a world that was an unstable mix of vestiges of feudalism and harbingers of Renaissance art and thought. In the dramatis personae of royalty, Ferdinand and Isabella loom largest, mainly for their expulsion of Moors and Jews from Spain, which, the author concludes, sealed off any Islamic involvement in the dawn of European domination of the world. This work's stylishness should find a ready readership during the quincentenary of Columbus' voyage. —*Gilbert Taylor*

Lopez, Barry.
The Rediscovery of North America.
Univ. Press of Kentucky, $15 (0-8131-1742-9). 64p.

Naturalist Lopez sees a link between the Spanish conquest of the New World and the current environmental crisis. In both cases, the search for material wealth—gold and riches for the Spanish, exploitable natural resources for contemporary abusers of the environment—becomes the reason for wanton destruction of both native civilization and nature's ecology. This 1990 lecture pointedly presses Lopez's convictions by making political and scientific comparisons between these historical events and current questions on just what type of disaster the world is facing. Lopez's rhetoric occasionally verges on an overly flowery style that might be more effective when spoken; nevertheless, his arguments emerge persuasively and pungently through this self-conscious poetry. —*John Brosnahan*

Maier, Frank.
Sweet Reprieve: One Couple's Journey to the Frontiers of Medicine.
Crown, $20 (0-517-58161-2). 256p.

When Maier's illness of several years was finally identified as a rare hepatitis, it had already severely damaged his liver. The first attempt at the ensuing transplant was abortive, and the later, successful operation was followed by a substantial rejection episode. The former *Newsweek* Chicago bureau chief takes the reader through both a medical case history and his persevering, strong-willed wife Ginny's emotional growth as a result of the attendant strains and uncertainty. He has much to say about relations with his doctors, nurses, and other medical personnel—anecdotes in which heart-warming elements are balanced by accounts of errors in processing and potential errors in treatment, the latter usually caught just in time by alert, outspoken Ginny. Written at the suggestion of one of his doctors and completed shortly before he died, Maier's winning, human account has much to offer actual and potential transplant patients and their families as well as anyone interested in contemporary medicine. —*William Beatty*

Marks, Richard.
Three Men of the Beagle.
Knopf, $22 (0-394-58818-5). 288p.

This story is potentially so gripping it is a shame that chance has thrown us only a few nuggets of fact and a writer who can flesh it out with only modest competence. The facts are these: in 1830, the ship carrying Darwin on his famous voyage stopped at the southern tip of South America, got itself involved in an incident with the local population, and found itself four "hostages" no one wanted. The aristocratic and devout captain, Fitzroy, fascinated by the extremely primitive nature of these Indians (they had no social structure, no housing, no clothes, no religion, no art, no morality) and believing that education would bring out the natural goodness of these people (virtuous Anglican!), determined to take them to England and teach them a new language, manners, and the catechism. He did, and two years later they were returned, self-conscious and uncertain, to their home. One of the three who survived the voyages was a boy of 14 when he was picked up, and his story forms the heart of the drama. The other two men of the *Beagle*—Fitzroy and Darwin, both young at the time of the tale—represent the two halves of the Victorian "character": sentimental toughness on one side, scrupulous and modest honesty on the other. With so much going for it, it is a pity Marks couldn't do more. Still, once picked up, his is a difficult book to put down. —*Stuart Whitwell*

Massie, Robert K.
Dreadnought: Britain, Germany, and the Coming of the Great War.
Random, $35 (0-394-52833-6). 1,004p. index.

Think "massive" when you think of Massie. But think "eminently readable", too. In his previous books, *Nicholas and Alexandra*, a dual biography of the last czar of Russia and his consort, and *Peter the Great*, about the czar who

History

turned Russia from Eastern- to Western-facing, Massie marshaled copious detail into splendidly dynamic narratives and won a vast popular readership. He now proceeds undaunted to tackle what is arguably an even more complicated historical subject: the story of the German naval challenge to Britain's turn-of-the-century hegemony of the seas—a situation that precipitated World War I. Following the defeat of Napoleon, Britain's dominion over the oceans of the world continued decade after decade; but in the meantime, the kingdom of Prussia was amalgamating all the German sovereignties into a mighty empire that soon sought to extend its power over sea as well as land. The race was on for bigger and better battleships and more colonies. Massie doesn't forget the impact of personalities on history and richly portrays the figures prominent in shaping this competition—foremost among them King Edward VII of Britain and the nephew he couldn't abide, German Kaiser William II. Once again, Massie makes history not merely palatable but scrumptious. —*Brad Hooper*

McCullough, David.
Brave Companions: Portraits in History.
Prentice Hall Press, $20 (0-13-140104-1). 272p. index.

Historian McCullough has been much praised for his work on the Panama Canal in *The Path between the Seas* and on Theodore Roosevelt in *Mornings on Horseback*. His latest contribution to historical literature is a collection of biographical essays written for periodical publication on an occasional basis over the past two decades. The individuals from the far and near past McCullough chose to highlight range widely over fields of knowledge; some are well-known figures, others decidedly not. The linkage between them is that they led lives of "active discovery." Scientist Louis Agassiz, lawyer Henry Caudill, artist Frederic Remington, photographer David Plowden, and writer Harriet Beecher Stowe are among the subjects of these elegantly rendered portraits, each a jewel of popular history. —*Brad Hooper*

McIntyre, Loren.
Amazonia.
Sierra Club, $40 (0-87156-641-9). 164p. index.

Following his visually stunning *Exploring South America* (Clarkson Potter, 1990), this eminent explorer-photojournalist, who has been traveling in South America since 1935, has drawn into one volume the best photographs taken on his numerous explorations in the Amazon Basin. Entailing parts of six nations, Amazonia is about as far removed from the experience of most North Americans as you can get, but this vast rain forest, home to flora and fauna and other natural features that are amazing to behold, is dwindling in size in the face of "development." McIntyre's spectacular photographs and sensitive textual narration usher the reader along the entire course of the mighty Amazon, in the process asserting the bold beauty of this region and lamenting its shrinkage. The moral of the book is that the Amazon Basin is not there to be tamed, but to be lived with as a partner. —*Brad Hooper*

McPherson, James M.
Abraham Lincoln and the Second American Revolution.
Oxford, $19.95 (0-19-505542-X). 256p. index.

The eminent Princeton historian, winner of the 1989 Pulitzer Prize for *Battle Cry of Freedom*, tenders a series of seven essays originally presented individually as lectures or papers. In light of the newly renewed interest in the Civil War generated by the magnificent PBS series, these pieces of brilliant writing should be welcomed by the serious reading public, since the twofold topic under discussion is Lincoln as leader and the 1861–65 war as revolution. McPherson's point, underscoring the collection as a whole, is unequivocal: "The Civil War changed the United States as thoroughly as the French Revolution changed that society." And from various approaches—Lincoln's abilities as commander-in-chief, the revamping of the South's social order following defeat, among others—McPherson presents cogent, supportable ideas to prove his complex assertion. *—Brad Hooper*

Meiselas, Susan, ed.
Chile from Within: 1973–1988.
Norton, $39.95 (0-393-02817-8); paper, $19.95 (0-393-30653-4). 143p.

Chile's recent episode of agony is these photos' subject. Taken "on the run" by Chileans risking their lives by doing so, these shots show—candidly and frighteningly—various manifestations of and eruptions against the oppression of General Pinochet's 1973–88 dictatorship. Heartsick faces reveal the fear under which Chile existed; street brutality and evidence of the more private kind—torture—produce disturbing viewing. Textual accompaniment, some by noted Chilean novelist Ariel Dorfman (now a resident of the U.S.), not only fills the reader in on facts about this dismal period but also helps the graphic photographs conjure the atmosphere of terror which was the very foundation upon which Pinochet's regime rested. A pictorial cri de coeur. *—Brad Hooper*

Murray, William.
The Last Italian: Portrait of a People.
Prentice Hall Press, $19.95 (0-13-508227-7). 256p.

To be read as a supplement to any of the numerous travel guides on Italy, Murray's 16 essays, some of which have appeared in the *New Yorker,* force the reader to focus on the problems confronting the peninsula. His writing offers perceptive commentary on Italy's many ironies, such as the fate of the natives, who have given up their traditional homes at the centers of famous cities to move into "modern" apartments in the sprawling ghettos surrounding their old neighborhoods; or that curious Italian trend of "reverse archaeology," whereby ancient objects, the remnants of past civilizations, are now being boxed and stored in the basements of many buildings, hidden again from human appreciation. Murray's Italian heritage and obvious love of his adopted country are apparent in this book, but throughout it, he rails against uncontrolled technology, materialism, and ecological devastation. It is these concerns that feed the passion behind his words. *—Kathryn LaBarbera*

History

History

✔**Naipaul, V. S.**
India: A Million Mutinies.
Viking, $22.95 (0-670-83702-4). 520p.

There are a million stories as well as mutinies in the naked country of India, and Naipaul takes his readers on a journey that shows how persisting divisions have assaulted the nation since its independence. Naipaul is something of an outsider in India; he was born in Trinidad of Indian immigrants but has toured his ancestral homeland on many occasions since his initial visit in 1962. His familiarity with the country and the people is quite evident, but Indian citizens nevertheless feel compelled to give Naipaul explanations that they feel he may need as a nonresident. Since Naipaul begins his account pretty much in medias res, these descriptions and explanations will also help his readers to sort out the castes, sects, ethnic and religious groups, and political parties that ever seem at odds, fighting for their rights. Naipaul's interviews with a broad range of people across the country's vast social and economic layers expose these divisions with intimacy and urgency. Indeed, the whole subcontinent seems like a vast plane of tectonic plates, shifting and colliding without warning, fracturing the country even further. Whether the results are seen as a process of restoration or merely as a path to further destruction, Naipaul covers the details with insight into both the momentous historical forces at work and the individual human lives at risk. —*John Brosnahan*

Paul, Jim.
Catapult: Harry and I Build a Siege Weapon.
Villard, $18 (0-394-58507-0). 272p.

Free-lance writer Paul confesses he's "always been a rock-thrower." And after finding a nice chunk of Red Creek quartzite that was just begging to be thrown but was a little too heavy for him, he called his best friend, Harry, and suggested they build a catapult. Some smooth talking, and promising to shoot only mock rocks (a promise broken) and to give a lecture afterward (a promise kept, but badly), earns a grant from the Headlands Center for the Arts, and the two San Franciscans are off on an adventure of whimsy and exploration, bolstered by know- and learn-how. Paul's easygoing narrative combines historical information with personal anecdotes, moving from Roman ingenuity to recollections about his father's golf game with charm and intelligence. What Paul had said would be an investigation into "catapult consciousness," the weapon maker's mind, turned out to be a lesson in understanding friendship and the art of creation as well; but mostly, as he shows, it was a lot of fun. —*Eloise Kinney*

Peele, Stanton and others.
The Truth about Addiction and Recovery: The Life Process Program for Outgrowing Destructive Habits.
Simon & Schuster, $22.95 (0-671-66901-X). 384p. index.

This book provocatively goes against everything most Americans have come to believe in the last 10 years about addiction and recovery. Specifically, it attacks the disease model of addiction, contesting the argument that addictions have biological or hereditary bases, or are lifelong illnesses. What's more, it slams the 12-step recovery program pioneered by Alcoholics Anonymous and subsequently conscripted as the only way to recover from everything from narcotics to sexual compulsion, from love to gambling. To the disease model and the 12 steps, the authors counterpose their "Life Process Program," which emphasizes positive behavioral changes within the context of an individual's everyday life. A lot of the program is commonsensical, emphasizing setting goals and finding new coping skills, family and community support, and a new perspective on problems. Although this regimen may not be appropriate for the severely addicted, it could greatly aid people with more moderate problems. In all, a powerful argument and a viable blueprint for lifelong change that constitute a much-needed—although sure-to-be-controversial—alternative to prevailing wisdom. —*Mary Ellen Sullivan*

✔Popescu, Petru.
Amazon Beaming.
Viking, $25 (0-670-82997-8). 388p. index.

An astonishing tale of exploration from the fecund density of the Amazon jungles to the rarefied peaks of the Andes. Loren McIntyre, well-known photographer and explorer, was on assignment for *National Geographic* in 1969 when he heard that members of the Mayoruna, an elusive tribe thought to be extinct, had been sighted. McIntyre's guide fell ill, and he ended up alone in the rain forest. Immediately contacted by the Mayoruna, or "cat people," he excitedly followed them into the jungle, slowly recognizing that he was their captive, participating in a ritualized journey back to "the beginning," a time before the intrusion of the "civilizados." McIntyre also realized that, in spite of his rational rejection of the possibility, the tribal chief was conveying information to him telepathically, "beaming" thoughts and explanations. McIntyre's startlingly improbable and suspenseful adventures are inlaid with provocative meditations on the nature of time and the Mayorunas' perception of their world. After his life-altering experience and dramatic escape, this indefatigable explorer and visionary went on to discover the true source of the Amazon high above the forest of the Mayoruna but within range of their ancient language of thought and memory. Popescu offers an arresting narrative of courage and discovery in the world's most mysterious land. —*Donna Seaman*

Powers, Ron.
Far from Home: Life and Loss in Two American Towns.
Random, $22 (0-394-57034-0). 317p.

Noted columnist Powers spent a great deal of time observing and pondering the sad levels to which a pair of towns—Cairo, in Illinois, Kent, in Connecticut—have been reduced. Cairo, "a violent and sorrowful" place, drew Powers' interest because of its sordid history of unfulfilled expectations. Cairo is located at the confluence of the Mississippi and Ohio rivers, and in its early

History

days was thought to have the potential for being the colossal trading center Chicago eventually became. Powers was familiar with Kent because he and his wife owned a weekend house there. What he came to realize was that he was part of an influx of city dwellers eroding the charm of New England villages by buying vacation property there and turning them into bland suburbia. Powers involved himself in the lives of the citizens of Cairo and Kent and learned about how they were trying to dig themselves out of their unhappiness. His perceptive commentary on the evolution—or, more accurately, the devolution—of U.S. towns in the twentieth century, particularly as affected by the growing ubiquity of the automobile, ensures a place for this study on public-library history shelves. —*Brad Hooper*

Powledge, Fred.
Free at Last? The Civil Rights Movement and the People Who Made It.
Little, Brown, $27.95 (0-316-71632-4). 687p.

Birmingham, NAACP, Little Rock, Atlanta, CORE, Greenville, SCLC, Oxford, Nashville, SNCC—these historic battlegrounds and participating groups are all here in this informative, cogent, and accessible history of the modern American civil rights movement. The lengthy text by veteran journalist Powledge is primarily chronological in construction, the coverage spanning from the pre–World War II existence of the southern black, through the major human, often brutal events—marches, demonstrations, burnings, shootings—and court decisions of the 1950s and 1960s, to the current status of blacks in the American system. Throughout, Powledge provides brief profiles of key players in the struggle—Floyd McKissick, James Farmer, Rosa Parks, James Meredith, Martin Luther King, Jr., etc.—injecting perspective on their personal struggles into the bigger picture of the fight for desegregation and true freedom and equality, all of which is set into the context of the long-range impact of the American Civil War. The setting for this important tale is usually the South, but Powledge doesn't shy away from discussing the subtler forms of northern or midwestern racism or acknowledging the startling fact that the Kennedy administration, despite its otherwise laudatory image in the cause, was in fact responsible for appointing racist judges to the federal bench. A salient mix of oral history and fact, much in the tradition of Hampton's *Voices of Freedom*. —*Martin Brady*

Robinson, Judith.
The Hearsts: An American Dynasty.
Univ. of Delaware, $49.50 (0-87413-383-1). 441p. index.

See p.34.

Royster, Charles.
The Destructive War: William Tecumseh Sherman, Stonewall Jackson, and the Americans.
Knopf, $30 (0-394-52485-3). 503p. index.

At the outbreak of civil war in 1861, few Americans could guess at the horrors soon to be loosed upon their land. The savage fury of the war, Royster observes, surprised nearly everyone; and as that fury steadily mounted, they found themselves unable to either explain or control it. Indeed, for reasons they only dimly understood, but which were evident from the outset, both sides actively sought to increase the level of destructiveness and violence. Royster attempts to comprehend, and make comprehensible, this grimly enigmatic aspect of the conflict by focusing on the deeds and personalities of the two men who came to epitomize the then-new concept of total war: generals Thomas ("Stonewall") Jackson, and William Tecumseh Sherman. In what is more rumination than a historical account, the author conveys a sense of elegiac sadness and achingly poignant insight as he shows how and why Americans inflicted such cruelties on each other. Recommended for all Civil War collections. —*Steve Weingartner*

Russell, Jeffrey Burton.
Inventing the Flat Earth: Columbus and Modern Historians.
Praeger, $12.95 (0-275-93956-1). 132p. index.

As an expert on the intellectual history of the medieval world, Russell has amassed convincing evidence for what he calls the "Flat Earth Error," the myth that all of Europe believed the earth was flat until Columbus bravely proved them wrong. Russell traces the origin of this deeply ingrained misconception by first demonstrating its falseness. He describes the prevailing perceptions of the cosmos during the medieval era and analyzes contemporary maps, noting that objections to Columbus' voyage were based on concern about distance, not fear of sailing off the edge of the earth. Having established the fact that educated people knew the earth was spherical, Russell traces the origin of the Flat Earth Error to nineteenth-century writers, particularly Washington Irving, "the most dramatic perpetrator of the Flat Error." He examines the appeal of the myth and its remarkable persistence. Russell packs a punch in this slender, clearly written, and engagingly argued volume, contributing to the discussions aroused by the quincentenary of Columbus' first voyage. —*Donna Seaman*

Russell, Sharman Apt.
Songs of the Fluteplayer: Seasons of Life in the Southwest.
Addison-Wesley, $18.95 (0-201-57093-9). 160p.

Russell's debut collection of essays is a fine contribution to the literature of the modern American Southwest and "constructed" life-styles. Russell and her husband moved to New Mexico's Mimbres Valley 10 years ago to live off the land in an adobe house they planned on building themselves. Russell's candor about reality versus dream is refreshing as she recounts their loss of naïveté. Her topics range from illegal aliens to modern trading posts and Navajo weaving to water rights and the tricky logistics of irrigation. She achieves just the right mix of fact and metaphor, humor and poetics. The most moving pieces are the more personal: a proud account of giving birth at home; a glowing paean to her father, a test pilot who crashed in the Mojave Desert in 1956; and an appealing theory about Kokopelli, "a prehistoric hunchbacked fluteplayer drawn on pottery and scratched in rock walls" all over the

History

Southwest. The prose here is poised and respectful, each word given the appropriate space and time. —*Donna Seaman*

Salmoral, Manuel Lucena.
America 1492: Portrait of a Continent 500 Years Ago.
Facts On File, $50 (0-8160-2483-9). 240p. index.

The Mendoza Codex, "published" in 1549, was a collection of drawings done by Mexican artists that depicted the everyday life of the Aztecs before the Spaniards arrived. Just before the Codex was loaded on to a ship bound for Spain, a narrative was added. Salmoral's book harkens back to the Mendoza and many other codices produced in the early years of the Spanish presence in the New World. Like its predecessors, *America 1492* is a compendium of ancient information and illustrations concerning the three major or "high" native cultures: Aztec, Mayan, and Incan. Blended with that, however, are more recent findings about pre-Columbian Americans plus tidbits about the less developed Amerindian nations from the Arctic Circle to Tierra del Fuego. Rituals for birth and death, breakfast menus in Cuzco, midnight revels in Tenochtitlán, examples of jewelry and ceramics—all render an intriguing look at the diversity of life in the Americas circa 1492. —*Cynthia Ogorek*

Salsitz, Norman and Salsitz, Amalie Petranker.
Against All Odds: A Tale of Two Survivors.
Holocaust Publications, $24.95 (0-89604-148-4); paper, $12.95 (0-89604-149-2). 398p.

The authors, who were wed in 1945, are both Polish Jews: Norman Salsitz was from the town of Kilbuszowa, his wife from Stanislawow. They survived the Holocaust by a combination of cunning and luck. Their stories are similar—ghetto confinements, false identities, tales of brutality, and miraculous, nimble-witted escapes. Norman Salsitz was taken to a slave labor camp, was shot in the hand, and escaped in 1940. Uncommon physical endurance enabled him to withstand the work details, beating, and shootings perpetrated by the Germans. With false documents and the ability to speak fluent Polish, he eventually succeeded in becoming an officer in the Polish army. Of the 2,000 Jews from Kilbuszowa, only 9 survived. Amalie Salsitz lived in a ghetto for almost a year before she escaped. Her mother, father, and sister were killed (12,000 Jews were machine-gunned to death in one day in the Stanislawow cemetery). With false papers, she fled to Krakow, posing as a Polish Gentile. She held such jobs as a live-in maid and governess for a German family with three children and as an assistant office manager at a construction company. At one time, she was employed cleaning toilets at the Gestapo headquarters. This is an incredible story, well told. —*George Cohen*

Sante, Luc.
Low Life: Lures and Snares of Old New York.
Farrar, $24.95 (0-374-19414-9). 360p.

Sante isn't interested in uplifting tales about New York's hardworking immigrants who pulled themselves out of the slums into the ruling classes.

Instead, he's intrigued with New York's underworld, called the "Big Smear" by tramps, the wild and dangerous "circus and jungle" that was New York in the Bowery, Hell's Kitchen, and the waterfront between 1840 and 1919. Sante begins by describing the geography and physical history of Manhattan and then delineates the horrors of nineteenth-century slum living. Once he's sure his readers have the scene firmly fixed in their minds, he introduces the cast: street vendors, petty thieves, con artists, suckers, drunks, whores, gangsters, and crimps ("operators who specialized in drugging and robbing sailors"). Anecdotes follow one right after another, flavored with the peculiarly theatrical parlance of the times and focusing on the legendary figures of sleaze and crime. Sante delves into the logistics of each vice—drink, drugs, prostitution, and gambling—and he analyzes the genealogy of gangs and the collusion of cops and politicians. Gritty and vivid social history conveyed with insight, irony, and panache. —*Donna Seaman*

Schama, Simon.
Dead Certainties: Unwarranted Speculations.
Knopf, $21 (0-679-40213-6). 368p.

Schama, author of *Citizens*, examines two cases in which tragic death and historical evidence have been linked and disputed. The death of English General James Wolfe while routing the French from Quebec in 1759 is the first and better-known instance; the murder of Boston real estate speculator George Parkman, whose body was discovered at Harvard Medical College with a chemistry professor charged with the crime, forms the second case in which rumor, evidence, and legend have obscured what really might have happened. The link between these two tales is historian Francis Parkman, who debunked the legend of Wolfe's death and who was the nephew of the deceased George Parkman. Schama aims in both instances to get to the real story by unconventional means; he becomes a literary detective in pinpointing suspects, outlining motives, checking alibis, and vetting competing versions. Going from the literal to the metaphorical in the blink of an eye, Schama seductively illustrates the fragile relationship between what is presented as truth and what is presented as history, with a nebulous boundary between the actual event and the story of that event. —*John Brosnahan*

✔Schlereth, Thomas J.
Victorian America: Transformations in Everyday Life, 1876–1915.
HarperCollins, $25 (0-06-016218-X). 416p. index.

What a wonderful book, even if it has nothing to do with repressed sexuality but instead conveys more of our kinship to the past than the relating of names and events that the word *history* commonly connotes. Profoundly American, it extends to everyday life the historical value formerly assigned to presidents, generals, and canonical artists. Tangibly, the transformations of the subtitle are largely innovations in material culture: California bungalows, the skyscraper, the American-style department store, fast-food lunches, streetcars and interurbans, the time clock, phys ed in the public school curriculum, snapshots, Jell-O, Pillsbury flour ... The list goes on, and it can be mislead-

History

ing, for Schlereth is no wry compiler of trivia. His analysis of social context reveals truly profound, intangible transformations in how and where Americans spent their time during four pivotal decades. His summaries of the theoretical literature are models of concision; e.g., a few paragraphs on the emergence of middle management convey as much as volumes of academic monographs. For a book that has no plot—no wars, no great men rising from obscurity—this is astonishingly hard to put down. —*Roland Wulbert*

Sergeant, Harriet.
Shanghai: Collision Point of Cultures 1918/1930.
Crown, $25 (0-517-57025-4). 384p.

Shanghai was an anomaly in China: an international metropolis. Suddenly open to foreigners and their opium in 1842, the city was quickly cut up into settlements exempt from Chinese law. These enclaves of British, White Russians, and Japanese were magnets for "the dispossessed, the ambitious, and the criminal." Sergeant re-creates the sizzle of that stylish, freaky, corrupt, and licentious era, from its filthy, disease-ridden streets to its lavish nightclubs, ostentatious homes, and infamous brothels. Through determined research, numerous interviews, and travel, Sergeant unearthed amazing stories of flamboyant individuals such as Victoria Litvanoff, a notorious madam; Du Yuesheng, a powerful gangster; Silas A. Hardoon, a fabulously wealthy Iraqi Jew and one of the few foreigners with any respect for or interest in Chinese culture; and Basil Duke, a Brit recruited for the beleaguered Shanghai police force. From millionaires to beggars, from the glamour of the Shanghai film industry to the brutality of a rickshaw-puller's life, Sergeant reveals the blatant prejudice and greed that fueled this legendary period in Shanghai history until the Japanese dropped their bombs and the Communists muffled it with tyranny. Frank and unflinching, vivid and compelling, this volume has wide appeal. —*Donna Seaman*

Shapiro, Mary J.
Ellis Island: An Illustrated History of the Immigrant Experience.
Macmillan/Collier, paper, $49.95 (0-02-584441-5). 288p.

Another fine volume linked to the renovation of Ellis Island. While Wilton Tifft's photodocumentary focused on the island itself, this jam-packed history, written by a curator of the Ellis Island Immigration Museum, concentrates on the people who flowed through the daunting immigration facilities. Descriptions of grueling voyages and the "chaos, confusion, and noise" of the island usher us into an overview of the peak years of immigration, 1880–1924. Photographs and quotes, culled from the thousands of pictures, letters, memorabilia, and recorded oral histories sent to the museum by immigrants and their descendants, grace every page. The fate of individuals and families in their chosen land is chronicled through personal histories and anecdotes, demonstrating how the legions that landed on Ellis Island spread out across the nation. Superbly detailed and vivid, this will be relevant to almost everyone. —*Donna Seaman*

Smith, Wayne S. and Reagan, Michael.
Portrait of Cuba.
Turner, $34.95 (1-878685-07-4). 192p.

Cuba is on our mind. How long can the seemingly dinosaurian Castro hold out in a world gone un-communist? Smith, a professor of Latin American studies at Johns Hopkins and director of that institution's Cuban studies program, here provides an outstanding overview of Cuban history, which moves quickly through the island's colonial period and difficult separation from Spain to the book's particular focus: the context in which Castro gained power, his effect on Cuba over the 30-year run of his dictatorship, and the significance to Cuban welfare of Soviet involvement and continued U.S. hostility. With a bounty of fascinating period photographs from earlier decades of this century and lovely ones of contemporary Cuba taken by well-credentialed professional photographer Reagan, this book is distinguished by its cogency and balance in viewing a land so close to the U.S. but so unknown by us. It amounts to the perfect answer for the general reader needing background on a place that is likely to be increasingly in the news as Castro ages and the Cuban way of life continues to fray. —*Brad Hooper*

✓Spiegelman, Art.
Maus: A Survivor's Tale II: And Here My Troubles Began.
Pantheon, $18 (0-394-55655-0). 136p.

Spiegelman completes *Maus*, the cartoon biography of his father that, more than any other single work, brought American attention to the comic book (aka the graphic novel) as a serious art form. In the five chapters that tell the rest of Vladek Spiegelman's passage through the Nazi Holocaust, he arrives and perseveres through some 10 months in Auschwitz and then, during the last months of the war, through frantic Nazi attempts to "clean up" the last Jews before the Reich crumbles. Finally, he is freed and united with his wife, Anja. As before, Vladek's story is told in his own words as tape-recorded by Art and punctuated by the old man's latter-day obsessions with frugality, his health, and the imagined untrustworthiness of everybody else. Art's reflections about his work and dealings with Vladek's cantankerousness also intrude into the narrative, leavening the horrifying heroism of Vladek's life with the funny-awful stresses of Art and Vladek's father-son relationship. Amid the vast wash of Holocaust testimonies, Spiegelman's achievement is, on account of its format, unique and also one of the most approachable, accessible, and immediately moving of them all. —*Ray Olson*

Steegmuller, Francis.
A Woman, a Man, and Two Kingdoms: The Story of Madame d'Épinay and the Abbé Galiani.
Knopf, $23 (0-394-58806-1). 288p. index.

Few centuries reveled in the sheer joy of knowledge and exchange of bon mots and wisdom as the eighteenth century—particularly in France, where the establishment of salons and promiscuity among the nobility were generally accepted as matters of little consequence. Here is the little-known story

History

of two minor writers-cum-wits in prerevolutionary times who maintained a friendship via correspondence. Translating not only the actual letters between the Neapolitan abbé Galiani and Parisian Madame d'Épinay, but also fleshing out the period personalities from primary and secondary sources, breathes vivacity into what could have been a dull narrative. Famed historical characters also become three-dimensional—Voltaire, Diderot, Mozart, and French royalty. —*Barbara Jacobs*

Toland, John.
In Mortal Combat: Korea: 1950-1953.
Morrow, $25 (0-688-10079-1). 672p. index.

The Pulitzer Prize–winning author of *The Rising Sun*, among other military histories too numerous to mention, here turns his exhaustive attention to the Korean War. As with previous efforts, Toland covers his topic in an episodic fashion, now employing straightforward historical narrative that chronicles the unfolding of events from the lofty heights of the author's perspective, then descending, as it were, into the trenches to describe the war from the point of view of individuals who were caught up in it. This is the tried-and-true Toland formula, fast-paced and enthralling, and it works extremely well as popular history. Yet it has its drawbacks; simply put, the flow of history in this big book is exceedingly broad but shallow. Many important aspects of the war are neglected (the war in the air, for instance); moreover, in striving for objectivity, Toland adopts a mushily value-relative stance toward the antagonists that seems an absurd contrivance, given what we now know about communism in general, and North Korean communism in particular. Nevertheless, this qualifies as a major study of the Korean conflict, and is therefore highly recommended for military collections of all sizes. Notes, bibliography. —*Steve Weingartner*

Vadrot, Claude-Maria and Ivleva, Victoria.
Russia Today: From Holy Russia to Perestroika.
Atomium Books, $31.95 (1-56182-004-0). 160p.

See p.252.

Viola, Herman J. and Margolis, Carolyn, eds.
Seeds of Change: A Quincentennial Commemoration.
Smithsonian, $39.95 (1-56098-035-4). 280p.; paper, $24.95 (1-56098-036-2). 280p. index.

A generously illustrated, handsomely designed collection of essays produced as an accompaniment to a Smithsonian exhibition that opened on Columbus Day, 1991. The book and the exhibition both aim to stimulate awareness of the massive changes Columbus' voyages brought to both Old and New Worlds. Since the five-hundredth anniversary of Columbus' voyage, scholars have been reassessing the clichéd view of Europeans "discovering" the New World. Instead, they are studying this pivotal event as an encounter, albeit a violent one, between cultures. Their essays examine life in the New World before and after the invasion of the Spaniards, covering the decimation wrought by disease and war as well as the short, brutal path from genocide to slavery. The authors identify five "seeds of change"—sugar, maize, disease, the horse, and the potato—transported between the two worlds, and they analyze each as a catalyst for cultural transformation or destruction. Their fresh perspective also considers environmental damage as a negative aspect of the seminal encounter. An inviting, accessible, and provocative overview of the controversial issues associated with the Columbian quincentennial. —*Donna Seaman*

Weatherford, Jack.
Native Roots: How the Indians Enriched America.
Crown, $20 (0-517-57485-3). 320p. index.

Weatherford follows his ironically titled presentation of the impact of native Americans upon the rest of the world, *Indian Givers*, with an exposition of Indian influences upon U.S. development. Since we tend to see native Americans' role in the nation's construction as a matter of getting out of the way of the European juggernaut, Weatherford's book is a mother lode of surprises. In each of 19 accessible, even exciting chapters, Weatherford demonstrates how deeply Indians have affected a particular aspect of U.S. culture, including exploration, forestry, the fur trade, agriculture, warfare, fishing, and geography. Indeed, Indians pioneered civilization itself in central North America, as the great pyramid of Cahokia in southern Illinois—site of a city that "around A.D. 1250 . . . was larger than London and ranked as one of the great urban centers of the world"—now mutely and ingloriously testifies. A valuable corrective to the sentimentality with which we regard the first U.S. settlers and developers. —*Ray Olson*

✔**Weintraub, Stanley.**
Long Day's Journey into War: December 7, 1941.
Dutton, $26.95 (0-525-93344-1). 716p. index.

Weintraub chronicles the diverse course of events worldwide—as well as the activities of individuals caught up in those events—on the day that Pearl Harbor was attacked and America entered World War II. From the moment the day begins just west of the International Dateline, Weintraub conducts an episodic tour of global conflict that ranges from the battlefields of Russia and Africa, to such focal points of governmental power as the White House and the palace of the Japanese emperor, to venues of incipient onslaught in Malaya, Hong Kong, the Philippines, and, of course, Pearl Harbor. With apologies to the author, Mars himself might have drawn up the itinerary for this journey, which shows us not only a war in progress, but a war in the making and a war just beginning. Among the people we encounter along the way are Roosevelt, Churchill, Hitler, Rommel, and MacArthur—to name but a very few of the host of players, great and small. Thrilling, intensely gripping, filled with the kind of drama befitting a tale of epic, and epochal, proportions, this is without question one of the best and most important Second World War–oriented books to emerge in the past 10 years. —*Steve Weingartner*

History

Wilkinson, Alec.
The Riverkeeper.
Knopf, $20 (0-394-57313-7). 224p.

Wilkinson, a staff writer for the *New Yorker,* reports on unfamiliar ways of life, like the hard toil of cane cutters in his acclaimed *Big Sugar.* Here he explores the personalities, cultures, motivations, and legacies of people whose livelihoods depend on river and sea. "The Blessing of the Fleet" introduces us to the Portuguese fishermen of Provincetown, Cape Cod. The title piece is set on the Hudson, "a complicated river," that is now protected by America's only official river keeper, John Cronin. His vigilance exposed Exxon's diabolical abuse: tankers were flushing their petrochemical-tainted holds and loading up with fresh water, stolen water that was then sold to Aruba. The final section is a fascinating study of the history and culture of Angoon, a tiny Tlingit town on Alaska's Admiralty Island. Wilkinson has raised matter-of-factness to an art form; his Hemingwayesque sentences unleash the sheer force of reality, creating bursts of fresh vision and comprehension. Adept and engaging investigations that expand our perception of America. —*Donna Seaman*

Wiser, William.
The Great Good Place: American Expatriate Women in Paris.
Norton, $20.95 (0-393-02999-9). 352p.

See p.105.

Woodward, Bob.
The Commanders.
Simon & Schuster, $24.95 (0-671-41367-8). 398p. index.

Fans and foes of Woodward's tales from Washington's power salons can probably agree that, with eyes on the keyhole and ears to the wall, he does deliver the inside goods. So it is with this story of George Bush's national security team and how they made their two biggest decisions by far: to wage war against Manuel Noriega and Saddam Hussein, respectively. The Pentagon's point men in the planning and preparation of each invasion have been, of course, Richard Cheney, the defense secretary, and Colin Powell, chairman of the Joint Chiefs. Woodward mobilizes seemingly every fly on the wall (400, he claims) willing to talk about how these two major posts were filled, the occupants' strong personal relationship, and the meetings building up to the serious step to unsheath the sword. Besides divulging that Cheney twice drove drunk in his youth, not many of Woodward's details meet the salacious standards he set in *All the President's Men, The Final Days,* and *Veil.* The scoop frontloaded into the book's prologue and dutifully hyped by the daily and electronic press—that Powell favored relying on economic strangulation to eject Iraq from Kuwait—won't be sensational in historic terms, but it does play on the seductiveness of eavesdropping on power gossip. Hence, more interesting than military plans and policy—cursorily discussed anyway—is discerning who has confided to Woodward. The media-savvy Saudi Arabian ambassador, Prince Bandar bin Sultan, blabs early and often, as does William Crowe, Powell's predecessor and apparent source of the Powell-as-Hamlet revelation. —*Gilbert Taylor*

✔Yevtushenko, Yevgeny.
Fatal Half Measures: The Culture of Democracy in the Soviet Union.
Little, Brown, $21.95 (0-316-96883-8). 368p.

Not everyone who rattled the Soviet authorities in the days before glasnost was a saint, and one or two sought to make themselves taller by cutting down Yevtushenko. But the articles collected here tell of an equally daring, if less loud-mouthed, resistance. There is a telegram sent to Brezhnev criticizing the invasion of Czechoslovakia in 1968, a letter supporting Solzhenitsyn (1967), and stories of his subtle differences with the saintly Sakharov and of his successful attempt to persuade a tormented Shostakovitch not to sign a piece of government propaganda. Here, too, is an absurd tale that could have been lifted from a novel by Joseph Skvorecky: Robert Kennedy pulling Yevtushenko aside (he is on a tour of the U.S.), taking him to the bathroom, turning on a shower, passing on sensitive information; Yevtushenko relaying the information; and finally, Yevtushenko being called to the Soviet embassy and questioned by two heavys who talk about "accidents" happening on the streets of New York—all of which turns out to be nothing really, a little overzealousness perhaps, almost a joke. . . . Yevtushenko's intellect is no more massive than his courage, but it is substantial, and these pieces give a thoroughly nonsensationalized picture of what it was like for those who learned all manner of strategies to survive and frustrate a system that did not want them. —*Stuart Whitwell*

Humor

Barreca, Regina.
They Used to Call Me Snow White: Women's Strategic Use of Humor.
Viking, $18.95 (0-670-83801-2). 204p.

An appreciation and celebration of women's wit. Barreca analyzes the differences in men's and women's humor in relationship to the old double standards because "to see the way wit functions is to see a map of our culture: to focus on things we've seen but not necessarily processed." Barreca skillfully illuminates the sexual politics of humor, describes the differences in men's and women's perceptions of what's funny, discusses the pervasiveness of jokes about sex, and analyzes the nature of women's comedy. Anchoring her study on the "Good Girl/Bad Girl" motif, Barreca artfully dissects TV sitcoms, movies, and books. Her sources include everything from the ironic screenplays of Anita Loos to "The Patty Duke Show," Dorothy Parker to Lily Tomlin, Mae West to Murphy Brown—and her examples are hilarious. Amid myriad funny comebacks, Barreca praises the curative qualities of comedy and suggests that an injection of levity into the rhetoric of the "F-word"—

Humor

feminism—would benefit everyone. Wise, liberating, and merry. —*Donna Seaman*

Barry, Dave.
Dave Barry's Only Travel Guide You'll Ever Need.
Ballantine/Fawcett, $18 (0-449-90651-5). 192p.

The popular humor columnist's take on traveling again showcases his scattergun style, which is really best indulged in smaller doses than a whole book's worth. But don't take our word on that, for each Barry book rockets to the top of the best-seller lists as if it were a Madonna disc in *Billboard*. Folks like Barry's farrago of non sequiturs, deliberate stupidity, heavy-handed ironies, flippancy, and lampshade-hat silliness. And don't get us wrong, lots of it's funny enough. It's just that it's tiresome at lengths longer than one newspaper column, just as many standup comics really flog their welcome to death if you have to put up with them for longer than 10 minutes on Carson. —*Ray Olson*

Blount, Roy.
Camels Are Easy, Comedy's Hard.
Villard, $21 (0-679-40053-2). 320p.

Blount, author of the novel *First Hubby* and previous volumes of humor, serves up a collection of wry essays, funny verses, and even "punny" (and challenging) crossword puzzles, the latter first appearing in *Spy* magazine. In typical Blountian fashion, *The Atlantic*'s wisecracking contributing editor tackles youthful reminiscences, books and movies, the Gulf War, governmental credibility, raccoon hunting, travels to South America, food, Reagan, and a host of other interesting topics. Perhaps best of all are his profiles of film director Jonathan Demme and the late comedienne Gilda Radner. There are 61 pieces in toto, all but two of which originally appeared in a host of national publications. A solid, popular purchase for the library. —*Martin Brady*

Dunn, Nora.
Nobody's Rib: Pat Stevens, Liz Sweeney, Babette, and Some Other Women You Know.
HarperCollins, paper, $9.95 (0-06-096498-7). 224p.

Many will remember Dunn from "Saturday Night Live." She refused to appear on a show with guest host and woman-hater Andrew Dice Clay and "coincidentally" was not asked to return for another season. The show misses her characters, including vapid talk-show hostess Pat Stevens and lounge-lizardette Liz Sweeney, among others. Fortunately readers can once again have a moment with Pat, Liz, and some new characters in this very funny collection of comic vignettes. It helps a little if you remember Pat and the others from TV, thus allowing you to visualize Dunn in these roles, which is always a treat. But even if you come green to the book, there are laughs aplenty. Take some of these quotes from the irrepressible Stevens: "Style is contrast: firm, man-made breasts with a soft, cashmere cardigan." When an animal-rights activist corners Pat and yells, "That animal you're wearing is endangered," Pat coolly replies, "No it's not, it's dead." Dunn even writes as a man, a driftwood artist who must ponder such questions as whether to make his piece abstract or representational—"Will it serve as a doorknob . . . a headboard? Is the woodshape bushy or curly? If so you may have a squirrel on your hands." Television's loss is publishing's gain. —*Ilene Cooper*

Fulghum, Robert.
Uh-Oh: Some Observations from Both Sides of the Refrigerator Door.
Villard, $19 (0-679-40103-2). 250p.

"If you notice phrases, ideas, and anecdotes that closely resemble those that appear elsewhere in my writing, it is not a matter of sloppy editing. I'm repeating myelf. I'm reshuffling words in the hope that just once I might say something exactly right." While Fulghum's self-indulgent luxury is the envy of us all, it's hard to argue with the incredible success he's had with this and previous books—*All I Really Need to Know I Learned in Kindergarten* and *It Was on Fire When I Lay Down on It*—which compile the author's brief, pithy (he hopes) musings on the mundane mysteries of life. Not all of it *is* pithy, however, and sometimes Fulghum comes off as Andy Rooney crossed with Richard Bach. But come to think of it, there's a formula for bestsellerdom if ever there was one. Some of the topics under discussion here include fireflies, hiccups, love and lust, the Cinderella fable, the stuff people put on their refrigerator doors, the delights of meatloaf, places like Pocatello, Idaho, and Moab, Utah, and, of course, the ubiquitous use of the exclamation *Uh-Oh*. Exactly why Fulghum's friendly fulminations are so popular may be an elusive proposition, yet ours is not to wonder why. The word to libraries? Buy! Buy!! —*Martin Brady*

Griffith, Bill.
From A to Zippy.
Penguin, paper, $12.95 (0-14-014988-0). 255p.

George Herriman's "Krazy Kat" was the great cult comic strip of the twentieth century's first half, and Bill Griffith's "Zippy" is the great cult comic strip of its second. They're alike in that both are about the constancy of character in an inconstant world. Kat would love Mouse and Mouse despise Kat though the landscape of Coconino County changed utterly from one panel to the next. The pinhead (Zippy, that is) will embrace pop culture and Griffy (his pal and creator) deplore it though each sound bite births a new fad (or worse, births again an old one). Although it concentrates upon the Zipman's syndicated daily manifestations during 1988–90, this biggest-ever collection of his follies and wisdom also draws from his comic book and calendar appearances. If you're into prime time, if you're into mass consumption . . . leveraged buyout . . . real estate . . . Elvis lives!—then you've got to let this acrocephalic in your life. —*Ray Olson*

Humor

A Harvard Education in a Book.
Putnam/Perigee, paper, $7.95 (0-399-51665-4). 192p.

Leave it to publications like *Mad* magazine and the *Harvard Lampoon* to topple (or try to) icons and idols across the U.S. This time, the target is none other than Harvard University itself, as *Lampoon* editors purport to give those who didn't matriculate in this Cambridge institution a Harvard education . . . or at least the ability to drop correct names knowledgeably. In reality, it's an alternative college catalog, covering photo tours, history, study skills, courses offered, dorm life, dating, and the like. Yes, the parody's pretty sophomoric; witness the description of Chaucer's *Canterbury Tales*: "A bunch of people go on a religious retreat and tell each other dirty stories." But in a very sober and serious age, with gloom and doom headlining every news page, it's a comfort to indulge in something completely silly. —*Barbara Jacobs*

McManus, Patrick F.
Real Ponies Don't Go Oink.
Holt, $16.95 (0-8050-1651-1). 198p.

Another collection of McManus' humorous essays from his column in *Outdoor Life* magazine. The cast of characters remains the same: wife Bun, who is always trying to get McManus to fix something around the house; and buddies Eddie and Retch, who are always trying to drag the author out to the field and stream for some hunting and fishing misadventures. Of course, Bun usually fails in her task; otherwise, McManus might be just another wimpy Dave Barry (who's a total nerd at these manly pursuits), or, even worse, another smarmy Bob Greene, whose idea of a great target is probably a cheeseburger in some airport hotel, for God's sake. No, McManus is a real man, and in his world real men confront nature on nature's terms: with rod, reel, and rifle (just to make the battle a bit more even). The author's fans will appreciate these comic escapades in the great outdoors for their humor and humanity and just because they feel they're probably not as klutzy as McManus always seems to be. McManus' previous book is *Whatchagot Stew*, a cookbook by a writer who doesn't cook but who sure can write funny. —*John Brosnahan*

✔O'Rourke, P. J.
Parliament of Whores: A Lone Humorist Attempts to Explain the Entire U.S.
Atlantic Monthly Press, $19.95 (0-87113-455-1). 256p.

A civics textbook to end all civics textbooks, *Parliament of Whores* drops a neutron bomb on Washington, D.C., savaging human nature as revealed in the workings of the three branches of government, the federal budget and bureaucracy, major cabinet departments, and various special interest groups, not to mention the 1988 presidential election. At the root of O'Rourke's gonzo brand of Republican conservatism is his almost visceral belief in original sin: people are slime; everything they (we) do is slimy; even the most sincere effort to "do good" is inevitably overwhelmed by the Law of Unintended Consequences. In a screed that owes much to three Jonathans (Swift, Edwards, and

Winters), O'Rourke, a *National Lampoon* alumnus and *Rolling Stone* contributing editor whose previous books include *Republican Party Reptile* and *Holidays in Hell*, aims his misanthropic but very funny darts at the "sheer, boring, gray dullness of government." Conservatives will guffaw gleefully; liberals will giggle guiltily; the Bored Majority will snore with a silly smile on its collective face. —*Mary Carroll*

Sarrantonio, Al, ed.
The National Lampoon Treasury of Humor.
Simon & Schuster/Fireside, paper, $10.95 (0-671-70833-3). 446p.

The humor of *National Lampoon* is an acquired taste that many do not appreciate. But the devoted audience—a certain brand of white, middle-class, hormone-addled men—has been staunch enough and large enough to support the monthy humor magazine for 20 years. If you're not a member of this elite group, you may find this collection of "classic pieces" rather vulgar, rude, and offensive, not to mention racist and sexist. But if you are a fan, then you will no doubt find the humor here irreverent, outrageous, absurd, and hilarious. Contributing writers include John Hughes (the successful teen-flick maverick) and P. J. O'Rourke (*Holidays in Hell* and the recent *Parliament of Whores*). Among the comic pieces are "How Your Parents Had Sex," "Six Fantasies of Richard Nixon," "Nancy Reagan's Guide to Dating Do's and Don'ts," "How to Talk Dirty in Esperanto," and "The Love Song of J. Edgar Hoover." —*Benjamin Segedin*

Literature & Language

Baker, Nicholson.
U and I: A True Story.
Random, $18 (0-394-58994-7). 192p.

Novelist Baker's homage to his master, John Updike, takes the form of a recounting of the self-tussles Baker underwent formulating and fashioning an essay on what makes the older writer so important to him. The thing was, though, that Baker was so gaga over Updike's novels—their style, their view of life—that getting his ideas presentable proved immensely difficult. Baker's mind tossed and turned before he could put pen to paper; he wrestled with the very notion of why and how writers are influenced by others of their ilk. Actually producing the essay took a backseat to Baker's obsession with enlightening himself on his obsession with Updike. And what the reader gets out of all this is an energizing, heartfelt, sprucely written—to say nothing of humorous—book on why book lovers love books. —*Brad Hooper*

✔Burchfield, Robert.
Unlocking the English Language.
Hill & Wang, $18.95 (0-8090-9490-8). 202p. index.

Dictionaries incite roots? In this wonderfully written collection of essays, Britain's most accomplished living lexicographer explodes the myth that dictionaries are dull, uncontroversial volumes. Drawing both from classic literary works and from his own career experiences, the author illustrates how language has changed in this century and how modern political and ideological pressures can make defining words a hazardous occupation. A defender of the historical approach to language, Burchfield attacks modern linguistic theories that block out past meanings of words and past patterns for putting words together. In both his erudition and his wit, the author manifests a love of words that makes this a delightful book for serious students of language. —*Bryce Christensen*

Camus, Albert.
Between Hell and Reason: Essays from the Resistance Newspaper Combat, *1944–1947.*
Wesleyan Univ., $35 (0-8195-5188-0). 170p. paper, $14.95 (0-8195-5189-9).

In a faraway land called France, in the faraway days following World War II, journalism was more than the relaying of verified information. It was the art of discussing public matters and shaping them with a pen. Of course, there will be many who won't be interested in the journalistic pieces of Camus: better to leave him as the philosopher of the absurd and that most gripping of existentialist novels, *The Stranger*. But Camus was much more, and in this remarkable series of brief documents we get an inspiring picture of a man blessed with sanity and courage. After the war, he, like many others, wanted the country purged of its traitors, and this is where these pieces begin. As time went on, however, Camus began to realize the dehumanizing value of violence even in the cause of justice, and so became the champion of principles rooted not in broad abstractions but in the concrete life of the individual. Camus was one of the most sane and honest men of the century, and this document records for the first time in English his complete editorials for *Combat*, which will serve as a warning to revolutionaries even in the centuries to come. —*Stuart Whitwell*

Carver, Craig M.
A History of English in Its Own Words.
HarperCollins, $22.95 (0-06-270013-8). 288p. index.

The author of the *Atlantic*'s popular column of word histories proffers more than 750 of them sorted neither topically nor by place of root origin but chronologically, according to when they first showed up in English. This procedure eventuates in six periodic chapters representing old English, middle English, early modern English, English during the apogee of the British middle class, American English, and the twentieth century. Within each chapter save the first, words are presented in order of first appearances in print. Carver leads off each chapter with a synopsis of linguistic influences during its period. Although it is more scholarly than many another popular etymological tome, its approach can't but win it the approbation of historically minded readers, and it is an ideal complement to the popular TV series and book, *The Story of English*. —*Ray Olson*

Conarroe, Joel, ed.
Six American Poets.
Random, $25 (0-679-40689-1). 320p. index.

The six are Whitman, Dickinson, Stevens, W. C. Williams, Frost, and Langston Hughes—presented in that order. So accurately has editor Conarroe read the temper and politics of contemporary taste in poetry that those half-dozen seem unassailable, their work *the* core of the canon of American poetry. As Conarroe points out in his judicious and temperate introduction, the six are easily envisioned as "three pairs of nearly polar opposites"— gregarious Whitman and reclusive Dickinson, lovingly materialist Williams ("No ideas but in things") and hyper-aesthetic Stevens, the pensive individualist Frost and the passionately communitarian Hughes. (These bipolarities invite at least one alternate way of reading the book, by the way: as a progression of two American poetic sensibilities, the humanitarian-libertarian [Whitman-Williams-Hughes] and the hermetic-idealistic [Dickinson-Stevens-Frost].) Conarroe presents mostly the most admired and familiar poems of all six, making his effort arguably the one historic American poetry collection every library ought to own. —*Ray Olson*

Crumley, James.
The Muddy Fork and Other Things: Short Fiction and Nonfiction.
Clark City Press, paper, $12.95 (0-944439-39-X). 248p.

James Crumley calls the assortment of journalism, short fiction, and novel excerpts that make up this collection "literary orphans" and notes that many of the nonfiction pieces were never published in the magazines by which they were assigned." Never trust editors. Whether he's lambasting boosterism in Houston, celebrating the joys of driving mountain roads, or profiling stuntman and movie heavy Roy Jenson, Crumley brings an unbuttoned iconoclasm to his diverse subjects that is immediately appealing. The short stories and novel excerpts, while occasionally less successful, still possess the toughness and vitality that have made Crumley's mystery novels (especially The Last Good Kiss) cult favorites among the hard-boiled set. Fans will also be pleased to find included here a lengthy and revealing interview with Crumley in which his no-nonsense answers reveal a personality every bit as cantankerous as those of his fictional detectives. (Q: "What about booze? It's important in your books." A: "It's important in life.") This isn't the new Crumley novel we've been anticipating for years, but it makes a tasty appetizer while we wait. —*Bill Ott*

Cullen, Countee.

My Soul's High Song: The Collected Writings of Countee Cullen, Voice of the Harlem Renaissance.
Doubleday, $27.95 (0-385-41758-6); paper, $14.95 (0-385-41295-9). 608p.

Countee Cullen (1903–46) was a seminal writer in the Harlem Renaissance, the blossoming of black arts centered in Harlem in the 1920s and 1930s. He matured early—publishing major poetry while still in college—and was roundly touted in the literary circles of his day. As reaffirmation of Cullen's important place in U.S. literature—and, as significantly perhaps, to introduce his works to readers unfamiliar with his gifts—this compilation boasts an extensive selection of Cullen's poetry, his one novel (*One Way to Heaven*, 1932), his translation of the Greek tragedy *Medea*, as well as essays, travel pieces, and speeches. His work was as concerned with beauty as it was with commenting on racial problems; and his espousal of the loveliness of the poetic line and the prose sentence with social critique results in a beguiling iron-fist-sheathed-in-velvet-glove effect. Gerald Early's lengthy but trenchant introduction places Cullen in the context of black writing of the time and spells out his specialness. —*Brad Hooper*

✔Dubus, Andre.

Broken Vessels.
Godine, $19.95 (0-87923-885-2). 155p.

Short-story writer Dubus explores themes drawn from his own life as he describes his childhood, his development as a writer, and the automobile accident in 1986 that left him a self-described cripple. Dubus' survival of these spiritual and physical assaults is poignantly and realistically portrayed in these essays, which date from 1977 to 1990 and document the condition of his life during this turbulent period of critical success, medical crisis, and marital failure. While Dubus affectingly comes to terms with his disability, the real heart of this volume lies in the writer's contemplation of his art. For it is in his writing that Dubus truly confronts the challenges he has faced in his past and will meet in his future as a creative personality. Body and mind battered, Dubus still endures both as a man and as a writer. —*John Brosnahan*

Dunn, Jane.

A Very Close Conspiracy: Vanessa Bell and Virginia Woolf.
Little, Brown, $29.95 (0-316-19653-3). 352p. index.

"In all close relationships there is a conspiracy of sorts, a 'breathing together'—with the added sense of concealment, of closedness, where the rest of the world cannot come," Jane Dunn observes in her engrossing study of two remarkable sisters. Quoting extensively from letters and diaries, she tries to breathe with Virginia Woolf and Vanessa Bell, to explore their conspiracy of sisterhood. Her first four chapters examine the sisters' childhood, in which they closed ranks against the world in order to provide comfort and support through sudden deaths, sexual abuse, and emotional tyranny. The last seven chapters explore various themes—art and writing, marriage, lovers, children, death—of an adult alliance characterized by artistic encouragement and sometimes rivalry. Seeing all of life through the lens of sisterhood seems forced and narrow at times, making, for example, Dunn's discussion of lesbianism incomplete. Mostly, however, Dunn's is an interesting biography of a complicity, for "the essential reciprocity in the sisters' natures cannot be revealed in an individual treatment where each had to stand alone. Wherever you cut Virginia Woolf—open her diaries, her letters, her fiction—there is Vanessa. And when Vanessa faced the depths of despair and doubted her existence, it was Virginia to whom she turned." —*Ryn Etter*

Ehrlich, Gretel.
Islands, the Universe, Home.
Viking, $19.95 (0-670-82161-6). 196p.

A scintillating set of essays by the author of *The Solace of Open Spaces* (1986) and *Heart Mountain*. Ehrlich's books record a quest for understanding how life, in its infinite forms, works. She meditates on the properties of rock, water, snow, heat, stars, and time while tending to her Wyoming ranch, sleeping outdoors, and exploring mountains, islands, deserts, and forests. Ehrlich observes the world with every fiber, sense, and emotion, and she articulates her discoveries in radiant language that leaps from the visual to the visionary, from the tactile to the abstract. And yet, while ardently pursuing understanding and expression, she sometimes stops to ask: "How can I shut out the longing to comprehend?" This dichotomy is at the heart of each essay as Ehrlich writes about the seasons, the "apocalyptic gaiety" of the West's 1988 forest fires, animals and plants, scientists and holy men. She travels to remote Shinto shrines in the mountains of Japan and the Channel islands, while her inner journey traverses the universe. An exquisite and affective volume. —*Donna Seaman*

✓Epstein, Joseph.
A Line out for a Walk: Familiar Essays.
Norton, $21.95 (0-393-02955-7). 333p.

At that moment when lesser writers begin bench pressing answers about the matter at hand, the quotatious (his word) Epstein raises questions about unexpectedly related topics. "Waiter, There's a Paragraph in My Soup," for instance, segues from autobiography to city bookstores to the problems of desultory reading to concrete reading habitats to novelistic accounts of the act of reading to ... Epstein is that ideal conversationalist, the consummate straight man. His questions provoke in us, his readers, really interesting answers that we are convinced he would love to hear. The playfulness, reminiscent of S. J. Perelman, of this author in whose presence we would so surely shine initially disguises his moral and political depth. The set piece topics that cannot upset us too much, like feminism and racism, are here along with smoking and fame and student evaluations—issues that upset us more than they should. This acknowledged master of the familiar essay will captivate readers who want to escape life momentarily and guide readers who, like Flaubert, want to live it more profoundly. —*Roland Wulbert*

Literature & Language

✔**Fabre, Michel.**
From Harlem to Paris: Black American Writers in France, 1840–1980.
Univ. of Illinois, $35.95 (0-252-01684-X). 464p. index.

Much has been written about American expatriate writers in Paris, the so-called Lost Generation, but this has traditionally been an all-white group. Fabre uses a wider lens, revealing an ongoing tradition of black American writers in France. With great sensitivity and clarity, he analyzes the appeal France had for black writers. Parisians rarely displayed the routinely overt discrimination practiced by Americans; instead, they welcomed and respected black writers, musicians, and artists. Cosmopolitan Paris was a relief from the claustrophobia of Yankee puritanism, and black writers felt free of the constraints of literary preconceptions. Fabre tracks the changing impressions the Americans had of France over the years, evolving from an image of the land of liberty to recognition of France's oppressive African colonial policies. The list of individuals profiled in this thoughtful, eye-opening study is a veritable who's who of black American literature from Victor Sejour to Langston Hughes, Claude McKay, Jessie Fauset, Gwendolyn Bennett, Richard Wright, James Baldwin, Chester Himes, Alex Haley, James Emanuel, and dozens more. By discussing the effects of both world wars and the ideologies of the Harlem Renaissance, the French Negritude movement, and Black Power in Paris, Fabre enriches our understanding of black history, culture, and art on both sides of the Atlantic. A must for all literature collections. —*Donna Seaman*

Galeano, Eduardo.
The Book of Embraces.
Norton, $19.95 (0-393-02960-3). 288p.

Using the same style and technique that transformed New World history in his *Memory of Fire*, Galeano now examines his own life in a series of commentaries on personal and political experiences. Sometimes these appear as folkloric stories, sometimes they are almost aphoristic in their brevity. Galeano touches on a multiplicity of subjects: his friendships with Pablo Neruda and Julio Cortázar, his long exile from his native Uruguay, the death of his grandmother, and automobile traffic in Los Angeles. As offhand and limpid as these observations might appear in isolation, together they make a powerful collective statement, as the author reconstructs a whole world out of his imagination. —*John Brosnahan*

Gordon, Mary.
Good Boys and Dead Girls: And Other Essays.
Viking, $19.95 (0-670-82567-0). 258p.

Novelist Gordon considers other writers and their works as well as social and religious issues in this collection of essays. The pieces of literary criticism and appreciation are, in the main, book reviews, most often Gordon's contributions to the *New York Times Book Review*. Here Gordon mixes admiration and appreciation for writers of her own generation as well as for such figures of the past as Edith Wharton and Ford Madox Ford. Gordon hits more controversial ground—and the heart of her own career—in the second section, which considers sex, the women's movement, and the Catholic church, sometimes separately and often all at once. Gordon's opinion on abortion and the tactics of the pro-choice and the pro-life forces show her ready to challenge assumptions from her own or any other tradition with fearlessness and honesty. The book closes with passages from her journal that again examine Gordon's own as a writer, woman, and mother. —*John Brosnahan*

✓**Green, Michelle.**
The Dream at the End of the World: Paul Bowles and the Literary Renegades in Tangier.
HarperCollins, $22.95 (0-06-016571-5). 400p. index.

The Moroccan city of Tangier was carved up by the Western powers after World War II, creating an international zone rife with easy money, easy sex, and easy drugs. Expatriate writers like Paul Bowles thrived in the exotic, occult, licentious, and decadently paradisiacal atmosphere. Green's vivid, detailed, and quote-soaked account of the literary life in Tangier from the 1940s through the early 1970s captures the hypnotic power of the place and the baroque personalities of those enthralled by it. The reserved and resilient Bowles and his fleetingly brilliant and debilitatively neurotic wife, Jane, resided in the center of a spiral that, over time, included the flamboyant heiress Barbara Hutton, William Burroughs, Tennessee Williams, Truman Capote, Allen Ginsberg, Francis Bacon, and a host of local characters. Green follows the twisted trails of the group's complicated sexual adventures, dedicated consumption of narcotics and alcohol, rivalries, intrigue, and literary achievements with perseverance and insight. Sensitive to both the shifting political climate of the city and the bold yet vulnerable souls of its foreign literati, Green has created a frank and vibrant group portrait. —*Donna Seaman*

Henderson, Bill, ed.
The Pushcart Prize, XVI: Best of the Small Presses, 1991–1992.
Pushcart; dist. by Norton, $28.50 (0-916366-71-5). 575p. index.

This annually published reader containing 56 recent essays, short stories, and poems, carefully selected from small literary journals across the country, is a regular favorite of readers. It's also a must-have for libraries, for this diversified anthology genuinely reflects the state of the literary arts in the U.S. today, unlike established, mainstream literature collections, which lean toward certain trends and/or biases in taste. The editor's thoughtful arrangement—interspersing two to three poems between each coupling of fiction and essay—encourages readers to tirelessly proceed through the volume as they would a novel: from front to back. Among the more well known names included are Ursula K. LeGuin, Marvin Bell, William Stafford, Mark Halliday, Joyce Carol Oates, Gwendolyn Brooks, Diane Williams, and James Merrill. And Edward Hoagland's inventive introductory essay, rich in metaphor about the writer's anguished struggle to say something new, captures the very essence of what the writers represented here have trium-

Literature & Language

phantly succeeded in doing: re-visioning experience in a way that challenges the mind, moves the heart, and stirs the soul. —*Mary Banas*

Hillerman, Tony, ed.
The Best of the West: An Anthology of Classic Writing from the American West.
HarperCollins, $25 (0-06-016664-9). 544p.

Hillerman briefly deserts his popular Navajo mysteries to edit this collection of western fact and fiction, much of it "odds and ends" from the personal library of Jack Rittenhouse, "book lover, author, reviewer, publisher . . . editor . . . and, for the past four decades, operator of his own antiquarian book dealership." Rittenhouse, a Michigander who reviewed books and collected library fines in Fort Wayne, Indiana, in the 1930s, has been documenting western history since World War II. He and Hillerman are both members of the Westerners, a group with corrals "in most places west of the 100th meridian" at whose meetings members trade western myths and memories. *The Best of the West*'s nonfiction sources run from 500 B.C. to the late nineteenth century; fictional selections by Harte, Crane, Scarborough, Davis, Stegner, and Norris are included (with apologies for omitting Doig, McMurtry, Zollinger, Calvin, Harjo, and Didion). Hillerman's subject groupings (e.g., explorers, settlers, Navajos, Hispanics, cowboys, miners, women, travel, and the military) make sense, and his juxtapositions encourage a thoughtful response. —*Mary Carroll*

Jerome, John.
The Writing Trade: A Year in the Life.
Viking, $20 (0-670-82885-8). 232p.

Jerome has been writing for 30 years, 20 on a free-lance basis. He's produced numerous magazine articles and seven books tackling bread-and-butter subjects such as skiing, automobile racing, and running as well as more personal investigations, including *Staying with It*. In this quietly seductive volume, he lets us in on the everyday life of a writer. He's modest, self-critical, and wry, confessing to fits of anxiety over finances and frustration with his style and the necessity of having to set aside creative projects for money-makers. But he also articulates the pleasures of writing: the "feeling of having gained a new understanding," the mystery of the emergence of ideas, and the satisfaction of massaging sentences into the perfect state of suppleness and clarity. Jerome describes his work habits, including a daily walk in the woods, and discusses the irrationalities of the publishing industry. A frank, often bemused account of the writing life that will intrigue dedicated readers and writers. —*Donna Seaman*

Konwicki, Tadeusz.
New World Avenue and Vicinity.
Farrar, $19.95 (0-374-22182-0). 212p.

A collection of essays, sketches, and reminiscences by one of Poland's most popular writers. (His most recent novel is *Bohin Manor*.) Published officially by Poland's government press in 1986, the text frequently addresses the state censor, adding a daring and taunting dimension to the wide-ranging commentary. Konwicki is, by turns, cranky, urbane, swaggering, self-critical, sad, and funny. He shares memories of his family, his job on the staff of a literary weekly, a dramatic hospital stay, and his experiences writing and directing films. He lampoons his literary efforts, bemoans the bewitching futility of writing, tells anecdotes about his cat, and dissects his tendencies toward boredom and loneliness and the amalgam of ambition, shyness, and pride that he perceives at the heart of his personality. Self-criticism wends its way into larger concerns, and the result is a self-portrait that reflects its social context. —*Donna Seaman*

Nathiri, N. Y., ed.
Zora! Zora Neale Hurston: A Woman and Her Community.
Sentinel Books, $24.95 (0-941263-21-5). 112p.

In this gracious tribute, novelist, folklorist, anthropologist, and "wandering minstrel," Zora Neale Hurston is remembered as liberated, flamboyant, bold and outspoken, brilliant, and enigmatic. The central piece is a concise biography of Hurston by journalist John Hicks, who conveys her electricity and creativity. Hurston ignored the social confines of race, sex, and poverty when she left home at an early age and worked her way to Howard University, a scholarship to Barnard College where she became the first black graduate in 1928, and on to Columbia, which brought her to New York and the Harlem Renaissance. Hicks follows Hurston's roller coaster career from her fame as a writer and folklore collector, to her lonely death in 1960. Other essays include a revealing history of Hurston's hometown, Eatonville, Florida, the oldest African American municipality; a discussion of Hurston's use of dialect and description of her books; and a celebratory piece by Alice Walker, responsible in part for the revival of Hurston's work. Numerous photographs and family reminiscences round out this fresh and informative volume. —*Donna Seaman*

Paz, Octavio.
The Other Voice: Essays on Modern Poetry.
HBJ, $16.95 (0-15-170449-X). 160p.

A series of essays from the 1990 Nobel Prize winner for Literature is bound to be of interest, and Paz is a fine essayist. His pace is slow, and he tends toward thoughtfulness rather than sensation, so these are not the sort of pieces that one can gobble up while swigging down some over-hot coffee on the way to somewhere else. And what does he discuss? Art (capital *A*), democratic liberalism, post-Baudelairean poetics, the dangers of individualism—everything, in short, that one would expect to be on a modern poet's mind. There is tremendous continuity between these high-minded and serious pieces, in part because there is no showing off. Paz is worried about the market-driven nature of contemporary art (and what serious person is not?), and worried, too, about the silliness of postmodernism and the failure of modern academics. But he is also hopeful, as every writer must be at some

Literature & Language

level, that something will be reborn in the future. "Every poet wishes to be read in the future, and in a profounder and more generous way than in his own time. It is not a thirst for fame; it is a thirst for life." —*Stuart Whitwell*

✔**Percy, Walker.**
Signposts in a Strange Land.
Farrar, $25 (0-374-26391-4). 428p.

A posthumous collection of nonfiction from novelist, essayist, and curmudgeon-philosopher Walker Percy (1916–90). Speeches, interviews, and essays (some published for the first time) investigate various aspects of Percy's lifelong interests: the South; science, language, and literature; and morality and religion. Stretching from a 1935 piece on movie magazines to Percy's last lecture, this collection displays the author at his charming, incisive, plain-speaking best. Witty, pithy, even devilish, Percy is equally at ease writing about the salubrious characteristics of bourbon as he is discussing race relations or the failure of science to achieve a coherent theory of man. Percy's consciousness is stretched like a net on a triad of poles: the rationality of science (he was a physician), the open-mindedness of an artist, and the faith of a Catholic. We get glimpses into his life when he writes about being orphaned at 14 and adopted by his bright and generous Uncle Bill, not to mention his feisty personality in "Questions They Never Ask Me," a caustic and amusing self-interview. The essays analyze Faulkner, the Civil War, the act of writing, man's unique capacity for language, and the modern malaise. Percy's masterful reasoning and reasonableness, his confident intelligence, his integrity and humor are uplifting and cleansing, while his topics are of enduring interest. —*Donna Seaman*

✔**Perutz, Kathrin.**
Writing for Love and Money.
Univ. of Arkansas, $17.95 (1-55728-211-0); paper, $9.95 (1-55728-212-0). 127p.

This brilliant book—which will take the reader in completely and make him or her laugh out loud—can be read either as a straightforward account of the narrator's experiences as ghostwriter of a "commercial novel" or as rather clever fiction. This will not worry the reader, though, until the book is closed, and since one of the themes Perutz addresses is the meaning of truth in fiction, this subversive ambiguity is appropriate. The narrator, Kate, is a promising author whose career is interrupted by marriage and children. She reenters the marketplace by bearing the monstrous literary offspring of "Jacqueline Knightsbridge," a pen name concocted to get placement at eye level on supermarket shelves. Knightsbridge is the creation of a dynamo Kate comes to call the Frog; her collaboration with him turns into sour grapes. Although Kate's travails may especially amuse publishing insiders and would-be writers, they will prove to be wonderfully entertaining for nearly anybody. —*Anne Schmitt*

✔Rushdie, Salman.
Imaginary Homelands.
Viking, $24.95 (0-670-83952-3). 432p.

This collection of Rushdie's essays written between 1981 and 1991 offers querulous opinions on any number of subjects political and literary, including the *Satanic Verses* controversy and Rushdie's stunning volte-face when he announced in late 1990 that he was embracing Islam as a result. Here Rushdie displays his unpredictability in full cry, whether he is objecting to censorship in Pakistan, attacking the governments of Indira Gandhi and Margaret Thatcher, or traveling with Bruce Chatwin through Australia. Much of the volume consists of book reviews for various periodicals and newspapers, in which the writer outlines his dissatisfaction with Christoph Ransmayr's *The Last World*, eulogizes Raymond Carver, and applauds Thomas Pynchon's return to print (after 17 years) in *Vineland*. The comments on Indo-Anglian literature and culture are notable for some stinging anticolonialist taunts, while Rushdie's musings from seclusion close the book on a sober and solemn note. —*John Brosnahan*

Russell, Sandi.
Render Me My Song: African-American Women Writers from Slavery to the Present.
St. Martin's, $18.95 (0-312-05288-X). 288p. index.

This welcome volume concisely covers its subject. From Lucy Terry's earliest recorded rhyme in 1746, to Ntozake Shange's novels of the 1980s, Russell surveys the development of black women's literary traditions in America. We see the emergence of Phillis Wheatley and Frances Harper from the grip of slavery; we hear the addresses of Alice Dunbar Nelson and Angelina Grimké to a predominantly white audience; we explore dire urban realities with Lorraine Hansberry and Margaret Walker; we experience the rise of black power in the works of Angela Davis and Nikki Giovanni; and we watch the explosion of new voices from South and North in Alice Walker, June Jordan, Toni Cade Bambera, and Rita Dove. Single chapters examine that unique genius Zora Neale Hurston, chart the development of the great Gwendolyn Brooks, and trace the evolution of Toni Morrison's craft. Extensively footnoted and with an excellent bibliography, this is a vital book for general collections. —*Pat Monaghan*

Safire, William.
Coming to Terms.
Doubleday, $25 (0-385-41300-9). 400p.

Fans of Safire's widely syndicated "On Language" columns will rejoice in this compilation of essays first published in newspapers in 1988–89. Drawing on the use (and misuse) of language as expressed by media personalities and politicians, in legend and literature, Safire regales readers with such linguistic distinctions as verb usage with *neither/nor* constructions, the origins of phrases such as "gilding the lily" (it's "*painting* the lily" per the Shakespeare text), and the etymology, spelling, and ongoing development of hundreds of terms and phrases (*bimbo, arbitrage, hermeneutic, wimp, timeframe, plugged nickel, exchange of views,* Moslem versus Muslim, Qaddafi versus Khadafy, etc., etc.). Safire quotes from the classics, analyzes the lingo of executives, presidents, clergy, sports personalities, and others, and submits his own work to the helpful correctives of his many fans, whose follow-up letters are appended to each piece. (Essays are, with a few exceptions, alphabetically arranged.) Like the previous Safire compendiums, this one will be welcome in the public library. —*Martin Brady*

Sanders, Scott Russell.
Secrets of the Universe: Scenes from the Journey Home.
Beacon, $19.95 (0-8070-6330-4). 256p.

Sanders' essays are in many ways classically personal. They dwell on practices too familiar to notice. Like good conversationalists, they encourage dialogue. Sanders' meditations on the way heterosexual men look at women are insightful, observant, conversant with the literature. More than that, however, they both legitimize and stimulate the reader's thoughts on the topic, something more pompous writings cannot do. Sanders may be a bit too correct and morally cautious for some readers, but he is not diffident about his subjects. He never apologizes for the "trivial" status of the topics (yard ornaments, signs along highways, local cafés) from which he educes universal meaning. He doesn't rely on anxious humor (a mainstay of newspaper humorists who address everyday life) to broadcast his knowledge of what convention considers an incongruity of matter and manner. He doesn't strain for profundity. He indicates topics that deserve more thought than they are accorded by convention, gives us some orientation, and invites us to pursue them on our own. —*Roland Wulbert*

Trillin, Calvin.
American Stories.
Ticknor & Fields, $19.95 (0-395-59367-0). 294p.

Everyone has a story to tell, but some stories are more interesting than others. It also helps if you know how to tell them. Leave it to Calvin Trillin to find the extraordinary in the ordinary. His travels for the *New Yorker* have culminated in a collection of tales that bring out the eccentricities and peculiarities that embody America in all its shortcomings and glory. Trillin's true-crime stories, tales of murder in middle America, engrossing and full of surprises, are narrative gems worthy of a Capote. His profiles of the weird and infamous detail the less-than-conventional lives of such folks as the controversial drive-in movie critic Joe Bob Briggs; ice cream entrepreneurs and aging hippies Ben and Jerry; oddball showmen Penn and Teller; and Miami crime reporter Edna Buchanan. Poignant and funny, Trillin's reportage is irresistible. —*Benjamin Segedin*

Vonnegut, Kurt.
Fates Worse Than Death: An Autobiographical Collage of the 1980s.
Putnam, $22.95 (0-399-13633-9). 240p.

Like *Palm Sunday*, this is a gathering of speeches and articles—what used to be called "fugitive" writings, presumably because they hadn't been brought to the justice of book publication before—stitched together by what their author calls "breezy autobiographical commentary." Launched by such occasions as the death of the army buddy with whom he endured the firebombing of Dresden (the central event in his fiction as well as his life), a trip to "freedom fighter"–ravaged Mozambique, and the request to lecture upon "The Legacy of Strategic Bombing" at the National Air and Space Museum in Washington, these would-have-been ephemera are full of a characteristic Vonnegutian sweet-and-sour tone and humor. But they are also, more than his novels, transparent vehicles for his rage at the ongoing beastlinesses of humanity and his ultimately unquiet resignation to the healing of nature and time at the price of human extinction. Any admirer of the novels can't help but be enthralled. *—Ray Olson*

Woolf, Virginia.
A Passionate Apprentice: The Early Journals, 1897–1909.
HBJ, $24.95 (0-15-171287-5). 398p.

This is a mixed bag of journals and diaries printed in their entirety, kept by Virginia Woolf (then Virginia Stephen) from age 15 to 27. The earliest entries consist of abbreviated observations of people, places, and events, followed by exercises in extensive essay writing; more detailed reminiscences of people and places from her childhood follow, ending with travel journals and essays. Despite Woolf's 1908 comment that "When I read this book . . . I am struck by the wildness of its statements—the carelessness of its descriptions," still, her work is instructive if only because she ran, even in her younger days, in circles that included the prominent figures in the world of art, literature, politics, law, and education. While these are journals, Woolf, even as a youngster, was fully aware of an invisible reader who made her "put on her dress clothes such as they are." But, mostly, the modern reader herein becomes a partner to Virginia Woolf teaching herself to write—and as the journals progress, we easily discern her signature style (of understatement and contrasting imagery) taking shape. *—Allen Weakland*

Yardley, Jonathan.
Out of Step: Notes from a Purple Decade.
Villard, $19 (0-394-58910-6). 288p.

Book reviewer, columnist, Pulitzer Prize winner, and champion of clear thinking, Yardley has collected the best of his *Washington Post* essays from the past 10 years. Armed with a vigorous vocabulary, streamlined sentences, a boxer's pace, and deadly accuracy, he hits his targets squarely, dispersing the usual drivel about literature, art, education, the media, and sports. Yardley criticizes the self-indulgence of new fiction, the pandering of college administrations that allows courses on TV's long-running "M*A*S*H*," the insatiable appetite for titillating public confessions conducted by the "blow-dried sob sisters of videoland," and all that is smug, insular, and self-serving. Yardley isn't afraid to object to vulgarity or insist on the value of dignity, restraint, integrity, and thinking for yourself. He calls them as he sees them, helping his readers shake off the lull induced by the platitudes of commerce and the status quo. —*Donna Seaman*

Music

Bachmann, Robert C.
Karajan: Notes on a Career.
Pantheon, $25 (0-679-40628-X). 371p. index.

It is sad that the most remarkable passages of a biography about the most remarkable of modern-day conductors should have nothing to do with music. But the truth is, this is what everyone wants to know about Karajan: What, precisely, was the nature of his cooperation with the Nazis? Bachmann is careful but cruel: Karajan's defenders may have made excuses for him, but the facts are that Karajan joined the party early in the 1930s and, like all the artists who profited from the absence of prominent Jews, turned a blind eye to evil and came under the protection of Göring. Yet all his life Karajan never seemed to understand that there were any moral complications in this. Frankly, there is little evidence of outright anti-Semitism. But what is revealed in this portrait is perhaps more chilling: a devotion to beauty and serenity so complete that moral sensibility is blocked altogether. Karajan extends our concept of evil by revealing its cold, mechanical beauty. He did so much for music, yet in the future readers will not be so easily seduced by the aristocratic genius of one who dreamed of heaven as he strolled the borders of hell. —*Stuart Whitwell*

✔Brendel, Alfred.
Music Sounded Out: Essays, Lectures, Interviews, Afterthoughts.
Farrar, $25 (0-374-21651-7). 258p. index.

Pianist Brendel, the author of *Musical Thoughts and Afterthoughts* (1976), returns to print with a collection of essays on music, composers, and the life and role of the performer. As an acclaimed interpreter of Mozart and Beethoven, Brendel not unexpectedly covers both their solo compositions and their concertos; but he also examines works by Liszt, Schumann, and Busoni. Brendel discusses the art of building a program, champions the cause of live recordings, and examines performance styles, both his own and other pianists'. In a less serious vein, Brendel attacks the problem of not allowing the humor in music through by playing certain works with too much solemnity, a topic that allows his natural wit to amuse and instruct his readers. Revealing discourses on both the art and the craft of making music. —*John Brosnahan*

Dalton, David.
Mr. Mojo Risin': Jim Morrison, the Last Holy Fool.
St. Martin's, $24.95 (0-312-05900-0); paper, $14.95 (0-312-05899-3). 129p.

"Mr. Mojo Risin" was Jim Morrison's anagram for his name, one of the many identities forged by the self-proclaimed "Lizard King" on the overheated anvil of his ego. Dalton, longtime editor of *Rolling Stone*, has written a volcanic account of Morrison's frantic life, his prose exploding like fireworks as he rattles off the pertinent facts. For example, his first mystical experience at age 6; his father's career as a navy officer; his adulation of Rimbaud and Baudelaire; his stint at UCLA Film School that developed his flair for cinematic performance; and his taste for low life. Dalton writes: "He was too good to be true. A teenybopper idol, an underground hero, a Beat poet, a shaman, a dreamboat, a rock star, a wild man who pissed on your rug, a visionary, a stud, your drinking buddy and on and on." Aided by numerous photos, Dalton takes in the whole frenzied era as he describes Morrison's intuitive genius, the intensive collaboration among the Doors, their explosive success, and Morrison's rapid decline from a brilliant performer and acidhead *Vogue* sex symbol to a burned-out, paunchy drunk. Timed to capitalize on the publicity generated by Oliver Stone's film, *The Doors*, this volume will have staying power for rock fans. —*Donna Seaman*

✔Escott, Colin and Hawkins, Martin.
Good Rockin' Tonight: Sun Records and the Birth of Rock 'n' Roll.
St. Martin's, $19.95 (0-312-05439-4). 256p.

For 20 years, Escott and Hawkins have plugged away on their exhaustive, anecdotal chronicle of the little Memphis label that launched Elvis—and Johnny Cash and Carl Perkins and Roy Orbison and Jerry Lee Lewis and Charlie Rich. They've published it at least twice before, but they've kept on researching and revising 'til it's almost perfect. (No cigar, though: Elvis' second flip side, "I Don't Care If the Sun Don't Shine," just ain't from Disney's *Cinderella*. But wait a minute! Dig this description of Jerry Lee Lewis when he entered the Sun studio for the first time, age 21: "He was barely educated, twice married, once jailed, and good for nothing much other than pounding the piano." Okay, White Owls on me, guys.) They've interviewed everybody who'd talk to them: if not the stars, then the studio staffers who worked with them. Most important, they've talked with Sun's proprietor Sam Phillips, the nonmusician whose taste for raw, exciting music that married black blues to white honky-tonk country turned out to be indispensable to perfecting rock 'n' roll. He never became a big-time player in the music biz, which is another fascinating strain in Escott and Hawkins' narrative, but if anyone could be called r 'n' r's father ("pappy" seems more fitting, though), it's he. Tricked out with photos of Sun's stars and staff—which is to say, with faces that just plain take your eyes into custody—this book's as glorious a bit of Americana as blue suede shoes. —*Ray Olson*

Music

Flippo, Chet.
Everybody Was Kung-Fu Dancing: Chronicles of the Lionized and the Notorious.
St. Martin's, paper, $13.95 (0-312-06349-0). 320p.

Be it in a profile of ex-con and rhinestone cowboy David Allan Coe or former soul superstar, the Reverend Al Green; an obit of Bill Haley (of "Rock around the Clock" fame) or troubador Phil Ochs; or an interview with pre-Bonfire Tom Wolfe, pop chronicler Flippo covers the vast ground of pop music and youth culture with authority. In almost two decades' worth of articles published in *Rolling Stone* and elsewhere, he's proven to be a cutting-edge reporter, as much participant as observer, whether hobnobbing with Mick Jagger or John Lennon, talking with Jerry Lee Lewis about Elvis, or hanging out with Dylan on the set of *Pat Garrett and Billy the Kid*. Also in this collection are accounts of the making of George Romero's grisly zombie flick, *Dawn of the Dead*; of convict-turned-literary-star-turned-murderer Jack Henry Abbott; and of the famous crowd tragedy at the 1979 Cincinnati Who concert. *—Benjamin Segedin*

✔**Fluegel, Jane, ed.**
Bernstein Remembered.
Carroll & Graf, $32 (0-88184-722-4). 160p.

This tribute to the great Leonard Bernstein should find an avid library audience. Bernstein, one of the most versatile and talented American musicians of the century, was also a fascinating subject for the camera, and the proof of his photogeneity is here in some 400 shots that span his early years in Boston, his great successes as symphony conductor and pianist, his equally great achievements as composer of classical music and works for Broadway and the ballet, and even his notoriety as a "personality." Among the photographers represented are Cartier-Bresson, Eisenstaedt, and Henry Grossman. In addition, there's a preface by violinist Isaac Stern and an introduction by critic Donal Henehan. A beautiful book about a beautiful man and an important artist. *—Martin Brady*

Lees, Gene.
Waiting for Dizzy.
Oxford, $21.95 (0-19-505670-1). 304p. index.

Lees' third collection of his marvelous jazz journalism may seem less focused than the first two (*Singers and the Song* and *Meet Me at Jim and Andy's*), which concentrated, somewhat loosely, upon jazz singing and the jazz life-style, respectively. It also seems to contain more pieces that are fundamentally interviews, fewer that combine, in Lees' virtuosic manner, such conversations with memoirs, musico-sociological lore, and the kind of technical information about playing music that nonplaying jazz fans just eat up. But these articles are still lovely and poignant and funny and vivid. They fall roughly into three groups. The first includes profiles of some relative oldtimers, most notably the evergreen, amazingly vital octogenarian altoist, trumpeter, composer, and arranger Benny Carter. The second comprises sketches of three great guitarists: Herb Ellis, Lenny Breau, and Emily Remler. The third includes the title piece and, as the invocation of Dizzy Gillespie implies, consists of portraits in bop. —*Ray Olson*

Previn, André.
No Minor Chords: My Days in Hollywood.
Doubleday, $22.50 (0-385-41341-6). 256p.

The revered days when movies were really movies, stars were truly glamorous, and studio heads absolute gods of the Hollywood universe here receive a reality check—and a down-to-earth jolt in André Previn's account of his decade-plus in Los Angeles. It's a breathless collection of anecdotes, occasionally organized, more often not, about celebrities some readers might only vaguely recall—Errol Flynn, Vincente Minnelli, Sam Goldwyn, Johnny Mercer, Ava Gardner. These snapshots from the viewpoint of a now-world-known musician reveal egos and eccentricities not far removed from those of today's idols, and stories such as Jascha Heifetz's auctions of gifts and Minnelli's peacock brouhaha in *Gigi* will evoke grins as well as grimaces. More important is the story of the maturation of a wide-eyed German emigré into a master musician with a genuine love for all beings, large and small. Sighs, too, accompany the biography, since many will nod to the question, "Where are the movies of yesteryear?" —*Barbara Jacobs*

Reed, Lou.
Between Thought and Expression: Selected Lyrics of Lou Reed.
Hyperion, $18.95 (1-56282-993-9). 192p. index.

There are very few rock lyricists whose work even makes sense, let alone reads well, without the music to clear up ambiguities and set moods. Reed, whose first group, the Velvet Underground, was the house band at Andy Warhol's Factory in the late 1960s and was the seminal influence on 1970s punk rock and remains the fountainhead of the rock avant garde, writes lyrics that don't just make sense. They are better than most American poetry being written these days, and that despite the fact that, when they're just words on a page, they *do* lose the rhythmic life the music gives them. The subjects of his songs are the mean streets, marginal people, and the struggle for love amidst and against squalor, violence, and pain. It is no surprise whatsoever that one of Reed's literary heroes is Hubert Selby, Jr., author of the scabrously compassionate "underground" classic, *Last Exit to Brooklyn*. It is a surprise, a pleasant one, to find Reed's loose and humane interview with Selby concluding this collection, along with his talk with Vaclav Havel, who—like many modern Czech artists, the author-president says—is a longtime fan of Reed and the Velvets. —*Ray Olson*

✔Rosenberg, Deena.
Fascinating Rhythm: The Collaboration of George and Ira Gershwin.
Dutton, $24.95 (0-525-93356-5). 320p. index.

Any lover of great American popular song ought to love this book, which, Rosenberg maintains, isn't a biography. Well, it may not be one Gershwin's

Music

life story, but it is the life story of a vital relationship, of the way Ira and George were a single songwriter. Inevitably, Rosenberg relays many biographical details about each brother singly as well as both together. But after the first chapter, the processes behind their achievements and the structures of their songs become the foci of her attention. She shows, through musical examples so simple and clear that even those only marginally literate in music will follow them, how George could develop an entire suite of songs from a mere cell of music—a one- or two-bar phrase, a pentatonic scale, etc.—and how Ira could fashion lyrics that match the music's invitation to boundless variation, to a kaleidoscope of meanings and nuances. A fine addition to any American music—to any American—library. —*Ray Olson*

Stroff, Stephen M.
Discovering Great Jazz: A New Listener's Guide to the Sounds and Styles of the Top Musicians and Their Recordings on CDs, LPs, and Cassettes.
Newmarket, $18.95 (1-55704-103-2). 208p. index.

Here's something rather wonderful, even subversive, hiding out as just another entry in a novices'-guide-to-music series. Stroff's book is based upon an earlier, self-published effort "to present a straightforward, easy-to-read history of jazz as concisely as possible." Stroff is the soul of brevity, fair-mindedness, catholicity of taste, and good prose manners as he not only describes jazz's stylistic developments but also gives pretty much equal weight to each period of the music and each significant player. This is almost unheard of in jazz writing, which abounds with scribes who ignore or slander whole periods and any musicians of which they disapprove (on nonmusical more often than musical grounds). Moreover, Stroff, a musician himself, gives very cogent reasons for appreciating the customarily pooh-poohed likes of Benny Goodman, Ramsey Lewis, and Cleo Laine and for taking the godlike status of, say, Eric Dolphy or John Coltrane with a smidgen of salt. His record recommendations are darn good, too. —*Ray Olson*

Taraborelli, J. Randy.
Michael Jackson: The Magic and the Madness.
Birch Lane, $21.95 (1-55972-064-6). 592p.

Can Michael Jackson be as weird as everyone thinks? Well, if even half of this new book is true, the answer is a resounding "yes," and the blame can be put squarely on the shoulders of the superstar's father and on Jackson's early-career life-style. Taraborelli, who last time out took on Diana Ross in *Call Me Miss Ross*, recounts how Jackson's ambitious father, Joe, started his kids off singing in strip joints. On the road, Joe would brag about his exploits with women, a direct contradiction to what Michael's mother, Katherine, a strict Jehovah's Witness, was saying about sex. Michael's brothers weren't much better; they'd bring girls to the room and fool around while Michael was in the next bed. Supposedly, as a joke, Michael was locked in a room with a prostitute, then instructed to lose his virginity. One might conclude, then, that it was only a short step from being sexually traumatized to craving plastic surgery. Taraborelli also tells us plenty about Papa Joe's verbal abuse of

Michael as well as his efforts to control all aspects of his children's lives. Taraborelli provides just what readers of this kind of book are looking for—lots of juicy details and the opportunity to say "You've got to be kidding!" over and over again. The book doesn't stint in giving the reader a glimpse of Michael's genius, yet it's impossible, upon concluding, not to feel deeply sorry for this boy-man. Jackson, in this telling, becomes yet another celebrity burdened with all the things that money can't buy. —*Ilene Cooper*

Troy, Sandy.
One More Saturday Night: Reflections with the Grateful Dead, Dead Family, and Dead Heads.
St. Martin's, $24.95 (0-312-05938-8). 288p.

Troy, a San Diego attorney, is a Dead Head supreme who has attended concerts and kept track of the Grateful Dead for 20 years. Now he puts it all together in a photo-packed tribute to the band's sustained energy, creativity, and ability to make people happy. The text begins with a breathless account of the Dead's various configurations and notable performances, including the 1978 concert at the pyramids and the Portland show that seemed to usher in the eruption of Mount St. Helens with "Fire on the Mountain." Band members, managers, soundmen, artists, spouses, friends, and other Dead Heads share memories of acid trips, the Dead's Haight-Ashbury headquarters, collaborations with other musicians, commitments to worthy causes, and philosophies of music and life in 16 lively interviews. A must for all rock-'n'-roll collections. —*Donna Seaman*

Whitaker, Bob.
The Unseen Beatles.
Collins Publishers, $40 (0-00-215953-8). 160p.

Can there actually be another cache of never-before-seen photos of the Beatles? The answer is essentially yes. Some of Whitaker's photos *have* been seen previously, then, most notably the cover of the *Revolver* album and the infamous "Butcher" cover that appeared only in the initial printing of the *Yesterday and Today* album. But otherwise, this collection of some 150 photos has, until now, lain in state on the photographer's farm. In 1964, the young Whitaker caught a break when assigned to cover the Beatles' first tour of Australia. Beatles manager Brian Epstein liked his work so much that he invited him along on subsequent tours and then back to England. The photos here—mostly in black and white with occasional color—are by and large candid, so the overall quality is uneven, though many will indeed satiate those Beatles fans who always want to see more of their heros. Whitaker has also included some rare shots of the Lennons (i.e., pre-Yoko) and Harrisons mugging goofily for the camera at home. A must for those who remember the Fab Four when. —*Martin Brady*

Occult/New Age

Bache, Christopher M.
Lifecycles: Reincarnation and the Web of Life.
Paragon House, $18.95 (1-55778-350-0). 237p. index.

There are certainly enough books available on reincarnation to fill up several New Age bookstores, but Bache offers something the others don't—an explanation that not only purports to define how reincarnation works, but also shows why adopting this perspective can be both life affirming and life changing. Though he begins with the now-requisite "case studies" of people claiming to have lived before, Bache quickly moves on to a more philosophical discussion that engages while it disarms. To his credit, he doesn't duck the hard questions: How does chance figure into the scheme of things? Is there a place for reincarnation in Christian thought? Just who is in charge of this whole rebirth roulette, anyway? Admittedly, some of Bache's answers are simply his own, but the quality of his thinking goes well beyond what is usually offered on the subject. An essential addition for the 133 shelves. —*Ilene Cooper*

Broughton, Richard S.
Parapsychology: The Controversial Science.
Ballantine, $22 (0-345-35638-1). 416p. index.

Because Broughton is the director of research at the world-renowned Institute for Parapsychology in Durham, N.C., one would assume a certain biased interest to be present in his book. Instead, the author brings a healthy skepticism to his subject and the dispassionate interest and discourse of the scientific investigator. Yet he still turns out a lively, fascinating exploration of documented cases of paranormal experiences in everyday life, focusing on psychic dreams and precognitive experiences. Broughton describes how psychic, or psi, phenomena are scientifically measured, reviews in great detail the history and evolution of the field of parapsychology, and packs his volume with dramatic case histories that will captivate even die-hard skeptics. Although Broughton's book is not exhaustive or convincing in its purported demonstration of scientific principles that "prove" the existence of the paranormal (much of his "evidence" is highly subjective, and his arguments are vague), the author is one of the first to clear up much of the confusion that exists over his field's terms, goals, and techniques. A clear, no-nonsense, up-to-date look at a perennially favorite topic of readers. With notes and bibliography. —*Mary Banas*

Brown, Karen McCarthy.
Mama Lola: A Vodou Priestess in Brooklyn.
Univ. of California, $24.95 (0-520-07073-9). 388p. index.

Brown is a white academic, a professor of sociology and anthropology of religion at Drew University to be exact, who set out to study urban voodoo in the Haitian community in Brooklyn and has ended up as a voodoo initiate. Her research brought her to Mama Lola, a spiritual leader and part of a family that includes five generations of healers, most of them women. Brown's engrossing, intimate, penetrating, and frequently mystifying book embraces the keen observations of a scholar as well as personal, dramatized narratives relating pivotal events in the lives of Mama Lola and her family and of Brown's interaction with them as they "serve the spirits." She describes the eerie experience of possession, the complexity and enigma of the spirits' personalities and messages, the importance of mother-daughter relationships, and voodoo's emphasis on survival in the here and now. By focusing on voodoo's influence on family life, gender roles, and social change, Brown shares her unique understanding of its vitality and meaning. A triumph of ethnography, imagination, and integrity. —*Donna Seaman*

Donner, Florinda.
Being-in-Dreaming.
HarperCollins, $18.95 (0-06-250233-6). 303p.

Admirers of Lynn Andrews and Carlos Castaneda will be pleased with this book. Those who like to know more precisely what's fiction and what simply reads like fiction may be more skeptical about the "young UCLA student meets mysterious Mexican woman, travels with her, and encounters sorcerers in modern Mexico" plot. Donner's third book continues her descriptive journey into spirit realms and self-discovery. It'll probably be as popular as her previous *Shabono* and *The Witch's Dream*. —*Ryn Etter*

Siegel, Lee.
Net of Magic: Wonders and Deceptions in India.
Univ. of Chicago, $60 (0-226-75686-6). 472p. paper, $19.95 (0-226-75687-4).

Siegel is a professor of religion, an adventurer, and a magician who transfixes you with his word magic. This book, a striking study of Indian magic past and present, is a veritable bag of literary tricks containing the vividness of a travelogue, the scholarship of history, and the creativity of fiction. As he records his experiences with magicians all across the subcontinent, he conjures up the pungent, nearly overwhelming swirl of smells, sights, and sounds that clog India's febrile cities and towns. Siegel befriends various Maslets, a Muslim subcaste of street performers who are masters at crowd control and the execution of tricks rich in metaphysical implications, and describes the precariousness and freedom of their lives. He also goes behind the scenes of the elaborately staged productions of Hindu magicians who dress like maharajahs. As he reveals the secrets of famous tricks and dissects the link between magicians and holy men, Siegel also ponders our need for deception and our pleasure in illusions. An entrancing and masterly book that will fascinate anyone interested in the practice of magic, the mystique of India, or the spectacle of humanity's infinite inventiveness and gullibility. —*Donna Seaman*

Williams, Ben and others.
The Black Hope Horror: The True Story of a Haunting.
Morrow, $19 (0-688-05176-6). 224p.

Truth proves once again to be stranger than fiction in this account of a six-year ordeal undergone by the Williams family, who unknowingly built a house over a graveyard. The haunting began on moving day when a black snake stuck its snout up through the decking. The Williams' uneasiness and that of close neighbors grew as they encountered armies of ants, belligerent crows, asthma attacks, vicious family fights, sinkholes, localized storms, and shadowy black figures. Then the bodies were discovered. The only thing more gruesome than living through this ghostly nightmare was the legal terror all the families encountered when they tried to sue the developer. Gripping and ever so real. —*Cynthia Ogorek*

Parenting

Caron, Ann F.
"Don't Stop Loving Me": A Reassuring Guide for Mothers of Adolescent Daughters.
Holt, $19.95 (0-8050-1136-6). 224p. index.

This valuable guide spotlights the psychological aspect of a little girl's transition to adult female. It provides mothers with insights into the volatile behavior of teenage daughters, practical information on risks, and thoughtful advice on a range of problems. Caron is sympathetic and knowledgeable, the hard-earned result of going back to school, convinced there was more to understand about her two daughters than the information available to her. The results—on trust, limits, peer pressure, the "Don't worry, it won't happen to me" syndrome—are worth reading. She covers the big problems of anorexia, bulimia, drugs and alcohol, and the touchy subjects of underage drinking, sexuality, peer friendships, and mother-daughter relations. Never underestimating the complexity of the hazards faced by mother and daughter, Caron urges vigilance as well as affection and support. She backs her advice with information from formal studies, her own and other mothers' experience, and interviews with teenage girls, whose comments add a special poignancy. —*Virginia Dwyer*

Feiden, Karyn.
Parents' Guide to Raising Responsible Kids: Preschool through Teen Years.
Prentice Hall Press, paper, $9.95 (0-13-650813-8). 240p. index.
Smith, Dian G.
Parents' Guide to Raising Kids in a Changing World: Preschool through Teen Years.
Prentice Hall Press, paper, $9.95 (0-13-650821-9). 272p. index.

While these two new books in the Children's Television Workshop series sometimes crisscross over the same territory, they are quite different. Feiden views the subject of child rearing from a developmental perspective, concentrating on how parental responsibility and discipline change as children move from preschool into the teenage years. Invoking some of the best-known experts (Ginott, Brazelton, Elkind), the author explains how parents can set limits and foster values while still allowing their children to become strong, self-reliant, and responsible. Concrete suggestions to help adults guide young people through a variety of situations—peer pressures, school stresses, problems with drugs, alcohol, or money—add to the book's value. An annotated resource list is appended.

Though Smith's book is filled with advice on parenting, too, she is less interested in disciplinary strategy than in the nature of the family today and the increasingly complicated sociological issues it faces. Stressing children's need for good role models and solid values, she urges parents to think carefully about the values they are passing along in their families. Child care, single-parent households, drugs, and changes in sexual mores are among the concerns she explores, providing reasoned counsel to foster a better understanding of today's challenges and help adults confront them more effectively. Resources. —*Stephanie Zvirin*

Fishel, Elizabeth.
Family Mirrors: What Our Children's Lives Reveal about Ourselves.
Houghton, $19.95 (0-395-44261-3). 287p. index.

"The most complex challenge of parenthood," Fishel argues, is "confrontation with the words and puzzles of our own childhood." Drawing on family systems psychology, her book studies the "loop of influence" connecting parents and their young children to the parents'"families of origin." Childhood experiences in this first family affect the new parents' choice of a parenting style (Fishel's spectrum runs from traditionalist through rebel and compensator to synthesizer) and their ability to cope effectively with classic parenting problems (e.g., separation, anger, and self-esteem). *Family Mirrors* gracefully blends psychological theory, expert opinion, and literary insights with the memories and experiences of "on-the-job trainees"—160 parents Fishel studied through personal interviews, a detailed questionnaire (reproduced in an appendix), and parenting group discussions. It is a hopeful book, arguing that parents can come to terms with their pasts and change unhealthy family patterns in the present and future. One small reservation: Fishel's own family is so *very* intact—two parents and two sons, with four healthy grandparents until the author's father-in-law died as she was completing this book—that she may understate the difficulty of resolving intergenerational issues in families disrupted by divorce, disease, or death. —*Mary Carroll*

Leonard, Joan.
Tales from Toddler Hell: My Life as a Mom.
Pharos/World Almanac, $14.95 (0-88687-542-0). 112p.

These 16 short, entertaining essays (several published previously in *Parents* and other mass-circulation magazines) are by turns humorous, inventive, and bittersweet. A latecomer to motherhood (she started in her late

Parenting

thirties), Leonard colorfully juxtaposes in each essay the cosmopolitan, carefree life she and her husband once led with the jarring and draining reality of caring for two very active toddlers. She takes us on fascinating visits to both the exotic and the chaotic, such as Venice (where stairs compete with baby strollers), two-hour airplane rides that seem to last two decades, the family dinner table, and the maternity ward after the birth of her second child (a moving tribute to mother-love's amazing power to increase exponentially like the biblical loaves and fishes). A charming collection that speaks to parents (and nostalgic grandparents) everywhere. —*Mary Banas*

Levine, Katherine Gordy.
When Good Kids Do Bad Things: A Survival Guide for Parents.
Norton, $19.95 (0-393-03019-9). 320p.

Caring is the basis of the step-by-step strategy offered in this book for dealing with troubled teenagers. Parents of adolescents who have serious problems, such as substance abuse or violent behavior, will appreciate this guide because it confronts issues beyond messy rooms and pierced ears. The author, a social worker who has been a foster parent to almost 400 children, outlines problems and solutions with warmth, honesty, and guts. Her "caring response" approach involves a parent-child alliance and provides an alternative to tough love. Caring intervention, if necessary, is also discussed. How to find professional help and the importance of self-care during trying times conclude this intelligent guide. Listings of self-help groups and suggested reading are included. —*Betsy Levins*

Miller, Mary Susan.
The School Book: Everything Parents Must Know about Their Child's Education, from Preschool through Eighth Grade.
St. Martin's, $24.95 (0-312-05578-1); paper, $14.95 (0-312-05508-0). 416p. index.

Miller offers a comprehensive guide that answers both basic and complicated questions parents ask about school. Formatted in classic, Dr. Spock–like question-and-answer style, it advises parents on working with the school system from preschool through junior high. In addition to covering common problems such as doing homework, Miller addresses more serious concerns, including sex and drugs. A terrific tool for parents in helping their children get the most out of school. —*Tracie Richardson*

O'Neill, Hugh.
Here's Looking at You, Kids! The Romantic Adventures of Mom and Dad.
Prentice Hall Press, $17.95 (0-13-201153-0). 208p.

Much-published humorist O'Neill, whose writings have appeared in *Parents*, *McCall's*, *Reader's Digest*, and *Glamour* magazines, here displays his unique brand of sophisticated wit in 23 delightfully thought-provoking essays on the pride, joy, and day-to-day catastrophes known only to parents. In what amounts to a series of cautionary tales, the author accurately portrays what life with kids entails, shattering illusions—many his own—

along the way. This is an especially good primer for today's numerous upscale, later-in-life parents, who, thinking themselves financially and emotionally prepared for a blissful family life, need their eyes opened to the blitzkrieg that awaits them. Through imaginative literary, corporate, and military metaphors, O'Neill shows how children are the most cunning creatures on earth, and instructs parents, via hilarious scenes drawn from his own life, on how to appear to be in control in a Disneyesque world filled with chaos—and cuddles. —*Mary Banas*

Shelov, Stephen P. and others.
Caring for Your Baby and Young Child: Birth to Age Five.
Bantam, $32.50 (0-553-07186-6). 704p. index.

This is the first in a three-volume set outlining the care of children from birth to age 21. Written and edited by pediatricians, it is a definitive resource—a comprehensive, encyclopedic manual of basic care, physical and emotional development, and health emergencies and common complaints. In all, some 125 topics are covered, from the simplest (e.g., how to diaper your baby) to the most serious (e.g., children with AIDS). Although priced quite a bit higher than many other books on its subject, the tome's caliber and volume of information make it worth the investment. —*Tracie Richardson*

Smith, Dian G.
Parents' Guide to Raising Kids in a Changing World: Preschool through Teen Years.
Prentice Hall Press, paper, $9.95 (0-13-650821-9). 272p. index.

See p.154.

Philosophy & Psychology

Asbell, Bernard and Wynn, Karen.
What They Know about You.
Random, $20 (0-394-55791-3). 384p. index.

Subtitled *The Most Significant, Surprising and Amusing Discoveries the Experts Have Made about You and Your Behavior*, this is a compendium of some of the best of the 33,000 (!) studies conducted each year by psychologists, psychiatrists, sociologists, and public-opinion pollsters. Asbell and Wynn have not only unearthed the most entertaining findings, but freed them of their often wretchedly wordy, overblown academic prose. The topics address every aspect of life from the language of eye contact to erotic response, attitudes toward aging and physical appearance, and the entire carnival of human emotions, impressions, and orientation. The tests used range from the silly— people hiding in public rest-room stalls to see who washes their hands—to subtle attempts at discerning sense of self. Readers will enjoy the quizzes and the "Look Yourself Up" sections and will find confirmation of their own

Philosophy & Psychology

experiences as well as revelations and lots of tidbits to chuckle over. All studies are cited in full at the conclusion of the text. An irresistible reflection of our private and public selves. —*Donna Seaman*

Baumeister, Roy F.
Escaping the Self: Alcoholism, Spirituality, Masochism, and Other Flights from the Burden of Selfhood.
Basic Books, $22.95 (0-465-02053-4). 288p. index.

Contrary to recent popular opinion, Baumeister theorizes that beneath self-destructive acts or even recurring failures, many individuals desire not to harm the self but to escape from the heavy burden of self-consciousness that exists in contemporary Western society, particularly prevalent since the human potential movement of the 1960s and the "Me" attitude of the 1970s. Rather than wanting to inflict pain or punishment on themselves, the alcoholic, masochist, bulimic, or suicidal actually seek release from the overwhelming awareness of self that encompasses tremendously high expectations of one's own performance and achievement and an obsessive concern for how one appears to others. The author cites spirituality and religious exercise as a positive form of escape, promising some relief from the ego's domination, while offering the possibility of a transformative experience. A fascinating study—both provocative and enlightening. —*Alice Joyce*

Bolles, Edmund Blair.
A Second Way of Knowing: The Riddle of Human Perception.
Prentice Hall Press, $18.95 (0-13-471582-9). 240p.

What is perception and how does it work? Some scientists, called *physicalists* by Bolles, postulate mechanical explanations based on the laws of physics; they try to understand our brains as some sort of organic computers. The humanists, on the other hand, emphasize sensory experience that involves a leap from physical reflex to subjective description, leading to the statement: "Conscious meaning rather than objective knowledge is the fruit of perception." Like all good popular science writers, Bolles patiently dissects the sequence of thoughts behind scientific theories and pinpoints their major differences. He poses many intriguing questions about the relationships between perception and awareness, analysis, language, and culture, as well as the link between neurology and psychology, and then explains the difficulties involved in trying to answer them. Laid-back and conversational, Bolles approaches his stunningly complex topic with panache, curiosity, and a healthy respect for enigmas. —*Donna Seaman*

✔Brown, Norman O.
Apocalypse and / or Metamorphosis.
Univ. of California, $22.50 (0-520-07298-7). 250p.

Here's one professor emeritus who hasn't mellowed with age. The author of that Marx-and-Freud-conflating New Left bible *Life against Death* writes as prophetically as he did in the 1950s. Oh, he may not shock us today as much as in his 1960 announcement to Columbia University's Phi Beta Kappas that he was eagerly awaiting the "blessing" of madness (a decade later, Lionel Trilling was still incensed), and his writing may have become more academic (see his interpretations of Islam and Spinoza herein). But Brown is writing academically *about* prophecy, and he has by no means abandoned the Dionysian, free-associative style of his 1960s intellectual bombshell, *Love's Body*. He has not changed substantially, but his constituency has. The vision that captivated 1960s intellectuals now flourishes in the burgeoning, largely female New Age, neo-pagan, and spirituality movements. Brown's prophecy of spiritual rebirth has come true, but not among the readers who once championed him. It's unfortunate that readers who know him have forsaken mysticism, and readers who value mysticism do not know him. Some matchmaking is in order. —*Roland Wulbert*

Kherdian, David.
On a Spaceship with Beelzebub: By a Grandson of Gurdjieff.
Globe Press Books, $24.95 (0-936385-20-0); paper, $12.95 (0-936385-10-3). 288p.

Kherdian recounts the story of his spiritual journey from the 1960s to the 1990s. The book centers on his encounter with and reaction to the teachings of Gurdjieff and the so-called Fourth-Way of spiritual enlightenment, an influential cult responsible, in part, for the popularity of the enneagram, EST, and Biosphere II. Initially suspicious of Gurdjieff, Kherdian becomes a follower even while rebelling against the group's structure. He breaks away to join a smaller band of Gurdjieff disciples living on an Oregon farm and then leaves again to live in upstate New York, where he realizes the value of what he has been taught. Kherdian's story is easily accessible and interesting to follow, particularly since it provides insight into the Gurdjieff method. Glossary of terms. —*Mary Deeley*

✔May, Rollo.
The Cry for Myth.
Norton, $22.95 (0-393-02768-6). 317p.

Recipient of numerous awards for his contributions to the field of psychology and author of *Discovery of Being: Essays on Existential Psychotherapy*, May has now turned his attention to the role myths play in our lives. Theories surrounding myths have been seeping out of the confines of theoretical psychology and academia through the teachings of Joseph Campbell and are finding a large, receptive audience. May takes things a bit further, stating that "contemporary therapy is almost entirely concerned with the . . . individual's search for myths" and that our materialistic culture is bereft of functioning myths and heroes of either sex. Citing the high incidence of depression, drug abuse, and even suicide in our society, May argues that people are suffering from a lack of meaning in their lives. He goes on to explain how myths provide a sense of significance and connection to an order higher than ourselves. This is a slippery concept—one that many may dismiss as fanciful—but May is not alone in believing that psychology must include a spiritual dimension. His theory is well presented in lively interpretations of

Western myths, which, in his definition, include not only the classic Greek tragedies, but also the Horatio Alger tales, Fitzgerald's *Great Gatsby*, Ibsen's *Peer Gynt*, and the original "Sleeping Beauty," which is titled "Briar Rose." May's thinking is supple, compassionate, and grand, aimed at those who are able to see everyday problems as reflections of universal experiences. —*Donna Seaman*

Moir, Anne and Jessel, David.
Brain Sex: The Real Difference between Men and Women.
Carol Publishing Group/Lyle Stuart, $17.95 (0-8184-0543-0). 228p. index.

Many people confuse the equality of the sexes with sameness, arguing, for instance, that women could be just as good at math if they were encouraged at an early age. The authors beg to differ, flatly stating that "the sexes are different because their brains are different." After anticipating and countering the myriad objections to such a stance, they proceed to explain the mechanics of sex differentiation in the womb and the role male hormones play in the sexing of the brain. The provable variations in the layout and organization of male and female brains involve the distinction in functions located in each half of the brain and the link between them. Noting that dissimilarities manifest themselves immediately, Moir and Jessel sail through numerous examples of behavioral, emotional, and intellectual differences between the sexes at various life stages; they also analyze a selection of case studies that point to a prenatal hormonal source for homosexuality. Two dozen pages of notes support their lucid, entertaining, provocative, and potentially controversial claims. —*Donna Seaman*

✔Ornstein, Robert.
The Evolution of Consciousness—of Darwin, Freud, and Cranial Fire: The Origins of the Way We Think.
Prentice Hall Press, $25 (0-13-587569-2). 336p. index.

Every few years one comes across a book that will change one's thinking forever, and this is one such book. Ornstein's thesis is that we have to change the way we think about the human mind and the way we use it. Indeed, he believes change is imperative, for the brain is adapted to life as it was 40,000 or so years ago, and the planet today is too crowded, too polluted, too fast-changing for us to try to get along using mechanisms that no longer work. Why do people cancel vacations because of a single terrorist action and ignore the murders all around them? Why do they get angry about spending $25 for a paperback and shrug their shoulders at losing $2,000 on the purchase of a home? Ornstein, the author of the classic *Psychology of Consciousness*, examines the most recent findings of those who work on the brain and finds that we have, quite literally, many "minds" within us, each operating independently and with very little governance. The rationalizing work of the mind occupies only one or two percent of its activity, and "consciousness"—highly touted as our finest biological adaptation—would have been a hindrance if it had not been given a very minor role. The truth is, Ornstein is saying, that we have to recognize that we are biological creatures and not conduits of mystical or rational truth. We need to teach both children and politicians how the mind really works, need to explain to journalists how sensationalism affects and misleads the brain, need to think of humanity as one interlocking organism rather than a patchwork of nations, tribes, or individuals. The only evolution from now on is conscious evolution, for we have stepped beyond the realm of our biologically given nature and for better or worse have the future in our hands. A most incredible work of synthesis and insight, so far outstripping the dancing Wu Li philosophies of New Age physicists as to make them laughable. This could be the first work of a new Bible, read again and again by those looking for a wise and intelligent future. —*Stuart Whitwell*

Robbins, Anthony.
Awaken the Giant Within: How to Take Immediate Control of Your Mental, Emotional, Physical & Financial Destiny!
Summit, $20 (0-671-72734-6). 539p.

Management textbooks discuss motivation in terms of equity and expectancy, reinforcement and goal-setting, to teach present or future managers how to motivate others to perform job-related tasks effectively. Writers and lecturers like Robbins have a different audience and a different goal: They offer individuals dissatisfied with their lives analysis, advice, and techniques intended to help them "be all (they) can be." Robbins, author of the national best-seller *Unlimited Power,* heads a complex of companies that market his concepts through in-person and videotaped seminars, audiotapes, management and financial counseling, and franchise operations. His concepts include slogans like CANI! (Constant And Never-ending Improvement), a trademarked science called Neuro-Associative Conditioning, and strong emphasis on understanding and, where appropriate, changing one's life values, rules, references, and identity as the key to improving one's life. It is easy for satisfied or contented people to poke fun at self-help books and tapes, but millions of Americans seem to find them helpful. Robbins' system is somewhat elaborate, but his advice builds on common sense and on psychological and sociocultural reality. —*Mary Carroll*

Rose, Phyllis.
Never Say Goodbye: Essays.
Doubleday, $18.95 (0-385-41692-X). 160p.

A celebrated biographer, Rose raises philosophical questions about the perplexities of contemporary life. Why does torture exist? What are the values of motherhood, of loneliness? Is it better to give than to receive? (Not really, she concludes.) Her meditations, first published in venues like the *New York Times* and *Atlantic*, are splendid examples of the classic essay, often originating in observations about her daily life and frequently contradicting received wisdom. But they are by no means museum pieces. As a good modernist should, Rose finds a voice that embraces clashing perspectives without resolving them and that sustains tension between the general and the particular. Her personal experiences are sometimes too adventurous (the car trip with the transvestite) or reverent (remembering her favorite teacher at

Radcliffe) to subordinate themselves entirely to the universals they illustrate. At those times, she blurs the distinction between essay and short story and provides some of the pleasures and insights that attract readers to the contemporary essay. —*Roland Wulbert*

Sayers, Janet.
Mothers of Psychoanalysis: Helene Deutsch, Karen Horney, Anna Freud and Melanie Klein.
Norton, $24.95 (0-393-03041-5). 336p. index.

Four women—Helene Deutsch, Karen Horney, Anna Freud, and Melanie Klein—helped establish modern psychoanalysis, by adding to Freud's emphasis on patients' oedipal relationships with their fathers an equal concern with mother. Gripping, novelistic accounts of the foremothers' lives make up the book. Interweaving biography, psychological analysis, and interpretation of each woman's theories, Sayers creates memorable characters whose differences become clear. Seeing Deutsch's independence and Klein's arrogance, we understand how each came into conflict with the Freudian establishment; discovering Horney's childhood idealization of her own mother, we realize how it colored her evolution of the "womb envy" theory; learning of Anna Freud's analysis by her own father, we come to understand her limitations and gifts as a theorist. A useful, deeply intelligent book. —*Pat Monaghan*

Plants & Gardening

Dickey, Page.
Duck Hill Journal: A Year in a Country Garden.
Houghton, $19.95 (0-395-57783-7). 275p. index.

Dickey's journal both informs and inspires as she muses on planning and planting a formal garden, a project she has enthusiastically cultivated over the past nine years. The Duck Hill gardens exist amid additional acres replete with horses, dogs, chickens, and geese. In a month-by-month format (over a time span of one year), chapters feature plants selected for various gardens that constitute Duck Hill's overall plan: an herb garden, the main garden, and a white garden, among others. With regard to color schemes, a wonderful quote from Gertrude Jekyll indicates the author's own individualistic tendencies: "The business of a blue garden is to be beautiful ... it should be beautiful first ... then just as blue as may be consistent with its best possible beauty." Dickey's gifts for rich description and astute observation will reward amateur and experienced gardeners with plenty of knowledgeable advice. Watercolor sketches and line drawings illustrate the text. —*Alice Joyce*

A Garden for All Seasons.
Reader's Digest Press, $30 (0-276-42011-X). 432p. index.

This comprehensive book "draws on the secrets of English gardening to help American gardeners achieve a beautiful landscape through the seasons."

Containing techniques for planting, propagating, pruning, and maintaining more than 1,000 plants, the book also has more than 1,200 color illustrations (photographs and drawings). Also, it features a plant selector guide that is color-coded by seasons, and several photographic layouts show such plants as clematis, roses, dwarf conifers, rhododendrons, and primulas to best advantage. If a gardener could have just one flower how-to book, this would be a good candidate. —*George Cohen*

Hillier, Malcolm.
The Book of Container Gardening.
Simon & Schuster, $24.95 (0-671-72253-0). 192p. index.

Hillier (author of *The Book of Fresh Flowers* and *The Book of Dried Flowers*) continues to amaze even the most experienced of home planters by pulling together more than 40 container designs well identified in terms of soil, site, watering, and plants. Showcase creations aside, Hillier's a master of practicalities: types of containers (go for the patina of age, not modern plastic), site selection (from sunny to shady as well as specific locations like doorways and steps), and container decorating and plant care (down to the basics of repotting). Color photographs seem to bloom off the pages. In the end, this is a guide that acquits itself as more than just coffee-table decoration. Plant lists appended. —*Barbara Jacobs*

Owen, Jane.
Eccentric Gardens.
Villard, $24.95 (0-394-58447-3). 160p. index.

Readers of traditional lore should expect the unexpected in this collection of inspired English landscapes. There will be the temptation, as well, to lift more than a few ideas from the 25 genuinely picturesque gardens, featuring whimsical follies to biblical allegory. Aesthetic influences include surrealism and contemporary site-specific sculpture, while interviews with the creators contribute entertaining and enlightening insights. These "eccentric gardens," captured in striking color photographs, yield many lovely day-trips—without the necessity of a transatlantic flight! —*Alice Joyce*

Poetry

✔Ackerman, Diane.
Jaguar of Sweet Laughter: New and Selected Poems.
Random, $18 (0-679-40214-4). 288p.

Ackerman inhales the world with every sense, cell, and pore and exhales in words that chime, sing, and ring. She's a deep breather and a deep thinker; her images are fresh, immediate, and memorable. This selection of new work and poems from earlier volumes, including *Lady Faustus*, accentuates Ackerman's range of voices and moods. She can be teasing, flirtatious, and funny, as well as smart, scientific, tender, sad, wondrous, and ecstatic, but always sensual and richly feminine. In these glorious new poems, she writes of hummingbirds, penguins, deer, Halley's comet, the Amazon, Antarctica, waves, flying, teaching, and loving. The poetic forms are varied, elegant, and contoured, with rhythms sure and exhilarating as a ride in an expertly banked plane or sled or fast boat. "Drenched with life," Ackerman frees the exotic from the familiar, finds the familiar in the exotic, the large in the small, the personal in the vast. A must for poetry collections of any size. —*Donna Seaman*

Ammons, A. R.
The Really Short Poems of A. R.
Norton, $17.95 (0-393-02870-4). 176p.

Filled with sharp irony and passionate insight, the more than 100 poems in this collection span the career of one of the deans of contemporary poetry. These "really short," intellectually stimulating sound bytes shed new light on the poet's wit and wisdom. Natural sights become visions: "It was so windy / last night the snow / got down nowhere / except against something." Sex is bewildering: "One failure on / Top of another." And learning about life is learning about irony: "The smart gain / knowledge / and learn to / express / themselves to join / the world of power / where / it pays to / know / little and say / less." Throughout, Ammons makes you laugh and forces you to think hard about the way humans relate to natural phenomena and to themselves. From such simple, short expressions emerge complex, often confounding ideas. New readers of poetry as well as those with an active interest in lyric verse will love this volume. —*Thomas Phelps*

Balaban, John.
Words for My Daughter.
Copper Canyon, paper, $10 (1-55659-037-7). 80p.

There could not be a more timely winner in the National Poetry Series. Questions of human inhumanity should never be left aside, of course, but, in the post-Vietnam era, fewer poets are choosing to address such subjects. John Balaban, however, has not forgotten what he saw as a conscientious objector doing medical service in Asia: "the 9-year old boy, naked and lacerated ... yelling 'Dau, Dau,' while I, trying to translate / in the mayhem of Tet for surgeons who didn't know / who this boy was or what happened to him, kept asking / 'Where? Where's the pain?' until a surgeon / said, 'Forget it. His ears are blown off.'" In this splendid title poem, Balaban addresses his child: "I suspect I am here less for your protection / than you are here for mine, as if you were sent / to call me back into our helpless tribe." The apparently simple narratives are deeply emotional and accessible. Balaban's translations of Bulgarian and Vietnamese poets alternate with his own fine work in this excellent collection. —*Pat Monaghan*

Baranczak, Stanislaw and Cavanagh, Clare, eds.
Polish Poetry of the Last Two Decades of Communist Rule: Spoiling Cannibals' Fun.
Northwestern Univ., $39.95 (0-8101-0968-9); paper, $14.95 (0-8101-0982-4). 204p.

This excellent anthology introduces the American reader to the wealth of passionate poetry produced in Poland since 1970. The range is great: from Nobel laureate Czeslaw Milosz to the young aphorist Ryszard Krynicki; from the distinguished older poet Wislawa Szymborska to Ewa Lipska, from the "generation of '68." Editor Baranczak, himself one of the best known of the émigré poets, contributes a sterling introduction in which he defines the change from a state of censorship—and resultant self-censorship—to one in which poets are challenged to express their meanings directly and without irony. This straightforward stance is best melded, he argues, to a "Single Observer" voice, in which ordinary details convince the reader of the poet's vision. The selected work, however various, is accessible and frequently moving, as in Krynicki's short poem: "Poor moth, I can't help you, / I can only turn out the light." —*Pat Monaghan*

Boyle, Kay.
Collected Poems of Kay Boyle.
Copper Canyon, $19 (1-55659-038-5); paper, $10 (1-55659-039-3). 144p.

Some poetry seems written on the waters, some carved into stone. Kay Boyle's fits the second category. There is something so unmovable, so crystalline, about her lines that they seem sculpted rather than written: "Not a land, or like other lands, with trees coming out and the grasses growing / or of waters shriveling in the wind like the faces of old women." Welcome at last to Boyle's collected works: it is a long overdue volume, for Boyle has been active in American poetry since James Joyce picked fights in Paris bars for Ernest Hemingway to finish. Though she has long been an important teacher of poetry in San Francisco, her own work has not been granted the stature it deserves. Perhaps this collection of every published Boyle poem will rectify that. Certainly it will give lovers of classic beauty many thrilling moments: "I, bereft, was awakened by fountains of light / Spraying over the granite monuments of clouds, over the towers and cornices, / Over this toppling architecture of storm." —*Pat Monaghan*

✔Budbill, David.
Judevine: The Complete Poems, 1970–1990.
Chelsea Green, $24.95 (0-930031-47-4). 320p. paper, $14.95 (0-930031-48-2).

For 20 years, David Budbill has been writing about his small-town and rural Vermont neighbors—tree-farm laborers, mechanics, junk ("antique") dealers, hardscrabble farmers—some of the most direct and clear-eyed poems of the half-century, at least. Previously appearing in three collections and one play, the work is gathered together with poems written since *Why I Came to Judevine* was published. Budbill's poems are prosaically straightforward and easy to read, but they have the rhythmic life of the best of Jeffers and are as

165

large-souled and democratic as Whitman. Although as full of New England salt as Frost's, they are far more compassionate, more Christian in the finest sense of the word. For Budbill's personae are the poor and oppressed, and he is as staunchly their advocate—an angry protester of the way weekenders and land speculators have dispossessed the people of northern Appalachia— as Sandburg ever was of "the People, yes." He is emotional, as in his sudden vision of nuclear holocaust in "Corot's Pool"—but not sentimental: his greatest single character, foul-mouthed Acadian laborer Antoine LaMotte, is as gross—and as vital—as Chaucer's Wife of Bath. Many are going to say *Judevine* is as good as Masters' *Spoon River Anthology*. Okay, but off the mark: *Judevine* may be better thought of as the book James Agee was ultimately too pious and too distanced from his subjects to write. *Judevine* is a great book. —*Ray Olson*

Carey, Michael.
Honest Effort.
Holy Cow! Press, $14.95 (0-930100-38-7); paper, $7.95 (0-930100-39-5). 96p.

Move over, Wendell Berry! A new poet is turning over the possibilities of contemporary literature set in America's farmland. Unlike Berry, however, Michael Carey sets his poems in the real world of today's farmers, complete with bankers and bureaucrats as well as cows and corn. Carey farms an 800-acre spread in Iowa for his living. So there is no romanticism here, in his world of rain-threatened harvests to which the farmer must respond, "if not soon, then never," even while the muse calls the poet. Sometimes the weather does not hold: "nearly Christmas and the bins / still hungry for grain." Sometimes the temptation to give up, sell out, is strong: "Work your back off in the fields / until you can't think straight, / and then, well, then . . ." But the sensuality of country life recalls the poet again and again from its hardship: "my breath shooing flies / my soul in the heavens." Carey's is a strong, sure, welcome voice. —*Pat Monaghan*

Collins, Billy.
Questions about Angels.
Morrow, $18 (0-688-10774-5). 64p. paper, $8 (0-688-10731-1).

These poems stick in the memory like burrs. Nothing in their pleasant, slick surface suggests that they'll hang on so. At first reading, they seem slight, cagey, a bit too polished and coy. The subjects seem derived from art rather than life; we note the death of allegory in one poem, bemoan innocence lost with Dick and Jane's arrival in another. Yet days later, the poems echo in the mind: the wolf who reads fairy tales until he enters one seems familiar enough to have been a dream or a late-night TV image; the history teacher who protects his students by lying about the past creeps into casual conversation. The sense of the poet's personality is unshakable. Edward Hirsch, who selected this book for the 1990 National Poetry series, calls Collins an "American original." He's right. —*Pat Monaghan*

Dubie, Norman.
Radio Sky.
Norton, $17.95 (0-393-02957-3). 64p.

This final collection in a trilogy that began with *The Springhouse* and *Groom Falconer* is a bold adventure into realms of the surreal. The poems included here are both fresh and disturbing, with images stimulated by real and imagined events, or the real and imagined combined through a smoke-screen of poetic vision. Plucking many metaphors from characters of the past, Dubie sets a tone that leads the reader from darkness to light. While the poet seems almost obsessed with death, with vast numbers of graves and sweeping burial plots, his magic comes with resurrected visions of our world, as mean spirited, as unjust, or as unfeeling as it might be. Current events such as Tiananmen Square are evoked through images of Christ raising Lazarus from the dead in Renaissance paintings. Our relationship to nature is truly discovered in "A True Story of God" as Thoreau contemplates moose nose, a delicacy sliced off for the bride of the hunter. These are bold poems, disturbing yet thoughtful. —*Thomas Phelps*

Halpern, Daniel.
Foreign Neon.
Knopf, $19 (0-679-40636-0). 84p.

While Daniel Halpern has not yet entered the inner circle of great American male poets—where the likes of Ashbery, Merrill, and Merwin currently reside—his seventh collection may spur his induction into that rarefied realm. Several of these poems examine the lives of the artist (Caravaggio and Count Basie, to name only two), while others explore landscapes, both real and conjured. The title poem compares the calm of the smooth-edged rustic life with the "high-contrast cities / lit-up at night in foreign neon." Halpern forces us to search our conscience for motives, not answers. Writing in a cool yet mysterious idiom, he poses choices that demand emotional reaction. Halpern, the editor of *Antaeus*, deserves reading. His new collection makes an excellent addition to the contemporary American poetry shelf in most public and academic libraries. —*Thomas Phelps*

Henderson-Holmes, Safiya.
Madness and a Bit of Hope.
Writers and Readers/Harlem River Press, paper, $9.95 (0-86316-136-7). 120p.

That this poet is also a performer is obvious in every one of her taut lines. Rarely does a spoken voice come through as clearly as in these poems of urban rage and hope. Henderson-Holmes explores the orchestral color of words and uses images rhythmically. In the splendid long poem, "Rituals of Spring," written for the seventy-eighth anniversary of the Triangle Shirtwaist Factory fire in New York, she pictures the trapped girls as spring flowers falling to earth, then cuts back to reality: "and the girls / were girls not angels jumping, / not goddesses flying or hovering / they mashed, they broke into / large pieces, smell them in the rain / and the sidewalks / opened in shame to meet the

Poetry

flowering girls." A vivid, visceral work that deserves a wide audience. —*Pat Monaghan*

✔Ignatow, David.
Shadowing the Ground.
Univ. Press of New England, $20 (0-8195-2195-7); paper, $9.95 (0-8195-1197-8). 80p.

"I obey traffic signals. I am cordial to strangers, I answer my / mail promptly. I keep a balanced checking account. Why can't I / live forever?" Those concluding lines from one of the short poems in this crystalline collection exemplify the book's excellence. All the poems deal with, one might say, death. But, in fact, they deal with life: how one feels as it wanes. Sometimes Ignatow is eager to get it over, to move to the next stage; sometimes he is angry at lost powers; sometimes he reaches a mystic realization that he dies only because he's lived. This wonderful collection should last as long as humans are mortal. —*Pat Monaghan*

Larsen, Deborah.
Stitching Porcelain: After Matteo Ricci in Sixteenth-Century China.
New Directions, paper, $8.95 (0-8112-1161-4). 64p.

This intriguing and well-wrought book offers a narrative-in-lyrics based on the life of Matteo Ricci, an Italian missionary who lived in China from 1583 until his death in 1610. From journals, from histories, from Asian and Western poetry, Larsen has stitched together a faint narrative thread that draws us through vividly pictured moments of Ricci's life: his rough crossing to China, where he dressed as a Buddhist monk to show his vocation; the loss of his friend, Joao Barrados, swept overboard on the river Gan; his prostration before the Dragon Throne when, at last invited to meet the emperor, he found only an empty room. Upon that narrative Larsen hangs lovely imagistic verses: Ricci, changing into mandarin clothes, says, "My ankle-length silks smell of the rain / . . . Dusk is my purple belt, daylight my high black hat." An unusual and very effective first book. —*Pat Monaghan*

✔McGrath, Thomas.
Death Song.
Copper Canyon, $17 (1-55659-036-9); paper, $10 (1-55659-035-0). 140p.

Following a long illness, McGrath died in September 1990, leaving *Death Song* as a testament to his unique vision. Much of his work focuses on nature and on its relationship to humankind, but he clearly transcends the narrow limits usually implied by the term *nature poet*. At once celebratory and hushed, affirmative and realistic, everyday and mysterious, earthbound and cosmic, his work defies category. For example, in "Loon," the brief but explosive poem that closes the volume, McGrath addresses "Something crying on the empty lake / A cry with long legs / A cry that goes far into the forest; / Into the weedy bottom and deep of the lake; / Out to the stars: and back," revealing each individual's connection with the grandness of the cosmos. *Death Song*, full of poems that leave the reader breathless with their beauty and intelligence, will certainly establish McGrath as one of our most important and distinctive poetic voices. —*Jim Elledge*

✔McNeill, Louise.
Hill Daughter: New & Selected Poems.
Univ. of Pittsburgh, $24.95 (0-8229-3685-2). 140p. paper, $12.95 (0-8229-5456-7).

Praised for her early work by Archibald MacLeish, Louis Untermeyer, and Stephen Vincent Benet, Louise McNeill outlived but has not outlasted them. For decades, her work—like that of all too many women writers—has been out of print, her substantial reputation all but vanished. Welcome, then, is this major collection, which should appeal to both scholarly and lay readers. The former will hail the rediscovery of this major poet, the careful and eloquent introduction by Maggie Anderson that places McNeill in her historical context, the useful bibliography. The latter will relish the poetry: clear, classic, passionate lyrics. Appalachian hillfolk speak many of the poems, telling their life stories—of the unrepentant runaway wife, the proud dying pauper, the thrifty pioneer. McNeill is no poet of a bygone age, however, for her later poems lament the earth's endangerment by nuclear force: "I sat by the window and trod my loom, / And I saw the shape of a gaunt mushroom / Grow up the iceberg and spread to the sky; / And I wove in my cloth that the world would die." She is a poet of deep ecology and deep humanism and extravagant, melodic genius. —*Pat Monaghan*

Nemerov, Howard.
Trying Conclusions: New and Selected Poems, 1961–1991.
Univ. of Chicago, $16.95 (0-226-57723-3). 152p.

Howard Nemerov published his *New and Selected Poems* in 1960. This collection, including 23 new poems written while Nemerov was poet laureate, covers the period from 1961 through 1991. It contains a wide variety of verse in terms of both theme and style. There are short, humorous poems like "Imprecated upon a Postal Clerk," longer, more intricate works like "By Al Lebowitz's Pool," and the wonderful meditative prose poem "The Thought of Trees." Nemerov is clear, accessible, and often fun to read. This representative selection of his work deserves a wide audience. —*Bill Gargan*

Neruda, Pablo.
Selected Odes of Pablo Neruda.
Univ. of California, $40 (0-520-05944-1); paper, $12.95 (0-520-07172-7). 375p.

For anyone who's written poetry or wanted to, for anyone who professes to love it, this bilingual selection of the Chilean laureate's renowned "elemental odes" is a must-read. In clear, simple, resonant lines, Neruda sings the praises of this ordinary, transient, luminous world. Artichokes and seaweed, sex and panthers, storms and stamp albums are observed and lauded in turn. Each crisply translated poem is expansive, taking up pages and pages of text—but because of their curious format, only a few words per line, they are also spare and lean. What is most memorable about these poems is the abundant love that gleams through every line. Praising a chestnut lying on the ground, Neruda sees it as an "intact delight / an edible rose," imagining the brave nut leaping to the earth to open a new world of life, to become "the ancient but new dimensions / of another chestnut tree in the earth." There is nothing so unimportant that the poet's love does not encompass it. —*Pat Monaghan*

✔Poulin, A.
Cave Dwellers.
Graywolf, $18.95 (1-55597-139-3). 121p.

Although a highly acclaimed translator, anthologist, and editor, Poulin is best known for his poetry. In his eighth collection, he delves into extraordinary as well as everyday experiences, from seeing angels everywhere ("Angelic Orders") to waiting for the mail to be delivered ("My Mailman"). He reveals in the process that all human experience is imbued with meaning. But Poulin is no didactic versifier. His work is rooted deeply in emotion, focusing on the individual's relationship to the cosmos. In "The Angels of Radiators," the narrator, whose wife and daughter are asleep, expresses concisely and brilliantly his feeling of utter loneliness: "I'm alone in this old house / lost in landscapes somewhere / between the points of stars, / my furnace fails like heaven." Poulin tracks the relationship of the individual to the universe even in the larger events of U.S. history, as in "American Centaurs," which on one level is about the Conquistadors but, on another, explores our inability to achieve grace. Clearly among the best poets of his generation, Poulin deserves much more attention than he has previously received. A must-buy. —*Jim Elledge*

✔Rebsamen, Frederick, trans.
Beowulf: A Verse Translation.
HarperCollins, $18.95 (0-06-438437-3). 160p.

As splendid as Allen Mandelbaum's recent translation of *The Odyssey* was, it provided nothing like the shock of this magnificent translation of *Beowulf*. One assumes that no self-respecting college professor will want his students to be without it—or that anyone will really dare to say they prefer the relatively characterless, schoolboyish translations that have come before. Because really serious readers can learn Old English without too much trouble, renditions in Modern English haven't taken the poetry of the original very seriously. But what a shock now that someone has! With the subtle rules of alliteration, stress, and pause in place—and with a translator bold enough to invent his own vigorous and imaginative compound nouns—the poem suddenly takes flight and carries us to the highest mountains of achievement. True, because this is not boy's-stuff adventure, some of the passages are difficult; but not as difficult as, say, Milton or Shakespeare, beside whom the unknown poet of this epic certainly belongs. Can anything more be said? *Stuart Whitwell*

✔**Rich, Adrienne.**
An Atlas of the Difficult World: Poems, 1988–1991.
Norton, $17.95 (0-393-03069-5). 64p. paper, $7.95.

More than 100 years have passed since Walt Whitman heard America singing. Now Adrienne Rich "wrestles for the soul of her country / as she wrestles for her own being." In her thirteenth and possibly most moving book, Rich listens as did Whitman to this nation's song. But her patriotism comes harder than Whitman's ecstatic connection. Rich's America includes "the desert where missiles are planted like corn . . . the breadbasket of foreclosed farms . . . the cemetery of the poor / who died for democracy." The poet, "bent on fathoming what it means to love my country," finds its meaning in her love for the land's natural beauties and the beauty of its women "turning the wheel or working with shears, torque wrench, knives, with salt pork, onions, ink and fire." There is more to this book—occasional poems, portraits, explorations of Jewish heritage—but the title poem is worth the price of admission. —*Pat Monaghan*

Shange, Ntozake.
The Love Space Demands: A Continuing Saga.
St. Martin's, $15.95 (0-312-05892-6). 80p.

There are many excellent poems in this book, but the last four—a sequence entitled "I Heard Eric Dolphy in His Eyes"—are so exhaustingly powerful that the remainder of the book fades behind them. The sequence, a "choreopoem" designed for musicians and dancers that explores the "magic and limitations of Afro-American urban life," springs to life on the page. In "Crack Annie," an addicted mother sells her child's virginity—and her future—promised for a "whole fifty cent of crack," then sees "an unknown / virulent blues / a stalkin talking no answer but yes to me / blues" in little Berneatha's eyes. In "Open up / this is the police," a pregnant woman eats an ounce of cocaine to protect her man from a police bust, then feels her heart break for "Esmereldita [who] floats cherubic / yeah / in placenta waters / streams of tears" and whose death is ensured by her mother's action. We are seared by the pain in these poems; Shange's passion transforms the reader from spectator into witness. —*Pat Monaghan*

Soto, Gary.
Home Course in Religion: New Poems.
Chronicle, paper, $8.95 (0-87701-857-X). 77p.

> *"I didn't catch on right away*
> *That meanness was part of the family."*

There's anger and fragility in the casual idiom and rhythms of Soto's clear, intense poems. Without nostalgia or self-pity, he remembers the way things look to a small child ("My younger brothers sucked the nostril holes / Of Tinker Toys") and to a teenager ("I couldn't believe my life. I was a Mexican / Among relatives with loud furniture . . . I wanted out"). Arranged chronologically, circling back to repeat crucial experiences and obsessions, the poems make up a kind of memoir (reminiscent in many ways of Tobias Wolff's *This Boy's*

Poetry

Life). The nuns would be proud of him, Soto says, those who made him write I WILL NOT TALK BACK a lot of times on the blackboard ("Now I'm quiet. . . . And the people I like best are quiet"). As a boy, he can barely suppress his rage against his bullying, small-minded stepfather. Now middle-aged and a father, Soto knows that "family won't go away." —*Hazel Rochman*

Stafford, William.
Passwords.
HarperCollins, $21.95 (0-06-055293-X). 112p. paper, $10.95 (0-06-096587-8).

Some poets are revered, some admired, some envied. William Stafford is loved. His generous presence fills his books as surely as it has filled so many classrooms with hopeful writers. One picks up Stafford expecting not to be overwhelmed by craft or overpowered by emotion but to be moved gently toward a humanitarian vision. Little aphorisms point the way: "When we talk, truth / is what we mean to say," and "a birthday is when you might not have been born." Anecdotes, too, reveal their human mystery: "One time I asked Agnes to dance. How she / put up her arms—I thought of that this morning / fifty years later." In this, his ninth volume, Stafford shares his journey into age, his meditations on memory, his calm sense of death as part of life. It is all we expect of a Stafford collection. —*Pat Monaghan*

Strand, Mark.
The Continuous Life.
Knopf, $18.95 (0-394-58817-7). 160p.
Strand, Mark.
Selected Poems.
Knopf, paper, $10.95 (0-679-73301-9). 152p.

Strand's selection as the nation's Poet Laureate brings renewed attention to his work. *The Continuous Life* is his first collection of new poems in 10 years; its publication coincides with a new edition of his *Selected Poems*, which first appeared in 1980.

The latter remains an excellent choice for public libraries. A magical realist in verse, he transforms the everyday into peculiar moral fables: guilt becomes a dirty hand caked with a "sad dirt / made of sickness / and human anguish," which must be cut off; literature is so nourishing that, "ink runs from the corners of my mouth . . . / I have been eating poetry." Despite its glassy brilliance, however, Strand's work is often bleak, painting the body as a prison of memory: "A scar remembers the wound. / The wound remembers the pain. / Once more you are crying." These poems reveal a yearning toward death that takes constant effort to outwit, for "in that final flowing of cold through your limbs . . . you love what you are." Strand's recent work, in *The Continuous Life*, is lighter, often playful, especially his prose-poem explorations (a sestina with no line breaks!) and classical eclogues. If you can acquire only one, though, select the richer, more profound *Selected Poems*. —*Pat Monaghan*

✔**Walker, Alice.**
Her Blue Body Everything We Know: Earthling Poems, 1965–1990, Complete.
HBJ, $22.95 (0-15-140040-7). 397p.

What a splendid gift Alice Walker makes here to her readers! Not only one of America's major novelists, Walker is also a poet of note. In this welcome edition of her complete earlier work, joined to new, previously uncollected poems, we see a quarter century of impressive artistic development. Her first poems are tiny, spare renderings of Africa: "The fresh corpse / Of a white rhinoceros / His horn gone / Some Indian woman / Will be approached / Tonight." Then the middle period, in which Walker struggles to join her natural animism with her political ideals; less effective than her later work, these poems stand as testimony to a complex period in America's history. Politics and spirituality come together in her breathtaking latest poems, including the ravishing paean to Gaia that is the title poem: "We have a beautiful / mother / Her green lap / immense / Her brown embrace / eternal / Her blue body / everything / we know." An important collection from a powerful poet. —*Pat Monaghan*

Popular Culture

Benton, Mike.
Horror Comics: The Illustrated History.
Taylor, $21.95 (0-87833-734-2). 152p. index.

The first of a projected series, each installment of which will treat a different comic book genre. Benton's text is rather once-over-lightly but not too superficial. He has his facts down, and he describes different comics artists' styles and such events as the mid-1950s anti-horror comics crusade accurately. You won't be misled by anything he says, even if sometimes you wish he'd say it better. He adds visual as well as historical interest with boxed inserts into the main text—little précis of such subjects as "The Other Comics Codes" (i.e., precursors of the industry-wide code adopted in 1954) or particularly piquing quotations from the likes of Stephen King, once a horror-comics-addicted kid (figures, doesn't it?), and meretricious anti-comics zealot Fredric Wertham. The volume concludes with valuable advice to collectors and an annotated checklist of 50 years worth of major horror comics. All this information is nice, but face it, the pictures—reproductions of outstanding horror comics artwork over the years—make this a browsing item supreme. —*Ray Olson*

Blonsky, Marshall.
American Mythologies.
Oxford, $21.95 (0-19-505062-2). 288p. index.

Blonsky, a distinguished semiotician and a leading analyst of contemporary American culture, here opens a new window on many of our country's icons

Popular Culture

by showing us in his canny, inimitable way how we as a culture are viewed by foreigners stretching from Moscow and Milan to Hong Kong and Tokyo, as well as by many of our own implausible yet much-admired "representatives." He spoke firsthand with and observed luminaries and celebrities from a variety of fields—film directors, politicians, academicians, TV anchors, actors, writers, models, and designers—including Giorgio Armani, Umberto Eco, and Americans Vanna White, Merv Griffin, Stephen King, Eva Gabor, and Ted Koppel, among others. What emerges is a loosely structured yet revealing hodgepodge of wide-ranging ideas and insights, many of them dripping with irony. Reading this challenging deconstructionist writer is a mind-bending adventure that will entertain, annoy, shock, anger, titillate, and utterly baffle readers. Aimed at a scholarly audience, this is fascinating to read just as Thomas Pynchon is—to see a mind fabulously spinning its own ornate yet tangled web of conceit. Contains 30 halftones. —*Mary Banas*

Boswell, David.
Fun with Reid Fleming, World's Toughest Milkman.
Eclipse Books, $32.95 (1-56060-108-6); paper, $12.95 (1-56060-109-4). 173p.

Take Danny DeVito's haircut, Karl Malden's nose, W. C. Fields' disposition, and Arnold Schwarzenegger's strength. Put them all together, and you've got Reid Fleming, world's toughest milkman. He's the kind of guy who, after sailing his milktruck (god knows from where or how) into a swimming pool, not only lives but bobs to the surface spluttering with rage, "Kids! There's been kids in this water!" The cartoon creation of Canadian David Boswell, Fleming is a churl of epic proportions and an absolutely staggering gall. There being poetic justice and then some in Boswell's alternate world of working-stiff's revenge, Reid's girlfriend Lena, a TV star and multiple divorcée ("I lost count after two"), can match him barb for barb. Reminded of a party they're going to, he says, "Okay, I promise not to pass out in the punch bowl," and she fires back, "You have to wear a *suit* if you want to do that." The *Toronto Globe and Mail* has said Boswell's surly deliveryman "makes a virtue out of gratuitous violence." Don't know about that, but he does make it outrageously funny. —*Ray Olson*

✔Briggs, Joe Bob.
The Cosmic Wisdom of Joe Bob Briggs.
Random, $16.95 (0-394-58890-8). 270p.

Joe Bob—that good ol' boy, cable-syndicated "drive-in critic" and authority on schlock from Grapevine, Texas—wants to share with you his thoughts on just about anything from Jessica Hahn, Abdomenizers, and "Love Connection" to zombie talk shows like "The McLaughlin Report," Marion Barry, and the dangers of electric appliances. To call Joe Bob irreverent would be missing the point. Offensive? Perhaps. In bad taste? Very likely. Joe Bob Briggs is downright and deliciously amoral—and proud of it. How can you not like someone who could defend the prairie dog hunters' right to carry AK-47 Kalishnikov semiautomatic assault rifles? Or openly wonders at the naiveté of anyone who bought bonds called "junk" and was then surprised when the bottom fell out of them. He wonders, too, about sex addicts, volunteers to be on the ayatollah's hit list, and has a healthy contempt for lawyers. This homespun humor makes Dave Barry's seem prudish in comparison. Usually about three pages long, Joe Bob's pieces are just the right size to be the perfect companion for approximately 62 visits to the powder room. Joe Bob has fluffed the feathers of more than a few feminists, fat farmers, fundamentalists, "fetus fans," and frequent flyers, and, we hope, will continue to do so. —*Benjamin Segedin*

✔Callahan, Bob, ed.
The New Comics Anthology.
Macmillan/Collier, paper, $19.95 (0-02-009361-6). 288p.

"Prior to this point in history, comic strips were created by often exceptionally talented men and women as a way of entertaining nitwits and kids," editor Callahan overstates, but now "graphic literature [is] one of the most challenging new art forms." Although his subsequent encomia of several classic strips undercut his rap against the bad old comics, partaking of the feast his anthology provides compels agreement with his assessment of the new ones. He sorts the volume's riches into four stylistic-topical chapters. Two exemplify basically humorous genres, one consisting of spoofs and japes reminiscent of the high jinks of vaudeville (e.g., Art Spiegelman's brilliant melding of tough-guy crime fiction and cubist art clichés, "Ace Hole, Midget Detective"); the other, of the bad attitudes, ghoulish humor, and ugly visual affect that mark them as "punk funnies," the comics analog to, say, the music—and the looks—of the rock group the Ramones. The other chapters highlight two kinds of realistic comics, concerned, respectively, with such global problems as war, terrorism, and crime, and with everyday events, most often those of the artists' own lives. The contributors constitute an honor roll of American and European comics creators—the likes of Harvey Pekar, Jacques Loustal, Drew Friedman, Aline Kominsky-Crumb, Linda Barry, Eddie Campbell, Muñoz & Sampayo, etc. —*Ray Olson*

Daniels, Les.
Marvel: Five Fabulous Decades of the World's Greatest Comics.
Abrams, $45 (0-8109-3821-9). 287p. index.

Purveyors of such cultural icons as the Amazing Spider-Man and the Incredible Hulk, Marvel Comics gets the coffee-table treatment in this colorful, attractively designed volume. Marvel's story begins with the introduction of the superheroes, the Sub-Mariner and the Human Torch, in 1939, during the so-called golden age of comics. But the publisher's greatest success came in the 1960s when it updated the genre with such revisionist heroes as Spider-Man and the Fantastic Four. Daniels' behind-the-scenes look at the development of Marvel, his profiles of the line's foremost heroes and villains, and biographies of leading writers and artists will entice Boomers who grew up with Marvel's 1960s titles as well as young fans of today's line dominated by those superpowered mutants, the X-Men. But the book's strongest appeal lies in the generous samplings of artwork spread throughout. These really tell the Marvel story, and as a coda there are reprints of four classic stories

Popular Culture

demonstrating, with the help of Daniels' annotations, the Marvel style. 'Nuff said! —*Gordon Flagg*

Frank, Reuven.
Out of Thin Air: An Insider's History of Network News.
Simon & Schuster, $24.95 (0-671-67758-6). 417p.

With his text framed by the television coverage of the American presidential nominating conventions from 1948 onward, Frank narrates the evolution of television news programming as well as his own career in the medium. From 1950, when he joined NBC as a newsreel editor, until he stepped down as NBC News president—for the second time—in 1988, Frank was in a privileged position to observe how news broadcasting changed for better or worse, not only on his own network but throughout the industry. All of the legendary figures are here—Huntley and Brinkley, Ed Murrow, Charles Collingwood, Roger Mudd—along with some of the scandals—Charles Van Doren and "The $64,000 Question," corporate bloodbaths, and the evening a telecast of *Heidi* preempted the final moments of a football game that turned out to be too close to call, especially when viewers demonstrated that they'd really rather be watching those American gladiators than that Swiss brat. Along with the anecdotes, however, Frank supplies a more sober consideration of the news business and allows his readers a behind-the-scenes look at how the news is made and reported. —*John Brosnahan*

Fraser, James.
The American Billboard: 100 Years.
Abrams, $49.50 (0-8109-3116-8). 192p. index.

This is a treat—a big rectangular book with big type on a big, brash topic. Billboards are as American as apple pie. Built on a scale fit for a huge highway-laced country and its sprawling cities, billboards have graced (or defaced) our streets and roads for a century, selling everything from bread to tobacco, liberty bonds to Coppertone, cars to politics. Fraser, chief librarian at Fairleigh Dickinson University, connects the history of billboards to trends in society at large, graphic arts, and the advertising industry. Billboards have been created in every style, from designs by artists such as Maxfield Parrish and N. C. Wyeth in the early days, to slick photography, cryptic messages, and optical illusions. Fraser concludes with a peek into the future, which may bring high-tech billboards and special effects. A visually stimulating look at one conspicuous manifestation of popular culture. —*Donna Seaman*

✔Fussell, Paul.
BAD; or, The Dumbing of America.
Summit, $19 (0-671-67652-0). 208p.

Curmudgeonly critic Fussell does his reputation proud in this encyclopedia of features of modern-day America that fall so far short of their reputations that they magnify the quality of badness. That is, they are BAD, "if not . . . because pretentious, [then] because banal, stupid, or subadult." Unsurprisingly leading Fussell's list is advertising, "the *sine qua non* of BAD . . . for

BAD depends upon and arises only out of it." Other targets of Fussell's rage, despair, and acid wit—airlines, airports, architecture, food, hotels, public sculpture, restaurants, television—don't surprise, either, since everyone relies on them being less satisfying than their proprietors and boosters say they'll be. Besides those obvious subjects, Fussell goes after the less often remarked inadequacies of American banks, beliefs, books, ideas, music, objects (mostly collectibles), and poetry. His most disturbing criticism is reserved for things that threaten to destroy our national integrity (BAD colleges and universities, BAD people [politicians and evangelists]) and even our lives (BAD engineering, BAD naval missile firings). Unfortunately, he sees "The Future of BAD" as "immense" and advises the "only recourse is to laugh. . . . If you don't, you're going to have to cry." Good satire, and like all good satire, very entertaining and very disquieting. —*Ray Olson*

✔Garber, Marjorie.
Vested Interests: Cross-Dressing and Cultural Anxiety.
Routledge, $35 (0-415-90072-7). 427p. index.

In an absolutely fascinating look at gender-bending in the arts and in everyday life, Garber convincingly argues that "the transvestite makes culture possible, that there is no culture without the transvestite." From Peter Pan to Elvis Presley, *Tootsie* to *Twelfth Night*, Garber examines how clothes do make the man (or woman). Well researched and wonderfully illustrated, Garber's book covers such topics as dress codes, religious habits, sailors, high and low fashion, cross-dressing for success, detective fiction, racism, lesbian-gay liberation, Freud, and Little Red Riding Hood and the Wolf. Her study of cultural unease and the constructs of power even leads her to those bastions of patriarchal privilege, Harvard's Hasty Pudding Club and Kissinger and Reagan's all-male society, the Bohemian Club—both of which regularly feature cross-dressing revues. Garber's work is scholarly, witty, perceptive, and provocative—a sheer delight to read, consider, and discuss. It's one of the best works of cultural criticism around—absolutely first-rate. —*Ryn Etter*

Hook, J. N.
All Those Wonderful Names: A Potpourri of People, Places, and Things.
Wiley, paper, $10.95 (0-471-53011-5). 304p. index.

If your name books are dog-eared, too old to list the names of the children of celebrities such as Mel Gibson, and short on humor, you need this funny, trivia-filled, and delightful new volume from word aficionado Hook, who has updated and expanded his earlier *Book of Names*. Hook begins with "The Names People Give Their Defenseless Children," a look at traditional and offbeat first names, and then provides an amusing and informative look at the surnames and genealogy of various ethnic groups, celebrating the most common (Chang, Smith, and Johnson) and one-of-a-kind names (Kwasimady). The origins and whimsy of place-names get a thorough treatment through anecdotes and thematic groupings such as "Towns That Brag about Themselves" and noisy (Roaring Gap, North Carolina) or peaceful (Loveland, Colorado) towns. Finally, Hook dredges up the forgotten names of

Popular Culture

early automobiles (Okay) and the stories behind the names of major league baseball teams. A terrifically enjoyable, affordable resource. —*Donna Seaman*

Lichter, Linda and others.
Watching America: What Television Tells Us about Our Lives.
Prentice Hall Press, $22.95 (0-13-026824-0). 352p. index.

Claiming to be the "most comprehensive study of life on television that has ever been conducted," this smart, descriptive, and alert overview of TV plots, themes, topics, and characters focuses on television's "impact on our collective consciousness." The authors tracked the fluctuations in attitudes toward women, minorities, business, and crime through analysis of a random sampling of episodes from 620 prime-time continuing series and concluded that in its early years, television promoted the status quo but quickly became "an agent of social change." Television's creative elite, based in New York and L.A., are, for the most part, more liberal than their shows' viewers and tend to work from a cynical, antiestablishment perspective. Lichter and her coauthors discuss the "sexing" of television, TV's view of the workplace and family life, and the latent politics of dramas about cold-blooded crimes. They avoid gross generalization and overstatement, preferring honest ambiguity, attention to nuance, and acceptance of the fact that television, like all storytelling, both reflects and alters its audience. An exceptionally balanced, observant, and human assessment of what has become our homes' hearth. —*Donna Seaman*

✔**Marcus, Greil.**
Dead Elvis: A Chronicle of a Cultural Obsession.
Doubleday, $25 (0-385-41718-7). 256p. index.

On August 16, 1977, Elvis Aron Presley was found dead in a bathroom in Graceland, a victim of a (accidental?) drug overdose. He didn't stay dead for long. His second coming arrived practically before the first one had gone. Marcus, author of the acclaimed *Mystery Train* and *Lipstick Traces*, offers a series of essays, written since 1977, culled and updated from such journals as *Rolling Stone*, the *Village Voice*, and *Artforum*. Picking up where he left off in the concluding essay in *Mystery Train*, he makes a case for Elvis as a true American original. Well versed in American literature and the archetypes they reveal, Marcus is quick to show dead-on connections between Elvis and a gamut of cultural icons and traditions. References to Melville's white whale and Abraham Lincoln's Second Inaugural Address are not out of place here, and they are often followed by quotes from the *National Enquirer*, Camille Paglia, or Roy Orbison. Marcus is fascinated by the deification and mythologizing of Elvis and the attempts by others (e.g., pop-pathobiographer Albert Goldman) to tear him down. Definitely not for the indiscriminate Elvis fan, *Dead Elvis* is provocative reading, revealing much about the American psyche and its hybrid traditions. —*Benjamin Segedin*

Panati, Charles.
Panati's Parade of Fads, Follies, and Manias: The Origins of Our Most Cherished Obsessions.
HarperCollins, $25 (0-06-055191-7); paper, $12.95 (0-06-096477-4). 528p. index.

Panati loves to collect quirky information about our lives and relay it with wit and panache, even making death funny in *Panati's Extraordinary Endings of Practically Everything and Everybody*. Here he gives American popular culture a big, affectionate bear hug. He characterizes mass culture as entertainment striving for "neither complexity nor profundity," seeking "only to reach and delight as many of us as possible. At a net profit." He explores the origins of popular culture, nostalgia, fads, and leisure time and then, beginning with the Gay Nineties, dances his way through a century of "fads, follies, and trends," fairs and expos, dance crazes, popular songs, best-selling books, and radio and television hits. Each item is described and creators, when possible, identified. The chapter titles set the tone for each decade: "The Innocent Oughts" for 1900–09, "The Tender Teens," "The Soaring Twenties," "The Swing Thirties," "The Fantasy Forties," "The Fabulous Fifties," "The Schizophrenic Sixties," "The Self-seeking Seventies," and, in a grand finale, "The Spendthrift Eighties into the Payback Nineties." A terrifically enjoyable panorama of Americana. *—Donna Seaman*

Peacock, John.
The Chronicle of Western Fashion: From Ancient Times to the Present Day.
Abrams, $29.95 (0-8109-3953-3). 224p. index.

A former senior costume designer at BBC television, John Peacock offers a convenient quick-reference of Western costume from ancient Egypt to 1980. Presented chronologically, the 8 to 10 illustrations per page are lavishly colored and use color schemes appropriate to each period. All illustrations are labeled with country of origin and wearer's societal status. Every century is followed up by concise captions corresponding to the illustrations. Included is an illustrated glossary (85 line drawings accompany 182 terms). Unfortunately, this costume chronology ends short of 1980, the advent of one of costume's more interesting decades; however, it will prove helpful to anyone trained or untrained in costume history and design. Highly recommended for public libraries. *—Janet Lawrence*

Reidelbach, Maria.
Completely Mad: A History of the Comic Book and Magazine.
Little, Brown, $39.95 (0-316-73890-5). 216p. index.

Mad is now such an American institution that it's hard to recall what a splash it made when it debuted in 1952. The impudent, anything-goes approach developed by *Mad* creator Harvey Kurtzman inspired (some would say warped) a generation of humorists—its influence shows up everywhere from the underground comics of the 1960s to today's *Naked Gun* movies. Kurtzman left shortly after the comic book switched to a magazine format, and his successors developed the formula that turned *Mad* from a cult into an enormous popular success. In researching her chronicle, Reidelbach spoke with most of the *Mad*men behind the magazine. However, the "authorized biography" approach glosses over the magazine's formularization (a current issue of *Mad* looks pretty much the same as one from 30 years ago) and its shift from irreverence to irrelevance as subsequent generations turned to such competitors as the *National Lampoon* and "Saturday Night Live." Still, for those of us who haven't picked up an issue since adolescence, the hundreds of samples of art reprinted from the magazine's run show that our memories aren't wrong— *Mad* at its best was as funny as we remember it. —*Gordon Flagg*

Tebbel, John and Waller-Zuckermann, Mary Ellen.
The Magazine in America, 1741–1990.
Oxford, $35 (0-19-505127-0). 512p. index.

Readable histories of the American magazine are seldom seen. Mott's Pulitzer Prize–winning *History of Magazines* (Harvard, 1938), four volumes long, stops at 1905. Tebbel and Waller-Zuckermann review the same period briefly, then follow the unprecedented growth of mass-market publication from 1919 to 1945 and conclude with developments since then, notably the alternative press scene and "The Triumph of the Business Press." They recount the evolution of periodicals devoted to women, blacks, class consciousness, muckraking (i.e., investigative reporting, often of high caliber), intellectuals, and genre fiction. Chapters on photojournalism, advertising and circulation, and design and marketing illuminate the technological and administrative aspects of magazine journalism. The narrative pace is rapid, and repeatable facts are profuse: for example, the magazine holding the world record for consecutive annual increases in circulation is . . . *National Geographic*, 103 years a-burgeoning. —*Roland Wulbert*

Visser, Margaret.
The Rituals of Dinner: The Origins, Evolution, Eccentricities, and Meaning of Table Manners.
Grove Weidenfeld, $19.95 (0-8021-1116-5). 455p. index.

A captivating discussion of eating customs, old and new, told with subtle wit. University of Toronto professor Visser (author of the acclaimed *Much Depends on Dinner*) interweaves scholarship with elegant writing in examining worldwide aspects of table manners, including the ancient and frightening (cannibalism) and the new and trendy (today's servantless household), all set forth with references to fact and fiction and peppered with hundreds of interesting tidbits of information. Visser quite willingly inserts opinions here and there, as in her examination of different classes of airline food and her insistence that children try all types of foods. Move aside, Miss Manners, here's a more thoughtful, less contentious contender for your position. —*Barbara Jacobs*

Wigginton, Eliot and others.
Foxfire: 25 Years.
Doubleday, $24.95 (0-385-41345-9); paper, $14.95 (0-385-41346-7). 364p.

Fans of the Foxfire movement will find much to ponder in this oral history of both the school and the publications whose educational philosophy sparked 25 years of experimentation and achievement among the residents of Appalachia. Those new to the Foxfire experience may be left a bit high and dry, however, since most of the accounts are too anecdotal and uncritical to give a fair assessment of either its techniques or its objectives. For those familiar with Foxfire and its founder, Eliot Wigginton, this volume will function as an excellent souvenir. Wigginton and his many students recall their learning experiences and reacquaint readers with some of the more fascinating stories and characters constituting the Foxfire legend. In typical Foxfire style, these memories are accompanied by numerous photographs. —*John Brosnahan*

Religion

Allen, Paula Gunn.
Grandmothers of the Light: A Medicine Woman's Sourcebook.
Beacon; dist. by Farrar, $19.95 (0-8070-8102-7). 256p.

Allen draws on various Indian traditions to tell the stories of female spiritual figures—"the Great Goddess in a variety of guises." The 21 tales come not only from her own Laguna Pueblo and Lakota peoples, but also from the Aztec, Ojibwa, Maya, Lummi/Nootsac, and Dine. "Stories connect us to the universe of medicine—of paranormal or sacred power," Allen explains. Hers "tell how the cosmos was formed and the ways of magic" and work as "ritual maps or guides" for those who want to walk the path between the mundane and the spirit worlds. Allen acknowledges great differences among Indian communities in North America but stresses the "similarities in world view and spiritual understanding." Given Allen's reputation as poet, storyteller, and scholar, and given the renewed, continuing interest in matrifocal traditions, this book has a built-in audience. —*Ryn Etter*

Anderson, Sherry Ruth and Hopkins, Patricia.
The Feminine Face of God: The Unfolding of the Sacred in Women.
Bantam, $20 (0-553-07561-6). 245p. index.

What makes this book intriguing is not so much its thesis—that women's spiritual experiences differ from those of men—which is almost a commonplace today. No, its strength is in the voices of the American women who revealed their inner journeys to the authors. A few of the speakers are ministers or otherwise publicly associated with spirituality; most are women you might meet at the grocery store. All speak of finding a way through the limitations of traditional religion and into a new, freer space that both demands and consoles. The bravery of their search is inspiring, the strength of their visions is inspiriting. —*Pat Monaghan*

✔**Bryan, Michael.**
Chapter and Verse: A Skeptic Revisits Christianity.
Random, $21 (0-394-57509-1). 336p.

Common knowledge, especially that put forth by the media, maintains that fundamentalist Christians are boobs at best, charlatans at worst. Certainly, Jim and Tammy, Jimmy Swaggart, and their followers haven't done much to dispel that image. Bryan, a skeptic and lapsed Methodist (not necessarily in that order), decided to enroll at Baptist Criswell College in Dallas, to see if thinking people can believe in the inerrancy of the Bible. Though friends told him he would either quit or convert, Bryan did neither. Instead, he found that his tour through the evangelical world made him look at difficult questions and forced him to deal with people that did not fit into the fundamentalist stereotypes. Bryan is particularly good when he's describing the varied cast that makes up the faculty and student body of Criswell. Though we may not agree with their views, these are people who (for the most part) do read, think, and live in the modern world. In depicting his subjects so evenhandedly, Bryan challenges our own beliefs, and although it's doubtful whether many will change their religious affiliations based on this book, it certainly forces us to look behind the popular image of fundamentalism. —*Ilene Cooper*

Cornwell, John.
The Hiding Places of God: A Personal Journey into the World of Religious Visions, Holy Objects, and Miracles.
Warner, $19.95 (0-446-51468-3). 294p. index.

Cornwell brings an appropriate touch of disbelief to an exploration of contemporary religious phenomena. Even so, he clearly comes away from some of his encounters profoundly moved and vaguely disturbed. All readers will find a little bit of themselves in his journey; hence, they will keep turning pages to see how everything comes out. What happens when Cornwell meets Briege McKenna, whose healing powers and ability to discern the human heart are legendary? Is the stigmatic he meets in Montreal a fraud? Cornwell comes to the conclusion that he cannot "prove" unequivocally that the phenomena he witnesses are supernatural, but he has a profound respect for the mystery inherent in each and the feeling that he may have found God even while he was questioning his manifestations. For anyone who has ever wondered about religious appearances and miracles, this book will prove fascinating. —*Mary Deeley*

Couliano, I. P.
Out of This World: Otherworldly Journeys from Gilgamesh to Albert Einstein.
Shambhala, paper, $15 (0-87773-488-7). 280p.

From the proverbial dawn of civilization on, visiting other worlds—be it heaven, hell, the planets, etc.—has been a "top priority" of humankind. And to the observer, not the participant, it appears that such trips are in and of the mind. Couliano states that the potential for such "mindspace" adventures "is infinite, for there is no end to our imagining more space" and that, throughout history, there has been a "surprising unity in the variety" of experiences among shamans, witches, magicians, and visionaries. In geographical and chronological chapters, Couliano charts the similarities and differences between reports of otherworldly journeys, from the Egyptian coffin texts and their depictions of the kinds of characters one will meet up with (e.g., the "big Dog-face") because of earthly transgression (including working too hard!) through Tibetan Buddhism, Iranian ecstatics ("It is impressive how frequently crimes derive from pollution and to what extent punishment is olfactory"), Jewish mysticism, Christian apocalypses, and contemporary out-of-body experiences. There is a wryness behind the erudition that makes this comprehensive, extensively researched exploration entertaining as well as vastly informative. —*Eloise Kinney*

Diamant, Anita and Cooper, Howard.
Living a Jewish Life: A Guide for Starting, Learning, Celebrating, and Parenting.
HarperCollins, $24.95 (0-06-271508-9). 331p. paper, $9.95 (0-06-273025-8). index.

Written from a liberal, or non-Orthodox, perspective, this sparkling text conveys some of the joy of what it calls "doing Jewish." It is written as a kind of handbook to help those who are perhaps new to the faith or rebuilding for themselves as adults the traditions with which they were (or were not) brought up. It would also make an excellent introduction for anyone unacquainted with Jewish customs. Ideas for further reading are offered at the end of every chapter, and the text is sprinkled with humorous and inspiring quotes from other sources. Choice, as opposed to obligation, and the importance of integrating personal meaning and a celebratory mood into ritual religious observance are stressed. Discussing the Sabbath, for instance, the authors give a menu of suggestions for blessings and ceremonies from which a family could tailor-make its own routine for dinner on Friday night. The book is especially strong in suggesting ideas that will be fun for parents to share with children. —*Anne Schmitt*

Feuerstein, Georg.
Holy Madness: The Shock Tactics and Radical Teachings of Crazy-Wise Adepts, Holy Fools, and Rascal Gurus.
Paragon House, $24.95 (1-55778-250-4). 384p. index.

Feuerstein has put together a fascinating look at spiritual leaders, both past and present. He documents the strange behavior and methods of such widely diverse characters as Baghwan Rajneesh and the apostle Paul, pointing out the similarities in their reactions to the spiritual dimension. Feuerstein also touches on the context in which the "holy fool" operates, particularly in relation to discipline and discipleship. The book's third section deals with the significance of this spiritual behavior. More interesting is the

Religion

examination of five contemporary gurus and clowns: those who have followed the exploits and cults of Gurdjieff, Crowley, Rajneesh, Trungpa, and Lozowick will appreciate the concise histories of these people and their disciples. —*Mary Deeley*

Godwin, Malcolm.
Angels: An Endangered Species.
Simon & Schuster, $19.95 (0-671-70650-0). 255p.

Godwin has put together a beautifully illustrated volume for anyone with a passing interest in angels, in folklore and tradition about heavenly beings, or in religious art. Part one deals with the groups of angels (e.g., Seraphim, Principalities, etc.) and individual figures such as archangels Michael and Raphael. Godwin also deals with hell's angels (no, not the ill-tempered bikers of Altamont fame, but those who hang out with Satan). Each individual or group is concisely identified, with a discussion on the meanings of their names and salient features of the legends surrounding them. Part two concerns itself with the interaction of angels and human beings, from the earliest Jewish writings to the New Age. Using Scripture, art, and eyewitness accounts, Godwin presents a fascinating journey devoted to answering the question, What and who are angels, really? His conclusion is thought provoking. —*Mary Deeley*

Goldman, Ari.
The Search for God at Harvard.
Times Books, $19 (0-8129-1653-0). 272p.

In 1985 Goldman, an Orthodox Jew and a religion reporter for the *New York Times*, was given a sabbatical to study comparative religion at the Harvard Divinity School. The result is this book, an examination of the school and its students. Goldman confronts the teachings of Christianity, Buddhism, and Hinduism; in the process, he develops a fuller understanding of himself and his own religion. "In many ways," he writes, "the year at Harvard helped knit together the many diverse facets of my life, my stormy childhood, my disordered education, my passion for journalism and the powerful, mystical pull faith continues to have on me." With candor, Goldman gives the reader a chance to look inward and do some of his or her own introspection. —*George Cohen*

✔Marty, Martin E.
Modern American Religion, Volume Two: The Noise of Conflict, 1919–1941.
Univ. of Chicago, $29.95 (0-226-50895-1). 444p. index.

This second volume of *Modern American Religion* by the redoubtable University of Chicago professor is a cultural history, with the emphasis on the American aspect of religion during the decades under discussion. Americans of original stock, Anglo-Saxon Protestants, appeared to peak in power during Prohibition and then subside into factions during the Great Depression. Modernists, fundamentalists, liberals, and realists all contributed to the divisions within the national Protestant churches. The struggle was seldom deadly, but there was friendly fire within the ranks. The participants unwittingly solidified the pluralistic tradition in our nation. Some of the more colorful were Baptist politician William Jennings Bryan, Princeton fundamentalist J. Gresham Machen, renowned preacher Harry Emerson Fosdick, and perhaps the leading charismatic preacher of his day, Reinhold Neibuhr. (Some of the churchmen such as Gerald L. K. Smith, Francis Townsend, and Father Charles Coughlin were also the leading bigots.) Marty's volume includes all groups—Lutherans, Presbyterians, Methodists, Baptists, Mormons, Jews, Catholics, Orthodox Christians, and Jehovah's Witnesses are all described with compassion and clarity as to their multifarious goals and activities. Marty also rightfully includes native Americans, whose religion was considered nonexistent by our government. In sum, a valuable contribution to history in the process. —*Eugene Sullivan*

✓Sewell, Marilyn, ed.
Cries of the Spirit: A Celebration of Women's Spirituality.
Beacon, $35 (0-8070-6812-8). 308p. paper, $16.95 (0-8070-6813-6).

There are many occasions to reach for this book. Looking for a poem to read on a special occasion—anything from New Year's Day to a wedding? Hoping for a collection that, while wide ranging and representative, reads easily because it's organized to stress connections among the works? Seeking poems that, while elegant and well wrought, speak directly to the heart? This fine volume meets all those needs and many more. It will circulate far more than most anthologies, even of women's poetry, because its focus is on the spirituality of women's experience. It includes some of the great statements of the century: Muriel Ruckeyser's "No more masks!" and Nikki Giovanni's "Black love is Black wealth." It also includes less pivotal works that are consistently fine: philosophical but passionate, specific but universal. A book that many, without realizing it, have been waiting for. —*Pat Monaghan*

Simmons, Thomas.
The Unseen Shore: Memories of a Christian Science Childhood.
Beacon, $17.95 (0-8070-1018-9). 173p.

To write honestly about oneself in a clear and forthright manner, especially when it involves often painful childhood memories, is noteworthy. Simmons, a poet, humanities professor, and father of two, was raised as a Christian Scientist by devout and caring parents. His brother and sister easily rebelled at the teachings of Mary Baker Eddy; Simmons, on the other hand, devoted to his mother, tried to reconcile his bodily desires, hurts, and illnesses with the Christian Science practice—that is, that prayer and belief will open themselves to God's perfection, and the needs of the body will go away. And yet, the bruised limbs and, ultimately, the bruises of the heart would not go away. Simmons' beautifully written book, while admitting the cruelties of his parents, evidences tolerance and compassion despite the pain. The image of him riding his motorcycle on the seaside cliffs of Northern California, boldly defying bodily harm, and his last-time visit to a dying mother, are juxtaposed at story's end with the image of Simmons rowing his boat through the rain

Religion

and fog of a Maine harbor toward unknown islands in the future. —*Eugene Sullivan*

Spong, John Shelby.
Rescuing the Bible from Fundamentalism: A Bishop Rethinks the Meaning of Scripture.
HarperCollins, $16.95 (0-06-067509-8). 260p. index.

Spong, an Episcopalian bishop, is tired of the fundamentalist wing of the Church claiming the Bible as their own. He doesn't agree with their narrow interpretation, but his own, more liberal view is sure to provoke discussion and at times cause consternation. He discusses issues that have been raised elsewhere (Is the virginity of Mary based on a mistranslation of the Greek word in the Bible?) and brings forth new interpretations that have only been whispered about (Was Paul gay?). His appraisal of Paul's character is perhaps the most controversial of his positions, but his problems with the Bible and the harsh God it depicts, even in the New Testament, won't be well received in many circles. Spong is not writing to discredit the Bible, the book with which he says he has had a lifelong affair. Rather, he wants to bring it into the twentieth century by focusing on its eternal truths rather than the historical, philosophical, and scientific aberrations that have caused some to discount it entirely. Though he reaches a bit on the Paul issue, Spong offers interesting, well-thought-out ideas that should do what he intends—get people thinking about the Bible. —*Ilene Cooper*

✓Wiesel, Elie.
Sages and Dreamers: Biblical, Talmudic, and Hasidic Portraits and Legends.
Summit, $25 (0-671-74679-0). 443p.

Wiesel roams around the Bible like more ordinary folk tramp around a shopping mall. He stops and examines a particular icon, decides what he buys about a particular biblical tale, and in general enjoys the goods. Based on a series of lectures, this collection's focus is 25 Jewish figures whom Wiesel loves because "despite their grandeur, or thanks to it, they remain close to us everywhere and always." The subjects are mostly men—Noah, Rabbi Akiba, The Ostrowitzer Rabbi—though Ruth and Esther get a nod. These figures each represent a specific era, but Wiesel shows, in surprisingly accessible, even colloquial, prose, that their problems and dreams are not so very different from our own. As Wiesel develops his arguments, shifting his focus as one tilts a prism, readers may very well wish they had him in their living rooms, all the better to argue back. (Certainly such colloquy would be well within the tradition of Talmudic debate.) Before they begin arguing with Wiesel, even in their heads, many readers will want to consult the original texts; unfortunately, the glaring omission of chapter and verse citations will make some of them difficult to find. Still, this is a rich, provocative volume— the kind of book that gets the blood racing. —*Ilene Cooper*

Science & Nature

✔**Ackerman, Diane.**
The Moon by Whale Light and Other Adventures among Bats, Penguins, Crocodilians, and Whales.
Random, $20 (0-394-58574-7). 192p.

The latest news from the animal world by Ackerman—nature writer, poet, adventurer, and artist extraordinaire. Sent on "thrilling and nourishing journeys" by the *New Yorker,* Ackerman accompanies various animal experts, not to say fanatics, on field trips into the deserts of Texas and Antarctica, the waters off the coasts of Hawaii and Patagonia, a Florida alligator farm, and a San Diego penguin nursery. Hair-raising escapades are undertaken in pursuit of knowledge about maligned and misunderstood creatures. Take bats, for instance: Ackerman assures us that they are "sweet-tempered, useful, and fascinating." Alligators are "passive, otherworldly, and . . . make tender mothers and languorous sensual swains." Ackerman contrasts her tactile experiences with animals—nuzzling with a baby penguin, swimming eye-to-eye with a whale—to the myths and superstitions that surround them and attempts to imagine the world as they perceive it. Unavoidably, the glow of wonder bursts into the glare of hard facts about humanity's destructiveness versus the needs of other earth dwellers, but Ackerman's keen delight in the tenacity of life and her spirited participation in its pageant offer implicit hope and joy. Her other recent works include *A Natural History of the Senses* and *Jaguar of Sweet Laughter. —Donna Seaman*

Adams, Douglas and Carwardine, Mark.
Last Chance to See.
Harmony; dist. by Crown, $19.95 (0-517-57195-1). 240p.

Adams, of *The Hitchhiker's Guide to the Galaxy* and Dirk Gently fame (*Dirk Gently's Holistic Detective Agency*), brings his stellar wit and keen sense of irony to this report from the endangered-species front. He first met zoologist and wildlife author Mark Carwardine on an expedition to Madagascar to look for the aye-aye, a rare lemur. The sight of this gentle, ancient, and threatened creature inspired Adams to continue the quest to see other creatures who are nearing extinction, kept alive only by the extraordinary efforts of dedicated, even fanatic scientists. They travel to Komodo Island to see the dragons, Zaire to visit the white rhinoceroses and mountain gorillas, New Zealand to look for kakapos, China to check on Yangtze River dolphins, and Mauritius in pursuit of rare birds and bats. Their travels are complicated by thuggish officials and dilapidated vehicles, but they succeed in their mission and report firsthand on the surviving members of these protected species. Adams brings all the whimsy of his novels to this chronicle with vigorous descriptions, hilarious characterizations (especially of himself), thoughtful observations, and a fresh, critical perspective. A book that makes you laugh and cry and wish our species had evolved a bit further in the foresight department. —*Donna Seaman*

Asimov, Isaac.
Atom: Journey across the Subatomic Cosmos.
Dutton, $21.95 (0-525-24990-7). 280p.

If you've been searching for a basic text on how the atom works, this is it. For the uninitiated, ions, isotopes, quantum theory, electrons, photons, positrons, protons, and neutrons—not to mention the seemingly endless array of subatomic particles—can be confusing. Asimov puts all of this into some semblance of order, even if, after a while, one can again confuse a quark with a pion in the process of giving it a wrong lepton number. (That is, of course, if you're talking about matter and not antimatter.) Still there's a particular, messy fascination to investigating how the atom works. First off, it's amazing that one can even penetrate something as small as the nucleus of an atom. But then, there are the so-called "atom smashers" (more formally called particle accelerators), which destroy atoms. By looking at the wreckage that flies out, scientists get an idea of how an atom is put together. One scientist compared this activity with hitting a watch with a sledge hammer, then looking at the crushed remains to see what made the watch tick. If that turns you on, so will the prolific Asimov's latest. —*Jon Kartman*

Bass, Rick.
Winter: Notes from Montana.
Houghton, $18.95 (0-395-51741-9). 144p.

Bass, a Texan, and his friend, Elizabeth, from Mississippi, set out to find the ideal place to write and paint, a "place of ultimate wildness." Their dream drives them all the way to the edge of the U.S.: a Montana valley along the Yaak River in the center of two million acres of national forest where a few hardy souls live without electricity, phones, or paved roads. They arrive on the brink of winter as caretakers of a haunted ranch complete with a three-story lodge, greenhouse, barns, and cabins. Bass learns to chop wood, anticipating the hard winter with thrills of fear and pleasure. He watches owls, deer, coyote, the snow, the northern lights, and the huge moon; he has nightmares and moments of boundless joy. This entrancing and candid journal celebrates life in the wild and the magnetism of the written word. Bass, a petroleum geologist and environmentalist, is also author of *Oil Notes* (1990) and other books about the outdoors. —*Donna Seaman*

✓Casti, John.
Searching for Certainty: What Scientists Can Know about the Future.
Morrow, $22.95 (0-688-08980-1). 416p.

The import of scientific predictions has rarely been explained more engagingly—or more provocatively. From the meteorologist's observatory to the political scientist's lecture hall, Casti investigates the logical and mathematical possibilities for forecasting the future. Computer programming—lucidly interpreted for novices—provides the most fully developed illustrations, but developmental biology, climatology, investment finance, and military aggression also receive illuminating attention. In a style refreshingly light and humorous (science without tears?), Casti manages to sidle up to some troubling and sobering conclusions. Rigorous analysis exposes gaps in all scientific (or quasi-scientific) forecasts, including many relied upon by financial experts and political pundits. For readers inspired to learn more, Casti includes a "Dig Deeper" section with technical references. —*Bryce Christensen*

Close, Frank.
Too Hot to Handle: The Story of the Race for Cold Fusion.
Princeton, $24.95 (0-691-08591-9). 370p.

One of the most spectacular nondiscoveries of all time, cold fusion, makes a strange yet compelling tale. Himself a distinguished physicist, Close traces the tangled events that led first to a stunning public announcement by two chemists at the University of Utah that they had created fusion (the source of the sun's nuclear energy) in room-temperature beakers, and then to the eventual discrediting of their claim. After a brief overview of the nature of fusion and its potential for meeting the world's energy needs, the story (complicated by several subplots) moves from an obscure laboratory in Utah into the halls of Congress, as various groups jockey for control of what they suppose will be untold power and wealth. With lucidity and balance, Close exposes the haste, self-delusion, and carelessness that prompted the two Utah chemists first to boast of an amazing triumph, then to hide and distort evidence demanded by skeptics. This is a book to clarify not only the scientific process but also the political, economic, and cultural pressures under which scientists work. —*Bryce Christensen*

✓**Cone, Joseph.**
Fire under the Sea: The Discovery of Hot Springs on the Ocean Floor and the Origin of Life.
Morrow, $23 (0-688-09834-7). 320p. index.

Cone lures readers into his exciting account of the recent and momentous discovery of seafloor vents by comparing it to a detective story. The riddles to be solved are the very essence of science: "How is the earth put together?" and "How and where did life begin?" Cone plots the course of the inspirations, revolutionary theories, controversies, breakthroughs, and proofs that led scientists to the seafloor's hot springs and an understanding of the forces that create them. This is a tale of serendipity, politics, and greed, involving a cast of brilliant and courageous thinkers, explorers, and inventors of incredibly sophisticated equipment. It is also a testament to some astonishing natural phenomena: as seawater circulates through the seafloor, it's heated to temperatures exceeding 660 degrees Fahrenheit; it then gushes out into the cold, dark ocean, building towers of minerals and sustaining remarkable, improbable, and previously unknown life-forms nurtured by chemosynthesis. The closing chapters explain how this unique ecosystem may contain the secret to the origin of life. Popular science writing at its best. —*Donna Seaman*

Science & Nature

Cooke, John.
The Restless Kingdom: An Exploration of Animal Movement.
Facts On File, $39.95 (0-8160-1205-9). 224p.

Morris, Desmond.
Animalwatching.
Crown, $35 (0-517-57859-X). 256p.

The fact that each of these authors uses the word *pleasure* in his introduction can be taken as a good sign. Pleasure is what they experience when studying animals, and pleasure is what they give to their readers.

Cooke focuses on how animals move on land and in air and water, discussing only the "new, the remarkable and the improbable" to be sure his audience stays enraptured. His descriptions of the mechanics of the locomotion of hummingbirds, leopards, caterpillars, swallows, whales, kangaroos, ghost crabs, horses, snakes, rainbow trout, and penguins, to name only a few, are detailed, comprehensible, and guaranteed to amaze. He places these marvels of movement within an evolutionary context, tracing the development of certain physical features and their advantages. Nearly 200 color photographs and two dozen line drawings illustrate the text.

Best-selling (and prolific) animal behavior expert Desmond Morris synthesizes his vast knowledge in this energetic celebration of animal life. He shares his observations of how animals form social groups; outsmart predators through escape, visual and chemical defenses, distraction, and even self-mutilation; and how they feed, use tools, handle conflicts, mate, and parent. Morris' explanations of the particulars of the gestures, appearances, and habits of animals deepen our perception of the lives of creatures great and small and offer intriguing comparisons to our own instinctive behavior. Lavishly illustrated with color photographs. —*Donna Seaman*

Dwyer, Augusta.
Into the Amazon: The Struggle for the Rain Forest.
Sierra Club, paper, $10 (0-87156-637-0). 264p.

Dwyer, a Canadian journalist living in Rio de Janeiro, grew curious about the Amazon and set off on an often-adventurous investigative journey. She visited the rubber tappers of Acre, from whom she heard firsthand accounts of the deadly conflict over the rain forests, and became friends with Chico Mendes shortly before he was murdered. From there she traveled east to Pará, where she witnessed the harsh lives of river dwellers suffering from the devastation caused by the construction of the giant Tucurui Dam. As Dwyer crisscrossed the region, she saw and heard evidence of the haste with which technology and industry have been forced on the people of the Amazon, resulting in violence, poverty, oppression, epidemics, and the obliteration of traditional ways of life as well as natural resources. Dwyer places the destruction of the rain forests within the context of Brazil's politics and frantic economy, and reveals details of the life-and-death struggle against the greed, brutality, and stupidity of the region's exploiters. —*Donna Seaman*

Science & Nature

Eldredge, Niles.
The Miner's Canary: A Paleontologist Unravels the Mysteries of Extinction.
Prentice Hall Press, $20 (0-13-583659-X). 256p. index.

The canary of Niles Eldredge's title once served as an early warning system for odorless, poisonous gases. The health of the canary reflected the hazard posed to miners. In his new book, renowned paleontologist Eldredge takes the decline of song birds in his own backyard as a sign of the state of our global environment, and he finds the global miner's canary not at all well. This book goes beyond the alarm sounded so many times before over the loss of biological diversity; in clear and understandable prose, it provides a general history of extinction that uses the paleontologist's perspective (in which vanishing species are a fact of life) to throw light on today's local and global environment. Eldredge demonstrates how global climate change, which affects the size and location of habitats, underlies much of the extinction that went on in remote geological time. He then argues that humans—"loose cannons" in the rain forests—by altering habitats pervasively, have become new agents in the destruction of ecosystems, though he admonishes us not to be so vain as to think we are ever the sole cause of anything in nature. A mass extinction is now under way, and because we are part of the global ecosystem, our own survival as a species is at stake. No question the canary is ill. "Tomorrow," warns Eldredge, if we do not take the proper measures to salvage the environment, "it may well be dead." Important reading. —*Philip Herbst*

✔**Ellis, Richard.**
Men and Whales.
Knopf, $40 (0-394-55839-1). 528p. index.

A comprehensive history about the unbalanced relationship between men and whales that is on as grand a scale as its cetacean subject. Ellis, a marine artist and author of *Dolphins and Porpoises*, among other titles, begins his fascinating, complex, and disturbing study with detailed descriptions of nine families of whales. He then brings humanity onto the scene. Once the myriad uses for the oil, meat, and bone of the whale were discovered, the "long, gory history of whaling" began. The first to hunt whales were the Basques, but the profitable sport spread rapidly around the world in spite of its danger and noisomeness. While the need for oil and meat was understandable, the huge demand for baleen, or whalebone, for three centuries of corset-wearers was ludicrous, causing the suffering of laced-up women as well as the terrible deaths of thousands of whales. One might think that the discovery of petroleum would have at least slowed the slaughter, but instead technology made it even easier to find and kill whales. The statistics are astonishing: 267,194 sperm whales were killed during the period 1964–74; 29,000 blue whales, the earth's largest animal, were murdered each year until they became too scarce to hunt. Ellis' account of the "save the whales" movement records the dawning of sanity, but the current moratorium on whaling is shaky at best and may be too late for some species. This magnificent, abundantly illustrated volume covers every imaginable aspect of whaling, making it an invaluable resource for libraries. —*Donna Seaman*

Foreman, Dave.
Confessions of an Eco-Warrior.
Harmony; dist. by Crown, $19.95 (0-517-58123-X). 240p.

Well, not really confessions. Foreman, founder of Earth First!, the leaderless, unorganized group of activists most famous for spiking trees in old-growth forests slated to be cut down for lumber, neither admits to anything actionable nor relates much of his personal life in these pages. He does verify that spiking trees is indeed something that radical environmentalists do, and he explains how and why they do it in practical, ethical, philosophical, and even what may be called religious terms. In fact, his explanation is somewhat repetitious in this set of position papers and exhortations that's been given the guise of a monograph. Few readers caught by his rhetorical flare and passion will mind the many replays, and a great many will feel challenged by Foreman's acute questioning of the morality of progress and the primacy of *Homo sapiens* among Earth's creatures. He repudiates the anthropocentrism upon which all civilizations and virtually every religion rest their claims to moral and ethical legitimacy, proposing in its stead that all species, all constituents of the Earth, are of equal value and that only a human order that does not destroy any of the rest of the Earth is ethical and moral in any meaningful sense. —*Ray Olson*

Gohau, Gabriel.
A History of Geology.
Rutgers Univ., $35 (0-8135-1665-X); paper, $12.95 (0-8135-1666-8). 253p.
index.

If astronomy was the first science to cross horns with the theologians, geology was not far behind. If astronomers looked into the realm of God, geologists did something even more disturbing by actually analyzing God's handiwork. Gohau relates the history of geology from the first attempts to understand how this planet is put together and the failure to find conclusive evidence of the biblical flood to the modern era of plate tectonics. Today geology is undergoing a rapid revolution since confirmation in the late 1950s and 1960s that the continents are gradually moving and sliding up against one another, thereby creating earthquakes, mountains, and volcanoes. Much like the study of life, once differentiated into botany and zoology—terms now soundly replaced by the broader *biology*—the study of this planet is now more properly called geoscience in that its concerns are more global than a term connoting the mere study of rocks. Readers will find out pretty much everything they ever wanted to know about the history of this rapidly evolving science. —*Jon Kartman*

Goldsmith, Donald.
The Astronomers: Companion Book to the PBS Television Series.
St. Martin's, $24.95 (0-312-05000-0). 352p.

This companion to the recent PBS TV series makes an excellent basic astronomy and cosmology text. It traces recent research in both fields, providing easily read explanations of such strange phenomena as quasars and black holes and the history and current theory of how stars work.

Goldsmith, an astronomer himself, obviously knows many of the colleagues he mentions, professionally if not on a first-name basis. In the preface, Goldsmith voices his hopes that the book will spur future scientists into these fields, despite such risks (no doubt quite surprising to many readers) as suffering from the effects of a lack of oxygen while at work studying the stars through the newer telescopes on some of the world's higher mountains, such as Mauna Kea in Hawaii. —*Jon Kartman*

✔**Gould, Stephen Jay.**
Bully for Brontosaurus: Reflections in Natural History.
Norton, $22.95 (0-393-02961-1). 524p.

Evolutionary biologist Gould's fifth collection of essays is his best yet. Witty, charming, and always splendidly rational, Gould offers discussions of "evolutionary change and the nature of history" within the context of a wide range of topics, including Joe DiMaggio's 56-game hitting streak, male nipples, the origin and perpetuation of the "QWERTY" format of typewriter keyboards, the mania for dinosaurs, and the surprising characteristics of kiwis and a frog that carries its young in the stomach and then gives birth through the mouth. Gould's focus in each piece is on the value of details and the understanding of the "cascade of consequences," as well as the importance of being aware of the subtle biases of expectations and mindsets. Gould brooks no sloppy thinking, no wishful seeking for confirmation of moral beliefs in nature, no confusion from legend and unexamined assumptions. He tirelessly and creatively tests Darwin's theory, offering unexpected juxtapositions while leading us down serpentine, sometimes difficult, but always rewarding paths of thought. Gould is a superb teacher, nurturing thought and wonder, exemplifying the "power and beauty of reason" and sharing his "dream that excellence in one activity might be extended to become the pattern, or at least the goal, of an actual life." —*Donna Seaman*

Hann, Judith.
How Science Works.
Reader's Digest Press, $24 (0-89577-382-1). 192p. index.

If constant questions such as "Why does it rain?" or "What makes a balloon go up?" can't be answered by nonscientist parents, then it's time to supplement conventional education at home. This first volume in a series, written by a science journalist and BBC-TV personality, does indeed make sense of all those queries, with chapters focusing on the world of matter; energy, force, and motion; light and sound; air and water; electricity and magnetism; electronics and computing. More than enough projects are designed to satisfy inquisitive minds of all ages, and most use simple kitchen and household equipment (thermometers, wood, wires, and candles, for example) for experiments ranging from measuring boiling points to creating a radio. Introductions to each subject include overviews of major scientific discoveries. (Unfortunately, necessary templates and patterns require a microscope for magnification and duplication.) —*Barbara Jacobs*

Hartmann, William K.

The History of the Earth: An Illustrated Chronicle of an Evolving Planet.
Workman, $35 (1-56305-122-2). 241p. paper, $19.95 (0-89480-756-0).

Hartmann has produced a string of popular science books illustrated with his and Ron Miller's vibrantly imagined paintings, often of sights no one has ever seen. Here he shows and tells us the story of the earth's coming-of-age. In a relaxed, conversational tone, he explains how we've been able to learn about the earth's history from rocks and stars. Drawing on the latest theories from the fields of cosmology, evolutionary biology, astronomy, and geology, he postulates the origins of the earth, the moon, and life itself. The paintings depict fantastic landscapes, seascapes, and long-extinct plants, animals, and insects. Moving into our times, Hartmann describes catastrophes such as volcanic eruptions, earthquakes, and asteroid/comet impacts, and speculates on the disproportionate effect we have had on the biosphere. An excellent, up-to-date, and visually exciting introduction to earth science. Hartmann's other titles include *Out of the Cradle: Exploring the Frontiers beyond Earth* and *In the Stream of Stars.* —*Donna Seaman*

✓Jordan, William.

Divorce among the Gulls: An Uncommon Look at Human Nature.
North Point, $17.95 (0-86547-426-5). 212p.

What makes these remarkable essays constitute "an uncommon look at human nature" may, for many, be their biologist-author's pronounced zoomorphism; i.e., the provocative, compelling, persuasive, and charming way he demonstrates the profoundest likenesses of humans to the other animals, even some of the humblest. In "Cockroach Memoirs," for instance, from his observations of one of the most disdained creatures that ever crawled, he extrapolates meaningful concepts of human intelligence—indeed, of what intelligence qua intelligence is (to wit—but drastically boiled down—intelligence is a trait coincident with biology). In virtually every essay—whether on the mockingbird, the medfly, gulls, the roof rat, his groundlevel conference with a farmer on the alfalfa weevil and the tiny wasp that is its nemesis, or the everyday slaughter of experimental animals—he reminds us of how intimate is the kinship of humans to the rest of creation, especially the animals, and he considers the moral and ethical responsibilities the web of correspondences among us and the animals entails. This is all wonderful, all distinctive. But perhaps the really uncommon thing about Jordan's "look" lies in his sublime skill as storyteller and writer. He relates his own and other scientists' telling actions and reactions with great humor and flare and describes the behavior of critters absolutely grippingly. His philosophical essays are thus ultimately grounded not in science alone, but also in warm human interest. —*Ray Olson*

Lerner, Eric J.
The Big Bang Never Happened.
Times Books, $21.95 (0-8129-1853-3). 544p. index.

For anyone interested in cosmology or physics, this is a must read, a book that marks a possible turning point in the history of science. During most of this century, the big bang has been the theoretical cornerstone of our understanding of the universe. As the title clearly states, Lerner, a plasma physicist, tries to demonstrate that this cornerstone isn't: that the electromagnetic forces on plasma, and not gravity, explain the origin and structure of the universe. Unfortunately, he goes beyond physics and tries to link cosmology with human culture and society, not to mention life itself. In this respect he is guilty of attempting to devise a Theory of Everything, which crime, as he views it, he ascribes to big bang backers such as Stephen Hawking. Time will tell whether Lerner's theories wind up in scientific sanitary landfills along with Ptolemy's crystal spheres and the idea of a universal ether. But coupled with recent understanding of previously assumed chaotic physical events (which are really not that chaotic), the possibility that the big bang never happened could presage a new era in physics. Stay tuned. —*Jon Kartman*

Lorenz, Konrad and others.
Here I Am—Where Are You? The Behavior of the Greylag Goose.
HBJ, $26.95 (0-15-140056-3). 203p. index.

Pioneering ethologist Lorenz, famous for his work with the imprinting mechanism of newborn ducks and geese, has pulled together decades of work with his species of choice, the greylag goose. Fascinated by waterfowl since childhood, Lorenz offers careful, even intimate observations of the social behavior of this species, which has resulted in what he describes—"without immodesty"—as "the most complete investigation to date of the ethology of a higher organism and its social system." Beginning with his first pet goose, Martina, Lorenz relates anecdotes about specific geese that are both entertaining and informative. The conflicts and drama of these closely watched geese mirror our own social struggles to a surprising degree as they experience squabbles and rivalries, stormy love affairs, jealousy, and grief. Once he has familiarized us with the personalities and activities of his subjects, Lorenz analyzes their "behavioral repertoire" of displays and vocalizations associated with hatching, preening, feeding, and courting. A fitting summation of Lorenz's lifework, this volume exemplifies his unique mix of rigorous scientific inquiry and good, old-fashioned intuition. —*Donna Seaman*

McMullen, Jeanine.
A Small Country Living Goes On.
Norton, $19.95 (0-393-03039-3). 272p.

Creativity permeates Jeanine McMullen's life. Her BBC radio program "My Small Country Living" uses sound in unusual, sometimes outrageous ways, with her editing bringing to life the work of country people, from Wales to

Science & Nature

Cornwall. Besides cherishing the skills of the past, when people coaxed the best from local products (e.g., Irish linen makers), McMullen also exhibits her own penchant for keeping alive older and exotic breeds of animals on a small farmstead in Wales, from Anglo-Nubian goats to "badger-faced" sheep to chickens feathered in lace, all of which are named, loved, and documented. McMullen effectively recounts her bittersweet struggle to manage her menagerie and to capture the sounds of others who make a small country living. McMullen's appreciation for quality in living is supplemented by a wicked sense of humor. —*Virginia Dwyer*

✔Montgomery, Sy.
Walking with the Great Apes: Jane Goodall, Dian Fossey, Biruté Galdikas.
Houghton, $19.95 (0-395-51597-1). 278p.

This is an exciting book. Montgomery provides an outstanding, popularized synthesis of the long-term, close-range study of large primates conducted by three renowned women, all protégées of anthropologist Louis Leakey, who believed "that women are better observers than men." The author also conveys a fine sense of the diverse personalities of the three: Jane Goodall of England, who has observed chimps at Gombe in Tanzania for 30 years (see her own *Windows on the World*); American Dian Fossey, who lived among the mountain gorillas of Rwanda for 18 years until her brutal murder in 1985; and Canadian Biruté Galdikas, who for 17 years has made her home among the orangutans in a swamp jungle in southern Indonesian Borneo. Montgomery describes the unconventional Leakey's faith in his chosen researchers and spells out the resistance put up by the scientific world about these women, who not only studied their subjects in the wild, but also gave them names and, at times, interfered in the natural order of things to help the apes. Montgomery likens their studies to a vision quest: "Whether it was voiced or subconscious, sustained or abandoned, each woman had to have felt the ancient longing to become one with the animals." A selected bibliography and list of organizations that support the trio's work are appended to a splendid, well-written account, enhanced by scattered photos, that will draw in readers unfamiliar with the research projects as well as those who have been following them through the years. —*Sally Estes*

Morris, Desmond.
Animalwatching.
Crown, $35 (0-517-57859-X). 256p.

See p.190.

Norris, Kenneth S.
Dolphin Days: The Life and Times of the Spinner Dolphin.
Norton, $21.95 (0-393-02945-X). 288p. index.

Norris has been studying dolphins for decades. His fascination stems from the driving curiosity of pure science as well as a practical concern: How can tuna be netted without killing hundreds of thousands of dolphins each year? By focusing on the beautiful and "dainty" spinner dolphins who frequent the clear bay waters of Hawaii, Norris and his crew of inspired researchers decoded the logistics of dolphin schools. Vivid descriptions explain the dolphin's language of leaps and spins, clicks, barks, and whistles; the syntax of caresses, mechanics of echonavigation and breath, and the myriad aids to synchroneity, an essential element of life on the move. Norris' delightful and enlightening accounts of dolphin society are in disturbing contrast to his eyewitness report on the deadly disorientation and fear experienced by dolphins caught in giant tuna nets. His confidence in our ability to invent a netting method that allows dolphins to escape is utterly convincing, as is his cynical recognition that the will to achieve this is drowned by social and economic imperatives. Absorbing and provocative. —*Donna Seaman*

Palmer, Tim.
The Snake River: Window to the West.
Island Press, $34.95 (0-933280-59-9). 326p. paper, $17.95 (0-933280-60-2).

An in-depth report on the state of the West's mighty Snake River and a discussion of the "core issues of its management." Palmer, who traveled sections of the 1,056-mile-long river and its environs with canoe and bicycle, analyzes the damage done by irrigation, diversion, and damming, but he also offers hope that new approaches and priorities will contain future destruction. Moving smoothly from description to data, Palmer conveys the majesty of the river as it flows through mountains, desert, canyons, and farmland, nurturing great forests and beleaguered wildlife such as bald eagles and salmon, and then explains the problems associated with silt, hydropower, and wastewater. In dissecting the conflicts over land and water rights, Palmer asks sensible questions about what is gained and what is lost when dams are built and wetlands drained, focusing on long-term habitat concerns rather than temporary political and economic agendas. An excellent resource for understanding the incalculable importance of a great river. —*Donna Seaman*

Paulos, John Allen.
Beyond Numeracy: The Ruminations of a Numbers Man.
Knopf, $22 (0-394-58640-9). 320p.

From *A* (*algebra*) to *Z* (*Zeno's paradoxes*), mathematics has rarely been so entertaining as in this delightful survey. Exploring more than 70 topics, Paulos not only demystifies mathematics, but also conveys something of the intellectual pleasure the subject affords. Often witty, occasionally profound, and never dull, the author brings formulas to life with fascinating anecdotes and humorous illustrations. Since each entry is an independent essay, readers can browse or jump around as their interests lead them. Some of the topics are classical (e.g., the Pythagorean theorem and Platonic solids), but others are close to today's frontiers (e.g., fractals and chaos theory). Professionals may regard it as frivolous, but this is an ideal book for readers who suppose that mathematics is distasteful or boring. Paulos provides a list of suggested readings for the adventurous. —*Bryce Christensen*

Science & Nature

Porritt, Jonathon.
Save the Earth.
Turner Publishing, $29.50 (1-878685-05-8). 208p. index.

This is an ambitious book that attempts to engage ordinary people who care but don't know much about environmental problems. Ugly realities of land, air, and water degradation and their human consequences are shown while the text also suggests ways to end them. Its most effective weapon is the graphic presentation: a fine collection of color photos, eye-grabbing charts and graphs, and luscious typography. These display the sordid connections among poverty, politics, and pollution while also stating what can and cannot be remedied. Delightfully framed commentaries by those involved in environmental reform range from Paul McCartney to indigenous tribal leaders. Also included are quick takes on successful actions and organizations—in erosion control, land reform, or successful farming. The book also includes an action packet with a short list of specific commitments individuals can successfully undertake, and three mail-in cards—to the 1992 United Nations conference on the environment; to President Bush; and one requesting information on 11 environmental organizations. This effective presentation of problems and remedies warrants a shared exploration and, hence, use in most libraries.
—*Virginia Dwyer*

Raup, David M.
Extinction: Bad Genes or Bad Luck?
Norton, $19.95 (0-393-03008-3). 192p. index.

The author of *The Nemesis Affair* returns to his quest for the why and how of extinction. Raup discusses the many difficulties inherent in studying this essential but elusive topic and then explains the descriptively named models most commonly used to analyze *speciation*—the division of evolutionary lines into species—and extinction, both mass extinctions and "background" disappearances. These models—the Gambler's Ruin, Broken Stick, and Field of Bullets—make use of information gleaned from fossils and statistics on considerations such as geographical distribution, body size, and minimum viable populations. Raup concisely identifies key generalizations, cautions against emotional biases, and narrows the debate down to three extinction modes: random extinction, the classic "survival of the fittest," and "wanton extinction," which is selective but not preferential. His carefully stated conclusion is that life on earth experiences this wanton extinction and that meteorite impact has been the central catalyst. A challenging amalgam of wit, reason, and intellect, bound to fuel debate and attract popular-science buffs.
—*Donna Seaman*

Raymo, Chet.
The Virgin and the Mousetrap: Essays in Search of the Soul of Science.
Viking, $18.95 (0-670-83315-0). 182p.

Raymo is a teacher, science columnist for the *Boston Globe*, and author of books such as *The Soul of the Night* as well as a novel, *In the Falcon's Claw*. He is also a seer who gazes raptly at computer images of DNA molecules and sees an echo of the magnificence of gothic architecture such as the rose window at Chartres. His successful search for the soul of science leads to informative and inspiring elucidation of the links, or "invisible harmonies," between science and human experience, between knowledge and spirituality. Raymo writes fluidly and imaginatively about an intriguing range of topics including astronomy, the biochemistry of memory, "space-bugs," our propensity for violence, and animal rights. Attuned to the value of metaphor, he draws on the works of van Gogh, Ted Hughes, and, entertainingly, Dr. Seuss for the poet's view, while he also discusses the dangerous aspects of inquiry in essays on radium and genetic engineering. Eminently satisfying. —*Donna Seaman*

✔Reisner, Marc.
Game Wars: The Undercover Pursuit of Wildlife Poachers.
Viking, $19.95 (0-670-81486-5). 294p.

We don't usually think of dangerous, covert operations when we think of game wardens, but risky undercover work is a way of life for Dave Hall of Louisiana's Department of Wildlife and Fisheries. Reisner, environmentalist, investigative reporter, and author of *Cadillac Desert*, tells Hall's astonishing story with flair. Hall has stalked big-time poachers for 25 years using a winning combination of "surveillance, subterfuge, and criminal psychology" to pull off complex sting operations that rival the cleverest Hollywood creations. International trade in illegal wildlife is a huge business that is often linked with drug traffic and some frighteningly rough characters. Since Hall and his agents were always wired, transactions for alligator hides, walrus and elephant tusks, and tons of poached fish were taped, adding chilling authenticity to Reisner's dramatic account. Hall's investigations took him from the Louisiana bayous to the bars of Nome, Alaska, from the French Quarter to the heavily guarded home of a Jewish gangster in Jersey. The numbers of animals killed and dollars exchanged are overwhelming, even sickening, and Reisner places the blame squarely on the biggest customers: Japan and the countries of Asia. Suspenseful and angry, this is a hugely entertaining exposé. —*Donna Seaman*

Restak, Richard.
The Brain Has a Mind of Its Own: Insights from a Practicing Neurologist.
Crown/Harmony, $18 (0-517-57483-7). 224p. index.

Restak's earlier books include *The Brain* and *The Mind*, and his newest combines the two in challenging and invigorating ways. He maintains a stereoscopic view of humanity, watching our behavior and emotions correspond to the incredible biology of our brain. There are two recurring themes in this elegant series of essays: first, the indivisibility of mind from brain, and second, the moral and societal implications of the discoveries being made about how the brain functions and to what degree genetics are involved. Restak baffles and thrills us with his unravelings of such subtleties as the meaning of free will and "changing our minds," the value of anxiety, and the myth of reasonableness in life-threatening situations. Both philosopher and doctor, he asks us to consider the fact that "our activities, habits, and interests not only define our personalities in the psychological sense, but actually affect the physical structure of our brain." Complex as this sounds, Restak manages to keep it simple, presenting each concept and concern in explanations that unfold like a bud that blooms. A resonant and important work. —*Donna Seaman*

Rheingold, Howard.
Virtual Reality.
Summit, $22.95 (0-671-69363-8). 384p.

Rheingold explains just what computer-generated artificial worlds are and how they will affect everyday life at the office, in the home, in the classroom, and in the research laboratory. This "virtual reality" is the result of complex simulation programs that allow the operator to experience a wholly artificial world. Rheingold describes some of his own experiences in cyberspace and also profiles the work of the people who have pioneered the frontiers of science. With applications ranging from medical research to adventure games or even simulated sex, the possibilities of the technology are astounding. Rheingold covers both the processes of human perception and the engineering research that make these altered states realizable. —*John Brosnahan*

Schullery, Paul.
Pregnant Bears & Crawdad Eyes: Excursions & Encounters in the Animal World.
Mountaineers Books, $18.95 (0-89886-293-0); paper, $12.95 (0-89886-292-2). 186p.

If this book is any barometer of ecological consciousness, it's remarkable how much we've changed our outlook in but a few years. It used to be that bears were considered nothing more than vicious killers, but Schullery talks about the female bear's motherliness in being able to delay gestation: the fertilized egg just stops developing until she's ready for the pregnancy to proceed. Although most of us regard a new road in the forest as a rape of nature, Schullery points out that many creatures use it as a pathway, new species of plants spring up in the disturbed soil, and many scavengers get a boost in food intake from road kill. He even debunks Bambi, saying that trying to learn about nature by viewing the movie is like learning race relations by watching "Amos 'n' Andy." The little kiddies see Bambi, and when they hear about a forest fire, think thousands of Thumpers and Flowers get turned into well-done sirloins. Most, however, walk away from the fire, which, he points out, is, in the long run, beneficial to both the forest and the resident wildlife. —*Jon Kartman*

✔Sesti, Giuseppe Maria.
The Glorious Constellations: History and Mythology.
Abrams, $95 (0-8109-3355-1). 496p. index.

Sesti has filled a gap in the history of astronomy and explored the juncture of science and mythology by explicating the "archaeology of the stars." This large, splendidly illustrated volume (672 illustrations in all) begins with an overview of the evolution of astronomy from the keen observations of the Sumerians through the contributions of the Egyptians, the Greeks and Romans, the Islamic empire, and the Renaissance revolution. The creation of the animals and figures of the constellations is documented with contemporary star maps from each era, which are then compared with the actual location of the stars. An exquisite 94-page section is devoted to color reproductions of the grand anthropomorphic celestial fresco in the Villa Farnese in Caprarola, Italy. Painted in 1575 by an unknown artist, it is "the finest representation of Western astronomy." The remainder of the book focuses on the symbolism and mythology of 48 ancient constellations and the Milky Way. A beautifully designed treasury of the art, myth, and science of the stars. —*Donna Seaman*

Shapiro, Robert.
The Human Blueprint: The Race to Unlock the Secrets of Our Genetic Script.
St. Martin's, $22.95 (0-312-05873-X). 352p. index.

Drawing upon his own education and experience, many interviews, and a broad knowledge of the subject, Shapiro produces an informative and intriguing book. His imaginative approach—especially his use of everyday analogies—and his clear style will appeal to many readers. He begins with the work of Mendel and Morgan but presents this frequently discussed material with liveliness and some unusual touches. Much of the rest of his story deals with James Watson, director of the Human Genome Project, and other leaders in the scientific disciplines involved. The history Shapiro relays includes notably understandable presentation of the discoveries and hypotheses about the makeup, production, errors, and purposes of some of the billions of human genes. Shapiro then suggests possibilities for the near and distant futures and considers their scientific, social, political, and ethical elements. Wingerson's *Mapping Our Genes* covers some of the same ground but approaches the subject on a more individualized level by illustrating genetic diseases with case histories. Both books are valuable treatments of their common subject. —*William Beatty*

✓Sheldrake, Rupert.
The Rebirth of Nature: The Greening of Science and God.
Bantam, $21.95 (0-553-07105-X). 272p.

Sheldrake, a biochemist with a philosophical and theological bent, has a unique and creative view of the universe. One of his previous books, *A New Science of Life*, introduced the morphic field hypothesis that suggests that "invisible regions of influence," including a sort of collective unconscious for each aspect of nature, guide nature's growth and evolution. Here Sheldrake continues to pursue the implications of this Jungian vision in terms of religion and science and how it can change our perception and treatment of the earth. In a deft summation of the ways civilization has taken us away from our ancestor's animistic view of the world, Sheldrake questions the assumptions that unchanging laws of nature exist, or that the concept of God can't include a sense of sacredness in nature. He reasons that if evolution is the path life follows and we are part of nature, our beliefs will also evolve, enabling us to change and survive. A beautifully written, deeply felt, and sinuously argued challenge to many habits of thought. —*Donna Seaman*

Stone, Judith.
Light Elements: Essays in Science from Gravity to Levity.
Ballantine, paper, $8 (0-345-36608-5). 224p.

In this wonderful collection of her monthly *Discover* magazine columns, Stone's sharp wit is aimed at those who are, if not scientifically illiterate, at least apprehensive about science. (With good reason. If recent surveys are accurate, most citizens of this country are so scientifically ignorant they think Chernobyl is either Cher's maiden name or a ski resort and that DNA is a food additive.) Yet she also cuts through the ivory tower implication that only the gifted can understand scientific concepts. Stone shows that science is not all that fearsome as she considers such curiosity-piquing matters as the scary idea that cow manure may lead to the demise of life on this planet, how plants are used for national defense, and the profile of a company that offers mummification to those about to shuffle off their mortal coils. If more of us spent some time reading essays like hers, we'd know what the ozone layer is. That is, if we really want to know. —*Jon Kartman*

Swain, Roger B.
Saving Graces: Sojourns of a Backyard Biologist.
Little, Brown, $17.95 (0-316-82471-2). 152p.

Despite his book's subtitle, Swain's essays aren't all about critters one might find in the south 40 that one probably doesn't have, anyway. Swain, however, lives on a large New England spread that affords the luxury of and space for keeping beehives, observing birds going after the blueberry patch, and other events few urbanites ever see. Besides the fauna in *his* backyard, he champions some of the natural world's more despised creatures, such as wolves, bats, and wasps. He also strays a bit to contemplate animals one definitely won't find in the backyard, such as the so-called Jesus Christ lizard (a South American reptile that can "walk" on water) and the leatherback turtle. Nostalgia as well as biology is on hand, as Swain swears he can recall his early years by merely seeing a horse chestnut and conjuring the days he'd fill his pockets with the oversize seeds. He also celebrates the joys of drinking water, an event most of us take for granted. This is a gentle natural-history book without any great message, just understanding of and joy in the natural world. —*Jon Kartman*

Thomson, Keith Stewart.
Living Fossil: The Story of the Coelacanth.
Norton, $19.95 (0-393-02956-5). 256p. index.

In 1938 a strange, large, scaly, oily fish was hauled up in a net off the coast of South Africa. Marjorie Courtenay-Latimer, curator of the local natural history museum, was notified, realized its rarity, and contacted J. L. B. Smith, a chemistry professor by day and Africa's only ichthyologist by night. With just a sketch to go by, Smith made an educated and imaginative leap and identified the creature as a coelacanth ("SEEL-uh-kanth"), a fish thought to have been extinct for 80 million years. Smith's revelation made headlines, but confusion, greed, and political and scientific rivalries hampered research efforts. Thomson, a world-famous coelacanth expert, engagingly tells the amazing story of the discovery and study of this "living fossil." He explains its evolutionary connection to the first land animals, what is known about its biology, and what questions remain unanswered, including the pressing issue of population—overfishing may render this unique, relict species extinct, a painful irony. Brisk and engrossing, this is a winning mix of science and adventure. —*Donna Seaman*

Wallach, Bret.
At Odds with Progress: Americans and Conservation.
Univ. of Arizona, $24.95 (0-8165-0917-4). 255p. index.

Hard on the closing of the frontier came the opening of the conservation movement of the 1900s. One early skirmish pitted no-development preservationists, exemplified by the now legendary John Muir, patron saint of the Sierra Club, against the equally legendary Gifford Pinchot, prophet of managed land use and moulder of the U.S. Forest Service. It's no different now, and Wallach insightfully examines the tension in seven geographical instances. The tension actually stems from the ambivalence within each of us, says the author, created by the desire of bettering our lives—progress—versus our abhorrence at battering the land in its pursuit. And the tension is resolved, or rather rationalized, through three disguises: the disguise of efficiency, of social welfare, and of ecology. Into this original typology he fits the successes and failures of the conservation movement, be they the creation of the national forests or the depletion of the Ogallala aquifer, and with doses of Dillard-like naturalism he has cut a conservationist gem that soberly contrasts with the eco-alarmism that is so much the fashion in this genre. —*Gilbert Taylor*

Ward, Peter.
On Methuselah's Trail: Living Fossils and the Great Extinctions.
Freeman, $18.95 (0-7167-2203-8). 207p. index.

The history of life on Earth has been punctuated by frequent mass extinctions. (Many may wonder, Who's next?) Ward takes a unique tack by exploring species that have survived and in some cases prospered throughout the many millennia since life began. Although he avoids dealing with the one most of us are best acquainted with—our urban neighbor the cockroach—he covers a wide range of animals whose ability to survive ice ages, changes in the level of the oceans, and encounters with comets and asteroids is downright remarkable. It's amazing that a creature like the horseshoe crab (which isn't a crab at all but is more closely related to insects and spiders) has seen many species come and go and has survived relatively unchanged. The text drags a bit when Ward chronicles his detailed exploration through the fossil-bearing rocks. But

Science & Nature

there is a captivating message here: few species, in point of fact, survive the upheavals this planet has endured; the fate of *Homo sapiens* is by no means ensured. —*Jon Kartman*

Westbrock, Peter.
Life as a Geological Force.
Norton, $21.95 (0-393-02932-8). 256p. index.

Most of us think of geology as the study of rocks, inert matter at the mercy of glaciers, volcanoes, water, and wind. The traditional viewpoint sees a world in which purely physical forces influence and shape life-forms, hence the division between geology and biology. But Westbroek asks us to look at things from a different, more inclusive perspective. What if living things don't adapt to the physical environment, but instead modify it, adapting it to their needs? Beginning in his native Holland, a land much affected by a conspicuous life-form, i.e., man, Westbroek takes us on a global journey of observation, pointing out the myriad ways life, usually in its least visible forms, directs earth's complex dynamics. His prose is animated and strongly imagined as he describes plate tectonics, the recycling of matter, and the essential roles of various microorganisms in places as diverse as Java, Scotland, and Florida. A cogent and vivid presentation of some of the exciting discoveries made when scientists look at the whole picture, instead of data divided into arbitrary fields. —*Donna Seaman*

Wheelwright, Jean Hollister and Schmidt, Lynda Wheelwright.
The Long Shore: A Psychological Experience of the Wilderness.
Sierra Club, $20 (0-87156-625-7). 224p.

Almost 40,000 acres of Southern California coastline was home, for the better part of a century, to the Hollister family. Several generations of women grew up there, in intimate connection with the cycles of the cattle-ranching season. The latest two of these generations, a mother and daughter who are both Jungian analysts, faced the eventual necessity to sell the wild lands. Out of the pain of separation has grown this dual memoir, in which each records the life they recalled and explores the meaning of wilderness to the soul. Because these women know the hypnotic monotony of days in nature as well as the momentary, intense metaphysical connections, this book is a far cry from the shallow meanderings of city folk vacationing in the wild. This is a wilderness as it has been lived, unrecorded, through eons. An important contribution to natural history. —*Pat Monaghan*

✔**Whynott, Douglas.**
Following the Bloom: Across America with Migratory Beekeepers.
Stackpole, $19.95 (0-8117-1944-8). 210p.

In the midst of rational-technological society, hidden from it and indifferent to it, a secret and romantic confederation perpetuates a form of life centuries old, the life of migratory beekeepers, whose story is retold masterfully in Whynott's account. A thousand of them in America forkload their hives on flatbeds, follow the bloom north in the summer and south in the winter as their charges make honey and pollinate America's crops. They shape rivers of bees (which initially try to bump intruders away), handle them without gloves, exchange combat stories (not for the squeamish male reader). Like John McPhee writing on oranges, Whynott demonstrates that an accomplished and fervent author can tell readers more than they would have believed they wanted to know about a seemingly mundane subject. In this enthralling book, bees—with their evolutionary and social history, their place in everyone's life, their scholars—and the migratory beekeeping business—with its legends (e.g., Lorenzo Langstroth's discovery of bee space), its most unforgettable characters, and the tracheal mite that endangers it—are captured in prose that, although factual, evokes transcendental contemplation and daydream. —*Roland Wulbert*

Social & Political Issues

Astin, Helen S. and Leland, Carole.
Women of Influence, Women of Vision: A Cross-generational Study of Leaders and Social Change.
Jossey-Bass, $25.95 (1-55542-357-4). 221p. index.

Female leaders—there still aren't many, but their ranks are swelling rapidly, thanks to the women's movement and social change. This book looks at who the female leaders of the past three decades are, how they got there, and how they've influenced their worlds. The authors, both respected researchers, take an academic approach, almost literally as they interview mostly women in academia, from the president of the University of Chicago to the dean of the Harvard School of Education to presidents of women's colleges and groups nationwide. The resulting profiles are of strong, intelligent women who beat the odds against their advancement through a combination of factors. The authors look at what these factors are, what qualities these women share, how they emerged as leaders, and how they are breaking ground for the future. Astin and Leland also consider women who may not be in defined leadership positions yet who still wield influence. Their overall approach is thoughtful, intelligent, and probing—going beyond the stereotypes to get at some of the real issues for and experiences of women who are or could be leaders. Although the text is a bit stiff in format, the authors' effort is a wellspring of information—and inspiration—for women in all fields and at all levels. —*Mary Ellen Sullivan*

Bartimus, Tad and McCartney, Scott.
Trinity's Children: Living along America's Nuclear Highway.
HBJ, $21.95 (0-15-167719-0). 296p.

The story of Interstate 25 is a chronicle of how the U.S. government always gets its way, whether it's commandeering a prep school in the pristine wilderness of New Mexico for a nuclear laboratory or denying that the noise from one of its jets has caused a horse to maim a woman. I-25 has always

Social & Political Issues

Social & Political Issues

been a "military" highway. Once an Indian path, then the Spanish *jornada del muerto*, it is now the connector from White Sands, New Mexico, through Colorado to the MX missile sites in Wyoming. Traveling the route, the two authors interviewed residents and workers and delved into the history—good and bad—of the road since the early 1940s and the dawn of the nuclear age. But even a silver lining theory—that good things can and do come out of nuclear research—doesn't dispel the cloud of death shrouding the territory along I-25. Glossary, notes, bibliography. —*Cynthia Ogorek*

Barzun, Jacques.
Begin Here: The Forgotten Conditions of Teaching and Learning.
Univ. of Chicago, $19.95 (0-226-03846-7). 216p.

Scholar, critic, cultural historian, and champion of the written word, Jacques Barzun has been speaking and writing about teaching, reading, and learning for decades. This high-voltage collection of essays attacks the attitudes and inflated verbiage of educational theory and challenges us finally to face up to the failures of our schools. Barzun's diagnoses and prescriptions are based on common sense and a no-frills approach. In uncompromising language he discusses teaching teachers to teach, the need for history and geography classes, the role of art education, the distortions of textbooks and multiple-choice tests, and the essentiality of reading and writing, "the means of learning and thinking." Freshly edited and newly introduced, these essays argue for reform at every level, from elementary school to college. Barzun's clear and rigorous thinking shapes each piece into a beam of light slicing through the layers of habit and thought cliché that are strangling our schools. An arsenal of reason and eloquence for those willing to fight for change. —*Donna Seaman*

Bell-Scott, Patricia and others, eds.
Double Stitch: Black Women Write about Mothers & Daughters.
Beacon, $19.95 (0-8070-0910-5). 271p.

Stitching together memories of motherhood and daughterhood, the writers in this anthology use the metaphor of quilt making to explore the textures and nuances of these sometimes joyful, sometimes turbulent relationships. This confluence of fiction, personal narrative, essay, and poetry offers generous views into the heart of these women's unromanticized struggles with the cycle of poverty, sexism, racism, incest, alcoholism in the family, and their struggle to discover their own identities in a white patriarchal society. An informative introduction by Patricia Bell Scott and Beverly Guy-Sheftall, two of the six editors, familiarizes the reader with the collection's structural metaphor—quilt making—through a brief history lesson on its significance in African American society. Alice Walker, Audre Lorde, Bell Hooks, Sonia Sanchez, and 43 other women stitch together personally revealing and empowering memories—"patchwork"—of the legacy of strength, determination, and spirituality cultivated by years of learning to survive, passed down from mother to daughter. A truly powerful collection, long overdue. An excellent catalog of suggested readings is included along with brief biographies of each author. —*Christine Schlenker*

Bennett, Madeline.
Sudden Endings: Wife Rejections in Happy Marriages.
Morrow, $22 (0-688-09428-7). 220p. index.

A smoothly written and painfully clearheaded assessment of one of the tragic realities of modern life: when a man suddenly and seemingly inexplicably leaves wife and family. Bennett is herself a victim of "aggressive abandonment"; she draws achingly on her personal experience and that of other women, all of whom were married at least 10 years (in Bennett's case, 25), then woke up one morning to find hubby either gone or announcing that the marriage was over. Bennett has desperately wanted to identify the causes for her husband's behavior, particularly because she never saw it coming. Within context, the psychological terms used—*bad object rage, bonding crisis, projective identification*, etc.—will click with intelligent, interested readers, as Bennett discusses probable causes (often male trauma of some kind, not always the typical midlife crisis), the devastation caused to all concerned (especially the children), the often callous behavior and financial game-playing of husbands in flight, the difficulties of bringing into the emotion-charged arena professional counselors interested in saving the marriage, and a legal system that, in its current construct, embraces a "no-fault" approach to divorce without reasonably protecting obviously disadvantaged abandoned spouses. Bennett also provides (with the benefit of hindsight) advisories on how to spot the conflicted husband before he acts rashly. (She further notes, ironically, the collusion of other women when he does.) A solid selection for any medium to large library. —*Martin Brady*

✔Bing, Léon.
Do or Die.
HarperCollins, $19.95 (0-06-016326-7). 204p.

Bing has been writing about gang life for the past four years and has earned the trust of various members of South Central L.A.'s notorious and factious Crips and Bloods. Her revelatory interviews with gang members of various ages and experiences immerse readers in the highly specific language, routine, and mentality of gangbangers. What emerges is a bleak social landscape wracked by violence for violence's sake and drenched in fatalism, alienation, and suffering. In conversation after conversation, African American homeboys and homegirls tell the same story: to live is to fight, the only world that matters is the 'hood, earning respect is the goal, and killing people is a thoroughly acceptable means to that end. Bing, keenly observant as well as consistently unsentimental, unflappable, honest, and coolly courageous, visits gang members at home and in jails. While she does amass predictable tales of crime and murder, she also assembles heartbreaking portraits of startlingly articulate, complex, and fierce individuals. A searing investigation into a realm that must be understood and confronted. —*Donna Seaman*

Social & Political Issues

Social & Political Issues

Bobo, Kim and others.
Organizing for Social Change: A Manual for Activists in the 1990s.
Seven Locks, paper, $19.95 (0-932020-93-3). 288p. index.

Prepared by longtime fulminators of citizen activism, this big, handsome paperback advises how to get the grassroots stirring. The authors say the activism they suggest should be on behalf of a recruitable majority and should have three animating principles: to "win real ... improvements in people's lives," to "give people a sense of their own power," and to "alter the relations of power." The first of the three major divisions of their text addresses choosing a winnable issue, developing strategy and tactics, and giving structure to an activist organization. The large second part discusses specific organizational skills (e.g., developing leadership, using the media, and working with other action organizations such as churches and unions); the third part covers the means of and tools for supporting an organization (e.g., fund-raising, administrative systems, computerization). The guide is personably, literately written and contains a generous final section of annotated resources, including the words to what might be called the activist hit parade ("Solidarity Forever," "We Shall Not Be Moved," etc.). Manuals don't come much better than this. —*Ray Olson*

Brown, Peter.
Minority Party: Why Democrats Face Defeat in 1992 and Beyond.
Regnery Gateway, $21.95 (0-89526-530-3). 258p. index.

A clumsy stylist, Brown isn't going to win any writing kudos. But for plain speaking as he details how and why the Democrats will, if they're not more responsive to changes in the electorate, lose control of the House and Senate as well as the Oval Office, he deserves some kind of prize. U.S. voters are now mostly suburbanites and younger than the Democrats' hard core. They're bullish on family values, bearish on crime. Upwardly mobile, they fear new taxes. They are not personally racist and believe the 1960s civil rights movement conquered institutional racism. They're patriotic and believe the U.S. has a special role in world politics that greenlights actions like the Persian Gulf War. Independent and entrepreneurial, they despise rewarding the shiftlessness of those on welfare who, as they see it, won't work. Not union members, they don't buy the class analysis Democrats customarily invoke to rally the troops. Moreover, they're not all white but include most Asian Americans and increasing numbers of Hispanic citizens, despite Democrats' assumption that all "persons of color" are their constituents. If this all makes them sound like Bush's bunch, well, that's the Democrats' problem in a nutshell, for these voters will prevail, especially since, Brown says, the newest round of reapportionment will be much harder for Democrats to finagle in their favor. Must reading for political animals. —*Ray Olson*

Carter, Stephen L.
Reflections of an Affirmative Action Baby.
Basic Books, $22.95 (0-465-06871-5). 356p. index.

Carter, professor of law at Yale University, believes that affirmative action policies as they stand in this country are ineffective and dated. He contends that even black professionals must constantly prove their worth to their white colleagues, are often forced to maintain unrealistic standards of excellence in their professions, and are pressured to maintain "correct" political stances. To confront these racist attitudes, the author calls for direct, open communication between professionals, black and white, for only between equals can genuine solutions to difficult problems be found. Highly recommended for the social science shelves. —*Jane Jurgens*

Cetron, Marvin and Davies, Owen.
Crystal Globe: The Have and Have-Nots of the New World Order.
St. Martin's, $25 (0-312-06325-3). 464p. index.

Surveying the trade balances, budget deficits, and interest rates of the present, two futurists ply their prognosticating trade in the sphere of global economics. Country by country, they spew forth percentages and decimal points—those "damn dots," as a former chancellor of the British exchequer called the numerology of the dismal science—to venture a diagnosis of the planet's economic health 10 years hence. Their chart says Africa will continue to fester as an AIDS-infested abscess; lassitude will dissipate the dynamism of Japan, Inc., as its new generation works less and plays more; North America, including Mexico, will recuperate under salutary free-trade pacts; and the formerly communist countries will limp along as long-term convalescents. Backed by an encyclopedic torrent of facts, these conclusions seem plausible. But will Israel truly be at peace, will Washington actually displace New York City as a financial center, and will anglophone Canada really be absorbed by the U.S.? Like any good astrologists, Cetron and Davies interpret the economic zodiac in so many ways that some predictions will inevitably be proven while others will be forgotten. The only certainty is that stack weeders can't safely consign this tract to the flames until the year 2000, its advertised expiration date. —*Gilbert Taylor*

Cobban, Helena.
The Superpowers and the Syrian-Israeli Conflict.
Praeger, $19.95 (0-275-93944-8); paper, $12.95 (0-275-93945-6). 208p. index.

Middle East analyst Cobban's "historical case study of how things were in the Israel-Syria theater during the years 1978–1989" was largely completed before Iraq's invasion of Kuwait, but the events of the past year make this book more, rather than less, relevant. Most Americans think the "occupied territories" are the West Bank and the Gaza Strip (ignoring the formerly Syrian Golan Heights). Cobban's focus, then, on these two heavily armed nations and their superpower relationships could hardly be more timely. Her thorough summary of the context and development of the Syria-Israel conflict during this period of confrontation in Lebanon and of massive arms buildup is followed by an insightful analysis of shifts in the power relationships between Israel and the U.S., Syria and the USSR, and, of course, the superpowers themselves. Seeking to understand both the "relative immunity" of the Israel-Syria conflict to the late 1980s trend toward peaceful resolution of conflict in other parts of the Third World and the "seemingly anomalous strategic stability" between Syria and Israel in this period, Cobban offers hope that intelligent diplomacy by these nations and by the superpowers can move this troubled region "beyond crisis management." —*Mary Carroll*

Cockburn, Andrew and Cockburn, Leslie.
Dangerous Liaison: The Inside Story of the U.S.–Israeli Covert Relationship.
HarperCollins, $24.95 (0-06-016444-1). 416p. index.

While the historic relationship between the U.S. and Israel is today in the midst of some difficulties, Israel has been a staunch ally since shortly after its formation in 1948—in more ways than one might imagine. Israel's survival and perseverence in a Middle East that has been hostile to its existence is due in part to the secret alliance between the intelligence organizations of Israel and the U.S. The Cockburns examine the history of Israeli covert activity from the country's origins to the present day, revealing shady goings-on and ethically questionable practices that would make Oliver North seem like a boy scout. The U.S., not unaware of such policies, benefited from Israel's deals with regimes it was forbidden to do business with, as well as received intelligence about governments the U.S. did not have access to (namely those nations behind the Iron Curtain). The Mossad, the Israeli equivalent to the CIA, acted as a subcontractor, and, in such places as Latin America, did our "dirty work"—that is, trained Nicaraguan contras, death squads in Honduras, and even members of the Medellín drug cartel in Colombia, all under the guise of anti-communism. The Cockburns also explore the Israeli relationship with South Africa and other African nations, including Ethiopia and Idi Amin's Uganda, and they cover Israel's wars. Extensively researched, *Dangerous Liaison* suffers from what might be considered too much information, making it somewhat difficult to keep all the players straight without a scorecard. But the revelations here are startling, controversial, and will no doubt be hotly contested. —*Benjamin Segedin*

Davis, Flora.
Moving the Mountain: The Women's Movement in America since 1960.
Simon & Schuster, $23 (0-671-60207-1). 662p. index.

Davis sees feminism as one continuous movement with, so far, two waves of radical change, the first of which began in the late nineteenth century and finally won women the vote in 1920. The second wave is the subject of this comprehensive history. Davis focuses her effort on action, not theory, by asking, "How did feminists achieve what they did?" Her goal is to capture "a sense of the excitement, the craziness, the sheer creative chaos" of the movement over the last 30 years. She succeeds by telling the inside story of Kennedy's Commission on the Status of Women and the ironic way Title VII, the banning of sex discrimination in the workplace, was added to the 1964 Civil Rights Bill. Davis chronicles the rapid rise of grass-roots organizations, the founding of NOW, and the invention of consciousness-raising. As younger, more radicalized women got involved, issues cropped up in every aspect of life, from women's health, the abortion controversy, and violence against women to matters of education and employment. Davis examines landmark decisions, the mutually effective relationship between the movement and the media, and the question of why there are still so few women in Congress. Davis' conclusion is that we've won half a revolution. Her energetic, thorough, and forward-looking narrative will help win the other half. —*Donna Seaman*

DeSantis, John.
For the Color of His Skin: The Murder of Yusuf Hawkins and the Trial of Bensonhurst.
Pharos, $18.95 (0-88687-621-4). 272p.

Racism runs deep in U.S. society. The feelings that racial incidents inflame (anger and guilt) and the reactions they can cause (violence, defensiveness, panic) often create a battle storm aggravated by government's unwillingness to address the *nature* of racism and the oppressive socioeconomic system that maintains it. As a traveler through this storm, DeSantis must be commended. In this book, he journeys through the murder of young African American Yusuf Hawkins by a young white mob of residents in the Brooklyn community of Bensonhurst. After giving a brief history of race and ethnicity in Brooklyn, DeSantis uncovers events leading to the murder, the murder itself, the investigation, the activism, the trial, and the aftermath. DeSantis' account is a focused study—moving adroitly from one character to the next—in which the reader is never separated from the larger context. Chronology is observed, however, the characters are the key, and DeSantis treats them all, from Hawkins' father Moses Stewart to triggerman Joey Fama, from activist reverend Al Sharpton to self-serving defense attorney Elizabeth Holtzman, with sensitivity and understanding of their complex human situations. —*Angus Trimnell*

✔**Dublin, Max.**
Futurehype: The Tyranny of Prophecy.
Dutton, $19.95 (0-525-24968-0). 288p.

Modern fortune-tellers here run head on into an intelligent skeptic. Dublin, a Canadian sociologist, disputes the predictions as well as the moral authority of John Naisbitt, Alvin Toffler, Herman Kahn, James Burnham, Henry Kissinger and all the other secular prophets who have made a living by telling us what tomorrow will bring. Dublin is particularly unrelenting in his attack upon the claims to scientific expertise and numerical precision made by twentieth-century seers. Because policymakers and legislators often rely on scenarios for the future, such scenarios can become self-fulfilling in ways that compromise the freedom of individuals and of democratic governments. Fixation on supposed waves of the future may create a sterile uniformity in culture and thought, Dublin warns. As an antidote to contemporary credulity, the author reminds readers of the need for ethical reflection and historical perspective. —*Bryce Christensen*

Social & Political Issues

✔**Ehrenhalt, Alan.**
The United States of Ambition: Politicians, Power, and the Pursuit of Office.
Times Books, $23 (0-8129-1894-0). 320p.

Among the many memorable lines in *Butch Cassidy and the Sundance Kid*, the one that resounds through contemporary consciousness is Sundance's query about the huge, mysterious posse that dogs the duo during the movie's big chase sequence—to wit, "Who are those guys?" Ehrenhalt answers that question as it applies to the new generation of politicians. Bolstering his argument with case studies of political change at the city council, county commission, state legislative, and congressional levels, he gives the answer the Kid should've got: "They're professionals pursuing their trade." Unlike the possemen, today's pols aren't hired guns. They're self-chosen—entrepreneurs whose specialty is campaigning and whose rationale is the belief that government is good (which is why virtually none are thorough conservatives). They are animated by the egalitarianism, individualism, and candor that became standards of public service in the wake of the elitism, cabalism, and deceit perceived to have eventuated in Vietnam and Watergate. But they won't be led and they won't defer, which means they're often incapable of the give and take necessary to such matters as formulating a budget. In Ehrenhalt's accomplished hands (oh, he could have made his argument with fewer of them, but his case studies are little gems of political history), these guys are more intriguing than they'll probably ever be on the news. —*Ray Olson*

✔**Faludi, Susan.**
Backlash: The Undeclared War against American Women.
Crown, $24 (0-517-57698-8). 544p. index.

Pulitzer Prize–winning journalist Faludi's fiery, scintillating cultural report starts with a big bang. She declares that the man shortage (virtually dooming educated women over 30 to spinsterhood), the dire poverty brought upon women by no-fault divorce laws, the infertility epidemic (aka the biological clock syndrome) afflicting women over 30, and the emotional depression and burnout rampant among single and career women all "have one thing in common: they aren't true." Blasting to smithereens (with genuine statistical evidence) the claptrap upon which those Reagan '80s myths were based is, however, just her opening salvo. In the three fat succeeding parts of her scrupulously and exhaustively documented tome, she notes the 1980s rise of not just anti-feminism but downright misogyny in popular culture, politics and public discourse, and the everyday lives of American women. This is all delicious reading for its contentiousness, its rooting out of lies and hidden agendas, and its scoring of points against misogynist spokespersons including (their characterizations are in accord with Faludi's depictions of them) sad-sack male feminist turncoat Warren Farrell, phony scholar Allan Bloom, and inane New Age "masculinist" huckster Robert Bly. Her book is not an analysis but a presentation of evidence that can only properly be refuted by factually sounder evidence that she is sure does not exist. What does exist is male overreaction to women's tiniest gains in social, economic, and political equality, as well as male violence, mendacity, and powermongering. This almost literally dynamite book deserves the largest possible readership, not least because it tells what so many, looking about them with candid eyes, see so clearly: male sexism, not feminism, is running rampant, despoiling every ideal worth professing. —*Ray Olson*

Fiske, Edward B.
Smart Schools, Smart Kids: Why Do Some Schools Work?
Simon & Schuster, $22.95 (0-671-69063-9). 270p. index.

Fiske, education correspondent for the *New York Times*, presents an optimistic overview of some alternatives to what he calls the outmoded "factory model" of public school education that predominates in this country. He looks at schools that have decentralized management, adopted shared decision making, rearranged their schedules, and developed new standards of accountability. In practice this might mean, for example, a new role for the principal, a longer school year, or children being evaluated on the basis of a videotaped performance rather than a written test. In the "factory model," children sit passively and wait for the teacher to fill them up with knowledge, like so many widgets in an assembly line. Fiske offers new technology—computers in the classroom—as one of the components that can help the teacher become a coach instead. His anecdotal evidence of new approaches already in place in schools across the U.S. is attractive, if not conclusive, proof of his thesis that these are the essential steps toward a comprehensive restructuring of the nation's educational system. Fiske admits that there is no consensus among teachers or administrators regarding the solution to the schools' problems, and he looks for political support from universities and the corporate community. —*Anne Schmitt*

Flynn, John C.
Cocaine: An In-depth Look at the Facts, Science, History and Future of the World's Most Addictive Drug.
Birch Lane, $18.95 (1-55972-060-3). 192p. index.

Believing that what the average American hears—"just say no" and lurid details of the nation's ghetto-crack problem—isn't nearly adequate, Flynn can't say enough about cocaine. First off, he says that viewing cocaine as just another part of the nation's drug problem is outrageous and does a major disservice. It is the most highly addictive drug, he argues, quickly and insidiously stimulating the body's pleasure receptors and capable, in some cases, of causing almost instant addiction. In his book, he delves into the science of cocaine, along the way imparting the drug's infamous history from Sherlock Holmes' rhapsodies to Sigmund Freud's experiments to several addicts' ravages. He concludes with a discourse on social action and recommendations for dealing with U.S. drug problems. Never clever or cute, Flynn's serious book is a good step up from and beyond the cocaine reporting of the popular media. —*Mary Ellen Sullivan*

Social & Political Issues

Fontana, Vincent J. and Moolman, Valerie.
Save the Family, Save the Child: What We Can Do to Help Children at Risk.
Dutton, $19.95 (0-525-24989-3). 320p. index.

This is a fiercely angry book: angry at the political hypocrisy, interagency squabbling, and public indifference that make child abuse a "sometime" issue. It is also a hopeful book, however. Fontana, author of the 1973 best-seller *Somewhere a Child Is Crying* and veteran of more than 20 years at New York Foundling Hospital and its affiliates, feels the time has come for a "total, integrated plan" to pull together federal, state, city, professional, community, and family resources around new strategies to prevent abuse. We know enough about the roots of child abuse, Fontana argues, to support families at risk before they become abusive. Every family needs more help and support from its community, the parents, employers, even the media, to function healthily. And government agencies at all levels need to bring together in every neighborhood a "complete package of essential human services" so that teams of professionals (in medicine, child care, education, and law) can work together to "stop the hurting and start the healing." Fontana's second book is an eloquent and impassioned plea for America's children. —*Mary Carroll*

Forst, Martin L. and Blomquist, Martha-Elin.
Missing Children: Rhetoric and Reality.
Lexington, $22.95 (0-669-24418-X). 301p. index.

Two seasoned experts in criminal justice and social policy here provide the first-ever thoroughly researched, well-documented discussion of the true nature and extent of our nation's missing children problem. Their wholly credible findings are both eye-opening and reassuring. The media, politicians, and special-interest groups, argue the authors, have greatly exaggerated the number of American children abducted by strangers each year. Annual estimates are that 105 children in the U.S. and Canada are kidnapped and killed by strangers, while the thousands of other missing children are runaways or victims of parental abductions. The authors meticulously examine the legal, political, and social issues related to all types of missing children and take great pains to define each legal category of "missing" children. Included are numerous case histories, easy-to-digest statistics, carefully drawn historical parallels to modern-day crimes, the cold, hard facts about why law enforcement's hands are tied in the search for missing children, and the reasons behind the public's distorted perceptions of how much—or how little—child-search organizations have really contributed toward solving this new social problem. A lucid, groundbreaking, information-packed handbook that belongs on every library's shelves and in the hands of all who confront this problem every day, including parents. —*Mary Banas*

Fried, Charles.
Order and Law: Arguing the Reagan Revolution: A Firsthand Account.
Simon & Schuster, $19.95 (0-671-72575-0). 245p. index.

One of the Reaganauts who fought the agendas and orthodoxies he brands as "left-liberal," Fried did battle at the U.S. Justice Department. On the legal front he took on the Supreme Court, which in his view had become a target-rich environment occupied by enemies such as employment quotas, *Roe* v. *Wade*, and rubbery judicial edicts that promoted the "welfare-bureaucratic state." Attacking the latter may account for the trench-warfare tenor of Fried's story—laying the strategy for bringing up test cases, arguing with colleagues even more doctrinaire than he, and defeating the liberal opponents of Reaganism, whom he viewed as using the courts for promoting socioeconomic goals inimical to individual freedom. Whatever one's position on that charge, Fried's clarity of expression is well suited to nonlawyers. —*Gilbert Taylor*

Garment, Suzanne.
Scandal: The Culture of Mistrust in American Politics.
Times Books, $23 (0-8129-1942-4). 336p. index.

Special prosecutors, inspectors general, investigative reporters, congressional staffers—these are the characters who, since their crudescence in the post-Watergate reforms, have been censorious in the ceaseless quest to eradicate moral turpitude from public life. Thanks to their diligence and dedication, the government is daily saved from sinking into a den of iniquity, and this tome catalogs dozens of their noble and selfless conquests, which saved us from the baleful likes of malefactors named Bert Lance (corrupt banker), Hamilton Jordon (cocaine snorter), Richard Allen (Reaganite bribe-taker), Raymond Donovan (same), Geraldine Ferraro (spouse of real-estate shark), Theodore Olson (liar to Congress), and Oliver North (same). The members of this group share one thing in common: *none of them* was ever legally convicted of *anything*, yet they all spent *years* fending off the original charges. By then, though, the press is onto the next case, having satisfied its absolutist ethic of the public's right-to-know, hardly aware of the tenet's collision with the often and unctuously proclaimed right of privacy. Is the government run more honestly as the result of these inquisitions? No, says Garment; instead, we get ever more draconian strictures on official behavior. Of course, scandalmongers express benign and generally accepted purposes for their actions—ridding the public morals of sexual harassment, for instance. The treatment meted out to Supreme Court nominee Clarence Thomas (unfortunately, too late to be included in this book) was a bomb thrown at our depraved political culture. —*Gilbert Taylor*

✓Garreau, Joel.
Edge City: Life on the New Frontier.
Doubleday, $22.50 (0-385-26249-3). 526p. index.

As in his first book, *The Nine Nations of North America*, this senior writer for the *Washington Post* uses demographics to explain American life-styles.

Social & Political Issues

Here, he posits that the American city as we know it—Manhattan, for example—has become obsolete (in fact, the last one built was Detroit). These days, Americans live in Edge Cities, which surround our old downtowns and surpass them in population and the amount of office, retail, residential, and most importantly, parking space. "Ample free parking is the touchstone distinction between Edge City and the old downtown." Garreau's aim is not to attack developers and residents of sprawling strip malls and office parks, but rather to explain the population shift of the last 20 years as a tribute to American individualism and determination to control the quality of their lives. In 1978, for example, women went to work in extraordinary numbers (and bought cars to get there). Businesses had to respond to the needs of mothers who could not afford the time it took to commute into the city. In response, CEOs moved their offices to accommodate the needs of this new work force, and Edge Cities were born. The author sparks his text with humor, e.g., the developer's rallying cry: "1 worker = 1 car = 1 parking space." Individual chapters discuss the Edge Cities that have sprung up around New York, Boston, Detroit, Atlanta, Phoenix, Dallas, Houston, Los Angeles, San Francisco, and Washington, D.C. Sure to be the subject of features in the "Living" sections of many major newspapers. —*Kathryn LaBarbera*

Geoghegan, Thomas.
Which Side Are You On? Trying to Be for Labor When It's Flat on Its Back.
Farrar, $19.95 (0-374-28919-0). 267p.

Millions of Americans can't spell the word *union*; this ignorance is a cause as well as an effect of the devastating drop in U.S. labor union membership (from one-third to one-sixth of the work force) over the past 30 years. Labor lawyer Geoghegan argues that most Americans (even those who *support* labor) don't realize that the legislation and court decisions of the decades after World War II are more important than global economic trends in shifting the current balance of bargaining power from labor to management. This is not another 1960s activist's memoirs; without ever quite *deciding* to make labor law his specialty, Geoghegan went from Harvard Law to the United Mine Workers reform-slate staff and then became involved in many of the most interesting labor fights of the past quarter-century. Vivid anecdotes and solid analysis blend in this important contribution to the debate on the future of America's economy (and its democracy). —*Mary Carroll*

Gordon, Suzanne.
Prisoners of Men's Dreams: Striking Out for a New Feminine Future.
Little, Brown, $19.95 (0-316-32106-0). 352p. index.

A funny thing happened to the feminist revolution on the way to the marketplace: it got waylaid. Gordon contends that today's suit-wearing woman, who works late hours while paying others to raise her children, was not the goal two decades ago. Even less did mid-century reformers aim at a world where one third of the workers go without health insurance, millions work at more than two jobs just to squeeze by, and women nightly go home to the "second shift" of housework, which leaves them feeling like they're "walking a tightrope." In documenting this bleak view of a social movement's co-optation, Gordon does not, thankfully, blame feminists for the disappearance of values traditionally nurtured by women, although who *is* to blame is a bit unclear. Gordon isn't strong on solutions, either, although she acknowledges the obvious fact that women retreating en masse from the workplace to garden and suckle simply isn't possible. Yet by documenting the problem in excruciating detail, and with the help of testimony by hundreds of women, Gordon enters into public debate the frustration of balancing freedom and economic independence with friendship and nurturance. An important book. —*Pat Monaghan*

Gunn, Christopher and Gunn, Hazel Dayton.
Reclaiming Capital: Democratic Initiatives and Community Development.
Cornell, $24.95 (0-8014-2323-6); paper, $9.95 (0-8014-9574-1). 184p. index.

The wealth gap between the haves and have-nots is ever-growing, and people in communities across this rich nation are finding their quality of life plummet and basic needs (shelter, health care, transportation) dangling beyond their grasp. In a time when faith in a beneficent capital class is justifiably waning, the Gunns have compiled this informative, useful survey of the "whys, whats, and hows" of community development through community empowerment. *Reclaiming Capital* focuses beyond "gross" and "net" to the surplus product that the Gunns call "social surplus." Any substantive community progress must follow grass-roots initiatives to procure and use this surplus. Development banks, credit unions, and collectives are discussed as well as more theoretical points of economy and society. These are accompanied by a varied, full bibliography. This book could be such a powerful tool (when accompanied by more "hands-on" guides) that its advanced terminology and sometimes difficult, abstract language should not be a barrier to acquisition. This book serves well for community discussion groups and should be available to all public library patrons. —*Angus Trimnell*

Halberstam, David.
The Next Century.
Morrow, $16.95 (0-688-10391-X). 224p.

In this lucid but jolting extended essay, Pulitzer Prize–winning commentator Halberstam reviews and ruminates on the major issues facing the U.S. today—issues that not only are agents of our current social, political, and economic climates, but that also must be faced squarely if improvement in our national life is to occur. While no doom-and-gloomer, Halberstam nonetheless sees the need for improvement. The "unraveling" of communism and the termination of the cold war leads him to ponder the giant that the U.S. must now come to understand more clearly: Japan. Citing reasons behind Japan's economic superiority leads Halberstam to launch stiff words against our own educational and industrial systems. He offers no quick solutions but instead presents revisionist philosophical underpinnings. Given Halberstam's best-selling status, this pungent little book should garner widespread attention. —*Brad Hooper*

Heller, Mark A. and Nusseibeh, Sari.
No Trumpets, No Drums: A Two-State Settlement of the Israeli-Palestinian Conflict.
Hill & Wang, $18.95 (0-8090-7393-5). 135p. index.

Brought together by the Foundation for Mideast Peace to work through possible solutions to the technical issues any serious Israeli-Palestinian negotiation will need to address, Heller and Nusseibeh are Harvard Ph.D.'s (the former in political science, the latter in philosophy) affiliated with Tel Aviv University and Bir Zeit University, respectively. They approached their collaboration with doubt and profoundly different histories, perceptions, and attitudes but had a common goal: to establish an agenda and suggest practical steps that could allow a viable Palestinian state to coexist with a secure Israel. Heller and Nusseibeh discuss specific security arrangements, the location and practical effect of borders, relocation problems (for both Palestinian refugees and Israeli settlers), local and region-wide agreements on water usage, and the significance of Jerusalem to both Israel and Palestine. By spelling out the complexity of a two-state settlement and outlining practical agreements that could make it a reality, *No Trumpets, No Drums* makes a major contribution to an essential dialogue. —*Mary Carroll*

Hewlett, Sylvia Ann.
When the Bough Breaks: The Cost of Neglecting Our Children.
Basic Books, $22.95 (0-465-09165-2). 336p. index.

In this landmark study, economist Hewlett, former director of the Economic Policy Council, takes a hard-eyed, bottom-line-oriented look at the increasingly fractured lives children in the 1990s are being forced to lead because of divorce, poverty, absentee parents, violence, neglect, and a host of other societal ills. Her solution? Political leaders and corporate America *must* develop practical policies and programs (and provide the financial means) to help take care of our nation's children, for doing so will "add to the productive capability of the economy" in the long run, she argues. To bolster her argument, Hewlett jam-packs her book with hard-to-ignore facts, statistics, cause-and-effect scenarios, and, always the economist, dollars and "sense" perspicacity. This is one solid, meaty book, almost encyclopedic in its recitation of studies and intriguing cost-benefit analyses of some very urgent human dilemmas. Very accessible and utterly convincing—a "must" for all libraries. By the author of *A Lesser Life: The Myth of Women's Liberation in America.* Notes. —*Mary Banas*

Hine, Thomas.
Facing Tomorrow: What the Future Has Been, What the Future Can Be.
Knopf, $22 (0-394-57785-X). 253p. index.

Hine, author of *Populuxe*, states that "the present seems to be working so badly we can't bear to think about the future." But think, and act, we must, if there is to be a future, and Hine believes we are at a point where individual actions and a reasoned, "subtle" shaping of our goals are necessary to provide for one. In a sober, intelligent voice, Hine examines the history of the future—from a biblical prophet's warnings to General Motor's Futuramas, which, naturally, urged automobile consumption as the way to go—and the present, with technological advances, from computers to biotechnology, affecting every aspect of life. In chapters exploring the environment, including work and home, utopias, the homeless and Yuppies, the irony of increasing illiteracy in the "information age," space travel, and more, Hine offers both a description and a prescription, ways to balance the ideas that "nothing is new" and "everything changes" and to use what amazing tools we have to expand our options, not limit them. Includes readings and source list. —*Eloise Kinney*

Hite, Shere and Colleran, Kate.
Good Guys, Bad Guys: The Hite Guide to Smart Choices.
Carroll & Graf, $18.95 (0-88184-686-4). 288p.

The battle of the sexes, round four, as refereed by Hite and Colleran. Round one: *The Hite Report: A Nationwide Survey on Female Sexuality.* Round two: *The Hite Report on Male Sexuality.* Round three: *The Hite Report on Women and Love.* This time, though, the authors are writing not about sex, not about love, but about that nebulous contemporary phenomenon, the relationship, as they ask why women are stereotyped as such emotional wimps when it comes to men. With the help of 15 years of statistical research, the authors transform themselves from George Gallup, Jr., into Ann Landers, lending a mutual shoulder to cry on, whispering comforting justifications, and supplying any number of retorts and rejoinders for masculine swinishness. Quote after quote from the victims documents the miserable condition of male-female relations, from the pressing question of how far a woman should go on the first date to who should provide for birth control to the universal demonstration that all men are scum. There's also a militant feminist cast to this tome, in its suggestions that not only is it okay not to have a man in your life, but that maybe women should rely solely on other women for friendship— and perhaps more. And although the book proclaims itself a roadmap for relationships in the 1990s, it was originally published as a paperback in Great Britain in 1989 and really seems to be mired in the sexual politics of the 1960s, even if the main sexual topic in this updated edition is now the threat of AIDS rather than the exact location of the G-spot. (Maybe what Hite and Colleran need are one or two of Robert Bly's wild men to show them what *real* sensitivity is.) —*John Brosnahan*

Hoeveler, J. David.
Watch on the Right: Conservative Intellectuals in the Reagan Era.
Univ. of Wisconsin, $24.95 (0-299-12810-5). 348p. index.

For Americans beginning to debate the historical significance of the Reagan years, Hoeveler identifies the key intellectual issues by examining eight prominent conservative thinkers. Only one of the figures considered—Jeane Kirkpatrick—has assumed direct political responsibilities. But all eight helped create the cultural zeitgeist that put Ronald Reagan in the White House. Because he focuses on political controversy, the author looks not at academic intellectuals but rather primarily at public polemicists, such as

Social & Political Issues

William F. Buckley, George Will, Michael Novak, and R. Emmett Tyrrell. Himself a historian, Hoeveler treats his subjects with sympathy but critical intelligence, exposing not only personal contradictions and inconsistencies, but also internal tensions and paradoxes in the conservative movement itself. Readers will find insights not only into the disputes that separate conservatives from liberals, but also into the internecine wars between neoconservatives and paleoconservatives, between libertarians and traditionalists. —*Bryce Christensen*

Hutchinson, Earl Ofari.
The Mugging of Black America.
African American Images, paper, $8.95 (0-913543-21-7). 120p.

A candid, firsthand account of the realities, myths, and lies that define blacks as perpetrators of crime, the victims of crime, and the casualties of the criminal justice system. Hutchinson has written an angry book that explores the roots of crime in slavery, the failures of the Reagan-Bush administrations, the damage done to the black image in the media, the drug crisis, and the problem of "black on black" crime. The author offers some solid guidelines for community organization and action, stating that the answers lie within the community itself, e.g., community protection councils, police-community partnerships, innovative and aggressive educational and support programs, all of which will encourage and guide the individual and the community toward self-esteem and self-sufficiency. Contains statistical information and bibliography. —*Jane Jurgens*

Ishihara, Shintaro.
The Japan That Can Say No.
Simon & Schuster, $18.95 (0-671-72686-2). 148p.

This is the approved, public translation of the little book that caused such a flap when a "vile, error-filled" (says Ishihara), Pentagon-funded, secret version of it was leaked while it circulated amongst congresspersons. The military bureaucracy represented Ishihara's argument for an independent Japanese defense policy as evidence of a renewed "yellow peril" to white, Christian America. Reading Ishihara as he wants to be read, it's hard not to nod in agreement not only with his ideas about Japan assuming its fair share of defense but also with his criticisms of U.S. racism in Asian relations, of the greed and shortsightedness of U.S. business executives, of U.S. policy toward the Philippines (he, like that nation's rebels, advocates redistributing the land), and much else. No crude Uncle Sam basher, Ishihara is much harder on his own country for its toadying to the U.S. when it should, by his lights, be negotiating as an equally powerful partner due to Japan's high-tech industrial might. Indeed, the author envisions Japan and the U.S. constituting a "Group of Two" that ought to be, as one chapter subtitle styles it, "The Major Players in the New Era" born out of the collapse of communism. To further that partnership, Ishihara forwards plenty of suggestions for Japan's use and "An Agenda for America" that often sounds strikingly like what many homegrown critics have been telling us for years. —*Ray Olson*

Social & Political Issues

✓**Kotlowitz, Alex.**
There Are No Children Here: The Story of Two Boys Growing Up in the Other America.
Doubleday, $21.95 (0-385-26526-3). 336p.

Three years ago, Kotlowitz wrote a series of *Wall Street Journal* articles profiling the squalid living conditions in a Chicago housing project, with special focus on two brothers who lived there. This volume expands the author's original pieces into a full-blown account and features extensive new first- and secondhand research. The reader witnesses two years in the lives of Lafeyette and Pharoah Rivers (12 and 9, respectively) and their mother, LaJoe, as they fight the daily battle against drugs, violence, and the treadmill economic existence of welfare. Here in the Henry Horner Homes, friends die from gunshot wounds, LaJoe's older son, Terence, goes to prison for armed robbery, the Department of Public Aid investigates the family's eligibility claims (with an eye toward cutting them off the dole), gangs and cocaine are on the loose, unmarried teenage girls become mothers many times over, and young black males are the statistical fuel line that feeds a shocking school drop-out rate. While Kotlowitz quite correctly puts all of this into the greater context of the 1950s public housing debacle, the sorry state of Chicago's public schools, and the continuing problem of the lack of male role models in the African American community, he doesn't really offer solutions. And while there are bright spots even among the poverty and waste—Lafeyette manages to avoid serious trouble, Pharoah proves to be a wizard at spelling, and both receive educational assistance from Kotlowitz himself—the plight of the ghetto-bound as a whole remains stagnant, while the projects face nearby gentrification and new-money business schemes that threaten to displace them. In its liberal-minded spirit, this true-life story grasps the universal by exposing the particular. Alas, it also appears to prove the claim that, 25 years after LBJ's Great Society initiatives were begun, money's not the solution to societal ills. —*Martin Brady*

✓**Kozol, Jonathan.**
Savage Inequalities.
Crown, $20 (0-517-58221-X). 288p. index.

In what must be the most depressing book of the year, the man whose National Book Award–winning *Death at an Early Age* was one spur to the alternative education movement of the late 1960s reports that the life-wasting, de facto segregation he observed 25 years ago in Boston's schools is still with us. In chapters concentrating upon the appalling schools of East St. Louis, North Lawndale and the South Side in Chicago, the South Bronx and Central Harlem in New York, Camden (N.J.), Washington, D.C., and San Antonio, Kozol challenges repeatedly the current wisdom that putting more money into public schools will do no good. At the least, more money will fix busted toilets, decaying ceilings and walls, broken windows and stairs, or heating and cooling systems that either don't work or work erratically, turning some classrooms into sweatboxes, others into refrigerators; it will at least begin to make these schools minimally comfortable places for learning. At

Social & Political Issues

best, money distributed equitably might give poor children, who are over-whelmingly black and Hispanic, something approaching the level playing field in life that gets so much political lip service. But there's no sign that such evenhanded school financing is forthcoming. Kozol has to admit, and he does so almost apologetically, that despite "a deep-seated reverence for fair play in the United States," in education "we want the game to be unfair and we have made it so; and it will likely so remain." Well, the pledge of allegiance says we stand for liberty and justice; it doesn't say we stand for equality, does it? —*Ray Olson*

Lang, Susan S.
Women without Children: The Reasons, the Rewards, the Regrets.
Pharos, $18.95 (0-88687-532-3). 288p. index.

Lang, author of *Extremist Groups in America* and a forthcoming book on teen violence, is a keen observer of social trends and issues. She will endear herself immediately to readers of this sensitive and frank study in the way she avoids the negative implications of the word *childless*, using the decidedly upbeat term *child-free* instead. While Lang does explore the sorrow and grief infertile women experience, her interviews and research uncovered a high degree of satisfaction and happiness in women who, for one reason or another, have not had children. Lang moves smoothly from the societal context, such as a discussion of women and careers, to the articulate and eye-opening attitudes and goals of individuals. She examines the many reasons and circumstances behind a woman's deliberate decision not to have children or more passive postponement of pregnancy until it's too late. By avoiding generalizations and accepting ambivalence, Lang illuminates the sometimes surprising and stereotype-shattering feelings of child-free women, particular-ly as they grow older. Her investigation embraces the whole of human experience and offers invaluable perspectives on the meaning of family, marriage, love, and freedom. —*Donna Seaman*

Lasch, Christopher.
The True and Only Heaven: Progress and Its Critics.
Norton, $25 (0-393-02916-6). 576p.

The publication of *The True and Only Heaven* could not have come at a better time in American politics—a period when traditional liberal ideas have lost favor at the polls. Lasch—author of the respected *Culture of Narcissism*—offers a thoughtful study concerning the ideas of progress as they developed in liberal thinking in the political and economic arenas of the last century and a half. Contrasted with liberal progress is populism and its ideas on limita-tions, both political and economic. Writers such as Thomas Carlyle, Ralph Waldo Emerson, and William James are cited here as men who cautioned society against unrealistic expectations. Calamities of war, environmental decay, destructive trends in the family, dangerous court intrusions altering societal values, and insatiable consumerism speak to the need for restraint and the importance of heeding thinkers like Emerson, who preached workmanship, morality, loyalty, belief in heroes, and a healthy skepticism of progress. The lower middle class, despite being narrow and parochial, according to Lasch, still seems to support these values. Any book that ranges across such broad cultural developments is bound to have contestable ideas. Is abortion only a class issue? Is Emerson of heroic stature? And just what *is* the new class? Lasch's sociological jargon may bog down some readers, but otherwise this book is highly recommended. (Perhaps politicians will read it and have something different to say in the next national campaign.) —*Eugene Sullivan*

Maltz, Wendy.
The Sexual Healing Journey: A Guide for Survivors of Sexual Abuse.
HarperCollins, $19.95 (0-06-016661-4). 352p. index.

Sex therapist and family counselor Maltz, who was a date-rape victim in graduate school, speaks to other sexual abuse survivors in this sexual healing self-help guide. The symptoms of sexual abuse are listed before wide-ranging case histories back up checklists and questions that accompany the logically arranged information. As with so many other behavior problems, the first key to recovery for the victim is to acknowledge the sexual abuse experiences. The author's ultimate goal is to help readers achieve an intimate, caring, respectful relationship with a sexual partner. In order to help with this, various intimacy and touching exercises are included. Not written in a quick-fix, pop-psychology style, this is a thoughtfully composed introduction to a serious problem, which may require professional therapy. Includes an extensive list of helpful resources.
—*Sue-Ellen Beauregard*

Marsh, Dave and others.
50 Ways to Fight Censorship: And Important Facts to Know about the Censors.
Thunder's Mouth, paper, $5.95 (1-56025-011-9). 144p. index.

With the aid of 25 other contributors credited as "friends" on the title page, rock chronicler Marsh proffers practical ways for anyone of school age on up to defend freedom of speech. His 50 suggestions begin with "The Single Most Important Thing You Can Do—Speak Out!" They proceed through such "Things You Can Do by Yourself" as voting, teaching children how to spot censorship, writing letters to several different kinds of influential recipients (e.g., legislators, newspapers, movie moguls), getting to know the major censorship groups, supporting and/or joining anticensorship organizations, getting involved with one's library, even running for office against an anti-free-speech incumbent. The last 20 suggestions are for "Things You Can Do with Others," from organizing voter-registration drives to bringing lawsuits against censors. Each suggestion's entry includes a rationale for doing it, how-to advice, and, often as not, both the story of someone who succeeded at it and a little list of helpful resources. For lovers of the First Amendment, this is the book of the year, maybe of the decade. —*Ray Olson*

Miedzian, Myriam.
Boys Will Be Boys: How We Encourage Violence in Our Sons and What We Can Do to Stop It.
Doubleday, $20 (0-385-23932-7). 368p.

An important, ground-breaking exploration of how and why American males are increasingly turning to violence and what we, as individuals and as a society, can do about it. Lucid, well researched, and highly practical, this very accessible book will appeal to a broad spectrum of readers, including parents and teachers. Miedzian convincingly demonstrates, drawing heavily on research studies in psychology, sociology, and anthropology, how violence can be greatly reduced in our society, although not completely eradicated. Her discussion is surprisingly objective and well tempered in view of the complexity of volatile issues surrounding her topic. She tackles with equanimity such contributing factors to male aggression as family upbringing, heredity, acculturation, and mass marketing and provides specific recommendations for change both at home and in the schools. Many of the ideas and programs the author describes are very innovative and offer workable solutions, particularly the parenting curriculums now being tried in some inner-city elementary schools on the East Coast. A penetrating study that's certain to become a standard work in the fields of social psychology and cultural anthropology. Contains notes, statistics, and an extensive bibliography. —*Mary Banas*

Miles, Rosalind.
Love, Sex, Death, and the Making of the Male.
Summit, $20 (0-671-74492-5). 262p.

What do Jack the Ripper, Adolf Hitler, and Jeffrey Dahmer have in common? They're men. And they kill. Those two facts are, feminist scholar Miles contends, deeply connected. This disturbing work should be required reading for all those infatuated with the contemporary men's movement, for Miles poses profound questions about the male sexuality and power that movement seeks to revalorize. She ponders the Nussbaum-Steinberg murder case in New York, when "public attention focused on the woman Nussbaum. Why did she stay with Steinberg? Why did she fail to inform the police? One question never seemed to arise. No one, but no one, asked why HE did it." Miles asks, and she answers that our society so confounds maleness with violence that the nonviolent male feels unmanly. Men torment each other in schools, business, and politics, endlessly comparing themselves and their rivals to an imagined omnipotence. If she's short on solutions—to wit, a single page that includes allowing men to "honor their emotions as much as they do their anatomical attributes" (so who's stopping them?)—Miles is long on articulation of the problem. —*Pat Monaghan*

Miller, Henry.
On the Fringe: The Dispossessed in America.
Lexington, $18.95 (0-669-24905-X). 192p. index.

Vagabonds, transients, and hobos tramp through these pages, which reach from the present all the way back to the Black Death of the 1350s. From that vast sweep of time, Miller selects a few episodes and describes the customs and mores of the natives and legal constraints on their movement. For example, he debunks the myths of the Old West, stripping the mask from the jut-jawed Marlboro man who stares stoically into the distance, asserting that he was just a wage serf who didn't even own his own horse. He was part of the vast "residuum" of surplus labor needed by every economic epoch, a figure alternately envied by society for his perceived freedom or stigmatized for his loose morals and marbles. Miller proceeds to describe the convulsive atmosphere of the Great Depression and then ties his themes into a happening of great social significance—San Francisco's 1967 Summer of Love. The coverage of that subject, along with a narrow case study of Bay Area street people in 1973, constitutes the hook of originality public libraries look for. —*Gilbert Taylor*

Millman, Marcia.
Warm Hearts and Cold Cash: The Intimate Dynamics of Families and Money.
Free Press, $19.95 (0-02-921285-5). 240p. index.

Much of sociology is devoted to analyzing and explaining popular observation. Millman, chair of sociology at the University of California at Santa Cruz, has previously examined obesity in the U.S. in *Such a Pretty Face* (Norton, 1980) and health care delivery in *The Unkindest Cut* (Morrow, 1977). Now she considers the role of money in family life. Because money can be counted but love cannot be measured, the two often become confused. Millman spent several months observing court battles over contested wills and divorces. She contends that the key to helping dysfunctional families is to observe how they handle, use, spend, or withhold money. Like her earlier works, this book is perceptive, fascinating, and thorough. —*David Rouse*

Mones, Paul A.
When a Child Kills: Abused Children Who Kill Their Parents.
Pocket, $21 (0-671-67420-X). 297p.

Mones, a children's rights advocate, presents a disturbing look at the crime of parricide. In his studies of children and their parents, the author has found that when a child murders one or both parents, the abuse of the child by the parent was usually severe. In eight separate case studies, he deals with boys and girls who kill their fathers or mothers and children who kill both parents or who hire others to commit the parricide. Mones observes that the crime of parricide is committed less by daughters than by sons on either parent, bearing out the statistic that only "10% of all violent crimes are committed by women." Included are an essay on "The Legacy of Child Abuse" and a final plea for better, more effective strategies of intervention. Disturbing reading but highly recommended. —*Jane Jurgens*

Social & Political Issues

Nixon, Nicholas and Nixon, Bebe.
People with AIDS.
Godine/Imago Mundi, $45 (0-87923-908-5); paper, $25 (0-87923-886-0).
160p.

One review of the exhibition to which this book is adjunct remarked that the depiction of persons with AIDS has become a grisly minor industry among artists. From the ruck of AIDS pictures, Nicholas Nixon's rise secure in their artistry and their power. A photographer whose technique is acceded to be practically peerless, Nixon uses a big old view camera and black-and-white film to produce images of incredible clarity, tonal richness, and composure. His work before this series was also marked by fineness of composition. Not that these portraits of 15 AIDS sufferers taken at regular intervals to disclose both the ravages of disease and the persistence of personality are not well composed. Rather, their formal properties are overwhelmed by those ravages and that persistence. Nixon shot his subjects very close, so that they register with as much immediacy as possible—the next best thing to being present in the flesh. They are distinctive persons—even if the accompanying text consisting of their own and others' (lovers, parents, siblings) statements is necessary to make them really come to life—and confronting them in the predicaments they're so horrifyingly, visibly in is to face the death that stalks us each. Will we look this bad? Will we look this good—enduring, present to the end? (All proceeds from this book will be given to the Hospice at Mission Hill in Boston.) —*Ray Olson*

Prothrow-Stith, Deborah and Weissman, Michaele.
Deadly Consequences.
HarperCollins, $22.50 (0-06-016344-5). 224p. index.

This is one of the first book-length studies of violence among young adult males, aged 15 to 24, to treat its subject as a public-health issue. This innovative approach to an intractable social problem that's been "talked to death" offers new hope and fresh, workable solutions. The author is the former public health commissioner of Massachusetts and is currently a top administrator at the Harvard School of Public Health, where she is concentrating on designing a wide-ranging violence prevention curriculum for implementation in schools nationwide. The first half of this clear, straightforward book reviews the roots of violence, especially among the highest risk group—poor, young black males. This standard discussion of how TV and other popular media, family environment, and the community setting influence violence is enlivened by gripping, real-life vignettes, hard-hitting facts and statistics, and accessible psychosocial interpretations. The volume's second half details the programs and activities that are being tried in a range of settings to stem the growing tide of violence. Should be on every library's shelf. —*Mary Banas*

✓**Rifkin, Jeremy.**
Biosphere Politics: A New Consciousness for a New Century.
Crown, $20 (0-517-57746-1). 416p.

Driven to extreme measures in a futile quest for security, humanity has sought to dominate its environment by what Rifkin calls the enclosure (the exploitation, privatization, and commodification) of the global commons ("the land masses, oceans, atmosphere, electromagnetic spectrum, and gene pool"). No longer content with serving nature, humankind was determined to control it. To accomplish this daunting task, it was necessary to create the nation-state, the military-industrial complex, the multinational corporation, and all the apparatus that goes with them. Rifkin depicts modern man as Icarus, who, in his arrogance, attempts to become like God, thus bringing the world to the brink of annihilation. Technology, in its endeavor to give us autonomy, Rifkin writes, has isolated us instead, severing our ties with our past and with the earth, resulting in the suppression of our senses and an unprecedented environmental crisis. "The more we possess, the more we are possessed," he writes. According to Rifkin, only the current movement to reopen the global commons offers salvation. Rifkin, author of the acclaimed *Entropy*, offers a history, science, and economics lesson in an immensely provocative examination of the state of things and how we got there. —*Benjamin Segedin*

Sabato, Larry J.
Feeding Frenzy: How Attack Journalism Has Transformed American Politics.
Free Press, $22.95 (0-02-927635-7). 336p. index.

Sabato, a professor of government at the University of Virginia, provides an intriguing analysis of how today's press has abdicated its role as public watchdog and become something of a bloodthirsty bulldog eager for sport and spectacle. Sabato's emotionally loaded discussion clearly is aimed at John Q. Public, but even logical readers will be persuaded by the author's well-founded argument that the democratic process is being undermined because meaningful news and commentary on issues of real consequence are increasingly overshadowed by political pseudoscandals à la Gary Hart, Geraldine Ferraro, Jim Wright, et al. As a result, he says, even when the press does attempt thorough, balanced coverage, politicians avoid speaking openly for fear of being misrepresented; thus, the public is further deprived of the facts it needs to make informed choices. *Feeding Frenzy* is based on frank discussions with more than 150 broadcast and print journalists and dozens of political insiders and consultants and includes numerous quotes, case studies, and a brief history of modern American political journalism. Crisp, colorful, and unfailingly provocative, this information-packed volume is certain to spark much interest and discussion. —*Mary Banas*

Sander, Joelle.
Before Their Time: Four Generations of Teenage Mothers.
HBJ, $19.95 (0-15-111638-5). 168p.

An engrossing oral history, as told to researcher-therapist Joelle Sander, of the lives of four related black women from succeeding generations who all became teenage mothers. In recording these women's struggles, Sander breathes life into the dry statistics on teenage pregnancy we hear so much about in the media and shows with powerful immediacy the day-to-day dilemmas these "mothers too soon" face. Here we meet firsthand a great-grandmother, a grandmother, a mother, and a daughter from the New York City area whose family dynamic becomes painfully clear in a repetitive cycle of violence, poverty, neglect, and teenage motherhood that typifies the lives of many other young, unwed mothers nationwide. This innovative approach to a significant social issue is more emotionally potent and hard-hitting than any research study could ever hope to be. We glean important insights into how and why some women become caught in the emotional web of adolescent pregnancy. In all, a wrenching, documentary-style account. —*Mary Banas*

Shames, Stephen.
Outside the Dream: Child Poverty in America.
Aperture, $29.95 (0-89381-468-7); paper, $19.95 (0-89381-475-X). 88p.

From 1984 to 1989, photographer Shames traveled the nation taking pictures of children living in severe poverty. This selection from that project is, to an image, sobering, even appalling, as in the photo of a preadolescent boy shooting up drugs, in a sequence showing a man badgering his wife as their child cowers, and in the shot of a little boy seated among old men eating Salvation Army handouts. Writer-teacher Jonathan Kozol's introduction passionately and somewhat despondently acquaints us with the magnitude of child poverty in the U.S., and the afterword by the president of the Children's Defense Fund, which will receive a donation for each copy of this book that is sold, pleads that we do something to help. It all constitutes an eloquent, affecting volume, but one that, unfortunately, will probably be perused only by "bleeding-heart liberals," ignored—out of impotent despair and shame more than callousness—by everyone else. —*Ray Olson*

Simon, David.
Homicide: A Year on the Killing Streets.
Houghton, $24.95 (0-395-48829-X). 599p.

Though Baltimore is one of the smaller big cities, its murder rate per capita—some 250 total per year—ranks it up there with larger urban sinkholes such as Detroit or more notorious death camps such as drug-war-ring Washington, D.C. (the numbers are held down by Baltimore's first-rate trauma centers). For one year, *Baltimore Sun* reporter Simon became an unofficial member of the Baltimore Police Department's Homicide Unit, accompanying jaded but dedicated detectives along the murder beat. What Simon witnessed won't surprise many—an overworked, understaffed, sometimes politically self-conscious force dealing with violent death stemming from pathetic, poverty-induced domestic squabbles, disputes over drugs and drug turf, and, in general, the horrific senselessness of daily life in the urban maelstrom. The latter is perhaps best represented by one case that consumes the time of many of the principals in this chronicle: the unsolved murder of 11-year-old Latonya Wallace, stabbed and left for dead in a Baltimore back alley after paying a visit to the local library. Simon's exhaustive account is certainly comprehensive—we learn in detail how the cops go about their jobs following the trinity of homicide investigation: physical evidence, witnesses, confessions. More important are the insights into their personal lives and how they deal with all the horror. The writing is gritty, sometimes almost beautifully so, though the sheer length of the book may wear down less ambitious readers. Even so, Simon scores big for, if nothing else, his moxie. —*Martin Brady*

Slater, Philip.
A Dream Deferred: America's Discontent and the Search for a New Democratic Ideal.
Beacon, $19.95 (0-8070-4304-4). 222p.

Part joyful prophecy, part jeremiad, *A Dream Deferred* recalls all those impassioned social analyses that made the sixties the sixties—the works of Herbert Marcuse, Norman O. Brown, Paul Goodman, Theodore Roszak, and Charles Reich, not to mention Slater's own best-seller on the hollowness of American individualism, *The Pursuit of Loneliness*. Slater's new book's undergirding argument is that democracy is inevitable, that the "megaculture" of authoritarianism that has prevailed for centuries is giving way to the megaculture of democracy. ("Megaculture" is pretty much what in the sixties we used to call, thanks to Thomas S. Kuhn's *Structure of Scientific Revolutions*, a "paradigm." Plus ça change, plus c'est la même chose.) The U.S., however, is becoming more authoritarian, Slater says, backing up that assertion in 10 chapters of lively complaint that form the book's diagnostic middle section. Each of the 10 takes up a different symptom of authoritarian reaction—militarism, the widening gap between rich and poor, dualistic (*us* v. *them*) official thinking, so-called fundamentalist Christianity, the growth of official secrecy, etc. But if Slater is an impressive diagnostician, so good that his book constitutes an excellent summation of the American progressive political critique, he's not at all prescriptive. He hasn't the foggiest about how to keep the U.S. from goose-stepping down the tubes while the rest of the world effervesces with new freedom. He just hopes the U.S. recaptures its flagging democratic spirit. So do we all. —*Ray Olson*

Smith, Joan.
Misogynies.
Ballantine/Fawcett Columbine, $16.95 (0-449-90591-8). 192p.

This collection of vituperative essays analyzes the depiction of women in books, newspapers, movies, even the Bible. British journalist Smith takes on such films as *Psycho*, *Dressed to Kill*, *Jagged Edge*, and *Fatal Attraction*, finding a particularly insidious strain of sexism in these more "mainstream"

Social & Political Issues

slasher epics, which epitomize "the marketing of female fear as a commodity." In Smith's view, Scott Turow's *Presumed Innocent* is a "lengthy piece of character assassination designed to strip away the glamorous veneer from the single, successful woman and expose the corruption underneath." About Alfred Hitchcock, Smith states, "The stimulus for [his] sheer nastiness to women undoubtedly lies in his solitary and intensely Roman Catholic childhood." And about *Sophie's Choice*, she says, "The model of female sexuality constructed by Styron has nothing to do with real women but exists to legitimize masculine sexual fantasies which are violent, vicious, and ultimately lethal." But men aren't the only ones who get it in this hyperbolic, paranoid, yet compelling thesis. Smith goes on to lambaste Mrs. Thatcher, whose "success lies in her ability to perform a trick, one which is both clever and successful but nevertheless dishonest. . . . [She] has disguised herself as a man . . . who reminds her colleagues that underneath it all she is a capricious, bossy female who is quite prepared to beat them about the head with her handbag." Finally, Smith offers a lengthy examination of the case of Peter Sutcliffe, the Yorkshire Ripper, whom she sees as only an exaggerated form of "men who beat their wives, destroy their self-respect, treat them like dirt." To be sure, Smith is a passionate writer, but what disturbs most about her tirade is the lingering possibility that it's really other women whom she hates and fears the most. —*Martin Brady*

Turner, Stansfield.
Terrorism and Democracy.
Houghton, $21.95 (0-395-43086-0). 259p. index.

The vexatious hostage problem Turner confronted as President Carter's director of the CIA was the seizure by Iranian "students" of the U.S. embassy and staff in 1979. That crisis seems to haunt the memoirs of all of Carter's lieutenants, and this one is no exception. Turner recalls that his recommendations were either to mine Iranian harbors or make a deal with the captors, and here he elaborates the case for bargaining by citing a string of incidents in which presidents stretching back to Jefferson made concessions to free U.S. citizens. The key precedent for his thesis is the Pueblo incident in 1968, in which the U.S. retrieved the crew of a ship captured by the North Koreans by confessing to illegal spying, and then repudiated the statement once the crew was free. But when Turner suggested the same solution to Carter's problem, "the President immediately and peremptorily said, 'You know we can't do that, Stan.'" With Khomeini intransigent, options inevitably whittled down to the rescue mission that ended in humiliating disaster in April 1980, and Turner's post mortem is a withering indictment of the military's failure. Whether or not his acerbic conclusions are intended to deflect criticisms of his own performance at the CIA, they underscore a chronic weakness that supports his position: the U.S., to this day, cannot reliably resort to rescue in lieu of bargaining with terrorists. Thus Turner's work is likely to incite at least as much controversy among military and intelligence experts as did his 1985 book, *Secrecy and Democracy,* but the general public ought to appreciate his skill at simplifying a contentious subject without distorting it. —*Gilbert Taylor*

✓**Wachter, Robert M.**
The Fragile Coalition: Scientists, Activists, and AIDS.
St. Martin's, $19.95 (0-312-05801-2). 288p.

Wachter was the program director of last summer's sixth International Conference on AIDS in San Francisco and as such, the one most responsible for the shape the great confab eventually took. In this book, written with limpid ingenuousness rather than writerly grace or aplomb, he tells the story of that remarkable event, which constantly threatened to degenerate into a shouting match between scientists and activists or disintegrate on account of U.S. travel restrictions on HIV-positive foreigners. For more than a year, the young physician-academic was up to his eyeballs in politics, striving to create a rapprochement—no, a collaboration—between researchers who wanted to exchange meaningful scientific information and ACT-UPers (members of the AIDS Coalition to Unleash Power) who wanted to use the conference to dramatize the urgent needs of people with AIDS. He succeeded almost beyond his fondest hopes, bringing scientists and activists to realize their common ground as battlers against an unprecedentedly gruesome pandemic and against the bigotry and callousness that foster it. He succeeded perhaps, one can't help thinking, because of the magnanimity and modesty that characterize his account, in which he seems never to be the crucial player in any of many, many dramatic crises and in which he voices his own oh-my-gosh reactions to such things as being called by the White House and getting a bodyguard assigned to him. Surprisingly enthralling, often profoundly moving, this is an absolutely essential addition to AIDS literature. —*Ray Olson*

✓**Whitney, Catherine.**
Whose Life? A Balanced, Comprehensive View of Abortion from Its Historical Context to the Current Debate.
Morrow, $20 (0-688-09622-0). 256p. index.

The subtitle of this superb popular history of the U.S. abortion conflict is problematic. Mixing the chronicling of public events with the stories of ordinary women active on both sides of the struggle, the book is admirably comprehensive. It is, however, hardly balanced—i.e., utterly disinterested— in its final effect. Whitney does not find virtue and reason residing in both pro-choice and antiabortion camps in equal proportions. She never impugns antiabortionists' motives or personalities; indeed, the antiabortionist activists upon whom she focuses are notably sympathetic. But the pro-choice foot soldiers are sympathetic, too, and the results of antiabortion activism—the picketed and fire-bombed clinics and their verbally and physically abused clients, the teenagers dead from back-alley abortions undertaken when parents wouldn't consent or couldn't be asked to consent to legal abortion, the parishioners excommunicated for not being politically correct, the medical research and humanitarian foreign aid defunded because it might "encourage" abortion, etc.—as well as the dishonesty of antiabortion propaganda most decidedly are not. The antiabortion movement ultimately appears as deeply misogynist (none of its leaders are women, and its basic assumption is that the life of a fetus is more important than the life of the woman bearing it), antidemocratic, and irresponsible. Highly, unreservedly recommended. —*Ray Olson*

Wilcox, Fred A.
Uncommon Martyrs: The Berrigans, the Catholic Left, and the Plowshares Movement.
Addison-Wesley, $18.95 (0-201-52231-4). 272p. index.

The first Plowshares Movement demonstration occurred in 1980. Invading General Electric's plant in King of Prussia, Pennsylvania, eight of the antiwar activists hammered on the nose cones of nuclear warheads in order to turn those atomic swords into plowshares. *Uncommon Martyrs* is almost a hagiography of these quintessential American Catholic leftists who take Christian teachings literally to heart. Jean and Joe Gump learned their politics in Chicago's radical community. Brian Wilson grew up in a family sympathetic to the American Nazi party but was radicalized in the military in Vietnam. Second-generation Irish American John Grady married third-generation Irish American Teresa after earning a master's in sociology at Fordham; they read Simone Weil, formed antiracist organizations, and met Catholic radicals Dorothy Day and Thomas Merton. They also met Daniel and Philip Berrigan, the subjects of Wilcox's first two chapters, who regard Plowshares as a contemporary avatar of their radical 1960s ideals and tactics. They and their disciples may be political saints, but their politics and courtroom testimony are nothing if not theatrical, and their collective story is at times an unrestrained page-turner. —*Roland Wulbert*

✔Wolf, Naomi.
The Beauty Myth: How Images of Female Beauty Are Used against Women.
Morrow, $21.95 (0-688-08510-5). 327p.

Beauty has been defined in different ways in different times and places, but currently it is epitomized by models 23 per cent thinner than the average woman. Semistarvation diets, extreme exercise regimes, and dangerous, painful surgery are all suffered to achieve a look rarely found in nature. Wolf tracks the development of the latest "official" body type and its emotional, physical, and political ramifications in this bold, passionate, uncompromising, and well-substantiated examination of the fashion imperative. Women have made great progress in the struggle for equal rights, but many experience a backlash of insidious self-criticism and obsession with conforming to the status quo of beauty. Wolf looks back to earlier "ideals" foisted on women and finds that "the beauty myth is always prescribing behavior and not appearance." The behavior dictated to women in our consumer culture is a perverse sort of punishment for success that demands "professionalism" in all realms including looks. Women commit themselves to the requisite thinness and the attempt to thwart the signs of age with a grim, almost cultist fervor. Wolf bemoans this denial of life, pleasure, and that which is truly feminine. She lambastes the glamorization of violence in "beauty pornography" (which has nothing to do with sex, only power), and cites distressing statistics on sex crimes and eating disorders. The pervasiveness of the "ideal" infects women with debilitating insecurities that block the joy and freedom of healthy sexuality and perpetuate the inequality of the sexes. Better than a shelf full of self-help books, this is an invigorating and provocative analysis that will be widely read and discussed. —*Donna Seaman*

✔**Yergin, Daniel.**
The Prize: The Epic Quest for Oil, Money, and Power.
Simon & Schuster, $24.95 (0-671-50248-4). 781p.

A history of our oleaginous age—the prize referred to is petroleum, of course. Its distillates power our cars, heat our homes, propel our ships, put aloft our planes, and enshroud everything in plastic. Unfortunately, the citizenry is only dimly aware of the facts. It takes the effects of some foreign convulsion, such as the quadrupling of oil prices following the Arab embargo of 1973–74 or the war against Iraq, to remind us of the facts; then we sit up and echo the Talking Head's plaintive question:"My God, how did I get here?" Answers abound in Yergin's globe-girdling story that spans the period from the industry's 1859 birth in the upper tributaries of Pennsylvania's Allegheny River right up to its modern epicenter in the sandy wastes of Armenia. In between he covers the industry's critical technical and commercial moments. The author's grand emphasis, however, is less on the buccaneers who turned black gold into bucks than on how oil has been transmuted into the symbol, for any country blessed with or dependent on the viscous stuff, of national power and sovereignty. With many vignettes enlivening Yergin's factual account, this monumental work is both historically significant and tremendously readable. —*Gilbert Taylor*

Sports & Recreation

Aaron, Henry and Wheeler, Lonnie.
I Had a Hammer.
HarperCollins, $21.95 (0-06-016321-6). 352p. index.

Aaron's saga, as told to journalist Wheeler, is a significant piece of sports biography. Though the text moves along deliberately with a minimum of style, the long-overdue story it relates probably tells as much about America and baseball in general as it does about Aaron in particular. Hammerin' Hank was born in Mobile in 1934—poor, black, but crazy about baseball. His tremendous gifts as a hitter brought him to the attention of local scouts, and a stint in the old Negro Leagues with the Indianapolis Clowns brought him to the attention of the Boston Braves (who were soon to move to Milwaukee, and later to Atlanta). Curiously, Aaron's incredible career—which saw him, from 1954 to 1976, break Babe Ruth's all-time home run record, win the Most Valuable Player Award, and appear in many All-Star games, two World Series, and one League Championship Series—seemed to go unnoticed, until the public realized that this was the man who would shatter the Babe's revered mark.

Suddenly, Aaron was receiving hate mail (some of it republished here to good effect) and undergoing the kind of daily scrutiny that would destroy lesser men. But persevere Aaron did—as he had for two decades prior, quietly achieving greatness in the game and striving to express his points of view on racism without jeopardizing the gains he saw African Americans making in the national pastime. Some would perhaps criticize Aaron for not speaking out more boldly, but that wouldn't be giving him credit for being a man of his time. In fact, through example, Aaron led. This is an important, if often unexciting, work, enlivened by many comments from Aaron friends, acquaintances, and colleagues. —*Martin Brady*

Angell, Roger.
Once More around the Park: A Baseball Reader.
Ballantine, $18.95 (0-345-36737-5). 400p.

Angell is well known for his baseball classics (e.g., *The Summer Game, Late Innings, Season Ticket*), which are collections of his work for *New Yorker* magazine (where he is also the fiction editor). Most of the essays gathered here have appeared in other books—in his introduction, Angell calls this a "re-collection"—but five are in book form for the first time. Highlights include an overview of baseball's representation in cinema, a painful account of Pirate pitcher Steve Blass' inexplicable career-ending inability to throw strikes, and a young Vermont couple's mutual love for the game. Angell's fine reputation is deserved and secure; he's observant, analytical, amusing, empathetic, and a fine enough writer to reflect those qualities on paper. It would have been better if there had been more new material here, but recycled Angell is still better than new work from most anybody else. —*Wes Lukowsky*

Creamer, Robert W.
Baseball in '41: A Celebration of the Best Baseball Season Ever—in the Year America Went to War.
Viking, $19.95 (0-670-83374-6). 318p. index.

Readers have endured many published strolls down baseball's Memory Lane recently. And just as one readies a plea of, "Enough already!" Creamer appears. The acclaimed biographer of Babe Ruth and Casey Stengel here eschews the rose-colored lenses favored by many of those who delve into baseball's past. Creamer's premise is simple: 1941 was baseball's greatest season. He presents a sound argument. It was the year DiMaggio hit in 56 consecutive games and Ted Williams batted .406 (the last to hit over .400); there was a high-pressure, season-long pennant race between the Brooklyn Dodgers and the St. Louis Cards, and though the Yankees won the World Series, it was a competitive and exciting set of games. Creamer carefully leads readers through the season, maintaining suspense while placing all the events in their appropriate baseball context. Creamer also injects enough of the volatile world political climate to cast a pall over the on-field excitement. The 1941 season meant a great deal to Creamer. He was 18 going on 19, and with war looming, was about to leave his childhood behind. Highly recommended. —*Wes Lukowsky*

Cromartie, Warren and Whiting, Robert.
Slugging It Out in Japan: An American Major Leaguer in the Tokyo Out-field.
Kodansha, $19.95 (4-7700-1423-6). 277p.

In 1983, at age 29, Cromartie decided to test baseball's free-agent market. Little did he expect that the high bidder would be Japan's Tokyo Giants. With the expectation high for his performance, Cromartie had to adjust to both a new society and a new role as a team leader. Though he struggled at times, he flourished over the long haul. Cromartie is refreshingly candid. Though Japan has its problems, he says, at least it didn't have Jerry Falwell begging for money. (This comment is typical of Cromartie's humorous, slightly cynical worldview.) In the early sections of the book he skims over his years with the Montreal Expos, but the prime focus here is the Japan experience. Cromartie offers brief profiles of his teammates, comments on the differences between American and Japanese playing styles, and reflects on the positive and negative aspects of Japanese culture. Excellent reading for baseball fans. —*Wes Lukowsky*

✔Dickey, Glenn.
Just Win, Baby: Al Davis and His Raiders.
HBJ, $19.95 (0-15-146580-0). 242p. index.

Davis, the guiding light of the Los Angeles/Oakland Raiders, is a troubling—troubled?—soul. Football has been an obsession. In terms of on-field success, it's been a magnificent obsession. In his quarter century at the Raider helm he's produced three Super Bowl champions and numerous serious contenders. But Davis seems destined never to become a revered elder statesman of football as did, say, George Halas. Though the word *admire* is often employed in discussions of Davis, so is *detest*. Dickey, a Davis observer for more than 20 years as a columnist for the *San Francisco Chronicle*, openly admires his subject. He recounts Davis' coaching savvy, his shrewd personnel moves, his ability to judge talent (and personality), and his courage in standing toe-to-toe against the NFL when he wanted to move from Oakland to Los Angeles. He also asks the question "What price success?" as he ponders Davis' isolation, paranoia, and monomaniacal pursuit of Raider wins. In the recent *Slick*, Davis' other biographer, Mark Ribowsky, obviously cared little for his subject but found too many proponents to dismiss him completely as an amoral, Machiavellian manipulator. While Ribowsky portrays an ambitious man pursuing success, Dickey sees an ambitious man trapped by success at the expense of all his other personal relationships. Good reading for football fans. —*Wes Lukowsky*

Fedo, Michael.
One Shining Season.
Pharos; dist. by St. Martin's, $16.95 (0-88687-608-7). 176p.

Baseball fanatic Fedo went on the road in search of old baseball players whose careers stretched from sometime in the 1940s to sometime in the 1970s. He found 'em, too—some retired, others still plugging away at nonsports

Sports & Recreation

careers, some content to forget the glory days, others basking in what's left of the limelight. The hook to Fedo's journalistic pursuit is based on the fact that each of these guys—Walt Dropo, Willard Marshall, Wes Parker, Roger Wolff, Ned Garver, Stan Lopata, Bob Hazle, Dave Nicholson, Barney Schultz, Billy Grabarkewitz, and Lee Thomas—all had fairly mediocre careers with the exception of at least one year in which their talents carried them to a notable level of achievement. Fedo's search for the clues as to why those big years happened—what set them apart from all the other seasons—reveals much about the players, their teammates, and the game itself. Fedo also draws out of his interviewees their feelings about their beginnings (baseball and otherwise), retirement, and the nature of today's game with its pampered, high-salaried stars. A sure winner for public library sports shelves. —*Martin Brady*

Feinstein, John.
Hard Courts.
Villard, $22.50 (0-394-58333-7). 456p.

Feinstein may be forever haunted by the success and attendant controversy of his first book, *A Season on the Brink*, which explored Bob Knight and Indiana basketball. Nevertheless, this is a solid effort that will appeal to and generally please tennis fans (though it may leave some of the more knowledgeable buffs vaguely unfulfilled). Feinstein spent a year on the pro tennis circuit, interviewing dozens of players, coaches, linesmen, ballboys, trainers, and assorted hangers-on. The insights are old news: McEnroe is hyperactive and disorganized; Martina is often nice, sometimes bitchy; players get huge appearance fees in addition to tournament winnings; Agassi occasionally quits in secondary matches. Interviews with the less famous fare better, if only because readers have little prior knowledge of them (they hence seem infinitely more interesting than the overexposed stars). On balance, an entertaining read, though not the tour de force one might have hoped for. —*Wes Lukowsky*

Fireovid, Steve and Winegardner, Mark.
The 26th Man: One Minor Leaguer's Pursuit of a Dream.
Macmillan, $18.95 (0-02-538381-7). 256p. index.

Fireovid spent parts of five seasons—very small parts—in the majors, the last in 1986. When that season opened, he was back at the Triple A level, the top minor league. He was 33 and no longer a young prospect. This is a diary of the 1990 season, when Fireovid was still harboring a dream that was fading fast. His wife and three kids are supportive, yet the author asks himself if he's depriving them by pursuing his dream. Confident of his ability, he wonders why he never gets called to the "Show," yet he never whines or succumbs to bitterness. Fireovid may not have been much of a major league pitcher, but his book is a first-rate experience for baseball fans, who will appreciate this intelligent young man's reflective review of his career. —*Wes Lukowsky*

✔**Golenbock, Peter.**
The Forever Boys: An Intimate Look at the Hidden Lives of Ex–Major League Ballplayers as They Played One More Time.
Birch Lane Press, $19.95 (1-55972-034-4). 384p.

Best-selling sportswriter Golenbock, author of *The Bronx Zoo, Number 1,* and *Personal Fouls,* which exposed the scandal-ridden North Carolina State basketball program, returns to the baseball field with this pleasant examination of the Sun Belt Senior League in which most of the players are former major leaguers and all are over 35. Golenbock wintered with the St. Petersburg Pelicans from November 1989 through February 1990. He hung out in the clubhouse, stayed in the same hotels, and rode the buses. And talked. And listened. What emerges is a love of baseball. By and large these players were not superstars, and many never made the big, never-have-to-work-again money being tossed around today. They probably should be getting on with their lives, but when the chance to play again came, well … Golenbock captures their wistfulness, their determination, and their refusal to let the inner child fade away. For all Golenbock's prior success, this may well be the best work he's ever done. —*Wes Lukowsky*

Hauser, Thomas.
Muhammad Ali: His Life and Times.
Simon & Schuster, $24.95 (0-671-68892-8). 640p. index.

Former heavyweight boxing champion Ali is, arguably, the most recognizable person in the world, his ring exploits, combined with his personality, having provided an endless supply of grist for the press. Hauser, whose award-winning *Black Lights* was an empathetic view of the fight game, does a thorough job in researching Ali's life, from his Louisville youth to his current semiretirement in Michigan. Hauser's technique is to allow those involved with Ali to speak for themselves while the author provides background, context, and segues. The Ali who emerges is as complex as one would expect, often exhibiting great personal fortitude yet at other times appearing gullible and as easily led as a child. Ali's current physical condition is of great interest to many, and Hauser's evenhanded exploration of the man's health is both disturbing yet somewhat hopeful. And though Ali cooperated fully on this project, it is not the fawning hero-biography one might expect from such an arrangement. A serious sports bio that will substantially reward a large audience. —*Wes Lukowsky*

Helm, Mike.
A Breed Apart: The Horses and the Players.
Holt, $22.50 (0-8050-1326-1). 320p.

If universities offered classes in thoroughbred horse racing, this would be the textbook. Helm sought out a pair of unusually candid and articulate trainers (Bill Morey and Chuck Jenda), a jockey (Jack Kaenel), a specialist in maintaining racing surfaces, a veterinarian, a steward, a couple of horse owners, a racing secretary, and even a successful handicapper or two, which must surely have been the hardest to find. He then bounced between them through an entire racing season to ask endless questions, transcribe the answers, and absorb an impressive quantity of information. It all comes out in these pages, and the result is the most comprehensive primer imaginable on the fascinatingly complex game of racing. The book is highly recommended for anyone thinking of becoming involved with the sport, even as a recreational bettor. For those with a more serious intent, it should be considered mandatory. —*Dennis Dodge*

John, Tommy and Valenti, Dan.

TJ: My Twenty-six Years in Baseball.
Bantam, $19.95 (0-553-07184-X). 320p.

Tommy John's 26-year stint as a major league pitcher began when Kennedy was president and ended in 1989 with Bush in the White House. It was a career that encompassed some of the most significant developments in the game's history, among them, free agency and big money, the designated hitter, artificial turf and domed stadiums. Although it includes a little background on John's life, this book is more an occasional memoir than an autobiography. Nicely structured around the pitcher's preparations for his last season, the text both charts his baseball-playing progress and reveals the subtle—and sometimes not-so-subtle—changes the game has undergone. The wonderful anecdotes, insight, and analysis are all delivered with the same crafty intelligence that was John's greatest asset on the mound. —*Wes Lukowsky*

Johnson, Dick and Stout, Glenn.

Ted Williams: A Portrait in Words and Pictures.
Walker, $24.95 (0-8027-1140-5). 224p.

Williams, whose career spanned from 1939 to after the 1960 season, was the greatest hitter of his baseball generation. Though he appears frequently in the baseball record books, his name would appear with much greater regularity had he not lost five prime seasons to military duty during World War II and the Korean conflict. Drawing solely on previously published accounts—mostly from the seven daily Boston newspapers that were active during Williams' career—Johnson, the curator of the New England Sports Museum, and Stout re-create and analyze Teddy Ballgame's on-field exploits and private battles. Augmenting the text are essays by such notable writers as Donald Hall, George V. Higgins, and David Halberstam. In addition to the more than 175 black-and-white photographs, readers can look forward to a 25-page statistical analysis. Williams youthful anger and passion were responsible for much of the controversy that swirled around him; they also helped generate tremendous interest among baseball fans. More than 30 years after he last swung a bat, the Splendid Splinter is as splendid (and fascinating) as ever. —*Wes Lukowsky*

✔**Lamb, David.**
Stolen Season: A Journey through America and Baseball's Minor Leagues.
Random, $20 (0-394-57608-X). 285p.

Lamb, a respected journalist who established his credentials in such global hot spots as Beirut and Vietnam, took an unpaid leave from the Los Angeles Times to explore baseball's minor leagues—those modern outposts of the game that in themselves provide a childhood of memories. After buying a somewhat dilapidated mobile home, Lamb headed off in spring 1989 to "steal a season from adulthood." Lamb presents a baseball drama in which the stakes aren't million-dollar contracts or world championships; the participants simply want another day or week or season living with the game they love. In revealing subtle truths about others' lives, Lamb discovers much about himself. And, at a time when so many pop psychologists tell us we are irrevocably doomed to assume the unhappy burdens of childhood, it's exhilarating to recognize that good memories are a part of our makeup, too. A success as either a stylish baseball travelogue or a journey of the heart. Highly recommended. —*Wes Lukowsky*

Lott, Ronnie and Lieber, Jill.
Total Impact: Straight Talk from Football's Hardest Hitter.
Doubleday, $19.50 (0-385-42055-2). 384p.

Lott was arguably the best defensive back of the 1980s. He also played on the best team of the era, the four-time Super Bowl champion San Francisco 49ers. After the 1990 season, he left his heart in San Francisco but moved his bank account to Los Angeles, where he's now menacing pass receivers for the Raiders. This is more of a professional memoir than an autobiography, and readers who want to vicariously experience the mental, physical, and emotional toll the NFL extracts need look no further. Lott, a very aggressive player, is just as forceful in print, analyzing and critiquing players, teams, coaches, owners, and the league. He's often positive, occasionally negative, but always credible. An intelligent, thought-provoking glimpse into the NFL by a perceptive insider. —*Wes Lukowsky*

✔**Miller, Marvin.**
A Whole Different Ball Game: The Sport and Business of Baseball.
Birch Lane, $21.95 (1-55972-067-0). 437p. index.

Twenty-five years ago, when the Major League Baseball Players Association was born, the minimum salary was $6,000. Due in large part to first executive director Miller's leadership, the minimum is now $100,000, and dozens of players earn more than a million per season. Miller recounts the formation of the union within the context of the attitudes of the time, when most fans, even then, failed to understand the reasons why men playing a boy's game needed a union. Miller clears up that issue early with a brief baseball history lesson. Overall, his memoir is told fondly and with humor, but more importantly, with candor. His portrayals of owners and commis-

Sports & Recreation

sioners are reasonably evenhanded—though Bowie Kuhn takes a pounding—and offer rare insights into a complex process. Miller is not now a household name, yet his importance to the current economic structure of baseball (and other professional sports) can't be denied. This excellent, timely volume may find a surprisingly wide library audience. —*Wes Lukowsky*

Mills, George R.
Go Big Red! The Story of a Nebraska Football Player.
Univ. of Illinois, $19.95 (0-252-01825-7). 234p.

The author played football for Nebraska in the mid-1970s. He was not a star; he lettered in just two seasons and was a part-time starter only during a portion of his senior year. He never played professional football and went on to coach high school football and sell real estate. He's not famous. So why read his book? Mills' experience in college football was more typical than the stars of the team. For every Heisman hopeful there are dozens of players on the same team who just want to play or make the traveling squad or keep their scholarships or move up to third string. Mills, his vision clarified by a decade and a half away from the experience, is able to place his athletic experience in an appropriate perspective. It was, on balance, a good experience, but he acknowledges its drawbacks. Anyone who's been disgusted by the recent revelations concerning college sports and its abuses may want to read Mills' story. It's an eloquent statement of sports' value as an environment for learning about one's limitations. —*Wes Lukowsky*

Mullarkey, Karen, ed.
Baseball in America: From Sandlots to Stadiums, a Portrait of Our National Pastime by 50 of Today's Leading Photographers.
Collins Publishers, $45 (0-00-215731-4). 224p.

From the publishers of the impressive and popular *Day in the Life of . . .* series of photo books comes a colorful, wide-ranging, and endearing collection of pictures portraying the glory and charm of America's favorite pastime. The more than 200 photographs capture the game from all angles—from Little League parks in the boonies to women's softball, from Latin American barrios to the minor and major leagues. The photos come in all shapes and sizes—from sharp full-page and double-page spreads to modest but poignant insets—and focus on all the appropriate people and sights. There's future Hall-of-Famer Nolan Ryan in muscular wind-up, a gorgeous double-pager of Wrigley Field *in medias res*, Harlem kids warming up, fans in Eugene, Oregon, buying their hot dogs, big-league umpires in a laid-back moment at a video arcade, silly shots of silly mascots, and much, much more. The helpful captions provide perspective throughout, and along the way readers are treated to five enjoyable photo-essays and brief interviews with well-known baseball lovers such as Charles Kuralt. Almost as good as a box seat behind home plate. —*Martin Brady*

✓**Nelson, Mariah Burton.**
Are We Winning Yet? How Women Are Changing Sports and Sports Are Changing Women.
Random, $18.95 (0-394-57576-8). 256p.

The author, an award-winning journalist and former college athlete, examines the effect of women on sports and, conversely, sports' effect on women. Though a narrower thematic focus may have increased its impact, this is nonetheless a stimulating series of essays that touch on virtually all areas of female sports participation. The opening chapter chronicles women's first view of male-dominated sports: fathers who promoted softball more than baseball; leagues that refused them entry; and peer groups that categorized female athletes as "not ladylike." Nelson also looks into financial discrimination against scholastic girls' programs. She offers comparisons of both emotional and physical strength between the sexes and delves into the issues of lesbianism and homophobia. Someday women athletes will be afforded the same opportunities as their male counterparts and will be measured by the same standards. It is a long process but one that this effort may facilitate. A serious book that raises important issues to which there are no simple answers. —*Wes Lukowsky*

✓**Oppenheimer, Judy.**
Dreams of Glory: A Mother's Season with Her Son's High School Football Team.
Summit, $19.50 (0-671-68754-9). 320p.

About this time last year, Bissinger's *Friday Night Lights* appeared. It was a revealing—some critics say negative—study of high school football in football-crazy Texas. This book is an examination of high school football in soccer-crazy Bethesda, Maryland. The two books will probably be compared and Oppenheimer's praised for its generally sunny outlook. Both deserve praise, both are honest, both reveal a special reality. The Odessa, Texas, of *Friday* is an isolated, economically depressed, blue-collar city. There's not a lot to focus one's attention on in Odessa, and the subsequent community pressure foments a different level of football intensity. Bethesda, however, is a suburb of Washington, D.C. Its residents are white collar, well-educated, and affluent. The children of Bethesda view football as an intriguing, exciting interlude in a life pregnant with future successes, while for too many of Odessa's children high school football may be their best opportunity for establishing a sense of self-esteem. That contrast doesn't detract from Oppenheimer's achievement—a book filled with humor, the joys and frustrations of being 17, and the exhilaration of competition. Excellent. —*Wes Lukowsky*

Parker, Robert and Parker, Joan.
A Year at the Races.
Viking, $35 (0-670-82678-2). 175p.

Novelist Robert Parker, his wife, Joan, and photographer William Strode chronicle a year's progress in Cot Campbell's Dogwood Stable, following the

Sports & Recreation

horses, including a promising young colt named Summer Squall, from the sales rings of Keeneland and Saratoga to the training center at Aiken, South Carolina, and on to the tracks of New York, Maryland, and Florida. Parker's text is lively, accessible and keenly observant, though the commentary is by no means expert. Many of Strode's photographs serve primarily to illustrate the text, yet none of those depicting the magnificent thoroughbreds can be less than lovely and few are routine. Several—a faraway view of steeplechasers loping past towering trees, for example, or one of flat racers stepping onto the track through early morning fog, or cooling out on a sun-dappled backstretch—are arresting in their beauty. The Parkers and Strode clearly became enamored with the world they entered, as much for its stretches of serenity and the offhand elegance of its inhabitants as for its spurts of adrenalin-stirring activity. The success of their collaboration is that they seduce the reader as well. *—Dennis Dodge*

Pavel, Ota.
How I Came to Know Fish.
New Directions, paper, $9.95 (0-8112-1165-7). 160p.

If you think this is just another book by another insane fisherman, think again. (Pavel [1930–73] really was insane, though, and spent years in various European psychiatric institutions after a mental breakdown during the 1964 Winter Olympics.) These autobiographical stories recount the fishing experiences of Pavel's youth, as he watches war come over his land and then yield to peace and a polluted river. Most of us think of fishing as a weekend hobby, a life-and-death struggle only for the fish. For Pavel, fishing (and the occasional episode of deer poaching) meant food and survival, especially during the Nazi occupation of Czechoslovakia. One chapter details fishing from a pond—the carp in it went to the German troops—forbidden to mere anglers who, if discovered, were sentenced to immediate death by the gestapo. In such stories, Pavel gets at the roots of fishing better than Hemingway ever did. We who climb aboard our high-powered bass boats with electronic gizmos should read this book, if only to remind ourselves of the necessities from which fishing arose. *—Jon Kartman*

Rosenfeld, Harvey.
Roger Maris: A Title to Fame.
Prairie House, $19.95 (0-911007-12-2). 320p. index.

Roger Maris hit 61 home runs in 1961, breaking Babe Ruth's previous, seemingly unassailable record of 60 set in 1927. Though Maris had other good seasons—he was a solid hitter, excellent base runner, and superb outfielder— he never approached the magnificence of that banner year again. Maris finished his respectable career with the St. Louis Cardinals, went about his life as a businessman, then contracted cancer and died in 1984. In conjunction with the 30-year anniversary of Maris' home-run feat, Rosenfeld has written a sympathetic but never sacharrine biography. By most accounts, Maris was the salt of the earth—a North Dakota boy who wanted to play ball and be left alone. The media circus surrounding his pursuit of Ruth's record frustrated and annoyed him. His desire for privacy violated, he grew sharp and sullen with the press, a behavior little tolerated by hard-bitten New York scribes. Rosenfeld does a good job in setting the record straight: as most fans have come to realize, Maris was an honorable man and consummate team player. In these days of whining superstars, it's refreshing to read about a player who conducted himself with dignity and pride. —*Wes Lukowsky*

✔**Rybczynski, Witold.**
Waiting for the Weekend.
Viking, $18.95 (0-670-83001-1). 213p. index.

The author of the original and acclaimed *Home* (Viking, 1986) much more than satisfies the interest his readers may already have in a subject. Like some artists, he compels interest in subjects cowled in familiarity. In the essays herein, he examines the two-day weekend (unilaterally instituted by Henry Ford only 65 years ago), the changing meaning of leisure, blue laws (so named because of the blue paper of legal documents in New Haven), the biology of leisure (the seven-day week is perfectly adapted, as it happens, to the circaseptan rhythm of many bodily functions), the first calendar (Egyptian), etc. His theorizing about the place of leisure in our lives hews close to historical particularities and sometimes aspires to prophecy. It can also be wise: he notes that the response of political and religious authorities to the 200,000 New Yorkers attending nickelodeons weekly in 1908 "was common in the history of leisure: when too many people had too much fun, someone eventually objected. Play is rarely 'harmless.'" —*Roland Wulbert*

Schwartz, Jane.
Ruffian: Burning from the Start.
Ballantine, $18 (0-345-36017-6). 288p.

Ruffian was arguably the best thoroughbred filly of all time. She was unbeaten in her first 10 starts and had, in fact, actually led all the way in every race. But on July 6, 1975, she met Kentucky Derby winner Foolish Pleasure in a match race at Belmont Park in New York. Tragically, Ruffian shattered a leg in the race and, despite intense veterinary measures, had to be destroyed. Schwartz, whose work has appeared in *Sports Illustrated* and the *National*, uses the doomed filly's life as a basis for a pointed look inside thoroughbred racing, which, much like boxing, is a sport with a glittering facade and a hard, unsentimental heart. Again, as in boxing, the touchier the business, the more interesting its practitioners, from the owners to the stable hands to the grooms to the jockeys. Each has a story and a reason for devoting his life to a sport, and it's worth noting that few do it for the money. Schwartz captures this addictive life-style effectively, both the heaven and the hell of it. —*Wes Lukowsky*

Sports & Recreation

✔**Sheed, Wilfrid.**
Baseball and Lesser Sports.
HarperCollins, $19.95 (0-06-016531-6). 292p.

Some three dozen collected essays of sport—mostly baseball—by a highly regarded novelist, essayist, and biographer. Sheed's been watching America's favorite pastime avidly for years—moreover, he has keenly observed and/or admired the players (DiMaggio, Greenberg, Mays, Rose et al.), the great writers (Red Smith, Halberstam, Angell, Boswell, etc.), the movies (*Field of Dreams, Bull Durham*), the issues (money, Sabermetrics), and the controversies (e.g., Shoeless Joe Jackson). He writes eloquently on all of these topics, incisively critiquing and whimsically reflecting on both the simplicities and mysteries of the game. (Sheed's chapter on ballplayers who aren't in the Hall of Fame but maybe should be will find an interested audience for sure. There is also a particularly good piece on Howard Cosell.) Informed and classy sportswriting, backed up by the esteemed Sheed name. —*Martin Brady*

Slaughter, Enos and Reid, Kevin.
Country Hardball: The Autobiography of Enos "Country" Slaughter.
Tudor Publishers, $18.95 (0-936389-23-0). 208p.

Enos ("Country") Slaughter was an outfielder for the St. Louis Cardinals and New York Yankees from the late 1930s through the 1950s. His competitive spirit was legendary. So was his occasional orneriness. The latter, and allegations of racism, kept him out of the Hall of Fame until 1985. In this as-told-to biography, Slaughter complains some about his delayed election to the Hall, grouses a little about the "puny" (in spirit) modern ballplayers, and has a go at a couple of detested rivals from his past. But mostly, he speaks of the game he played, the fun he had playing it, and how he admired and respected the men he competed with and against. An enjoyable sports memoir from a player who enriched the game in a way very few can claim. —*Wes Lukowsky*

St. John, Bob.
Heart of a Lion: The Wild and Woolly Life of Bobby Layne.
Taylor, $19.95 (0-87833-744-X). 197p. index.

The late Bobby Layne is a pro football legend. He led the Detroit Lions to a pair of world championships in the 1950s and almost single-handedly revived an impoverished Pittsburgh Steelers franchise. Layne was the quarterback who set the standards for leadership, competitiveness, and clutch play, yet, despite his Hall of Fame stature, he probably wouldn't fit in with today's cookie-cutter NFL image. Layne was the original late night carouser and party animal of whom it was said, "He danced every dance." Yet Layne always came to play and was not averse to loudly chastising teammates who were not as focused on the field. Yet none resented it because of the respect Layne commanded. Great subject, fine book. —*Wes Lukowsky*

✔**Strawn, John.**
Driving the Green: The Making of a Golf Course.
HarperCollins, $25 (0-06-016659-2). 352p.

What Tracy Kidder did for houses, John Strawn does for golf courses. While the question of how a golf course is designed and constructed may seem a bit arcane for many general readers, Strawn—like Kidder, John McPhee, David Macaulay, and others—turns the process into a technological adventure, appealing to our innate fascination with how things are made. On every level, the creation of Ironhorse Country Club in West Palm Beach, Florida, captures the imagination: as a case study on negotiating with bureaucracies ("In Florida you need a permit to get a permit"); as a testament to the special genius of the golf course architect, in this case, Art Hills ("At Ironhorse, the canvas was blank. Every swale, every mound and bunker grew first on a drafting table in Toledo, Ohio."); and as yet another reminder that behind every project is a *deal* ("Stay on the right side of the money . . . don't pay until it's all done the way you want."). Finally, though, it's the details that win us over: golf courses have lakes, Strawn notes, largely because digging them is a cheap way to get dirt. Think about that the next time your five-iron to the green finds a watery grave. —*Bill Ott*

Wetherell, W. D.
Upland Stream: Notes on the Fishing Passion.
Little, Brown, $19.95 (0-316-93172-1). 216p.

Attempting to explain why people go fishing, Wetherell tries to prove that fly fishing for trout is the highest form of fishing. Well written, his text detailing his passion for trout fishing will hit the soul of anyone who has spent any time in piscatorial pursuits. But the modern angler recognizes that no one fish is the best and no one type of angling is the best. A true fishing purist gets the same joy out of catching any fish. Period. The modern angler knows that sometimes fly fishing is the best way to catch fish, and sometimes other forms are the best. It would be nice in this era of shrinking fishing habitat if we could all go to a nearby stream and catch lots of fish. Perhaps this was possible in years past, but no longer. Wetherell can condemn large bass fishing boats of 200 horsepower driven by anglers using dozens of electronic gizmos to catch fish—but that, whether he likes it or not, is fishing in 1991. The solitary angler with a fly rod catching trout out of a stream is, in a larger sense, an image of a time for which we all yearn, a time that has passed. —*Jon Kartman*

Whitford, David.
Extra Innings: A Season in the Senior League.
HarperCollins, $19.95 (0-06-016459-X). 255p.

The Senior League was, on the surface at least, a good idea. Old—but not too old—ex–big leaguers would play a three-month season in Florida from November to February. It could be a tourist attraction and would fill the time between the end of the World Series and the start of spring training. Alas, the league limped through the 1989–90 season with dreadful attendance, an idea whose time was yet to come. Whitford's effort compares favorably with Peter Golenbock's similar *The Forever Boys*. Veteran fans will enjoy catching up on the lives of Scipio Spinks, Rollie Fingers, and Bill ("Spaceman") Lee while rooting for a return of forgotten skills. Some, like Fingers, came back for the money; others, like journeyman shortstop Toby Harrah, just wanted to play because ... well, just because. Whitford eloquently chronicles dozens of life stories with empathy and humor. Whatever the fates dealt these middle-aged athletes, it's refreshing to see how they embraced an opportunity to get out and play one more time. Highly recommended. —*Wes Lukowsky*

Wills, Maury and Celizic, Mike.
On the Run: The Never Dull and Often Shocking Life of Maury Wills.
Carroll & Graf, $19.95 (0-88184-640-6). 333p.

Wills was an outstanding shortstop for the Los Angeles Dodgers in the 1960s—he's tenth on the all-time base-stealing list, and in 1962 he stole 104 bases (an incredible record at the time). As good as he was as a player, Wills was equally bad as a manager, his Seattle teams of 1980 and 1981 being touchstones of ineptitude. After he was fired, he became a cocaine addict: Wills snorted away a personal fortune and nearly lost his life. Finally, Wills says, he got sick and tired of being sick and tired. He's currently immersed in the lifelong struggle to stay sober. Baseball fans will enjoy the revealing anecdotes of Wills' playing days—they make up a large portion of the book—but mostly this is an honest attempt by a man to face his shortcomings and understand them. —*Wes Lukowsky*

Travel

Adams, Alice.
Mexico: Some Travels and Travelers There.
Prentice Hall Press, $20 (0-13-202326-1). 240p.

Popular and critically acclaimed novelist Alice Adams recalls the pleasures and vicissitudes of her many visits to Mexico. Her recollections embrace some 20 years of travel and observation in a country upon which "we all impose our own preconceptions." Adams' Mexico is a land of sun and "marvelous ... magically buoyant" sea, of towns trivialized by junk-stocked tourist shops and dominated by opulent churches. Adams is sensitive to Mexico's long-burning fever of faith as she contemplates the stark power of Mayan ruins and muses on the wealth of the Catholic church and the poverty of its worshipers. On a more personal level, she describes various hotel keepers, hired drivers, irritating tour groups, and her own treasured travel companions. Adams' prose is sneaky: poised, graceful, even ladylike, it lulls you, working under your skin until you suddenly recognize the depth of her insights into this enigmatic land. —*Donna Seaman*

✓Cahill, Tim.
Road Fever: A High-Speed Travelogue.
Random, $17.95 (0-394-57656-X). 288p.

Is there any reason to drive from the tip of Tierra del Fuego to road's end at Prudhoe Bay, Alaska, in 23 days—15,000 miles through blizzards, deserts, jungles, clogged cities, war zones, and rural areas infested with hijackers? Yes! To spawn a top-shelf page-turner for adventure and travel fans alike. Canadian "professional adventure driver" Garry Sowerby convinced General Motors and other firms to put up money, equipment, and logistical support in return for publicity. Author-codriver Cahill devotes half the book to a year's preparation: "The essence of our adventure was to avoid adventure at all costs." Sowerby might say they achieved this, but thanks to Cahill's writing, readers will gleefully disagree. Cahill drives the story with the smooth assurance Sowerby drives a Chevy Sierra through the Andes. He's funny, terrifying, and insightful describing Central American borders run by teenagers with automatic weapons and sheer drops off narrow mountain roads. His descriptions—whether of a garish Las Vegas PR extravaganza, the rape of the rain forests, or fatigue-induced temporary madness—are simply fine writing. —*Thomas Gaughan*

Corn, Charles.
Distant Islands: Travels across Indonesia.
Viking, $21.95 (0-670-82374-0). 264p.

Indonesia is hard to grasp. An archipelago of over 13,000 islands, it embraces numerous geographies, peoples, and cultures. The recipient of centuries of Arab, Asian, and European immigrants, conquerors, and proselytizers, Indonesia manages to keep deep ethnic and religious distrust and contempt at a low simmer. Corn regales us with history, observation, and anecdote as he gamely boards stifling and crowded trains, buses, and boats, traveling from island to island, city to village. He mulls over the republic's many paradoxes, particularly its dual passion for religion and prostitution. "Facility with the silent language of sensuality" is one trait shared by the diverse islanders. Corn travels from Jakarta, a "brooding, hot labyrinth of a city," to Java on to Bali, Australia's playground. His itinerary includes Sumba, Nusa Tenggara, Timor, Flores, Borneo, Banda, and the Moluccas, or Spice Islands. He visits with Malays, Bugis, Dayaks, Bataks, the Minangkabau, and the Acehnese. His adventures are varied and amusing and informative in a subtle, penetrating manner, giving us a key to understanding the people of this volcanic, watery, and kaleidoscopic world. —*Donna Seaman*

Ford, Peter.
Around the Edge.
Viking, $19.95 (0-670-82827-0). 331p.

While a reporter covering Central America, Ford decided to travel the Caribbean coastline from Belize south to Panama, hoping to accomplish his journey either on foot or by boat. This coastal sojourn would be fraught with rather awesome difficulties. Ford's travels occurred while hostilities between the Nicaraguan Sandinistas and the contras were an all too real fact of life, and although he had obtained permission to cross the border, his journal contains a riveting account of the passage from Honduras into Nicaragua. Additionally, the author remains attentive throughout the narrative to historical details that illuminate the Garifuna culture. Originally created by the mingling of an African slave colony with Carib Indians, the Garifuna migrated from the island of St. Vincent to Belize, Honduras, Guatemala, and Nicaragua, mainly in coastal settlements. *Around the Edge* is a gripping account of Ford's tenacious resolve to travel through a remote area in spite of the most adverse conditions. —*Alice Joyce*

Frater, Alexander.
Chasing the Monsoon.
Knopf, $21 (0-394-58310-8). 288p.

The year 1987 would find Alexander Frater, chief travel writer for the *London Observer*, awaiting the arrival of a monsoon in Trivandrum, at India's southernmost tip. While he was a young boy living on the New Hebrides Islands, a framed print of The Wettest Place on Earth hung beside his bed. Steep hillsides, tigers, and temples were pictured, blanketed in all-encompassing sheets of rain. Frater grew to share his father's passion for meteorology, progressing from exultant experiences with local hurricanes, to a thorough fascination with the image of Cherrapunji, Assam, the remote village depicted in the bedside print. Letters written by a family friend confirmed accounts of amazing rainfalls recorded in the fabled town, said to be the Indian monsoon's end point. When the passing of years brought the death of Frater's father, and later, his mother, he decided to follow the monsoon along its northward path. This pilgrimage, of sorts, would culminate in Cherrapunji itself. The adventure was to present one particularly difficult challenge. Political unrest had made Assam off-limits to foreigners, with permission for travel flatly denied. *Chasing the Monsoon* provides a total immersion in the rich scents and sights of India. Although glimpses of fearsome devastation occur, the overriding theme remains the monsoon's legendary power to rejuvenate and renew life. Readers are promised a thrilling journey. —*Alice Joyce*

Frerck, Robert and Reid, Alastair.
Eternal Spain: The Spanish Rural Landscape.
Abrams, $75 (0-8109-3252-0). 176p.

"If I were to think of a single image for what drew me to Spain and the people of Spain, it would be one of coming into a valley in the mountains, seeing a single man working in a field, stopping for one of those quintessential Spanish conversations." Narrow in height and long in width, this striking volume's format is perfect for displaying the more than 64 spectacular full-color, double-page, wide-angle shots of Spain's landscapes as well as for showing smaller photographs that zero in on details—architecture, sculpture, people, fiestas, etc.—and are artfully arranged on the pages with the smoothly written text. The combination provides an appreciative and lyrical sense of

Spanish life, culture, and history as a whole and region by region. A book truly to be savored in remembrance or in anticipation. —*Sally Estes*

Travel

Greene, Graham.
Reflections.
Viking, $19.95 (1-871061-19-9). 320p.

With the great British writer having recently died, interest in Greene will be renewed, a situation that will be reflected in greater public library demand for his works, at least for the time being. Consequently, this gathering of previously uncollected essays should be given careful consideration for purchase. These pieces—70 of them, each relatively short—range chronologically throughout Greene's writing life (as well as his incessant globe-wandering life), from 1923 to 1988. They fall generally into the category of travel writing, but for Greene, that particular genre meant not only sharing sights and smells but also feeling free to comment on the political agendas at play in whatever country or region in which he happened to find himself. Combining sensitivity to the uniqueness of place with a comfortably eloquent style, Greene is a travel writer to be relished. —*Brad Hooper*

Hansen, Eric.
Motoring with Mohammed: Journeys to Yemen and the Red Sea.
Houghton, $19.95 (0-395-48347-6). 240p.
Horwitz, Tony.
Baghdad without a Map and Other Misadventures in Arabia.
Dutton, $18.95 (0-525-24960-5). 240p.

Two young and often irreverent American travel writers unveil the mysteries of the Middle East.

Hansen's story begins more than 10 years ago when he was shipwrecked on an island off the coast of Yemen. There he buried his personal notebooks in the sand, where they remained until the author returned to retrieve them in 1988. With Mohammed as his chauffeur and guide, Hansen journeys around North Yemen (North and South Yemen were reunited in 1990) trying to reach the island again and to find what remains of his boat and his desert fantasy existence. The real discoveries, however, occur in Hansen's observations of daily life in the Islamic world, where both Arabs and Westerners coexist but where their separate cultures mix as well as oil and water. Whether confronting government officials, assessing the political climate, or chewing *qat* (a Yemeni drug that seems part tobacco and part marijuana) with the locals, Hansen proves both revealing and entertaining.

Horwitz reached the Middle East with the excuse that previously landed him in Australia and Cleveland—his wife took a job there, and he decided to tag along. Headquartered in Cairo, Horwitz embarked on trips throughout the region in search of adventures and stories he could write up. Among the more notable accounts are the suicide missions to Iran, Iraq, and Libya, where an American Jewish journalist might not expect to find an especially warm welcome. But for all the hazards, there are also rewards, particularly a monumental *qat* hangover in North Yemen. Horwitz mixes insight and humor in these observations that illustrate on an everyday level both the contradictions and the idiosyncrasies of the Arab world. —*John Brosnahan*

Hofvendahl, Russ.
A Land So Fair and Bright: The True Story of a Young Man's Adventures across Depression America.
Sheridan House, $22.95 (0-924486-10-4). 320p.

Hofvendahl's travels at 16 seem right out of Woody Guthrie. When he jumped ship in 1938, he headed east through Canada, south to New Orleans via New York, and across to San Francisco. He rode the rails often, and here he tells of catching freights on the fly, of panoramas viewed from "side-door Pullmans" or from open gondolas snaking down California peaks. There were also times without shelter, food, or water. Hofvendahl remembers, with feeling, exquisite regional cooking; a blond, blue-eyed Danish shipmate; farmers clinging to their land with hard work and shrewd moves in hard times; black men who stretched his understanding; and women who provided pleasure and learning. Good-byes were an important part of the author's education: to hobos who shared common dangers; to strangers who helped as they could; to some who would have been friends. A rare and exhilarating true-life tale. —*Virginia Dwyer*

Horwitz, Tony.
Baghdad without a Map and Other Misadventures in Arabia.
Dutton, $18.95 (0-525-24960-5). 240p.

See p.249.

Iyer, Pico.
The Lady and the Monk: Four Seasons in Kyoto.
Knopf, $22 (0-679-40308-6). 352p.

Travelogues, be gone. In their stead, a new genre is appearing: autobiographical peregrinations that expose the state of the writer's heart and mind in addition to revealing parts of a land foreigners would not normally see. A modern-day Thoreau, Iyer journeys to Kyoto for 12 months, absorbing sights, sounds, and philosophies of the East. As an extra, he meets (and falls in love with) 30-year-old Sachiko Morishita, a Japanese wife torn between traditional fealty to family and the yearning to be free. The evolution of that friendship flows in and out of oriental scenery and the Japanese fascination with all things Western, of fractured communication, of ceremonies and celebrations. All told with a remarkable ear for dialogue and an uncanny sensitivity to people and places. —*Barbara Jacobs*

Jenner, Michael.
Journeys into Medieval England.
Viking, $29.95 (0-7181-3440-0). 256p. index.

In an almost ideal realization of the tourist's guide for armchair and actual traveler alike, Jenner first proffers, in an introduction and nine regional chapters, just enough words on medieval England's architectural and engineering achievements to whet appetites to see them. Then he devotes far more of each chapter to gorgeous color photos of precisely the structures and features he mentions. Therewith, he plants the urge to bodily confront and experience these churches, castles, and ruins, to be sure, but he also thoroughly satisfies those who can't do that. Even those who still don't want to "do" medieval Britain must allow that these are pictures of great distinction, especially in their veristic attention to the textures of grass, stone, wood, and flowing water. A lovely book to browse whether or not you use it to plan a trip. —*Ray Olson*

Latham, Aaron.
The Frozen Leopard.
Prentice Hall Press, $20 (0-13-946021-7). 256p. index.

Latham has written a thrilling account of an African sojourn, a book that overflows with luminous imagery and glorious moments of spiritual connection. While suffering from writer's block and an overwhelming malaise that weighed heavily on his soul, Latham, the author of *Urban Cowboy* and *Crazy Sundays: F. Scott Fitzgerald in Hollywood*, embarked on this journey to Kenya with his family, hoping for some form of release or at least some answers. He would find the beauty of the land, the proud bearing of the Masai people, and the magnificence of the animals all working their wonders. Sharing the resultant experience includes evocative portrayals of the scientists and settlers who devote their lives to preservation of the many vanishing species and the wild landscape. Moreover, Latham recounts his personal journey through the convolutions of his own psyche toward a serene resting point where delayed grieving is finally met head-on. —*Alice Joyce*

Laufer, Peter.
Iron Curtain Rising: A Personal Journey through the Changing Landscape of Eastern Europe.
Mercury House, $19.50 (1-56279-015-3). 213p.

Winston Churchill's iron curtain speech in March 1946 marked the beginning of one tragic act in the drama of Eastern Europe; the startling events of the past two years are clearly the first few scenes of a new act whose later developments cannot be predicted with certainty. Readers who want to understand the human impact of these initial scenes—and the issues at stake in developments to come—should read Laufer's on-site examination of the eight countries of Eastern Europe over the months since the collapse of the Berlin wall. Laufer covered these nations for ABC and CBS, and based on his descriptions of scruffy $12 hotel rooms, he also spent time there as a free-lance journalist. With no ax to grind, Laufer captures the complex motivations of those who participated in these revolutions, as well as the ambivalence of many Eastern Europeans toward the economic model (as distinct from the political model) offered by the West. His anecdotes humanize issues few Americans grasp. His book is readable, entertaining, enlightening, and a good addition to collections on this potentially explosive part of the world. —*Mary Carroll*

Travel

Louis, Victor and Louis, Jennifer.
The Complete Guide to the Soviet Union.
St. Martin's, $29.95 (0-312-05837-3); paper, $18.95 (0-312-05838-1). 624p.

Vadrot, Claude-Maria and Ivleva, Victoria.
Russia Today: From Holy Russia to Perestroika.
Atomium Books, $31.95 (1-56182-004-0). 160p.

Two books aimed at making Russia more accessible, one through detailed travel information, the other with color photographs. Though both books were written before the dismantling of the Soviet Union, they still contain valuable and fascinating information for travelers of both the real-life and the armchair variety.

The Louises' travel guide is almost a standard for foreign visitors. In its third revision and expansion, the hefty volume, with two columns of small type per page, provides relevant facts about all Soviet locations recommended by Intourist, more now than ever before. A brief "General Information" section is followed by 500 pages of alphabetical listings of towns, cities, and out-of-town places of interest. Each entry includes historical overviews, descriptive information, and sight-seeing, hotel, restaurant, and transportation suggestions. Specific car trips are also recommended.

The Soviet Union's astonishing variety and immensity come across loud and clear in the Louises' book, but if a picture really is worth a thousand words and readers are looking for armchair adventures, the photographs in *Russia Today* will do the trick. Vadrot, a French journalist, and Ivleva, a Soviet photographer, traveled far and wide, capturing the "Soviet Union's amazing current history without neglecting the eternal images of Russia." Their pictures reveal the "most secret aspects of Russian life," recording the fervency of prayer, the pride of artists, and the vibrancy of young people as they embrace the fashions of the West. A fine introduction to a country of contrasts, conflicts, and diverse cultures. Though published before the failed coup of August 1991, this book reveals the spirit of contemporary Russia that both prompted and quelled the coup. —*Donna Seaman*

Malcolm, Andrew H.
U.S. 1: America's Original Main Street.
St. Martin's, $29.95 (0-312-06480-2). 260p.

You might think a book about a road would be pretty dull, but this one captures much about what this country once was, still is, and, perhaps, what it will become. U.S. 1 was one of the first blacktop roads linking this country from border to border, in this case from Canada to the tip of the Florida Keys. In colonial times, it was known as the King's Highway, and since that time such famous personages as George Washington, Paul Revere (on his famous ride), Benedict Arnold, and Jefferson Davis have ridden upon it, as have troops of the Revolution, the War of 1812, the Civil War, and other wars to end all wars—not to mention millions of civilians known only to friends and acquaintances. Thinking more contemporarily, the Charles Kuralt of his "On the Road" series would fit quite well into the book's spotlighting of modern-day sights and people. Malcolm can be pretty tiresome at times, bemoaning the explosion of shopping malls and traffic jams on the route, or worse, the fact that a new interstate blots out the old U.S. 1. But he convinces us that, although U.S. 66 may have been the star of an old TV show, we really ought to go get some kicks on U.S. 1. —*Jon Kartman*

Travel

Modzelewski, Michael.
Inside Passage: Living with Killer Whales, Bald Eagles, and Kwakiutl Indians.
HarperCollins, $19.95 (0-06-016533-2). 208p.

The Inside Passage is the waterway from Seattle to Alaska, but for some it is also a spiritual passage back to our place in nature. Modzelewski was all set to follow his pro-football-playing father onto the gridiron, but found himself writing poetry instead and dreaming of a paradise: "a northern island with an evergreen forest full of wild animals; cold, clear sea streaked with salmon; dark, brooding skies." Providentially, he meets Will Malloff, who lives on such an island and is willing to share it with a novice. On his very first kayak trip, Modzelewski finds himself gliding over schools of fish beneath the shadow of an eagle and in sight of a whale, a seal, mountains, and a full moon facing a setting sun. Not bad. Malloff is a fascinating man—a healer, boat builder, and teacher—and Modzelewski quickly learns survival skills. He ingenuously expresses his joy in solitude, snow, storms, stars, and interactions with animals. Writing an alone-in-the-wilderness book is becoming almost a rite of passage, like the coming-of-age first novel—an interesting reflection of our times. —*Donna Seaman*

Moorhouse, Geoffrey.
On the Other Side: A Journey through Soviet Central Asia.
Holt, $19.95 (0-8050-1229-X). 192p.

Beginning his journey near the Pakistan border where he stopped in his *To the Frontier,* Moorhouse now enters Soviet Central Asia in 1989 on a trip sponsored by the National Geographic Society. While there are no color photographs to set the scene for the author's experiences, the descriptions in Moorhouse's splendid style are worth more than a thousand glossy pictures. What camera could portray the effect of a beauty contest in a Kazakh village in which a segment of traditional dancing is followed by the leather-skirted contestants dancing to a disco beat? Or could a photograph explain the situation of German-speaking Soviet minority settled in the middle of a vast Asian wilderness? Well, Moorhouse can accomplish all of this with ease even if he becomes a bit brutish about the accommodations and service, which are often less than adequate even by his well-traveled standards. The exoticism and the conflicts of this immense region are so expertly caught in this account that the author's quirks and quibbles are more than excusable and indeed add a bit of petulant fun to this amazing and revealing voyage. —*John Brosnahan*

Travel

✔**Raban, Jonathan.**
Hunting Mister Heartbreak: A Discovery of America.
HarperCollins, $25 (0-06-018209-1). 384p.

English critic and travel writer Raban follows his 1981 best-seller *Old Glory: An American Voyage*, a conjuring up of Mark Twain's Mississippi River life, with another account of impression-gathering in search of the American character. Intent on re-creating the American experience, Raban took the first step in that direction by setting out from his native country not in the comfort of a wide-body jet but on a steamship, thus enabling him to more closely imagine the immigration process from Europe in the nineteenth and early twentieth centuries. Once disembarked on the New World's shores, Raban traversed the U.S. in its vastness and multiformity, from big-city department stores to small-town diners, from proud South to booming Northwest. In holding up a mirror to our faces, Raban forces us to wince on occasion, but more often he induces chuckles of recognition as we admire our resourcefulness. At once limpid and rousing, this unique travel book is sure to be as popular as its predecessor. —*Brad Hooper*

✔**Scheer, George F.**
Booked on the Morning Train: A Journey through America.
Algonquin, $21.95 (0-945575-40-8). 384p.

Wondering "what remained of the great tradition" of cross-country train travel, Scheer spent six weeks jouncing, swaying, and rocking on Amtrak trains. Starting in North Carolina, he traveled to New Orleans, St. Louis, Austin, San Antonio, L.A., Santa Fe, Durango, Kansas City, Seattle, and many other points north, thinking about the world outside the train windows, the community inside the cars, and the realm of the mind. Scheer talks to everyone: honeymoon couples, Amtrak staff, late-nighters in the lounge car, and whomever he's seated with at meals. He admires sleepy stations at night, mulls over train history, and shares facts about the mechanics of track and locomotive and the design of sleepers. He takes side trips and relates local lore and conversations with sax players, geologists, trout fishermen, and an Indian of the Laguna Pueblo who asks, "What is life when it's done but memories?" Scheer's memories take the pulse of America from the still-romantic vantage point of a window seat on a fast-moving train. —*Donna Seaman*

Schmidt, Jeremy.
Himalayan Passage: Seven Months in the High Country of Tibet, Nepal, China, India & Pakistan.
Mountaineers Books, $22.95 (0-89886-262-0). 320p.

Schmidt and a friend of his, along with their wives, navigated the mountains of the Himalayas from Tibet to the tiny kingdom of Sikkim. Christening the rather vast trip provisions with the name Mount Equipment, these experienced mountaineers were well prepared in every way for their seven-month journey. On foot treks and mountain bikes, their travels would yield moments of euphoric communion with majestic and breathtaking Himalayan vistas. They would also endure incredible "adventures"—traveling in darkness along dangerous, twisting roads, in buses or trucks so overcrowded that bodies would pile atop each other helter-skelter for endless hours of torturous discomfort. At times, while ill, they spent days staying in clamorous, unsanitary lodgings, waiting for bureaucratic red tape to unravel and hopefully allow the desired passage. For readers concerned with the earth's remaining wild and remote areas of great natural beauty, Schmidt provides an illuminating view as he relates the vast similarities and differences of these other cultures, other faiths, other peoples, dwelling in ancient sites bombarded by an "explosive confrontation with the twentieth century." —*Alice Joyce*

✓Settle, Mary Lee.
Turkish Reflections: A Biography of a Place.
Prentice Hall Press, $19.95 (0-13-917675-6). 256p.

Writer Settle returns to visit Turkey, where she lived for three years in the 1970s and where she set her novel *Blood Tie*. Traveling around the country, Settle evokes both the past and the present, recounting the historical landscape and relaying her own personal odyssey. Settle captures the remains of Ottoman legend in her pictures of ruined monuments and in her quotations from Turkish literature; she also briefly fills in the history of the country in the twentieth century, when wars, territorial squabbles, and ethnic unrest have disturbed the peacefully slow pace of life. But the charm, hospitality, and beauty of the Turkish people create the strongest impression here, as Settle reunites with old acquaintances and is introduced to new friends at every step of her journey. —*John Brosnahan*

Taber, Sara Mansfield.
Dusk on the Campo: A Journey in Patagonia.
Holt, $19.95 (0-8050-1473-X). 256p.

In this beautifully written account of time spent in Patagonia, Taber reveals a region in Argentina that to this day projects a uniquely enigmatic image and allure for the adventurous traveler. This is an insider's view of the isolation and loneliness of a remote, seemingly unforgiving land. While initially doing research, the author and her husband spent 18 months in a whale camp, cut off from other people for months at a time. Returning five years later as a doctoral student, Taber gathered oral histories from many Patagonians—strong, proud people who shared their struggles, dreams, and triumphs. An account of an inward journey as well as one of distance, readers may find themselves transfixed by the fortitude and independence in these recorded voices, lured, as Sara Mansfield Taber was, to search for the key to surviving solitude and hardship with abundant faith and grace. —*Alice Joyce*

✓Tisdale, Sallie.
Stepping Westward: The Long Search for Home in the Pacific Northwest.
Holt, $19.95 (0-8050-1353-9). 272p.

"I've only recently come to realize that my ancestors stayed here in spite of all that keeps me here—in spite of the mountains, and the storms, the high

255

True Crime

plains and the wild coast. It was a land that seemed meant for solitude and isolation, the singular existence of the single man, and it had to be turned into a world of commerce and families." Tisdale's insightful meditation on living in the Pacific Northwest builds on this rich irony in our pioneer heritage. The very things we now bemoan in the Northwest—the loss of old-growth forests and the plethora of dams, for example—are natural outgrowths of the first settlers' need to tame the wilderness. Torn between her respect for the pioneer spirit and her wish to preserve what is untouched in the natural world, Tisdale brings fresh insight to her analysis of such familiar issues as clear-cutting and the spotted-owl controversy. Her focus, though, is finally more philosophical than polemical: "When we join ourselves to a place, we join air and land as though they were clothes to wear." The clothes of the Pacific Northwest have rarely been displayed as vividly as they are here. —*Bill Ott*

Winchester, Simon.
Pacific Rising: The Emergence of a New World Culture.
Prentice Hall Press, $24.95 (0-13-807793-2). 500p. index.

The sun rises first in the Pacific; now, it seems, the economic, political, and cultural sun is rising there, too. Have the world's interests shifted from the Atlantic to the mighty Pacific, with its diverse and varied inhabitants? Winchester provides a sourcebook of entertaining anecdotes, history, opinions, and speculation on the ocean that has "given the world everything from silks to silicon" and the people who seem to have traded their grass outfits for three-piece suits, all while the world was looking the other way. Spiked with insights gleaned from personal explorations, this fact-filled foray into what Melville called "the tide-beating heart of the earth" is highlighted with odd gems of information, all wryly observed and reported. While bemoaning all that is implied in the name change from "South Seas" to "Pacific Rim," Winchester brings to life the old ways and the inevitable new, charting the many links that draw the islands together as well as the rifts, physical and economic, that keep them apart. Includes maps and a list of further reading. —*Eloise Kinney*

True Crime

Anastasia, George.
Blood and Honor: Inside the Scarfo Mob, the Mafia's Most Violent Family.
Morrow, $22 (0-688-09260-8). 349p.

It's a perverse, enduring irony that the word *honor* gets so badly abused in so many books about the Mafia. Maybe Mario Puzo's operatic blockbuster, *The Godfather*, which described a perverse sort of honor among thieves and killers, is to blame. "Forget any fancy or idealistic notions about 'men of honor.' If they existed at all, they died a generation ago," writes *Philadelphia Inquirer* reporter Anastasia in this account of the brief, incredibly violent reign of Philadelphia mob boss Nicodemo ("Little Nicky") Scarfo. Based largely on the testimony of confessed murderer and extortionist Nick Caramandi, who generated millions for Scarfo before being marked for death, *Blood and Honor* is the story of a madman. Scarfo reveled in "whacking" people and insisted on doing it in public; the more witnesses, the better he liked it. He also delighted in pitting "family" members against one another in small intrigues that often proved fatal. *Blood and Honor* will find a large audience, but Mafia buffs will be taken aback. The book's most startling and important revelations concern absences: of honor, intelligence, cunning, style, and competence. Scarfo, Caramandi, and the dozens of other hoods discussed were/are low-rent bozos whose sole strength was viciousness. The only remotely shrewd insight is Caramandi's—it's hard to swindle an honest person. —*Thomas Gaughan*

Baumann, Ed and O'Brien, John.
Murder Next Door: How Police Tracked Down 18 Brutal Killers.
Bonus Books, $19.95 (0-929387-61-9). 250p.

From the grisly to the brilliant, the logic of murder is showcased by two Chicago crime reporters who detail cases from all over the world. In a few pages, Baumann and O'Brien retrace the often confounding machinations of criminals and the pit-bull detective work it takes to locate minute pieces of data that solve puzzles. But these amazing stories don't stop with solutions. Truth being stranger than fiction, the things murderers have gotten away with are often more confounding than the crimes they have committed. Absolutely fascinating. —*Cynthia Ogorek*

Egginton, Joyce.
Day of Fury: The Story of the Tragic Shooting That Forever Changed the Village of Winnetka.
Morrow, $20 (0-688-09085-0). 306p.

The attraction of some true crime accounts lies in showing the effects of violence upon the well-to-do and sheltered, thereby "proving" that money, even if it often seems to buy happiness, can't buy security from madness and horror. This recounting of the day in 1988 when a deranged young woman, Laurie Dann, rampaged through wealthy Winnetka, Illinois, shooting children, certainly offers that kind of allure. But journalist Egginton's exhaustive round-up of the experiences and reflections of dozens of the men and women caught up in that emergency does more than coddle resentment of the rich. It demonstrates a community of caretakers reacting to a crisis with consummate professionalism, compassion, and grace. Police, school administrators and teachers, paramedics, nurses, doctors, psychiatric social workers, and clergy all behaved awe-inspiringly well. Of course, they could only mitigate the day's traumatic effects, they could only repair—not make better—those affected, including themselves. And yet, would that other targets of similar violence, the children of the less well heeled, could have their wounds and pain so well assuaged. That is the sober thought with which one closes this book, and it is probably the reaction Egginton intends. —*Ray Olson*

✔**Fletcher, Connie.**
Pure Cop: Cops Talk from the Street to the Specialized Units—Bomb Squad, Arson, Hostage Negotiation, Prostitution, Major Accidents, Crime Scene.
Villard, $22.50 (0-679-40036-2). 304p.

"Cops are consummate storytellers. They turn street grit into powerful poetry." Fletcher follows her successful *What Cops Know* with another dose of cop talk, an oral history of the Chicago Police Department made up of raw data organized into seven sections: "Bomb Squad," "Arson," "Prostitution," "Crime Scene Investigation," "Major Accidents," "Hostage/Barricade Incidents," and "The Street." This is the kind of stuff for which Elmore Leonard would pay dearly, as cops tell it like it is—crude and colorful, bloody and bold. Succeeding in winning the trust of Chicago police—who don't usually open up to any outsider, especially a journalist—Fletcher provides an outlet for typically tight-lipped cops to spin a good yarn. And they do. They love to tell their experiences with blood-and-guts, and they spare us nothing as they jump at the opportunity to set the record straight. Accordingly, here are rare accounts of highly specialized units and undercover vice squads as well as of walking a beat on the mean streets. Raunchy and dramatic, these anecdotes will find a large audience wherever true-crime and crime fiction thrive. —*Benjamin Segedin*

Franklin, Eileen and Wright, William.
Sins of the Father: The Landmark Franklin Case: A Daughter, a Memory, and a Murder.
Crown, $22 (0-517-58207-4). 353p.

On September 22, 1969, Eileen Franklin's best friend, Susan Nason, disappeared from her suburban San Francisco home. Three months later, the bruised, strangulated body of the eight-year-old victim was found in a nearby wooded area. With no suspects and few clues, the unsolved case remained open until 20 years later, when Eileen Franklin began recalling bits and pieces of that brutal murder, which she had witnessed. The rapist and murderer was none other than Franklin's burly, alcoholic father, George, who had been verbally, physically, and sexually abusing his wife, five children, and others for years. This book is a wildly fascinating chronicle of this well-publicized case (George Franklin was convicted and sentenced to life imprisonment in January 1991), detailing both Eileen's stormy life and her father's long history of violence. Mixing Eileen's first-person insights and reflections with third-person narrative, Wright spins an evenhanded account of this stranger-than-fiction episode. In the hands of a writer less skilled, this could have devolved into a titillating soap opera, but Wright manages to remain objective. —*Sue-Ellen Beauregard*

✔**French, Thomas.**
Unanswered Cries.
St. Martin's, $18.95 (0-312-05526-9). 320p.

By keeping his cool—simply describing what happened and restraining the impulse to goose readers' emotions—newspaper journalist French has crafted

True Crime

a true-crime narrative as compelling as any in the genre. It's about the 1984 stabbing-bludgeoning murder of 35-year-old Karen Gregory in little Gulfport, Florida—a messy crime in which the obvious suspect wasn't picked up for an uncommonly long time, mostly because he was too well known as a good guy to local police. Said suspect was a young fireman, given to being the neighborhood watchman, who indeed told police he'd gone outside to investigate movement around the victim's house after hearing her scream—but who, like the rest of the neighbors, didn't report the scream at the time. His ultimate apprehension, two trials, subsequent appeals, and the psychological effects the crime and its aftermath had upon the families and friends of victim and culprit alike are the meat of the book, and French lets readers do the chewing. Chew we do, because such roiling issues as survivors' rights, courtroom etiquette (severe for the prosecution, almost obscenely lenient for the defense), and how the cronyism of firefighters and police can shield criminals among them are the leitmotivs of this absorbing document. —*Ray Olson*

McClung, Kevin and Rivele, Stephen J.
Dark Genius: A Child Prodigy in the Shadow of the CIA.
Knightsbridge, $22.95 (1-56129-142-0). 442p.

Philip Roth once announced that it was no longer possible to write fiction because reality was simply too outrageous for the novelist to surpass. *Dark Genius* is a compulsively readable proof of that proposition—at least in the subgenre of out-of-control intelligence agencies. As a second-grader in Silicon Valley in 1965, coauthor Kevin McClung was enrolled in MGM, Mentally Gifted Minors, an experimental educational program. Kevin's gift was for invention and, according to this book, his work was regularly monitored by CIA agents, who even measured his skull, unknowingly aping Nazi eugenicists. By age 21, he was designing and building lethal fountain pens and other devices of death and terror for the likes of Idi Amin, Quaddafi, and Salvadoran death squads. Dark Genius elicits a sequence of responses, including utter amazement and shock. Spooks E. Howard Hunt, Richard Secord, and Frank Terpil, Mafiosi Santo Traficante, Hell's Angel Sonny Barger, and Richard Allen (Reagan's national security adviser) appear in the book and indirectly intersect with McClung's work in amazingly unlikely spots. Evidence of CIA drug trafficking to fund wars on nearly every continent produces first horror, then disgust. But don't let horror and disgust keep you from buying this; it's sure to circulate. —*Thomas Gaughan*

McDougal, Dennis.
Angel of Darkness.
Warner, $19.95 (0-446-51538-8). 384p.

From 1970 to 1983, Randy Kraft kidnapped, drugged, and murdered 67 young male hitchhikers. McDougal's book is the ghoulish chronicle of how this most prolific serial killer was ultimately brought to San Quentin's death row, and it's not a reassuring story of modern police sleuthing. Containing enough graphic descriptions of mutilated bodies to satisfy the most voyeuristic reader, it's almost a catalog of repeated perversion. McDougal seems to

True Crime

dump bodies throughout the book as casually as Kraft dumped them along Southern California freeways. He tells us something about each victim, however, driving home the point that these men, some of whom lived on the fringes of society, were just human beings whose bad luck it was to accept a ride from the wrong stranger. McDougal's ultimate gift lies not in his ability to portray the suspense of chase and capture, but in his showing the killer as everyone thought of him. By tracing Kraft's life—through thousands of interviews and conversations—a puzzling picture of a likable, hardworking, upwardly mobile superachiever emerges. Therein lies the horror, however, as we wonder how someone so normal-seeming could become society's worst nightmare. —*Tracie Richardson*

✔**McGinniss, Joe.**
Cruel Doubt.
Simon & Schuster, $25 (0-671-67947-3). 576p.

The bare facts: Bonnie and Lieth Von Stein were savagely attacked in their North Carolina home; Lieth died of stab wounds and severe beatings; Bonnie survived, inheriting Lieth's two-million-dollar estate; Angela, Bonnie's daughter, was in the adjoining bedroom but was not attacked; Bonnie's son, Chris, was away at college in Chapel Hill. The few pieces of evidence: a burned map, written in Chris's handwriting, giving directions to the Von Stein house; a blood-splattered paperback; a mysterious bag. The suspects: James Upchurch, a college friend of Chris' and the charismatic leader of a group of college kids who spent long hours role-playing Dungeons & Dragons and taking drugs; Neal Henderson, a burly genius and college dropout. The unfolding scenario: a fascinating tangle of conflicting evidence, conflicting loyalties, and a mother's unwavering, at time almost irrational, belief in her child's innocence. *Fatal Vision* author McGinniss was brought into this case at the request of Bonnie Von Stein, and his literary prominence may explain the high level of accessibility he received from victims, investigators, and suspects. Chris was lost in drugs and medieval fantasies. He was failing college, and his rich stepfather was unsupportive. Suspects Upchurch and Henderson never quite receive the character detailing the Von Steins get, but both men's testimonies reveal copious discrepancies. McGinniss is clearly sympathetic to the family, yet is objective enough to stress that they seldom appeared either likable or grieving and that the evidence, though circumstantial, is daunting. The sense that many facts remain hidden is quite inescapable. This is just the kind of blood-stained, family tragedy that never fails to attract a crowd. —*Peter Robertson*

O'Brien, Joseph F. and Kurins, Andris.
Boss of Bosses: The Fall of the Godfather: The FBI and Paul Castellano.
Simon & Schuster, $22.95 (0-671-70815-5). 340p.

Are these guys for real? They might as well be Brando, De Niro, Pacino, and Pesci, with life imitating gangster movies, as the true-crime reportage of these two FBI agents testifies. O'Brien and Kurins spent years investigating the Gambino family, the most powerful clan of the so-called Cosa Nostra, and their illustrious godfather, Paul Castellano, chieftain from 1976 to 1985. With painstaking diligence and perseverance, the two agents masterminded a break-in of the Castellano's mansion and planted a bug in his innermost sanctum, allowing them to monitor hours of incriminating conversation. What they heard was immensely invaluable, revealing the family's reach into everything from garbage in Nassau County to pornography in Times Square, from unions to wholesale meat, from liquor, nightclubs and restaurants to extortion, bribery, and murder. The Mob under Castellano, while no doubt corrupt, still operated under a code of loyalty and honor, ethics of sorts, spawned from a Byzantine web of intrigue, alliances, and archaic ritual. The younger, flashier, more violent breed of Mafiosi, with their interest in the heroin trade, smelled weakness and finally whacked Castellano in 1985, abruptly ending many of the age-old traditions. O'Brien and Kurins developed a respect for Castellano, even an awe, the result of the intimate bond acquired from years of surveillance, listening to personal conversations, and harassing his foot soldiers. Castellano was finally arrested, and, as relayed in a sensitive, touching chapter here, the two agents went out of their way, violating the bureau's own guidelines, to take the declining boss to his favorite restaurant for a corned beef on rye. —*Benjamin Segedin*

Olsen, Jack.
Predator: Rape, Madness, and Injustice in Seattle.
Delacorte, $19.95 (0-385-29935-4). 370p.

Hot on the heels of Olsen's Edgar Award–winning *Doc: The Rape of the Town of Lovell*, which depicted the disgustingly unorthodox practices of a Wyoming gynecologist, comes *Predator*, a biographical exploration of a sociopath who raped more than 50 Seattle-area women at knifepoint. In compact, understated chapters that are chilling in their straightforward portrayal of perversion, Olsen details the life of pseudonymous Mac Smith— his dysfunctional family, early sexual experimentation, and bent toward crime, all of which contributed to a world view where women were whores and he wasn't raping them, but "stealing their time." While Smith continued to stalk women, a young Seattle man, Steve Titus, was arrested, tried, and convicted for one of Smith's rapes and saved from prison only by the Pulitzer Prize–winning efforts of journalist Paul Henderson. Titus' ruined life is yet another symptom of the terrible sickness spawned by Smith. Olsen doesn't simply tell the story of one sexual psychopath; he makes understandable (but not forgivable), and thus more horrifying, the creation of such a creature, the relative ease with which he was able to operate, and the many barriers leading to his conviction: for one, victims too traumatized to press charges. Ultimately, Olsen shows, the system works, but only after it has been jump-started like an old car after a long, freezing night. —*Eloise Kinney*

True Crime

Rule, Ann.

If You Really Loved Me: A True Story of Desire and Murder.
Simon & Schuster, $22.95 (0-671-68835-9). 448p.

By the age of 33, junior high dropout David Arnold Brown—overweight, acne-scarred, chain-smoking, and in less-than-perfect health—had been married six times to five different women, had fathered three daughters, and had parlayed his technological wizardry into a thriving business retrieving lost computer data. Then one night in March 1985, Brown's third (and fifth) wife, Linda Bailey Brown, was murdered in her bed, and Brown's eldest daughter (by his first wife), 14-year-old Cinnamon, was charged with the crime and sent to the California Youth Authority prison in Ventura. But the case still rankled the Orange County prosecutor's office. Suspicions were aroused even more when, soon after, Brown cashed in on four insurance policies taken out in Linda's name and then subsequently married the deceased's dishwater-blond moppet sister, 17-year-old Patti. The case was reopened in 1989, and authorities eventually secured a murder conviction on Brown, even though he never pulled the trigger (apparently, Cinnamon really did, with possibly an assist from Patti). This bizarre tale of greed, lust, and mind control—Brown is a first-rank sociopath who, Manson-like, fed on the psychological inadequacies and sexual naïveté of down-and-out teenage girls—should hold the attention of the many true-crime fans in public libraries. Veteran crime journalist Rule has scored big in the genre previously with the best-selling *Small Sacrifices*, *The Stranger beside Me*, and *Possession*. —*Martin Brady*

FICTION

General Fiction

Abe, Kobo.
Beyond the Curve.
Kodansha, $18.95 (4-7700-1465-1). 240p.

The first collection of short fiction by one of Japan's premier writers. Each ingenuously simple tale is shrouded in a haze of paranoia and surrealism, a sort of Kafka-esque atmosphere of uncertainty and conspiracy. Abe's protagonists are victims, trapped in the inevitability of a nightmare. A man comes home, discovers the corpse of a stranger in his room, and immediately feels guilty. Another character finds himself inexplicably turning into a plant, while a third is awakened by a family of intruders who take over his life. Memory loss, the evaporation of rationality, estrangement from the everyday—Abe's world is stark and arbitrary. He dramatizes alienation and helplessness with grim humor and finesse, creating poignant satire. Abe's novels include *The Ark Sukura*, *Secret Rendezvous*, and *The Woman in the Dunes*. —*Donna Seaman*

Abel, Robert.
Ghost Traps.
Univ. of Georgia, $17.95 (0-8203-1252-5). 168p.

Abel's stories are about the joyous unpredictability of life. His prose is so energetic and direct that anything seems possible, and everything seems new. Although his characters may appear uncertain, vulnerable, or cautious, they are also willing to be propelled along in one direction or another by unknown forces. They are ordinary people in slightly extraordinary circumstances, but Abel looks at their lives so generously that each event crackles with meaning. In "Appetizer," a man fishing an Alaskan stream unexpectedly meets one bear and then another. Although this is something that has happened to him before, he immediately focuses on whatever mysterious core it is that holds him together and becomes a part of this new action, catching fish for the bears. "With a bear at your side, it is not the simplest thing to play a fish properly, but the presence of this huge animal, and especially her long snout, thick as my thigh, wonderfully concentrates the mind. She smells like the forest floor." Be here now, she says. This is a beguiling collection of stories by an ardent realist. Winner of the Flannery O'Connor Award for Short Fiction. —*Frances Woods*

General Fiction

Adams, Alice.
Caroline's Daughter.
Knopf, $22 (0-394-56825-7). 320p.

Alice Adams is back with a new novel reminiscent of her best-selling *Superior Women*. Women, both superior and otherwise, are once again the focus in this pop-psych soaper. Caroline has had three husbands—the most recent a loving companion of 25 years—and five (yes, five) daughters. She has just returned to San Francisco from a five-year sojourn in Portugal with Ralph and is in for a rough year, coping with his heart attacks and death and the various difficulties of her precocious, passionate daughters. Each of the young women is described in firm detail, covering appearance—weight, hair styles, and clothes—as well as more abstract matters of sexuality and ambition. There's dark-haired, intense Sage, a ceramicist married to a cheating creep; Liza, married to a kind psychiatrist, mother of three, and a fledgling writer; Fiona, a successful if trendy restaurateur; Jill, a corporate lawyer; and Portia, Ralph's only daughter, a bit fey and unformed. The women play musical chairs with lovers and husbands, gain and lose fortunes, gossip, cry, worry, and forgive. Within the entertainingly busy plot, Adams finds space to reflect on the conflicts of career and love, children and achievement, as well as the hateful decadence of the 1980s, AIDS, and the plight of the homeless. On another level, this is a keen critique of San Francisco, with its precariously steep hills, earthquake threat, street people, fog, and provincial snobbism. In sum, a hearty and satisfying read sure to please popular-fiction fans. —*Donna Seaman*

Aiken, Joan.
Jane Fairfax.
St. Martin's, $17.95 (0-312-05884-5). 256p.

Aiken is an accomplished writer of more than 50 novels, short stories, plays, and children's books, not to mention the daughter of famed writer Conrad Aiken. With the highly stylized *Jane Fairfax*, a companion novel and a tribute to Jane Austen's *Emma*, Aiken reaches the height of her craft. The novel is an uncommonly good imitation of Austen's witty and evocative use of language and of her powerful rendering of the manners and mores that shaped nineteenth-century society. Aiken here retells Austen's story from the point of view of Jane Fairfax, Emma's friend and rival. The emotional world of willful, much-indulged Emma is richly contrasted with that of poor, humble, sweet, talented Jane. Attesting to Aiken's immense talent, the novel can stand on its own and will be relished even by those who have never read *Emma*. Highly recommended. By the author of *Mansfield Revisited*, a sequel to Austen's *Mansfield Park*. —*Mary Banas*

Alvarez, Julia.
How the Garcia Girls Lost Their Accents.
Algonquin, $16.95 (0-945575-57-2). 308p.

Four sisters and their experiences of life and love in both the Dominican Republic where they were born and the U.S. where they now live. The Garcia girls represent an immigrant family that honors traditional ways and changed realities in a not-always-comfortable mix of old and new. Love and sex figure prominently as areas the sisters are all too willing to explore despite their father's vigilance, and the stratagems and connivances performed in the name of romance are often truly astounding and hilarious. Visits with relatives in the mother country play up these divergences from the old order, while lingering moral confusion adds a confrontational edge to the sisters' predicament. Perhaps a bit too episodic to build to a real climax, these stories nevertheless expose the pangs and joys of being a woman and becoming an American. —*John Brosnahan*

✔Amis, Martin.
Time's Arrow.
Crown/Harmony, $18 (0-517-58515-4). 138p.

Amis continues to unsettle his readers with surreal, twisted perspectives. His last novel, *London Fields*, sported an aspiring murder victim searching for a perpetrator; his latest challenges our sense of time and narrative. *Time's Arrow*, a technical marvel, shoots us into the past as it reveals the true identity of a man called Tod Friendly. As Tod lies in a hospital bed, his consciousness distances itself from the present and assesses his life in reverse, like a film run backwards. Every action is reversed and every conversation inverted. This voice, this estranged soul, watches Tod create food and beverages at meals, get paid for bringing items into stores, and grow younger. As his American identity is stripped away, his hideous past as a German doctor and executioner at a Nazi extermination camp is revealed. Amis' time reversal is brilliantly effective and extremely disturbing. Life in reverse is jarring: you don't gain intimacy, you lose it; children grow smaller and smaller and finally disappear. But for Tod, whose real name is Odilo Unverdorben, this warped perspective is protection from the appalling truth. He sees the maniacal labor of the camps as a huge healing process that pulls Jewish and Gypsy souls down from the smoky sky and bakes them back to life in the awful ovens. This denial, this wishful lie, evokes the naked monstrosity and incomprehensible horror of the Holocaust with fresh shock and terrifying recognition. Amis has created a haunting masterpiece of conscience, awareness, and the failings of memory. —*Donna Seaman*

Arnold, Jean.
The Scissor Man.
Doubleday, $18.95 (0-385-41508-7). 304p.

A richly textured coming-of-age story set on a lush jungle island off the coast of Central America and filled with a subtle symbolism that underscores the conflicting strains of emotionalism and reason at war within the maturing protagonist, 13-year-old Octavia. Born into an eccentric household headed by a Mayan physician wedded to an American who's disconsolate over her dull, restricted lifestyle, Olivia, the youngest of four children (including one deceased), struggles to find meaning and acceptance in a world ruled by superstition, fear, and anger. Compounding Olivia's confusion over her own blossoming sexuality is the sexual exploitation of her retarded older sister, the beautiful Maribel. Relief from household tensions seems certain with the eagerly awaited arrival from the States of Olivia's Uncle Clo and handsome cousin Julian, but an unexpected turn of events spells disaster for the family, especially Olivia. Arnold, the author of two previous novels (*Fausto's Keyhole* and *Prettybelle*), has a gift for perceptive characterizations and vivid narration. An unforgettable, beautifully articulated tale. —*Mary Banas*

✔**Atwood, Margaret.**
Wilderness Tips.
Doubleday, $20 (0-385-42106-0). 247p.

If anyone ought to have a best-selling book of short stories, it's Margaret Atwood. Each of these 10 is a virtual novel-in-miniature, with middle-class protagonists (not all women, by the way) reminiscing, in extended flashbacks and rueful-wistful bursts that interrupt their everyday routines, about significant experiences from their youth (the way-back-then of the 1950s and 1960s). Lois recalls her summer camp friend Lucy, who disappeared on a canoe trip ("Death by Landscape"). Successful TV interviewer Susannah comes to see her life as a succession of abandonments by the men who nurtured her, beginning with her father, lost in World War II ("Uncles"). Julie remembers breaking off her first great affair, with a married professor when she was a student ("The Bog Man"). Richard, a literature professor whose own career's now downward bound, reviews 30 years of his encounters with Selena, a brilliant poet who tragically preceded him in decline ("Isis in Darkness"). These are some of the more somber of Atwood's involving stories. Others (see especially the collection-concluding "Hack Wednesday") are, if hardly frivolous, full of the humorous mutterings of the middle-aged soul that will spark instant recognition and wry appreciation in many an aging Baby Boomer. Wonderfully brainy, savvy, and consequential tales. —*Ray Olson*

Ballard, J. G.
The Kindness of Women.
Farrar, $19.95 (0-374-18110-1). 286p.

Ballard makes it difficult to like him. Following the success of *Empire of the Sun*, he has again used the material of an autobiography to fashion a novel, this time about the years of his adult life, focusing above all on the kindness of women who have helped him face the tragedies and peculiarities that have made him such a strange and fascinating writer. The kindness of women generally takes the form of allowing the novel's narrator, Jim, to adhere as closely as possible to the moist recesses of their bodies, soothing his disoriented, violence-ravaged heart and mind with their maternal, pornographic, equally vulnerable genitals-breasts-and-hips softness. The childhood in war-torn Shanghai, the threat of nuclear World War III, the violence of psyche-fragmenting scientists, the implosive psychedelia of the 1960s—these may have been enough to drive any brilliant and sensitive writer back into the earth-warm body of the goddess, though, and if Ballard makes it difficult to like him, this story of an extraordinary flight from the Apollonian horror of Nagasaki into the chthonic but forgiving arms of Hera/Aphrodite is a moving one, powerfully reproduced. —*Stuart Whitwell*

Banks, Iain.
Canal Dreams.
Doubleday, $19 (0-385-41814-0). 208p.

Banks' quirky, stylish first novel, *The Wasp Factory*, offered more than a hint that a new talent was on the horizon. The playfully subversive sf works—*The Player of Games* and *Consider Phlebas*—he has since written have done nothing to blunt that view. *Canal Dreams* wavers between past and near future, as the mind and body of young Japanese cellist Hisako Onoda come to an unusual fruition, bringing international fame after years of poverty and stifled emotions. Fame brings world tours, but Hisako's fear of flying results in boat trips and a slow touring schedule. One such trip finds Hisako in love with a younger Frenchman, an officer aboard the liner on which she is traveling. Banks delights in teasing his readers. Languid scenes of underwater diving are set against erotic reveries, and the tricky cross-cultural sallies between crew and passengers demonstrate Banks' sure way with language. The ship is soon stranded on a Panamanian lake as war breaks out. Such is the insidious level of suspense working here that the reader is almost relieved when the revolutionary forces storm the ship, commence killing, and take hostages. Naturally, Onoda is unaware that her whole life—her solitary devotions, martial-art discipline, physical waywardness, and late-blooming sensuality—have unwittingly created a killing machine. The Scots-born Banks joins Martin Amis and Ian McEwan among the vanguard of the new British subversive novelist. —*Peter Robertson*

Banks, Russell.
The Sweet Hereafter.
HarperCollins, $19.95 (0-06-016703-3). 272p.

Banks has made a name for himself with such darkly affecting works as *Continental Drift.* Only a writer of his stature and talent could attempt a book like this one—in which 14 children are killed in a school bus accident in Upstate New York—and make it bearable to read. As it turns out, he never convincingly accomplishes what seems to be his goal here: to portray "what happens to a town that loses its children." Part of the reason for that failure, however, is the strength of his characters, especially the four, distinctly different individuals who tell the story: we care about them as people, and we pay less attention to the group dynamics, though we do get the point that there must be someone to blame, someone to ostracize in order for the town to move on. Banks deserves applause for making us see how grief can manifest itself in countless unsuspected ways; he also earns our respect for describing the accident only once and with few horrifying details. —*Deb Robertson*

✔**Barnes, Julian.**
Talking It Over.
Knopf, $22 (0-679-40525-9). 288p.

Put three people in front of a mirror; then break the mirror in three places. Have the three put the pieces back together; the mirror will look largely the same, except for the cracks, though in fact, the picture will be completely different. Julian Barnes' latest novel is an elaborate, almost metaphysical exercise in mirror breaking. Three thirtysomething characters—plodding Stuart, flamboyant Oliver, enigmatic Gillian—reflect on their tangled relationship. We listen to the pompous Oliver heap scorn on his friend Stuart, who marries Gillian. It becomes easy to hate Oliver, whose bravado requires deceit to keep it afloat. He tells us Stuart is rather dim. Stuart agrees. But, of course, he isn't. He's methodical. And his heart is eventually broken and calcified by Gillian and Oliver. Events receive multiple interpretations. The roles of lover, husband, voyeur, and emotional foundation cross over, run parallel, then intersect. And along the way, Barnes wields his customary wit like a paring knife. The novel is awash in luxuriant verbiage that illuminates, amuses, and distracts, the distractions being what saves Barnes from becoming yet another tired, albeit talented chronicler of English mores. We are allowed, encouraged even, to form opinions concerning our threesome, then to have these opinions shattered, like the metaphysical mirror, as events reveal heretofore unseen weaknesses and strengths. Another tour de force from a flamboyant writer who delivers substance as well as style. —*Peter Robertson*

Bawden, Nina.
Family Money.
St. Martin's, $17.95 (0-312-06351-2). 240p.

Family and money can be a bad combination, bringing out the worst of one and inflating the importance of the other. Bawden examines both and very much more in this perfectly fashioned and keenly felt novel about a London widow and her children. Fanny is adjusting well to widowhood and the simplicity of solitude, but her peace is shattered when she intervenes in a deadly street fight and is knocked unconscious. Feeling "papery," she can't remember the circumstances of the attack and feels disoriented and detached from her grown children, Harry and Isabel. When she begins to exhibit seemingly eccentric behavior and arranges to sell her house, Harry and Isabel fret peevishly and offer little understanding or help. Meanwhile, Fanny is being harassed, even threatened, by one of the men involved in the fatal fight, but, in a triumphant reclaiming of control over her life, she faces her fears alone. Bawden's engagingly complex characters waltz around issues of inheritance, aging, independence, generosity, and trust, blind to each other's needs, but able, finally, to simply love each other. A gem from one of Britain's best. —*Donna Seaman*

Beattie, Ann.
What Was Mine.
Random, $20 (0-394-40077-X). 237p.

At first glance, Beattie's latest collection of stories—including two previously unpublished novellas—reprises the writer's familiar themes and style. Beattie's portraits of contemporary life, however, are less cool emotionally, more tangled psychologically, and more complex than the author's reputation as a minimalist master would presume. A Christmas Eve accident reopens the rift between a divorced alcoholic mother and her grown son; an embittered housewife engineers a practical joke that announces with savage force the end of her marriage; and the rivalry between two brothers is exposed in an artist's installation piece. With few exceptions, these stories reveal a deepened tone and a persistent indeterminacy that Beattie conveys and captures in her characters' minds and actions. —*John Brosnahan*

Begley, Louis.
Wartime Lies.
Knopf, $19 (0-679-40016–8). 208p.

Begley's marvelous and disturbing novel is told from the point of view of Maciek, a Jew and an only child who lives in an unnamed town in eastern Poland at the start of World War II. With his mother having died in childbirth and his father having disappeared, Maciek is being raised by his Aunt Tania. Posing as Catholic Poles and carrying forged Aryan papers, they travel to Lwów, then to Warsaw—where they meet Maciek's grandfather—then on to a village where they work on a farm, always barely escaping the trains to Auschwitz. The reader of this novel by a gifted writer reaches a better understanding of the destruction of the European Jews in a world gone mad. More important, unlike so much Holocaust fiction, *Wartime Lies* neither trivializes nor exploits the horrors of this most inhuman era of our history. —*George Cohen*

Belloc, Denis.
Neons.
Godine, $17.95 (0-87923-869-0). 102p.

Belloc's story of a young man's coming-of-age in Paris seems prompted by the same sociosexual stirrings evident in Annie Ernaux' *Cleaned Out.* In Belloc's version of young Denis' experiences, however, the sordid details of his entry into the low life of Pigalle are a bit more disturbing and lurid (although the economic and emotional compulsions seem to stem from the same frustrated source for both characters). Since Denis has chosen sex (or has the choice forced on him) as his profession, some explicitness is justified and necessary. Just how Denis became a male hustler is retold in a series of episodes that begin with his boyhood, describe his jail sentence for theft, portray his daily routine on the job, and finally ponder his future as a painter. Belloc renders all of this in undecorated prose that bluntly and vividly replicates Denis' life and the ambivalence that tears him apart. A haunted and violent slice of life on the seamy side. —*John Brosnahan*

General Fiction

Bellow, Saul.
Something to Remember Me By.
Viking, $21.95 (0-670-84216-8); NAL/Signet, paper, $5.99 (0-451-16870-4).
240p.

A trio of short works by one of this country's premier writers appears together in simultaneous hardcover and paperback publication. All three tales have been published separately. The novella *A Theft* first saw print as a paperback original in March 1989. It concerns the marital and extramarital relationships of the delightful main character, Clara Velde. *The Bellarosa Connection*, also first published in paper in 1989, is a superbly affecting story about a man who fled Europe during the Nazi horror with the help of celebrity Billy Rose. The short story "Something to Remember Me By," introduced in the pages of *Esquire* magazine in 1990, is a beautifully comic-poignant recollection by a father to his child of a disturbing incident from his own childhood. Recommended for libraries where the three stories are unavailable in their original form. —*Brad Hooper*

Berberova, Nina.
The Tattered Cloak and Other Novels.
Knopf, $21 (0-679-40281-0). 352p.

The American debut of Nina Berberova, 89, who, like her characters, fled Russia for Paris after the Revolution. Her recently rediscovered short novels (fewer than 100 pages) emit the melancholy and loss of displaced persons, wrenched from lives of light and warmth and thrust into the hard toil of poverty and hopelessness. In "The Resurrection of Mozart," Maria Leonidovna waits anxiously in the countryside outside of Paris for her husband while entire villages limp slowly away just ahead of the approaching edge of war. In "The Waiter and the Slut," a widow without family or funds struggles to wrest finery from rags so that she can attract a man. Lonely, broken, trapped people "waiting for love to help," can't connect with the beauty and poetry remembered from their past. Berberova writes tenderly, instilling meaning in objects like a large, ancient, moth-eaten cloak and the routine of survival. Moody, precise, and proud, these tales pinpoint the sorrow of life shadowed by exile and war. —*Donna Seaman*

Berney, Louis.
The Road to Bobby Joe and Other Stories.
HBJ, $18.95 (0-15-177870-1). 154p.

A masterfully crafted debut collection of 12 short stories by a promising new writer. Set primarily in his native Oklahoma, Berney's stories deftly explore the dreams and disappointments of ordinary, working-class people desperately fighting for a way out of their hardscrabble existence. The title story tugs at the heart with its realistic depiction of a sister's agonizing decision to escape to a better life with the six-year-old niece she's raised, on the eve of her no-good brother's release from prison. "This Is a Band" expertly captures the lingo and illusions of a talentless garage band that believes they're headed for fame by making it with a nympho groupie who has been with rock bands that have succeeded. "Swimming," a sadly tender story, evokes the lost youth and innocence of a 60-year-old retiree who has outlived all his relatives and who now witnesses the demise of his familiar childhood haunts. Berney's tales are wonderfully rich in atmosphere and, remarkable in light of their compactness, paint indelible portraits of some fascinating true-to-life characters. —*Mary Banas*

Billington, Rachel.
Theo and Matilda.
HarperCollins, $21.95 (0-06-016483-2). 368p.

When Theo and Matilda decide to buy a condominium complex in the English countryside, they both feel they have been there before. They have— four times—in a romance spanning nearly 1,400 years and centered on a spot of land that has seen the rise and fall of a humble monastery, a country manor, a Victorian mansion, and a contemporary mental hospital. Billington intelligently and humorously charts the evolution of Theo and Matilda's wills and interests, and their journeys toward and away from God, tempered always by their passionate love for one another. The novel is peopled with charmingly troublesome characters—from a demented midwife to a manipulative doctor—all of whom also change with time, while retaining vestiges of their former selves. Theo and Matilda are not always happy, not always even likable, and though their love seems ill-fated, touched again and again by tragedy, they are just living, as best they can, albeit again and again. Though the Matilda incarcerated in the asylum wonders why she should "be voyeur to the humiliations wrought by time," Billington skillfully shows that humiliations are coupled with successes, despair with true love, and that all's well that never ends. —*Eloise Kinney*

Binchy, Maeve.
The Lilac Bus.
Delacorte, $20 (0-385-30494-3). 336p.

This novel comprises eight vignettes—scenes from the lives of people who travel home together each weekend from Dublin to the village of Rathdoon. On the bus, like commuters, they say hello and make dutiful, pleasant conversation, but they reveal little of their private lives, especially their reasons for traveling home so often. As Binchy examines Nancy, Dee, Mikey, Judy, Kev, Rupert, Celia, and Tom, she moves from character study to cops and robbers. For example, Nancy, a parsimonious, unpopular girl, is made to see how her penny-pinching reflects a meanness in her spirit. The source of Nancy's revelation is Celia's mother, Mrs. Ryan, the owner of the local pub, whose drinking has become a frightening problem. Celia must force her mother to realize her addiction and convince her to take the cure. Then there's the character Kev, who has become unwittingly involved in high-level burglary and office theft and comes home each weekend to escape the planned heists. Some of the situations portrayed come to rather pat resolutions, the characters aided by the counsel of family and friends. Other tales are less predictable—and richer due to a tinge of ambiguity. Sentimental in an unmistakably Irish way, Binchy's stories never fail to bring a smile despite the common troubles they portray. —*Denise Perry Donavin*

Bosse, Malcolm.
Mister Touch.
Ticknor & Fields, $21.95 (0-89919-965-8). 502p.

This dark, apocalyptic tale by the acclaimed author of *The Warlord* might more accurately have been titled *Yuppies Get Their Comeuppance*. In an inimitable style—a quirky blend of gutter slang/dialect and know-it-all bluster edged with refinement—Bosse depicts a nightmare world in which the mighty have fallen and the derelict have risen in the wake of a viral epidemic (V70, a successor of AIDS) that in a matter of weeks has eradicated almost all human life from the face of the earth. Only a small group of 150 people—mostly minority gang members—have survived and roam the Greenwich Village area, along with wild, ravenous dogs, led by a now-blind former Wall Street arbitrageur (Mister Touch), who escaped criminal conviction on charges of insider trading thanks only to the plague. Calling themselves the Skulls, they seek refuge in Arizona where, in scenes disturbingly reminiscent of *The Lord of the Flies*, they attempt to rebuild civilization according to their own rules. Intense, captivating drama filled with dark irony. —*Mary Banas*

Boyd, Blanche McCrary.
The Revolution of Little Girls.
Knopf, $19 (0-679-40090-7). 192p.

As early as eight years old, when she climbs out of a tree knowing she has to put her shirt back on after playing Tarzan, southern redneck tomboy Ellen Lorraine realizes she is at odds with a world that is "suspicious of girls who [do] not want to play Jane." Her believable yet picaresque search for self-acceptance and maturity takes her from a "haunted" South Carolina plantation to Harvard and a failed marriage, from psychedelic drugs and screenwriting in California to a shaman in Peru's Nazca Plains, from a love relationship with a lesbian psychiatrist to the borders of insanity. Boyd weaves the tapestry of her novel on a loom where the warp is always the South, and the weft is the lives of unique characters who are picked up and dropped again and again as they create the pattern of Ellen's life. Laugh, cry, share Ellen's anger, and ultimately her optimism in this exceptional, impossible-to-put-down, not-to-be-missed novel that stands assuredly in the company of *Cress Delahanty* and *Rubyfruit Jungle* as a fine woman's coming-of-age story. —*Marie Kuda*

Brennan, Karen.
Wild Desire.
Univ. of Massachusetts, $22.50 (0-87023-751-9). 192p. paper, $9.95 (0-87023-752-7).

Brennan, winner of the 1990 Associated Writing Program Short Fiction Award, is a writer of many voices, many moods. She moves facilely from poetic, fantastic prose (as in "Building a House," where the narrator takes her

General Fiction

children's nightgowns to use for a roof and tells them stories of a head-on collision with a truck) to clever, wry vignettes (as in "Looking for Love," where a middle-aged woman strolls though a grocery store seeking not just dinner, but dinner guests). Brennan writes simply, too, often depending on understatement—a bored housewife describes the beginning of an affair by stating, "I was never very good at duplicity and so it went downhill from there"—but the stories themselves are tinged with a desperation born of the unlivability of the characters' lives. These tales of women and men eking out an emotional existence in the best and worst of times go straight to the heart of the matter, which is most often broken, shattered, unfixable. —*Eloise Kinney*

Brookner, Anita.
Brief Lives.
Random, $19 (0-394-58548-8). 262p.

After a brief detour for *Lewis Percy*, a sympathetic portrait of a bachelor set adrift after his mother's death, Brookner returns to the world she knows best—the inner lives of women, viewed here in terms of several key issues: "proper" wifely behavior, motherlessness, and widowhood, all of which are pondered by the seemingly mousy Faye, a club singer in her youth who marries an attorney, then retires quietly to the suburban household and dinner parties demanded by her husband's business affairs. With reluctance but with an inescapable sense of duty, she regularly visits Julia, the wife of her husband's partner. Julia is another familiar type—the woman so firmly convinced of her right to the spotlight that others, both male and female, indulge and encourage her prima-donna status. Brookner's story focuses upon the odd friendship, but more particularly on Faye's growing realization of the truth about her marriage and her destiny. Once again, Brookner's knowledge of women's friendships and enmities is revealed in the sharpest, most exacting of terms. —*Denise Perry Donavin*

✔Brown, Larry.
Joe.
Algonquin, $19.95 (0-945575-61-0). 360p.

This is one of those books that demands to be read, reread, talked about, and relished. Larry Brown, author of the acclaimed Vietnam novel *Dirty Work*, as well as two collections of short stories, *Facing the Music* (Algonquin, 1988) and *Big Bad Love*, has written a big bad novel that encompasses the human condition within the narrow framework of poor "white trash" in rural Mississippi. Joe Ransom is a middle-aged redneck with a soul. He fights and spits, drinks beer by the gallon from a cooler embedded in his truck, and endures bad relationships with women. But within the society he inhabits, he is a moral man, more or less following the rituals and established "codes" of fair play. Unfortunately, he is involved in a classic feud, the roots of which are never revealed, that threatens to destroy him. Also destined to cross paths with Joe is the nomadic Jones family. Gary Jones is a hardworking and painfully naive teenager. His father is pure evil, his mother nearly insane, and his siblings barely human. Joe offers Gary work, fueling hope that these

General Fiction

two very different men will learn enough from each other to save themselves. In telling the stories of these and other characters, Brown especially illuminates the rules by which civilized life is lived in rural Mississippi, and they are as clear and stratified here as anywhere. Even the jailed and jailer treat each other with a strange courtesy. The authenticity of Brown's voice and the seamless world he creates are breathtaking. His themes of love and redemption, hope and dignity, weakness and strength are universal, and the telling is mercilessly compelling. —*Deb Robertson*

Brown, Rebecca.
The Children's Crusade.
Seal Press, paper, $8.95 (1-878067-04-4). 128p.

From the author of *The Haunted House* comes a disturbing portrait of childhood that moves from realism to parody to an allegory centering on the ill-fated Children's Crusade in 1212. The territories are defined and the battle lines are drawn as the story of an intense child custody suit is related. Family relationships are seen in brutal, uncompromising terms, with children as victims. This original work is unyielding and tough, with the style and themes of the author's previous work recalled. —*Jane Jurgens*

Bufalino, Gesualdo.
Lies of the Night.
Atheneum, $18.95 (0-689-12124-5). 176p.

Winner of the 1988 Premio Strega, Italy's top literary award, this taut tale revolves around a single night. Four men are imprisoned in a fortress on a tiny, rocky island pummeled by the pounding sea. Convicted of treason, they are condemned to die the following morning. But the governor makes them an offer: he leaves them four sheets of paper, a pen, and a sealed box. If just one of them, anonymously, writes down the name of their secret leader, reputed to be close to the throne, he'll let them all live. They're put together in a room with an infamous yet God-fearing brigand who encourages them to spend the night talking about themselves, recounting their "most memorable hour." Their stories abound in adventure, lust, and revenge, yet each prisoner struggles with his fear of death and of having lived a pointless life. Bufalino captivates and teases by questioning the value of morality, loyalty, and truth, and then rewards his readers with a clever, twisted conclusion. —*Donna Seaman*

Burke, Martyn.
Ivory Joe.
Bantam, $19.95 (0-553-07182-3). 320p.

Melding a traditional narrative with the distinctive, wisecracking asides of his adolescent protagonist, Christie Klein, Burke delivers a warm, engaging look at growing up wild in 1950s Brooklyn. Christie and her sister, Ruthie, are well acquainted with their father Leo's hobbies—drinking, playing cards, and throwing wild parties. As charming as he is irresponsible, Leo vainly struggles to maintain the fine line separating the legitimate business operations of his garment factory and his obligations to the Mob. His ex-wife, meanwhile, is busy managing black singer Ivory Joe and his group, the Classics. As the band sets off for a concert tour in the Deep South, Leo finds himself drawn into the group's affairs when the Mob decides to move into the music business. All the raucous goings-on don't prevent Christie and Ruthie from plotting to reunite their estranged parents. The combination of the immensely likable Klein family and the wealth of colorful details on the workings of the Mob and the music business make for grand entertainment. —*Joanne Wilkinson*

Burman, Edward.
The Image of Our Lord.
St. Martin's, $17.95 (0-312-05876-4). 304p.

To the "sophisticated," secular minds of the twentieth century, the medieval obsession with holy relics often seems absurd. Yet, as Burman's exciting first novel shows, reasonably intelligent men of the fourteenth century regarded these relics with utmost seriousness; they venerated them and also appreciated the immense political power that came to those who possessed them. Two young men, Jacques Fournier and Nicholas de Lirey, are assigned the seemingly mundane task of interrogating an aged, heretical knight. They quickly become enmeshed in a web of intrigue and betrayal involving King Phillip the Fair of France, the papacy, and a secretive order of crusading knights. Jacques, a low-born but proud and relentless monk, and Nicholas, a dispossessed knight, are both strong, well drawn, and appealing characters whose relationship develops from antagonism to mutual respect. Burman weaves a tale with numerous twists and turns; yet the story is always credible, and his grasp of both the facts and the spirit of the age is superb. Burman, a teacher who recently turned to writing full time, appears to have a very bright future. —*Jay Freeman*

✔Busch, Frederick.
Closing Arguments.
Ticknor & Fields, $19.95 (0-395-58968-1). 288p.

Marcus ("Goblin") Brennan is a small-town lawyer in upstate New York, a Vietnam vet, and a very troubled man. His wife has been trying, patiently, to help him overcome his post-traumatic stress syndrome, and she's hoping that the unveiling of a war memorial will somehow appease Brennan's demons. Meanwhile, their marriage has turned strained and platonic and their two children are courting tragedy in the form of drugs and AIDS. Enter Estella Pritchett: sexy and petite but surprisingly strong, a social worker specializing in child abuse and accused of murdering her lover. Brennan takes the case and immediately, inevitably, gets involved with Estella and her dangerous brand of sadomasochism. Busch has Brennan narrate, maintaining a relentless intensity. The focus pivots from hair-raising accounts of Brennan's capture and torture by the Vietcong to pained scenes with his family, violent sex with Estella, childhood memories of being abused by his father, and the taut courtroom battle. Busch delves unflinchingly into the dark, bleakly

General Fiction

erotic, and terrifying realm of intimate violence, masterfully peeling back each layer of deception, brutality, and suicidal desire. Leaving the turgid confines of domestic dramas like *Harry and Catherine* behind, Busch has ventured boldly and surefootedly out into forbidding territory. A gripping, sorrowful, and potent work. —*Donna Seaman*

Cameron, Peter.
Far-Flung.
HarperCollins, $19.95 (0-06-016717-3). 192p.

Cameron's second collection finds him still obsessed with difficult moments in white middle-class lives, still limning them with the restraint his emotion-stifling characters personify and which, as a literary device, ironically emphasizes their affective desolation. These 12 stories' personae are nearly all substantially older than those in *One Way or Another*, and the lovers' and families' breakups they endure are generally more complicated and unfold over more time. But if there's been development in the maturity of Cameron's characters and in the ambitions of his little narratives, there's no change in his sweet, parsimonious, Hemingwayesque style. It's a joy to read, although it sometimes seems to have insufficient range to express the complications of mature adult emotions. The book's contents appear in three sections, the first consisting of seven freestanding stories (one featuring protagonists from Cameron's novel *Leap Year*); the next, of two stories about a gay male couple split when one of them, a diplomat, is posted to Africa; the last, of three stories about members of the same eccentric Indiana family. —*Ray Olson*

Camp, John.
The Empress File.
Holt, $18.95 (0-8050-1545-0). 288p.

Longstreet, Mississippi, is an old, tough river town run by a crooked mayor and council. When a redneck cop mistakes a black youth for a purse snatcher and kills him, the crime is whitewashed. Black activists in Longstreet hire Kidd to "take the town down." Kidd, a semi-amoral, tarot-reading, artist/computer hacker/con man/hard guy, enlists LuEllen, a professional burglar and his sometime lover, and Bobby, a never-seen genius hacker, to help drive the crooks out of office and steal all their money. With this second Kidd novel, Pulitzer Prize–winning journalist Camp has a winning series on his hands. Kidd is a fascinating, quirky enigma. He and LuEllen lie to everyone, allies and victims alike, con some people, and terrorize others. Camp's writing never intrudes, it simply carries the story. His knowledge of computers, burglary, classic stings, and human nature rings true, and his reporter's sensibilities create vivid, interesting locales. —*Thomas Gaughan*

Caraganis, Lynn.
Cousin It.
Ticknor & Fields, $19.95 (0-89919-945-3). 224p.

In incredibly perky, bordering on demented prose—like a *Seventeen* magazine article gone slightly berserk—Caraganis' novel, set in the 1950s, details the concerns of 17-year-old orphan Vickie Fowler. After quarreling with her cousin about Liberace, Vickie moves into a posh ranch-style home owned by her cousin Itzel. In between sipping Cokes and listening to Patti Page, Vickie is visited by an increasingly bizarre cast of characters who don't seem to fit her Pollyanna-like view of the world. She deals with her gay cousin, lecherous nephew, abrasive aunt, and bratty next-door neighbor as if they were simply experiencing severe lapses in etiquette and continually tries to engage them in conversations about clothes and cosmetics. The schizy dialogue and overly vivacious heroine give this loopy novel its distinctive charm. —*Joanne Wilkinson*

Carroll, James W.
Memorial Bridge.
Houghton, $22.95 (0-395-51136-4). 483p.

Carroll's fine reputation rests on eight novels written in quick succession, including the best-selling *Mortal Friends* and his most recent work, *Supply of Heroes.* He opens this chronicle of twentieth-century America in the post-Depression Chicago stockyards, where the hero, Sean Dillon, locates the cause of a massive flood of the entire place: a bloated human corpse blocking a pipeline. The horror of this incident doesn't stop Dillon from falling in love with Cass Ryan, the red-haired niece of the murdered man. Their life together gets more intriguing, as Dillon finishes his law degree, gets a job in the FBI during World War II, and takes his wife and son Richard on a rapid rise to Pentagon power. The novel climaxes as Dillon takes charge of military intelligence at the beginning of the Vietnam era. The author's signature moral conflicts surface most notably when Dillon's son is jailed for dodging the draft, and the hero uses all his connections and experience in FBI and Pentagon matters to free the boy. Dillon is great at beating the odds, and struggle—be it personal or professional—is what drives him to rise above his peers. In this lengthy, but gripping, novel, Carroll takes these struggles and sets them against the great events of modern American history, emphasizing the eternal conflicts between father and son, husband and wife. A page-turner, certain to draw a large audience. —*Kathryn LaBarbera*

✔Cartier, Xam.
Muse-Echo Blues.
Harmony; dist. by Crown, $18 (0-517-57793-3). 192p.

Cartier has brought the power and emotion of jazz to prose and written a dazzling tone poem that sings, shouts, and wails the blues of African American life. Kat is a young composer living in San Francisco and going through a dry spell—she can't get in touch with her muse. Daydreams at the keyboard fill her mind with "real-seeming fantasies" about a woman named Kitty in the 1940s, her sax-playing lover, Chicago, and his mother, Lena. Scenes from the past play in variation to the present. In each era, Cartier stalks the politics of fashion and attitude and exposes double-edged cynicism, snaking anger, and detonating humor. Pages are peppered with the names of jazz giants like Billie Holiday, Lester Young, Duke Ellington, Sarah Vaughan, Dexter Gordon,

General Fiction

and Cecil Taylor. Cartier creates cinematic streams of action pulsing with graceful motion and a bass line of jive with its rhymes and wordplay, feints and jabs. She choreographs the dance of tension between men and women and dramatizes the struggles of artists. An unerring, bittersweet, and virtuoso performance. —*Donna Seaman*

Chabon, Michael.
A Model World and Other Stories.
Morrow, $18.95 (0-688-09553-4). 288p.

Happily, Chabon's meteoric rise to critical acclaim with his debut novel, *The Mysteries of Pittsburgh*, will be a sustained phenomenon, lighting the realm of literature with his perfected, glistening prose. Chabon's sentences are put together like patterns found in nature: the design of a butterfly's wings or the whorl of leaves in a tree. And they contain life like the pulse of a young man in love or the queasy rush felt during an argument. Each of the six stories in the first part of this collection emits its own gentle, moody, humorous atmosphere, whether set in Pittsburgh, France, or L.A. Chabon takes us to a wedding, a funeral, a chance encounter with an ex-lover in a café, tracking the alternating currents of tension and affection in conversations and the faint sourness of regret. The second section is a series of stories about the youth of one Nathan Shapiro, who copes with puberty and his parents' divorce with instinctive compassion, wit, and wistfulness. If we had to compare Chabon to another, it would be Salinger. —*Donna Seaman*

Chafets, Zev.
Inherit the Mob.
Random, $19 (0-679-40263-2). 256p.

The first foray into fiction by the author of *Members of the Tribe* is half hard-boiled, half warmhearted, and altogether funny. Chafets has raided the world of old-time mobsters and bourbon-drinking journalists for a cast of gleefully gutsy, sharp-tongued characters. William Gordon, who grew up as Velvel Grossman, is a Pulitzer Prize–winning journalist who never gave much thought to the shady and lucrative business his father and uncle conducted— until Uncle Max dies. Gordon is told that he has inherited his uncle's fortune if he can collect it from Max's former partner, a stereotypical Sicilian godfather. Unable to resist temptation and deaf to his father's warnings, Gordon enlists the help of his crazy friend Farrell, a veritable encyclopedia of gangster lore. Things quickly get out of hand, and Gordon's father hightails it down to Miami for reinforcements: a bunch of geriatric Jewish gangsters up for one last grand caper. In a hilarious showdown, wit triumphs over might, and Chafets wraps up a terrific bit of comedy. —*Donna Seaman*

Chase, Joan.
Bonneville Blue.
Farrar, $16.95 (0-374-11539-7). 183p.

A collection of 11 atmospheric short stories by an award winning novelist, whose two previous books are *The Evening Wolves* and *During the Reign of the Queen of Persia*. Chase's naturalistic fiction contains a powerful, almost cloying immediacy, emphasizing the entrapment of her characters' gritty lives. The title story is set at the height of the Vietnam War, in a rough, rundown neighborhood filled with draft evaders, antiwar protesters, and mostly working-class couples fighting hopeless, private wars. The desperation of the lives of the central characters, homemaker Irene and her mechanic husband, is symbolized by their pampered shiny blue Bonneville car, which sits on their street in constant readiness yet takes them nowhere. "The Harrier" similarly depicts emotional and environmental blight as a housewife in a small town yearns fruitlessly for sexual fulfillment in the arms of a younger man, a hippie beholden to no one. In "Crowing," a young female caretaker witnesses an astonishing, frightful display of pent-up anger by a deceptively placid and doddering old man on whom life has played its cruelest trick. Achingly moving fiction by a master of the art. Highly recommended. —*Mary Banas*

✔Cheong, Fiona.
The Scent of the Gods.
Norton, $19.95 (0-393-03024-5). 224p.

Cheong's debut is as lyrical and bittersweet as a fruit tree blossom falling silently to the ground. Set in Singapore during the violent turmoil of the 1960s, it tells the story of an extended family of Chinese descent. Su Yen, the youngest member of the household, narrates. She is a gentle, watchful child with an innocent sensuality that sensitizes her to the memory- and secret-rich atmosphere of their large, immaculate house. Her grandmother is head of the family that includes Su Yen and her two cousins, all orphaned when their parents were killed in a car accident, and a slew of aunts and uncles. Su Yen's older male cousins call her "Chief" and are loving and protective but gradually rebel against their grandmother's attempts to live by Chinese traditions. Su Yen slowly becomes aware of sex, the tension of pent-up emotions, and the impulse to break out of her obedient quietness. Her inner evolution is matched by outer chaos as Singapore's lush beauty is marred by violence and tragedy invades her home. A haunting and graceful coming-of-age tale deepened by its insight into cultural conflicts. —*Donna Seaman*

Chernoff, Maxine.
Plain Grief.
Summit, $19 (0-671-72463-0). 221p.

All too often, holidays fail to deliver the advertising world's promise of a blissful family scene. Chernoff, known for her earlier five volumes of poetry as well as a collection of stories, begins this first novel on Thanksgiving Day in Chicago, with the grim reality of a failing marriage being bombarded by accompanying crises that will unfold in the six-day span of time that follows. Sarah Holm, while grieving her father's recent death, has tired of silently suffering her professor husband's infidelities and has taken a lover herself. During the holiday dinner, she discovers 15-year-old Carrie has run away with her cousin, taking off cross-country on a bus trip. Deciding to follow her

General Fiction

daughter to California provides Sarah with the impetus for a final break in the marriage. The author portrays characters with an engaging degree of depth as well as humor; Sarah's widowed mother Ivy, alcoholic sister Mae, lover Jeremy, and her two children each come to deal with their own "plain grief" in ways that are both very real and very true. This perfectly rendered picture of a marriage as it is dissolving ultimately conveys a promise of release rather than an endless submersion in pain. —*Alice Joyce*

Chin, Frank.
Donald Duk.
Coffee House, paper, $9.95 (0-918273-83-8). 176p.

Eleven going on 12, Donald Duk undergoes a full-scale identity crisis. And it's not just his name—or even worse, that his mother's name is Daisy. It's the whole dichotomy of being a Chinese American that Donald's fighting, with his decision to become thoroughly American and to deride his Chinese heritage. Since Donald lives in San Francisco's Chinatown, this isn't going to be easy. Moreover, his father owns a—What else?—Chinese restaurant and is a performer in the Cantonese opera. In school Donald's teacher is much too interested in making Donald an example of a multicultural stereotype. What saves Donald from this ethnic muddle? Well, a sense of humor helps a lot, as does Donald's generally loving and understanding family. Chin makes his young hero both a believable kid and a potent symbol of the immigrant experience, in which the road to success is paved with both gold and potholes. Chin is also the author of *The Chickencoop Chinaman* and *The Year of the Dragon*. —*John Brosnahan*

✔**Cisneros, Sandra.**
Woman Hollering Creek and Other Stories.
Random, $18 (0-394-57654-3). 163p.

Cisneros can tell stories—all kinds of stories, and they're genuinely funny, revealing, poetic, and cleverly insightful. Despite the author's claim that "the people they're really for are the Latinos," these stories will find a much wider audience. "Barbie-Q," a two-pager, is a comic nostalgia piece: two little girls struggle with having only one outfit apiece for their Barbies, and no Kens, until they come upon a toy warehouse fire sale that supplies riches beyond their wildest desires. "So what," they say, "if our Barbies smell like smoke when you hold them up to your nose even after you wash and wash and wash them. And if the prettiest doll . . . has a left foot that's melted a little—so?" "Little Miracles, Kept Promises" is a series of letters to saints, asking for help, offering thanks, from "help me find a man" to "Thank you. Our child is born healthy!" Each letter is a story in itself, ricocheting the reader from snickering at folly to empathizing with heartache. Other stories leave humor behind: "Never Marry a Mexican" simmers with rage; "Eyes of Zapata" stands just on the border of realism, with the spirit of the general's wife soaring through history. There are 22 stories packed into this slim volume, and each is remarkable. —*Deb Robertson*

Cooper, J. California.
The Matter Is Life.
Doubleday, $18 (0-385-41173-1). 224p.

A collection of moralistic tales from the author of *Family*. These are the sort of stories your mother or aunt would tell you to make some point about the evils of selfishness. The narrators are folksy, a little scolding, and very blunt, the tales they tell dramatic and extreme, embracing the many trials and tribulations of African-American life. Some are positive enough, like the feisty narrative of a woman in her nineties attending the funeral of a peer, or the tale of a young girl and her brothers who try to earn money working in an onion field. Several focus on self-centered, vain women who care only for their looks and possessions: one ends up pathetically overdressed with the puffy face of a drinker and no friends, while another, in a graphic depiction of the degradation of drug addiction, utterly destroys herself. Cooper's fables are gritty and authentic, her message of heart and soul clear and insistent. —*Donna Seaman*

Coover, Robert.
Pinocchio in Venice.
Simon & Schuster/Linden Press, $19.95 (0-671-64471-8). 330p.

Old Pinocchio returns to his native Venice in disgrace. Hollywood has made a travesty of his film bio, he has lost his magnum opus when his computer was stolen—hard disk, floppies, and all—and, worst of all, his human body is turning back into wood. Only the nose seems to be unchanged. Pinocchio's transformation from puppet to man and his decay back to a pile of splinters are dazzlingly captured in Coover's raunchy postmodern frolic. Beneath the surface of bawdy baroque description there lies a more substantial portrait of humanity beset by age, loneliness, lust, and illness, Pinocchio holding on to the memories of the past while being assaulted by all the cruelties the modern world can muster. Coover uncovers the terror and wicked laughter that arise in the process of becoming, being, and dying with an uncommon honesty that is tearful in more than one sense. —*John Brosnahan*

Costello, Mark.
Middle Murphy.
Univ. of Illinois, $16.95 (0-252-01795-1). 128p.

The stories in this collection trace the first 40 or so years in the life of one Michael Murphy, who first appeared in *The Murphy Stories*. In the first tale, "Young Republican," he grows up and leaves his Decatur, Illinois, home. The remaining stories are all about returning, or, in a sense, never having really left. In "The Soybean Capital of the World," Murphy makes a picaresque and drunken journey back to Decatur, to be met by his disapproving father. A common thread in the stories is Murphy's sense of having failed his parents. "The Roaring Margaret" relates how the expectations of parents hover over both Murphy's first marriage and his second. "Forty Hour Devotion" shows

Murphy returning to Decatur with his pregnant second wife and 13-year-old son to visit his now-widowed mother, and the reaction each has when the boy's stepfather accuses him of stealing. The two final stories deal with Murphy's attendance at his mother's death. Densely written and carefully observed, these stories expertly chart the subtleties of human relationships. Another strong entry in the Illinois Short Fiction series. —*Mary Ellen Quinn*

Crook, Elizabeth.
The Raven's Bride.
Doubleday, $19.95 (0-385-41775-6). 384p.

Sam Houston endures as one of the most fascinating and powerful political figures of nineteenth-century U.S. history. As a teenager, he left home to live for three years with the Cherokee Indians; he remained a lifelong proponent of Indian land rights. Under the tutelage of Andrew Jackson, Houston rose to the governorship of Tennessee; after he resigned under a marital cloud, Houston moved on to Texas where he became a founding father and hero of the struggle for independence from Mexico. Little is known of Houston's first wife, Elizabeth Allen, who left him after only 11 weeks of marriage. Nevertheless, Crook, a Texan herself, has written an absorbing and emotionally stirring first novel based on their ill-fated relationship. Crook shows us the familiar but still immensely attractive Houston—volcanic, courageous, yet emotionally vulnerable. By Crook's own admission, the character of Elizabeth is largely her literary invention; nevertheless, she emerges as a flesh-and-blood personality with a strength and presence that is bound to win over readers. A first-rate piece of historical fiction as well as a frequently moving love story. —*Jay Freeman*

Danvers, Dennis.
Wilderness.
Poseidon, $18.95 (0-671-72827-X). 255p.

Alice White is beautiful. She lives alone, picks up men for one-night stands, and works as a travel agent. She's also a werewolf. Since the age of 13, she turns into a wolf on the night of every full moon. Her psychiatrist doesn't believe her, just like no one believed her after she tore a young man's throat open when he tried to rape her. No one could explain the murder, but everyone thought her story was the result of shock, so she learned to keep her secret to herself, locking herself in the basement every month, suffering in her solitude both as a woman and as a wolf. Finally, Alice lets herself fall in love and dramatically reveals her animal self. Danvers relates this sensitive and elegant variation on the werewolf theme simply and patiently, and, with suspense and sympathy, he explores the interface between animal and human, magic and mundaneness, and the expansive, courageous, and freeing aspects of love. Utterly seductive and fulfilling. —*Donna Seaman*

General Fiction

Davies, Robertson.
Murther & Walking Spirits.
Viking, $21.95 (0-670-84189-7). 357p.

The hero of Davies' new novel dies in the opening sentence, an irresistible example of this esteemed writer's typically wry style: "I was never so amazed in my life as when the Sniffer drew his concealed weapon from its case and struck me to the ground, stone dead." Connor Gilmartin, editor of a Toronto newspaper's entertainment section, is a corpse, but his mind, or soul, remains mysteriously alive. His shaken murderer hastily dresses while his still-naked and remarkably cool-headed companion, Gilmartin's wife, takes charge. Gilmartin, unsure about what exactly a recently deceased person is supposed to do, amuses himself by watching the adulterous pair and attending his own funeral. Then he goes to the movies. To his surprise, he finds himself subjected to a private screening of a film set in New York in 1774. It's about a Tory widow who flees to Canada. Gilmartin is startled to recognize the widow as his great-great-great-great grandmother. The inexplicable screening continues with films set in Wales divulging the fascinating and complex stories of his grandfather's ancestors. The films convey more than sight and sound, making our hero eerily privy to his relatives' thoughts and feelings. Davies has great fun with this device, giving full rein to his sense of drama, love of gritty, historical detail, and delight in satire. A sage and witty interpretation of the afterlife that asks "Do we die and learn?" We do, in any case, certainly enjoy Davies' humor, warmth, and wisdom. *The Lyre of Orpheus* was his previous novel, while *The Enthusiasms of Robertson Davies* collects his essays.
—*Donna Seaman*

Davis, Donald.
Barking at a Fox-Fur Coat.
August House, $19.95 (0-87483-141-5); paper, $9.95 (0-87483-140-7). 224p.

Seventeen humorous, original tales based on the author's childhood and family experiences in rural North Carolina. Davis, a professional storyteller, has refined his craft into a perfect blend of the oral tradition and creative fiction, resulting in some highly memorable and endearing characters. Each yarn cleverly highlights a set of human foibles, such as ignorance or gullibility, and ends with an ironic twist in the tradition of O. Henry. All 17 tales, which are intended to be read in sequence, focus on the fictional character Uncle Frank of Iron Duff, North Carolina, a gruff, worldly-wise, yet smart-alecky old geezer who's always pulling the leg of his nephew and other assorted relatives and friends. The title story, for instance, has Uncle Frank regaling listeners with details of a foxhound who can follow the scent of a fox that has been dead half a century. In the sidesplitting yarn "Uncle Frank Invents the Electron Microphone," Uncle Frank cleverly scares two squirrel hunters from his property—without losing their humongous family's votes in the upcoming election—by divulging "top secret" facts about a high-tech, CIA-planted recorder that can tape sounds going as far back as the dawn of time and still echoing in the valleys of Iron Duff. Only one tale, "Uncle Frank and the Talking Cat," falls short of its promise. A wholesome, hilarious, and highly entertaining collection that will be well thumbed throughout the years to come. —*Mary Banas*

Davis, Rebecca Harding.
Margret Howth: A Story of Today.
Feminist Press, $35 (1-55861-030-8); paper, $11.95 (1-55861-036-7). 304p.

For some 40 years a successful radical writer, Davis (1831–1910) discussed the gender, race, and class issues of her time in dozens of novels and short stories. Historians and literary critics, Jean Fagan Yellin imparts in her afterword, believe Davis "introduced the industrial revolution into American literature and helped launch the literary movement of American realism." In *Margret Howth*, Davis observes "the commonplace" with kinship and understanding. She presents industrializing America as a society hungry for physical and spiritual necessities, for roses as well as for bread, as she explores the failures of capitalism and the saving power of spiritual values in the lives of mill and clerical workers, women and men, blacks and whites. An artificially happy ending fascinatingly reflects the power dynamics of gender and money, for Davis evidently rewrote to meet her male editor's call for less gloom and more sunshine. Like Davis' more famous *Life in the Iron Mills* (1861), *Margret Howth* is essential reading for anyone interested in the literary or social history of mid-nineteenth-century America. —*Ryn Etter*

Davis-Gardner, Angela.
Forms of Shelter.
Ticknor & Fields, $19.95 (0-395-59312-3). 276p.

Davis-Gardner's second novel is a writer's reminiscence of the painful facts surrounding a difficult coming-of-age. Always harboring the futile hope of finding the jazz-musician father who left her mother years earlier, Beryl Fonteyn, narrator and protagonist, is now ensconced in Chicago, but not far enough from the simmering anger of the deep disturbances of youth in North Carolina. She recounts life with her seriously depressed mother, a manipulative stepfather with an obsession for beekeeping, and a younger brother who takes refuge in religion. The idyllic childhood of myth constantly evades Beryl in this very real, compassionate, at times harrowing, yet beautifully lyrical portrayal of the peaks and valleys of growing up in a dysfunctional family. —*Benjamin Segedin*

Dazai, Osamu.
Self Portraits.
Kodansha, $18.95 (0-87011-779-3). 208p.

The rebellious, self-absorbed nonconformity that informs those autobiographical short stories earned Dazai the adulation of Japanese postwar youth and the enmity of critics. Son of a wealthy, politically prominent landowner, he joined the Communist underground briefly, overcame drug addiction, may have been clinically paranoid, raised his legitimate and illegitimate children in poverty, and in 1948 drowned himself in the Tamagawa Canal at the age of 39. The Hemingway influence evident in the earlier stories disappears with time, but Dazai's fascination with the West remains constant. Although each story stands on its own, the collection, with its first-person narrator who changes over time and its recurring characters and places, has the appeal of a novel. It's a page-turner, set at the heart of twentieth-century history, depicting prewar life among Japan's rich and famous, mobilization for the Second World War, Allied air raids on civilian populations—all of it told matter-of-factly. The photographs and background information compiled by translator McCarthy further distinguish an altogether exemplary book. —*Roland Wulbert*

Denker, Henry.
Payment in Full.
Morrow, $19.95 (0-688-10450-9). 384p.

A veteran novelist tackles the emotional issue of interracial adoption with warmth, sensitivity, and compassion. During the height of the Depression, Rebecca and David Rosen, a childless Jewish couple, open their home and their hearts to Elvira Hitchins, the recently orphaned eight-year-old daughter of a black domestic. Lacking a viable point of reference and a supportive social network, the Rosens nevertheless manage to overcome racial, cultural, and religious tensions in order to forge an extraordinary family unit. As Elvira matures into an exceptionally bright and talented young woman, she and her foster parents confront ignorance and bigotry with a daunting combination of humor, pride, and common sense. A heartrending tribute to the ultimate triumph of love, respect, and courage in the face of cruelty and prejudice. —*Margaret Flanagan*

Denton, Bradley.
Buddy Holly Is Alive and Well on Ganymede.
Morrow, $20 (0-688-10822-9). 360p.

Denton, author of *Wrack and Roll*, is back with more wild and crazy, action-packed satire. Oliver Vale has a metaphysical link with Buddy Holly: he was conceived in a car to the tune of "Heartbreak" the day of Holly's death. His young, unwed mother raised him with a fateful belief in the spirituality of rock 'n' roll and left him her extensive record collection, multivolume diary, and satellite dish when she died. Years later, Buddy Holly appears on every television on earth, performing in a glass bubble on the surface of Ganymede, a satellite of Jupiter. He seems disoriented and keeps asking for Oliver. Fearing the wrath of the authorities, Oliver takes off for Holly's grave in Lubbock, Texas, to try and figure it all out. Denton juggles Oliver's charmingly peculiar childhood memories with elaborate chase sequences featuring a foulmouthed fitness freak, an angry G-man in a Jag, a giant Doberman pinscher cyborg, and inept but well-meaning aliens. An energetic, empathic, and quintessentially American pop-culture fantasy. —*Donna Seaman*

Dexter, Pete.
Brotherly Love.
Random, $22 (0-394-58573-9). 272p.

Dexter's title is one of the few instances of humor in this unrelentingly sorrowful tale of mobsters in Philly. The brothers Flood don't know the meaning of the word *love*. Phil and Charley are two Irish tough guys running a labor union and competing with the Italian syndicate. Charley's son Peter narrates, beginning at the tender age of eight, when he watches his baby sister die after being hit by a neighbor who loses control of his car. The tragedy leads to a brooding but rapid disintegration of the family. Peter's mother cracks up and is taken away, and his father defies the wishes of his brother and their superiors by murdering the driver of the car that killed the baby. Charley then vanishes and Peter, silent and wary, finds himself living with his cruel uncle—who turns out to be his father's killer. In spite of Phil's insisting that they're now brothers, the bond between Peter and Phil's despicable son, Michael, is one of deep distrust and dangerous rivalry. Hushed, methodical, and brutal, the story spans 25 years. Peter is soul-dead and seeks pain to feel peace, while Michael enjoys the suffering of others. As they spar in an ever-tightening circle, they are surrounded by a ring of corpses until they can do nothing but join them. A masterfully devastating work by the award-winning author of *Paris Trout*, and *Deadwood*. —*Donna Seaman*

Dickinson, Charles.
Rumor Has It.
Morrow, $18.95 (0-688-10225-5). 256p.

A fast-paced tale of newspaper skulduggery. It's Halloween, and there are more tricks than treats at Chicago's number-two paper. The *Bugle* is closing and employees are angry, but editor Danny Fain wants to leave on a high note with an explosive story. Glancing out the train window on the way to work, he sees what appears to be a hit-and-run accident involving a child in a ghost costume. Instead of calling the police, he sends out a reporter. Meanwhile the newsroom is in an uproar over the paper's closing. Dickinson juggles a series of vignettes, rapidly sketching a vivid set of characters including the paper's overpaid movie critic, a reporter cursed by his nickname, and a calculating TV executive. Everyone reacts to losing their jobs differently—some traitorously, some valiantly—and many sacrifice sound judgment for sensationalism. Dickinson, author of *The Widows' Adventures*, provides top-notch entertainment with a deep emotional pitch. —*Donna Seaman*

Dobyns, Stephen.
After Shocks / Near Escapes.
Viking, $19.95 (0-670-83914-0). 268p.

A beautifully written portrayal of how the 1960 Chilean earthquakes changed forever the lives of the Recabarren family. Lucy Recabarren was eight years old when the quakes struck, and now she is divorced, with a daughter of her own, but she remembers with great clarity the sounds ("the objects in the house began to whisper together"), the incredible sights, and, most of all, the destruction of all normalcy. The novel haunts with its imagery; for example, young Lucy listens in terror from her sickbed as the barking of dogs, the crying of birds, and the distant ringing of church bells signal the arrival of yet another quake. Dobyns explores the themes of death and loss with eloquence and wisdom, skillfully reconciling a child's speculation with an adult's knowledge of how personal walls can tumble as quickly as real ones: Manfredo stops speaking, Uncle Walterio won't stop eating, unmarried Great-Aunt Clotilde prepares for death by putting on a wedding gown, and Aunt Dalila seeks an affair with her husband's brother. Lucy ultimately comes to understand why her loved ones "slip away, like people at a party who have to leave early." —*Eloise Kinney*

Dorrie, Doris.
What Do You Want from Me? And Fifteen Other Stories.
Knopf, $19 (0-679-40092-3). 176p.

The second set of short stories from Dorrie, author of *Love, Pain, and the Whole Damn Thing* (1989) and a filmmaker best known for the acclaimed *Men*. Dorrie writes of her native Germany, a chilly, nervous place; L.A., where "only whores and Europeans walk"; and New York, where everyone marches "head down, toward some imaginary goal." Her stories are quick and stark, studies of men and women frozen in inarticulate conflict or confusion. The characters are usually lonely women in their thirties, thrown into unexpected situations. In "The Sofa," two ex-lovers with their new cohorts run into each other in a furniture store; "I'm Sorry" is the story of a young German woman who brings her Jewish American lover home, and conversely, "Los Angeles" is about a German woman who comes to L.A. to surprise her American lover. Dorrie's world is edgy, creepy, and peopled by loners who accept, even seek, the intrusion of strangers. Cultural differences add an unusual dimension to this strong collection. —*Donna Seaman*

✔Dorris, Michael and Erdrich, Louise.
The Crown of Columbus.
HarperCollins, $21.95 (0-06-016079-9). 384p.

The first novel to appear under both Michael Dorris' and Louise Erdrich's names is unlike anything either of them has done in the past. While this story of a native American professor's discovery of a crown hidden by Columbus possesses all the grace and subtlety one expects from the authors of *A Yellow Raft in Blue Water* and *Love Medicine*, it is also a thrilling adventure story and a probing examination of how we interpret history. Initially, Dartmouth professor Vivian Twostar is a reluctant Columbus scholar, agreeing only to do an article for the school's alumni magazine as a way of padding her vitae. But then she comes across an uncataloged cache of papers in the Dartmouth library that sets her on the trail both of the mysterious crown and of Columbus' heretofore undiscovered private diary. Using alternating first-person narrators, the story moves from Vivian to Roger Williams—her lover, the father of her newly born daughter, and the author of an epic poem about the

General Fiction

life of Columbus. Vivian's search takes her, Roger, their child, and Vivian's teenage son to the Bahamas, where the novel's multilayered conflicts are resolved in a stunning evocation of history as felt life. Dorris and Erdrich have managed a remarkable feat here. Paralleling Vivian's transformation of a pedantic, tenure-building essay into a vehicle for personal catharsis, they have woven the seemingly limited concept of a quincentenary-celebrating novel into a myth-shattering vision that connects past with present and the native American experience with the lives of all of us. Finally, the enigma of Columbus—Is he Vivian's "pillager" or Roger's ambiguity-laced epic hero?—becomes meaningful insofar as it fuels our own journeys of self-discovery. —*Bill Ott*

Dovlatov, Sergei.
A Foreign Woman.
Grove Weidenfeld, $16.95 (0-8021-1342-7). 128p.

Many authors fall in love with their characters; only a few are so entranced they enter their fiction under their own names. Like Dovlatov the author, Dovlatov the character is certainly a little in love with Marusya Tatarovich, a child of the Soviet *nomenklatura*, the philanderer in her marriage to a medical student, the philanderee in her relationship with a popular singer. Marusya decides (she doesn't quite know why) to take her son by the singer and emigrate to the U.S. Neither Jewish nor a dissident, Marusya is as "foreign" among the Russians "of the third wave" in Queens as in the multiethnic, government-sponsored jewelry workshop she attends in Lower Manhattan. She interacts, pleasantly or not, with the men of the neighborhood, including Dovlatov; the women there, in general, disapprove of her, especially when she takes up with a middle-aged Hispanic man. Marusya considers returning to Russia, which gives the author (a prison guard and journalist in the USSR who came to the U.S. in 1978 and had five other novels published in translation before his death in 1990) an opportunity to tweak Soviet diplomats and intelligence types, as throughout the book he has fun with various immigrant tendencies. A funny, sad, and tender novel. —*Mary Carroll*

Dufresne, John.
The Way That Water Enters Stone.
Norton, $18.95 (0-393-02924-7). 176p.

When water enters stone it "trickles through crevices, runs along channels, gathers itself in pools, and stands there." It patiently erodes and destroys the stone. "And there's nothing the stone can do." So, too, do these stories—set in the East and the South, among people with debilitations that keep them from "normal" life—seep into our subconscious with their primal nature, making us accept the cruelty of humans and of the natural world. The most "epic" of the stories, "The Fontana Gene," covers several generations of the Fontanas of Louisiana: "They have what folks used to call a curse, but now we know better. What the Fontanas have is bad water in the gene pool." The dynasty is plagued by madness, physical birth defects, and a propensity to produce only male children, but the rapacious Fontana gene battles back each generation in a reverse Darwinism: "survival of the sorriest." Dufresne's voice carries the precocious child's tone that many southern writers have used to great advantage: matter-of-fact, unflinching, unself-consciously clever. —*Deb Robertson*

Eberstadt, Fernanda.
Isaac and His Devils.
Knopf, $22 (0-394-58496-1). 368p.

What's a father to do when he sees his son fulfilling the dashed hopes of intellectual glory that the father himself once tried to grab onto and then rejected for marriage, family, and a steady job as a high-school teacher? And what is the son to do when he tries to march to the beat of a different drummer without alienating his father and without following in the same footsteps his father had wanted to tread? Eberstadt, the author of *Low Tide*, examines this relationship in the story of Sam Hooker and his son, Isaac, each character wrestling with the values he has chosen or has thrust before him. Since the two really care for each other, their mutual frustration becomes both affecting and humorous. Both battle over their love for one another and their right to pursue their separate lives. Eberstadt sets her story in rural New Hampshire, which provides a suitably atmospheric background for these psychological investigations. Sometimes the minor characters become a bit too intrusive (Sam's wife—and Isaac's mother—proves to be a rather unsympathetically drawn stereotype), but Eberstadt's style brings a vivid and refreshing originality to the novel's major scenes. —*John Brosnahan*

Edgerton, Clyde.
Killer Diller.
Algonquin, $17.95 (0-945575-53-X). 275p.

Wesley Benfield, Edgerton's wayward youth from *Walking across Egypt,* is 10 years older and a good deal wiser (though far from perfect). Wesley is in a halfway house for "borrowing" a white Continental. The detention/training program is on the grounds of a North Carolina Baptist college, and its director is very interested in his own political potential and physical image. When Wesley starts up a band with a few other youthful offenders, they are told to perform only gospel music; so they sing the blues whenever college administrators are not eavesdropping and make desperate plans for their escape to freedom and fame. Edgerton's characters are irresistible; his sense of humor is a blessing, especially when aimed at self-righteous religious folk. Some of the best lines are given to a young retarded boy whose sense of logic is irrefutable yet irritating to Wesley, who is teaching him masonry. The boy likes bricklaying but will not learn how to shake hands, saying, "I don't want to meet anybody. I already know everybody I want to know." Edgerton is one storyteller well worth knowing as this funny, pointed coming-of-age tale well demonstrates. —*Denise Perry Donavin*

Edwards, Louis.
Ten Seconds.
Graywolf, paper, $8.95 (1-55597-150-4). 176p.

Eddie has an epiphany as he watches a high school track meet: 10 seconds of spontaneous insight into his past, present, and future. In the present, he's a 26-year-old oil refinery worker, living in a small, Louisiana town, married to Betty, and the father of two children. He loves his honest, upright, and "good" wife, but finds domesticity stifling and adventures, no matter how harmful, essential. Edwards guides us through Eddie's starkly honest memories, presentiments, and fantasies in a fluent stream of consciousness that flows over the rocky terrain of love, sex, friendship, childhood, parenthood, and freedom. He delves into the nuances of sexuality and the emotional spectrum between love and alienation, desire and anger with tremendous insight and integrity. Eddie's rich inner monologue reveals the conflicts found within African American society as a whole and one man's full heart. A strikingly poignant and polished debut. —*Donna Seaman*

✔Elkin, Stanley.
The MacGuffin.
Simon & Schuster/Linden, $19.95 (0-671-67324-6). 263p.

Elkin's sentences tilt, bump, and swerve like a carnival ride. He tackles things from oblique, fractured angles that accentuate the world's weirdness. Here he has a grand time toying with Hitchcock's famous device: the MacGuffin. A Hitchcock MacGuffin is the catalyst that drives the plot, like the search for secret documents or the plans for building an airplane. It's actually of no importance; what *is* important is what the MacGuffin makes people do. Elkin's hero, Bobbo Druff, commissioner of streets in a no-name, medium-sized midwestern town, has his own personal MacGuffin. Fifty-eight years old and veteran of numerous operations, Druff is feeling tired and pessimistic and is convinced that he is being spied on, that some sort of conspiracy is afoot. It might have to do with his son's Lebanese girlfriend who is killed crossing a street, an Oriental rug–smuggling operation, or simple political malice. Whatever the cause, it makes this funny-looking, self-dramatizing, and unlikely romantic hero act quite extravagantly. He takes a mistress, has enigmatic arguments with his overly vigilant chauffeurs, and frets about his oddball son. He thinks of his MacGuffin as a guardian angel, or "the spirit of narrative in his life"; a force that makes you "learn to live fast or die" but doesn't save you from the crushing routine of life. A wily, funny, and disarming novel: Elkin at his best. —*Donna Seaman*

Engberg, Susan.
Sarah's Laughter and Other Stories.
Knopf, $18 (0-394-58556-9). 193p.

"Sarah's Laughter" is a magnetic novella that pulls you into the intricacies of personality and painful love. Thomas Burden, 77, is, indeed, burdened by deep cynicism, fear, and loneliness. Formerly a book editor for a newspaper, Thomas feels drained by a lifetime of judgments and pronouncements. His inclination to withdraw from the messy business of life was exacerbated by his divorce from Sarah, a lovely, nurturing woman with a far sunnier perspective. Engberg inhabits Thomas' curmudgeonly mind, tracking the slow, reluctant thaw of his hardened heart. This exquisite knack for psychological nuance shapes each of the richly modulated stories in this collection. In "On the Late Bus," a 15-year-old shuttles sullenly between the homes of her divorced parents and suddenly wonders if she can make something besides trouble. "Smart Baby" is the story of a woman on the brink of menopause who dreams about a talking baby and tries to sort out her feelings for a male friend. Each tale is rounded and succulent and, like fruit, nourishing and germinal. Engberg's last book was *A Stay by the River*. —*Donna Seaman*

Ephron, Amy.
Biodegradable Soap.
Houghton, $18.95 (0-395-57227-4). 159p.

Ephron's screenplay technique influences her novels (her last was *Bruised Fruit*). She's a minimalist, doling out bite-size chapters, or scenes, of two pages or less that keep to the surface of things. The effect is one of detachment, an appropriate stance for this slender, pointed tale of life in La La Land. Claudia has become "obsessed with waste" and mired in the paradoxes of ecological thought. Which is worse, cutting down trees to make paper bags or using plastic bags that won't biodegrade? How can they shower California with an insecticide that can take the paint off cars? What does it do to people? What can she safely feed her young daughters? Meanwhile her husband moves out and takes up with a gorgeous Italian actress who couldn't care less about the hole in the ozone layer. Friends tell Claudia to date, get collagen shots to smooth out her crow's feet, and exercise with Billy, everyone's favorite personal trainer. But Billy gets shot by an angry husband who considers sex somewhat beyond the scope of aerobics, and Claudia keeps her wrinkles and her integrity. Ephron's deadpan humor elicits grimaces rather than laughs: her scenario is all too absurd and accurate. —*Donna Seaman*

Epstein, Joseph.
The Goldin Boys.
Norton, $19.95 (0-393-03022-9). 288p.

Epstein is known for his masterful essays, collected most recently in *A Line Out for a Walk*. This volume of short stories, his first book of fiction, is a winner. All nine tales are set in Chicago and told with a solid, almost courtly charm. Epstein's characters are Jewish and speak and think with that uniquely Jewish lilt of teasing inquiry. The author's favorite device is to create a story within the story by having his narrators describe the life of someone who fascinates them. In "No Pulitzer for Pinsker," it's an eccentric and inappropriately cocky classmate; in the title story, the son of a hardworking shopkeeper marvels at the wealth and ease of the Goldin family and their abrupt slide into tragedy. Epstein contrasts the gritty world of wheeling and dealing with the more abstract realm of academia, and he compares the grace of natural talent with the diligence of sustained effort. These stories capture life's essences, such as the particulars of a day's routine, the force of personalities, and the transforming love for a child. Spirited and memorable tales from a multifaceted writer. —*Donna Seaman*

Ernaux, Annie.
A Woman's Story.
Four Walls Eight Windows, $15.95 (0-941423-51-4). 112p.

Another unadorned and powerful novel from the award-winning, best-selling French author of *Cleaned Out.* In pure, simple, and restrained language, the narrator tells the story of her recently deceased mother. Taken out of school to work at age 12, her mother was determined to live a better life, and eventually she and her husband were able to purchase a small grocery and café. Handsome, robust, and blunt, she was an energetic businesswoman and a loving mother and wife with a lively interest in the world and respect for reading, fashion, and proper behavior. The narrator, struggling to remain objective, follows the more difficult course of her own relationship with her mother, from puberty to her mother's last day. Ernaux describes the eerie decline age brings, exacerbated in this case by Alzheimer's, with the calm and honesty that follow deep grief and reflection. —*Donna Seaman*

Escamill, Edna.
Daughter of the Mountain: Un Cuento.
Aunt Lute, $18.95 (0-933216-83-1); paper, $8.95 (0-933216-82-3). 212p.

Setting plays a central role in this impressive debut novel about the changing face of the American Southwest. Through the vehicle of Maggie, a young mestiza living in a poor border town surrounded by desert and mountains, we learn in a series of stories, or *cuentos*, told by Maggie's grandmother, a Yaqui Indian, about the Yaquis' vanishing folkways and loosening hold on the land they love. We also observe, along with Maggie, the overwhelming growth of her small town and the incursion of "undesirable" elements that force Maggie to search inside herself for a positive vision of the future and for control of her destiny. Her grandmother's *cuentos* thus prove to be invaluable guideposts. Written with a spare elegance that underscores the stark beauty of the desert setting, this novel captures with eloquent simplicity a life lived in harmony with both humanity and nature. —*Mary Banas*

✔Feinberg, David B.
Spontaneous Combustion.
Viking, $19.95 (0-670-83813 0). 226p.

The sequel to the award-winning *Eighty-Sixed* is less novel than performance. It's the further adventures of B. J. Rosenthal, who thinks of himself as "the most neurotic personality in Manhattan" but is actually a pretty typical smart, middle-class, Jewish, gay American male. His wit has bounced back from the AIDS deaths that had knocked the wind out of his sails by the end of *Eighty-Sixed*. Unfortunately, his physical well-being has not: fairly shortly into this book, he discovers he's HIV-positive (i.e., carrying the AIDS virus). Still, during the book he suffers more from the ever-increasing volume of pills he's obliged to take than from illness. And his wry, daft, pop-culturally allusive humor remains healthy despite the increasing body count among his friends. Reading more like a Christopher Durang play than a conventional novel, this is direly and passionately funny, perhaps the best sustained work of gay male humor ever published. —*Ray Olson*

Fergus, Charles.
Shadow Catcher.
Soho, $19.95 (0-939149-55-9). 320p.

In 1913, a train expedition visits native American reservations for the purpose of encouraging Indians to accept American citizenship and to enter the "mainstream" of American culture. Included in the expedition are James McLaughlin, an inspector for the Bureau of Indian Affairs, and his young stenographer, Ansel Fry. Through the insights of these two men, Fergus provides a series of fascinating and haunting images of Indian life in transition, while offering a unique perspective on the clash of white and Indian cultures. Fergus treats his characters, white and Indian, historical and fictional, with respect and affection while avoiding preaching or facile sentimentality. In his first novel, he displays a fine grasp of both language and subject matter as he brilliantly chronicles the struggles of a traditional culture to adapt to the modern world while holding on to a cherished heritage. —*Jay Freeman*

Fielding, Joy.
See Jane Run.
Morrow, $19.95 (0-688-08867-8). 364p.

A woman experiences an attack of amnesia on a downtown Boston street when she goes out on a shopping errand. Who is she? Why is she carrying no purse and no identification? Why is her dress covered with blood? And why is $10,000 stuffed into her coat pockets? The woman really begins to lose her mind when her husband, a handsome surgeon, reclaims her at the hospital and returns her to her suburban home, where she will be able to reconstruct her life from square one. Or can she? Why is her amnesia persisting, even though her nightmares seem to unveil her past? Did she really have an affair with her neighbor's husband? And is it possible that her husband is deliberately sedating her with pills and shots to permanently cloud her memory? Fielding certainly knows just what questions to ask in the suspenseful unraveling of this character's mind, and the author is almost as good at supplying the answers to what's really being hidden by all the deceptions. Fans of Fielding's past psychological thrillers, which include *The Deep End*, will enjoy this latest one right down to the last agonizing revelation. —*John Brosnahan*

Figes, Eva.
The Tree of Knowledge.
Pantheon, $20 (0-394-58765-0). 154p.

John Milton's daughter tells all about her life with her notoriously misogynistic father in Figes' historical novel. Deborah Milton is now an old woman and the widow of a poor weaver, but she vividly recalls the times and personality of her famous parent for the people who are now interested in Milton as a literary figure and man. Figes herself is interested not only in the Miltons, father and daughter, but in the condition of women in general in the late seventeenth and early eighteenth centuries and beyond. The intellectual and social chauvinism exhibited in Deborah's education and life assume a symbolic value here, the book evoking a set of relationships between men and women and between social classes that has stifled talent and imagination over the years and centuries. Figes is also the author of *Nelly's Version.* —*John Brosnahan*

Fraser, George MacDonald.
Flashman and the Mountain of Light.
Knopf, $22 (0-679-40071-0). 376p.

The natives are revolting, and the English hold on the Punjab region of India is slipping. The Sikh army is well organized, even though the Punjab's rulers are an unruly covey of squabbling, booze-soaked degenerates. The situation calls for diplomacy, derring-do, and determination. Who can save the situation by mingling with said degenerates, learning their secrets, and, oh yes, wrestling the priceless diamond from the belly button of the ruler's slatternly sister whilst "rogering" with aristocratic glee? None but Harry Flashman, hero of eight previous adventures, which were, by Flashy's own admission, "as fine a catalogue of honours won through knavery, cowardice, taking cover and squealing for mercy as you'll ever strike." Imagine the bastard offspring of a gene pool mixing P. G. Wodehouse, Tom Sharpe, and Rudyard Kipling let loose on the Victorian era's wars and women, and you get some idea of the loony mayhem that Fraser brings to the Flashman chronicles. Of course, actually sitting down and reading one of the books is an infinitely better idea. —*Peter Robertson*

Freeman, David.
A Hollywood Life.
Simon & Schuster, $19.95 (0-671-72738-9). 320p.

Rarely in literature does Hollywood look real; stereotypes are too strong to overcome. Freeman, however, not only understands the beast, but re-creates it vividly. His style holds no sentimentality, no aspiration—survival is supreme. Megastar Carla Tate is center stage here, a character reminiscent of Natalie Wood (and a few others)—raised on Hollywood, avoiding the pitfalls of her models, and attaining stardom from childhood through death. Here is

Hollywood, from L. B. Mayer's back-lot empire to today's wheeling and dealing between independent producers and bond holders, screenwriters and actors. Freeman's narrator, a prodigy director, becomes the psychological focus. Gabe Burton is liaison between star and audience. Desperately dealing with the death of Carla, his one-time mistress and lifelong influence, Gabe tells a tale that seems sincere. But how much should readers believe from a grieving man who adored the woman he immortalizes? This gem of contemporary narrative offers much more than readers of commercial fiction may be expecting. —*Denise Blank*

Freeman, Judith.
Set for Life.
Norton, $19.95 (0-393-03027-X). 352p.

A graceful and strong second novel by the author of *The Chinchilla Farm*. Once again, Freeman has created characters a reader can trust and care for. Phil is seriously ill and in need of a heart transplant. He has a deep, loving bond with his 16-year-old grandson, Luke, who is distressed at the thought of losing his grandfather. Preoccupied, Luke goes for a drive across the Idaho landscape, loses control of the car, and is killed. His young heart fits perfectly into his grandfather's grief-stricken body. As Phil regains his health, he has the eerie sensation that Luke's spirit remains in his heart. Meanwhile, 16-year-old Louise has run away from her neo-Nazi stepfather and abruptly intrudes on Phil's quiet, brooding life. As they try to reach out to each other, Freeman charts the tricky paths of recovery from sorrow and fear and the healing power of simple things. This paean to elemental, down-to-earth values is rooted in keen and subtle perceptions of the complexity of emotions and the vagaries of life. Magnetic and stirring. —*Donna Seaman*

✔**Fuentes, Carlos.**
The Campaign.
Farrar, $22.95 (0-374-11828-0). 222p.

Why is it that Latin Americans write such magnificently *literary* historical fiction? Well, in part, because theirs are historical novels of *ideas* rather than sentiment, just as readable as the romantic English-language type, but appealing more to the head than the heart. This distinguished Mexican writer's latest novel is certainly a prime example of just that quality. The less-than-clean separation of Latin America from Iberian control is an abiding theme of the fiction of the area, and Fuentes focuses here on Argentina's complicated transition from colonial to free status. The protagonist is one Baltasar Bustos, a young man of certain privilege—the son of a wealthy ranchowner on the pampas—who performs an amazing act of defiance against the Spanish colonial regime. He sneaks into the house of the judge of the superior court of the viceroyalty of La Plata and substitute's the magistrate's newborn child with the child of a black prostitute. In the process, he not only causes the house to catch on fire, killing one of the babies, but also catches a glimpse of the judge's wife and falls in love with her. To assuage himself of guilt and to attempt to gain her love, Baltasar joins the independence army and follows the lady of his dreams all over South America. This is not, however, a romance but a riveting inquiry into the conflict between ideals and practicality, between an altruistic political life and a self-absorbed personal one. To be read alongside of, and admired with, Gabriel García Márquez's novelized life of Simón Bolívar, *The General in His Labyrinth.* —*Brad Hooper*

Gabaldon, Diane.
Outlander.
Delacorte, $20 (0-385-30230-4). 640p.

While on her second honeymoon in Scotland just after World War II, Claire Randall returns alone to a nearby *henge*, an ancient circle of stones, to gather a plant specimen that interests her. (After spending the war as a nurse in France, she has taken up the housewifely hobby of plant pressing to please her husband, an Oxford don.) As she picks the plant, she accidentally touches one of the stones, and it screams. Suddenly, it's the year 1743, and she is in the war camp of Scottish insurgents, a battlefield nurse once more—or is she a witch? Whatever the case, Claire's life is in peril. Should she go back to the twentieth century or stay with the passionate James Fraser? This is escape fiction at its best, and Claire's decision won't surprise any reader with an adventurous soul. —*Cynthia Ogorek*

Gammon, Catherine.
Isabel Out of the Rain.
Mercury House, $18.95 (0-916515-96-6); paper, $10.95 (0-916515-97-4). 192p.

With urgency this first novel plunges into the despairing psyche of a nameless woman, revealing, through an alcoholic haze, the festering wound left by the worst transgressions of the father. Gammon proceeds to weave a dense pattern of intertwined lives as the reader is swept dizzyingly in time and place from Saigon to New York, Berkeley to Guatemala and back again. Gritty and compelling, these characters could comfortably inhabit a Sam Shepard play replete with disintegrating families whose lives are consumed by booze or frozen in denial. Isabel, a teenage runaway, has taken refuge with Russell, a stranger who recalls a daughter left behind yet never seen. Their seemingly ordered existence erupts when Cheyenne surfaces with bloodied shirt, memories of murder, and enough drunken ramblings to illuminate long-buried secrets. It remains for the enigmatic Santana to appear, embodying those forces which in the end will connect and clarify unraveling lies. A richly textured portrayal of damaged lives. —*Alice Joyce*

Gervais, Paul.
Extraordinary People.
HarperCollins, $19.95 (0-06-016618-5). 224p.

Tolstoy's fertile observation that each miserable family is distinctive and potentially fascinating again yields artistic fruit in this fine first novel. Sam Beeler's is a miserable family. Father Gerald is cold and remote. Mother Meg is funny and lively but crawls into the bottle when she realizes Gerald won't change. Brother Cliff envies Sam, mocks his parents, cross-dresses on the sly, and spies on the man showering next door. Sam yearns for the normalcy of the family's summer-vacation neighbors when he's a boy and of a loved professor and his wife when he's in college. He never achieves it (in fact, he turns out gay, confirming his own non-normalcy), so he forges a career about as far away from the other Beelers as he can get—as an enologist in Italy. They keep calling him back, however, as each sickens and dies and also breaches the wall Sam's built around his need to love them. Except in one flashback chapter, Gervais writes from Sam's calm, retrospective viewpoint and writes utterly convincingly, too, leaving shrouded many mysteries of why the Beelers are the way they are, but showing them to be as complicated, suffering, repulsive, and appealing as you and I. —*Ray Olson*

Gibson, Mary Ellis, ed.
Homeplaces: Stories of the South by Women Writers.
Univ. of South Carolina, $29.95 (0-87249-784-4); paper, $14.95 (0-87249-785-2). 311p.

Gibson has gathered together eight writers who manage to shed a radiant light upon contemporary southern culture and mores. Stories selected for this anthology include Elizabeth Spencer's "First Dark," a sympathetic exposé of genteel, small-town life: although the narrator reveals "something so recklessly fecund about a south Mississippi spring," nature's extravagance is shown to be stultifying when the lovers choose to walk away from the place where they sought "connection with the past." Family relationships figure prominently in these works, along with the repercussions that result from tense relations between races. In Toni Cade Bambara's story "Madame Bai," the protagonist lives in the racially charged atmosphere of Atlanta, in the time before Wayne Williams was charged with murdering black children there. Alice Walker's "A Sudden Trip Home in the Spring" follows Sarah Davis from her college dorm (where white girls thoughtlessly compare her black-skinned beauty to "a poppy in a field of winter roses") back to her rural Georgia hometown for a funeral. And Ntozake Shange's spirited young heroine learns, on becoming a woman, an unfortunate lesson that leads her mother to instill extreme caution into Indigo's trusting, rather fantastic approach to life. With clear and resonant voices, these collected stories assume a penetrating stance on issues of class, race, and gender. —*Alice Joyce*

Gifford, Barry.
Sailor's Holiday: The Wild Life of Sailor and Lula.
Random, $20 (0-679-40149-0). 350p.

"Ain't it somethin', though, Dal, how it's just one weird thing happens after another?" That's Marietta Pace talking to her best friend, Dalceda Delahoussaye, about the latest in the string of bizarre events that continue to bounce against her life and the life of her daughter, Lula. What is it this time? Well, it could be Lula's boy, Pace, being kidnapped in New Orleans, or it could be Lula getting back together with Sailor Ripley after he got out of prison (see

Gifford's *Wild at Heart*), or it could be Marietta rekindling her youthful romance with the notorious gangster Santos, or it could be Pace getting involved with the Rattler brothers (that would be Smokey Joe and Lefty Grove Rattler, so named by their pa, Tyrus Raymond Rattler). Frankly, it could be a lot of things. These four interconnected novellas take Sailor and Lula through the middle 20 years of their lives, and the world proves to be just as "weird on top" as it was when they were kids. But Sailor and Lula at midlife are every bit as "wild at heart" as ever, and that means more of what made the first book the quirkiest, tenderest, most warm-hearted love story in years. *Sailor's Holiday* isn't as accomplished a work as *Wild at Heart*: the novella structure is a bit disjointed, and the first story, "59° and Raining," while thematically connected to what follows, is altogether different in tone, a kind of Jim Thompson–like look at a pair of soulless dead-end kids. Still, all the elements that make Gifford one of our most appealing writers are in evidence here: staccato dialogue that's as tender as it is tough, an absolutely unhinged sense of humor, and, best of all, a wonderful mix of noir sensibility with a romantic soul. "Ain't much left in this lonesome world got no doubt in it," Gifford has a philosophical waitress opine. And, yet, he gives us Sailor and Lula, who keep right on living in that lonesome world and rising above it. —*Bill Ott*

Gilbert, Sarah.
Dixie Riggs.
Warner, $18.95 (0-446-51527-2). 208p.

All Dixie Riggs wants from life is to get married and have Buck Speed's children. And to become a world-famous fashion model. And to know for sure if white trashiness is genetic, or if her redneck mother, LeDaire, grabbed the wrong baby so long ago. Oh, yes, in the meantime, she wouldn't mind figuring out exactly who mailed those lurid photos of her posing in skimpy lingerie to Buck Speed's highly religious father. Dixie gets all and tells all, in a delight-fully fresh and funny voice that rings with the sublime righteousness of the truly innocent. Is it Dixie's fault that Buck, an aspiring televangelist, makes her pray after sex, thus driving her into the open arms of his best friend, Donnie? Or that Sparkle, Dixie's best friend, deserves to be beaten up after horning in on Buck? Gilbert's portrayal of Dixie's revenge is raucous and comic, even in its flashes of introspection: "If you're poor, you're probably always going to be making sleazy mistakes. And if you're just lucky enough not to be poor, you're probably going to make the same mistakes but wear better clothes making them." —*Eloise Kinney*

Gittelson, Celia.
Biography.
Knopf, $19 (0-394-58712-X). 259p.

Raphael Alter has found his niche: he writes about other people's lives. It's a safe, vicarious existence that lets him hibernate in his messy lair of an apartment, sifting through the paper trail left by his bolder subjects. His latest is Max Leibert, a recently deceased poet who roared through his allotted years with abandon. Gittelson's clever setup ushers us into the life stories of these two opposite yet complementary personalities. Max's character is created by interviews, letters, journals, and poems, while Alter (as in *alter ego*?) pursues his research under siege: the building he inherited from his father is sliding into dangerous dilapidation, rousing anger and fear in his poor, troubled, and elderly tenants. On the bright side, his inquiries lead him to Chloe, a lovely, skittish woman who was Max's last lover. In a dramatic denouement, Alter is altered by love and freed from his isolation. At one point, Alter's books are called "delicate and humane"; Gittelson could have been describing her own novel, which is that and much more. A particularly worthy Book-of-the-Month Club alternate. —*Donna Seaman*

Godden, Rumer.
Coromandel Sea Change.
Morrow, $18 (0-688-10397-9). 224p.

An Indian resort hotel on the coast of the Coromandel Sea is the setting for Godden's latest novel of romance, love, tragedy, and, rare for Godden, politics. What begins as a social comedy pitting the Anglo-Indian tradition against the far greater historical force of Indian culture itself ultimately descends into far deeper and personal emotional exercise as the love of a honeymooning English couple heads for the rocky shoals of marital disaster. The couple's differences stem from their opposing reactions to the Indian people and country and especially to the charismatic charms of a young man who is running an unorthodox campaign for the Indian parliament. Godden deftly sketches in the atmospheric background details and then allows her large cast of characters to enact the changing commitments and startling revelations that will make up the drama. If on occasion Godden telegraphs her intents too far in advance and illustrates a less than compassionate treatment of the novel's villains, the sheer enchantment and propulsion of her storytelling make these minor technical quibbles. —*John Brosnahan*

Godwin, Gail.
Father Melancholy's Daughter.
Morrow, $21.95 (0-688-06531-7). 512p.

Godwin, the author of *A Southern Family*, studies another family—this time that of an Episcopalian rector in Virginia's Shenandoah Mountains. As a young girl, Margaret experiences the loss of her mother and later the death of her father. These traumatic episodes undoubtedly mark Margaret's character as she grows into a woman and belatedly tries to contend with the heritage of her missing parents. While Godwin's psychological depiction is affecting, the social comedy and setting of her story are much more richly realized. The religious conventions of small-town, upper-middle-class life are captured in riotous detail, the rector contending with his unruly flock and family. In fact, some of the minor characters are so vividly portrayed that their problems and predilections often swamp the more immediate and presumably momentous questions that Godwin's narrative probes. —*John Brosnahan*

299

General Fiction

Godwin, Parke.
Sherwood.
Morrow, $20 (0-688-05264-9). 384p.

Godwin, known for a body of superior science fiction and fantasy, is even better known for his imaginative historical fiction. Here, in the first of two volumes devoted to the subject, he tackles the legend of Robin Hood, Anglo-Saxon resistance leader at the time of the Norman Conquest. Imaginative embellishments, like making the Sheriff of Nottingham a certain Ralf Fitz-Gerald, a young Norman knight trying to cope with the new land and its people, are handled with skill, scholarship, command of language, and excellence of characterization. A historical novel that is not only certain to be in demand but is also highly recommended for the virtues that leap from every page. —*Roland Green*

Goldstein, Rebecca.
The Dark Sister.
Viking, $19.95 (0-670-83556-0). 260p.

If you relish the sonorous prose of Henry James, you'll follow Goldstein's demanding novel with pleasure and surprise. Goldstein, echoing the famous Jamesian style, has constructed a psychological and metaphysical drama tinged with the chill of a ghost story and the threat of madness. At the center is Hedda—38, Jewish, conspicuously tall, skinny, flat-chested, and author of seven notorious novels, each featuring a beautiful JAW (Jewish Angry Woman), an annihilator of men. But her eighth book is taking a new direction, precipitated by Hedda's sudden departure from New York for a lonely old house on the New England coast. Here she finds herself inexplicably writing about William James, Henry's older brother, and a pair of strange, spinster sisters. Alice is an archetypal Victorian old maid, while Vivianna is a voluptuous, self-taught astronomer, fascinated by "darkened stars." As Hedda's book spins off into some hilarious asides concerning the plight of women in misogynistic societies, a parallel tale about Hedda's weakening grip on reality, her sister Stella, and their traumatic past emerges. A sinuous, demanding, and brilliantly inventive performance. —*Donna Seaman*

Gordimer, Nadine.
Crimes of Conscience.
Heinemann; dist. by Trafalgar Square, paper, $8.95 (0-435-90668-2). 121p.

Betrayal is a dominant theme in these dark, beautiful stories by a great South African writer—betrayal, and also its opposite, the unexpected good that people find in themselves. In Gordimer's superbly crafted fiction, the astonishing reversals of story always grow from character and circumstance and from how apartheid affects individuals in their complex interaction. All but one of these 11 tales have been collected before—in *A Soldier's Embrace* (1980) and *Something out There* (1985)—but this small paperback in the African Writers series provides an excellent introduction to some of the author's best work over the last 15 years. Just right for book-discussion groups, the collection ranges from the well-known "Town and Country Lovers" to the more recent "A City of the Dead, a City of the Living," in which a Soweto woman finds herself attracted to a fugitive who threatens her family's safety. —*Hazel Rochman*

✔**Gordimer, Nadine.**
Jump and Other Stories.
Farrar, $19.95 (0-374-18055-5). 296p.

In her eighth collection of stories Gordimer writes with an insider's intensity about people caught in the savage particulars of southern Africa today; at the same time, the surprise of the stories and the slash of their endings make the words resonate with the revelations of an ever-widening universe. "Once upon a Time" sets the Sleeping Beauty myth in a prosperous Johannesburg suburb where a white family wants to live happily ever after. Desperate to shut out suffering and violence, they imprison themselves; they build their own concentration camp with razor-bladed coils around every wall. The act of storytelling is always part of the stories: how we imagine—or suppress—alternative lives for ourselves and others. In "The Ultimate Safari," Gordimer sets exotic travelogue adventure against the stark narrative of an orphan refugee child from war-torn Mozambique, who envies the game-park animals their food and their home: "We wanted to go away from where our mother wasn't and where we were hungry. We wanted to go where there were no bandits and there was food. We were glad to think there must be such a place; away." Writing like this will not let readers get away. —*Hazel Rochman*

✔**Gould, Lois.**
Medusa's Gift.
Knopf, $19 (0-394-58229-2). 204p.

Gould is one of American literature's best-kept secrets—a name not recognized by the majority of the reading public, but admired and even adored by discriminating fiction lovers. Her explorations of the ways women find to express passion, fantasy, and power have led her from creating credible Eva and Isabel Perón-type figures in *La Presidenta* (1981) to the enigmatic American woman resident on a lovely Greek island in *Medusa's Gift*. Mystery and rumor swarm around Magdalene; some islanders believe her to be a famous actress who supposedly drowned two decades previously but who faked her death to flee both country and limelight. In fact, a film historian comes to the island to write the life of Magdalene, and from their encounters much of Magdalene's past is aired—until her ugly death (and even then, some people believe she didn't die *this* time, either, but continues to live on some other Aegean island). Gould takes a situation that in lesser hands could have descended into cliché and renders it rich and resonant not only by her savory style and brilliant sense of composition, but also by her dexterity in carving strong female characters with a firm yet sensitive hand. To pick up this novel is to refuse to put it down unfinished, and those who appreciate Gould will flock to obtain a copy.—*Brad Hooper*

Graham, Winston.
The Twisted Sword.
Carroll & Graf, $21.95 (0-88184-693-7). 512p.

Graham concludes the enormously popular Poldark saga with an epic adventure revolving around Napoleon's defeat at Waterloo in 1815. When Ross Poldark undertakes a government assignment to assess the strength of Bonapartist sentiment in Bourbon, France, he and his beloved wife, Demelza, are swept into a giddy Parisian social whirl, belying the ominous threat of war. Meanwhile, young Jeremy Poldark, a lieutenant in the British army, and his bride enjoy a carefree honeymoon in Brussels. As fate and fortune conspire to reunite the Poldarks on the bloodiest of battlefields, life among their familiar band of friends and relatives in Cornwall continues to amuse and intrigue. Devoted fans will not be disappointed in this fond adieu to one of historical fiction's most endearing and enduring couples.—*Margaret Flanagan*

Graver, Elizabeth.
Have You Seen Me?
Univ. of Pittsburgh, $17.95 (0-8229-3682-8). 200p.

In a series of 10 short stories, Elizabeth Graver portrays her young characters catching glimpses of the adult world they are growing into. "The Body Shop" begins with Simon as he sorts eyes and hands, attaches legs, and patches joints, helping his mother with the business of transforming old mannequins. The story weaves around his childhood discoveries and ends with his mother's death and with his adult realization that he cannot create a flawless world for his daughter just by patching together body parts. "The Boy Who Fell Forty Feet" cannot cope with his father's death, choosing to compare himself with the children in his class and to a woman he witnesses pinned down by a crane in a building site. The title story concerns 11-year-old Willa, who arranges old milk cartons so the missing children can stare each other down. All the stories begin somewhere in the middle with the revealing of an essential detail. The author then builds a whole piece by retracing her characters' histories in a fluid, seamless narration that takes them in the directions indicated from the beginning. This graceful, affecting book was the winner of the 1991 Drue Heinz Literature Prize. —*Amy Gibson*

✓Gray, Alasdair.
Something Leather.
Random, $19 (0-394-58963-7). 256p.

In order to get to the beginning of the story, which really comes closer to the end, the reader must traverse author Gray's playfully subversive cross-section of Glasgow life, from the postindustrial wasteland of the sixties, through the transitional seventies and eighties, and on to the culturally reborn nineties. It all leads up to the purchase of "something leather" by divorcée June, who puts her new toy to good use in an orgy/bondage encounter with Senga and Donalda, proprietors of the leather shop, and Harry, a fourth woman who avidly joins the frolic. Along the way, we are bombarded with crisp one-liners; dialogue that fizzles, explodes, and meanders like real-life wordplay; and a series of seemingly unrelated, totally bizarre scenes set against the angry squalor of Thatcher's "free enterprise Britain." There isn't any reason why three generations of working men talk war stories in a boiler room, or a comedian laments love and the dearth of classic jokes. They just do, and it all works in its own wayward way, insidiously endowed with brutal clarity. Gray brings both verve and venom to this searing examination of freedom, hard won and usually hard compromised. *Something Leather* isn't just a remarkable novel; it would make a great movie, preferably directed by Bill (*Local Hero*) Forsyth. —*Peter Robertson*

Green, Julian.
The Distant Lands.
Marion Boyars, $29.50. 902p.

Once upon a time—in the 1930s, specifically—a young man of southern American parentage, though himself a resident of France since birth, abandoned a novel he'd just begun, having decided the subject had been "scooped" by the new best-selling American novel, *Gone with the Wind*. Julian Green went on to write a distinguished body of other fiction, which in fact earned him membership in the hallowed French Academy. Recently, Green went back to the novel set in the American South he'd given up on decades before, and finished it; it became a smash in France and is now being published in the U.S. This 1,000-pager takes its sweet time in providing what eventually becomes a compelling drama of the 1850s South, as 16-year-old Elizabeth Escridge arrives from Britain to live on the plantation of her rich Georgia relatives and subsequently finds herself up to her pretty little neck in domestic embroilments and romantic entanglements. Less melodrama than colorful and careful historical fiction, Green's opus is a delicious immersion into time and place. Reminiscent of the historical novels of Anne Rice in its lovely rather than laborious attention to details of the past, *Distant Lands* is stylish and fluid, with an abundance of characters who attract with their humanness. —*Brad Hooper*

Greene, Graham.
The Last Word and Other Stories.
Viking, $17.95 (1-871061-23-7). 160p.

A collection of stories spanning Greene's long and illustrious career. The older of these 12 tales were omitted from Graham's earlier anthologies, the most recent of which was *Collected Short Stories*. The newer stories are from the last few years, and one has never been published before. All find Greene at his best: each piece is stark, almost melodramatic, paced like a chess game with life in check, and viewed through Greene's usual lenses of religion, morality, destiny, aloneness, and alienation. In "The Lottery Ticket," a traveler's prize leads to murder in a small, sour Mexican town; an old boozy poacher saves a village from a German invasion in "The Lieutenant Died Last"; and the title story is a chilling view of the future's obliteration of the beliefs of the past. "A Branch of the Service" combines espionage with gastronomy, and Greene's 1920s detective story "Murder for the Wrong

Reason" is tinged with irony and futility. Another treasure from a master still going strong at 86. Greene's last novel was *The Captain and the Enemy*. —*Donna Seaman*

Greene, Harlan.
What the Dead Remember.
Dutton, $18.95 (0-525-93378-6). 192p.

Imagine the limpidity of Tennessee Williams' short stories wed to the outsider friendships of a Capote or McCullers novel. Imagine the story at hand is still about youth, sex, and love, and you've got this effortlessly readable novel. Its four parts report its narrator's most important summers in Charleston, South Carolina. During the first, he's 13, and, although he wants to join a circle of beautiful boys, he befriends Stevie, who's retarded, instead. During the second, he's 14, and the golden boys plot to humiliate him, but . . . "One at a time,' I said, and they obeyed." He doesn't return until he's a grown gay man with a promiscuous youth behind him. He dabbles in Charleston gay life, discovers some of the boys of old in it, but then takes up with Stevie again, becoming his and his caretaker-sister's boon companion until the story's cataclysmic climax and cruel but tragically credible ending. A terrifically sad and lovely piece of work. —*Ray Olson*

Griffith, Patricia Browning.
The World around Midnight.
Putnam, $22.95 (0-399-13590-1). 256p.

Narrator Dinah Reynolds has returned temporarily to Midnight, the "town where Texas still is," to publish her late father's weekly paper, the *Midnight Citizen*. When a semifamous Christian rock singer's plane crashes in Claude Sanders' Swiss chard field, all manner of strange events commence. All the yellow cats in town disappear. Dinah's daughter-in-law, Traci, runs off with Midnight's number-one realtor and marries him, causing her state trooper son to get drunk and start shooting at Midnight's lone red light. Back in North Dallas, her husband, Dude, meets another woman. Bobby Joe Daniels, her high school flame and the Christian rocker's manager, returns to Midnight and rekindles old feelings. Grandmother Lilly decides to marry another resident of the Happy Acres Nursing Home, outraging Dinah's strictly Baptist mother. There are hints of miracles at the crash site. At the eye of this maelstrom, Dinah struggles for balance with grace and a delightful sense of humor, humanity, and human foibles. Midnight is a quirky, sweet-spirited, winsome place that readers will come to care about. —*Thomas Gaughan*

Grumley, Michael.
Life Drawing.
Grove Weidenfeld, $17.95 (0-8021-1438-5). 192p.

An excerpt from this little novel was one of the best things in the first *Men on Men* anthology. The whole recounts the sexual awakening of Mickey McGinnis, a white Iowa youth—athletic, no sissy—who upon graduating high school, circa 1960, heads down the Mississippi to a black male lover in New

Orleans. The relationship founders when Mickey yields to another man's advances, after which he heads to Hollywood, where he sleeps around and tries to break into the movies. That doesn't pan out, so he goes home and starts college. And, the reader is quite convinced, develops into Michael Grumley (a conviction encouraged by novelist Edmund White's introductory characterization of the novel as autobiographical). The book shimmers with the truth of sexual realization despite rather delicately avoiding explicit details about body parts and couplings. What it lacks that Grumley might have added had he not died of AIDS in 1988 is some recognition of the ambiguities, fears, and social abrasions Mickey must feel but which are bypassed in favor of sweet sensuality and wonder-filled self-discovery. —*Ray Olson*

✔**Grunwald, Lisa.**
The Theory of Everything.
Knopf, $20 (0-394-58149-0). 320p.

Alexander has dreamed of an angel ever since his mother showed him a ghost and then disappeared. Now 30 years old, Alexander has devoted his life to physics and the formulation of mathematical concepts to explain the mysteries of the universe. When he finally completes years of grant-supported work—his Theory of Everything—his carefully controlled life spins off into chaos. The agent of change is his enigmatic mother, who reappears and leads him into the realm of the occult. While his extraordinary theory is splashed across the pages of *Time* and *Newsweek*, Alexander goes off to work with a reclusive alchemist in New Jersey. He doesn't learn how to make gold, but he does learn how to embrace life. Grunwald understands the age-old lure of the promise of magic, the quest for the key to life, and the impulse to bury oneself in abstractions to avoid the pain of existence. And she writes of it all with tenderness, poise, and grace. An exalted, entrancing, and lyrical novel, affirming the promise of the author's debut, *Summer.* —*Donna Seaman*

Hailey, Elizabeth Forsythe.
Home Free.
Delacorte, $19.95 (0-385-29914-1). 304p.

Like the movie *Down and Out in Beverly Hills*, *Home Free* is about a "bum" who is taken in by the wealthy in California. Protagonist Kate undergoes a maelstrom of transformation—personally and socially—after her film-director husband, Cliff, announces on Christmas Eve that he is leaving her for another woman. That same night, Kate meets, befriends, and eventually behomes a homeless family: Ford, handsome and lithe, with strong faith in God; his wife, Sunny, who, like Kate, is determined to find her place in the world; and their two likable children. The book offers moments of sheer human verisimilitude; these, combined with well-drawn characters and a plot that snares almost from the first page, make the book hard to set down. One is tempted, but not quite, to say *Home Free* is a "feel good" book. It is more strongly a "do something good" book. Though we can never quite get over the nagging feeling that Kate's idealism is implausible, Hailey proves that it is

General Fiction

possible to write serious fiction about such seemingly untouchable subjects as faith, hope, and charity. —*Eloise Kinney*

Hall, Rodney.
The Second Bridegroom.
Farrar, $19.95 (0-374-25668-3). 216p.

Australian novelist-poet-biographer Hall may not top the best-seller lists, but he deserves a place on library shelves. In this first novel in a trilogy, Hall tells of a convict transported to Australia in the 1830s who escapes from his master to live for a time with the aborigines of New South Wales. A native of the Isle of Man, where independence from Mother England and pre-Christian religion (including the myth of the goddess who takes a new husband each six months) retain their power, FJ is a printer, in his way a literary man, condemned to death for stealing William Caxton's hundredth book; his death sentence is commuted only when FJ convinces the court he is a forger, not a thief. Hall, who received Australia's most prestigious literary prize, the Miles Franklin Award, in 1982 for his third novel, *Just Relations*, has been compared with Faulkner, Joyce, and García Márquez; in *The Second Bridegroom's* world of ship and shore and wilderness, in its juxtaposition of native and settler, freedom and captivity, reality and the words we use to capture reality, comparisons to Melville and Conrad seem inevitable. —*Mary Carroll*

Hannah, Barry.
Never Die.
Houghton, $18.95 (0-395-51560-2). 152p.

Mississippian Hannah follows several distinctive novels and short story collections with another invigorating work that once more reveals him to be a prime descendant of the southern gothic school associated with Truman Capote, Flannery O'Connor, Carson McCullers, and others. Like his forebears, Hannah has a penchant for depicting grotesques—for simultaneous mockery of and sympathy for people afflicted physically, morally, or emotionally. In this case, the object of his uncompromising limning of peculiarities of personality is the small western town of Nitburg in the early years of the twentieth century—a place sunk in moral turpitude. In a string of short episodes, Hannah follows the desires and excesses of a group of Nitburg denizens, foremost among them the college-educated gunslinger Fernando. Fernando suffers some bad breaks at the hands of the man who runs Nitburg—old Judge Nitburg himself—and attempts to rid the place of vice and vermin. The resultant struggles are hilarious. —*Brad Hooper*

Hardie, Sean.
Table for Five.
Simon & Schuster, $19.95 (0-671-72329-4). 373p.

When Charlie Kavanaugh, itinerant TV director, is hired by Julia Cornwall, little does he suspect the dangers lurking behind the facade of an innocent documentary to be taped in Israel. When he begins to sense that all is not kosher with his producers, Charlie activates his own network in Israel and back in London, calling the plays of a double bluff that rescues not only Julia and himself from criminal prosecution, but also four well-known Israelis from certain death. A well-crafted thriller crammed with exquisite detail and outspoken characterizations. A must-read for the Israeli politics as well as the cloak-and-dagger romance. —*Cynthia Ogorek*

Hearon, Shelby.
Hug Dancing.
Knopf, $20 (0-394-58652-2). 288p.

A real charmer from the award-winning author of 12 novels including *Owning Jolene*. Hearon juggles an endearing tangle of characters, a heart-tugging plot, and amusing commentary on religion, guilt, and land use, Texas-style, with finesse. Romance and satire vie for center stage in the story of Cile Tait, a young woman of grit and passion. Cile lives in Waco, married to a dour Presbyterian pastor and mother of two ecology-minded "Amazons." She is also carrying on a lusty affair with Drew, a married man with two sons. He was her high school sweetheart who disappeared right after her mother drowned in a flash flood. His mother, an elder in the church, turns out to be responsible for that abrupt separation and, inadvertently, their steamy reunion. Their affair and declaration of their intentions to legitimize it spark a series of schemes, stalls, and manipulations. Hearon adds to the suspense with tornadoes and hailstorms, land deals and unexpected reconciliations. The music is country, the kids smart and savvy, the love conquering and sweet. Truly a feel-good read. —*Donna Seaman*

Hedges, Peter.
What's Eating Gilbert Grape.
Poseidon, $20 (0-671-73509-8). 335p.

Dramatists have invented dozens of devices to let audiences know what their characters are thinking but not saying. Hedges, who at age 28 has formed his own theater company and had his plays produced at the off-Broadway Circle Repertory Theater and at a number of regional theaters, has found an unconventional solution: he's written a novel. Narrator Gilbert Grape has a full load of problems. His family thinks "families are what other people have." His love life, such as it is, is a mess. The old-fashioned grocery where he works is losing its customers to a glitzy supermarket with its own lobster tank. And his town itself—Endora, Iowa, population 1,091—is losing its young people, burning down its elementary school, and rapidly turning into Anytown, U.S.A. This is a funny, touching, caring first novel whose characters are familiar and moving in spite of (or perhaps because of) their peculiarities. As 24-year-old Gilbert prepares for his retarded brother's eighteenth birthday party, ends his first sexual relationship and begins what he hopes may be his second, and wrestles with the mysteries of life and death, laughing and crying, loving and accepting others and loving and accepting himself, he takes a long step toward an adulthood delayed by the multifarious things "eating" him as the novel begins. Readers will wish him well. —*Mary Carroll*

Herrin, Lamar.
The Lies Boys Tell.
Norton, $19.95 (0-393-03010-5). 256p.

Ed is down to one lung and dying, but he has a plan: he intends to die in the bed and room in which he was born. This will take some doing, as he can barely walk and shouldn't leave his Kentucky home, and the bed would have to be moved from his sister's place in Georgia to his Alabama birthplace. Only one member of his determinedly unimaginative family can help him—his renegade son Larry. Ed convinces Larry to buy a van and spirit him away from his loving, worried wife and other children. Ed insists on total secrecy, placing Larry in the bizarre predicament of granting his father his dying wish while terrifying and infuriating his mother and siblings who believe he's kidnapped the old man out of spite. Driving slowly across the South, they retrace the tangled paths of their lives and heal old wounds. Herrin has fashioned a sort of Faulknerian on-the-road saga with tremendous delicacy and gentle irony. —*Donna Seaman*

✔Hersey, John.
Antonietta.
Knopf, $21 (0-679-40194-6). 304p.

Is there anything more satisfying than seeing an old pro do his thing superbly one more time? Of course not, so whatever you do, read this new product of a 50-year career of craftsmanly writing. Dramatically cast in five acts set in 1699, 1778, 1830, 1918, and "Last Year," it notes the highlights of 300 years in the life of the violin Stradivarius built after falling in love at first sight with his second wife, Antonia, in whose honor he names it. The instrument is filled with his passion and stimulates desire in all who hear it. If this sounds like the set-up for something cornball and vulgar, have no fear. Hersey's intelligence, wit, and stylishness—not to mention his well-informed musical taste—save the novel from foolishness while letting it exude charm, ribaldry, and humor with symphonic largesse. Symphonic variety, too, as Hersey changes style with each act. At first, he's magisterially omniscient in relating how Antonietta was made and how it changed Stradivarius. He assumes the personae of the Mozarts, father and son, for the epistolary second act; of a violinist who plays for Berlioz during the composition of the *Symphonie Fantastique* in the third; and in the fourth's overlapping interior monologues, of Stravinsky, Ramuz, and a Russian virtuoso who wields Antonietta as *Histoire du Soldat* is written. The last act assumes the form of a teleplay as it tells how an insider-trading wheeler-dealer acquires the Strad to give himself a cultural gloss. Desire (for sex in the first four acts, for money in the last), the love of music, and warm amusement with human folly abound. A scrumptious reading experience. —*Ray Olson*

Himes, Chester B.
The Collected Stories of Chester Himes.
Thunder's Mouth, $24.95 (1-56025-020-8); paper, $12.95 (1-56025-021-6)
446p.

This collection of 60 short stories gives a good impression of the author's achievement in this form. Calvin Hernton's introduction places Himes' work in the central context of African American writing and offers an explanation for his currently undervalued reputation as the author of novels and short fiction. With his stories depicting the struggles of black Americans against the pervasive aftereffects of slavery, Himes offers a pointed view of race relations in the U.S. from the 1930s through the late 1970s. Himes' experiences as a restaurant worker, prison inmate, and European exile surface in many of these pieces, and the writer explores the beleaguered humanity of his characters with understanding, wit, and compassion. —*John Brosnahan*

Hlasko, Marek.
All Backs Were Turned.
Cane Hill, paper, $8.95 (0-943433-07-X). 118p.

In this novel of exile set in an Israeli parolees' community called Elath during the early 1960s, the late, celebrated Polish author describes a cruel, chauvinistic society of outcasts in which women are the catalysts for men's violence. Dov Ben Dov, whose criminal record includes killing his wife's lover, and Polish expatriate Israel Berg have a symbiotic relationship: Dov's strength and reputation protect Berg, who takes the blame for charges against Dov to keep him out of jail. But in Elath, Dov becomes involved with his younger brother's fight with competing fishermen and with Berg's relationship with a German woman tourist. Violence, as casual as it is inevitable when honor is the ultimate value, spins out of control to an ironic ending. With its flat, compressed prose, the novel conjures a world that insinuates itself into the reader's consciousness. —*Michele Leber*

Hood, Ann.
Something Blue.
Bantam, $18.95 (0-553-07140-8). 272p.

Hood writes gentle, introspective novels. Like *Three-Legged Horse*, *Something Blue* is about creative people trying to figure out how to live. A triad of thirtysomething women in New York struggle with their dreams and uncertainties. Lucy earns her keep as a Whirlwind Weekend tour guide, rushing inexperienced tourists through quickie European visits, but her true calling is illustration. Her best friend, Julia, conceals pertinent information about herself, including the fact that her mother is the author of a young adult series about a Nancy Drew–like character named Vicky Valentine, whom Julia despises. Katherine is preppy and peppy but ran away from her lavish wedding to find out about passion. Hood's characters worry about their pasts, fear intimacy, and wonder about how to reconcile love and ambition. Emotional authenticity, artful details, and a happy wrap-up make this a perceptive, pleasing love story. —*Donna Seaman*

Hospital, Janette Turner.
Isobars.
Louisiana State Univ., $18.95 (0-8071-1710-2). 177p.

In memory, dream and fantasy, intimacy, misunderstanding, and isolation, the characters in these short stories glimpse patterns, seek meanings, struggle to understand. The past is ever present, and history—personal, familial, national, international—lies just beneath the surface of everyday events. Hospital, born in Australia, has lived all over the world; many of her characters, too, are citizens of several continents, dislocated, perhaps, but never quite rootless. Moving through space and through time, coping (as the 90-year-old professor in "To Be Discontinued" remarks, describing once more his single, youthful encounter with Einstein at Princeton) with randomness and indeterminacy, these characters demand the reader's attention and involvement. Like Hospital's first short-story collection, *Dislocations* (1987), which won the Fiction Award of the Fellowship of Australian Writers, *Isobars* is likely to satisfy award juries as much as it pleases readers. —*Mary Carroll*

Ignatieff, Michael.
Asya.
Knopf, $22 (0-679-40657-3). 320p.

A Canadian of Russian descent who now hosts the nightly arts program "Live at Night" on BBC television, Ignatieff told the *London Observer* early this year of his perhaps naive hope that his first novel would be, not a historical novel or a novel of ideas, but "the kind of book I used to devour under the covers, reading by flashlight." To a large extent, this debut novel meets its author's objective. *Asya* spans nine decades in the life of Russian Princess Anastasia Vladimirovich Galitzine Gourevitch and centers on issues of innocence and knowledge, fidelity and betrayal. But it is the character of Asya herself and her relationships with men—her father and brother, her husband and son, her friends and lovers—which capture the reader and provide the story's fascination. Asya travels—from a comfortable country house near Smolensk to the makeshift hospitals of the White Army after World War I, from an emigré apartment in Paris in 1919 to a hasty retreat from the City of Lights only hours ahead of Hitler's troops and their collaborators, from London under the blitz to London after V-E Day, and, finally, in her most astonishing leap of time, space, and faith, from a reclusive retirement in London to the USSR of Gorbachev and, perhaps, the husband she has not seen for 50 years. Ignatieff effectively uses Old Russia, Russia-in-exile, and New Russia (now not-so-new, of course) as the backdrop for a solid yarn, which is at once a story of love and a tale of survival. —*Mary Carroll*

Inman, Robert.
Old Dogs and Children.
Little, Brown, $19.95 (0-316-41897-8). 448p.

The author of *Home Fires Burning* has created another unforgettable southern tale inhabited by warm, striking characters, such as Bright Birdsong and her best friend, Flavo Richardson. The novel opens as the town

Bright has lived in all of her life prepares for Fitzhugh Birdsong Day in honor of her son, the governor, who is running for reelection. Throughout the story, Inman reaches back into Bright's six decades, blending past and present with the same potent beauty displayed in his first novel. We see Bright as a young girl visiting her father's sawmill, working at his side on a camp house, playing music, and being assured by her dad that he could solve everything. He couldn't, of course, but his inspiration has compelled Bright to make commitments and forge community change, especially regarding civil rights. Inman is a consummate storyteller. —*Denise Perry Donavin*

Iossel, Mikhail.
Every Hunter Wants to Know: A Leningrad Life.
Norton, $21.95 (0-393-02985-9). 288p.

Within this bold, occasionally wayward collection of stories is a deliberately rambling coming-of-age tale that, fraught with childhood bravado and fear, rings painfully true. Set against the politically quixotic Brezhnev years (the "time of stagnation"), Soviet emigrè Iossel's first work follows young Yevgeny Litovtsev on the awkward path to manhood and political awareness. We start with a first meeting with the West in the shape of an American named Bruce. Yevgeny is frightened, then seduced by the Westerner's self-assurance. Later we explore Yevgeny's past insecurities, some universally childlike, some unique to the turbulence of the Soviet Union. Throughout the book, we see Yevgeny caught between shifting ideologies, as he stands in line with his grandfather in Red Square, as Stalin falls from grace, as another boy taunts him, as he stands up for his views and is chastised for doing so. All this confusion leads inexorably to the protagonist's eventual immigration to the U.S., where TV is endless, rock 'n' roll is king, and things are not exactly what he expected but unequivocally different. Iossel's prose is vibrant, and a sense of irony is seldom far from the surface. —*Peter Robertson*

Jen, Gish.
Typical American.
Houghton, $19.95 (0-395-54689-3). 296p.

A tempestuous novel about three young Chinese immigrants who come to America in the late 1940s: Ralph, his older sister Theresa, and her delicate friend Helen. Ralph and Helen marry, and the three of them set up house in a crumbling tenement and try to figure out their new country. Theresa, considered too tall and plain for marriage in China, is dutiful and self-sacrificing, earning her medical degree and contributing to the household without complaint. Helen had grown up expecting to be pampered, but discovers that she enjoys working. Ralph is governed by a dangerous mixture of ambition and naivete, which pulls them into a dizzying series of surprising events that takes them from rags to riches, city to suburb, and the halls of academia to "Ralph's Chicken Palace." Jen conjures an atmosphere of confusion and high emotion in which manic humor skitters across the rough grain of prejudice, cultural differences, greed, and sexual mores, while the realization of dreams alternately uplifts and destroys. —*Donna Seaman*

Johnson, Nora.
Perfect Together.
Dutton, $19.95 (0-525-93316-6). 336p.

Fran and Charlie are the perfect New York City couple: fashionable, professional, social, steady, and controlled, until Fran breaks the spell and says she wants to have a baby. Passion soars; Charlie is thrilled, but even after every possible medical procedure and a radical move to a house in the suburbs, Fran can't conceive. Their maid, however, has the opposite problem. Charlie manfully apologizes to all concerned and begs for forgiveness, but insists on keeping "his" baby, setting off a brilliantly orchestrated series of events that explores the treacherous waters of surrogate motherhood. As all hell breaks loose in more directions than a spilled box of ball bearings, Johnson chases down warped attitudes toward genetics, parenthood, and domesticity. Every convolution in the story line exposes arrogant, selfish, and thoughtless assumptions, while Fran gets off some real zingers. Ultimately, two irrefutable truths emerge: the shocking disparity between the sexual act and the responsibility for a new life, and the fact that when a child needs love, you give it without biological prejudice. Entertainment of the highest order.
—*Donna Seaman*

Jolley, Elizabeth.
Cabin Fever.
HarperCollins, $19.95 (0-06-016622-3). 224p.

This darkly introspective novel is a sequel of sorts to Australian writer Jolley's *My Father's Moon.* It continues the story of protagonist Veronica Wright, a British nurse who has survived the World War II bombings of London and who now travels to a medical conference in modern-day Manhattan, where she attempts to put her life back in order. Through an innovative flashback technique in which the heroine's fragmented recollections tumble willy-nilly onto the page yet eventually are knitted together by connecting threads of meaning, Jolley masterfully conveys Veronica's inner turmoil over her onetime affair with a married doctor, her decision to have a child out of wedlock, and her own emotional fallout from her stressful years of nursing the war's wounded back to health. *Cabin Fever* is not a traditionally plotted story but, rather, a kaleidoscopic series of snapshots that keep shifting to give us an ever-new angle on the main character and her hard-won insights into life. An engrossing tale of human interiors, with a very appealing heroine.
—*Mary Banas*

Jones, Douglas C.
The Search for Temperance Moon.
Holt, $22.50 (0-8050-1387-3). 320p.

For the reader immersed in Jones' detail-rich historical novel, the myths and realities of the Old West crackle like machine-gun fire; yet the lingering effect of this elegant, measured book is less frenetic, more like the echo from a single Remington reverberating in a lonely canyon. Jones never lets his narrative fall into a Michener-like morass of endless chronology. While nearly every banker, gunman, lawman, madam, breed, and half-breed who passes through the town of Ft. Smith, Arkansas, has a personal history that Jones takes unmistakable relish in recounting, he does so without sacrificing a moment of narrative intensity. The question under review is what happened to Temperance Moon, Ft. Smith's wealthiest madam and shrewdest businessperson. Was she, as the local authorities believe, simply gunned down on a lonely road—end of story? Her daughter, the resourceful Jewel, doesn't buy it. She enlists Oscar Schiller, a former lawman with a hot temper and a taste for good cocaine (rare in these parts), to investigate. Soon Oscar's eccentric team, including an Asian lawman with a talent for disguise and an alluring Creek woman, is on the job. Taking obvious delight in his colorful and complex characters, Jones offers a particularly unsentimental view of the post–Civil War West, revealing in the process that several of the evils we postindustrial types like to claim as our own were perfectly at home on the range. —*Peter Robertson*

Jones, R. S.
Force of Gravity.
Viking, $19.95 (0-670-83591-9). 268p.

An arresting first novel about madness. Emmet is gentle, wren-thin, and kind-hearted, living an obsessive, fearful existence in a dilapidated apartment building. He wears heavy clothing in the heat of summer, eats only carrots, lies to his shrink, and spends his sleepless nights walking with his dog. Memories of his childhood are surreal and eerie: his father hurling him off a cliff into a man-of-war-infested sea, clinging to a rocky precipice with his mother as the rising moon, "pulsing with a saucery light," glazes the desert. Emmet struggles to control his perceptions, but the very essence of objects is altered before his frightened eyes, and every exchange with strangers becomes fraught with menace and danger. Jones conveys the nauseating disorientation of insanity with restraint, grace, and respect for the absurd. Once Emmet is hospitalized, his craziness seems quite mild compared with the delusions of his fellow inmates. A tale full of sad magic and lingering hope. —*Donna Seaman*

Jönsson, Reidar.
My Father, His Son.
Arcade, $19.95 (1-55970-117-X). 256p.

The second installment in a proposed trilogy about the chaotic and comic life of Ingemar Wallis Rutger Johansson. The first book was *My Life as a Dog*, the source of Jönsson's Oscar-winning screenplay. As the saga continues, Johansson has joined the Swedish merchant marines, following in the footsteps of his ever-absent, dismayingly selfish father. After warning us that he has "a magnetic ability to adhere to life's exaggerations," our hero launches into a hilarious and highly doubtful account of foolhardy, life-threatening escapades both aboard ship and in port at locales ripe for trouble: Australia, South Africa, and Nigeria. These tales of sharks, thieves, mutilation, and insanity are told in flashbacks as Johansson engages in hopeless arguments with his passionate and unreasonable wife in Algiers. Jönsson's humor is aggressive, but he can turn a phrase with great delicacy, keeping you off balance between slapstick and pathos. Admirers of his previous novel and the film of the same name won't be disappointed. —*Donna Seaman*

✔Just, Ward.
The Translator.
Houghton, $21.95 (0-395-57168-5). 313p.

Ward Just's reputation for shrewd and worldly fiction has gained momentum with each book (most recently, *Jack Nance* [1989] and *Twenty-one: Selected Stories*), a trend that will be sustained by the release of his latest novel. In *The Translator*, a richly philosophical, provocative, and cosmopolitan work, Just explores the implications of expatriatism. Sydney Van Damm, a German living in Paris and graced with an innate sense of language and "oceanic patience," is a translator, content to interpret the thoughts of others. His marriage to an American is a close and articulate bond, tested harshly by the birth of their handicapped son and the tides of change in their homelands: America's economic woes and Germany's unification. When Sydney has to put aside his literary pursuits for more lucrative but risky work, he finds himself in a jam that can't be resolved with linguistic prowess. Just masterfully weds the emotions of his compelling characters to the political forces that inadvertently mold their lives, musing on the nature of art, war, corruption, grief, and responsibility along the way. A brooding and savvy performance. —*Donna Seaman*

✔Keillor, Garrison.
WLT: A Radio Romance.
Viking, $19.95 (0-670-81857-7). 368p.

With this book—his longest sustained story—public radio star Keillor proves he is also the dean of contemporary literary humorists. As the subtitle implies, this is a love story about radio; at any rate, it's about radio and it's a love story. In 1926, in Minneapolis, Ray and Roy Soderbjerg begin, as a promotional device for their restaurant, station WLT (stands for With Lettuce and Tomato). By gosh, it catches on. The brothers eventually close the kitchen and put their all into the "Friendly Neighbor" station. Well, Ray does, anyway; Roy's the dreamy inventor type and gets banished to Moorhead while Roy, Jr., becomes general manager. WLT's a honking success until 1950, when (womanizing) Ray's ironclad rule that employees shall stay outta each other's britches is disclosed to be rusted to a filigree and all-purpose writer Patsy Konopka starts forgetting to pull the pages of blue dialogue she scribbles to help her keep awake out of the finished scripts. But before that bitter (screamingly funny) end, young Francis With has fulfilled his ambition to work for the station. In fact, name fortuitously changed to Frank White, he becomes Roy, Jr.'s right hand and an up and-coming announcer. And he falls in love with actress Maria Antonio—that's the love story, unless you count Frank's love for radio as one (you certainly can't count the station staff's hilariously horny shenanigans as anything like romance; passion, maybe—romance, no way!). Anyone familiar with the tales of Lake Wobegon knows

Keillor's flare for making baggy-pantsed comedy out of everyday mishaps. From the safe-for-the-whole-family contents of those stories he here turns to lewder and cruder (but on other pages, more intellectual) occasions for laughter—and he's never been funnier! This is a comic masterpiece. —*Ray Olson*

Keneally, Thomas.
Flying Hero Class.
Warner, $19.95 (0-446-51582-5). 304p.

No one could accuse Keneally of writing the same book over again. This widely regarded Australian novelist has even written about the U.S. Civil War (in *Confederates*), and now he draws on a terribly frightening aspect of today's global—but hardly harmonious—community. Frank McCloud is manager of the Barramatjara Dance Troupe, an aboriginal group from Australia. A successful run of performances in New York behind them, he and his dancers embark on what should be a routine commercial flight to their next venue: Frankfurt, Germany. Routine it most definitely turns out not to be. Not long after takeoff the plane is commandeered by a Palestinian terrorist group; and Frank, along with two other men, are made targets for especial terror—Frank, because the Palestinians believe him to be an exploiter of the oppressed group of people of which his dancers are members. A plot situation that in less masterly hands could have never elevated itself above a movie-of-the-week-type thriller of limited depth and ingenuity does in fact stay straight on course, as not only a compelling drama carried by finely shaded characters, but also as an intelligent contemplation of issues the contemporary world has yet to reconcile. —*Brad Hooper*

King, Stephen.
Needful Things.
Viking, $24.95 (0-670-83953-1). 640p.

Full of the sharply realized physical details and the accurately juicy speech that make every word Stephen King writes worth reading, this novel is his version of Ray Bradbury's *Something Wicked This Way Comes* and its great forebear, Mark Twain's "Man That Corrupted Hadleyburg." In it, a mysterious Mr. Leland Gaunt opens a curio shop in Castle Rock, Maine (scene of *The Dark Half* and *Cujo*, too). Therein you may find your heart's desire—that is, the useless item you want so much it becomes a necessity. Quite quickly, Gaunt is doing landoffice business in such things as a 1956 Sandy Koufax Topps baseball card, a foxtail in perfect condition, and a flawless carnival glass lampshade—each for mere dimes and nickels, plus a promise to play little pranks upon a neighbor. In practice, the pranks have more dire consequences than their perpetrators can imagine. Eventually, the town is in ruins, many of its citizens are dead or damaged, and the hero who drives Gaunt away leaves in relieved disgust. Some readers might be a bit disgusted, or at least disappointed, too, for the cataclysmic ending is rather pat and predictable, and Gaunt is not as vivid as King's earlier monsters. But still, the tale is a good, fan-pleasing read that most resembles King's postapocalyp-

General Fiction

tic fantasy, *The Stand*, in that its parts are more enjoyable than the whole.
—*Ray Olson*

✔**King, Stephen.**
The Waste Lands.
NAL/Plume, $14.95 (0-452-26740-4). 512p.

Everything in the third installment of master fantasist King's longest sustained effort, *The Dark Tower*, is pumped up a couple notches—the action, the suspense, the cultural allusiveness, the inventiveness, and in fact, the volume, for loudspeakers blare earsplittingly throughout the tale's biggest, most spectacular, though penultimate, climax. Gunslinger-knight Roland of Mid-World and the two New Yorkers he snatched in *The Drawing of the Three* from our world (which Mid-World is like but only occasionally, *culturally* intersects, so that, for instance, both worlds have Z. Z. Top records) proceed ever nearer the Dark Tower, where lies the source of the shocking degradation of the culture of Roland's planet. Joining them, via another nailbiting passage from Earth to Mid-World, is 11-year-old Jake Chambers, another New Yorker who, in *The Gunslinger*, died out of Gotham and then, apparently, out of Mid-World, too. It turns out Jake both did and did not die, for in the decadently fluid time-space of Roland's planet (where the clocks don't tell time by any decipherable system), death can occur less than definitely. As usual—no, more than usual—for King, there's lots of mayhem, magic, and also sheer book-learning in this yarn. The well-acculturated and wannabe well-acculturated will revel in King's borrowings from everything from medieval riddles to eighteenth-century poet and hymnodist William Cowper to the Land of Oz to T. S. Eliot to Hollywood movies of the 1940s to post–World War II children's books to rock 'n' roll. The man's a pop polymath, and in *The Dark Tower* he's pouring everything he knows and loves into a vast romance of the imagination that is as quirky and spooky and funny and dazzling as the *Arabian Nights* or the great medieval romances of Europe. —*Ray Olson*

Klavan, Andrew.
Don't Say a Word.
Pocket, $19.95 (0-671-74008-3). 310p.

A secret is buried with the body of Elizabeth's drug-riddled mother. And as Elizabeth's mind decays, the imaginary friend who protects her becomes a creature of substance. But she tells no one—except Dr. Nathan Conrad, known as "the psychiatrist of the damned." Conrad, however, has problems of his own: the abduction of his daughter, Jessica, and the secret cameras and microphones that stop him and his wife from calling the cops. This is truly dark territory, every bit the equal of Thomas Harris' *The Silence of the Lambs*, even though Klavan, who garnered an Edgar under the pseudonym Keith Peterson and wrote the screenplay for the Michael Caine psychological thriller *A Shock to the System*, isn't the neogothic stylist Harris is. The book's good guys, the doctor and his family, are warmly drawn, while the investigating cop is simply a big, flatulent dollop of low-level humanity. Klavan's sinewy links between the killers, the messed-up Elizabeth, and the kidnapping are slick and ingenious. If you're foolishly trying to get to sleep after watching Jonathan Demme's celluloid treatment of *Lambs*, best forget it. Crack open Klavan's eerie masterwork instead. The rest of a long night awaits. —*Peter Robertson*

Koontz, Dean.
Cold Fire.
Putnam, $22.95 (0-399-13579-0). 384p.

The words *life line* suddenly echo in his head without warning. And Jim Ironheart is transported, traveling across the country to save lives seemingly at random. His existence is no longer his own, and his troubled adolescence becomes a shadow world that appears at night, in his deepest sleep. But his series of heroic acts soon comes to the attention of reporter Holly Thorne, whose instincts, both journalistic and womanly, are quickly aroused by the reclusive and troubled hero. The trail to solving the mystery of Jim and the dueling demons of his psyche leads back home, to a small California town, to familial death, and to childhood powers of imagination that create a safe fantasy, a psychic retreat that ultimately explodes in adulthood. Koontz is perhaps the least given to verbal pyrotechnics of the current horror masters. His work displays a subdued prose style; cultural sidebars are kept to a minimum; and blood spills are few and far between. But he also knows how to generate genuine terror without gore: a plane flight during which Jim wrestles with the dilemma of saving only his chosen targets or the rest of the passengers, or the final encounters with the warring spirit factions, which effectively jump from horror to high camp and back again. —*Peter Robertson*

Korda, Michael.
Curtain.
Summit, $19.95 (0-671-68684-4). 378p.

High drama in three acts. Robert Vance is a superb Shakespearean actor. He falls in love with an actress, Felicia Lisle, whose fastidious beauty conceals fierce passion. Unable to escape their marriages, they become Britain's favorite adulterous celebrity couple, playing the role of lovers both on stage and in private. Korda opens this page-turner with a prologue set 40 years in the future and hinting at dark, long-hidden secrets. He then flashes back to the 1940s when Vance and Felicia are stranded in Hollywood, broke after a disastrous attempt at taking *Romeo and Juliet* on the road in the U.S. Felicia, drinking and pill-popping, is on the verge of a breakdown, and Robby is anxious to return to London and serve in the RAF. Korda mines the vulgarity of Hollywood and the pretension of London theater for his robust, satisfyingly conflicted characters. Vance and Felicia simmer with guilt, resentment, and fear while the action becomes more desperate, abandoned, and tragic in true Shakespearean style. Korda brings you inside his characters: you are Vance playing Mark Antony, striding across the stage, sweating buckets, his mind a blank, or Felicia confronting her evil Uncle Harry with his "horsemen's hands." Having set his novel on stage, Korda can pull out all the stops—nothing is too theatrical. And it's a hit. —*Donna Seaman*

317

General Fiction

✔Kundera, Milan.
Immortality.
Grove Weidenfeld, $21.95 (0-8021-1111-4). 345p.

A meditative, sophisticated, and many-tiered novel by the master of articulated eroticism and philosophies of existence. Kundera orchestrates several story lines aimed at divining the meaning of immortality and the path to happiness. One strand concerns a novelist, disarmingly named Kundera, who finds inspiration in the sight of a woman waving to a lifeguard at a swimming pool. This gesture kindles his imagination, and he writes about Agnes, a woman who has stopped loving the world, senses only its aggressive ugliness, and feels "no solidarity with mankind." Kundera casts a brooding, melancholy eye on humanity's reductive obsession with image, the precariousness of our sense of self, and the difference between living and being. Scenes with Agnes play in a curious harmony with amusing scenes featuring the great poet Goethe, both during his lifetime and in the hereafter, where he converses with Hemingway on the nature of life and death. Much as Kundera tells us that happiness is not found in the pursuit of sexual conquests, recognition, or immortality, but in selfless, primordial being, he can't resist the urge to live consciously, eloquently, and creatively, and for that we are grateful. —*Donna Seaman*

Kunin, Vladimir.
Intergirl: A Hard Currency Hooker.
Bergh Publishing, $19.95 (0-930267-06-0); paper, $9.95 (0-930267-07-9). 192p.

Prostitution isn't a crime in the Soviet Union, but possession of *valuta*, or hard currency, is a serious offense. The intrepid Intergirls take their chances, however, trading sex for foreign currency at tourist hotels and business conventions. Intergirl Tanya is a classic whore with a heart of gold in this sorrowful tale. She loves her mother and labors long hours at her official hospital job but moonlights on the Intergirl circuit, hoping not just for luxury items and cash, but for escape via marriage to a foreigner. A Swede takes the bait and they marry, but her departure is marred by betrayals and threats, and life in Sweden is sterile and lonely. The persistent atmosphere of foreboding is brought to fruition in an explosive and tragic conclusion. Kunin's frank treatment of prostitution and the consequences of the corrupt economic system catapulted this gloomy little melodrama to bestsellerdom in the Soviet Union; it has also been made into a Soviet-Swedish film. —*Donna Seaman*

Kurzweil, Allen.
A Case of Curiosities.
HBJ, $19.95 (0-15-115793-6). 382p.

In 1983, at an auction in Paris, our unassuming narrator chances upon a modest box that will become his obsession for the next six years. The small, compartmental "box of curiosities," or *memento hominem*, holds objects that are meant to illustrate one person's life, in this case, that of eighteenth-century Frenchman Claude Page—student, artist, watchmaker, inventor, mechanical genius. Just as the items in the box draw the narrator in, they draw us in, because each is surrounded by a circle of meaning that is ever expanding. The story that the narrator unfolds may or may not be the "truth" about Claude, but it is an authentic tale of inquiry, desire, and creation. When Claude, exasperated and unsure of himself, complains that he is not in control of his diverse thoughts, his lusty teacher replies, "'Do not try. . . . The revelations you seek . . . arise from the violent copulation of opposing thoughts. . . . Belief, even if it is wrongheaded, will propel you closer to the act of creation." This wonderfully romantic tale of education and obsession is as moving as it is fresh and exciting. —*Frances Woods*

Labro, Philippe R.
One Summer out West.
Ballantine/Available Press, paper, $7.95 (0-345-36364-7). 272p.

A French exchange student at an East Coast college travels across the U.S. during the summer of 1955 to work for the forest service in Colorado, but his experiences in the West are hardly what he or his readers could expect. There's that dose of syphilis, for one thing, caught from a charming folksinger in an Indiana sunflower patch. Then there's the Hell's Angels assassination squad, to say nothing about the vicious organized brawl among camp workers. Mostly, however, this story is about the protagonist's discoveries—of his own emerging identity and of the mythical nature of the American West itself. Beginning as a wary and frail student, he grows into maturity both physical and mental, hitchhiking across the country and confronting a whole new breed of men and women who populate a rough and ready world. William Byron's translation of Labro's French original sometimes blurs the linguistic and cultural differences by making Labro sound too American, too early— even Labro seems to stretch the boundary between autobiography and fiction at times, as he did in *The Foreign Student*—but the essential quality of the author's adventures comes through in resounding fashion. —*John Brosnahan*

Laker, Rosalind.
The Golden Tulip.
Doubleday, $20 (0-385-41560-5). 592p.

An enchanting historical novel that follows the exploits of Francesca Visser and her family during late seventeenth-century Holland, as they move in the circles of Rembrandt, Vermeer, and William of Orange. Francesca's dream to become a master artist threatens to be thwarted by the devious Ludolf van Deventer, who manipulates her heavily indebted father into signing a mar- riage contract for her. Only her own determination and the constant support of Pieter van Doorne—the tulip grower who loves her selflessly—and her sisters guide Francesca toward her goal. The tales of her sisters are equally well crafted, as the stubborn Aletta learns to overcome fears brought on by a near-rape attack in childhood in order to care for a man she hardly knows, while Sybylla is nearly trapped by her conviction that gowns and jewels will make her truly happy. Laker weaves history and art appreciation into her

General Fiction

story thoroughly and unpatronizingly. An excellent choice for readers who enjoy more meat and less heat in their romance. —*Denise Blank*

Lazarre, Jane.
Worlds Beyond My Control.
Dutton, $17.95 (0-525-24976-1). 192p.

Considered a feminist because she writes so accurately and sensitively about being female, Lazarre has combined autobiography with fiction here and in her earlier works, which include *The Mother Knot* and *Some Kind of Innocence*. Narrated by Julia—a mother, a writer, and a teacher—this delicately balanced and lovingly nuanced tale takes the form, in turns, of both a journal and a novel. Julia is white, Jewish, 45, married to a quiet black man, and mother of two sons, one about to leave home, the other almost in high school. The issues in Julia's life are complex. She feels neither white nor black, hasn't been able to write since a set of stories alienated her best friend, and understands the need for restraint in mothering but suffers from it. She forces herself into silence until she realizes that she can love her sons without trying to control the world, and that if she must write, she must write. A fluid, unmasking, and gently funny articulation of the demands of art and motherhood. —*Donna Seaman*

Lee, Gus.
China Boy.
Dutton, $19.95 (0-525-24994-X). 322p.

Kai, or "China Boy," according to the bullies in his San Francisco neighborhood, is the only son and youngest child of an aristocratic couple from Shanghai who fled the Communists and landed in San Francisco's tough Panhandle district in 1944. Kai's mother was beautiful, passionate, and zealously protective of her son. She kept Kai inside for his first six years, instructing him in Confucian thought and Chinese traditions. But she dies, his father remarries, and Kai's world collapses. Kai's stepmother is white, chauvinistic, cold, and cruel. She will not let her stepchildren speak Chinese, eat Chinese food, or refer to their mother, and she literally throws her skinny, naive, and bewildered seven-year-old stepson out onto the streets. The Panhandle is a poor, black neighborhood, and Kai instantly becomes every tough guy's favorite punching bag. Lee conveys the spirit of Chinese and black cultures with fluent dialogue and telling description. The author's humor is rich and endearing, and when Kai starts standing his ground and fighting back, Lee has you up out of your seat rooting for him with all you've got. A jubilantly funny, heart-touching, and rousing debut novel. —*Donna Seaman*

Lee, Sky.
Disappearing Moon Cafe.
Seal Press, $18.95 (1-878067-11-7). 237p.

The Wong family tree provided at the opening of this Chinese Canadian family saga becomes indispensable as Lee skips back and forth in time, working up a certain amount of suspense and some confusion. The current of the novel pulses round and round this circuit of liaisons and births as family members battle over the issue of progeny. Mui Lan, who runs the Disappearing Moon Cafe in Vancouver's Chinatown, is desperate for a grandson. After five years, her only child's wife has not conceived, and, naturally, she blames her daughter-in-law. Because the old ways, finding a concubine or a second wife, are frowned upon in Vancouver, Mui Lan resorts to a scheme that manages to compromise everyone involved long into the future. As Lee conducts us through the ensuing tangle of love affairs, faked paternity, and a legacy of guilt, fear, and lies, she reveals the nastier aspects of Chinatown society and the destructiveness of sexual tyranny and dishonesty. A feisty, complex, and award-winning first novel. —*Donna Seaman*

Lefcourt, Peter.
The Deal.
Random, $19 (0-679-40152-0). 320p.

Charlie Berns is a B-movie producer so down on his luck his unpaid gardeners have torn out the shrubbery. Charlie is suicidally busy with a hose and the exhaust pipe of his Mercedes when his nephew, Lionel, materializes with a script he's written about Benjamin Disraeli and William Gladstone called *Ben and Bill*. It's literate, sensitive, and classy, and therefore hasn't got a chance of being produced, but Charlie has an inspiration. He's heard that Bobby Mason, a black karate champ and box-office superstar, is interested in doing a film about Judaism. In a hilarious sequence of evasive yet seductive maneuvers, Charlie convinces Mason that he has a script for a buddy movie about a black Jew commando and a British counterespionage agent. He snares a major studio and gets backing without showing anyone the actual script and then holes up with a drunk and mad screenwriter for a "rewrite" that turns the script into *Lev Disraeli: Jewish Freedom Fighter*. One absurdity leads to another: Charlie takes the production to Yugoslavia, where he hires a director who hates talking to actors; Mason is kidnapped by Macedonian separatists; and the home office is besieged by their new Japanese owners. Screenwriter Lefcourt's got the gift: his first novel plays with the speed, fakes, shots, and suspense of basketball at its hottest, and it's a genuinely funny and fresh satire of Hollywood. With only seconds left on the clock, Lefcourt's hero makes his shot and you hear applause as you turn the last page. —*Donna Seaman*

Le Guin, Ursula K.
Searoad: Chronicles of Klatsand.
HarperCollins, $19.95 (0-06-016740-8). 193p.

Klatsand, a small, quiet resort town on the Oregon coast, is the setting for Le Guin's latest, which offers a deceptively simple sampling of character vignettes. These symphonically interwoven prose poems limn the daily lives of ordinary people—"Nobody will ever know any of us ever existed. Except for Granddaddy. He's the only real one. . . . He was important. He has a biography. None of us will." Like pieces of a jigsaw puzzle, the separate stories, centering on different individuals, fit neatly together to provide an overall portrait of a remote community. Le Guin concludes with a demanding yet delicate stream-of-consciousness chronicle by the alternating voices of four generations of women, each tied to Klatsand in her own way. A lovely work to savor for the nuances and the elegant writing style. —*Sally Estes*

Levin, Ira.
Sliver.
Bantam, $19.95 (0-553-07292-7). 190p.

A master of horror and suspense, Levin makes fans wait entirely too long between novels. It's been 15 years since *The Boys from Brazil*. Unfortunately, although it's not unsatisfying, *Sliver*'s a slight reward for all that patience. It's short and seems shorter because it's written pretty breathlessly. Movie thriller nuts will spot its inspirations in *Rear Window* and *Gaslight*, for its plot brings together a voyeur whose voyeurism gets him into trouble and a heroine who falls for a man she comes to suspect is a murderer. But here voyeur and killer are one and the fortyish heroine is less winsomely vulnerable than young Ingrid Bergman. It's not fair to say much more about the plot, except that its mainspring is Orwell's concept, in *1984*, of Big Brother, which Levin scales down to fit *Sliver*'s setting in a new New York apartment building as sinister as the old brownstone of *Rosemary's Baby*. Although the way its final confrontation scene is resolved will strike many as far fetched, *Sliver* reaffirms Levin's mastery at putting his readers on edge and keeping them there till the last page is turned. —*Ray Olson*

✔Lively, Penelope.
City of the Mind.
HarperCollins, $19.95 (0-06-016666-5). 231p.

Winner of the Booker Prize and author of eight novels and numerous works for children, Lively possesses an acute sensitivity and an unfailing homing device for the perfect phrase. Her ongoing fascination with the organic nature of time has shaped many of her novels, but none on so grand a scale as this. Matthew Halland is a London architect and the adoring father of eight-year-old Jane. Divorced and lonely, Matthew filters each experience through his preoccupation with the end of his marriage. As he works on his projects, particularly an imposing tower of glass and steel named after the sixteenth-century explorer Martin Frobisher, he is keenly aware of the tide of construction, destruction, and rebuilding that has washed the city for centuries. He senses the history stored in old stone and brick and, as he takes his daughter to exhibits about dinosaurs and the stars, meditates on time before the existence of human beings. As Matthew befriends an artist who escaped the Holocaust, becomes entangled with a gangster and real estate mogul, and falls in love with a woman he meets in a sandwich shop, glimpses into the city's past, such as Frobisher's homecoming, the harsh life of a nineteenth-century street urchin, and the Nazi bombardment, are vividly imagined. Lively dramatizes the tenacity and complexity of life in the city as well as the simultaneity of the past and present in the mind. This masterful depiction of the subtleties of cognition and perception as well as a gentle love story is a stunning achievement. —*Donna Seaman*

Lively, Penelope.
The Road to Lichfield.
Grove Weidenfeld, $17.95 (0-8021-1134-3). 224p.

A flawless novel about the role of the past by one of Britain's best. As you read Lively's perfect sentences, certain phrases light up: e.g., "a scum of insects" on a windshield, a "landscape aching under a cold spring wind," or the "grey, foam-marbled sea." The physical world reflects the emotions of her reticent, disciplined, and often unhappy characters. Anne's father is dying. He lives in Lichfield, some distance from Anne's proper suburban household replete with two children and solicitor husband. On summer holiday from history-teaching duties, Anne drives to Lichfield alone to visit him in the nursing home and tidy up his vacant house. Her father drifts in a beautifully evoked limbo of dreams, memories, and confusion while Anne discovers how little she knew of him and falls in love with a neighbor. Like Lively's Booker Prize–winning novel, *Moon Tiger*, this earlier work (first published in England in 1977) explores the meaning of the past, as it is here linked to a meditation on marriages gone cold. —*Donna Seaman*

Llywelyn, Morgan.
Druids.
Morrow, $19.95 (0-688-08819-8). 448p.

Llywelyn is the much-acclaimed author of the best-selling epic novels *Red Branch* and *Lion of Ireland*, among others. With *Druids,* she is at the top of her form, weaving a spellbinding saga replete with the myth, legend, and history of the ancient Celtic tribes of Europe. It is a magical tale, yet utterly convincing, about the role the mystical druids—the thinkers, teachers, healers, and "Keepers of the Mysteries"—played in the life and culture of ancient Gaul. But more than this, it's the enchanting life story of the fictional Ainvar, a 15-year-old boy who unwittingly becomes the protégé of the chief druid of the Order of the Wise and the hope of the Carnute tribe in their battle against Caesar. Unlike other retellings of the Gallic wars, which focus on the conquest of Gaul by the Romans, this one inventively depicts one tribe, led by the valorous Ainvar, that withstood the mighty Caesar's assault. As ever, Llywelyn's skill at making ancient history come alive for a modern audience without sacrificing authenticity of fact or detail is nothing short of brilliant. A richly atmospheric tale filled with subtle flashes of humor, perceptive characterizations, and heart-stopping suspense. Not to be missed. —*Mary Banas*

Lord, Nancy.
Survival.
Coffee House, paper, $9.95 (0-918273-84-6). 176p.

Local color is the outstanding virtue of these Alaskan short stories. Their characters are young, recent arrivals to the forty-ninth state, and even if they do not live in Anchorage, they are seen from the perspective of that city. Anchorage is not the setting for writers who wish to re-create the image of

General Fiction

America's last frontier familiar to "outsiders" (i.e., non-Alaskans), and Lord is, at times, uncomfortable with the city's urbanity. Beneath its thin veneer, however, the real Alaska prevails, she protests, and when she allows herself to describe without preconceptions the people and customs she has observed, her discomfort vanishes, and she emerges as a genuinely entertaining storyteller with a personal vision of human isolation. Moreover, the wilderness she depicts escapes first impressions and, in its subtlety, is an authentic descendant of everything Jack London imagined. —*Roland Wulbert*

Lott, Bret.
Jewel.
Pocket, $20 (0-671-74038-5). 358p.

Jewel Hilburn is a plainspoken woman who tells her story and opens her soul and comes alive as few literary characters do. Her lessons came early in rural Mississippi: an orphan sent to a correctional school, she learned to take responsibility for her life. Her marriage to Leston was solid and loving and produced five fine children and a comfortable living during the relative prosperity of World War II. Then Brenda Kay was born with Down's syndrome, and Jewel's life split in two. There are echoes of Sue Miller's *Family Pictures* in the portrayal of the effects of an exceptional child on a family, but there is added depth and dimension here, as Jewel spends decades making what she can of her youngest child's life, while regretting what she is unable to give to the rest of her family. When jobs are scarce and doctor bills high in the postwar years, Jewel fixes on California to provide a better life for them all, and she works for what she wants despite the cost to the good man she loves. Jewel's story of a life and its legacy moves at its own pace with strength and dignity, captivating with its moments of aching tenderness and undertow of quiet power. —*Michele Leber*

Louie, David Wong.
Pangs of Love.
Knopf, $19 (0-394-58957-2). 256p.

A distinctive debut from a writer with a Chinese American perspective. Louie's potent stories exude a blunt stubbornness and a sense of warped detachment and almost hallucinogenic alienation. In the title story, the 35-year-old narrator's mother has lived in America for 40 years without learning English while he can only speak the Chinese of a child, making the difficult task of communicating across cultures and generations truly impossible, the sort of failure experienced by many of Louie's memorable characters. Conversations don't quite match up, and confusions are accepted like the weather. In "Birthday," a mother speaks in aphorisms that don't quite make sense, while in "Inheritance," a father says: "Here's an ancient Chinese tale that I made up a long time ago." Another ingredient in Louie's psychologically saturated world is the pall of political awareness: the shadow of nuclear weapons, global conflict, and the feeling of vulnerability contrasted with a blind desire to believe that America, the chosen country, is perfect and safe.

A strong new voice in the growing chorus of Chinese American literature. —*Donna Seaman*

Loy, Rosetta.
The Dust Roads of Monferrato.
Knopf, $20 (0-394-58849-5). 256p.

This translation of an award-winning Italian novel brings Everyfamily into our hearts. In Loy's spellbinding account of three generations of an unnamed clan from northern Italy, the narrator moves in and out of the present, disclosing family legend in the smallest amount of dialogue and yet moving provocatively from one generation to the next. The author's talent for characterization is noticeable immediately, as is her ability to portray sibling relationships. The nineteenth-century time frame, which contributes the forces of Napoleon and cholera, builds on the fundamental passion of the story. Of course, this novel chronicles love, marriage, childbirth, illness, war, and death, but it ultimately speaks out on the loss of purity—purity too good for this world. While celebrating human strength of body and soul, Loy forces us to look at the cycle of life and how it is that "life wins every time." —*Kathryn LaBarbera*

Mahfouz, Naguib.
The Search.
Doubleday, $20 (0-385-26459-3); paper, $8 (0-385-26460-7). 144p.
Mahfouz, Naguib.
The Time and the Place and Other Stories.
Doubleday, $19.50 (0-385-26471-2). 192p.

One short novel and a collection of short stories by the Egyptian Nobel Prize winner expand on the writer's characteristic world and style.

The Search examines the quandary of a young man who must decide on his path in life. With the death of his mother, who supported him with the earnings of her illegal brothel, he must either find a new source of financial support or begin to follow his mother's criminal activities. One way out of this life of crime may be to find his wealthy father, whom his mother left soon after their marriage. Traveling from Alexandria to Cairo in this quest, the young man finds himself relentlessly drawn into a situation he would rather avoid. Mahfouz's tense narrative inexorably probes his protagonist's psychological depths while also evoking a compelling portrait of Egyptian society.

In the introduction to the collection of Mahfouz stories, Johnson-Davies briefly considers the author's achievement as a short-story writer in the context of Egyptian and Arabic literature. Mahfouz's obsession with an almost Proustian sense of time becomes evident in these pieces, most of them written in the 1960s and 1970s when Mahfouz found it difficult to compose his acclaimed novels. The characters range from young boys to old men, each one beset by the realization that the pace of existence has quickly passed him by. The ever-present reality of death and a pessimistic view of society are other elements characterizing these remarkably poignant stories, which find Mah-

General Fiction

fouz at the height of his powers, both as a writer and as a social commentator. —*John Brosnahan*

✓**Mailer, Norman.**
Harlot's Ghost.
Random, $30 (0-394-58832-0). 1,334p.

The literary world's own Stormin' Norman, after the luxuriously wrought but discomfitting murder-mystery *Tough Guys Don't Dance* (1984), which was preceded by an excessively detailed excursion into the rites and habits of pharaonic Egypt in *Ancient Evenings* (1983), now presents an incredibly involving espionage thriller that takes the reader behind closed doors of the CIA to see how spy stuff really works. The narrator of this leviathan of a novel is agent Harry Hubbard, son of a famous agent, godson and protégé of another legendary figure in the agency, Hugh Tremont Montague, code-named Harlot. Harry's recollection of his father- and mentor-shadowed CIA career reaches back to the mid-1950s and extends to the mid-1960s, relating Harry's work during this height of the cold war, which included some career-threatening skulduggery in Berlin, working in Uruguay with the future-famous Howard Hunt (of Watergate infamy, to refresh your memory), and the planning of a Castro overthrow. Of course, the foregoing bare-bones plot description only hints at the richness this magnificent novel represents. Mailer's years researching the innerworkings of the CIA have obviously paid off in terms of the quantity of absorbing detail; characters are themselves Mailer-esque (meaning, of course, deliciously larger than life in their loudness of personality); and all of this delivered in a style that even with the vast number of narrative pages nevers flags in its beauty, sonorousness, and even songfulness. Hats off to one of our major contemporary writers, who has once more justified his lofty niche. —*Brad Hooper*

Malouf, David.
The Great World.
Pantheon, $22 (0-679-40176-8). 330p.

"The mystery of other people's lives, how little we know of one another" is Malouf's subject in this superb novel. The complex relationship of two Australians who meet in a World War II Japanese POW camp is Malouf's vehicle. Digger Keen is strong, courageous, contemplative, and phlegmatic— the ideal comrade-in-arms. Vic Curran, orphaned during the Depression when his alcoholic father died, causes the death of Digger's closest friend through his lack of discipline. Later, Vic's ministrations save Digger's life. After the war, frantic, never-satisfied Vic becomes a tormented, hugely successful entrepreneur who continues for 40 years to seek out Digger. Above all, *The Great World* is the artful development of perhaps a dozen finely drawn, wonderfully, strangely human characters thrown into the momentous events of the century: the Great Depression, World War II, the turmoil of the 1960s, the materialist 1980s. Already a success in Britain and Australia,

Malouf's latest book is masterful, and readers looking for quality fiction deserve to find it in their library. —*Thomas Gaughan*

✔**Manley, Joey.**
The Death of Donna-May Dean.
St. Martin's, $17.95 (0-312-05852-7). 272p.

Arguing with his mother shortly after he's come out to her, 17-year-old Jamie, protagonist-narrator of this extraordinary coming-of-age novel, has an epiphany (a word he knows and uses, by the way): ". . . all at once, for the first time in my life, I realized: I sound like a sissy. And I always have." And it's tough to be a sissy—i.e., gay—in the small northwest Alabama city of Genoa, where he's grown up in a trailer park and become part of the male-male sexual underground in the town's "Queer Park." So he kicks himself out of home and repairs to the house of the "town faggots," Keller and Thomas, intending to learn how to be a homosexual. In the dizzying adventures of the next few weeks, he learns instead to be himself, thanks to Keller's teaching by bad example (as Jamie's mother—who's genuinely on his side, after all—makes him see it). The novel's grittily detailed sex, screaming alienation (especially of Keller's drag-queen friends), and sharply pointed camp humor; the jaded innocence of Jamie's fellow gay teens; even Jamie's hallucinatory encounters with Keller's evil queen alter ego (Donna-May Dean); as well as the story's pervasive bruised atmosphere—all will ring true to gay men. As for nongay readers, they'll get an education, humbling and difficult, because Manley writes from inside gay experience, giving no quarter to hetero self-righteousness, ignorance, and brutality. —*Ray Olson*

✔**Marsh, Fabienne.**
The Moralist of the Alphabet Streets.
Algonquin, $15.95 (0-945575-47-5). 238p.

Meredith is the moralist of a Connecticut suburb with alphabetized streets. She has won a tough fight with leukemia, driving her foe into remission. Now, healthy again at 18, she's a year behind in school, sexually inexperienced, and preoccupied with right and wrong. This particularly long, hot, and unruly summer tests her theories of morality and encourages her tendency for frankness and affection-tinged cynicism. Her parents are in Europe; her "favorite human being," a young man named Custer, is involved with sexy Carmencita; one sister is reluctantly separated from her alcoholic husband, the other is trying to love a workaholic while being extravagantly courted by Custer's still-married stepfather; and her feisty grandmother is driving her crazy. As complications and betrayals multiply, Meredith's delightfully wry humor is sharpened as her capacity for compassion and love expands. The warm response to Marsh's first novel, *Long Distances* (1989), paved the way for her second success. —*Donna Seaman*

General Fiction

✔Marshall, Paule.
Daughters.
Atheneum, $21.95 (0-689-12139-3). 416p.

Acclaimed writer Marshall's fourth novel since her ground-breaking *Brown Girl, Brownstones* continues to explore the psyche of her own personal archetype: a black woman torn between her West Indian roots and the demands of life in America. The latest incarnation is Ursa Beatrice Mac-Kenzie, daughter of Primus MacKenzie, a politician on the fictional island of Triunion, and his American wife, Estelle. This dual heritage forces Ursa to confront the fact that both of these worlds are bisected by persistent barriers to freedom: entrenched racism, sexism, and corrupt political systems. Ursa is a small-bodied, very bright, and very controlled woman whose strong-willed parents loom large even in her adult life. As the novel opens, she has just made some hard, lonely decisions: she's quit a lucrative but morally objectionable job and had an abortion. Marshall takes us back and forth from Ursa's current New York City dilemmas to memories of her Triunion childhood. Marshall weaves her story with sure, steady strokes, driving home each scene and its significance to create a tensile, richly textured fabric of history, occurrence, personality, and perception. Supporting characters, particularly Ursa's mother, friend Viney, and her father's mistress, Astral Forde, offer vivid portraits of women coping with difficult relationships, single parenthood, and compromise. A carefully considered, graceful, and lingeringly ponderable tale. —*Donna Seaman*

Martin, William.
Cape Cod.
Warner, $21.95 (0-446-51510-8). 652p.

By using the reader-winning formula of James Michener and his own previous best-seller *Back Bay*, Martin combines elements of romance, suspense, and mystery to dramatize the stormy history of Cape Cod, "a peninsula resembling, in all its parts, a man's arm raised to strike a blow at the sea." The three-century saga opens with the arrival of the *Mayflower* and its long-suffering passengers. The ship's log contains information about what may have been a murder, and a feud has already erupted between two of the families. This rivalry is destined to continue through the years, perpetuated by struggles over power, land, and the whereabouts of the incriminating ship's log. The Bigelows are God-fearing, rule-loving, and self-righteous, while the Hilyards are independent, adventurous, and rebellious, and all are tenacious fighters and survivors. Tacking back and forth from the present, where the battle over land and the ship's log (now worth millions) continues, to the colorful, often violent past, Martin embraces the entire sweep of American history with unflagging relish for authentic detail and private moments. He creates generation after generation of feisty Hilyards and cruel Bigelows, pitting them against one another in religious and political skirmishes and joining them in risky love. They endure hardships and shipwrecks, scandal and imprisonment, shame and anger, and contribute their bit to the making of America: taming the wilderness, wiping out the Indians, whale hunting, overthrowing the British, slave trading, rum-running, and politicking. Martin roots for renegades, parents who love their children, and those who respect and value the land, celebrating valor, pride, and determination. American as apple pie, this has blockbuster written all over it. —*Donna Seaman*

✔**Mason, Anita.**
The Racket.
Dutton, $19.95 (0-525-93351-4). 224p.

British writer Mason's *The Illusionist* was short-listed for the prestigious Booker Prize, and her fourth novel has received rave reviews overseas. A comparison with the masterful Graham Greene is as inevitable as it is apt. Mason launches us into the decadent world of Brazilian politics and crime in this keyed-up, soul-searching drama of high-stakes morality. Rosa, the moral center of the tale, is a tough-minded and outspoken history teacher in an out-of-the-way state capital. Fabio, a weak and undefined young man drawn to crime and poetry with equal abandonment, is on the run from his brutal racketeer employer when he remembers his cousin. He appears on Rosa's doorstep just after she has been threatened by Roberto, a ruthless and powerful man running for political office. With an unfailing precision of language and emotional timbre, Mason constructs resounding psychological portraits and complex conflicts that reach into the darkest corners of greed and corruption. Superb suspense spiked with a sinuous, understated wit and a shrewd intellect. —*Donna Seaman*

McCammon, Robert R., ed.
Under the Fang.
Pocket, paper, $4.95 (0-671-69573-8). 383p.

The stories in this anthology are all based on the bright idea of Richard Matheson's 1954 novel, *I Am Legend*: to wit, a world in which vampires have gained the upper hand. And it must be said that these tales' authors have picked up the ball and really run with it. Matheson's yarn was told from the viewpoint of the last normal human in a Southern California city, and the vampires in it were pretty zombie-esque. The vampires in these stories are articulate and have retained, albeit somewhat attenuated, the personalities, institutions, and social distinctions they cultivated before they . . . changed. In the hands of a passel of horror pros, including coauthors Suzy McKee Charnas and Chelsea Quinn Yarbro, Chet Williamson, editor McCammon, and the expected (in a mass-market paperback original) majority of newer names, the vampire's exploits will disgust, horrify, appall, astound—in short, amuse the dickens out of horror fans. —*Ray Olson*

McCullough, Colleen.
The Grass Crown.
Morrow, $23 (0-688-09369-8). 875p.

The best-selling author of *The Thorn Birds* delivers the second installment in her projected series of historical novels about the demise of the Roman republics and rise of the Roman Empire. This lengthy tome picks up where *The First Man in Rome* left off. Now-middle-aged Gaius Marius and Lucius Cornelius Sulla, allied in the first book, have become dangerous rivals, and McCullough plays on their shared history as she introduces the next generation of ambitious, if morally bankrupt, Roman Senate seekers. A 100-page glossary summarizes Roman terms, expressions, and customs that were explained fully in the first book. Though tracking ancient lineage and following foreign terminology could prove difficult for anyone unfamiliar with the earlier book, die-hard historical fiction fans—and McCullough aficionados—will be eager to accept the challenge. —*Kathryn LaBarbera*

McNally, T. M.
Low Flying Aircraft.
Univ. of Georgia, $17.95 (0-8203-1378-5). 176p.

McNally's 14 intriguingly interconnected stories have a crystalline quality—they're hard, sharp-edged, faceted, and fragile. The characters are, for the most part, young and creative. There's a potter, a photographer, a journalist, a teacher, and a pianist, but they seem to function in a haze, to do what they do out of loneliness or by mere chance. Set in Arizona, Chicago, New England, and Nicaragua, these often enigmatic, secretive tales unwind slowly, full of weather and objects pregnant with meaning. McNally can convey the subtleties of actions both ordinary, such as a dog walking jauntily over the snow or a woman dancing, and extraordinary, like three people diligently filling a swimming pool with furniture, or two girls stretched out along a runway, hanging onto the lights as the rush of landing jets lifts them off the ground. These are haunting stories that revolve around the deep sorrows of desertion, abuse, and death, but they sing with an acceptance of the power and mysteries of pain, love, and the conflicting forces of flight and gravity. —*Donna Seaman*

McNamer, Deirdre.
Rima in the Weeds.
HarperCollins, $19.95 (0-06-016523-5). 288p.

Set in the early 1960s, when women's emerging notions of independence were popularized via TV sitcoms such as Marlo Thomas' *That Girl*, this bittersweet story presents the flip side of liberation. The protagonist doesn't spend much time throwing her hat in the air in celebration of her independence (à la Mary Tyler Moore) because her sojourn in the big city has left her pregnant, unmarried, and doomed to return to her small hometown of Madrid, Montana. Though she fiercely loves her new baby, she is, at first, exhausted by her responsibilities and by her father's stern disapproval. She takes a job as a waitress at the local steakhouse and begins to sort through the traumatic past events leading up to the pain-filled love affair that has left her bitter and ashamed. Written with an aching wisdom, this first novel slowly and methodically lays open one woman's fear and loneliness and then documents her refusal to give in. —*Joanne Wilkinson*

Michael, Judith.
Sleeping Beauty.
Simon & Schuster, $22 (0-671-64893-4). 539p.

Michael's newest glitz-and-grief tale begins when Anne Chatham is 13-years-old. Her mother is dead, and her father, part of a powerful family of real estate developers, isn't paying much attention, which makes it relatively easy for Uncle Vince to start molesting her without any interference. Two years later, Anne chooses a family dinner to disclose what their golden boy has been doing to her; the shocked family doesn't quite believe Anne, causing her to run away, put herself through school, become an important attorney (and sexual phobic), and finally reappear at her grandfather's funeral, ready to reestablish a relationship with her family. The book shoots off to a fast start but gets bogged down at times with the nuts and bolts of construction deals, while the subplot of Anne's archaeologist boyfriend finding a pharaoh's tomb seems to almost be from another book. It must be said, though, that Michael does this sort of thing much better than most of the competition: the characters, naturally larger than life, are still believable, unlike the Collins sisters' paper dolls, and the plotting is much less tortured than Krantz. You can put it down, but if you're in the mood for a big story with lots of interfamily squabbling and an ice-princess heroine (awakened in the last 10 pages), this will suit just fine. —*Ilene Cooper*

Michel, Sam.
Under the Light.
Knopf, $19 (0-394-58723-5). 240p.

Here are mean dads and neighbors, embarrassing moms and lovers, tragicomic animals, and loyal, adventurous friends, all bound together by the character of Harry Drake. The story "Reno, Reno, Reno, Reno" continues all the author's signature elements. There is Harry Drake and his friend, Tom, two boys who know everything and nothing; Harry's lonely mother and the yard man who becomes her lover; and a lovesick dachshund disfigured in an accident. The dachshund and the yard man's dog play out the humans' fates in a comedic way that softens the blows the humans face. Like many southern writers, Michel relies on the quirkiness of incident, but he places his quirks in the context of the stark realities associated with the American West. The result is both unsettling and engrossing. Harry Drake seems to beg comparison with Hemingway's Nick Adams—and he does have a consistent persona, even though he changes in age and circumstance from story to story. This is the first book for Sam Michel, who tells a story you haven't heard before and whose unique and distinctive voice evokes "the common folk" without straining. —*Deb Robertson*

Miller, Henry.
Crazy Cock.
Grove Weidenfeld, $18.95 (0-8021-1412-1). 224p.

Crazy Cock was written in the late 1920s when Miller was living in Greenwich Village and struggling with his need to write and his difficult, even psychotic marriage to June Mansfield Smith. The manuscript disappeared until 1988, eight years after his death. First titled *Lovely Lesbians*, this volume is part of Miller's grand "autobiographical romance," directly preceding *Tropic of Cancer*. It's set in the sleaze-soaked, bohemian Village. Tony Bring, an aspiring writer, is supported by his ravishing and wild wife, Hildred, who works in a local dive. She insists that her new "friend," Vanya, be allowed to move in with them. Tony, loath to lose her, is slow to accept the fact that she and Vanya are lovers, leading to a snarl of bizarre situations, lies, and confrontations. As his fury and dread swell to manic proportions, his heightened perceptions lead to an obsession with depravity. Through his eyes, the Village writhes with a grotesque and diseased energy. Miller tempers his baroque sensibility with irony, plumbing the depths of despair while lashing out at life's absurdity. A potent tale that holds its own with Miller's best works. —*Donna Seaman*

Mistry, Rohinton.
Such a Long Journey.
Knopf, $22 (0-679-40258-6). 384p.

Mistry, author of the collection of short stories *Swimming Lessons*, proves to be no less adept at engaging his readers with a longer narrative about a middle-class family in 1970s Bombay. The family of a Parsi bank clerk lives in a run-down compound and manages to struggle along in hard economic times. But the family's luck will change for the worse, and comedy will begin to edge into tragedy. Illness, youthful rebellion, political unrest, and deepening poverty converge as the clerk is drawn into a scandal that will reach to the upper levels of the Indian government. Mistry again sketches a memorable physical setting that helps to draw attention to the physical and emotional conditions of his characters, but a darker and deepening tone blots out even modest hope in their lives. —*John Brosnahan*

Moggach, Deborah.
The Stand-in.
Little, Brown, $19.95 (0-316-57751-0). 400p.

Jules Sampson is a serious if chronically underemployed British actress. She's also 11 years older than her struggling playwright-playboy boyfriend, Trev, and knocked a bit off balance by the vagaries of life: a demanding father, feelings of insecurity, and that old green flame, jealousy. So it doesn't take her long to feel more than unfulfilled as stand-in for the simple yet seductive Hollywood superstar, Lila Dune, and more than suspicious of Lila and Trev's relationship. Being Lila herself would be much more rewarding, Jules figures, and her burgeoning obsession leads her to gain and lose center stage in this spicy insider's view of the glamour and greed fueling the famous and the not-so-famous. This book just gets better and better: Jules' voice is appealingly intelligent and cleverly delusional, and her revenge—albeit short-lived—is almost perfectly calculated. —*Eloise Kinney*

✔**Monette, Paul.**
Halfway Home.
Crown, $20 (0-517-58329-1). 288p.

Monette follows his big AIDS novel, *Afterlife*, with a marvelous, melodramatic romp. It's about AIDS, too, since its protagonist-narrator has the malady and never lets us or himself forget it, but it's really about how Tom Shaheen, angry gay man who's made a career out of his repudiation of the family and the Catholic church that raised him, heals his life. His modest claim to fame is his scandalous and scabrous performance as "Miss Jesus"—a satiric gay Christ complete with muu-muu, crown of thorns, and cross upon which he writhes in ecstasy while nailing himself to it. AIDS has sidelined him, though, and he's moping over his life in a beach house owned by his theatrical patron. In short order, he's pulled up out of his funk when his hated, athletic brother shows up, wife and son in tow, running for their lives from the brother's crooked business partner. Another jolt comes when Tom realizes that his patron is in love with him, and what's more, he's in love with his patron. In the course of a story that, it's true, becomes soap-operatically sensational, the brothers settle their differences, Tom's new love blooms, and a host of amusing secondary characters and incidents blaze from the pages. This is the most compelling and endearing popular gay novel since Patricia Nell Warren's *Front Runner*, but since Monette's more than twice as good a writer, his book's that much better. —*Ray Olson*

Monikova, Libuse.
The Facade: M.N.O.P.Q.
Knopf, $23 (0-394-57250-5). 384p.

A slyly comical tale about a quintet of brilliant, eccentric, and rowdy Czech artists and archivists whose names begin with the letters of the subtitle. Podol, Orten, and Maltzahn are restoring the extensive frescoes of a large, Renaissance castle. They naughtily improvise decorative motifs, foregoing the requisite flora and cherubs for pointed images of modern life. The archivists are Qvietone, more interested in bugs than royal history, and Nordanc, who is gay and primarily interested in Qvietone. When the five stop work for the winter, they set out for Japan but end up stranded in Siberia, virtually held prisoner by a group of bored Soviet scientists. The Czechs find themselves acting out a fairy-tale scenario, trying to win their freedom by performing odd feats. Their trials include staging a hilarious version of a Gogol play and competing in an absurdly mismatched, uncoordinated hockey game. And that's only the beginning of their Siberian adventures. It takes a while to get the hang of this sometimes diffuse first novel, but it's well worth the effort. Monikova's intellectual, political, and aesthetic playfulness knows no bounds, and her slapstick is priceless. —*Donna Seaman*

✔**Morrell, David.**
The Covenant of the Flame.
Warner, $19.95 (0-446-51563-9). 452p.

Still best known as the only begetter of Rambo (in *First Blood* and two sequels), Morrell's no great shakes as a prosesmith—he gets stilted when the action lets up and makes tone-deaf word choices throughout—but oh, how he can plot! Not complicatedly, but with so much blood-splattering action and nerve-wracking suspense that you just can't skip a single page, and if you peek at the ending you deserve to be burned at the stake—for this book particularly, because it's about the forces of good and evil, of orthodoxy and heresy. To be specific, it's about the way the struggle between the Albigensian heresy and the Inquisition covertly blazes on in an environmental struggle and how ecological journalist Tess Drake gets involved in it when she meets an attractive and charismatic man who's mysteriously burned to death days after their meeting. To investigate his death, she teams up with New York detective Lt. Craig, and soon, with certain high-placed despoilers of nature being assassinated, and with bullets flying and fires flaring at every turn, the pair is fleeing from both sides. To say more about this utterly absorbing, epical thriller, except to note that it does not trivialize the moral and ethical questions it stirs in the reader, would be to spoil a yarn that ranks with the classics of its genre—with *Treasure Island* and *King Solomon's Mines*, for starters—and makes Indy Jones' exploits look like an aerobics class. —*Ray Olson*

Morrow, Bradford and McGrath, Patrick, eds.
The New Gothic: A Collection of Contemporary Gothic Fiction.
Random, $22 (0-394-58767-7). 336p.

Aficionados of dark and stormy nights, fog-bound castles, and moonlit moors will want to explore the exterior and interior landscapes mapped by this collection of new gothic fiction. The editors argue in their introduction that "an artistic vision intended to reveal the bleaker facets of the human soul" is as central to late-twentieth-century literature as to that of the eighteenth or nineteenth centuries. Their eclectic collection supports this theory with selections from predictably gothic authors such as Anne Rice, Joyce Carol Oates, Peter Straub, and Ruth Rendell and such not-so-usual suspects as Jamaica Kincaid, Martin Amis, John Hawkes, Robert Coover, John Edgar Wideman, and Jeanette Winterson. *The New Gothic* will introduce readers who relish the macabre to a variety of new sources. It belongs in most literature collections and should be brought to the attention of readers who snap up these authors' longer works. —*Mary Carroll*

Mortman, Doris.
The Wild Rose.
Bantam, $20 (0-553-07419-9). 784p.

Against a backdrop of cold war conflicts in Hungary, Mortman, author of the best-selling *First Born*, creates an epic romance worthy of high interest. Drifting occasionally into travelogue and music-history lecture, the author nevertheless remains focused on the story of Katalin Gáspár, who, under the guidance of her creative and politically active family, grows from a three-year-old prodigy to become an internationally renowned concert pianist. The plights of friends forced to emigrate from Hungary, her father's struggle to deal with a career crushed by prison camp brutality, her childhood sweetheart's rise in his adopted America—all swirl around Katalin's story, revealing Mortman's dexterous management of time and place. Occasionally, errors in music research show, but these minor detractions are easily forgiven. The author's admiration of the heritage she shares with her characters beams brilliantly through it all. —*Denise Blank*

General Fiction

Mosley, Nicholas.
Judith.
Dalkey Archive Press, $19.95 (0-916583-69-4). 298p.

A woman's descent into moral depravity is engineered by several Svengali-like men in Mosley's novel, which was first published in Great Britain in 1986 and is issued here in a revised edition. *Judith* also forms a part of an ongoing series of linked novels that explore the lives of an interlinked cast of characters. Judith herself is a Lulu-like creation, although Judith seems much too aware of her decline to become a symbol of moral innocence or ambiguity. She first tries a career as an actress before settling on a role as a London party girl and companion. She flees a drug-powered existence for an Asian ashram, but inner peace is had to find in a place where chicanery reigns. Finally Judith returns to England were she becomes involved with a band of peace demonstrators and a bomb explosion that brings her back to reality. Told as a series of letters whose length rivals those of Samuel Richardson, Mosley's novel makes Judith's experiences far from admirable but nevertheless totally compelling. —*John Brosnahan*

Muhanji, Cherry.
Her.
Aunt Lute, $18.95 (0-933216-66-1); paper, $8.95 (0-933216-63-7). 179p.

The title of this engrossing novel comes from the first sight we get of the central character: "This her," Brother says as he introduces his wife, Kali, to his mother, Charlotte. How the young, light-skinned, pregnant woman moves into her own identity (and the spirit of her namesake) and into the lives of the neighborhood women is the subject of this first novel which, in telling Kali's story, captures the fighting spirit of a whole generation of black women "born after slavery and before civil rights." A skillful creator of scenes and characters, Muhanji explores in richly textured and evocative prose the complexities of relationships—particularly the intricacies of black lesbian and gay lives—in Detroit in the 1950s, celebrating both individual identity and community strength. From its exquisite cover to the concluding glossary of street slang, an excellent offering from a strong writer. —*Ryn Etter*

✔**Murakami, Haruki.**
Hard-Boiled Wonderland and the End of the World.
Kodansha, $21.95 (4-7700-1544-5). 405p.

What can you say? Fantastic? Four stars? Murakami is supposed to be Japan's best-selling author, but this is no Danielle Steele. First, we have one of these "calcutec" guys (you know, the ones who take information in one side of their brains then pass it out the other, coded), then a pretty-in-pink granddaughter who takes him into a closet that leads past the dangerous Infra-Nocturnal Kappa things (INKlings), past a waterfall, to the professor—who, by the way, is working on a sound cancellation device—who will eventually get Mr. Calcutec in trouble with the System and the Semiotics. *Which*, by and by, turns out to be not so big a problem as the one in his brain: to wit, he is about to collapse into it and lose all consciousness of the world. And then there's the even-numbered chapters, where we find a guy who has just had his shadow removed and a guy who lives in a walled city "dream-reading" from the skulls of dead unicorns. Naturally, this guy wants to go back to the world he came from. And it turns out that this is Mr. Calcutec's world—in other words, that these two fellas are one and the same, going in opposite directions. The obvious antecedents of Murakami's work are *Gulliver's Travels* and *Alice in Wonderland*, and despite the superficial craziness of the story, there is a similar seriousness, even a heartbreaking poignancy toward the end. Yet, one wouldn't be surprised to hear that someone had read the whole book while holding their breath. *Hard-Boiled Wonderland* is sensational. It exposes the plastic food of postmodernism for what it is and gives us something modern, earthy, and exciting. —*Stuart Whitwell*

✔**Murray, Albert.**
The Spyglass Tree.
Pantheon, $20 (0-394-58887-8). 209p.

Murray has captivated readers with books such as the nonfiction *Stomping the Blues* and *Train Whistle Guitar*, a novel about the childhood of a black boy called Scooter. In *The Spyglass Tree*, Scooter has grown into an irresistible young man with a gift for learning. It's the 1930s, and Scooter has left his Mobile home, off to college on scholarship. As he takes to university life, he often thinks back on his charmed past. Adored without conflict by both his adopted mother, Mama, and Miss Tee, his natural mother, Scooter's ready intelligence was nurtured carefully by his teachers. As Murray relates various episodes in Scooter's life, he builds a keen, energetic portrait of Southern black culture. His characters are magnetic and gorgeous creations. Their talk is wise, poetic, sassy, and funny; their look and body language cinematically vivid. And Scooter is a prince, conducting himself admirably in every circumstance, no matter how dicey. Murray handles words like notes, stringing together as many as he can to net every possible nuance of meaning. Brilliant—in every sense of the word. —*Donna Seaman*

Nixon, Cornelia.
Now You See It.
Little, Brown, $17.95 (0-316-61170-0). 192p.

Nixon's chapters can stand alone as stories, but, taken together, they form a vivid family narrative set in the years between World War II and the Vietnam War. Ella, a German refugee, and her husband, Edward, a philosophy professor, have a relationship of great mystery to their children. They, along with their daughter, one of their three sons, and Edward's mistress, take turns advancing the tale, each revealing new aspects of the whole. Nixon's subtle storytelling skill is most evident when she assumes the daughter's voice; for example, the complex fabric of this family's life together is evoked in microcosm when the daughter tells of her attachment to an indifferent cat, who is happy to move to a childless neighbor's yard to avoid the tortures of the girl's older brothers. Both ordinary and extraordinary, Ella and Edward will be remembered as people you once knew. They are fully formed products of their experiences, and they remind us that depth of character is the happy by-product of aging. —*Deb Robertson*

Oates, Joyce Carol.
Heat and Other Stories.
Dutton, $21.95 (0-525-93330-1). 384p.

The first short story collection in five years from this prolific woman of letters. The 25 stories include several prize-winners, and all bear the salient characteristics of Oates creations: the articulation of frightening, overpowering emotional forces that bewilder and disorient, the link between sex and violence, and rapidly drawn yet authoritative psychological profiles. Many of these facile tales unwind beneath a pall of loneliness and hopelessness. Deftly drawn characters suffer losses of various kinds: the pitiful death of a premature baby, virulent estrangement between mother and daughter, or the disappearance of a lover. Other stories explore the aftermath of rapes, murders, suicides, or inexplicable attack like the disrobing and beating of a woman in a suburban wildlife preserve by a pack of vicious children. Oates can also be subtle; "The Swimmers" is a model of charged restraint. Her short fiction seems to well up from a subterranean source, seeping onto the page and into our minds. The stories are haunting and yet can be tedious; some insist on a claustrophobic, noxious horror, while others emit a chilling suspense and eerie suggestiveness. Oates continues to thrill her admirers, annoy her detractors, and woo new readers. —*Donna Seaman*

O'Neill, Joseph.
This Is the Life.
Farrar, $18.95 (0-374-27590-4). 214p.

Solicitor James Jones lets his work slide and his imagination run wild when former teacher and renowned barrister Michael Donovan seeks his aid in getting a divorce. Why would Donovan's wife, Arabella, leave such a talented, erudite man? Why did Donovan mysteriously lose his voice in the middle of a trial? And why has Donovan's eccentric father, Fergus, taken such an interest in the case? These, and other questions, plague Jones, tossing and turning him from sleep and all he holds dear: taking long baths, eating fast food, avoiding the amorous advances of a former girlfriend, and, mainly, taking an "undeflected, eventless route through the days." Jones' flights of fancy and visions of fame and honor are held in check by twinges of self-doubt—that, and the fact that nothing is really as he perceives it to be. O'Neill's first novel is a humorous imbroglio of a disgruntled man's fantasies, with Jones coming full circle in his tortured explication of much ado: "People do not have stories, they have lives; they have a spell of sticking around in the flesh, and then they are no more." —*Eloise Kinney*

Onetti, Juan Carlos.
Body Snatcher.
Pantheon, $22 (0-679-40178-4). 260p.

Originally published in 1964, this fine novel by an internationally acclaimed Uruguayan fiction writer is only now being accorded publication in English translation. Perhaps—let's hope—Onetti will one day soon be as widely appreciated in this country as, say, García Marquez or Vargas Llosa or any of the other major Latin American literary figures more widely recognized here. In *Body Snatcher* (which could be the book that does the trick), Onetti reprises as his setting the little fictional town of Santa María, mean home to sordid existences and failed prospects—Onetti's microcosm for analysis of the burst-dreams syndrome that has been the hallmark of Latin American history. Larsen, called the Body Snatcher, has come to Santa María to found a brothel, and soon a bawdy house in its midst becomes the town's primary civil issue. Comic and serious by turns, a novel to beguile and unsettle. —*Brad Hooper*

Osborn, Karen.
Patchwork.
HBJ, $19.95 (0-15-171292-1). 266p.

Poet Osborn's first novel is a haunting and purely told drama of kinship, womanhood, and the long aftermath of tragedy. Ash Hill, a rural South Carolina mill town, is the setting, and the relentless labor of maintaining the giant looms—keeping the streaming threads straight and the shuttles flying—serves as a metaphor for the grind of poverty and the toil of family life. The story runs from the Depression years to the present and is told in the voices of three sisters and a daughter. Rose is the moral center, a hardworking, religious, and steadfast woman who raises her own children, a niece, and grandchildren and tends to her two loony sisters, Lily and June. Lily is lusty, shameless, dishonest, and utterly self-absorbed. June is sweetly crazy and free of any memory of her troubled past. Finally, there's Sylvia, born to June but raised by Rose. Their tales are fluid and captivating sagas of love and betrayal, lies and hard truths, irresponsibility and loyalty. This is fine new fiction, deserving a place on the shelf and in the heart. —*Donna Seaman*

Oster, Jerry.
Violent Love.
Bantam, $18.95 (0-553-07127-0). 320p.

A dismembered corpse rises to the river's surface as a college crew rows past. The leading suspect is the husband of the deceased, a powerful journalist who takes up with another woman relatively soon after the body is discovered. But let's not forget the secret club full of well-heeled gentlemen engaged in pursuits that might best be described as Mapplethorpean. In fact, the brothers in chains could just be the real villains, and the less-than-grieving husband and his olive-thighed partner, merely eager lovers. Along with the mystery, Oster offers endless discourses on what's hip and what's not, heaping scorn on those who don't know the real names of Prince, Madonna, Cher, and Stevie Wonder. (Of course, Oster leaves himself wide open for picky readers to spot the occasional gaffe: Mike Rutherford is still a member of Genesis.) The mix of dark suspense and pop-culture cram course can be a little disconcerting, but don't let it put you off the book. This is a novel that must be finished: the nail-destroying conclusion is unforgettable. —*Peter Robertson*

Otto, Whitney.
How to Make an American Quilt.
Villard, $18 (0-679-40070-2). 179p.

Whitney Otto's first novel is a triumph of story and metaphor. Otto sees American quilts as emblems of American womanhood: expressions of vision, practicality, creativity, skill, friendship, love, and patience. She borrows the short, declarative phrases of a "how-to" book to tell the tales of a group of California women who have been quilting together for many years. The "instructions" include advice on quilt making as well as love: "Use only the highest-quality thread when piecing your quilt together." Then: "Think of how it all began with that first kiss." Each of the quilters brings her past to the sessions—memories of crushed hopes, passion and regret, love and loss, reconciliation and peace. There's the story of Hy and her sister, Glady Joe, who had very different marriages; the mythic tale of Sophia Darling, who abandoned her dreams; and the difficult lives of Anna Neale and her daughter, Marianna, whose mixed racial heritage leaves them in a no-man's land. Otto embroiders the personal over the historical, noting that quilts "are something handed down," like stories, personality traits, circumstances, and conse-quences. Otto has tremendous insight and compassion, understanding the rareness of a perfect marriage, the anger of thwarted lives, and the vagaries of love and motherhood. Her prose is as careful and precise as needlework, each word a perfect stitch, each contributing to this grand pattern of in-heritance, hard-won wisdom, and hope. A novel that will capture many hearts. —*Donna Seaman*

Paetro, Maxine.
Windfall.
Simon & Schuster, $19.95 (0-671-69028-0). 293p.

This novel follows its protagonist, Harriet Braintree (a literary agent for romance novels), through the ups and downs of a very 1990s romance. Paetro creates engaging characters who are mostly "thirtysomething," living in Manhattan, and struggling with family issues, career woes, and the *C* word (commitment). Harriet has to contend with a highly skittish, WASPish boyfriend *and* a multimillion-dollar inheritance complete with a magnificent if decrepit mansion, which further complicates her already tenuous love relationship. An enjoyable and, at times, fanciful romp that will have readers cheering on a wonderfully earthy and lovable heroine. —*Alice Joyce*

✔Palliser, Charles.
The Sensationist.
Ballantine, $15 (0-345-36958-0). 160p.

Charles Palliser follows up on his first novel, *The Quincunx,* with a short work absolutely unlike it—and absolutely unlike anything else, either. David is our sensationist, a man who thrives on sexual conquest. His liaisons seem to come out of an insatiable thirst for intimacy, but predictably these encounters leave him empty and unfulfilled. Finally he meets Lucy, a woman complex and mysterious enough to tease out his love, but just as terrified—and vengeful—as he is. On the surface, of course, this is an old story, but the difference is in the telling: unlike the lush prose of *The Quincunx,* the text here is spare and provocatively elliptical. This is masterful, careful prose, exceedingly balanced and assured, at once as direct as the searing emotion it means to convey and as awkward as that emotion leaves us. In this respect the work resembles that of Marguerite Duras, though in a quite masculine incarnation. A subtle, compelling, extraordinary piece of fiction. —*Patrick Comiskey*

Parks, Tim.
Goodness.
Grove Weidenfeld, $17.95 (0-8021-1390-7). 192p.

Young George Crawley's father, a missionary, is killed, while he, his mother, and his sister are allowed to go free when his mother agrees to renounce her religious faith. *Goodness* becomes a theme that haunts George's life. Growing up, the family stew consists of one unconventional sister, a weird aunt, and dotty old grandfather, who are forever catered to by his pious, widowed mother. Anxious to escape this household, George does in fact marry up. Shirley is from a wealthy London family. But life together alternates between black comedy and pathos as their upwardly mobile life-style—without children—is drastically transformed by the birth of a mentally retarded, physically deformed, blind baby girl. Parks is a writer of stunning talent creating discomforting situations amid characterizations of emotional complexity. —*Alice Joyce*

Pearson, T. R.
Gospel Hour.
Morrow, $19.95 (0-688-09480-5). 384p.

Faulkner wrote that the only subject worth writing about is the "human heart in conflict with itself," and Pearson knows his Faulkner and knows good advice. The heart in question belongs to Donnie Huff, a seeming dim bulb whose near-death experience in a logging accident ultimately carries him to witness his newfound faith in a seedy revivalist's tent meeting. After successfully bringing "infusement" to a few benighted seekers of solace, Donnie is pained to learn that he can't heal everyone's spiritual ills. Unlikely as this may sound, *Gospel Hour* is a laugh-out-loud comic masterpiece and a worthy follow-up to Pearson's trilogy about life itself in Neely, North Carolina. Burying dialogue in baroque yet earthy page-long narrative sentences and eschewing commas the way Donnie might kidney stones in his "tracts and ducts and byways," Pearson's prose recalls Faulkner. There are also echoes of Mark Twain in the storytelling and the nuggets of wisdom Pearson mines. The difference is sweet-spiritedness; like storyteller Garrison Keillor, Pearson is genuinely fond of his memorable characters. —*Thomas Gaughan*

Pelletier, Cathie.
The Weight of Winter.
Viking, $21.95 (0-670-84090-4). 395p.

Much of what happens in tiny, snowbound Mattagash, Maine, is both funny and not funny. Pelletier, who has written about this northern outpost twice before, does not give us a sneering outsider's point of view. Rather, we take our cue from two observant, reasonable, and therefore somewhat ambivalent Mattagashers—44-year-old Amy Joy Lawler, who would like to get her mother into the Pine Valley nursing home without anyone feeling sad or guilty, and 107-year-old Mathilda Fennelson, the oldest woman in Maine, who sits at Pine Valley and tells herself the story of Mattagash. Bundled up in coats that seem to have a life of their own, moving slowly over ice and snow, Mattagashers have a weight both literal and figurative that makes them difficult to categorize and certainly impossible to discount. Pelletier has the sympathy and wit to let her characters behave in outrageous or brutal ways without turning them into caricatures who can elicit only one response. When Amy Joy's dreams of escape get buried under another Mattagash winter, the sense of inevitability doesn't make her story any less interesting or any less meaningful. —*Frances Woods*

Penman, Sharon Kay.
The Reckoning.
Holt, $22.95 (0-8050-1014-9). 593p.

Penman lets her passion for history and the complicated relationships of royal families show through in this sweeping historical drama of the thirteenth century. Simon de Montfort of England and Llewelyn ap Gruffydd of Wales are about to forge an alliance based on the marriage of Llewelyn to de Montfort's daughter when Simon and one of his sons are killed in battle. The marriage is off, but the battle for Wales continues, with the Welsh prince pitted against his wily brother, Davydd. This internal bleeding weakens the ap Gruffydd grip, allowing Edward I of England to overcome the Welsh. Llewelyn is killed, Davydd is vanquished and executed, and the family is dispersed to prisons and convents around Britain. Thus does Wales pass into British hands. Penman has deftly finessed fact with fiction. A must read for fans of historical fiction, by the author of *Here Be Dragons* and *Falls the Shadow.* —*Cynthia Ogorek*

Piercy, Marge.
He, She and It.
Knopf, $22 (0-679-40408-2). 320p.

Enter the year 2059, when, after a nuclear holocaust and a great famine, strange and wonderful and terrifying technology alters the state of the Earth and of humanity. Jump back to the year 1599 in Prague, where Jewish mysticism (the kabbalah) weaves a spell—and a golem or artificial being—to protect a ghetto from Inquisition pogroms. In language simultaneously sci-fi futuristic and astoundingly humane, Piercy dazzles in wordplay and emotions with two tales. The first, a story of far away, features psycho-engineer Shira Shipman fighting to retain custody of her son, moving to Tikva (the "free" land), and falling in love with Yod, an illegal cyborg (a man-like machine). The second, a fable of long ago related by Shira's grandmother Malkah, centers on Polish rabbi Judah Loew and his fight to save his people via the golem Joseph. Piercy's language sings and entrances; the plots transcend the mere human-versus-machine theme to reach age-old philosophical issues with a touch of feminism. Piercy's reputation ensures high demand. —*Barbara Jacobs*

✔Pirsig, Robert M.
Lila: An Inquiry into Morals.
Bantam, $22.50 (0-553-07737-6). 416p.

It's been 18 years since Pirsig's *Zen and the Art of Motorcycle Maintenance* first spoke to the hearts and minds of thousands of truth-seekers. Pirsig is the same patient, disciplined, and hungry thinker, but now his stand-in narrator is named Phaedrus, after a Greek philosopher frequently referred to in *Zen*. He's traded in his motorcycle for a sailboat, his traveling companion, son Chris, for Lila, a woman he met in a bar, and his focus on values for a concentration on morals. While his physical journey takes him down the Hudson River, his philosophical quest leads to the creation of a "metaphysics of quality" to explain what he sees as the moral bankruptcy of our times. Phaedrus/Pirsig dissects our habitual assumptions and works out the far-reaching implications of viewing quality as "the primary empirical reality" and morality as "a very complex struggle of conflicting patterns of values" linked to evolutionary levels. In the course of this solitary and demanding effort, Phaedrus/Pirsig unveils and articulates arresting observations about native American mysticism, the mix of European and Indian values in "the American personality," and the Victorians as the "last static social pattern."

His meditations are interrupted by discordant exchanges with Lila, who's losing her tenuous grip on sanity. An underlying sense of alienation and sadness grows in intensity as Phaedrus/Pirsig declares the hippie revolution, in which he participated, a "disastrous mistake." Lila's disorientation recalls his own stark experience with insanity, bringing him full circle to ponder, once again, mysticism and its place in the moral order of the universe. Powerfully conceived and expressed, this philosophical novel is guaranteed to inspire debate. —*Donna Seaman*

General Fiction

Porter, Connie.
All-Bright Court.
Houghton, $19.95 (0-395-53271-X). 224p.

All-Bright Court is a colorfully painted but crumbling housing project for steel workers outside of Buffalo, New York. The population has changed from white to black in the 1950s, as many families leave the rural South in search of a better life. What they find is the exhausting, unhealthy labor of the plant and a slum showered with pollution. Porter's episodic and subtle but piercing novel tells the tales of several All-Bright Court families over a period of two decades. The Taylors are the focal point. As Mary Kate and Samuel raise their large brood, politics and world events affect their lives. The fight for civil rights, Martin Luther King, Jr.'s assassination and the ensuing riots, Vietnam, the moon walk, labor disputes—all work their way into the household's routines, fears, and dreams. Porter's dialogue is masterful, matching evolving styles and outlooks while capturing the mix of scolding and affection parents heap on children and the anger and sorrow harbored within. While episodes dramatize the differences between races, generations, and the unschooled and the well educated, Porter's vision confirms the universals: decency and love. An outstanding debut. —*Donna Seaman*

Prager, Emily.
Eve's Tattoo.
Random, $19 (0-394-57490-7). 193p.

Prager's latest novel is mesmerizing. The setting is Manhattan—a literary, artsy milieu where writer Eve Flick, who happens to be a WASP, celebrates her fortieth birthday by treating herself to a tattoo: a braceletlike band in the form of six digits . . . the number of a concentration camp victim she calls "Eva." Submerged in the literature of the Holocaust, Eve becomes a storyteller, relating the stories of women killed by the Nazis to friends and strangers alike. Becoming more obsessed with each passing day, Eve feels "Eva" has become a part of her. Perhaps not surprisingly, French Catholic lover Charles César finds her behavior a bit too much to live with (he was, in fact, born Jewish). And so goes this disturbing, ironic tale, grabbing hold of the reader from the first page, it never lets go, even after the final page is turned. —*Alice Joyce*

General Fiction

Pratchett, Terry.
Guards! Guards!
Penguin/ROC, paper, $4.50 (0-451-45089-2). 350p.

This eighth novel in Pratchett's Discworld saga takes us to the city of Anhk-Morpork, with its unionized criminals. This arrangement is fine with the captain of the night watch, but then an oversize dwarf arrives, and he is determined to clean up the city in the best Wyatt Earp tradition, even if he has to fight a dragon to do it. The zaniness sometimes gets out of hand, but the novel is good, rowdy fun and can be enjoyed independently of the rest of the series, which is emerging as the most ambitious humorous science fiction project since Douglas Adams launched his *Hitchhiker's Guide to the Galaxy*. —*Roland Green*

✔**Pritchett, V. S.**
Complete Collected Stories.
Random, $35 (0-679-40215-2). 232p.

Pritchett's *Complete Collected Stories*—not to be confused with his *Collected Stories* or his *More Collected Stories*, although the present volume includes the 29 and 24 stories, respectively, in those two books—presents 82 short stories written over the writer's 60-year career. This chronological arrangement of all of the author's tales begins with items in the 1930s and continues up to *A Careless Widow*, offering an amazing merger between striking characters and humorous observations of human nature. Whether he's exploring the macabre humor in a tragic highway accident or probing tender memories of childhood, Pritchett captures the reader's attention and imagination from the very first sentence right through to the end of each of these masterful miniatures. A dazzling record of an ever-stylish and always entertaining writer. —*John Brosnahan*

Ricci, Nino.
The Book of Saints.
Knopf, $19 (0-679-40118-0). 240p.

There's talk in Valle del Sole, a small Italian village lost in the Apennines: talk about the pregnant Cristina who lives with her seven-year-old son and his crippled grandfather; talk about her husband, who has lived in Canada for many years; and talk about Cristina's encounter with a snake—its evil presence is seen as proof of Cristina's doomed soul. Her son, Vitto, just old enough to sense the disapproval of his peers, begins to bow under the weight of the shame his mother should be feeling. Teased at school and scared by stories of a snake-headed baby, he betrays his friend, Fabrizio, when his own conscience and fear incapacitate him. The village rivalries, gossip, and church pressure crowd around the mother and her son, and even Cristina's final act of rebellion—escaping with Vitto to America—ends tragically when she dies at sea during childbirth. Ricci's first novel is enlivened by the Italian storytelling tradition; Vitto's priest, his teacher, and his grandfather supply rich texture with their talk of village history and patron saints. A sobering view of the suffocating influence of religion and superstition on the life of a young boy. —*Kathryn LaBarbera*

Robinson, Kathleen.
Dominic.
St. Martin's, $24.95 (0-312-06340-7). 439p.

It is the good old days of the Roman Empire, a time when survival means a quick wit, a quicker fist, and unexpected alliances. Four centuries after Christ, a dwarf is born in Gaul on the fringe of the empire. He is named Dominic by his loving parents who, unfortunately, die while he is young. Given to his uncle, Dominic is soon sold to a traveling circus. The crudeness of his new life is mitigated only by his ability to take delight whenever, wherever it comes. His adventures are as bold and lusty as the Dark Ages soon to be opening in Europe, yet his spirit remains grounded in the basic goodness of mankind. Dominic's faith is rewarded not only with solid friendships, but by a happy reunion with the very people who sold him into slavery. A charming man, a charming tale, and a delightful first novel. —*Cynthia Ogorek*

Robinson, Roxana.
A Glimpse of Scarlet and Other Stories.
HarperCollins, $18.95 (0-06-016331-3). 208p.

In these finely crafted stories, Robinson probes the most intimate human relationships, revealing all-encompassing maternal love, heart-thumping illicit love, enduring married love, and fierce rage that can fester and erupt. In the title story, a wife, recently reminded of her own distant affair, discovers and destroys a note from another woman in her husband's wallet, then realizes what else she has destroyed. In "Graduation," a mother, suffused with love and pride for her only child, is deprived of an important experience with him by her still-enraged ex-husband. Many of these characters are divorced, so the strains of second marriages and stepfamilies are frequent themes, but relationships between adults and their parents and between women friends also are movingly explored. While Robinson's characters are generally people of privilege living in the Northeast, class and place matter far less than the universality of their emotions. The prose here is exceptionally pure and clean and, occasionally, wonderfully evocative. Robinson's earlier books have been well received—the novel, *Summer Light*, and the biography *Georgia O'Keeffe: A Life*—but these gemlike stories may be her finest work. —*Michele Leber*

Robison, Mary.
Subtraction.
Knopf, $19.95 (0-394-53943-5). 288p.

Robison has been called a minimalist for her spare short stories, collected in *Believe Them*, and her pensive first novel, *Oh!*, but here she has broken loose in a haunting existential love story. Paige is a poet married to Raf, who, at first meeting, appears to be a low-life, philandering drunk. But he has his charm. He is a former philosophy major at Princeton and Rhodes scholar, and his wanderings and inebriations have a dark logic to them. He has disappeared, and Paige trails him to Houston, a place of menace and heat; everything's a bit off and pulled out of shape. Robison's prose is hard-edged, corrosive, perfect, punctuated with quick, cynical, and surprising dialogue. The story line, which pulls in a startling set of brilliant, out-of-control characters, is a set of spirals in which Raf and Paige go the rounds of being together and then apart, lonely and apprehensive either way. Sharply funny, sad, sexy, and acute. —*Donna Seaman*

Robson, Lucia St. Clair.
The Tokaido Road: A Novel of Feudal Japan.
Ballantine, $19.95 (0-345-37026-0). 576p.

A thoroughly absorbing tale about a feudal Japanese girl, Lady Kinume ("Golden Plum") Asano, who is determined to avenge her father's forced suicide at the hands of the ruling Lord Kira. With remarkable realism and immediacy, Robson—author of *Ride the Wind* and other tales—vividly depicts Kinume's quest along the perilous Tokaido Road for the one man whom she believes can help her—Oishi, the Asano clan's head samurai. Suspense and intrigue run deep as Lord Kira has Kinume, disguised first as a courtesan named Cat and then as a lowly traveler, trailed by his chief henchman. Robson writes with a spare elegance and crispness that make this elegiac story ring with poesy. Readers will especially thrill at the story's credible plot twists and lifelike characters, and be enchanted by the lore and legend of ancient Japan that Robson skillfully embroiders into the narrative fabric. —*Mary Banas*

Rofihe, Rick.
Father Must: Stories.
Farrar, $18.95 (0-374-15384-1). 166p.

Each of Rofihe's 16 stories is a puzzle you want to solve and you smile when you do. He drops you into scenes-in-progress and allows you to listen to thoughts and conversations. His language is simple and considered, his words and sentences short and to the point—but the point is subtle and elusive until the story's conclusion. Often his characters are peering into themselves, or someone close to them, trying to explain their eccentricities, not defensively, but patiently and tenderly. Communication in one form or another is the key to these quirky, playful, and warm tales. In the title story, a man wonders what a woman's son should call him; in "Boys Who Do the Bop," Noonie wishes he remembered the song's lyrics. A hearing-impaired woman plays the violin and dreams of a man who would always whisper in her ear in "Quiet," while a man wishes he had more stories to tell to his wife in "Six Quarters." A fresh, funny, and deeply felt collection from a promising new writer. —*Donna Seaman*

Roszak, Theodore.
Flicker.
Summit, $19.95 (0-671-72831-8). 544p.

This is an irresistible book that spends more than 500 pages pondering the nature of films and asking the question, Why do we love the movies? The story follows the enviable course of Jonathan Gates, born in the "high noon of Hollywood's Golden Age" (1939), raised on Joan Crawford and the Three Stooges, and brought to maturity on the offerings of the Classic, a West Los Angeles art-film house. His most notable traits are his passivity and his mutability. Fortunately, he has a knack for falling in with the right people. The right person, if one wants to become a well-known film scholar, is the brilliant proprietor of the Classic, Clare Swann. Before she becomes the next Pauline Kael, she teaches Jonny everything she knows about sex and the movies and then hands him a project that will become his obsession and the basis of his career—the rediscovery of the amazing films of Max Castle. Roszak (*The Making of a Counterculture*) has woven fascinating hunks of film and pop-culture history into this portrait of the young film scholar. For fun, he shows us the world of Andy Warhol and does great impersonations of Orson Welles and John Huston, but he also goes deep inside the art of film. Although Roszak is not a great prose stylist, he has written the perfect film buff's novel. —*Frances Woods*

✔Roziner, Felix.
A Certain Finkelmeyer.
Norton, $19.95 (0-393-02962-X). 384p.

A triumphant tale of art, love, and politics in the Soviet Union. Aaron-Chaim Mendelevich Finkelmeyer is a Moscow Jew with the gift of poetry (a mixed blessing in the post-Stalinist era). At first his poems work to his advantage—patriotic verse earns him a cushy post in the army—but he can't publish his genuine literary work. A mentor suggests that Finkelmeyer take up translation to make money since the latest cultural craze is the poetry of obscure ethnic minorities. Finkelmeyer travels to Siberia and meets a Tongor man who recites "songs" about hunting on the tundra. Finkelmeyer ends up using his Tongor discovery as a cover for publishing his own poems under a Tongor pseudonym. Soon he's living a precarious double life that sets off a deliciously complicated and pointed series of events. Roziner surrounds his hero with a cast of extravagant, eloquent, and soulful characters who, in the best tradition of Russian literature, consume huge quantities of vodka, talk all night about art, tell stories, fall passionately in love, and revel in duping the authorities. Itself a product of *samizdat* (underground) literature, this vibrant novel intertwines philosophy with fun, making its argument for art all the stronger. —*Donna Seaman*

✔Rush, Norman.
Mating.
Knopf, $23 (0-394-54472-2). 487p.

"Rich" is an easy description to bandy about in a review. But if rich means that a novel is extraordinarily stylish and intelligent, deeply resonant of place and character, and all of it delicately striated with humor, then Rush's novel is indeed rich. Following his widely applauded story collections, *Whites* (1986), Rush now relates the tale of an American female anthropologist in Africa, whose thesis research (on fertility) has already gone dead when she falls for

General Fiction

a man who is in Africa running a utopian community for unfortunate women. This novel, the story of their love, takes a while to get up a head of steam, but once the engines are cranking it becomes a splendidly eloquent evocation of Africa as well as universal male-female natures and differences. Each of the two main characters has enough idiosyncrasies to sink a battleship—all the better, for it makes them as warmly human as any two people encountered in any fiction in recent years. Wrought with both verve and soul, this novel is not to be missed. —*Brad Hooper*

✔Russell, Paul.
Boys of Life.
Dutton, $18.95 (0-525-93327-1). 320p.

In a laundromat in Owen, Kentucky, in 1978, 17-year-old Tony Blair, who drinks enough whiskey each day to blot out the nightmares he's had since his abused childhood, meets avant-garde filmmaker Carlos Reichart. Carlos sees in Tony exactly the boy he wants in his next movie—and in his bed. Tony's got nothing to stick around for except his younger brother, Ted, so he joins Carlos' oddball company and for the next few years lives in New York, first as Carlos' lover and star, then pretty much as a gay hustler until he meets strange but straiter-laced would-be singer Monica. She and he buy a car, escape Carlos, settle in Memphis, eventually marry. Then on the marquee of a theater besieged by outraged fundamentalists, Tony spots a movie title that has to be one of Carlos'. He buys a ticket and finds in the film—an orgy of homosexual sadomasochism—his brother, Ted, grown and beautiful, and to whose memory (!) the movie's dedicated. Tony returns to New York for a fateful, violent confrontation with Carlos. This outline hardly suggests the richness of Russell's second novel, a genuine seven-league advance over *The Salt Point*. Picaresque and symbolic, raffish yet lyrical, told in one of the most compelling and authentic vernacular voices in American literature—Tony Blair is the peer of Huck Finn and Holden Caulfield—*Boys of Life* is an awesome achievement. It is, to date, the great American novel of gay male experience. —*Ray Olson*

Rutherfurd, Edward.
Russka: The Novel of Russia.
Crown, $25 (0-517-58048-9). 768p.

Following the hugely successful format of his first novel, *Sarum: The Novel of England*, Rutherfurd again tackles a country's entire history. This immense yet intimate dramatization of Russia's conflictful past begins in A.D. 180 in a small village clinging to the edge of forest and steppe. Vulnerable and isolated, it's an easy target for the fierce, marauding horsemen of the south and east who leave their indelible mark on the land and its culture. As he works his way through the centuries and across Russia's vast landscape, Rutherfurd personalizes the conflicts and challenges of each era by focusing on the fortunes of different families. Tales of survival, adventure, and romance are infused with insight into ethnic distinctions, class structure, religious attitudes, economics, sexual mores, and political intrigue. Russia's most notorious and powerful leaders, Ivan, Peter, and Catherine, are portrayed and key, future-shaping events interpreted up through the 1917 revolution. Rutherfurd conducts this grand symphony with absolute authority, blending knowledge with imagination, fact and context with emotion and suspense, and leaves us with a deeper understanding of the roots of Russia's current, volatile situation.—*Donna Seaman*

Sapia, Yvonne V.
Valentino's Hair.
Fiction Collective Two; dist. by Talman, $18.95 (0-932511-45-7). 197p. paper, $8.95 (0-932511-46-5).

Sapia tells a story shaped by the tender relationship between a father and his young son, ignited by elements of fantasy and magic. Facundo Nieves is a Puerto Rican barber living in New York with a secret that haunts his dreams. While his friends and beloved son, Lupe, know of the time when Nieves cut Rudolph Valentino's hair, they do not know details of the encounter that followed. Nieves narrates this tale of lives overflowing with love and the palpable energy of passion. Rich in nuance and emotional resonance, this novel won the 1991 Nilon Excellence in Minority Fiction Award. —*Alice Joyce*

✔Sayles, John.
Los Gusanos.
HarperCollins, $22.95 (0-06-016653-3). 475p.

As a writer and filmmaker, Sayles has exhibited a versatile sensibility: on the one hand, his low-budget, independent films (*Return of the Secaucus Seven*, *Brother from Another Planet*, *Matewan*, *Eight Men Out*) penetrate the great social issues of our day, offering probing and personal insights; on the other hand, his film scripts have provided cheap and immensely effective B-movie entertainment (*Piranha*, *Alligator*). As an author, Sayles has been nominated for the National Book Award and has won the O. Henry Award for short stories. Now, with Los Gusanos, his third novel, Sayles gives us a panoramic epic of the Cuban tradition of rebellion and betrayal, a provocative account of the plight of Cuban Americans—and how neither Castro nor the yanquis offered the true liberation they sought. At the same time, it is a gut-wrenching adventure tale, reminiscent in scope of Conrad. Sayles' understanding of the culture is remarkable; he depicts a cast of characters intent on returning to a homeland they had fled or had never been to, distrustful of gringo assistance after the disastrous invasion at the Bay of Pigs. Following the noble, if naive, plans for another invasion of the island, *Los Gusanos* recounts the recent bittersweet history of the Cuban people, and their love-hate relationship with the U.S., through the lives of former Fidelistas, Batista supporters, drug and gun runners, and the CIA. —*Benjamin Segedin*

Schulman, Helen.
Out of Time.
Atheneum, $19.95 (0-689-12122-9). 224p.

The Gold family comes to life on the pages of Schulman's first novel. Various scenes from Ken's life and his premature death are re-created by mother, brothers, sister, and lover. Even a neighbor recalls the night she heard the impact—as a car crashed against a tree, a site where many lives had been taken in the past. Equivocal as to whether the tragedy was an accident or a suicide, the novel's format allows for family and friends to reminisce, each in their own words, on the irrepressible Ken, a beloved if impetuous youth. The author's richly descriptive voice is most knowing in her portrayal of Hannah Gold, abandoned by her husband, Jack, and left all too soon by her favorite son. The surviving children grapple with memories of their parents' turbulent marriage and long-nurtured sibling rivalries, bringing vivid glimpses of the idealism of the 1960s, nervous breakdowns, and AIDS to the narrative. Darting back and forth in time, the story of the Gold family is a bittersweet reflection on one family's growth and maturation as it comes to terms with the loss of one seemingly indispensable part of its whole. —*Alice Joyce*

Schwartz, Sheila.
Imagine a Great White Light.
Pushcart, $18.95 (0-916366-67-7). 287p.

Each year Pushcart chooses an "overlooked manuscript of enduring literary value" for its Editors' Book Award. This year's winner is a collection of nine short stories that resonate with the power of emotional truth. Schwartz captures the ritualized harping and exaggeration of Jewish family life at its most ludicrous, as spouses resolutely refuse to attempt to understand each other, and grief-stricken mothers turn on stubborn daughters. Guilt, anger, and resentment flash in tricky, double-edged, and sharply funny dialogue. In the title story, a man has committed suicide, leaving his mother and wife locked in a torturous relationship. "Out-of-the-Body Travel," set in the pot-drenched late 1960s, perfectly captures the confusion of a teenage girl when her parents break up; and drug addiction and family obligations are examined with great delicacy in "A Tough Life." Schwartz's stories are exceptional—strongly composed, heartfelt, forgiving, and vivid. —*Donna Seaman*

Schwartz, Steven.
Lives of the Fathers.
Univ. of Illinois, $16.95 (0-252-01815-X). 152p.

There are fathers here, in these 10 powerful short stories, and uncles and sons and fathers-to-be, their lives incomplete. Schwartz writes like a detective of the heart, tracking what is missing on paths choked by misunderstanding and the uncomprehended: a mother's nervous breakdown, an uncle's theft, a first, lost love. Each story is unique in time (from the fifties through the sixties to the present) and circumstance, but linked by Schwartz's ability to combine wit with sorrow and the unexpected with the commonplace. The title story involves an elderly man's love, which lasts beyond the duplicities of memory;

in "Down Under," the clean-up crew in a Philadelphia slum teaches the landlord's nephew a lesson about the shredding of dignity; and in "Madagascar," winner of the 1988 Algren Award, the son of a Holocaust survivor is unable to walk in, or away from, his father's footsteps. Schwartz, author of *To Leningrad in Winter*, writes with compassion and a keen understanding of the longing to make things right in a very wrong world. —*Eloise Kinney*

See, Carolyn.
Making History.
Houghton, $19.95 (0-395-59221-6). 276p.

From an up-and-coming novelist whom lots of discriminating readers are watching, a hospitable but still potent inquiry into the eternal double question of what people want out of life and how they go about seeking it. Specifically, See limns the lives of a Southern California family of the present day, lives that are centered on the husband and father, a businessman with international connections. Both spouses have been married before, so there are "their" kids and "her" child. The latter is injured in a minor car accident— minor in injuries, but major in launching this story of each family member's personal investigation into what's best for his or her own happiness and whom he or she needs and does not need to help find it. These people may not be like the family next door, but it is See's talent to make them appealing and their plights universal. A novel to learn from as well as enjoy. —*Brad Hooper*

Sexton, Linda.
Private Acts.
Little, Brown, $19.95 (0-316-78203-3). 328p.

A wealthier, more thoughtful, and sexier "thirtysomething" cast populates this new novel by Sexton. Here the watchword is *compromise*. The book features both men and women compromising to balance work and family, and they also compromise ideals and ethics to get what they think they want. Both Sy and Alexis are hard-driving corporate types desperate to make their mark. Sy never sees his wife, Maggie, and their two children. Alexis dumps her husband, Nicolas, for boring her and is ready to dump her next boyfriend until she misses an important promotion and is nearly caught "cheating" on the biggest deal of her career. Meanwhile, Nicolas and Maggie begin an affair that provides Maggie with her sexual awakening while threatening to destroy her family. In the end, Alexis wakes up and falls in love with her boyfriend, Jon, who isn't so sure he wants her anymore. Sy drops out of the rat race to head a small company and spend time with the family. Maggie blows off Nicolas, learns to enjoy sex with Sy, and decides not to go back to work but instead to write a novel about "people like all of us ... about what it feels like to ... compromise." Too clever? Well, she almost manages it: there are plenty of carefully plotted "types" to identify with in this literate, timely drama. But it's clear that only Maggie wins—so we know which compromises the author likes. —*Deb Robertson*

General Fiction

Shaham, Nathan.
The Rosendorf Quartet.
Grove Weidenfeld, $18.95 (0-8021-1234-X). 368p.

This gem of a novel tells about four German Jewish musicians who, for various reasons, emigrated from Berlin to Israel and became acquainted with each other as members of a symphony orchestra founded in Tel Aviv in 1936. Subsequently, first-violinist Kurt Rosendorf forms a string quartet of his own. His first choice is shy, sensitive Conrad Friedman, second-violinist, then Eva Staubenfeld, a beautiful and glacial violist, and finally, the self-centered and earthy cellist Bernard Litovsky. Together they make beautiful music. But although the novel contains many informative insights into what makes a polished and professional quartet work, it's the characters who count. The personal events in each player's life are so involved in the performance that in the end the reader can more fully appreciate the subtleties of chamber music as an art and craft. There's never a wrong note in this unusually fine novel. —*Theresa Ducato*

Shalev, Meir.
The Blue Mountain.
HarperCollins, $22.95 (0-06-016691-6). 384p.

Shalev, an Israeli journalist and author of children's books, has reached his country's best-seller lists with this bewitching novel about a band of pioneering Russian Jews who established a settlement in Palestine at the turn of the century. Three men and a woman pioneered the greening of the desert. Their colorful stories are told through the memories of Baruch, the loyal, loving, and orphaned grandson of two of the settlers, Feyge and her husband, Mirkin. Mirkin, a genius with fruit trees and soon widowed, raised Baruch after his parents were killed by Arab terrorists. Baruch grows up to be a devoted collector of the tales of his village, and his reminiscences lead to leaps back and forth in time, from father to daughter to son, anecdote to confession, recounting pivotal moments of love and passion. Shalev is a tease, offering tantalizing hints, leaving questions unanswered for pages and pages, luring you on with the scents of honey and fruit, barnyard and field, and the strong, often eccentric personalities of the villagers. A captivating, funny, and bittersweet drama of zeal and folly, commemoration and irony. —*Donna Seaman*

Shreve, Anita.
Strange Fits of Passion.
HBJ, $19.95 (0-15-185760-1). 306p.

A superbly crafted, intelligently written exploration of the complicities of an abusive relationship. A middle-aged, successful writer, whose career was made after she wrote a tantalizingly slanted article about an abused woman who murdered her husband, is compelled to visit the woman's daughter years later and to give the daughter all the notes from the story, many of them written by the murderer herself. As the daughter, Christine, begins to read, so do we, and the story of Maureen English's torment unfolds with a journalistic intensity. In alternating chapters, author Shreve presents interviews with the citizens of the small New England town where Maureen tried to hide from her husband, as well as Maureen's version of the events. The many voices are impressively distinct, and the points of view are always honestly presented. Hovering over the whole is the question of a journalist's integrity in piecing together the shattered bits of any story. This novel is as forcefully true in its depicting of a "real" situation in fiction as Susan Brownmiller's *Waverly Place* was in fictionalizing a true story. Highly recommended. —*Eloise Kinney*

✔Sidhwa, Bapsi.
Cracking India.
Milkweed Editions, $18.95 (0-915943-51-4). 289p.

Published in Britain to glowing reviews, Sidhwa's third work heralds a burgeoning literary talent. Seen through the perceptive, playful eyes of Lenny, an eight-year-old Parsi girl of upper-class origin, the novel traces the turbulent partitioning of India in 1947, as the Indian congress, under Nehru and influenced by Gandhi, shakes free from British influence. The Sikhs, Hindus, Moslems, and much less numerous Parsis jostle and ultimately murder each other for power. It begins gradually, with Lenny hearing loud-voiced debates from under dinner tables. Oddly, Lenny's first-person narrative reveals an unsettling lack of innocence (Sidhwa seems to view the woman-child's maturing as, by necessity, an accelerated process, given the harsh subservience of Indian women). Lenny is a playful yet knowing creature; as her life and her country fall apart, she reveals a stoic resilience. The novel's politics are effectively juxtaposed against a lush, sensual center, as the author's prose lingers on the hot, dry Lahore streets, the warm breezes against thin saris, the pungent smells of mango. A novel to savor. —*Peter Robertson*

Silko, Leslie Marmon.
Almanac of the Dead.
Simon & Schuster, $25 (0-671-66608-8). 763p.

Silko's Laguna, Mexican, and white ancestry and legacy of conquest shape her award-winning poems and novels, including *Ceremony* and *Storytelling*. This novel, 10 years in the making, stretches out as long and hard as the desert horizon to encompass the story of the native Americans of the Southwest and Mexico and their 500-year resistance to the European invasion. This is a world humming with death, vengeful magic, and criminality. At the center of the hectic and crowded plot is Lecha, an Indian psychic whose powers allow her to locate the dead and converse with snakes, and Seese, a white woman seeking help in locating her kidnapped baby. Lecha possesses an old almanac of prophecies, which she is transcribing with Seese's assistance under fairly crazy circumstances. As Silko slowly unveils this immense and convoluted mural, we are confronted with arms and drug dealing, pornography, lust, cruelty, suicide, the theft and desecration of sacred objects, and the entire tragic history of the crimes of the conquerors and the pain and anger of the conquered. —*Donna Seaman*

✔**Simmons, Dan.**
Summer of Night.
Putnam, $22.95 (0-399-13573-1). 560p.

Old Central school in Elm Haven, Illinois, is about to shut its doors, and the last class to attend is settling in for a languid, small-town summer. But this isn't any ordinary school; for one thing, the bell in its belfry has been summoning evil for centuries. In a shock-littered cross between *Our Town* and Clive Barker's *Buckets of Blood*, Simmons mixes typical small-town drama—baseball games, sexual awakenings—with haunting images of building horror: a ghostly truck moving down deserted roads; a monkey's corpse; voices on a dead radio; snakelike creatures who prowl underground; a truck full of roadkill that becomes its own killing machine. Hovering over it all is the squat, gothic shape of the school with its stark, cruel lines and mysterious history, which we learn from the son of the town drunk. Simmons is an awesomely talented writer; his measured yet image-strewn prose is about as resonant, as thoughtful, and as ultimately shocking as horror fiction gets. —*Peter Robertson*

Singer, Isaac Bashevis.
Scum.
Farrar, $19.95 (0-374-25511-3). 195p.

A blunt title for a tidy tale of deception and depression. Max Barabander is a secularized Jew living in Buenos Aires in the early part of the century. In his prime, rich, and in love with his dynamic wife, Rochelle, he's satisfied with life until their only child, a 17-year-old boy, dies unexpectedly. Rochelle withdraws into her grief, leaving Max impotent, frustrated, and desperate. After consulting unsuccessfully with doctors, he decides that a trip back to his native Poland will refresh him. But his past was a seedy one, and Max reverts immediately to his old "underworld mentality." He charms one woman after another, seeking a cure. He's out of control, one minute proposing marriage to a rabbi's daughter, the next agreeing to procure girls for prostitution in Argentina. He goes from shul to séance, from guilt to justification, adrift in moral turpitude like flotsam in a fouled sea. —*Donna Seaman*

✔**Skvorecky, Josef.**
The Miracle Game.
Knopf, $20 (0-394-57220-3). 416p.

For such a great work of fiction, this novel, centered in Prague, 1968, is astonishingly accessible. Mostly, this is because Skvorecky is such a fine storyteller and knows when to pick up and when to let drop the various threads of his tale. But it is also because the tantalizing images he uses are so forceful: they are dotted in fugal patterns throughout the story. One of the themes they carry is that nature herself is rather corny: her baroque sunsets and rococo clouds are at times decidedly vulgar. But vulgarity, as the irreducibly natural, is in part what helps the hero of this novel keep his sanity in the face of the barren rationalism of the socialist tyranny. If he were not both fighting to hide his gonorrhea (which officially does not exist) and to get the deliciously sensual teenager Vixi in bed, he would have to think more about avoiding his socialist responsibilities. As a teacher, as a writer, as a witness of a supposed miracle that the authorities have gone to great lengths to reveal as fraud, he finds himself in an absurd but cruel world, powerful in its ability to crush all aspects of hope. The names in this novel tempt us to believe that it is significantly autobiographical, but whether it is or isn't, it is an extraordinary tale, more solid, more real, than most of the fiction one encounters these days. —*Stuart Whitwell*

Slavitt, David R.
Short Stories Are Not Real Life.
Louisiana State Univ., $18.95 (0-8071-1665-3). 175p.

Slavitt's prior accomplishments encompass dozens of books of fiction, poetry, and nonfiction. The mastery implied by this record is evidenced in this volume. These stories reveal highly magnified, very real renderings of family histories and encounters—newly divorced (and newly married) men of middle age grappling with the struggles and muted passions accumulated in their 50-odd years, living lives of remarkable intention. Characters engage the reader with their poignant, often humorous predicaments: for instance, the professor of the title story ruminates on urban violence while critiquing his students' revelatory prose amid his own erotic fantasies. Reminiscences abound: an aging man about to become a grandfather recalls battles with his own father; others contemplate the right moves for healing wounds with grown daughters, young sons, ex-wives, or old friends. A writer entirely lacking artifice in the sense of stylistic trends, Slavitt is thoroughly in command of the language, offering clear, spare prose that illuminates characterizations through an infusion of candor and lucidity. —*Alice Joyce*

Small, David.
Alone.
Norton, $19.95 (0-393-02991-3). 512p.

In Small's fictitious universe, circumstances rule. His previous *River in Winter* is a powerful evocation of a life gone wrong, and here, in this long, involved drama, lives are mangled by intractable personalities, illness, and cowardice. Earl Dimes has survived a rotten childhood. His father has a volatile temper, his mother is chronically depressed and overtly favors his older brother, whose favorite activity is beating up his passive sibling. Earl hooks up with another set of bullies when he marries Linda, an Italian from Long Island. Her father, Phil, is hyperactive, bossy, inexplicably wealthy, well connected—and the novel's most enjoyable creation. Earl and Linda's marriage is loveless, held together by Phil's money and insistence, and their son. Numerous mishaps, misunderstandings, and tragedies occur, all explained with tense humor, compulsive attention to detail, and the gloom of a weary, self-obsessed loner. Small submerges us in a study of selfishness, inept parenting, the ravages of old age, and the pointlessness of life without love and then offers a ray of hope after everyone has hit rock bottom. An emotionally authentic, brooding, and veracious work. —*Donna Seaman*

Smith, Kay Nolte.
A Tale of the Wind: A Novel of Nineteenth Century France.
Villard, $22 (0-394-57835-X). 528p.

Mystery and suspense readers have recognized Smith's fictional gifts since her first novel, *The Watcher*, won a 1980 Edgar; four fine thrillers with contemporary settings followed. In this first venture into historical romance, Smith plunges the reader into the artistic and high bourgeois maelstrom of nineteenth-century France. From the opening of Victor Hugo's *Hernani* at the start of the three-day revolt of 1830 to the dress rehearsal of Rostand's *Cyrano* in 1897, Smith creates a densely textured tapestry of artistic, political, social, and personal change. Her plot is rich with historical detail (three bloody revolutions, the rebuilding of Paris, generations of aesthetic change) and with involving personal crises (unwed parenthood, trial, imprisonment and escape, loving cohabitation and loveless marriage, homosexuality, and suicide). Her characters—three generations of women who struggle bravely to define themselves in a society that considers them troublemaking rebels and the actors and artists, bankers and bourgeois who support or subvert those struggles—are lively, believable, and compelling. *—Mary Carroll*

✓Spencer, Elizabeth.
The Night Travellers.
Viking, $19.95 (0-670-83915-9). 355p.

Mississippian Spencer is a damned fine yarn spinner, as no one acquainted with her relatively long list of novels and short story collections can deny— and as further proven in her latest novel. Spencer has used her native South extensively in her fiction, as well as European settings with which she is almost as intimately familiar. *The Night Travellers*, though, is not as anchored in locale as it is in time and issues. The former is the years of the Vietnam War, the latter the antiwar movement and the consequences of destructive protest activities on movement members. To be specific, Spencer limns the life of Mary Kerr Harbison, who, when young, has hopes of being a dancer; an interruption of her intentions comes in the form of a young antiwar activist, Jeff Blaise. It seems that her life once partnered with Jeff will be as little her own as her previous existence was under her mother's criticism and even suppression. How Mary's life, once she is in exile in Canada as a result of Jeff's commitments to his cause, is ultimately structured is presented to the reader at once elegantly and grittily. Spencer's many fans will applaud, while new admirers will ask for her previous works. *—Brad Hooper*

Stewart, Mary.
The Stormy Petrel.
Morrow, $18 (0-688-11035-5). 256p.

The title of perennially best-selling romancer Stewart's latest refers to both a little seabird and a boat piloted by one of the two young men who intrude upon young professor Rose Fenemore's country-cottage holiday on one of the smaller Hebrides. Unfortunately, the Petrel pilot, although he's the handsomer, turns out to be a dicey character. It's the other gent, helming another boat, who's steadier, though plainer. Love—well, polite amative inquiry, anyway—has its way, but not before some exceedingly minor skulduggery and lots of rather formulaic description of Hebridean natural splendor. Stewart's a past master of the supergenteel romance, and her many fans will probably enjoy the book. Readers used to more suspenseful, sexier, or cleverer romantic fare may find it desperately tame. —*Ray Olson*

✓Strieber, Whitley.
The Wild.
Tor, paper, $5.95 (0-812-51277-4). 378p.

Bob Duke isn't much of a man. Once a bohemian and still a poet who can't quite seem to get published, he's tried to support his wife Cindy and son Kevin as a stockbroker and a computer consultant, but he's a bust. And now the wolf's at the door, figuratively in that eviction notices on both home and office have arrived but also not so figuratively, and therein may lie his salvation. Always a lover of the great canines, he's transfixed one Saturday by the stare of a wolf at the zoo, a gaze that seems to invade his soul. A few days later, he thinks he turns into a wolf for a few hours. Not much later, he knows he turns into a wolf. Cindy and Kevin know it, too, because the transformation happens before their eyes. The rest of Strieber's spellbinding fantasy is largely a chase, as Bob flees Manhattan with the police at his heels, then northward to join a wolf pack, which in turn has to flee snowmobiling hunters. It's not only a chase, though, but also something of an ecological fable, and a tour de force of sensuous narrative writing as, since Bob's dominant sense modality turns from human vision to canine smell, so—virtuosically—does Strieber's prose. Satiric, cautionary, exciting, and deadly serious by turns, this is a tale to make one howl with delight. —*Ray Olson*

Sutter, Barton.
My Father's War and Other Stories.
Viking, $19.95 (0-670-83777-6). 257p.

In these six quietly dramatic tales, we meet familiar, ordinary individuals who each cross one of life's many thresholds into maturity. Set in simple, small towns in America's Midwest, the stories nonetheless depict complicated lives and emotions and touch on universal truths through their stirring sense of realism. "Don't Stick Your Elbow Out Too Far" rests on an all-too-contemporary metaphor: buying a car is an important social and sexual "initiation rite," as the 24-year-old, soon-to-be-married narrator, a grad student on a visit home to Iowa, comes to realize. In "Happiness," three idealistic male friends take an unexpectedly perilous canoe trip, but what looms larger than their fear of death is the prospect of settling into comfortable middle-class lives—a tragically naive fear given the story's dark, ironic ending. The title story gently portrays two antiwar sons experiencing an "epiphany" about their father's World War II experiences at, appropriately, Christmastime. Engaging, traditional fiction filled with memorable, natural-sounding characters, a strong sense of time and place, and subtle symbolism. —*Mary Banas*

General Fiction

✔**Tan, Amy.**
The Kitchen God's Wife.
Putnam, $21.95 (0-399-13578-2). 415p

Tan's *Joy Luck Club* was a spectacular debut and a hard act to follow, but this second novel is magnificent. It's a natural offspring of the first book, delving deeper into mother-daughter relationships, the vagaries of luck, and the will to survive. The catalyst for the tale is a longtime friend's demand that Winnie finally reveal the whole truth about her life in China to her grown, American-born daughter, Pearl. She unveils her painful past in a great torrent of words, unburdening herself of old angers and fears, re-creating her violent, war-wrenched youth and the brutal tyranny of her first marriage. Abandoned by her mother, who fled the oppressive, hopeless life of a second wife, Winnie was raised indifferently by relatives who married her off to a savage man. As Tan traces the many twists and turns of Winnie's saga, she dramatizes the inhumanity of arranged marriages and the subjugation of women. Myriad details of everyday life conjure up the chaos in China during the 1940s as the ancient feudal order crumbled and the Japanese attacked. As events unfold, it becomes clear that the often unspoken yet unshakable loyalty and devotion of women friends sustained Winnie, made her triumphant liberation possible, and now have brought her closer to her daughter. A ravishing, vivid, graceful, and unforgettable tale of womanhood, endurance, and love, lit by gentle humor and the healing aspect of truth. —*Donna Seaman*

Taylor, Erika.
The Sun Maiden.
Atheneum, $18.95 (0-689-12130-X). 240p.

First novelist Taylor has captured a new side of Los Angeles with a character who is a regular person, not a reflection of the "industry." J. O., age 20, is muddling through as a waitress at a coffee shop where she meets her lover, an Israeli with a mysterious past. Other supporting characters include her landlord, who is building the car of the future, her wacky actress roommate, and a young busboy who is haunted by his pyromaniac brother. Threaded throughout is a search for the father J. O. has never met, a search that may make some readers wonder if Taylor has read too many young adult novels (or, perhaps, too few). However, the book is a fresh, observant, and humorous read and has an upbeat ending that clearly lends itself to another helping of a character that public library patrons will be happy to see again. —*Iva Freeman*

Thomas, Maria.
African Visas: A Novella and Stories.
Soho; dist. by Farrar, $19.95 (0-939149-54-0). 256p.

Occasionally in these mostly just sturdily written stories, the writing is so evocative and poetic that it flashes with the kind of relevance-to-life-and-everything that our professors said great literature should always have. All the stories are about Africa, Americans who love it, and the irremediable otherness with which Americans in Africa, even when they've "gone native," must live. Most are told from the perspectives of Peace Corps members. Only two—"Back Bay to the Bundu" and "The Visit"—aren't, and they are Hemingway correctives about old women, one who has settled in Kenya and one who visits her daughter's family in Nigeria. In the long story that opens the collection—a wondrous, nonportentous, comic *Heart of Darkness* entitled "The Jiru Road"—young Sarah Easterday tells of her days in drought-stricken Ethiopia just before the revolution against Haile Selassie broke out, tells of them with a virtually extraliterary immediacy and grace reflective of Thomas' prizewinning skills as a reporter. "The Blonde Masai," "Makonde Carvers," and "My Mermaid" are all episodes from the Peace Corps life, and "You Are the Sun" relays how the narrator and her husband, like Thomas and hers, decided to return to Ethiopia. Unfortunately, there will be no more of Thomas' wonder-filled stories; she accompanied Congressman Mickey Leland on the 1989 mission to the Ethiopia-Sudan border that ended in a plane crash in which all were killed. —*Ray Olson*

Thomson, Rupert.
The Five Gates of Hell.
Knopf, $22 (0-679-40401-5). 384p.

The lives—short and violent—of three toughs are inextricably interlaced in this surrealistic, impressive novel. Middle-class Nathan, gang leader Vasco, and Jed ("Spaghetti"), with his top hat and flaking skin, grow up fast under the shadow and influence of the Paradise Corporation, the town of Moon Beach's most affluent and corrupt business, a funeral home extraordinaire. The wealthy come to Moon Beach to die, and there are plenty of ways to do it, especially if you know Neville Creed, chairman of Paradise. Creed rewards loyalty until it is no longer needed, as Jed finds out when he is forced to commit murder and flee Moon Beach. And if revenge is a dish best served cold, the novel is the chilling, meticulous preparation of an unforgettable meal. Thomson, author of the well-received *Dreams of Leaving*, has an undeniable gift for storytelling, and his prose and imagery are striking, almost breathtakingly original: "Years later, in exile, he would watch the railway trucks from his hotel, and it would sink a well in him, and he would taste the same calm water." A dark, riveting thriller. —*Eloise Kinney*

Thon, Melanie Rae.
Girls in the Grass.
Random, $18 (0-394-57663-2). 288p.

Thon's enthusiastically received debut, *Meteors in August*, is a classic coming-of-age novel with a cross-cultural twist, a line of inquiry she follows with even more adroitness in this splendid short-story collection. The title story opens the volume, and its utterly charming, gentle vision of youth on the brink of sexual comprehension doesn't prepare you for the shock of the

General Fiction

second story, "Punishment." Here Thon yanks us back to 1858, where a series of brutal acts results in the hanging of a slave for the murder of her master's infant son. Each of Thon's potent tales involves a traumatic loss of innocence and the clash between the adult world and the fragile realm of childhood. She switches racial milieus fluently, writing about an exchange between a white waitress and a Latino dishwasher, or a young black boy overwhelmed by the energy of a revival meeting. While the exteriors vary, the interior ache is the same; but when Thon does offer resolution, like in the perfect, lyrical, funny, and sad "Chances of Survival," her expression of hope is absolute. An unusually rich and varied collection. —*Donna Seaman*

Thurm, Marian.
The Way We Live Now.
Bantam, $19.50 (0-553-07604-3). 304p.

Love is where you find it in Thurm's novels of multigenerational urban families, though it may be lost or diminished by death, divorce, or distance. Spike Goldman is perfectly content with second wife Leora and infant son Benjamin until ex-wife Suzanne comes to call, eventually becoming Ben's baby-sitter and Leora's best friend, insinuating herself back into Spike's life and even into his dreams. Meanwhile, Leora's father, Alexander Fine, struggling with grief and loneliness after the death of his wife of almost 40 years, is smitten with his black housekeeper, Ionie, who has just become guardian of her baby great-granddaughter. In these pages, babies are appealing, relationships between adult children and their parents are alternately difficult and tender, and the narrative may ramble off after a quirky character (e.g., Alexander's blind date whose husband left her for their daughter-in-law) loosely connected to the principals. Less centered than *Walking Distance* (Random, 1987) and *Henry in Love*, Thurm's latest still has enough gentle humor and familial love for an evening's pleasure. —*Michele Leber*

Toibin, Colm.
The South.
Viking, $18.95 (0-670-83870-5). 238p.

Irish journalist Toibin's first novel is a masterpiece of subtlety and nuance, especially since he writes from a woman's perspective. It is 1950 and Katherine, an artist from a wealthy family, has abruptly left her husband, her son, and Ireland for Barcelona. She soon becomes involved with Miguel, who also paints. They communicate best in bed since their languages are as different as their backgrounds. They befriend another wandering Irish painter, Michael, and all three move up into the Pyrenees. Here, their respective pasts emerge and clash: Miguel's participation in the failed war against Franco, Michael's poverty-stricken childhood and near-fatal bout with tuberculosis, and Katherine's ambivalence about her experiences during Ireland's "troubles." Katherine is a rare and fascinating creation. Positively regal, she loves Miguel without understanding him, but she finally emerges from her ruthless self-involvement to attain genuine maturity. Laconic and solemn, this gracefully episodic drama vibrates with bottled-up passions, the psychological fallout of war and suffering, and the struggle for inner peace. —*Donna Seaman*

Trevor, William.
Two Lives.
Viking, $21.95 (0-670-83933-7). 374p.

Trevor's nineteenth book of fiction is a pair of novels, each about a lonely woman living on memories, books, and fantasies. "Reading Turgenev" is the story of Mary Louise, a shy, inexperienced Irish farm girl who marries a shopkeeper she doesn't love. Elmer Quarry is 14 years older than Mary Louise but just as naive. His two shrewish, spinster sisters are appalled at his sudden marriage, and soon the newlyweds find themselves appalled as well. They each find solace—Elmer with drink, Mary Louise with her sickly cousin, Robert, who has a penchant for Turgenev's tales. It's a brief, romantic interlude, kept innocent by Robert's abrupt death. Mary Louise ends up in an asylum where she is content to daydream about what might have been. "My House in Umbria" is a bit more exotic, narrated by an Englishwoman who writes romances and owns a boardinghouse in Italy. Fifty-six, pretty, and plump, Emily enjoys her life, relieved to be free of her difficult past, but her peace is shattered when she is injured in a bomb blast on a train to Milan. Several other survivors move into her house to recuperate, including Aimée, an American child now orphaned. They take comfort in each other's company until Aimée's uncle arrives to take her back to the States. Again, Trevor explores grief, memories, and the keys to survival—"illusion, mystery, and pretense." These are haunting, sensitive, and richly imagined stories. Trevor moves slowly, laying his carefully chosen, humble words down like flagstones in a garden path, paving his way into the heart of loss and consolation. —*Donna Seaman*

✔Tyler, Anne.
Saint Maybe.
Knopf, $22 (0-679-40361-2). 352p.

Trust Anne Tyler to take a story that in other hands (say, the restless fingers of Joyce Carol Oates) would become a haunted gothic portrayal of dark impulses, and instead produce a whimsical tragicomedy that glows with human foibles and wistful goodness. Tyler's version of harsh but warming reality encompasses life over four generations of a Baltimore clan well stocked with eccentricities. The center of this family, both in age and spirit, is a teenager whose indiscreet revelations at the outset speed the plot along, the lad unwittingly prompting his brother's suicide, his sister-in-law's drug overdose, and the orphaning of three young children—huge events that will mold the young man's life irrevocably. But the doom in the character's guilty anxiety never builds to full-scale crisis level. Instead, his steady passage through life and into middle age is tempered by the forgiveness he earns and the support he gives to others, finally affirming himself. —*John Brosnahan*

Ullman, Alex.
Afghanistan.
Ticknor & Fields, $19.95 (0-89919-968-2). 288p.

Patrick, the travel editor of a New York–based fashion magazine, is in love with Irina, granddaughter of the magazine's colorful founder, Nicholas Kuratkin. He decides to propose to Irina, but his plan is put on hold when Kuratkin dies. In the aftermath, Patrick gets involved in the addled escapades of Irina's troublesome brother, Michael, and then is unceremoniously dumped by his hoped-for bride. Spurred by the pain of rejection, as well as a friend's romantic accounts of risky endeavors in Afghanistan, and hoping for adventure, he arranges for a working vacation in France and Switzerland. But Michael is also in France, where Patrick rescues him from a suicidal drug binge (quite an adventure in its own right) and, propitiously, frees himself from old restraints. Ullman is an assured and sophisticated first novelist with an innate understanding of charm and absurdity and the ability to infuse the most ordinary of actions with inscrutability and emotion. A richly expressive, often funny, wholly absorbing novel. —*Donna Seaman*

Vassanji, M. G.
Uhuru Street: Short Stories.
Heinemann, paper, $8.95 (0-435-90585-6). 144p.

An excellent British import—a set of stories about the Muslim Indian community of Dar-es-Salaam, Tanzania, by an award-winning writer who grew up in it. Like the Jews in so many European cities, the Indians of Dar are the African city's mercantile class. Unfortunately, also like the Jews, during times of extreme change—e.g., the 1960s to 1980s in which the stories are set—the Indians are the targets of majority xenophobia. Although only one story, the most tragic, is directly concerned with anti-Indian violence, ethnic-minority paranoia chills many of the other stories. These are about a recurring set of characters, mostly described by the same narrator at different times in his life between childhood and maturity. In a few stories, this narrator doesn't figure at all. "In the Quiet of a Sunday Afternoon," for instance, concerns a young man's dissatisfaction with the wife an arranged marriage has brought him and the temptation a young widow represents to him. Something of an urban African *Winesburg, Ohio*, Vassanji's book is a piquantly flavored dish of humanity. —*Ray Olson*

Vetter, Craig.
Striking It Rich.
Morrow, $18 (0-688-10609-9). 256p.

The narrator, a San Francisco writer, is fed up trying to make a living penning articles for *Playboy*, an experience he likens to "playing saxophone in a strip-house band." And since he's not getting along too well with his wife, Suzanne, he decides to do what most of us would do in the same situation: move to Wyoming and be an oil-rig "worm"—starting from the ground up to what proves to be dangerous heights. After all, he reasons, there might even be a story in it. There is one, and a raucous, funny tale it is: the oil-boom biz is no place for a 39-year-old journalist-in-disguise, and Wyoming is (at least according to Monday, the barmaid-turned-housecleaner who lives across the street) the kind of place where you take your date to look at a pit of dead dogs. Our hapless hero is bruised, boozed, and beaten—but he rises like the cartoon coyote, time and again, to get the job, the story, and even the girl. Author Vetter writes for *Playboy* as well as other magazines, and his semi-autobiographical first novel details the boom and bust of the contemporary Wild West with a gleeful eye for the absurd. —*Eloise Kinney*

Vizenor, Gerald.
The Heirs of Columbus.
Wesleyan Univ., $18.95 (0-8195-5241-0). 188p.

Vizenor returns to the native American trickster tradition that infused *Griever: An American Monkey King in China* in his latest novel, a sly, inventive, and teasing tale about the cultural clash between the Old World and the New. In a dazzling and disorienting web of outrageous explanations involving a blue radiance, hand talkers, and Mayan blood, Vizenor speculates on the true nature of Columbus' legacy to the people of the New World. The explorer's tribal heirs include Stone Columbus, who made a fortune on a floating casino called the *Santa Maria* and who regales the country with trickster stories on talk radio, a healer named Almost Browne, and Felipa Flowers, a lawyer turned poacher. The action centers on the alleged remains of Columbus and Pocahontas and the repatriation of Indian ceremonial objects kept in museums. A courtroom hearing takes off into virtual realities under the guidance of a computer shaman, the heirs create their own sovereign tribal nation that conducts genetic healing, and Vizenor keeps us off balance with his subversive humor and otherworldly pyrotechnics. Abstruse in places, but wickedly clever. —*Donna Seaman*

Von Herzen, Lane.
Copper Crown.
Morrow, $19 (0-688-10688-9). 288p.

Copper Crown in 1913 is a small Texas town rife with hatred. Two young girls are curious about passion, and circumstances dictate that they'll learn about it the hard way. Cassie is white and has to lie to her father so that she can see her best friend, Allie, who is black. When a series of racially motivated and sexually violent incidents escalates into an all-out orgy of revenge and murder, Cassie and Allie flee the blood-soaked town taking along a motherless baby. They are determined to make it in this world of prejudice and lust, where beauty is a liability and color the defining factor. As the two women work hard for success and independence, they continue to run into the wall of racism. Von Herzen adds a ghostly dimension to her dramatic social realism with a supporting cast of kindly spirits. Emotionally resonant and keenly sensual, this complex and unusual novel trembles with the forces of conflict and reconciliation, love and memory. —*Donna Seaman*

Warren, Patricia Nell.
One Is the Sun.
Ballantine, paper, $12.95 (0-345-37042-2). 512p.

Warren deftly weaves native American legend and history into an unusual and colorful feminist saga about a Mayan priestess, Earth Thunder, who escapes a temple massacre in the Yucatán and establishes a mystical site in Deer Lodge Valley in southwest Montana in 1857. This multitextured novel aims less for historical realism than for creating a mood and a sense of women's place in history, particularly in a matriarchal society. The author uses two 13-year-old protegés of the aging Earth Thunder—Helle, the granddaughter of a Bavarian countess, and River Singing, a Bannack Indian slave girl—as vehicles for imparting native American philosophy and mores to her readers. It's a beguiling, fanciful story that's short on plot but long on character and luminously embroidered with ancient teachings. A long, roomy novel meant for quiet musings. —*Mary Banas*

Weldon, Fay.
Darcy's Utopia.
Viking, $18.95 (0-670-83645-1). 235p.

Eleanor Darcy, a woman with a singular vision of a utopian socioeconomic community, plays influential adviser to her husband, Julian, the vice-chancellor of a university and a renowned economist (until some of his counsel is considered wrongheaded and lands him in prison). Readers meet Eleanor and her ideas as she is being interviewed by two journalists, Hugo and Valerie, who seem more interested in each other than in their interview subject. (In fact, they have launched an impetuous love affair and settled in at the Holiday Inn, leaving behind spouses and children.) Finally, though, we do learn of Eleanor's somewhat squalid background (she began life as Apricot—named after the color of her mother's negligee) and of her rise to her current position as headline-making philosophical theorist. Weldon's characters' outspoken views on marriage, religion, intimacy, and social values are more vehement than ever, and they combine with the author's wicked sense of humor, resulting in a complex, superbly unsettling piece of fiction. —*Denise Perry Donavin*

West, Paul.
The Women of Whitechapel and Jack the Ripper.
Random, $22 (0-394-58733-2). 404p.

West has captured the pompous savagery of Victorian Britain in this novel: a vivid horror story, brazen carnal exposé, and astute political treatise. With writing bold, brassy, and brilliant, West introduces the opportunistic artist, Sickert, and delves into the intimate thoughts and frustrations of the prostitutes he associates with, exhuming the feminist attributes of women who have little more than their cunning and female body parts with which to make their way in the world. Yet Marie Kelly, that "bonny connoisseur of lust from

Limerick ... a woman of uncommon tenacity and semieducated verve," rises above her station to protest a transgression perpetrated against her friend Annie Crook, whose only crime was to fall in love with a dull-witted prince, and from there the story proceeds, patiently and deliberately, into the realm of horror and brutality. The novel, based on fact embellished with the author's splendid imagination, stands out as a true literary achievement. —*Ivy Burrowes*

✔Wharton, Edith.
The Selected Short Stories of Edith Wharton.
Scribner, $24.95 (0-684-19304-3). 416p.

Editor Lewis, who won the Pulitzer Prize for *Edith Wharton: A Biography*, notes, with satisfaction, the "dramatic rise in Edith Wharton's literary standing in the past decade," a phenomenon that will be sustained by this collection of 21 of the author's best stories. Lewis' excellent introduction explains Wharton's appeal and provides a brief overview of her life and prolific literary output. Wharton wrote short stories for 46 years, drawing on an inexhaustible wellspring of imagination, insight, wit, and consummate artistry. Her stories range from satire to ghost tales, social realism to myth. Wharton was keenly attuned to the subtext of class distinction and its prejudices, absurdities, and tedium, as well as to the societal nonsense women had to hide behind. Adept both at inner monologues and the layers of hidden meanings in conversation, Wharton, with unerring timing, makes the most of the economy of short stories. A treasure for Wharton fans and all short story enthusiasts. —*Donna Seaman*

✔Wharton, William.
Last Lovers.
Farrar, $18.95 (0-374-18389-9). 368p.

When you read Wharton you must let go of your cool and skepticism. You must open your heart to the story as you did when you were a child. Wharton is a courageous writer, unafraid of deep emotions or the excesses of sentimentality or melodrama; indeed, he rediscovers their compelling simplicity and directness. His eighth novel is an exquisite love story set in Paris in 1975. Jack, 49 and an American, has walked out on his lucrative corporate career and troubled marriage to return to his first love, painting. He lives a disciplined, hand-to-mouth existence, struggling to express his long-suppressed feelings in his paintings. While working in a park (and blocking the sidewalk), an elderly blind woman walks into him, knocking him off his feet and getting herself smeared with paint. Mirabelle, 71, speaks precise, almost aristocratic English and is small, elegant, and radiant. They fall slowly, carefully, and improbably in love. Mirabelle's tremendous sense of life inspires Jack to paint with new vigor and freedom, while in his company she blossoms, loving for the first time since the traumatic event that blinded her in her youth. They live in an enchanted world of pure communion, bliss, beauty, and magic. Wharton holds us spellbound, enthralled and warmed by his vision of

General Fiction

innocence and soulfulness. For readers who want to extend this experience, we recommend Wharton's earlier books, including *Birdy*, *Scumbler*, and *Tidings*. —*Donna Seaman*

White, Edmund, ed.
The Faber Book of Gay Short Fiction.
Faber and Faber, $24.95 (0-571-14472-1). 608p.

Faber and Faber churns out anthologies of astonishingly high quality at an astonishing rate. But then, the firm has a habit of picking perfect editors for its gatherings. Witness this volume's compiler. Edmund White is undeniably the most famous living gay writer in English, the one most sought after for endorsements, opinions, and insights not just on gay literature but on gay culture generally. He is so because he both writes progressively better and better books and reads with fair appreciation virtually all the other gay male writers in English going today. The result is this fat, wonderful collection, which proceeds chronologically from that nineteenth-century closet case, Henry James, to such young contemporaries as David Leavitt and Dennis Cooper. In between James and the youngsters come stories and novel excerpts by—to mention only the most famous—E. M. Forster, Christopher Isherwood, Tennessee Williams, William Burroughs, Paul Bowles, Gore Vidal, James Purdy, James Baldwin, Armistead Maupin, Andrew Holleran, and Allan Gurganus. Don't get this for the gay lit collection, though. Get it for the lit collection, period. —*Ray Olson*

Williams, Philip Lee.
Perfect Timing.
Peachtree, $16.95 (1-56145-024-3). 320p.

One man's midlife crisis is the starting point for this funny and touching quest for the meaning of art and love and life itself. Musicology professor and would-be composer Ford Clayton, adrift when wife Jill takes the kids and leaves after his brief affair with a young harpist, sees a bag lady on a television documentary and recognizes her as Camille Malone—gifted pianist, fiery intellectual, and the love of Ford's college life. She told him, 20 years earlier, "Nobody ever forgets Camille Malone," and she's right (their first two sexual encounters are burned in his memory). Ford sets out to save her and find some answers for himself; along for the ride is Ford's born-again ex-con cousin Clarence Clayton, whose religious malapropisms strike a chord with Camille, who's teetering on the edge of madness. Interspersed flashbacks describe Ford's days as a student at the North Carolina conservatory at which he now teaches, surrounded by music and aching to be the Beethoven of his day, listening to Camille's dizzying, allusion-filled tirades at meetings of the Malone Society. (Old letters, from a box in his parents' attic, further illuminate his past.) In a controlled structure, Williams (*The Song of Daniel*, 1989; *Slow Dance in Autumn*, 1988) combines rollicking humor, sharp sweetness, artistic allusion, and humble wisdom in a seemingly effortless, virtuoso performance. —*Michele Leber*

Wilson, F. Paul.
Sibs.
Dark Harvest, P.O. Box 941, Arlington Heights, IL 60006, $20.95
(0-913165-61-6). 320p.

The death of Kara's twin sister makes the headlines: clad only in a garter belt, she crashed through a plate-glass window. The dead woman called herself Ingrid, but Kelly was her real name. And the things she was doing—the sex and the drugs—weren't the kind of things she usually did. Kara comes to New York to find the truth about her sister and to once again fall under the seductive spell of her former lover, NYC cop Rob Harris. *Sibs* pretty much teases the unsuspecting reader from start to finish. Wilson begins with what seems a lot like a mystery: a death that makes no sense, two terrified witnesses. But from there, the novel wanders into deeper, more psychological waters: Ingrid/Kelly was a victim of multiple personalities, and Kara's behavior is beginning to suggest that someone not very nice is entering her mind—someone kinky, someone frightening. By the conclusion, Wilson can't resist turning the narrative screws another notch, as psychological terror gives way to a scenario bordering on the supernatural. Readers possessing a cavalier disregard for genre definitions will relish this tough-to-categorize thriller, turning the pages long into the wee hours. —*Peter Robertson*

Wilson, Robley.
The Victim's Daughter.
Simon & Schuster, $19 (0-671-72618-8). 208p.

Lissa Cooper once discovered her husband, an emotionally disturbed Vietnam vet, dead from a self-inflicted wound—and now returning home for her fifteenth high school reunion, she finds her father has just been beaten to death. So begins this fascinating study of a daughter's grief. The small Maine town's investigation into who killed Raymond Cooper and why becomes a pivotal point around which many sharply drawn characterizations come to life: Willard Strand, tough, chain-smoking investigator from the state attorney general's office and his attractive new assistant, Eleanor Watkins; Lissa's old friend, Donnie Savage, an unhappily married local cop assigned to the murder; and old flame Goodwin Kimball, father of the baby teenage Lissa was forced to abort, now a successful, widowed doctor. There will be many secrets uncovered as the mystery of Raymond Cooper's secret life is examined in painful detail in this compelling debut novel by a well-known short-story writer and poet. —*Alice Joyce*

Wolf, Joan.
Daughter of the Red Deer.
Dutton, $19.95 (0-525-93379-4). 432p.

Traversing into prehistory, Wolf creates a quick-moving, enchanting tale of Cro-Magnon culture in the Pyrenees, which holds a powerful modern message concerning the battle of the sexes and the masculine/feminine faces of God. Alin, the Chosen One of the matriarchal tribe of the Red Deer, is part of a group kidnapped by Mar, son of a murdered chief, in his desperate attempt

General Fiction

to replenish the women of the patriarchal Horse tribe after a poisoned watering hole takes their lives. Men of the Horse little expect women to question and insult them, let alone hunt with them. Red Deer women are surprised to learn of arts defunct in their own tribe (sewing, drawing), and to find that, once in a while, it's nice to depend on someone. How Alin reintroduces Earth Mother to her new society, and how Mar leads her to discover the profound joy of love are all complicated when the Red Deer trace their women and demand their return. The resolutions perhaps indicate that our present-day quest for comradeship and spiritual fulfillment needs a different approach. An excellent choice for readers who want exciting epic without the Micheneresque qualities. —*Denise Blank*

Wolfe, Thomas.
The Good Child's River.
Univ. of North Carolina, $21.95 (0-8078-2002-4). 292p.

The manuscript for this previously unpublished novel was discovered by Wolfe scholar Suzanne Stutman. In her introduction, Stutman provides a context for the book both in terms of Wolfe's other novels and his turbulent and inspiring relationship with stage and costume designer Aline Bernstein. Wolfe was fascinated by Aline's accounts of her New York childhood. He transformed her memories into a series of highly charged, fictional family portraits revolving around a young girl named Esther. Various episodes, some written from a woman's point of view, explore the agony of parental oppression. Wrenching experiences of revelation are dramatized in chapters focusing on Esther and her father and cousin, while road trips trigger rhapsodies to the "lyrical and savage earth." This rescued novel is a torrent of words, a white-water ride through a magnificent canyon alternately sun-dazzled and cloud-shadowed. Wolfe has a mighty, exalted, and incantatory voice that seems to reach us from a much earlier, more potent time, an era long before our digital, humdrum, and packaged days. His stereotyping and excess may be offensive, but his genius for evocation cannot be denied. Add this to your Wolfe shelf without hesitation. —*Donna Seaman*

Yezierska, Anzia.
How I Found America: Collected Stories of Anzia Yezierska.
Persea, $24.95 (0-89255-160-7). 336p.

Yezierska (1880–1970) was one of the thousands of poor Russian Jews who immigrated to America in search of a better life only to be thrust into the poverty and ugliness of New York City's Lower East Side, but she burned with an "extraordinary rebelliousness of spirit" and channeled her energy into her short stories and novels about the immigrant experience. Her early stories were published, awarded prizes, and optioned by a movie studio, sweeping her up from Hester Street to Hollywood. But her fame and material comfort were short-lived, and she wrote in isolation and semipoverty until her death. This volume collects and resurrects all of her passionate, dramatic, and urgent short fiction. The resounding introduction offers succinct biographical and critical information. —*Donna Seaman*

Zhang, Xianliang.
Getting Used to Dying.
HarperCollins, $19.95 (0-06-016521-9). 304p.

Officially criticized by China for his acclaimed novel *Half of Man Is Woman*, Zhang has again written of the trauma of life under the Chinese communists. A heady mix of memory, imagination, and reality, *Getting Used to Dying* is narrated by a well-known, "rehabilitated" Chinese author on a trip to America. His observations of the vulgarly wealthy West play in counterpoint to his searing recollections of his years in labor camps. Originally imprisoned for writing poetry, the narrator comes close to death many times. Once he is taken to an execution ground expecting to be shot, only to be returned to camp after witnessing the death of his companions; later he is thought dead and dumped in a corpse-shed. After his release, the company of women is the only thing that brings him peace, although even sex is linked to death. Aptly dubbed the Chinese Kundera, Zhang writes about the spiritual and mental toll of oppression with great precision, irony, and anger. —*Donna Seaman*

Mystery & Espionage

Abella, Alex.
The Killing of the Saints.
Crown, $20 (0-517-58509-X). 288p.
Easterman, Daniel.
Night of the Seventh Darkness.
HarperCollins, $22.95 (0-06-017928-7). 464p.

The black arts provide the thread that connects these two thrillers, one set in Los Angeles, the other in New York. The question in both, though, is whether the occult should be treated as a legitimate defense or a bogus alibi.

In *The Killing of the Saints*, two Cuban Marielitos are accused of multiple murders in an aborted jewelry store robbery. The crimes were committed while the pair was high on cocaine and immersed in the sacrificial rituals of the Santería cult. Investigator Charlie Morell has the difficult job of establishing that being under the sway of Santería is a valid defense. It seems a doubtful proposition, and Charlie is suitably reluctant. Not just because the cult is deadly, but because Charlie himself is Cuban and has a hidden past, career, and family life to protect. It isn't easy, given the growing Marielito presence on the mean Los Angeles streets. Abella takes a while to mesh narrative gears, but eventually the tempo and the rhythms start to gel. Abella finds some startling new shadows lurking on the Los Angeles streets—no stranger to crime in its many forms.

The black magic in *Night of the Seventh Darkness* comes from Haiti rather than Cuba, but it is no less deadly. When ethnologist Rick and his Haitian wife, Angelina, return to their Brooklyn apartment after a trip to Africa, their house sitter, Filius, is nowhere to be found. In his place, there is a strange smell that emanates from under the floorboards. That's where the remains are found, some fresh, some long dead, and some, in the form of Filius, that look dead but aren't. We're not talking garden-variety street crime here, that's obvious even before Rick's tongue is cut out and Angelina empties Jewish cop Abrams' fish tank. Eventually Abrams, haunted by Angelina and undergoing his own crisis of conscience, tunnels underground to find ancient bones and parchments full of incantations. He's either falling in love or under a deep spell. *Seventh Darkness* crackles with just the right mix of the exotic, the erotic, and the hypnotic. But that's voodoo for you. —*Peter Robertson*

Albert, Neil.
The January Corpse.
Walker, $18.95 (0-8027-3206-2). 204p.

Dave Garrett, disbared Philadelphia lawyer, now makes a living performing routine investigations for insurance companies and suspicious spouses. Although he has a gun, he never takes a case where he thinks he may need one. But when he's hired to determine if there is any reason to believe that Daniel Wilson, presumed dead for the past seven years, is really alive, Dave soon finds it prudent to stay armed. Wilson had mob connections, and Dave learns that the organization has its own reasons for keeping tabs on whatever turns up—including some missing money. For every clue that suggests murder, other evidence surfaces that implies a deliberate disappearance. Dave is certainly one of the most sympathetic detectives to appear in some time. Working within the conventions of the hard-boiled genre, the author demonstrates a high level of skill in creating excellent characters and a fast-paced, riveting, and thoroughly contemporary plot. The ending is guaranteed to catch readers by surprise. —*Stuart Miller*

Alexander, Lawrence.
The Strenuous Life: A Theodore Roosevelt Mystery.
Knightsbridge, $19.95 (1-56129-023-8). 304p.
Hall, Robert Lee.
Ben Franklin and a Case of Christmas Murder.
St. Martin's, $17.95 (0-312-05383-5). 288p.

Famous Americans playing detective has become a common theme in the mystery genre. Not only is Eleanor Roosevelt a veteran sleuth, thanks to son Elliott's numerous novels, but Teddy Roosevelt and Ben Franklin are also avid crime solvers. Here, Teddy tackles his third case, and Ben embarks on number two.

The Strenuous Life is set in 1895 with Teddy as police commissioner of New York City. A book in three parts, the action moves from New York City to Fort Sill, Oklahoma, and back to New York, as Roosevelt the reformer connects with John D. Rockefeller and Geronimo in dealing with two of his biggest problems: the Marquis de Morès and a heist at the 71st Armory. The fare is fun, the faces familiar, and the wrap-up leads right into what must be the next T. R. mystery—something about the deposed queen of the Hawaiian Islands, a pineapple plantation, and a murder. *You* figure it out.

Set a century earlier, Hall's book is played off as a personal diary of the author's great-great-great-great-great-great-grandfather. Thus, the text is written in the English language of the times (1757), and the action takes place in a historically accurate London. The reader is taken in immediately by a flawless combination of setting, characterization, dialogue, and plot. It all begins with Cassandra Fairbrass, who intrigues Franklin with her tales of late-night visits from ghosts (in which our scientist hero does not believe). When ghost-speak leads to murder, Franklin is off to catch the poisoner of Roderic Fairbrass, Cassandra's successful father. Dubious banking practices and a mysterious servant from the West Indies, who arrives during the Christmas season, also play roles. Always an interesting fellow, Ben Franklin, even at age 50 and stricken with gout, leads the reader on a madcap chase through the streets of London as his sidekick (B. F.'s awe-inspired and much-loved illegitimate son, Nicolas, from the first book) provides a running commentary.

With the help of their larger-than-life heroes, these novels inspire in the American reader a sense of our shared heritage. —*Kathryn LaBarbera*

Allegretto, Michael.
The Watchmen.
Simon & Schuster, $19 (0-671-73643-4). 253p.

Allegretto won the Shamus Award for his Jake Lomax series, and with *Night of Reunion* and now *The Watchmen*, he demonstrates his skill at nondetective suspense thrillers. No one in the Caylors' suburban neighborhood south of Los Angeles is demonically possessed—the dogs, cars, and other animate and inanimate objects do roughly what one would expect them to do. In this ever-so-normal setting, however, Lauren Caylor's life suddenly begins to go terribly wrong. A very peculiar couple rents the empty house across the street. A man in a blue car follows Lauren when she drives away from her office. Another unknown man appears repeatedly in the background of the photos she takes of her daughter and second husband at Sea World. Worst of all, when he spots someone at the entrance of the restaurant where they're eating, her thoughtful, loving husband first panics and then begins lying to her. Allegretto's characters are believable and involving, and he builds tension by making ordinary incidents profoundly threatening. Readers *may* figure out what's going on (there seem to be only a few possibilities), but will keep reading to find out whether the likable Caylors survive their scary situation. —*Mary Carroll*

Ambler, Eric.
Waiting for Orders: The Complete Short Stories of Eric Ambler.
Mysterious, $18.95 (0-89296-241-0). 144p.

The great spy-yarn spinner has written scads of novels but only these eight short stories, seven of them while waiting to find out what his place in Britain's war effort was going to be. He also wrote *Journey into Fear*, arguably his finest novel, during this period, so these should be prime stuff. The first, however, an episode in the heroics of the anti-Hitler German underground,

Mystery & Espionage

isn't. But the other six are. Given the collective title, "The Intrusions of Dr. Czissar," they're Ambler's only detective fiction. In each, a scholarly, refugee Czech policeman horns in on Scotland Yard—upon Assistant Commissioner Mercer, to be precise—and irrefutably proves it has muffed a murder case. The humorless Mercer is never, and the reader is always, amused. The eighth story is part of a never-completed novel. In it, the newly deposed president of a Latin American republic deftly manages to save his life and the fortune he's embezzled during his tenure. Full of the ironic, worldly-wise wit for which Ambler's prized, it's the kind of characteristic performance that becomes its author's anthology piece. —*Ray Olson*

Barnard, Robert.
A Scandal in Belgravia.
Scribner, $17.95 (0-684-19322-1). 218p.

The ever-popular British mystery writer bases this novel on an extremely workable premise. A former cabinet minister is writing his memoirs—a project he feels should come easily to him, except for one stumbling block. He can't quit thinking about Timothy Wycliffe, a young man he knew when both of them worked in the Foreign Office back in the 1950s. The thing is, Tim was murdered, and the narrator—the former minister—cannot get on with penning his autobiography until the nagging question of who actually did Tim in is settled in his mind. He goes off to do a latter-day inquiry, which leads him to Tim's family, friends since grown old, and police officers involved in the case. This novel is much less lighthearted than the usual Barnard fare, more a serious political novel than his customary social satire. But the investigative tension is predictably taut—and the ending is a double shocker. —*Brad Hooper*

Barnes, Linda.
Steel Guitar.
Delacorte, $18.50 (0-385-30013-1). 272p.

Carlotta Carlyle and Dee Willis share a past of boyfriends, blues licks, and bad luck. Now Carlotta hacks at night, sleuths by day, and just about makes ends meet. Dee went higher, then fell lower, blues singer to burn-out. Now cleaned up and climbing back to the top, she's hunting for an old partner and lover on the dark side of Boston's streets. Is her motive concern for a friend or the impending lawsuit that alleges she stole her best songs? Soon Carlotta is adding Dee's woes to her already hectic routine of cabbing, playing volleyball, learning the riffs to old blues standards, and getting cozy with her current boyfriend, a low-level mobster. *Steel Guitar* allows Barnes free reign to talk the blues: Gibson guitars, Vox AC30 amps, Fender basses. The novel starts at a delta crawl but soon gets up to 12-bar speed. More than Grafton and far more that Paretsky—the two writers she is most often compared with—Barnes manages to overcome the too-tough tendencies of her detective with salvos of self-deprecating wit: Carlotta pausing in mid-tailjob to check out a shoe sale (best to stock up when your dogs are size 11); Carlotta stuffing her handbag with fresh shrimp at a party for music-biz types. You never know when your luck will run dry, but Barnes ought to be able to buy her own chrimp tor quite a while. —*Peter Robertson*

Beaton, M. C.
Death of a Snob.
St. Martin's, $15.95 (0-312-05851-9). 192p.

Tousle-haired village bobby Hamish Macbeth finds himself at loose ends over Christmas and foolishly agrees to a trip to a health farm on a remote island. The voluptuous owner is worried about mysterious threats and adds Macbeth to the ragtag bunch of distant friends she has staying for the season. You know the sort: ex-husbands, fervent left-wingers, vain philanderers, a plump, besotted couple—in short, a prime batch of murder suspects. Death arrives on cue, leaving the ever-beleaguered Hamish to set the world right. Beaton mishandles the plot a bit in this sixth Macbeth adventure, adding her crime scenario far too late for absolute fairness, but the characters and atmosphere are as irresistible as ever: dour Scots aplenty, slovenly sleuthing, frighteningly foul weather, the occasional bad pint imbibed at the local, and, of course, romantic misfires all over the place. Seldom a dull moment; in fact, there's even a truck determined to kill its owner. —*Peter Robertson*

Begiebing, Robert J.
The Strange Death of Mistress Coffin.
Algonquin, $17.95 (0-945575-56-4). 252p.

A woman's battered body is pulled from a river. Her husband vanishes. The accused killer also flees. And there's a scent of witchcraft. What have we here? More hard-boiled fare straight from the mean streets? Not exactly. This oddly compelling account of adultery, crime, and punishment takes place in a seventeenth-century New England village. Based loosely on an actual incident that took place in New Hampshire, the novel uses the death of Mistress Coffin to expose a network of suppressed passion that extends to all the principals. Richard Browne, the newly transplanted Englishman who investigates the strange death, finds guilt wherever he looks: the victim was purported to be having an affair with the accused, who is assumed dead but is actually living with Indians; the victim's husband harbors his own regrets about his treatment of his wife; and let's not forget the accused's wife, who has become a much-sought-after widow now that her husband is out of the picture. And there's even Browne himself, who is among the "widow's" eager suitors. Algonquin is not known for mysteries, and this is no ordinary whodunit. Just imagine *Peyton Place* as Hawthorne might have written it. —*Peter Robertson*

Block, Lawrence.
A Dance at the Slaughterhouse.
Morrow, $19 (0-688-10349-9). 309p.

The world of Lawrence Block's maverick P.I. Matt Scudder is a dark one indeed—and we're talkin' Manhattan as cesspool, friend. This time around Scudder is hired by a man who's convinced that his sister was murdered by her cable-executive husband. The hunch seems like a good one, but in the course of his investigation Scudder descends into the depths of kiddie porn and snuff films, which, it turns out, definitely tie in to the case at hand. Scudder mopes about meditatively (and entertainingly), attends his AA meetings, hangs out with tarty girlfriend Elaine, takes advice from cop friend Joe Durkin, raises a glass (of tonic water) with hired-killer pal Mick Ballou, and generally attempts to sort out the murky life he leads. The conclusion is a bloody, yet satisfying, one, with Matt teetering on the up side of the down side. Strong stuff from a real pro. —*Martin Brady*

Bowers, Elisabeth.
No Forwarding Address.
Seal Press, $18.95 (1-878067-13-3). 271p.

Sherry Hovey takes her fears and her young son and vanishes, leaving her husband confused but more concerned with running his new restaurant, her parents angry and oddly defensive, and her co-workers perplexed but not especially surprised, considering Sherry's weird mood swings and general air of paranoia. But her sister is worried and hires Meg Lacey to track down the missing mother and child. Meg meets the hubby, talks to his protective friends, sits on a plastic-covered couch, and watches Sherry's near-alcoholic father order his wife around. Finally, a cab driver comes through with the desired information. Meg meets Sherry, who is plainly suffering and quite terrified. Hours later, she is dead from a brutal beating. This second Meg Lacey mystery delivers on the promise of the first, *Ladies Night.* The Vancouver, British Columbia, setting is fresh, the plotting precise, and the feminist themes of urban and familial horror powerful yet nicely understated. —*Peter Robertson*

Boyer, Rick.
Yellow Bird.
Ballantine/Fawcett Columbine, $18 (0-449-90506-3). 336p.

Oral surgeon Doc Adams is in the middle of a murder case again. While visiting an old medical-school chum on Cape Cod, Doc and wife Mary hear what sounds like a gunshot coming from a neighboring house. They snoop around but find nothing. Later, a body turns up, and Doc, in his role as oral forensics expert, identifies it as a friend of his. Coincidence, or did the murderer orchestrate Doc's involvement? Finding the answer requires unraveling switched identities, flirting dangerously close to marital infidelity, and confronting the killer in a showdown at a South Carolina beach house. After seven installments, the Doc Adams series is one of the most consistently entertaining in the genre. The plots rumble along unobtrusively, leaving us to concentrate on the interpersonal dynamics among Doc, Mary, and brother-in-law Joe, a Boston cop. Domestic life is at the core of the Doc Adams mysteries, and it is portrayed in all its complexity and with all its pain and pleasures—from bruised feelings and bouts of ennui through good smells in the kitchen and hearty, sustaining sex. Crime set against the battleground of daily life. —*Bill Ott*

Boyle, Thomas.
Brooklyn Three.
Viking, $18.95 (0-670-83019-4). 253p.

Murder One. Manslaughter Two. Brooklyn Three. You wouldn't want to be charged with any of them, but according to Francis ("The Saint") DeSales, a cop sentenced to walk the Brooklyn beat, "no matter how it comes out in the wash, the wrong guy gets screwed." Emotions reach the boiling point when a "man of color" runs for mayor of New York, and watermelon-wielding borough residents of mainly Italian descent register protest. While attempting to keep matters under control on the civil unrest front, DeSales also finds himself involved in a case that slides backwards in time to the radical sixties and to the improbably named Bono Hendrix—big muscles, big gun, big ego, a taste for drugs, and a score to settle. Back on the campaign trail, a provocative video is delivered to the candidate's home, and DeSales fends off racist killers and news-hungry media, not least his go-getting journalist girlfriend. This gritty, compelling novel, the third in a trilogy that also includes *Only the Dead Know Brooklyn* and *Post-Mortem Effects*, comes hard at the reader from several directions: Francis is anything but saintly, Bono is truly frightening, and the citywide mob mentality sounds all too real. Murder and manslaughter may carry stiffer penalties than being sentenced to Brooklyn, but only just. —*Peter Robertson*

Brashler, Anne.
Getting Jesus in the Mood.
Cane Hill, paper, $8.95 (0-943433-06-1). 106p.

If life is a fatal disease, the characters in Brashler's 17 stories don't know it; more accurately, they know life's limitations, but strongly prefer them to the alternative. Like John Cameron Swayze's Timex, they take a licking but keep on ticking. There is abuse and confusion and fear in these stories, but there is also toughness and resilience and unexpected love. Brashler's people find what they need to get by: the unhappy, overweight "heroine" of the title story takes a kind of solace from the Lord that the New Testament never discussed; aging, incontinent Mary Rhinegold (one of several Brashler characters who figure in more than one story in this collection) locates the "Duck Blind" from which she aims to shoot down the buzzard death; children in strange, dysfunctional families somehow manage to become (more or less) adult. Brashler, coeditor of *StoryQuarterly* and of its 1990 anthology, *The American Story*, provides no fairy tales here, no traditional happy endings. Her stories are snapshots of people for whom simply staying alive and struggling to be an individual are victories. —*Mary Carroll*

Breen, Jon L.
Hot Air.
Simon & Schuster, $19 (0-671-68105-2). 187p.

When he isn't compiling mystery anthologies, Jon Breen trots out a nifty line of crime tales that, like William Murray's, sparkle with pony lore and beg reviewers to make comparisons with a certain British jockey-turned-crime-novelist. *Hot Air* is fourth out of Breen's starting gate. It's a brisk, witty, occasionally tense canter through a rum collection of suspects in the charming company of Jerry Brogan, retired race announcer and sleuth on the side. Brogan is invited to Surfside Meadows to help celebrate the retirement of his nephew, jockey Brad Roark, who is going out in style with a last race, a flight in a hot-air balloon, and, despite Roark's own objections, a gathering of relatives. The reunion is being organized by a retired game-show host who is worrying over a TV documentary on fixed game shows (this also worries Brogan, since his wife was once a contestant). On top of all that, Surfside Meadows is awash in battling business interests. Could things get worse? Well ... how about the sudden expiration of one of Roark's relatives? Breen is lots of fun, knows his nags, and deserves at least one review that doesn't mention the name of Dick Francis. (Whoops!) —*Peter Robertson*

Brett, Simon.
Mrs. Pargeter's Package.
Scribner, $18.95 (0-684-19286-1). 288p.

Just as Brett's chronically unemployed yet remarkably active actor/sleuth Charles Paris never quite runs short of either gigs or stiffs, so the author's other series hero, the plumpish, elderly widow, Melita Pargeter, never runs short of her late husband's grateful business acquaintances, or to put it another way, his fellow criminals. That Mr. P. was a crook, albeit a popular and very successful one, allows his long-pampered and protected widow much unorthodox aid in the solving of copious dark deeds. *Package* has Mrs. P. in Greece, surrounded by disco-loving, culturally suspicious, package-holidaying English types. It's hardly by choice. Her friend, Joyce, asked her along. Depressed over the death of a mysterious rich husband that no one seems to have set eyes on, Joyce hits the ouzo with vigor, then dies in a manner suggesting suicide to the local punters. Avoiding the treacly simpering typical of so many British cozy mysteries, Brett keeps us chuckling with a steady stream of dryly noted cultural tidbits, while still supplying a wide-ranging plot that hangs together elegantly over a breathless 300 pages. *Package* boasts a near-fatal accident, messages in invisible ink, a nosy widow (well, two nosy widows, actually, one expired, one very much alive), plenty of repressed Anglo-Saxon frolicking in the balmy Aegean sun, and gallons of sustaining retsina close at hand. One thing about Simon Brett: he seldom wastes a word. —*Peter Robertson*

✔**Browne, Howard.**
Scotch on the Rocks.
St. Martin's, $14.95 (0-312-05509-9). 176p.

On the side of a dirt road in rural Texas, the Dawson family, recently the victims of a farm foreclosure, find salvation in the form of a bootlegger's bounty of single-malt Scotch (more rare than gold in these Prohibition times). Meanwhile, con man extraordinaire Lee Vance finds the Dawsons—his latest batch of prime suckers—and they set out together for Kansas City, where the scotch can be sold for sixty-thousand dollars. But first they must avoid the perils of the road: bouts of infighting, Dawson's wife's wanton desires, a crooked cop who tries to shanghai the booze, a bank robbery in a town where they stop, Vance's various detours for gambling, and an auto mechanic with a savage thirst. It's a lot of aggravation, but sixty thousand is a lot of cash, especially in 1932. Browne's first novel, *Pork City*, also utilized period set pieces to tell a compelling crime story; *Scotch* is set in the same era but with a different locale—less urban grit, more rural dust. *Pork City* was just fine; *Scotch on the Rocks* is even better. —*Peter Robertson*

Bruno, Anthony.
Bad Business.
Delacorte, $19 (0-385-29968-0). 288p.

The fourth darkly comic novel featuring mismatched but affectionate FBI partners Cuthbert Gibbons and Mike Tozzi continues the series' steady improvement. Both are tough, good agents, but Gibbons is 58, inching reluctantly towards retirement and a spit-and-polish, rules-and-regulations guy. Tozzi is in his mid-thirties, impetuous, impatient, and oftentimes suspended for . . . impatience and impetuousness. Thomas Augustine III is the assistant U.S. attorney from New York in charge of narcotics prosecutions. He wants to be mayor of New York City but doesn't have the money to mount a campaign. So he forges an alliance with the underworld to subtly sabotage any cases involving their members. But his web of financial support weakens when he sets up Tozzi to be the patsy in a key organized-crime trial. The main story line is always juxtaposed against Gibbons' domestic struggles with his new wife, Lorraine, who is Tozzi's cousin and tempermental equal. Much of the humor is generated by Gibbons' stoicism in the face of the Tozzi family fire. Solidly entertaining. —*Wes Lukowsky*

Burns, Rex.
Body Guard.
Viking, $18.95 (0-670-83320-7). 262p.

Here's the third mile-high sleuthing adventure for the low-rent, near-destitute Kirk and Associates. The title is, of course, somewhat grandiose. Devlin Kirk and muscle-bound, trigger-tempered Butch are the whole detecting team, although this time out they have a young kid, Chris, along for the ride. Kirk places Chris on a Denver factory floor, after a worried executive has hired him to investigate drug use in the factory. The principal evidence seems to be several severely stoned employees wandering round, slowing the production process and endangering life and limb. For a while Chris can't get close to the hub of the action. Then suddenly he gets too close. Unexpectedly a second paying gig opens up: a man is being followed and urgently requires bodyguarding services. At least that's what he tells Dev. Butch naturally can't wait to crack skulls. As in the past two Kirk capers (*Suicide Season* and *Parts Unknown*), the plot is slow to jell, and the author insists on one too many buttresses between subthemes. Still, Burns' Denver is becoming a top-notch crime locale, and, once underway, this tale is executed with both ferocity and finesse. —*Peter Robertson*

✔**Butler, Gwendoline.**
Coffin and the Paper Man.
St. Martin's, $16.95 (0-312-05835-7). 208p.

The uneasy infiltration of the new rich into the heretofore stolid domain of the old poor, London's Docklands, leads to threatening graffiti on walls, sleepless nights in trendy basement flats, scattered outbreaks of violence, and, inevitably, murder. The Docklands are the beat, the home, and the ever-present concern of high-ranking copper John Coffin. Naturally, when a local girl is raped and killed, Coffin takes a personal as well as a professional interest. On the road to solving the murder, Coffin shows us the underside of urban redevelopment—tensions percolating beneath the urbane surfaces of refurbished terrace houses, grudges nursed in squalid allotment flats. And then there's the Paper Man, taunting Coffin and his bobbies with a rare kind of knowledge. Butler's *Coffin* chronicles continue to stake out new territory in the crossbreeding of two genres: the police procedural and the psychological thriller. As in the past (*Coffin in Fashion, Coffin on the Water*), the author manages the tricky feat of advancing her narrative entirely through understatement: oblique conversations eventually reveal everything. There is nothing overt, yet nothing is left to chance. In five Coffin novels, Butler has yet to put a foot wrong. —*Peter Robertson*

Campbell, Robert.
In a Pig's Eye.
Pocket, $19 (0-671-70327-7). 217p.

Jimmy Flannery is moving up in the world, which, if you're a Chicago sewer inspector, is probably a good thing. Now Democratic committeeman for the twenty-seventh ward, Flannery is munching donuts in a storefront and listening to voters' problems, almost all of which seem to concern teenage pregnancy. Soon the red-haired, anachronistic sewer man is dragged by his crusading wife, Mary, who just happens to be pregnant, into the middle of the volatile abortion debate. There's also the matter of the rotund man with Italian currency in his pockets who drops dead at Jimmy's health club. A simple heart attack? Maybe, but why do his eyes look so funny? Embroiled in yet another murder case, Flannery makes good use of his most reliable investigative tool—the age-old Chicago custom of favors begged and granted. Though *Pig's Eye*, the eighth work in the series, features a less coherent plot and a lot more moralizing than many of its predecessors, Flannery remains a beguiling blend of cunning, chivalry, and wide-eyed innocence in a city that is itself an uneasy juxtaposition of old political orders, new kinds of crime, and ever-changing neighborhoods. —*Peter Robertson*

Cape, Tony.
The Last Defector.
Doubleday, $20 (0-385-41572-9). 400p.

Cape follows his first and splendidly received thriller, *The Cambridge Theorem,* with a reprise of spy-guy Derek Smailes, who finds himself this time working for British intelligence at the United Nations in New York.

Smailes—espionage hero of great and compelling dimensions—is involved in enticing a Soviet arms-control expert to defect at a tense time when the U.S. and the USSR are on the verge of putting names to paper on a demilitarization treaty. Of course—given the nature of the genre—nothing proceeds smoothly; specifically, British agents are being offed, and Smailes is in hot water for their murders. His extraction from the sticky situation amounts to a fast, intelligent novel perfect for avid readers of Deighton and le Carré. —*Brad Hooper*

Charyn, Jerome.
Elsinore.
Mysterious, $18.95 (0-89296-361-1). 208p.

Holden's a New York legend. He shuns publicity, but it sticks to him like a cheap suit. A retired hitman, he's living in splendid isolation, romancing a famous artist's unstable wife whose DA father has just taken her to a spot in the country for some "rest." So Holden has some time on his hands when one of Manhattan's richest men, Howard Phipps, comes calling. Phipps wants Holden to help him retrieve some illicit dough obtained in the tycoon's younger days and now sorely needed, as his empire faces attack from surprising sources—including his lawyer, who is also his daughter. Charyn cavalierly pitches his trusting reader into this dense narrative thicket with very little explanation or background. The effect is initially disconcerting, but soon the enigmatic Holden proves to be a pleasant addiction, a veritable superman of crime. This is no ordinary mystery novel, to be sure, but those with a taste for the unconventional will recognize it as a baroque masterpiece of perverse wit. —*Peter Robertson*

Chesbro, George C.
The Fear in Yesterday's Rings.
Mysterious, $18.95 (0-89296-396-4). 224p.

Chesbro's Mongo novels have a recipe. Villains are larger-than-life, James Bond–like megalomaniacs who threaten civilization as we know it with some form of new technology. After a couple of incredibly harrowing encounters, the diminutive but redoubtable Dr. Robert Frederickson, aka "Mongo the Magnificent," cuts those evildoers down to size. Mongo, you see, is a dwarf. He's also a famous private eye, a former star circus aerialist, a former professor of criminology, an animal empath, and—surprise!—a neurotic overachiever. This time, the recipe is seasoned with a love interest—a gorgeous snake charmer from his circus days. The father-and-son villains deal in "bioweapons"; they have reverse-bred wolves and dogs to re-create the lobox, an animal that supposedly killed off Neanderthal man. Mongo is hunted by the deadly beasts and must use his unique talents to avoid becoming a lobox lunch before he can restore peace and order to the Midwest. Incredible as it may sound, this one is more credible than the last three or four Mongos. Here's hoping faithful fans aren't disappointed. —*Thomas Gaughan*

Mystery & Espionage

Clancy, Tom.
The Sum of All Fears.
Putnam, $24.95 (0-399-13615-0). 800p.

Clancy, like the real-life spies, soldiers, and politicians who read him, is coming to terms with a new world, one without a monolithic Communist menace. In *The Sum of All Fears*, so is Clancy's hero, deputy director of Central Intelligence Jack Ryan. And so are European and Middle Eastern terrorists. Ryan has engineered a Middle East settlement that provides a home for the Palestinians and security for all. Suddenly, the terrorists are without their East bloc and Arab patrons and without a reason for being. Serendipitously acquiring an Israeli nuke lost during the 1973 October War, Palestinian and German terrorists develop a plan to get even with the whole, unreliable world. *The Sum of All Fears* is big, complex, tautly plotted, and a not-impossible extrapolation from the *geopolitik* of today. As in earlier books, Clancy handles narrative, action scenes, and especially submarines and things naval with wonderful skill. Ryan's still better with machines than people, but his job stress is effectively developed. This is classic Clancy, and that's just about as good as it gets in his genre. —*Thomas Gaughan*

Collins, Max Allan.
Stolen Away.
Bantam, $21.95 (0-553-07133-5); paper, $9.95 (0-553-35233-4).

Collins, a prodigious crime author and writer of the syndicated "Dick Tracy" comic strip, has expertly mined the historical crime novel before, notably in his tales of Eliot Ness' early years. He's usually a taut plotter and a relentless researcher, though a somewhat limited stylist. In *Stolen Away*, he takes his best, most idiosyncratic fictional creation, smart-mouthed, semihonest, gam-chasing Chicago cop Nate Heller, and puts him square in the center of maybe the crime of the century—the Lindbergh kidnapping. As always, Collins locks his characters firmly into place: the youthful and emotionally beaten Lindy, the wise-guy Heller—in the picture because of suspected underworld connections to the kidnapping—and a dense forest of dopey police drudges screwing up the investigation and rubbing Nate the wrong way. Collins takes a while to develop the focus of his story, but the clues fall thick and fast: psychics predict the rising amount of the ransom, giving Nate the opportunity to bed a sultry young clairvoyant; a pompous Brooklyn professor becomes a scene-stealing go-between; and a rich society dame in a ratty, one-dollar Sears housecoat has another theory. Nate moves gamely through the various scenarios, cracking droll and wise, always aware of the sudden flash of a stockinged leg and the chance for a spot of honest graft. While Collins may overreach a bit here—his narrative is convoluted to the point of distraction—he has a good thing going in Nate Heller. —*Peter Robertson*

Cook, Thomas H.
Evidence of Blood.
Putnam, $19.95 (0-399-13668-1). 320p.

You can never go home again, but in Cook's white-hot novel, true-crime writer Jackson Kinley tries to—to the backwoods Georgia town of Sequoyah where his boyhood pal and local cop Ray Tindall dies of a massive heart attack in a lonely canyon. After the funeral, Kinley goes through his pal's old papers and relives his final days. He also recalls Tindall's affair and his obsession. The mysterious woman is the daughter of a murderer, executed 40 years ago for the killing of a young girl—a crime that has resonated through the years and now sends Kinley on a journey his profession has only partly prepared him for: the absence of a body, a green dress soaked in blood, small-town justice moving swiftly and dogmatically. . . . Cook himself is from a small southern town and is a true-crime writer (*Early Graves*) as well as a best-selling, Edgar-nominated author. He is also a master crime craftsman whose prolific and divergent output might blind the reader to just how good he really is. *Evidence* is slow to build but blistering by the climax. —*Peter Robertson*

D'Amato, Barbara.
Hard Tack.
Scribner, $17.95 (0-684-19299-3). 244p.

Cat Marsala's second appearance in print is set aboard a luxury yacht but retains all the familiar trappings of a locked-room mystery. The Chicago journalist accepts an assignment to do a life-styles-of-the-rich-and-famous story aboard the *Easy Girl* on a cruise across Lake Michigan. Not only does the weather take a turn for the worse, but so does the health of a crew member, discovered in a locked cabin with his throat cut. D'Amato's inventive approach to a classic mystery form resonates through all aspects of the book. The setting may be wet, but the humor is dry and the writing excellent. To assist landlocked readers, a glossary of nautical terms is appended. —*Elliott Swanson*

✔Dibdin, Michael.
Dirty Tricks.
Summit, $18 (0-671-69545-2). 248p.

After a decade or so of Margaret Thatcher, England is no longer the same: the wrong people are in charge and near-penniless academics have been reduced to the role of token intellectuals at bad dinner parties. On the other hand, such parties can have their compensations: for our narrator, for example, getting to drink the overpriced wine and being seduced by Karen doesn't seem half bad. Nor does the thought of her husband's substantial life insurance. So Dibdin (author of the tricky, subversive, neo-Dickensian *The Tryst*) draws us into this superficially farcical satire, undergirded by substrata of understated evil. His narrator is charming, frequently funny (Dibdin is awesomely skilled in the British school of apt but wicked wit), and very bad. Perhaps not as bad as the simple facts of this would-be multiple murder would indicate, but bad enough. Sexual boldness seems to be a British narrative trademark these days, and Karen is certainly ever available. But our hero, too, is greedy for the life he thinks should be his—sans wallies, sans lumpen proles/sluts like Karen, sans her dreary hubby, sans her virile new lover Clive—and in a twisted sort of way he gets his wishes, though in a quite unexpected manner. A droll delight from start to finish. —*Peter Robertson*

Dibdin, Michael.
Vendetta.
Doubleday, $18.50 (0-385-42120-6). 288p.

Despite winning back-to-back Golden Dagger awards in Britain, Michael Dibdin is only now emerging from near-obscurity on this side of the pond, thanks to the recent appearance of two critically acclaimed novels, *The Tryst* and *Dirty Tricks. Vendetta* makes it a hat trick for this multitalented writer. The novel stars Aurelio Zen of Italy's Ministry of the Interior, a much put-upon investigator who must contend with a home-ridden mother, a back-stabbing bunch of fellow cops, and an unrequited passion for a younger woman. There's also the case at hand: the multiple shooting of a rich industrialist and his three dinner guests, preserved on video by the dead man's home-security system. From the onset, Zen is tugged two ways: his superiors would clearly like the crime solved one way, while the harassed inspector finds himself forced to take things rather more personally, as he is ineptly tailed, robbed, and given cryptic messages. Dibdin cuts periodically to his killer: disturbed reveries, chillingly extended passion and pain. For the reader, the crime is clearly unsolvable, yet the occasional clue still manages to tantalize. The solution arrives fast and a bit pat, but Dibdin effectively blends the politics with the paranoia. —*Peter Robertson*

Donaldson, D. J.
Blood on the Bayou.
St. Martin's, $16.95 (0-312-05387-8). 240p.

A werewolf in the French Quarter? An unlikely premise, perhaps, but hardly any more unlikely than the daily parade of hurricane-drinking grandmas wandering down Bourbon Street wearing T-shirts promoting oral sex. Donaldson, author of the voodoo-drenched *Cajun Nights*, knows there's something in the air in New Orleans that melts inhibitions the way sweat soaks the starch out of a shirt collar—and he knows how to use that Big Easy atmosphere to give a mystery novel an extra charge. New Orleans Medical Examiner Andy Broussard and psychologist Kit Franklin are fast becoming one of mystery fiction's most engaging duos; here they are confronted with a serial killer whose bloody m.o. suggests a rampant case of lycanthropy (werewolfism). That the trail leads to some hungry alligators and to a childhood friend of Broussard's from the Bayou serves to make the gumbo all the more piquant. A forensic pathologist himself, Donaldson combines an insider's knowledge of modern medical technology with a real flair for making the reader's skin crawl. —*Bill Ott*

Doolittle, Jerome.
Strangle Hold.
Pocket, $20 (0-671-70754-X). 159p.

Doolittle's Tom Bethany returns, just as cynical and even more prickly than in the much-praised *Body Scissors*. This time, he's investigating the death of a rich young man who has named the ACLU as beneficiary on his life-insurance policy. The insurance company's right-wing president, Warren Westfall, is denying the claim, calling the death a suicide. Bethany's involved because his married lover is an ACLU attorney who was once sexually assaulted by the despicable Westfall. *Strangle Hold* is terrific! Fully a dozen characters, most notably the Harvard constitutional law scholar and the odious insurer, are wonderfully well developed. Doolittle's Boston is alternately gritty and charming, and his dialogue is as crisp as the leaves that fall in Harvard Yard in October. Best, though, is Bethany: he's Travis McGee without the pontification, Spenser with an *attitude*. His righteous thuggery against Westfall and his minions is startling, cruel, and ultimately satisfying. —*Thomas Gaughan*

✔Duffy, Brian.
Head Count.
Putnam, $19.95 (0-399-13669-X). 240p.

An African republic on the verge of collapse; a gaggle of out-of-work Eastern European terrorists helping to foment a coup; a wily cop battling bureaucracy and insurrection with the help of a childhood friend turned expatriate FBI agent—yes, it sounds like that special blend of cynicism and Third World politics that Ross Thomas has made his own, but, in fact, it's a delightful first novel by the most impressive newcomer to hit the thriller genre since the Berlin Wall crumbled. Humberto Gub, chief of detectives in the African capital of Fado, has his hands full—of severed heads. They keep turning up in the most indelicate of places: on the curb of the city's busiest street, on the diving board of the only fancy hotel, and even in Gub's refrigerator. In order to stop the flow of heads, Gub must address the larger issue—how to quell the insurrection and bring some sort of order to his imperiled country. Like Thomas, Duffy excels not only at dramatizing the machinations of international politics, but also at exposing the human absurdities that politicians invariably leave in their wake. Brian Duffy is a name to remember—the world can always use another Ross Thomas. —*Bill Ott*

Dunlap, Susan.
Rogue Wave.
Villard, $18 (0-394-58524-0). 272p.

The storm crashes over the boat. The drunken mate is washed overboard; the skipper vanishes in the storm. Investigation matches the blood type of the missing sailor with the driver in a hit-and-run that, years before, left a provocative artist with no short-term memory. *Rogue Wave* quickly draws the reader into a tight, sleek plot inlaid with several sections of quietly stated power. And Kiernan O'Shaughnessy—no longer a practicing medical ex-

Mystery & Espionage

Mystery & Espionage

aminer but hired here to draw the threads together—has the requisite romantic troubles: a valuable medical source is also a former lover, while passion seems to be stirring anew with the hunky ex-jock currently acting as her personal chef, roomie, and confidant. It is unfortunate that aspects of Dunlap's work echo other crime writers—the Bay Area locale (Marcia Muller), the in-depth forensic detail (Patricia Cornwell), and the plucky resolve of her female detective (an ever-growing list that only begins with Sue Grafton)—because her work stands very well on its own. —*Peter Robertson*

Easterman, Daniel.
Night of the Seventh Darkness.
HarperCollins, $22.95 (0-06-017928-7). 464p.

See p.369.

Elkins, Aaron.
A Glancing Light.
Scribner, $18.95 (0-684-19278-0). 368p.

Chris Norgren, museum curator and amateur sleuth, returns in another new mystery set in the intriguingly insular universe of classical art. When a stolen masterpiece surfaces in a shipment of inexpensive copies, Chris verifies its authenticity but questions the involvement of the seemingly innocent importer. During a business trip to Bologna, his suspicions are confirmed when he discovers the renowned art squad of the Italian carbinieri is conducting an investigation of a series of related thefts and forgeries. As the elaborate scam begins to unravel, Chris becomes the target of a desperately cunning colleague. An intelligent and superbly crafted caper from an acclaimed Edgar-winning author. —*Margaret Flanagan*

Emerson, Earl.
Yellow Dog Party.
Morrow, $19 (0-688-09635-2). 288p.

Emerson's thoroughly entertaining, consistently offbeat Thomas Black series features labyrinthine plots that, Ross Macdonald–fashion, expose multiple layers of old wounds and unresolved conflicts extending far back into the characters' pasts. This sixth in the series is no exception. It starts with a seemingly trivial premise that soon turns lethal: four Seattle businessmen, friends since high school, hire Black to track down and then arrange blind dates with the women of their dreams, who range from local newscasters to former nude models to the gal in an adjacent box seat at the Kingdome. It turns out that one of the businessmen has arranged the whole "dream woman" scenario to find someone who knows a dirty secret about his past. Black, with the help of longtime platonic pal Kathy Birchfield, sorts it all out with the requisite amounts of tough talk, hard-boiled sensitivity, and silly horseplay (an Emerson specialty). Fans of the series will be especially interested in the finale, which suggests that the Black-Birchfield alliance is soon to turn nonplatonic. In the best prime-time tradition, though, we'll have to wait till the next installment to satisfy our prurient interest. —*Bill Ott*

Estleman, Loren D.
Motown.
Bantam, $19 (0-553-07421-0). 304p.

This second in Estleman's Detroit trilogy (following *Whiskey River*) moves forward from running guns and booze in the 1930s to hanging loose in the 1960s, complete with bad clothes, afros, and candy-apple red GTOs. Estleman seems more intent here on paying homage to the Motor City than on writing a mystery. Place is more important for Estleman than action, though this time several workable plots merge forcefully toward the novel's conclusion. One car-obsessed ex-cop is lured into spying on a consumerist organization wreaking havoc on the auto companies by promoting the implementation of weird safety devices like airbags and seat belts. Meanwhile, a crooked cop is enlisted by some Mafia-linked hoodlums caught up in a nasty fight with black gangs over control of street crime, numbers, and prostitution. The other side of the dispute is captured in the dilemmas facing Quincy Springfield, a black hustler with a philosophic bent, who faces hard times, broken fingers, and the absence of a good woman. Details power the action: long, straight roads that run from ghetto to old money mansions and back again. And then there are the cars. The lure of a chrome-covered T-Bird ends one cop's career, but a canary-yellow Z28 Camaro gets him back in the game. —*Peter Robertson*

Evers, Crabbe.
Murderer's Row.
Bantam, paper, $3.99 (0-553-29088-6). 240p.

Retired-sportswriter-turned-sleuth Duffy House first appeared in *Murder in Wrigley Field*. At the conclusion of that entertaining case, ol' Duffy thought he was done with murder. Well, he's not, because someone bushwhacked the obnoxious owner of the New York Yankees, Rupert Huston. Baseball commissioner Granville Chambliss asks Duffy to investigate on the game's behalf. Duffy agrees and, in his curmudgeonly fashion, sniffs out killer and motive. Despite the light tone, silly names, and baseball anecdotes, this is a fairly suspenseful and tricky whodunit. Incidentally, half the team that is Crabbe Evers is William Brashler, of *Bingo Long* fame. Enjoyable summer reading. —*Wes Lukowsky*

Follett, Ken.
Night over Water.
Morrow, $22 (0-688-04660-6). 400p.

The eminently talented and versatile Follett succeeds his massive historical epic, *The Pillars of the Earth*, with a suspenseful World War II–era thriller. The primary action takes place aboard a transatlantic flight of the Pan American Clipper bound for New York. The cast of characters who board the sumptuous seaplane in Southhampton includes an aristocratic Nazi sympathizer and his family, a renowned Jewish physicist, an American film star, an affable jewel thief, a bored housewife and her lover, and a Russian princess. The celebrated wayfarers are blissfully unaware that Eddie Deakin, the all-American aviation engineer, is being forced to sabotage the flight in order to necessitate a dangerous crash landing off the coast of Maine. Eddie is placed in the untenable position of choosing between betraying the trust his crewmates have placed in him or risking the safety of his pregnant wife, who is being held hostage by a gang of vicious thugs. As the tension mounts, a variety of romantic subplots are hatched, uniting the hapless travelers into a cohesive unit bound by the vagaries of circumstance and love. Follett underscores this taut adventure with a wealth of authentic detail that successfully evokes the bygone elegance and glamour of the legendary luxury airliner. —*Margaret Flanagan*

Francis, Dick.
Comeback.
Putnam, $21.95 (0-399-13670-3). 320p.

A chance encounter with an embassy cohort leads career diplomat Peter Darwin to a Miami nightclub, where he befriends an elderly English couple. After a mugging attack in the street, the newly formed threesome travels back to England together, where more trouble awaits. Soon Darwin is helping the old lady's son-in-law save his veterinary practice. He's up against both a crumbling reputation (several valuable horses have died on the operating table) and a crumbling building—the result of an arson attack. For Darwin, the whole caper is a chance to use the tricks a diplomat learns by necessity: cunning, watchfulness, flattery, and bold-faced fibbing on occasion. It's also a chance for childhood memories to resurface—some warm, some cold—both of his splintered family and of the local racetrack at Cheltenham, where he dreamed of jockeying. Though Francis is renowned for streamlined narrative, it takes him a little longer than usual this time to shift into high gear. Still, once on track, he keeps his readers jumping. —*Peter Robertson*

Friedman, Kinky.
Musical Chairs.
Morrow, $18.95 (0-688-09148-2). 288p.

Someone's whacking the Jewboys of Texas. You mean, the Kinkster's old band? That shower of degenerate multiethnic hosebags who got kicked out of every low-rent watering hole between the left and right coasts? Yup, that's them. Naturally, Kinky's concerned. Not concerned enough to change lifestyle, quit firing up the old stogies, slugging down Jamesons, hitting on the lesbian dance teacher in the loft upstairs, and gleefully insulting every ethnic, social, and sexually orientated group under the sun. But concerned enough to start worrying, especially when guitar player Tequila meets his maker in Kinky's shower. The Kinkster organizes a reunion tour of the Jewboys, figuring that at least all the potential victims will be in one place. There's also a subplot about the male lover of the dance teacher's female lover, who may or may not be a psycho killer. In Kinky tales (this is the fifth in the series), the plot is either (a) an excuse for Kinky to talk or (b) actually worth paying attention to. This time Kinky definitely takes the A train. Not to worry, the best stuff is always Kinky in full verbal flow: on Oscar Wilde (good), Andy Warhol (bad), the little-known art style called rectal realism (best not to ask), and women (always very good, especially unattainable lesbians). Best line? Kinky getting a table at an eatery with the statement "Sirhan Sirhan, tablo for one." Special award? *Musical Chairs* may well contain the most references to the word *scrotum* in a nonmedical context. —*Peter Robertson*

Gash, Jonathan.
The Great California Game.
St. Martin's, $19.95 (0-312-06363-6). 288p.

Lovejoy's on the lam in the Big Apple. His attempt to pose as a Yank isn't working (he keeps calling everybody "Guv"), and the new culture both attracts and intimidates him (too much ice in drinks, too much direct conversation, too many knowing women), but when he isn't putting a value on a priceless antique piece (and figuring out a way to purloin it), Lovejoy's a beguiling blend of sangfroid and naïveté. Hired by sundry rich types to do some butlering, he spots a fake at a soiree and is soon eyebrow deep in an involved scam. There's talk of missing Conan Doyle manuscripts, but Lovejoy can smell a red herring when he steps on one, and as usual he's working to make sure the action comes his way. Gash's first-person narrative fairly sizzles (Lovejoy can cut the heart out of any twit or empty-headed bird in about three well-chosen words), and now that British telly has put Lovejoy in a miniseries, perhaps there's hope that PBS will soon hoist him fully into the crime limelight, where he definitely belongs. —*Peter Robertson*

✓George, Elizabeth.
A Suitable Vengeance.
Bantam, $19 (0-553-07407-5). 384p.

From the first favorable reviews of George's debut novel, *A Great Deliverance*, the comparisons to P. D. James have flown thick and fast. George, like James, has an enigmatic, high-ranking, emotionally guarded New Scotland Yard copper for a hero. Also in common with James, George plots with an icy precision, sinks moral land mines at will, and conveys a wealth of subtext and emotional undercurrent beneath clipped utterances and mannered British voices. George takes her enthusiastic readers straight to the bruised heart of her detective, the to-the-manor-born Thomas Lynley. Here, George goes back in time, before Lynley acquired his proletariat sidekick, Barbara Havers. Lynley brings his beloved Deborah to the ancestral home in Cornwall to meet his estranged mother; his drug-addicted brother, Peter; his mother's longtime lover; and Peter's wreck of a girlfriend, Sasha. Sundry others, including forensic expert Simon St. James, are along for the ride. The kills start with the nonsurgical castration of a local newspaperman. Then one of Lynley's party falls from a convenient cliff. George segues from tangled passions (Lynley and St. James battling like repressed English gentlemen for the hand of the fair Deb) to recreational drugs to industrial drugs (a late plot addition that ties in the two murders and a third surprise villain) to a spot of cross-dressing. George's library following is on the rise; this tale offers the evidence why. —*Peter Robertson*

Mystery & Espionage

✔Gercke, Doris.
How Many Miles to Babylon.
Women in Translation, paper, $8.95 (1-879679-02-7). 103p.

Middle-aged and opinionated, female Hamburg police detective Bella Block does not lightly countenance fools or departmental sycophants. Following a series of unusual deaths in the quaint village where Bella maintains a small cottage for summer peccadilloes, she's assigned to take a working vacation and do some low-profile snooping. The village's bucolic facade begins to crumble as Bella draws closer to the criminal—a woman out for revenge following a nightmarish act of sexual brutality. When the gap is finally closed, Bella reaches one of the turning points in her life. She must decide between maintaining her integrity as a police officer or siding with the criminal. There are five other Bella Block mysteries in print in Germany, which, unfortunately, have never been translated. Let's hope they reach the U.S. as soon as possible. This is an outstanding series, and, showcased properly, Bella has the potential to become one of the most memorable characters in police-procedural fiction. —*Elliott Swanson*

Gill, B. M.
The Fifth Rapunzel.
Scribner, $19.95 (0-684-19389-2). 288p.

The blows fall hard on the young shoulders of 18-year-old Simon Bradshaw. Both his parents die in an automobile accident, and then his mourning is disrupted by a woman with long dark hair, who interrupts the funeral service and later invades Simon's home. Simon falls in love with his enigmatic house guest, but she seems distracted by the mysterious pasts of Simon's parents—especially his pathologist father, whose evidence convicted a man accused of the serial killing of five long-haired prostitutes. Multiple Edgar nominee Gill confronts the reader with a daunting array of secret pasts and off-kilter characters. Chief Inspector Tom Maybridge, attempting to conduct the investigation, hangs suspended above the action like a hapless marionette. By virtually dispensing with the traditional role of the detective, Gill may offend some, but she will win over just as many by deftly whipping up a lush palate of narrative colors, essaying bit parts with panache, and blending the whole with exacting detail. A poignant exploration of the end of innocence. —*Peter Robertson*

Gorman, Ed.
The Night Remembers.
St. Martin's, $16.95 (0-312-05482-3). 240p.

Perhaps because his sinewy prose lacks the kind of Chandlerian flourish that draws a crowd, Ed Gorman's advance into the upper echelons of crime writers has been sluggish. His latest is more of the same—subtle, ironic, never flashy, a sad tale light on handwringing pathos. The wife of an ex-con whom aging Cedar Rapids sleuth Jack Walsh sent to prison hires him to set the record straight. Jack is hesitant. Then a woman's body is discovered in the man's gazebo. Suddenly, George Pennyfeather is a murder suspect all over again, and Jack takes the case. Meanwhile, Jack, widowed in his early sixties, finds his slow emotional rebirth threatened when his much-younger girlfriend discovers a lump in her breast. Whether dealing with personal crises or following the murderer's trail to a child-pornography business, Jack is the kind of sleuth who is forever dogged by somber truths and bitter ironies. He grows on you, and so does Gorman, who, although not a ground breaker, tills the genre's familiar soil with care. —*Peter Robertson*

Gosling, Paula.
Death Penalties.
Mysterious Press, $17.95 (0-89296-458-8). 304p.

A car accident leaves a man dead and a son traumatized. Widowed interior designer Tess Leland must care for her boy and deal with the financial ruins left by her quixotic, flamboyant spouse. It isn't easy, what with the break-ins and the anonymous phone calls demanding money (What money for God's sake?). The police say there's nothing to investigate, but intrepid young sergeant Tim Nightingale is soon sleuthing away on his own time. Ranking detective Luke Abbott initially puts Nightingale's suspicions down to too much Sherlock Holmes, but soon even Abbott is alerted to danger. Somewhere in the dead man's full life a little secret refuses to lie down quietly. Paula Gosling has garnered several awards and a loyal following. She also has a ready wit, a cast of cynical coppers you can't help but like, and plots with the exacting precision of an ordinance survey map. —*Peter Robertson*

Grady, James.
River of Darkness.
Warner, $19.95 (0-446-51554-X). 406p.

Grady's new novel rises above the formulaic approach of many spy thrillers. A CIA agent with knowledge of enough dirty deals to turn the entire organization upside down breaks and runs. A squeaky clean Annapolis grad is sent to hunt him down by the Naval Investigative Service. But in this upside-down world where betrayals are the norm, even the hunter makes a great target. Covert U.S. intelligence scenarios intertwine with the drug trade and other unconscionable activities and are rendered with frightening realism. Grady, author of *Six Days of the Condor*, presents a striking vision of the wheels driving some of the CIA's headline-making fiascoes. Through characters who have real depth, the novel engenders cause for concern about the actions of a secret army operating beyond the law. —*Elliott Swanson*

Granger, Bill.
Drover.
Morrow, $20 (0-688-09856-8). 288p.

In order to bring down a gambler who caused the suicide of a pal, Jimmy Drover must get friendly with a mobster. As a strategy, this has definite problems: after all, it was Mob connections that got the former Chicago

Mystery & Espionage

Mystery & Espionage

sportswriter kicked out of journalism. The sting on the gambler works fine, although he comes back for revenge. Meanwhile, Drover is swimming in darker waters; the fix, engineered by two Chicago traders, is on for the Denver–New Orleans football game, and Denver's skirt-addicted, ego-obsessed quarterback is in line for the fall. As game day draws near, the QB beds a very bad girl, a size-four model who spends much of her life on her knees doing lines in bathrooms; Drover falls for his ex, a stewardess with a tempting overbite; the traders start a rumor about the QB; the commissioner orders drug tests; and the traders lay off big-money bets with a Louisiana contact. Granger hasn't written dialogue that power-shifts like this in a while: street-level ironies, greed, cunning, stupidity, all unleashed in clipped utterances. He seldom overplays his hand, and the action is a blur of lies and locales (Drover jumps between Chicago, the East Coast, and New Orleans). In this first in a new crime series, Drover takes us into some weird places, both geographical and psychological, all far beyond the gridiron. —*Peter Robertson*

Gray, A. W.
The Man Offside.
Dutton, $18.95 (0-525-93310-7). 240p.

When former Dallas Cowboy star Rick Bannion refuses to squeal to the feds, he does the full stretch. Then he gets out, and trouble finds him again. The wife of a friend and former teammate asks Rick to convince a lowlife drug dealer to miss a bail hearing; Rick does the job, but his friend gets whacked leaving the courthouse. The feds show up again, anxious for Rick to tell them about his dead pal's drug-running cohorts, but Rick isn't ready to squeal this time, either. The only way out is to find the killer himself. Gray, author of three previous crime novels (including *In Defense of Judges*), understands perfectly the delicate balance of sudden violence, surprising tenderness, and dark-edged irony that drives the genre. He gives us stone killers who suddenly go soft, chumps who suddenly get smart, loyalty in hard places, mayhem where you least expect it. Like Elmore Leonard, Gray also possesses the rare gift of making the reader tremble with the anticipation of bloodshed and chortle at caustic, black-hearted humor, all within the space of one sentence. —*Peter Robertson*

Hall, Robert Lee.
Ben Franklin and a Case of Christmas Murder.
St. Martin's, $17.95 (0-312-05383-5). 288p.

See p.370.

✔**Hall, James W.**
Bones of Coral.
Knopf, $20 (0-679-40017-6). 320p.

Key West: "A succulent bauble dangling 150 miles from the safety of the mainland. Too far away to feel the real effects of the land. An outpost for the unstable, maladjusted, the just plain insane." There are plenty of all three in

Hall's latest thriller, which takes the idea of Florida as a metaphor for sun-dried craziness to new heights. In *Skin Tight*, Carl Hiaasen created what seemed to be the ideal Florida villain with his quack plastic surgeon, master of the lethal nose job, but Hall may have gone him one better with crime fiction's deadliest and most outrageous father-son combo: Douglas Barnes, retired military man and now operator of the Key West dump, into which he obligingly deposits various dangerous chemicals the navy wants to get rid of ("Whatever happened to the idea of getting tougher by being exposed to toxins?"), and son Dougie, a muscular, mentally retarded wacko whose notion of a good time is "munching and crunching" things, mainly garbage with a bulldozer or human beings with his hands. Into the Barnes boys' clutches falls Shaw Chandler, a fireman whose attempt to make sense of his father's suspicious death leads first to the rekindling of a high school romance and finally to a surrealistic showdown at the dump. The image of a frenzied Dougie munching and crunching with near-sexual abandon while Shaw and his lover bounce from trash heap to trash heap in an effort to evade the bulldozer's mechanical jaws is likely to remain with most readers for some time. Hall's vision of Florida in the grip of garbage and garbage collectors is more than just Paradise Lost; it's Paradise Berserked. —*Bill Ott*

Hammond, Gerald.
Let Us Prey.
St. Martin's, $15.95 (0-312-05891-8). 192p.

The body of a gamekeeper is found near a large quantity of strong poison used illegally to kill birds of prey. There are hints of a married woman somewhere on the horizon, and a local animal-rights fanatic and an unpopular falconer are shedding no tears. Then there's the victim's employer: a struggling landowner running a shooting syndicate. Local gunsmith-sleuth Keith Calder once again finds himself with an unauthorized killing in the heart of Scottish border country. Hammond's Calder chronicles feature an appealing lightness of tone and no shortage of tweedy country types wading through thick heather spouting shooting and farming lore. This time, the narrator is elderly solicitor Ralph Enterkin, who tires easily, distrusts cars, and whose plump wife, Penny, tending bar at the local hostelry, is privy to a wealth of information, sometimes gospel and sometimes gossip. The eccentric Enterkin teams with Calder to solve the mystery and add another winner to a first-rate series. —*Peter Robertson*

Hammond, Gerald.
Whose Dog Are You?
St. Martin's, $15.95 (0-312-05536-6). 192p.
Steed, Neville.
Wind Up.
St. Martin's, $16.95 (0-312-05998-1). 224p.

The trick is to make the reader care about a subject in which he or she normally has no interest. It isn't easy, but certain mystery writers seem to

Mystery & Espionage

relish the challenge of combining murder with an offbeat vocation or avocation. The resulting juxtapositions are something to behold. Take these two examples: a sleuth/antique dealer and a sleuth/dog trainer.

The antique dealer, Peter Marklin, specializes in toys. Along with his sultry, occasionally errant lover, Arabella, and his best pal, the cantankerous, Heineken-mooching Gus (an authority on the current prices of prewar, die-cast Dinky toys), Marklin somehow manages to keep unearthing antiques with a murderous history. In his latest adventure, the fifth in Neville Steed's series, the wisecracking threesome are on the trail of an attic full of stolen toys, a suspicious widow, and the murder weapon—a 1920 Mercedes Benz sculpted in bronze. Sure, if you happen to collect antique toys, you'll love this tale, but the amazing thing is you'll probably like it just fine even if you don't know a Dinky toy from a Tinkertoy.

Scots author Gerald Hammond has two series running, both of which employ offbeat premises. His best features gun collector/sleuth Keith Calder, but his latest, which began with Dog in the Dark, also has its moments. After exorcising several personal demons, retired soldier John Cunningham, married to the devoted Beth and ensconced on his newly purchased Northern Fife farmland, spends his time training, boarding, and raising dogs— spaniels by choice, pretty much anything by financial necessity. In the series' second adventure, John and Beth find a loose spaniel running wild, a dead body, and a sinister connection between the two. Dogs have more of a built-in audience than Dinky toys, but Hammond wants to tell you a lot more about spaniels than you think you want to know. Be prepared to change your mind on that.

These wildly different but equally appealing books confirm the notion that a skilled writer is capable of making anything interesting. —*Peter Robertson*

Hansen, Joseph.
A Country of Old Men.
Viking, $17.95 (0-670-83826-8). 175p.

This is the last Dave Brandstetter mystery; it says so right on the title page of the dapper, gay sleuth's third caper since retiring from the business of investigating insurance death claims that got him involved in the first nine cases Hansen wrote up. He's enticed into discovering who shot a druggie musician—a homicide with plenty of the wrinkles series' fans gleefully anticipate. There are also, of course, plenty of the pleasures of Hansen's terse, gritty evocations of urbanized southern California; of Dave's mouthwatering good taste in food and drink; and of cameo appearances by the series' repertory of Dave's fellow crime-busters and friends. Between age and AIDS, there are fewer of the latter, and a leitmotiv of Dave's swan song is his own physical winding down. He's just about worn out, and his creator voices his own weariness through a secondary character—an aging writer of successful mysteries who's trying to get an autobiographical novel he's been hawking for 20 years published at last. So don't be surprised if a Hansen self-life, with or without the veil of fiction, shows up in the not-too-distant future. —*Ray Olson*

Harrington, William.
Virus.
Morrow, $17.45 (0-688-09064-8). 352p.

Computer whiz Darius Whitney's first virus is really more annoying than sinister. It detonates within all the major airlines' reservation systems during the pre-Thanksgiving rush, causing big-time chaos. The former owner of a computer firm, Whitney wants his company back, and he wants the pencil-pushing MBAs who seized it to suffer. They do, since the airlines blame them for their software problems. But the Thanksgiving fiasco alerts computer-security expert Scott Vandenberg, who quickly recognizes Whitney's hand-iwork and is called in to supervise restoration and future protection. On a nastier level, the virus is also noted by certain drug smugglers, who try to persuade Whitney to tamper with air-traffic control systems and with the computers that monitor flights into the country. Author Harrington takes the time to explain every scientific move and theory, making it possible for anyone who's ever been in the same room with an IBM PC to follow the plot machinations and the science behind them. Readers who relished the real-life electronic cat-and-mouse maneuvers of Cliff Stoll's *The Cuckoo's Egg* are sure to snap up this fictionalized computer-espionage yarn. —*Peter Robertson*

Hart, Carolyn.
The Christie Caper.
Bantam, $18 (0-553-07404-0). 336p.

What better setting for a murder mystery than a convention of Agatha Christie aficionados? Hart's sleuthing bookstore owner, Annie Darling, has organized the week-long convention at a resort off the coast of South Carolina. There will be movies, panel discussions, costume balls, and trivia contests—and, to Annie's dismay, several murders. The book is full of stock characters—the magnetic yet evil editor, the hard-boiled agent, the British mystery writer who helps solve the case—but in the context of the convention, they all fit in swimmingly. A bonus for Christie-lovers is the continuous background chatter of the convention-goers ("wish she hadn't put Poirot in *The Hollow* . . . she didn't need him") as well as the allusions Annie makes as she tries to solve her own murders. For superbuffs, there is also the convention's big Christie Trivia Contest, reprinted for readers. The mystery itself is almost a sideshow here, but the whole Christie carnival, including a classic conclusion in which all the suspects are herded into one room, is one jolly romp. —*Ilene Cooper*

✔Harvey, John.
Cutting Edge.
Holt, $16.95 (0-8050-1264-8). 277p.

Here's the third salvo in Harvey's jagged-edged, street-level series set in England's industrial Midlands area and starring sartorially inelegant, culinarily inventive Nottingham bobby Charlie Resnick. The plot focuses on three brutal stabbings in which a doctor, a male nurse, and a student are all the recipients of suspiciously clever knife wounds. Meanwhile, a woman officer's obsessive tracking of a rape suspect, a fellow officer's squalid romantic life, and another's depressing family troubles all vie for center stage, as does Charlie's latest houseguest, a onetime jazz great now drinking himself into slow oblivion. Resnick himself is still suffering from his own open wounds, including failure in marriage. Harvey's previous Resnick novels, *Lonely Hearts* and *Rough Treatment*, drew superlatives from critics of every stripe; expect the flood of praise to continue with *Cutting Edge*. This is definitive procedural fare: detailed, precise chronicling of what coppers do. Yet the precision never overshadows the human side of raw truths exposed in a harsh narrative glare: guys drunk on lust and lager, wives retreating, husbands wandering, drunks forever repenting. It's all there in the daily lives of Charlie Resnick and pals. —*Peter Robertson*

Havill, Steven F.
Heartshot.
St. Martin's, $16.95 (0-312-05442-4). 240p.

Bill Gastner is widowed, 70, overweight, a little cynical, and damn good at his job as sheriff of Posadas County, New Mexico. When three local teens panic at the approach of a police car and die in a fiery crash, Gastner's dismay is genuine—he'd known the kids since they were tots. When $180,000 worth of cocaine is found in the ashes, Gastner sets aside his grief to investigate. His dogged inquiry into the cocaine distribution hierarchy will please both procedural buffs and those who like their justice meted out by lone wolves. Gastner is a unique and endearing protagonist who certainly deserves an encore performance. —*Wes Lukowsky*

✓Hiaasen, Carl.
Native Tongue.
Knopf, $21 (0-394-58796-0). 321p.

Terrorists feeding tourists to alligators, bass fishermen killing each other in a mad frenzy to catch the big one, hitmen with Weed Wackers for hands—in Carl Hiaasen's novels, the idea of Florida as modern Armageddon is exaggerated, distorted, magnified, and, finally, transformed into a uniquely powerful metaphor that captures a "culture in terminal moral hemorrhage." In his fourth novel, Hiaasen finds perhaps his most outrageous image of decay yet: a theme park gone berserk. Ex–muckraking newspaperman Joe Winder, giving in to the swirling chaos that surrounds him, has sold out to the bad guys by accepting a job writing PR for the Amazing Kingdom of Thrills, a Disney clone in Key Largo. Then he comes face to face with the proverbial "story of a lifetime": the planet's last two "mango voles" (read cuddly rats) are stolen from the Kingdom. Unable to check his reportorial impulses, Winder uncovers layer upon layer of dirt beneath the theme park's squeaky clean image: a Mob snitch posing as the new Walt Disney (with the help of the Federal Witness Protection Program); a slimy but immensely profitable racket involving making your own endangered species; and a golf course/condominium deal that will ravage what's left of the Key's wetlands. With the help of a raucous supporting cast—sort of a bent version of the rude mechanicals in *A Midsummer Night's Dream*—Winder hatches a plan to save the wetlands and destroy the Kingdom. It all comes together in a spectacular finale that combines the fury of *Day of the Locust* with the imagination of Hieronymous Bosch. Our stomachs churning, we emerge from this literary roller-coaster ride wondering if it's possible for Hiaasen to turn his surrealistic screws any tighter. —*Bill Ott*

✔**Higgins, George V.**
The Mandeville Talent.
Holt, $19.95 (0-8050-1412-8). 278p.

Much has been written about George V. Higgins' mastery of dialogue and ability to evoke the underside of New England life—the part you won't find in *Yankee* magazine. Now it's time to celebrate something else: his charmingly old-fashioned belief in order, in the notion that the world is understandable if only we think hard enough. Take the murder of Jim Mandeville, for example. It's been 23 years since Mandeville, a banker in a quiet Berkshires hamlet, was killed with his own shotgun. No leads, no motive, no suspects. (If this sounds familiar, it is: Higgins has returned to the scene of the crime described in his first novel, *The Friends of Eddie Coyle*.) More than two decades after the fact, disaffected New York lawyer Joe Corey, whose wife is Mandeville's granddaughter, has decided to start digging. With the help of former Defense Department troubleshooter Baldo Ianucci, Corey sifts through a morass of phone records, bank statements, and real-estate transactions to uncover a Mafia-engineered land scam of gargantuan proportions. The drama in this book comes simply from watching the protagonists' minds work. Higgins makes us believe that the paper trail of contemporary life actually leads not to obfuscation but to clarity. Such a position puts him miles from many of today's best crime writers, including Floridians Carl Hiaasen and James W. Hall, whose heroes can only make temporary dents in the fundamental chaos they find at the core of the modern world. Can the center hold? Who knows, but it's exhilarating to watch Higgins using every ounce of his brain to make us believe it can. —*Bill Ott*

Higgins, Jack.
The Eagle Has Landed.
Simon & Schuster, $21.95 (0-671-73310-9). 361p.
Higgins, Jack.
The Eagle Has Flown.
Simon & Schuster, $21.95 (0-671-72458-4). 335p.

The Eagle Has Landed was first published in 1975 and has since sold 15 million copies in 36 languages and was made into a successful movie. It introduced Liam Devlin, an IRA gunman, poet, scholar, and one of the most celebrated anti-heroes of fiction. For any espionage buffs who have forgotten, "the eagle has landed" was a message received by Heinrich Himmler, head of the Nazi SS, on November 6, 1943, telling him that a small force of German paratroopers had landed in England and were poised to snatch Prime Minister Winston Churchill from the Norfolk country house where he was spending a weekend. The novel is now being published for the first time in

Mystery & Espionage

its complete form as the author originally wished it—with 10 percent new material, according to the publisher. Higgins' fiftieth book, *The Eagle Has Flown*, is the long-awaited sequel. Devlin is back, along with Lt. Col. Kurt Steiner, who led the paratroopers and was thought to be dead from a bullet in the heart. Not so. Devlin is asked by the Germans to parachute into England and free Steiner from St. Mary's Priory, where he has been taken after being held captive in the Tower of London. This sequel involves a plot to thwart the assassination of Hitler in order to prevent the nation's takeover by Himmler and the SS. Higgins is truly a master of the genre and, although the sequel is a little farfetched, his millions of fans won't be disappointed. It's a long wait but worth it. —*George Cohen*

Hoyt, Richard.
Whoo?
Tor, $17.95 (0-312-85149-9). 192p.

A mystery about the spotted-owl controversy? Yes, indeed, and a fine one at that. Hoyt's John Denson novels have always used their Pacific Northwest locale effectively, but this time the author outdoes himself, not only with evocative descriptions of old-growth forests, but also with levelheaded analysis of the owl issue, which has made enemies of environmentalists, on the one hand, and residents of the region's many timber-dependent small towns, on the other. Denson lands right in the middle of one such small town, Sixkiller, Washington, and soon finds himself investigating the death of a Fish and Wildlife Service employee responsible for counting the spotted owls on federally owned forest land. Employing his usual mix of broad humor, freewheeling use of the absurd, and ingratiating iconoclasm, Hoyt tells a story with no easy or politically correct answers. We respond to the stubborn individualism of the loggers and the environmentalists, both of whom are portrayed as defending a vanishing way of life. In the end, the wily Denson saves neither loggers nor owls, but he makes us want to do both. —*Bill Ott*

✔**Hyman, Tom.**
Prussian Blue.
Viking, $19.95 (0-670-82996-X). 464p.

In a series of mishaps, similar to the ones that dropped like sooty raindrops on Cary Grant in Alfred Hitchcock's *North by Northwest*, intrepid journalist John Brady watches his life plunge headlong down the toilet. With the advance he received to write an exposé of a CIA bigshot used up, and with his resolution weakened by booze, sex, and alimony payments, Brady finds himself in jail, where the uncooperative bigshot has conspired to deposit him. Thanks to the help of his former lover, an imaginative and seriously oversexed Swedish film star, Brady manages to escape the pokey, but whether he will be able to outwit the agency boys long enough to unearth a secret society buried deep within the government is an open question. *Prussian Blue* is a delirious joyride from start to finish, what with kinky seductions, red herrings, a red bra or two, and even a crash course in piloting an aircraft. The author of a more conventional espionage thriller, *Seven Days to Petrograd*,

Hyman proves more than adept at the madcap side of the genre, cracking wise with reckless abandon and galloping through his helter-skelter plot like a riderless horse in the Grand National. Movie rights should be snapped up tout de suite. If only Hitch and Archibald Leach were still around. —*Peter Robertson*

Ing, Dean.
The Nemesis Mission.
Tor; dist. by St. Martin's, $20 (0-312-85105-7). 384p.

Ing's second technothriller is set in the same future as his best-selling *Ransom of Black Stealth One*. Like its predecessor, this book has Ing's mixture of technical expertise, brisk pacing, and superior characterization (notably, women). The plot involves a drug cartel driven from Colombia to Mexico and its plan to remove $1 billion of its cash reserves from the U.S. The key to the DEA's and the FBI's efforts to foil the drug lords is a sophisticated, high-endurance, high-altitude, solar-powered aircraft called *Nemesis* and its two pilots, an ex-marine and a female gymnast. Both their survival and the battle against the drug lords go down to the very end. If Ing continues to write at this level, the technothriller genre has acquired a major new name. —*Roland Green*

✓Izzi, Eugene.
Prowlers.
Bantam, $19 (0-553-07328-1). 304p.

"I did it for Favore, and the way I see it, he owes me. I go in owing him twenty-two dimes. I get out and find he kept the meter running. It ain't fair, Sal, a man shouldn't have to pay juice when he's locked up because he didn't rat out the guy he owes the money to." Ace thief Catfeet has a point. Trouble is crime boss Sal isn't long for this earth, and can't help much. Plus, Favore is poised to climb to the top of the Chicago crime heap, and Catfeet's affair with Femal, the lush black beauty in Favore's semilegitimate employ, isn't helping his case a lot. Izzi's getting slicker and cagier with each turn; he throws his catalog of criminals together with the usual delirious power, serves up another slick gambling set piece, and sucker-punches us with short angry bursts of gut-wrenching prison talk as his characters' motives are dissected. This time, though, Izzi has hidden a few of his moves; he doesn't telegraph who's really bad as opposed to just plain unlucky, and he hasn't given away who's going to end up still standing, much less solvent, when the last taut page is consumed. But there's plenty of what readers of *The Prime Roll* and *King of the Hustlers* have come to expect from this master chronicler of the urban underworld: bruised words, loyalties pulled taut like piano wire, urban truths, and knockout scenes—like the one in which hick weirdo Merle gets creatively anarchistic in sunny Florida supermarkets before Uncle Favore brings him back home to the Windy City for the onset of killing season. —*Peter Robertson*

James, Bill.
The Lolita Man.
Countryman/Foul Play, $17.95 (0-88150-198-0). 158p.

The Lolita killings, in which teenage girls are expertly murdered and clumsily raped, cross two police turfs, city and county. British inspector Colin Harpur works the city beat, sleeps with a dead copper's widow, and worries about a strange neighbor girl whose diary, written in a weird and wonderful kind of Brontë-speak, hints at her infatuation with a mysterious stranger called "Dark Eyes." Trouble is, Dark Eyes closely resembles a composite the police have compiled to describe the Lolita killer. Before solving the case, the doggedly unambitious, grudgingly adulterous Harpur must contend with both his rival cops from the county and his Machiavellian superior, whose rambling speeches are minor masterpieces of colloquial obscenity, ersatz emotion, and all-consuming self-interest. James, who has nearly as many pseudonyms as he does published works (his real name is James Tucker), seems to have hit his stride with this second entry in the Harpur series, following *You'd Better Believe It*. The rich, riotous dialogue is a particular delight, as is Harpur's confrontation with British bureaucracy. —*Peter Robertson*

Jones, Bruce.
In Deep.
Crown, $19 (0-517-58205-8). 320p.

A Columbian drug lord with a reluctant mistress; a burned-out Santa Barbara cop pushed from one case to another; an obese and impotent millionaire—What do they all have in common? They all have moms, of course. Only some feel a little stronger about the subject of motherhood than others. The kills Tully is investigating duplicate each other: athletic women, mothers, sexually attacked, abandoned on the beach, photographed, and abused by a policeman's billy club. Is the last why Tully's pulled off the case? And what about the naive guy caught in the center, hired by the cops to watch the drug guy, hired by the impotent millionaire to watch his straying wife, hired by the drug lord to watch the mistress (a job not exactly tough on the eyes)—he's a former cop, too, with his own problems. Bruce Jones is a TV and movie screenwriter, which may explain the remarkably sure touch he has with this first novel and the slew of graphic, galvanizing images it comes loaded with. Tully the cop is a rare find: battered and plucky, a loser going for the main chance, crippled in love, dreaming of an ideal girl and a small boat on the blue water to call his very own. —*Peter Robertson*

✔Kakonis, Tom.
Double Down.
Dutton, $19.95 (0-525-93326-3). 336p.

Inside a seedy Florida motel room, gambler Tim Waverly and his money man Bennie try to figure out how they're going to pay the vig (*interest*, for you nongamblers) they owe a Chicago big shot. Then the big chance appears— seven card, nothing wild, a rich Arab prince with a bottomless purse, all set up by Waverly's old college pal, himself in the toilet financially and unhappily married to a woman Tim would like all for himself. Kakonis' first two forays into crime fiction produced *Michigan Roll*, which starred the former academic, former felon Waverly, and last year's *Criss Cross*, in which Kakonis, a Michigan resident, ably demonstrated that Elmore Leonard has a serious rival camped out on his own doorstep. With *Double Down*, Kakonis once again rolls nothing but winners, throwing out a steady stream of brutally funny lines threaded through with steamy sex, sun-fried morality, and sneaky card lore. Like Leonard, Kakonis has effortlessly moved his cast of grifters from Michigan down south for the requisite burned skin, white-hot violence, languid interludes, and sweaty bodies made all the more slippery by tanning lotion and treachery. Clearly, this is among the best crime novels of 1991. —*Peter Robertson*

Kaminsky, Stuart.
Lieberman's Folly.
St. Martin's, $15.95 (0-312-05398-3). 224p.

Two Mexican whores slaughter their formidably built employer in Texas and abscond with a portion of the dead man's ill-gotten gains. Fast forward 10 years to Chicago and a Near North deli, where elderly cop Abe Lieberman kvetches with his long-toothed buddies and listens sympathetically to the fears of his best informer, Estralda Valdez, "the classiest prostitute on the Near North Side." Later, Hanrahan, Abe's liquored-up, love-crossed partner, falls for a timid girl in a Chinese restaurant when he should be watching Estralda, who gets viciously whacked. Like Kaminsky's award-winning series of mysteries starring Soviet cop Porfiry Rostnikov, the death and detection here is set in the context of the characters' emotional and spiritual growth. Abe faces up to advancing age, a growing if unorthodox blossoming of faith, and his overly brilliant daughter's marital woes. Hanrahan is perhaps an even more fully realized creation, his tidy house empty, waiting for the wife who will never return. Kaminsky can be terminally cute on occasion. When he isn't—and he isn't here—he's about as crafty and soul searching as a crime writer can be. —*Peter Robertson*

✔Kaminsky, Stuart.
Rostnikov's Vacation.
Scribner, $19.95 (0-684-19022-2). 256p.

Actually, the Soviet detective's vacation is more like a busman's holiday. The intrepid sleuth and all-round scourge of the Politburo is accompanying his ailing wife to a restful spot. There he encounters an American detective, another Russian detective who quickly expires, and another, who is tailing Rostnikov, as are two shadowy killers, one gigantic, one one-eyed. Ludicrously, Rostnikov's ghoul-like assistant, Karpo, is also supposed to be taking things easy; instead, he watches a red-haired woman fall from an apartment window, which leads to an American agent training a dull-witted Soviet assassin in the finer points of death. The third member of Rostnikov's team is the younger, harassed Tkach, posing as a computer expert to lure a team

Mystery & Espionage

of thieves. The lure works well. As always, plots tend to blur: Rostnikov gets under the collective skin of Soviet officialdom, and Karpo damn near steals the show. But each Rostnikov novel is a welcome trip, and Kaminsky's plotting is effortless: sweeping procedural brushwork and character evolution essayed with delicate strokes. —*Peter Robertson*

✓**Kellerman, Faye.**
Day of Atonement.
Morrow, $20 (0-688-08604-7). 384p.

Two shocks await L.A.-cop-turned-Orthodox-Jew Peter Decker as he visits his wife Rina Lazarus' in-laws from her first marriage. A woman he never expected to see again is there for dinner, and Noam, a teenage cousin, vanishes before the elaborate ceremonies of the High Holy Days are concluded. The family is thrown into chaos, fights over orthodoxy and conservatism are shelved, and Decker, even wearing his robes and yarmulke, is a cop with a mission once more. *Atonement*, like the three previous Decker/Lazarus books, mixes Jewish lore with a gripping crime plot. With Decker and Lazarus now married, Kellerman can't rely on the vicissitudes of their on-off courtship to keep things lively. Still, there's more than enough here to keep readers involved: freewheeling shifts from cutting fish to cutting bodies, elaborate revenge schemes devised to right unnamed wrongs, and the visceral tension that springs from watching the pious Decker forced to descend once again into the moral sludge. This graphic, pungent novel shows Kellerman at the gritty peak of her form. —*Peter Robertson*

Kelly, Susan.
And Soon I'll Come to Kill You.
Villard, $18 (0-394-58415-5). 224p.

It's not that hard to make enemies, even when all you do is innocently interact with the mainstream population. But when you've done as much dating and dumping as Cambridge, Massachusetts, free-lance writer Liz Conners has—and, on top of that, when you've written enough exposés of rapists and con men and crime lords to fill up several résumés—well, enemies are never in short supply. Liz's latest is abusive and inventive. He threatens her, he follows her, he taunts her—all more than enough to convince Liz's cop lover, Jack, that this guy is for real. And there's no shortage of subjects, given the plethora of serial rapists and killers—past subjects of Liz's articles—who are walking the streets or soon to be paroled. Kelly's books are a lot like Nancy Pickard's: New England settings, supportive cop boyfriend, endearingly plucky sleuth. Both authors cut to the chase fast and pick up the occasional dark angle on the way. Kelly might have developed her psycho's character a little better at the beginning, but she makes up for that at the end, with a stunning climax that comes flying at the hapless reader from out of nowhere. —*Peter Robertson*

Klein, Zachary W.
Two Way Toll.
HarperCollins, $19.95 (0-06-016420-4). 288p.

The blighted Boston neighborhood called the End haunts Boston sleuth and building manager Matt Jacob. His life and career haven't exactly climbed to Olympian heights since he left the area. He needs to smoke at least one joint most days, and flatfooting at a shopping mall isn't doing a hell of a lot for his self-esteem. Then a face from the past jettisons Jacob backwards. Through a collage of crossed signals. A small-time deal and congenital loser called Blackhead wants an old murder investigated. He would. He's the newest suspect. Blackhead isn't much of a client (although the drug connection seldom concerns the oft-toking Jacob), but the chance to pound the mean streets of the End appeals to the latent masochism never far from Matt's wounded heart. Naturally drugs figure in the action. So does the dead man's crusading sister and her benefactor, Jonathan Barrie, a self-proclaimed savior of lost souls. Jacob's descent into Beantown's nether regions is as somber, low rent, low key, and low life as the hard-boiled addict could possibly wish for. —*Peter Robertson*

Knight, Kathryn Lasky.
Mumbo Jumbo.
Summit, $17.95 (0-671-68448-5). 201p.

Calista Jacobs, the children's book illustrator–amateur sleuth, familiar from *Mortal Words* and *Trace Elements*, is back in action. This time, the setting is a desert, where Archie Baldwin (Calista's lover) has set up a significant archaeological dig only to be impeded by a New Age religious cult whose growing control over a small western town and its environs is becoming dangerous. Perhaps because Calista has been defined so thoroughly in the earlier stories, there is less acclaim in this tale over her amazing talents and good looks. Her "almost-fourteen-year-old" son, Charley, takes on the most dangerous and heroic roles as he wrestles with rattlesnakes, swamis, and a New Age priestess. The final wrestling match is, however, left to Calista, out for revenge after her son is kidnapped by these nefarious, sexually energized individuals, posing as messengers from God. One interesting twist: the most gullible of the believers is an older woman whose clear-sighted, teenage daughter sees right through the scam and falls for Charley, who helps her get the goods on the bad guys. —*Denise Perry Donavin*

✔le Carré, John.
The Secret Pilgrim.
Knopf, $21.95 (0-394-58842-8). 335p.

You can't trust John le Carré, but what do you expect from a spy? First, in *The Russia House*, he seemed to relish administering last rites to the dying espionage genre: "We must cut down the gray men inside ourselves, we must burn our gray suits and set our good hearts free." Yet now, little more than a year later, he can be found if not reviving the form at least offering an elegy of sorts to the very gray men he so recently damned. Appropriately enough for an elegy, the action of the novel takes place almost entirely in flashbacks, as veteran agent Ned, now head of British intelligence's spy school, listens to a commencement address given by his former boss, George Smiley. As the eternally world-weary Smiley philosophizes about the lot of the spy ("By being all things to all spies, one does rather run the risk of becoming nothing to oneself"), Ned personifies his mentor's larger truths by recalling the lost friends and alienated lovers that dot the map of his covert career. Overlaying it all there is the melancholy sense of sacrificing the personal for the abstract; Ned is left in the end with "the remnants of a life withheld." This theme has bobbed to the surface throughout le Carré's career, but here it receives its most poignant treatment. With the full weight of the Karla trilogy, *The Perfect Spy*, and *The Russia House* behind us, we feel both the irony and the sorrow driving Smiley's announcement that "for as long as rogues become leaders, we shall spy." But at the same time we feel with equal strength the bemused relief with which the retired Ned, staking his claim for a separate peace, utters the novel's prophetic last line: "I'm a newcomer to the overt world, but I'm learning." —*Bill Ott*

Leonard, Elmore.
Maximum Bob.
Delacorte, $20 (0-385-30142-1). 297p.

The latest Leonard's rather routine, especially following the bravura *Get Shorty*. But Elmore's routine equals other hard-boiled guys' best shots, so this opus is pretty hard to put down. Maximum Bob is a Florida judge famous for his tough sentencing and, among women who have to work with him, as a fairly crude lecher. Parole officer Kathy Diaz Baker is the book's protagonist, though. For a slight violation, her parolee Dale Crowe Junior gets one of Bob's stiff sentences, by which he's not too pleased. Moreover, Dale's uncle Elvin, just out after doing 10 years from Bob on a murder conviction, conceivably could be nursing a grudge. What's more, Elvin hooks up with rich Dr. Tommy Vasco, who's under house arrest for illegal drugs—a sentence given him by guess who. When a live and lively alligator shows up in the judge's backyard, swallowing his wife's dog and scaring its owner clean out of town, and then when shots are fired through hizzoner's windows, Kathy gets suspicious and suspiciouser. Leonard's trademark toughness, grit, and sleaze are on every page, and the tale's developments and ending are, as usual, sickeningly convincing. But the characters aren't as compelling and juicy as Leonard's best. Good enough, though, to make pleased consumers, if not fans, out of those who've never read Leonard before. —*Ray Olson*

Leuci, Bob.
Double Edge.
Dutton, $19.95 (0-525-93383-2). 320p.

D.C. cop Scott Ancelet is tough and more than a little jaded, but the body he finds in a park one morning while jogging—a young boy with body parts shaved and neck hideously slashed—gets to him. Despite a bulging caseload, he takes on the investigation of the execution-style killing, getting help from

Big Moe, his partner, and Cotton, a longtime snitch and drug dealer who Moe hates but Ancelet somehow trusts. Leuci's real-life cop career was the basis for the film *Prince of the City*, and there isn't any question that he knows cops inside out. Ancelet is a living, breathing slice of burned-out, heroic, screwed-up street truth with a badge and an attitude and a few dark fears. Leuci stresses the loner mentality of his cops (criminals are "beasts," lawyers pretty much the same). There isn't a plot move the reader can't see coming as Cotton and Ancelet zero in on a serial killer, but the grainy authenticity of the narrative renders such reservations irrelevant. —*Peter Robertson*

Lewin, Michael Z.
Called by a Panther.
Mysterious, $17.95 (0-89296-439-1). 258p.

Maybe it's because things are quiet in the Hoosier State, but Indianapolis sleuth Albert Samson is antsier than usual. He's even been reduced to hiring himself out as "mystery detective" at swank soirees, but then things start to explode. The Scum Front, a team of environmentally safe, politically correct terrorists, plant a series of fake bombs, safe as mother's milk but designed to highlight the group's cause. But one of the would-be bombs is stolen by some serious bad guys not afraid to turn "fake" into "real." Samson, the "go for it" shamus, is quickly hired by the Front. Given the choice between a cheap laugh and a spot of plot tightening, Lewin invariably goes for the yuks. This madcap novel careens along improbably, but the reader doesn't mind a bit. With the laconic but wildly funny Lewin and the equally wacky Kinky Friedman (see *Musical Chairs*) currently writing up a storm, crime seems a lot more comical of late. —*Peter Robertson*

Livingston, Nancy.
Mayhem in Parva.
St. Martin's, $16.95 (0-312-06410-1). 192p.

The sixth mystery featuring G. D. H. Pringle has the sprightly, retired tax inspector looking for his roots in the quaint village of Parva, undergoing the rigors of a local flower festival coupled with the restoration of ancient wall paintings in the village church—all accompanied by the rivalry between local matrons fighting to the death for social leadership. Pringle arrives just in time to be almost run over by a hearse, bearing to the graveyard the late Major Petrie Coombe-Hamilton, the local eccentric squire whose departure from this world has left his daughter ecstatic. Then, when one of the more disagreeable village matrons turns up as a corpse on the village green—after apparently having spent some time floating in the river—and then disappears again, Pringle's lady friend, Mavis Bignell, feels justified in her attitude that anywhere outside of London is dangerous ground indeed. A light-hearted and amusing mystery using the grand old tradition of murder-in-the-English-village to hilarious effect. —*Stuart Miller*

Mystery & Espionage

✔**Lovesey, Peter.**
The Last Detective.
Doubleday, $18.50 (0-385-42114-1). 336p.

With this intricate, masterful, many-tiered examination of police work, Doubleday launches a new hardcover crime series called Perfect Crime Books, which will supersede the overly cozy Doubleday Crime Club. In *The Last Detective*, modern forensic technology, complete with computers and genetic fingerprinting, clashes with the motives and methods of anachronistic copper Peter Diamond, whose rough-and ready ways have gotten him in heaps of trouble. Now Diamond, delightfully human, shrewd but often dead wrong, struggles against bureaucratic intervention in a murder investigation. Geraldine Snoo, whose corpse was found in a lake, was a former soap star who left behind debts, a history of neurotic behavior, and an indifferent husband who, through a bizarre series of events, has come into possession of two letters written by Jane Austen. Lovesey moves seamlessly between third-person narration and the first-person recollections of various witnesses. Clues are littered all over the place, but only a few matter and none makes any kind of sense until much later, after the wrong person is set to take the fall and a missing household possession points the way towards a whole new avenue of investigation, one the loathed technocrats in their white coats managed to miss. Everything meshes perfectly in this air-tight tale: Lovesey's books should be force-fed to fledgling crime writers who believe plotting is unimportant. —*Peter Robertson*

✔**Marshall, William.**
Faces in the Crowd.
Mysterious, $19.95 (0-89296-367-0). 336p.

An unholy collage of period mayhem, crowded streets, sideshow wonders, cheap thievery, cunning levels of gutter-level deceit, bold claims of fortune-telling and miracle cures. The beat is New York City circa 1880, the coppers are the cerebral Virgil Tillman and his sidekick, the large and pious Ned Muldoon. Marshall's beguilingly idiosyncratic prose and his way with an oddball setting have made his Hong Kong mysteries a prolonged delight. He's a true original. With his New York detective, his quirky sense of wayward logic and joyously splattergun method of creating period and place gets cranked to a new high. Ned and Virgil track death through the crowded streets, from one whore's disturbing vision just prior to falling to the sidewalk below, to another's subterranean basement dwelling—the sinister scene of an attempted drowning. The intrepid twosome, often abetted by droll disguises, wade through a nastily spiraling cacophony of evilen prostitution, thievery, pornography, and murder, stretching all the way from swank homes in Brooklyn Heights to paupers' graves in Potter's Field. Marshall is as intent on pitching his reader into the wild immigrant heart of the new city as he is on letting Tillman and Muldoon make their eventual pinch. —*Peter Robertson*

Martin, Lee.
The Mensa Murders.
St. Martin's, $15.95 (0-312-05126-3). 192p.

Fort Worth policewoman Deb Ralston, beset by her menagerie of kids, pets, and husband, returns in a case involving a serial killer with a profound hatred of smart women—though most of the Mensa members portrayed here seem more like social rejects than intellectual giants. The first two victims are troubled women, both believers in spiritualism, one badly overweight, one obsessed with romantic thoughts directed at the boyfriend of Deb's best pal. As in her earlier works (including *Deficit Ending*), author Martin scales twin plot hurdles, delivering a seamlessly efficient procedural and continuing to develop the chaos-strewn saga of Ralston's private life. The case wobbles between the boyfriend, the brainy types who meet over Trivial Pursuit once a week, and a practicing medium. Then a third death occurs without a Mensa link. Hovering over the proceedings is a lunatic with a fixation on green dresses and a distracting habit of confessing to every murder committed in the Dallas–Fort Worth area. Deb may have some problems—chief among them, untidy kids of wildly disparate ages and a cranky, unemployed, laundry-ruining helicopter pilot for a hubby—but at least she owns no green dresses. A believable sleuth in a superior series. —*Peter Robertson*

Mathis, Edward.
September Song.
Scribner, $18.95 (0-684-19262-4). 256p.

At this stage in the game (seventh work in the series, fourth published since the author's death), Mathis has largely dispensed with traditional detection and thrown his sleuth, the heroically flawed Dan Roman, into some very dark places, a kind of quasi-melodramatic-soap-opera-masquerading-as-mystery. Divorced from the younger and richer Susie, Dan's now borderline alcoholic and clearly obsessed. Susie isn't thinking clearly either. She's still drawn to Dan, especially in moments of panic, like when a man her testimony put away gets released from prison and starts following her around. This novel comes with a lot more sex and brutality than past Roman tales. Dan gets several batterings, and his new buddy, a former pro-ball player nicknamed Big Boy, gets to splatter the convict and his two sons quite ruthlessly. Mathis is good at this stuff. He's a more stylistically interesting, technically adept writer than either crime solving or bodice ripping generally requires, and his splicing of the two gives *September Song* some added potency—not to mention a few more solid whacks to the abused body and bruised psyche of his detective. —*Peter Robertson*

McBain, Ed.
Downtown.
Morrow, $20 (0-688-08736-1). 302p.

Master crime author McBain takes a short trip—24 feverish, cinematic, convoluted hours—into some strikingly new territory, producing a warped urban comedy of errors that recalls Martin Scorsese's film *After Hours.*

Mystery & Espionage

Hapless tourist and Florida orange grower Michael Barnes, relaxing in a Big Apple watering hole after conducting some business with an ad agency, has a few hours to kill before his flight. Then it starts: first some teasing conversation; then a heist with a girl and a phony cop and a ring; then a Good Samaritan posing as a film director; then a car theft. Barnes is moneyless, carless, credit-card-less, and somewhat underdressed for the snowbound streets of New York on Christmas Eve. And when the stolen car is found with a stiff inside, guess who's tailor-made to take the fall? As a tour de force of kinetic plotting, *Downtown* is pretty much in a class of its own, but McBain tops off the whole weird concoction with giddy layers of stop-start dialogue, an inflamed level of sexual awareness, and oodles of film lore. —*Peter Robertson*

McBain, Ed.
Widows.
Morrow, $18.95 (0-688-10219-0). 332p.

Homicide detective Kling's troubled girlfriend on the force is detailed to the hostage negotiating team. In a parallel plot, a murdered 22-year-old, blue-eyed blond leaves behind a packet of the sex fantasies she has received from her anonymous lover. Several of them are cited in full, as are the equally explicit letters sent to a wealthy old man who is murdered later. Detective Steve Carella puts two and two together, but before he can round up the usual suspects, the murderer kills the old man's wife and his ex-wife (also blue-eyed blonds). In subplots, crackheads murder Carella's father, and Carella's sister suspects her husband is cheating on her. This being the forty-third 87th Precinct novel, McBain no longer introduces the recurrent characters, doesn't tell us that Carella's wife Teddy communicates in sign language, or jokes about Meyer Meyer's name. As a result, the veteran reader does not wade impatiently through familiar preliminaries, and the newcomer just beginning the series is intrigued by the density of the 87th's little society. McBain's command of literary procedure is every bit the equal of his characters' command of police procedure. —*Roland Wulbert*

✔McCrumb, Sharyn.
Missing Susan.
Ballantine, $17 (0-345-36575-5). 304p.

Attracting death like a fresh carcass attracts flies, royalty-adoring forensic anthropologist Elizabeth MacPherson is off on a tour of England's most famous murder sites. The participants are a bunch of knowledgeable if smug Yanks. The guide is a stock English character—the catty, aloof, seemingly impoverished academic. In this case, he's also been paid rather well to kill one of his charges. The plot is bound tight. We know the killer, and we know the victim. We hate one of them and feel slightly sorry for the other. Edgar-winning author McCrumb spins the British cozy formula on its ear, slipping in the expected sly one-liner or two and driving her plot so far up a narrative one-way street that only a writer with her nerve and ever-ready wit would have a snowball's chance in hell of pulling the whole tricky caper off.

Mystery & Espionage

She does, thanks largely to a virtuoso ending that both satisfies and comes just that little way out of left field. —*Peter Robertson*

McCullough, David Willis.
Think on Death.
Viking, $17.95 (0-670-83493-9). 255p.

The first in a new mystery series featuring the Reverend Ziza Todd, this page-turner is set in the Catskill region of New York, where the members of the Smyrna Community, originally a utopian settlement, now operate a successful business manufacturing and marketing class rings. The death of Aunt Nan Quick, one of the last direct descendants of the founding family, brings together a large gathering of salespeople, company officers, and the few remaining Quick family members. When the skeleton of Llewelyn Quick, who mysteriously disappeared without a trace 20 years before, turns up piece by piece just before Aunt Nan's funeral, Ziza Todd, in residence to do research on the Smryna archives, decides to do a spot of sleuthing. As might be expected, moves are afoot to acquire the community's lucrative business, and no end of greedy vultures is at hand. McCullough skillfully manages his nifty plot, effectively using multiple narrators and putting to good use many classic mystery conventions—a house in the country, a fixed number of suspects, a long-lost corpse. Await the next Ziza Todd novel with anticipation. —*Stuart Miller*

McInerny, Ralph.
Judas Priest.
St. Martin's, $17.95 (0-312-06375-X). 208p.

Fans of Father Dowling will be glad to see him back in action, especially when he gets mixed up with an old friend from the seminary—an ex-priest who abandoned his collar for a steamy radio show cohosted by an ex-nun. As intriguing as this premise is, particularly when the former priest confesses to Dowling that his daughter wishes to enter a convent, devotees of the mystery novel will be a bit disappointed in some of McInerny's police proce-dures. With a little effort, this story could have been more plausibly rendered. As it is, adventure is not lacking, and Father Dowling's quick wit saves his pal's hide (though not necessarily his soul). —*Denise Perry Donavin*

✔Mosley, Walter.
A Red Death.
Norton, $18.95 (0-393-02998-0). 240p.

Mosley's *Devil in a Red Dress* heralded the arrival of a major new voice in crime fiction. Combining a black hero, Easy Rawlins, with a vivid depiction of Los Angeles' Watts district in the 1940s, Mosley staked out previously unexplored territory, displaying both the genre's flexibility and his own sure hand with period detail and character development. In this second install-ment in the series, the calendar has moved ahead to the early 1950s, and the good-natured (and aptly named) Easy is in a pickle. The IRS is after him for hiding income from the apartment buildings he secretly owns; a Red-hating

407

FBI agent strong- arms him into investigating a labor agitator; and the local police suspect him in two murders. Though a bit less focused than *Devil*, this solid second effort does nothing to dim Mosley's rising star. As before, the novel's greatest strength lies in the subtle evocation of the sense of community that connects the blacks living in Watts, most of whom are recently transplanted from the South and all of whom share the burden of isolation from the monolithic white power structure that surrounds them. Mosley uses the conventions of the hard-boiled novel to bring social history alive in the most human of terms. —*Bill Ott*

Muller, Marcia.
Where Echoes Live.
Mysterious, $17.95 (0-89296-418-9). 326p.

A variety of offbeat Californian locales and the dogged persistence of sleuth Sharon McCone have brightened Muller's mystery series, although the rigid political and moral correctness of her detective's cohorts at their San Francisco legal cooperative can get pretty far up many reader's noses. *Echoes* once again has Sharon gunning her battered MG out of town, this time to the stark, deserted territory near the Nevada border. There McCone finds an SF-based company buying up land, disturbing the environment (a move guaranteed to get the co-op team hot under their tie-dyed collars), and disturbing the few old timers still scraping a living from a place teeming with ghosts, pristine lakes, petrified woodland, and a long-abandoned town. For a company concerned with mining rights, Transpacific appears to be doing very little digging; suspicions are stirred further when a man with two identities floats lifelessly past the local redneck watering hole. This refreshing series is distinguished by no-nonsense plotting and a sleuth blessed with only the minimum of emotional baggage (two cherished cats and a recently returned lover dropping heavy hints concerning marriage and offspring). If we feel obliged to heap more praise on the Paretskys and Graftons, then let's save some applause for Marcia Muller. She's every bit as good, and she's been at the game a damn sight longer. —*Peter Robertson*

Murray, William.
I'm Getting Killed Right Here.
Doubleday, $18.50 (0-385-42117-6). 256p.

Murray's fifth Shifty Lou Anderson mystery may be the best of the lot, which readers of *Tip on a Dead Crab* and *The King of the Nightcap* will recognize as high praise indeed. This time the horse-playing magician inherits a nifty filly named Mad Margaret, only to discover he can't afford to keep her without taking on an unsavory millionaire and his knockout wife as partners. A fling with the latter leads to rather predictable trouble with the former, and before Shifty can pull a disappearing act, he is drawn into a murkier intrigue involving a decades-old water-rights swindle and a string of murders that may yet extend to him. Murray has few rivals in fashioning serpentine plots and vivid characters—and none in evoking the seedy allure of the racetrack. The combination makes his latest offering as irresistible as a hot tip from the trainer of a 20-to-1 shot. —*Dennis Dodge*

Norman, Geoffrey.
Sweetwater Ranch.
Atlantic Monthly Press; dist. by Little, Brown, $18.95 (0-87113-371-7). 288p.

Ex-ballplayer Big John runs a camp for tough, unlucky kids in the backwoods of rural North Florida, away from the collegiate spring tans and Latin heat of Miami. Not every kid turns out right: one runs away to live a paramilitary/survivalist life with his Pa, and another, a scumball from way back, hires an oily lawyer and sues the near-destitute John for tanning his sorry behind once too often. Enter Morgan Hunt, ex-con, ex-killer, ex–Green Beret, now working in tandem with Nat Semmes, John's lawyer. Finding the first runaway is straightforward, but finding the second, the crybaby, is a darker, danger-strewn journey. Edgar winner Norman reveals a fresh perspective on Florida here, looking to the remote north rather than the neon, tourist-infested glare of the cities or the lush tropical weirdness of the keys. Perhaps one reason Florida has become the locale of choice for so many top crime writers is the wealth of contrast available within one long hot, humid state. —*Peter Robertson*

✔Parker, Robert B.
Pastime.
Putnam, $19.95 (0-399-13628-2). 223p.

It's taken Robert B. Parker 19 Spenser novels to get around to revealing anything about his sleuth's past. Spenser has always been the archetypal hard-boiled hero: the man without a personal history. (As Susan Silverman, his longtime lover puts it, "I only know you from that first time we undressed in 1974.") That all changes here, as Spenser muses about his youth in Laramie, Wyoming, where he grew up with his father and three uncles (his mother died in childbirth). Two events prompt all this rummaging about in Spenser's memory chest: the appearance of a dog—left to Susan by her ex-husband—and the disappearance of Paul Giacomin's mother (see *Early Autumn,* in which Spenser became the then-teenage Paul's surrogate father after coming to the boy's aid during his parents' divorce). When Paul, struggling with his own ambivalence over the prospect of marriage, finds his mother missing, he turns to Spenser for help. Naturally, this is no simple missing-person case, and Spenser must extricate Mom from the middle of a big-time mess involving her boy friend's appropriation of a million dollars of Mob money. But what's really center stage here is a meditation on the thorny matter of fathers and sons —Spenser's relationship with his all-male household of father and uncles, Paul's bond with Spenser, and even the oddly touching love of chief mobster Joe Broz for his son, Gerry. And don't forget the dog, who gets the memory ball rolling by eliciting comparisons with a canine from Spenser's past. It all works remarkably well: Parker handles the nostalgia with a light hand and with plenty of his characteristic wit. For readers who have followed Spenser over most of the past two decades, this ruminative novel delivers just the sense of texture the series has been missing. —*Bill Ott*

Parker, Robert B.
Perchance to Dream.
Putnam, $19.95 (0-399-13580-4). 271p.

After extrapolating *Poodle Springs* from the bare-bones sketch in an unfinished Raymond Chandler manuscript, Parker starts fresh here, sort of, with an all new Philip Marlowe story. Almost the whole *Big Sleep* team is on board, except for the old general, who has thankfully passed on. Norris, the butler, hires Marlowe to find the voluptuous, lip-sucking Carmen Sternwood, who has gone AWOL from the sanitarium. The tougher, older sister, Vivian Sternwood (Lauren Bacall, for you film buffs), is once again thrown Marlowe's way, and the libidos are still a twitchin'. The plot segues from a sleazy sanitarium owner with a very powerful and kinky friend to some *Chinatown*-style stuff about water rights and plans to buy short, move water, and sell long. Parker has Chandler's frenzied wit down nicely, and he is equally skilled at re-creating the stylized L.A. landscape. Unfortunately, he cuts once too often to italicized passages from *The Big Sleep* itself, gumming up the plot and calling attention to the fact that this tribute, skillfully executed as it is, lacks the eloquent pathos of the real thing. Still, Parker plots with a little more scope and linear logic than Chandler ever managed, and he fires off enough smart-ass one-liners to keep most readers happy. It's true, he never ventures near the subterranean emotional depths that Chandler would occasionally explore, but, after all, sequels—even when they're written by the same person—rarely match the originals. —*Peter Robertson*

Peters, Elizabeth.
The Last Camel Died at Noon.
Warner, $17.95 (0-446-51483-7). 352p.

The last camel in fact dies on page one of this sixth entry in Peters' popular series, which finds the archaeologist family Emerson—narrator Amelia Peabody, husband Radcliffe, and 10-year-old son Ramses—stranded in the Nubian desert, six days away from the Nile with only two days' supply of water. In "an affectionate, admiring and nostalgic tribute" to Sir Henry Rider Haggard, Peters, author of 23 mysteries in her own name and 24 suspense novels as Barbara Michaels, rescues the Emersons from death by dehydration only to deliver them to a hidden kingdom, a secret oasis, a sort of Sudanese Shangri-La. The year is 1897, and Lord Kitchener is in the process of restoring the Upper Nile to British control. The Emersons' plans for a productive but boring winter excavating Nubian ruins vanish when they see an opportunity to locate explorer Willoughby Forth, an acquaintance from Emerson's single days who disappeared from Nubia 14 years earlier with his young bride. The Emersons are decidedly unstodgy Victorians—feminist, democratic, egalitarian, respectful of other cultures—and charming, witty, entertaining sleuths—which may help to explain why Peters is currently one of mystery fiction's hottest authors. —*Mary Carroll*

Peters, Ellis.
Flight of a Witch.
Mysterious, $16.95 (0-89296-404-9). 240p.

Peters' latest mystery revolves around the sheer beauty of 18-year-old Annet Beck, whom no one—including her ineffectual parents and the reader—knows very well. The story is told in the third person, primarily from the vantage point of Tom Kenyon, new sixth-form mathematics teacher in a small Shropshire village, who becomes a boarder at Annet's house and, like virtually every other man who comes in contact with her, falls in love with her at first sight. Did Annet indeed have a Rip van Winkle experience at the mysterious Hallowmount, where, it is said, a witch coven used to meet, or was her five-day absence a cover-up for something else? That's what Inspector George Felse would like to know when Annet is identified as being near the scene of a robbery-murder in Birmingham. Foreshadowing sends messages of the occult; the actuality of what happens, however, is quite mundane. Still, Peters maintains throughout an atmospheric sense of place, family secrets, and unrequited love that will draw readers along. —*Sally Estes*

Peters, Ellis.
The Summer of the Danes.
Mysterious Press, $16.95 (0-89296-448-0). 256p.

Something is rotten in the state of Gwynned. Owain Gwynned punished his younger brother, Cadwaladr, for his men's ambush and murder of a prince allied to Owain by seizing Cadwaladr's lands in South Wales; the prodigal brother has now returned to reclaim these properties with a force of Danish mercenaries from Ireland. Bangor and Carnarvon in Wales are a long way from the Benedictine abbey of Saints Peter and Paul, where the chronicles of Brother Cadfael, former crusader, herbalist, and sometime detective, are most often centered. But Cadfael here accompanies his former assistant Brother Mark on a mission of church diplomacy; by midbook, Cadfael and a beautiful Welsh runaway are held hostage in the Danish camp. The Cadfael chronicles, set in twelfth-century Britain, are always a blend of historical novel and mystery. *The Summer of the Danes* has the requisite murder by person or persons unknown (as well as the romantic subplot with which Peters—aka Edith Pargeter—usually spices the action), but this time out the historical novel outweighs the mystery, and Cadfael is more observer than sleuth. But only the most single-minded mystery buff will truly regret that this Brother Cadfael story is a bit less mysterious than most of its predecessors. —*Mary Carroll*

✔Pickard, Nancy.
I.O.U.
Pocket, $17.95 (0-671-68041-2). 174p.

Almost every endearing aspect of the previous Jenny Cain mysteries has been either ruthlessly customized or else outright jettisoned in this brave and downright uneasy series detour. The quasi-cozy style, the liberal helping of cute spousal patter (between Jenny and her cop hubby, Geof), and the academic background all fall by the wayside here as Pickard explores Cain history—Jenny's mother's protracted mental illness and death, her Dad's apathetic failure with the family clan dynasty, his affair, and his treatment of a shy, adoring woman beset by post-partum demons. At Mom's funeral, Jenny becomes seriously unhinged, her condition not helped by a firm push applied to her back as the coffin is lowered and cryptic messages found on the visitor's book. The trail leads Cain backwards, through industrial espionage in the seafood line to a succession of tight-lipped encounters with doctors, priests, and Dad's ditzy new wife. Pickard wades through these swamplike emotional backwaters with surefooted precision, her scenes of distress or revelation never sinking in melodrama, and the multiple shocks along the way handled with remarkable élan. Pickard may lose a few fans here—adoring readers tend to dislike change—but this heretofore winning series loses nothing by taking a turn into the darker alleyways of the soul. —*Peter Robertson*

Pronzini, Bill.
Breakdown.
Delacorte, $17.95 (0-385-29896-X). 240p.

For the purpose of cover, his name's Art Canino, and he's pounding Bud Lights in the Hideaway, a low-rent beach tavern near San Francisco. He's actually the Nameless Detective, and he's in the bar to watch another drinker, who just may know something about the hit-and-run death of Nameless' client. It could be a legitimate case, or it could be that Nameless is being set up for a fall. Pronzini's existentialist sleuth has accrued heaps of praise in the past, and this novel isn't likely to change the pattern. *Breakdown* packs enough fog-ridden beachfront detail, barfly bravado, and sorrowful shamus patter to last most writers a whole crime series. Style is all in these grim, impressionistic adventures of the archetypal loner detective, and Pronzini's retro-hip prose is made to order for the job. —*Peter Robertson*

Raleigh, Michael.
Death in Uptown.
St. Martin's, $17.95 (0-312-05849-7). 256p.

Why did ex–Chicago cop Paul Whelan choose the blighted Uptown district to set himself up as a sleuth? Well, the overhead is low, and the local cuisine is an eclectic mix (Whelan's favorite eatery claims Persian extraction but can serve up a pizza puff with the best of them). Maybe he just feels at home there, alongside the shell-shocked souls walking the streets, sleeping on rooftops in the summer heat, passing a bottle in a garbage-strewn alleyway. And dying way before their time. Whelan's old pal Artie Shears is the latest to go, battered to death in an alley, his idea to write a book on the homeless the last of many lost causes. As he investigates the murder, Whelan soon finds himself slogging the Uptown streets in the company of a tough cop in a bad jacket, a rival yet, begrudgingly, an ally. First-novelist Raleigh proves especially adept at integrating locale into narrative. This fine debut has a sleek start, a painfully slow middle, and a cunning gem of a conclusion, the kind that makes the reader backtrack to make sure one of the jigsaw pieces wasn't lost or hidden along the way. —*Peter Robertson*

Rendell, Ruth.
The Copper Peacock and Other Stories.
Mysterious, $17.95 (0-89296-465-0). 183p.

Rendell's novels—the magnificently dark psychological thrillers and the Inspector Wexford police procedurals—are so first-rate that saying her stories are inferior means only that on a crime-fiction scale of 10, they're 9s. In her latest collection of stories, eight of them fall into her psychological thriller vein, the remaining one being an Inspector Wexford piece. "A Pair of Yellow Lilies" is a perfect example of the former type. Young Bridget Thomas, secretary of her women's group, goes to her local library to do background research on the famous fashion designer who is sheduled to come to speak to the group. In the library, she discovers her purse has been stolen, and through an odd set of circumstances, she gets acquainted with the thief—and makes amends. The other seven stories falling into the suspense category follow the pattern established by this one: well-realized characters set in somewhat predictable situations. The last story, "An Unwanted Woman," features Inspector Wexford in a bizarre tale about a woman's daughter who refuses to live with her mother until the mother's new husband is removed from the scene. Of course, murder happens, and, in the brief space of the story, the malefactor is indeed discovered—but without the luxurious tension found in the Wexford novels. Rendell has a devoted and extensive following, and this collection of stories is a must purchase. —*Brad Hooper*

Roat, Ronald Clair.
Close Softly the Door.
Story Line Press, $18.95 (0-934257-48-5). 160p.

Are there enough cases in Lansing, Michigan, to keep a private dick busy? Readers will certainly hope so after racing through the initial caper of Stuart Mallory, the most likable of snoops. Mallory covers a good portion of western Michigan, described in wonderfully specific detail, while trying to protect a former flame from a brutal hood who wants her silenced before she can testify against him. A fortune in stolen coins serves to complicate matters, but the plot isn't the main attraction here. It's Mallory, a refreshingly fallible hero with a saving sense of humor. Roat's spare but carefully crafted prose is an additional bonus. The author fares far better than his character's beloved Detroit Tigers, whose misadventures are chronicled at regular intervals. In his first trip to the plate, Roat knocks one clean out of the park. —*Dennis Dodge*

✔Robinson, Peter.
A Dedicated Man.
Scribner, $17.95 (0-684-19265-9). 261p.

Devotees of the British police procedural, charming rural version, who haven't met Chief Inspector Alan Banks have been shortchanged. In his second adventure, following *Gallows View,* Banks establishes himself as one of the most entertaining coppers on the other side of the Atlantic. Robinson has obviously studied the genre carefully; his Banks' mysteries have it all—right down to the map of the small village (in this case, Helmthorpe, nestled under the shadow of Crow Scar in a Yorkshire dale) where charm and murder are served in equal portions. The victim, Henry Steadman, was a local man whose passion was industrial archaeology and who apparently had no enemies in the world—except his murderer, of course. Probe as he might, Banks can find no one with a suitable motive. As the investigation progresses, more and more is known about the victim, but that only reveals how much everyone seemed to admire him—or so they claim. Another murder of a village teenager narrows the field and eventually leads to an unexpected conclusion. This story makes you understand why readers get addicted to genre mysteries—when they are good, they are very, very good. —*Stuart Miller*

✔Ross, Jonathan.
Daphne Dead and Done For.
St. Martin's, $15.95 (0-312-05408-4). 192p.

A former high-ranking policeman, Jonathan Ross has been combining exacting procedural wisdom with spirited characterization in the chronicles of his oft-beset bobby, George Rogers. Things start badly for Rogers this time out. He's sworn off tobacco, and, to make matters worse, he receives a weird ad submitted to a local paper's personal column. The note leads to a missing person case, which is complicated further when the husband of the missing woman, Daphne, is bludgeoned and fried to a crisp as his semidetached house burns. The flighty Daphne seemingly has fared no better than she deserves—a slew of bedmates, a lot of cheap and costly thrills. In addition, her lawyer appears to have done a bunk with the firm's books not exactly in order. Ross barely wastes a second or a word in his latest work; Rogers and his snuff-snorting, Pernod-sipping, Bentley-loving partner are soon up to their armpits in lovers and late-lamenteds. The usually terse policeman has some trouble fighting off a local newswoman, hot on the trail of a juicy headline and strangely anxious for a bout on the living-room floor of Rogers' disheveled digs. First-rate procedural fare. —*Peter Robertson*

Rossiter, Elizabeth.
The Lemon Garden.
Carroll & Graf, $18.95 (0-88184-682-1). 256p.

Waking in a strange hospital, suffering from amnesia, actress Joanna Fleming has many questions to answer. Not only must she find out who she is, but also what caused her accident and why she feels so threatened. Why is her white evening gown in a ball on the floor of her closet? Why is there one diamond-and-onyx earring in her purse when she never wears earrings? And whom can she trust? The difficult and brooding Angelo Valente, stepson of her aunt? Her director, Frank Harmer? Or Roddy Marchant, her former lover? And, finally, what is it about the lemon garden that terrifies her so much? An intense and well-crafted thriller and a must-read for mystery lovers. —*Cynthia Ogorek*

✔Ruell, Patrick.
Dream of Darkness.
Countryman/Foul Play, $17.95 (0-88150-178-6). 208p.

As with such recent works as Margaret Yorke's *Admit to Murder*, Julian Symons' *Death's Darkest Face*, and Michael Dibdin's *The Tryst*, the best British crime writers are expanding their narrative horizons at a remarkable rate. Forget coy plotting and hamlets full of the baser sort. Erudite, expressive essays on English class and culture are now being artfully placed within disciplined, meticulous, disturbing crime novels. Writing here as Patrick Ruell, Reginald Hill continues the trend, mixing political exposé, psychological suspense, and an eerie dream vision. Oxbridge-bound Sairey Ellis can't shake the dreams she has had since adolesence—dreams that have to do with her mother's mysterious death in Uganda at the time of Idi Amin. Sairey's fears assume a more physical reality when her night vision of an Indian boy with a star-shaped scar, who seems, in the dream, to hold the secret of her mother's death, actually appears in England and is attacked. The story of Sairey's haunted nights and days alternates with selections from her father's memoirs, which detail his diplomatic career in Uganda during the Amin years. Ruell effectively uses these parallel narratives to slowly unravel the mystery of Sairey's mother's death. A gem of a book with a startling finale. —*Peter Robertson*

Sebastian, Tim.
Saviour's Gate.
Delacorte, $19.95 (0-385-29881-1). 320p.

His power base rocked, the Soviet general secretary must decide to fight or flee. His childhood friend, the envoy, journeys to Washington to request an unusual favor. Meanwhile, American David Russert is seconded into active service in Moscow as a wave of riots devastate the city, and information about the general secretary's plan begins to leak. A test run for the escape is spotted, an agent compromised, motives stirred like choice ingredients, and the players scramble to find sides and somehow cherish the battered remains of their personalities. Sebastian, author of *Spy Shadow* and *The Spy in Question*, may have hit on the most workable espionage scenario since the onset of glasnost kicked much of the stuffing out of the genre. Equipped with a gripping, contemporary premise, Sebastian manages to avoid the reliance on flashbacks that spy novelists, including le Carrè in *The Secret Pilgrim*, have been forced to rely on lately. The novel isn't without flaws, however. Sebastian overuses cultural sidebars, and his romantic angle is more narrative crutch than the elegant metaphor it's supposed to be. Yet *Saviour's Gate* seethes with understated power, as the plausibility of the premise takes hold of the reader's imagination and the logistics of the situation are tantalizingly presented. A welcome new slant on the weary old game. —*Peter Robertson*

Setlowe, Richard.
The Black Sea.
Ticknor & Fields, $21.95 (0-395-56927-3). 413p.

A basket is delivered by a rickshaw driver to the doorman at Singapore's elegant Raffles Hotel. Inside is the severed head of a Russian naval officer. So begins Setlowe's high-action thriller with a post-glastnost twist. The Russians and Americans are on the same side—the side of the victims. Here the bad guys are a band of Malayan terrorists looking for weapons and eager to drive the infidels out of Southeast Asia, thereby restoring rule by the faithful. To accomplish this goal, they're willing (and eager) to chop off the heads of the American passengers and Russian crew members they've taken hostage on the *Black Sea*, a Soviet cruise ship. Setlowe does an excellent job of elevating the genre, lacing his story with historical detail, graphic description, and quirky political insights. The characters, too, never take a backseat to the action, as is so often the case. Not that the action ever lags. Setlowe turns up the juice and races to a surprising conclusion that places his novel a few knots ahead and few fathoms deeper than much of his competition in the adventure-thriller field. —*Robert Seid*

Seymour, Gerald.
Condition Black.
Morrow, $20 (0-688-10631-5). 336p.

British espionage author Seymour's latest effort is powered by a chillingly authentic premise. His hunter is an FBI agent investigating the accidental shooting of a fellow operative by a young English assassin, codenamed COLT, who is in the employ of the Iraqi government and whose real target is a scientist working to undermine the Iraqis' quest for nuclear weaponry. While the distance between COLT and his hunter shortens, a financially troubled British scientist finds himself drawn inexorably into the profitable world of betrayal. The novel's COLT sections provide tense thrills, guarded motives, and workmanlike plotting, but few real surprises. When the focus turns to the British scientist, however, Seymour offers his readers a carefully documented glimpse of the day-to-day toil endured by a lower-middle-class family battling ruin. There is something strangely endearing about the agonized traitor, and this beleaguered scientist, struggling with both officialdom and conscience, evokes our sympathy as completely as Maurice Castle does in Graham Greene's *Human Factor*. —*Peter Robertson*

Simpson, Dorothy.
Doomed to Die.
Scribner, $19.95 (0-684-19381-7). 288p.

Behind large bay windows, a nanny lies on the kitchen floor, dark blood seeping from a head wound, two crying children upstairs. Domestic violence? Perhaps. The returning mother distraught at the evidence of bad child care? Less likely. The nanny's husband angry at an affair discovered and a possible divorce? That's more like it. As usual, endless scenarios play out for copper Luke Thanet. And most of them even make sense. But Perdita Master didn't just die from a head wound. She suffocated inside a plastic bag, giving the crime a far meaner edge. Thanet and loyal subordinate Mike Lineham plod gamely through the tenth procedural in Simpson's popular series. Unlike, say, John Harvey's Charlie Resnick series, which is filled with copious socioeconomic references that allow the reader to explore the milieu as well as the murder, the Luke Thanet novels are much more linear, with their focus clearly on detecting—but it's high-caliber detecting. Confirmed clue-sniffers should be ready for a surprise here: both the solution and the sinner are shockers, though eminently fair ones. —*Peter Robertson*

Smith, Julie.
The Axeman's Jazz.
St. Martin's, $19.95 (0-312-06295-8). 384p.
Womack, Steven.
Smash Cut.
St. Martin's, $18.95 (0-312-06467-5). 304p.

The success of James Lee Burke has spawned a host of other mystery writers eager to exploit New Orleans' rich mix of squalor and elegance. Here are two outstanding sequels to two acclaimed series debuts. *New Orleans Mourning* won Julie Smith last year's Edgar award, and Womack's *Murphy's Fault* was a *New York Times*' Notable Book of 1990.

In *Jazz*, cop Skip Langdon's aristocratic background, her familial unrest, and the Crescent City's tightly knit clan of powerful families are on the back burner. She forgoes a spot of romance in California and draws the lion's share of active duty on the case of a serial killer whose first victims belonged to the swelling ranks of recovering addicts—both the traditional kind and the new, more sinister sort: codependents who sit stroking teddy bears representing the inner child. After being forced to endure a painful session at Overeaters Anonymous (and recklessly pounding a shrimp po'boy on the way home), her suspect list gets a few choice additions from her stint with the teddy-bear nurturers: the frightening and sensual Alex, a young WASP couple too good to be true, and a lady with a strange new name and a taste for the dark side. A New Orleans mystery isn't complete without at least one interlude for beignets and café au lait at the Cafe du Monde and some sinister talk of forbidden voodoo practices along the way, and this has both.

In *Smash Cut*, a nuclear plant close to New Orleans is the planned site for a movie studio. Andrew Kwang specializes in the kind of films that Jack Nicholson won't make, despite the easy money—sleazy, bimbo-laden flicks like *Volcano Vixens*. However, the urbane and mysterious Kwang is rich, likes to draw on local labor, and has New Orleans businessmen lining up to offer him a hand (usually palm up). Only the volatile daughter of the governor is in the way of his proposed move to the city. They squabble in a public place, and she dies. Obviously, Kwang needs someone like free-lance PR expert Jack Lynch who, in turn, needs something to pull him out of his own personal nightmare—the loss of his high-powered banking job, of a lover, and of a murderous spouse. Lynch begins his work to clear Kwang's name with the surface scum of the B-movie industry, then dives headlong into the more

Mystery & Espionage

treacherous waters of Louisiana politics, where graft is king of the swamps. From there, it just keeps getting better. —*Peter Robertson*

Steed, Neville.
Wind Up.
St. Martin's, $16.95 (0-312-05998-1). 224p.

See p.391.

Stewart, Edward.
Deadly Rich.
Delacorte, $20 (0-385-29998-2). 576p.

Begin with a flashback: a punk kid throws the daughter of a famous juicehead actress from a balcony. He gets time in stir. Now fast-forward to a cleaned-up actress doing lunch with socialite pals. One demented member of the party spots the convicted killer working in the kitchen and, later that day, croaks in the department store where the punk kid's loyal mom works. Meanwhile, NYC cop Cardozo is dealing with his wife's death, the lure of the actress, and the first moves of a serial killer terrifying the well-heeled with letters to a gossip columnist. *Deadly Rich* is twice the length of most glittery suspense yarns, but Stewart, author of the previous Cardozo adventure, *Privileged Lives*, believes firmly in leaving no stone unturned: troweled-on forensic detail, traditional serial-killer methodology, and, of course, plenty of good old-fashioned sex and drugs. Early-hours-of-the-morning page-turning is pretty much guaranteed. —*Peter Robertson*

✔Stout, David.
Night of the Ice Storm.
Mysterious; dist. by Ballantine, $19.95 (0-89296-415-4). 304p.

In a decaying upstate New York town, on a night when freak weather drives most of the inhabitants into darkened houses, one young man goes out for a drink, meets a priest, spurns a sexual advance, and kills with ferocious brutality. A few nights later he attends a going-away party for a worker at the local paper, and a few things best left unsaid are mumbled in a wash of hashish and booze. The crime, however, remains undetected, because of police incompetence and/or official pressure. Twenty years later, on the eve of the newspaper's fancy reunion party, one liquor-riddled police reporter remembers the party conversation and promptly dies. With his secret lurking close to the surface, the killer is desperate. Stout, who won an Edgar for his first novel, *Carolina Skeletons*, eventually delivers a solution and a killer—both obvious yet totally unexpected—but not before exploring the troubled lives of several newspaper employees, including a frustrated woman reporter, a one-time cynical whiz kid now close to the career skids, and a loyal and plodding journalist lured by infidelity. Writing with the narrative density of Joyce Carol Oates, Stout delivers a dizzying montage of background detail, socioeconomic observation (mostly about the death throes of an industrial town), slowly building tension, and, at the end, teeth-clenching narrative pyrotechnics. —*Peter Robertson*

Taibo, Paco I.
The Shadow of the Shadow.
Viking, $18.95 (0-670-83177-8). 233p.

With "world music" standard on progressive radio stations, "world mystery" seems due for a U.S. breakthrough. Spanish-born Mexican Taibo, executive vice-president of the International Association of Crime Writers, is doing his part, with the remarkable private-eye novel *An Easy Thing* last year and now with this fascinating fictionalized version of the early 1920s effort by Mexican colonels and the same American oilmen who gave us Teapot Dome to "liberate" Mexico's oil-producing Gulf Coast. The novel centers, however, not on that failed conspiracy, but on four dominoes-playing friends who stumble across traces of the plot and its cover-up. These four characters—the romantic newspaper crime reporter, the detached attorney who rejects his own class to defend petty criminals, the poet who fought with Pancho Villa and writes patent-medicine jingles and poems-for-hire, and the Mexican-born Chinese anarchist labor organizer—are complicated men moving through a Mexico City awash in greed, corruption, and brutal violence. In brief chapters with the staccato click of a domino on a marble table, the narrative shifts from one protagonist to another, traveling around the dominoes table, around the city and its working-class suburbs, and deep into the heart of the puzzle. —*Mary Carroll*

Tapply, William G.
The Spotted Cats.
Delacorte, $17.95 (0-385-30233-9). 256p.

There are really two kinds of Brady Coyne mysteries: the first are set in or near Boston and involve the lethargic lawyer being forced to turn sleuth, though he would rather be fishing; in the second type, set in some suitably idyllic rural retreat, he actually is fishing, though the solitary poetry of man and fly rod is invariably violated by murder. This time the action begins on Cape Cod, where Brady has driven to spend a weekend with cranky client Jeff Newton. Things turn ugly when Brady is held at knifepoint, Newton is assaulted, and a collection of solid-gold leopard figurines is stolen. With Newton in a coma, Brady sets out to find the culprits. The search takes him, fortuitously, to West Yellowstone, Montana, which just happens to be fly-fisherman's heaven. What we have here, then, is a sampling of Brady in both his venues: a little New England ambience as an appetizer, followed by a trip to the wilds, where fish stories served with murder are once again the Blue Plate Special. Tapply has been juggling this formula through 10 books; like your favorite fishing hat, it may be a mite tired, but it's still damn comfortable. —*Bill Ott*

Thompson, Joyce.
Bones.
Morrow, $19.95 (0-688-09653-0). 352p.

Freddy Bascomb is an artist and a single mother struggling to support two children, Paige and Chaz. So when the Seattle police offer her the job of sketching "Bones," facial reconstructions of the Green River Killer's victims, she accepts. Her work and a burgeoning romance are put on hold when her alcoholic father, newspaperman Nick, is murdered. Before Freddy has time to grieve, the unknown assailant (a master of disguise) begins stalking her and her children, leaving clues in the form of chapters of a novel with Nick as one of the characters. The whirlwind of ensuing events leaves Freddy as the eye of the storm, calm, desperate, and seemingly benign. Thompson's prose is commanding and richly dense. She builds supportive friend and family relationships as believably as she does disintegrating ones, and her big scenes are often so horrifying, or so humanly sad, that the reader aches to be able to intervene on the characters' behalf. A fine, intelligent thriller. —*Eloise Kinney*

Turnbull, Peter.
And Did Murder Him.
St. Martin's, $15.95 (0-312-05813-6). 192p.

The best police procedurals depict minor societies in microcosm. In Turnbull's Glasgow P Division series, we follow the day-to-day movements and moral quandaries of a mixed bunch of career cynics and diehard idealists, all played out against the grim, dank backdrop of Scotland's largest city. Along with the crushing weight of compounded irony, a given night's detritus usually includes empty beer cans, the greasy remains of a fish supper, and the puked-up aftermath of too much reveling. This time there is also the scrawny corpse of a knifed teenage junkie found huddled in a doorway. The foot soldiers of P Division locate the victim's home, his friends, and his family, who take the boy's death stoically. Readers also witness two elderly women mugged for four quid and the harsh specter of a father watching his child go through drug withdrawal. Turnbull isn't flashy, which might explain why he's yet to get much acclaim on this side of the Atlantic. With just a shade more narrative style to go along with all the grit, that could change very quickly. —*Peter Robertson*

✔Vachss, Andrew.
Sacrifice.
Knopf, $20 (0-679-40283-7). 320p.

Vachss creates a secret world full of unreadable signs, prison-learned truths, and complex survival rules for saint/sinner PI Burke (no phone, no address, a slew of fake identities) and his secret army of street-raised, street-safe killers and survivors. Here, Vachss, in real life a lawyer specializing in child cases, fearlessly rips apart the simplified myths and inhuman realities of child abuse. Luke is a traumatized boy whose personality has fragmented with the endless, systematic assault of parents belonging to a satanic cult. One layer of Luke has evolved into a killer. The hunt for another child's body leads Burke to a voodoo artifact hanging near the scene of the crime and an alluring witch woman, whose knowing soul touches Burke's own. Vachss' killers aren't as well formed as usual; perhaps he's intent on targeting widespread evil as opposed to single lethal subjects: the love-starved child, the welfare-level lover of a weak and beaten woman, and Wolfe, the DA, whom the author half-heartedly portrays as driven mercilessly toward getting convictions. Vachss' clipped, blunt, occasionally overly melodramatic sentences may, in some way, be ripe for parody (à la Mickey Spillane), but they also convey the frightening impact of the somber, shocking, emotionally deadening hellholes that Burke, breaking every civilized rule, battles gamely through. —*Peter Robertson*

Valin, Jonathan.
Second Chance.
Delacorte, $17.95 (0-385-29912-5). 288p.

Cincinnati private eye Harry Stoner is summoned to the home of wealthy psychiatrist Phil Pearson, whose daughter, a student at the University of Chicago, has disappeared. Stoner soon realizes she's joined forces with her emotionally disturbed brother on a mission of vengeance. It seems they both believe their mother was murdered, and her killer, imprisoned for an unrelated act, has just been paroled. Stoner is the purest example of the hard-boiled PI in print today. As he honorably pursues his case, he's confronted by a foul world in which greed rules, love is a weapon, and families are conduits by which the sins of one generation are visited upon the next. Valin is as good as anyone working the mystery field today. A strong novel on many levels. —*Wes Lukowsky*

Wambaugh, Joseph.
Fugitive Nights.
Morrow, $22 (0-688-11128-9). 336p.

What happens to a New Centurion when his legs go? That seems to be Wambaugh's preoccupation in his two newest, *The Golden Orange* and this one. In both, his heroes are 50-ish cops with bad wheels, living almost indigently amidst the glitz of wealthy California resort towns. *Fugitive Nights* focuses on Palm Springs PD detective Lynn Cutter, who's awaiting his pension after blowing out a knee while serving as Mayor Sonny Bono's bodyguard. Penniless from Charles Keating's Lincoln Savings scam, Lynn housesits for absent millionaires, sometimes eats dogfood, and always drinks cheap scotch. He needs a job but all he knows is police work; doing anything physically active could threaten his pension. Enter beautiful private eye Breda Burroughs and diminutive patrolman Nelson ("Half Nelson") Hareem, who engage him on separate-but-intersecting quirky quests that range from the desert to Bob Hope's neighbor's house. Wambaugh really does seem preoccupied. Both *The Golden Orange* and *Fugitive Nights* share similar heroes, motivations, locales, saloons, and senses of humor. But it's okay. Wambaugh's plenty good enough to walk this beat twice. *Fugitive Nights* will delight his loyal fans and surprise new readers. —*Thomas Gaughan*

Wilcox, Collin.
Hire a Hangman.
Holt, $18.95 (0-8050-0980-9). 248p.

Within the first 12 hours after three slugs ruin the arrogant features of ace surgeon Brice Hanchett, the list of suspects is long enough to stretch all the way up the steep hills from Fisherman's Wharf to the swank Russian Hill abode where the shooting occurred. San Francisco cop Frank Hastings scrapes away the surface glamour—the Jaguars and the wood-panelled interiors—and quickly gets to the dirt: an indifferent wife, a bitter former wife, a spoiled son, an abused stepdaughter, and, as a weird outgrowth from Hanchett's lucrative medical career, a lethally crazed woman, one of many unsuccessful applicants for the good doctor's much sought after liver-transplant services. Wilcox gets compared with Hammett a lot—and deservedly so. He mines the noir angles of the city with the same restless eye, and his skin-tight plots make the same sudden jumps from the gutter to the high hills and back again. —*Peter Robertson*

✔Wilhelm, Kate.
Death Qualified: A Mystery of Chaos.
St. Martin's, $22.95 (0-312-05853-5). 438p.

In both her fantasy novels, such as *Cambio Bay*, and her crime mysteries (*Sweet, Sweet Poison*), Wilhelm is known for her complex plots and intellectually stimulating premises. Her latest combines the suspense of a murder mystery and courtroom drama with the inventive terrors of science fiction. Barbara Holloway, a young, brilliant lawyer and the story's conscience and catalyst, dropped out of the legal system for five years, disgusted with its compromises and unjust justice. She is also estranged from her widowed, lawyer father, but when he calls and says he needs her, she rushes home to Turner's Point, Oregon, a small town on the banks of a mercurial river. Her dad needs more than filial affection; he asks her to take over a difficult, seemingly hopeless case: the murder trail of their lovely, petite neighbor, Nell, accused of killing her husband, Lucas, who had disappeared six years ago after participating in a secret research project about adolescent perception. Why was he kept prisoner on a college campus, heavily drugged, his identity concealed? Barbara intuits her way through a mist of confounding clues that lead to chaos theories and fractals, new dangers and unimagined psychological horrors. As the case expands, dragging more and more people into its vortex, Barbara survives murder attempts, confronts an old enemy, falls in love, and comes full circle, back to her hatred of the system. Set in the evocative, rainy, rocky woods of the Northwest and the frontiers of madness, this dark, chilling tale is the work of a master. —*Donna Seaman*

Wiltse, David.
Prayer for the Dead.
Putnam, $19.95 (0-399-13607-X). 304p.

In the considerable wake of Thomas Harris' *Silence of the Lambs*, the demand for skin-crawling psychotic excess is palpable. Wiltse, author of *The Serpent* and *The Fifth Angel*, rises bravely to the occasion. His killer, a psychopath named Roger Dyce, drains his victims' blood ever so slowly, so that the young men's wasted remains look prematurely dead and bear a definite resemblance to his hated father and/or his much-loved grandfather. Clever and capable though he is, Dyce leaves clues: his hankering for a particular ethnic type, his foul-smelling house, the huge cooking pot in his kitchen, and the stack of bones beneath the floor. So Dyce must contend with former government agent Becker, currently receiving psychiatric help for the worrying level of pleasure he derives from tracking and executing serial psychos. *Prayer* is terrifically good: page-turning but never gratuitous terror, droll dialogue, quasi-Gothic undertones, and complex character detailing of both hunter and hunted. —*Peter Robertson*

Wolf, S. K.
MacKinnon's Machine.
Simon & Schuster, $19.95 (0-671-70051-0). 315p.

A. C. MacKinnon, former Special Air Services sergeant major, is living quietly on a remote New Zealand sheep station until an old buddy offers him a small fortune to train a commando squad to kill Quaddafi. Oddities about the assignment nag, but it's only when the training is complete and an attempt is made on his life that MacKinnon realizes the target isn't the Libyan leader. Enter reference librarian Ann Rowen, who helps MacKinnon divine the real target and thwart the operation. Wolf has produced a first-rate thriller with mayhem, tradecraft, globe hurtling, and *realpolitik* enough to satisfy the genre's aficionados. Her descriptions of the hazards of high-speed night driving through the Sinai, the rivalry between Mossad and Shin Bet, and low-intensity warfare techniques, and the small, telling details of locales on five continents are convincing. And she really knows librarians: Ann Rowen is smart, able, ingenious, tough-minded in a crunch, and passionate— a wonderful turn on the stereotype. —*Thomas Gaughan*

Wright, Eric.
Final Cut.
Scribner, $18.95 (0-684-19300-0). 256p.

The screenwriter hates the old European actor and the young hotshot star, both of whom are rewriting his words. The producer needs to turn a profit badly. The low-budget thriller is set in Toronto, and local policeman Charlie Salter is given the supposedly easy job of adviser, ruling on what color to make the cop cars, rooting out the predictable flood of creeping Americanisms that deluge the story line. Things aren't going well, with large, fragile egos on overload as a series of accidental mishaps gum up the works and send tempers a-flying. Enter murder. The Salter novels (this is the eighth) are warm, low-key tales, bittersweet "fiftysomething" narratives filled with culture clashes, romantic interludes, familial broadsides, cease-fires, and grudging compromises, all contained in admittedly slight yet enduring crime plots. *Cut* expands on the mystery quotient as Charlie hunts for a killer in a well-stocked pool, forsaking the chance for a spot of bass fishing and all the while managing to steer clear of a son bent on ballet dancing, a career move unlikely to find favor with Salter's elderly father. Another winner in an excellent series. —*Peter Robertson*

Mystery & Espionage

✓**Wright, L. R.**
Fall from Grace.
Viking, $18.95 (0-670-83130-1). 246p.

Following the Edgar-winning *Suspect*, Canadian author Wright continues to mine the territory of Ruth Rendell and others—the suspense thriller underpinned with enough psychological and emotional subtext to sustain even the best mainstream fiction. Her detective is once again Royal Canadian Mounted Police sergeant Karl Alberg, whose beat is a picturesque coastal town near Vancouver. He has his hands full here, what with finding a body while on a boat trip and contending with his college-age daughter's crusading for animal rights. The tangled plot reaches in a multitude of directions, each explored in lavish, psychological detail: a roadside zookeeper, whose treatment of his animals arouses Alberg's daughter's ire; his frustrated wife, dreaming of secret loves; the wife's brother and his wife, carrying their own emotional baggage; and, circling around them all, the disquieting figure of Bobby, the local bad kid now back in town after a spell in jail. Trouble follows Bobby, and violence is never far behind. In Wright's fiction, detection is served up as a delectable side dish. Several subtly dysfunctional lives are skillfully drawn together, and though crimes inevitably result (and must be solved), Wright prefers to linger behind her characters' emotionally closed doors. What she finds there never fails to amaze us. —*Peter Robertson*

✓**Yorke, Margaret.**
A Small Deceit.
Viking, $18.95 (0-670-83977-9). 200p.

They meet quite by chance in a remote guest house. The man calling himself Baxter is a proper, emotionally guarded judge, escaping for a day or so from an orderly existence and a timid wife. The man calling himself Brown is a convicted criminal and a killer, moving between con games, between shy women who shelter him, and between his own murderous urges. Both hear the other's false name. Both look up. Both recognize the other. Brown assumes the judge to be hiding from something sordid. He indulges in a spot of harassment. He gains little, drifting between the judge's home and the house of a lonely local woman with three children. The killing urge soon returns. Only a writer with Margaret Yorke's smooth cunning and deceptively simplistic narrative technique could whip a taut climax and a cathartic emotional release out of this disciplined, metronomic tale. She isn't showy, or graphic, or gothic. She just instinctively knows her British characters: the hidden emotions beneath a cold word out of place, the effect of a soul-freezing childhood. The best of the British crime mistresses manage so much more than death and denouement in their novels. For example, Yorke's deft portrait of the gently yet inexorably trapped judge's wife contains all the nuance found in the nongenre work of such authors as Penelope Lively and Anita Brookner. —*Peter Robertson*

Science Fiction

Anderson, Poul.
The Time Patrol.
Tor, $21.95 (0-312-85231-2). 464p.

This collection of nine novellas about the Time Patrol, charged with keeping their own future safe by watching the past, belongs in any collection where Anderson is popular. The stories are arranged in order of publication, which demonstrates the growth of both the writer and the concept. Anderson is a notable user of historical material as a springboard for science fiction and fantasy, and the novella is the length at which he has always done much of his best work. Alternate-history buffs will be an audience for this book, as well as the usual crowd of Anderson fans. —*Roland Green*

✔Anthony, Piers.
Tatham Mound.
Morrow, $22 (0-688-10140-2). 531p.

As his 60 sf and fantasy novels (including such popular series as Xanth, Apprentice Adept, and Incarnations of Immortality) testify, Anthony relishes a good story. Here he shifts from the imagined future to the past, from tales of robots and ogres and unicorns to stories of the native peoples of North America and their tragic confrontation with the invaders from Europe. Inspired by the discovery and excavation of an untouched native American burial site on the Withlacoochee River near Anthony's Citrus County, Florida home, *Tatham Mound* is narrated by Tale Teller, a Toco Indian from northern Florida whose disabled arm (injured in his first effort as a warrior) and skill at languages and, later, storytelling lead him to travel across much of the southeastern quarter of what is now the U.S, north to Illinois' Cahokia Mounds, west to the Mississippi River. In his travels—as translator, messenger, storyteller, and finally captive of the "Castiles tribe" of Hernando de Soto—Tale Teller has a higher mission: directed by the spirit of a Toco elder he must determine what danger threatens his people and find a way to warn them and avoid this threat. Tale Teller fails in his mission—his tribe, part of the Safety Harbor civilization in Florida, is decimated by the diseases the Europeans carry with them—but his 35-year journey and the tales of many tribes he gathers provide a moving portrait of the living worlds destroyed when Europe "discovered" America. —*Mary Carroll*

Anthony, Piers.
Virtual Mode.
Putnam/Ace, $15.95 (0-399-13661-4). 310p.

Anthony has had great success writing series—Xanth, Incarnations of Immortality, etc.—and this novel begins a new one. The author relies on a familiar plot device: a person from another reality enters our world, then returns to his own with a companion. In this case the companion is 14-year-old

Colene, who emerges as one of the better-drawn adolescent females in recent years. Anthony's "realism" manages to avoid sleaze, and the lighter parts of the narrative, while indeed light, are never frivolous. In addition, Anthony's pacing and world building are up to standard. While it is obviously too early to render a verdict on the series, let it be said that Anthony shows definite growth as a writer. Recommended for any collection where the author has a following. —*Roland Green*

Blaylock, James P.
The Paper Grail.
Berkley/Ace, $17.95 (0-441-65126-7). 371p.

Another of Blaylock's low-key but eminently readable quest tales, with a particularly admirable use of the Northern California setting. A somewhat absentminded museum curator goes in search of a Hokusai drawing, becomes involved with several eccentric relatives, and then has to beat off or outrun a contingent of oddly sympathetic and highly plausible rivals for the possession of the drawing (the paper grail of the title). Blaylock manages leisurely pacing without becoming stodgy, and is generally emerging as a serious talent in contemporary fantasy. —*Roland Green*

✔Brooks, Terry.
The Druid of Shannara.
Ballantine/Del Rey, $19.95 (0-345-36298-5). 432p.

With *The Scions of Shannara*, popular sword-and-sorcerer Brooks embarked on yet another fantasy trilogy detailing the adventures of the humans and trolls and dwarfs and elves and gnomes who populated his previous Shannara epics. In the second installment of this Heritage of Shannara series, the reader finds that the evil Shadowen still retain their hold over the Four Lands, continuing to drain the Lands of the magic that had been their charm and lifeblood. Consequently, the king of the Silver River dispatches a contingent of, ah, bizarre individuals to recover the lost magic, a process that involves the need to capture the Black Elfstone. The mythological and historical roots of all quest novels are brought to original fruition in Brooks' hands; sophisticated fabrication—a luscious fairy tale for grown-ups—results from his patient construction of a richly appointed world and three-dimensional citizenry. An automatic purchase for active sf collections. —*Brad Hooper*

✔Brunner, John.
A Maze of Stars.
Ballantine/Del Rey, $18 (0-345-36541-0). 397p.

Past, present, and future commingle comfortably in Brunner's fuguelike tale that follows the experiences of Ship, a sentient biotechnological wonder created by humankind not only to seed more than 600 planets among the 600,000 in the galaxy's vast Arm of Stars, but also to make unalterable sweeps through thousands of years to follow-up on how the colonized worlds have developed. "So it made its way from star to star, marveling insofar as it could

Science Fiction

at the differences a mere half millennium had wrought yet also at the resemblances. Where control had not been wrested from them . . . humans remained astonishingly human . . ." On most worlds Ship has become a legend or is forgotten or denied, and Ship's existence is a lonely one, with only relatively brief respites when it is able, under the constraints set upon it, to take on human passengers. The plot's concept and execution are fascinating: Brunner has built not one but many exotic worlds, each crafted in enough detail to be credible in both physical and societal features, and he has given the whole an immediacy through the interactions between Ship and assorted humans as well as events on various worlds that lead to Ship acquiring another passenger for a time. The conclusion, which reveals Ship's initial and continuing purpose, leaves the reader much to ponder. —*Sally Estes*

Cadigan, Pat.
Synners.
Bantam/Spectra, paper, $4.95 (0-553-28254-9). 435p.

This novel will undoubtedly be pushed most heavily at the cyberpunk audience, yet it deserves a wider readership. It is an intelligent extrapolation of the impact of the widespread use of "virtual reality" computer simulations—so realistic that they can appear real on both individuals and society. Cadigan's world is depicted with care and intelligence, and while most of the well-drawn characters find themselves on the fringes of society, there is not the relentless confusion of sleaze with realism that mars so much literary science fiction. Probably Cadigan's best book to date and recommended for any collection with a strong audience for cyberpunk or unconventional science fiction. —*Roland Green*

✔Card, Orson Scott.
Xenocide.
Tor, $21.95 (0-312-85056-5). 448p.

The continuation of the story of Andrew ("Ender") Wiggin, begun in *Ender's Game* and continued in *Speaker for the Dead*, finds another interstellar conflict in the making. On the planet Lusitania, a virus essential to the life cycle of intelligent natives is also deadly dangerous to human beings, live-stock, and crops. Ender and his foster family must battle with a marvelously wrought assortment of allies and enemies to find a way of controlling the virus without destroying both the planet and two nonhuman races (the Buggers are also breeding again, thanks to Ender's saving of the Hive Queen). The book is a triumph of Card the philosopher rather than Card the storyteller, and by no means resolves all of Ender's problems, but its ethical concerns and command of the English language put it nearly up to the standard of its predecessors. —*Roland Green*

Cherryh, C. J.
Heavy Time.
Warner, $19.⊙5 (0-446-51616-3). 330p.

This latest novel set in Cherryh's Merchanter universe is about equal part fiction, thriller, and mystery and maintains the high skill and success readers have come to expect from the author. Two asteroid miners, somewhat at loose ends, salvage a drifting ship and rescue its owner. However, it turns out that the owner may be a murderer, and that powerful figures lurking in the shadows want the whole matter covered up, if necessary by disposing of the miners. Cherryh remains near the top of the field in both world building and characterization, and her narrative technique is steadily improving. Highly recommended. *—Roland Green*

Cherryh, C. J.
Yvgenie.
Ballantine/Del Rey, $19 (0-345-36784-7). 288p.

The third of Cherryh's novels drawn from Russian folklore brings back Ksvi Chernevog, the evil wizard of the second book. He has returned in incorporeal form, ready to prey on the susceptibility of Eveshka's now-adolescent daughter, Ilyana. Eveshka, the former *rusalka* (devouring ghost), has a major battle to fight against both magical assault and adolescent rebellion, both of which are depicted with Cherryh's usual knowledge of folklore and skill in characterization. The saga as a whole is emerging as Cherryh's most significant work of fantasy and should have a place in any active collection. *—Roland Green*

Claremont, Chris.
Grounded!
Berkley/Ace, paper, $4.95 (0-441-30416-8). 323p.

The sequel to *First Flight* brings back Lieutenant Nicole Shea, now grounded because of the psychological consequences of her contact with the alien Halyant'i in the first book. You can't keep a good astronaut down, though, and Shea is one of the more notable female warriors in recent science fiction. She promptly finds herself involved in the intrigues of the aliens, her own superiors, and the Cobri family (who collectively make Donald Trump look like a model of rectitude). The book has just about every virtue one can reasonably ask from military or action science fiction. Highly recommended. *—Roland Green*

✔David, Peter.
Q in Law.
Pocket, paper, $4.99 (0-671-73389-3). 252p.

Aboard the new *Enterprise*, two powerful merchant families of the Tizarin race are to be allied by marriage. All is going smoothly, until Lwaxana Troi, mother of ship's counselor Deanna Troi, appears—and sets her sights on Captain Picard. Lwaxana Troi is followed by the alien known as Q, who has come in his usual malicious fashion to learn about human romance. This time, though, he has met his match—in Lwaxana Troi. David is an accomplished humorist, and he both knows and respects the "Star Trek" universe. This is the first "Next Generation" novel to reach the classic level of the older novels of Duane, Lorrah, Hambly, or Snodgrass. Highly recommended. —*Roland Green*

✔Dickson, Gordon R.
Young Bleys.
Tor; dist. by St. Martin's, $19.95 (0-312-93130-1). 456p.

This latest volume in Dickson's grand creation, the Childe Cycle, takes place not long after *The Final Encyclopedia* (Ace, 1985), to which this is the sequel. While the Splinter Cultures tend to keep the three varieties of humans rigidly segregated, Bleys Ahrens is half-Friendly and half-Exotic. Raised by his Exotic mother, exploited by his half-brother, and finally maturing under the stress of that exploitation, Bleys is prepared to challenge the dominance of even the Dorsai. This is a more tightly structured book than *Encyclopedia*, and proves the potential for more fine tales in the Childe Cycle, which is good news to Dickson's large audience. An indispensable acquisition for science fiction collections. —*Roland Green*

Dickson, Gordon R. and others.
The Harriers, Book One: Of War and Honor.
Baen, paper, $4.50 (0-671-72048-1). 257p.

The first installment of a new shared-world military sf series features three tales about the ragtag Petit Harriers, your classic down-and-dirty outfit that tackles the thankless but essential jobs the more elegant Grand Harriers disdain. Dickson and Chelsea Quinn Yarbro have written the lead story concerning a weird succession crisis in which the rivals for a petty kingdom are identical clones. Steve Perry contributes a story about the disintegration of a drug ring, and S. N. Lewitt deals with the fate of a high-ranking officer caught in dubious dealings on an Islamic planet. Not long on novelty, the stories yet abound with action and humor, and the authors display nice touches with both hardware and characters. Recommended for military or action sf fans. —*Roland Green*

✔Donaldson, Stephen R.
The Gap into Conflict: The Real Story.
Bantam, $18.95 (0-553-07173-4). 210p.

The author of the insanely popular Thomas Covenant series launches a projected five-volume sf saga with this little space opera about two hard men, one bad and one worse, and one "hardening" woman, Morn Hyland. The worse man, Angus Thermopyle, is an ugly, foul-mouthed space pirate who rescues the voluptuous Morn when the undercover cop ship she's on self-destructs. Actually, it offed itself on account of her. She got an attack of "gap sickness," a berserker reaction to traveling at the speed of light, and gave the suicide command. To keep her from doing in his ship during another attack, Angus gives her a "zone implant," which also puts her in his power—heh, heh, heh! Naturally, he uses the implant's controls to have his loathsome way with the

Science Fiction

proud beauty. From this living hell, the merely bad guy—another, lots handsomer space pirate, Nick Succorso—extracts her, thanks to Angus' cowardly (don't ask, Donaldson says that's what it is) desire to live, even in prison. Fortunately for Morn, Angus hands the implant controls to her just before the cops nab him. And that's the end of *The Real Story*. Next installment: *The Gap into Vision: Forbidden Knowledge*. —*Ray Olson*

Drake, David.
The Warrior.
Baen; dist. by Simon & Schuster, paper, $4.95 (0-671-72058-9). 288p.

The latest volume in Drake's popular Hammer's Slammers series about futuristic mercenary tank troops, this actually encompasses two pieces—a short original novel and a reprinted (but solid) novella, "Liberty Port." The main work is the tale of Sergeant ("Slick") Des Grieux, who is always reluctant to obey what he considers nonsensical orders, with disaster resulting for the Slammers' enemies and his own career. The story is hardly more than three action scenes run together, but they are action scenes that are outstanding, even for a series that has produced some of the best in military science fiction. Recommended where the Slammers have an audience. —*Roland Green*

Forward, Robert L.
Martian Rainbow.
Ballantine/Del Rey, $18 (0-345-34712-9). 352p.

In the twenty-first century, last-ditch holdouts of communism have seized the human colony on Mars. A general wins a reputation by reconquering the planet, then turns megalomaniac. His twin brother, a scientist, turns against him and finds a key to the fight in the two-billion-year-old body of a Martian creature. This is not up to Forward's usual highly skillful writing level, since it does not focus on the scientific puzzles that he handles with such adeptness. However, there is plenty of action and some fascinating military hardware. Fans of hard-science and military science fiction will both enjoy this novel. —*Roland Green*

Friesner, Esther.
Harpy High.
Berkley/Ace, paper, $4.50 (0-441-31762-6). 256p.

Tim Desmond and Glenwood High in Brooklyn, who first met in *Gnome Man's Land*, are back. They are in even more supernatural peril than before, as more ancient magical beings try to escape into our world. Tim and his friends, human and otherwise, are enlisted (blackmailed?) by the Russian witch Babi Yaga to train all her friends and allies to live in (and take over) the world. Tim and friends eventually prevail, although not until after a long struggle, which Friesner depicts with her usual folkloric expertise, wry but never silly humor, and gripping action scenes. Friesner continues to be the champion of humorous fantasy, and her books will continue to have readers in most fantasy collections. —*Roland Green*

Science Fiction

Gibson, William and Sterling, Bruce.
The Difference Engine.
Bantam, $19.95 (0-553-07028-2). 352p.

In 1842, the British government withdrew financial support for inventor Charles Babbage's "analytical engine," a device that shared much of the same architecture used in modern-day computers but was based on a mechanical punch-card technology. With loss of funding, the project died. Gibson and Sterling imagine what the Victorian era might have been like had Babbage succeeded in creating a working "Engine" and thus launched the Age of Information 100 years early. Aspiring to join the intellectual elite that makes up England's (and the world's) ruling class, paleontologist Edward Mallory finds himself in the middle of a political power struggle after becoming the chance recipient of an enigmatic set of Engine program cards. He comes into contact with characters ranging from Thomas Henry Huxley to Sam Houston while dodging thugs out to recover the cards at any cost. The book's strongest feature is the evocative prose used to describe this fascinating world. There are some significant problems with structure, and one can only conjecture that this might have been a much more cohesive novel as a solo work by either author. Flaws notwithstanding, it is an original effort and is recommended for most fiction collections. —*Elliott Swanson*

Jordan, Robert.
The Dragon Reborn.
Tor, $22.95 (0-312-85248-7). 640p.

The third volume of Jordan's outstanding Wheel of Time high fantasy saga will not disappoint readers. Rand al'Thor is definitely the dragon of the title, though a most reluctant one. His companions each have their problems, while Egwene, Nynaeve, and Elayne are deeply involved in the intrigues that are shaking the Aes Sedai (the order of female magic-workers) to the core. Meanwhile, wars, rumors of wars, great and small crises, and general attacks of nerves abound, all well drawn against a rich and living world. Jordan is earning a high place for sheer storytelling ability, and this book belongs in any collection where the saga has already found readers. —*Roland Green*

Kerr, Katharine.
A Time of Exile: A Novel of the Westlands.
Doubleday, $21.95 (0-385-41463-3). 436p. paper, $10.95 (0-385-41464-1).

The fifth of Kerr's novels of the Celtic realm of Deverry begins a new series about the Westlands. Lord Rhodry Aberwyn's half-elven blood leads him on a quest to the elves' homeland and the discovery that his destiny is heavily involved with theirs. As usual, the quest involves exploration of past lives and a good many encounters with strange beings on various planes of existence. Kerr's characterization, pacing, and world building are of a very high order, and her large audience will eagerly demand this demonstration of her gifts. —*Roland Green*

Lee, Tanith.
The Book of the Beast: The Secret Books of Paradys II.
Overlook, $19.95 (0-87951-417-5). 196p.

The second of Lee's novels of the Renaissance-flavored city of Paradys combines fantasy, historical fiction, and horror in a manner that few authors would attempt (or would be as successful in pulling off). The deceptively simple plot involves demonic possession, but it is handled in an entirely classic fashion (and what at first appear to be embellishments tend to emerge as integral parts of the story). Lee's poetic style and her use of historical material are also as accomplished as ever. Major author, major work, and needed in any substantial fantasy collection. —*Roland Green*

✔MacAvoy, R. A.
King of the Dead.
Morrow, $19 (0-688-09600-X). 252p.

This sequel to *Lens of the World* continues the story of Nazhuret, orphaned nobleman, trained optician, and unlikely but effective adventurer in the service of the King of Vestinglon. In this book he and his mistress, Arlin (a lady as deadly as they come with a blade), travel to the empire of Rezhmia, Vestinglon's ancient foe, to avert a new war. This proves more complicated than anticipated, with political intrigues, scientific puzzles, and outright magic all playing a part. MacAvoy's prose and world building are of the same high standard as the characterization. More and more one thinks of this series as in the same tradition as Wolfe's excellent *Book of the New Sun*. Highly recommended. —*Roland Green*

✔McCaffrey, Anne.
All the Weyrs of Pern.
Ballantine/Del Rey, $20 (0-345-36892-4). 416p.

McCaffrey brings her human settlers on the planet Pern full swing in this installment in her popular series, as the past and future meet. In *Dragonsdawn*, she took readers back to the settling of the planet, showing us how it all came about—the first devastating Thread attack, the genetic engineering of the dragons, and the need to abandon the landing site. Here, Lord Jaxom of Ruatha and his white dragon, Ruth, are leaders in the rediscovery of the Landing and the revitalizing of Avivas (the Artificial Intelligence Voice-Address System), which is still extant after 5,525 years of maintaining itself on minimum power. Avivas sets out to educate the Pernians in the sciences that have been long lost in order that they might end the Thread threat for all time. This is an exciting, full-bodied, richly detailed new chapter in the Pern chronicle as the knowledge of the first settlers is united with the wisdom of the descendants. It also mirrors human nature, setting the hide-bound traditionalists against those willing to learn new ways by building on the relearned capabilities. Once again McCaffrey's narrative flows smoothly, maintaining the world and characters she has so lovingly created and setting new challenges for them to meet. A must for Pern fans. —*Sally Estes*

Moorcock, Michael.
The Revenge of the Rose.
Berkley/Ace, $17.95 (0-441-71844-2). 244p.

We have not, it seems, had our final encounter with Elric of Melniboné; and as presented with Moorcock's mature skills, he is well worth meeting. Elric has returned to his birthplace, the Dreaming City, and is on a quest for his father's soul. The price of failure is being forever pursued by that soul, so it is not surprising that Elric is willing to accept help even from such a strange being as the woman called the Rose (she is on a quest of her own). There are characters with tragicomic overtones, plenty of action, and lyricism in much of the prose. This is superior to *The Fortress of the Pearl* and certain to please readers who have been following Elric's adventures now for nearly a generation. —*Roland Green*

Paxson, Diana L.
The Serpent's Tooth.
Morrow, $20 (0-688-08339-0). 394p.

This retelling of the legend of King Lear is a tribute to Paxson's imagination and scholarship. Lear is presented as an Iron Age British king who married three captive queens and had a daughter by each. Two of the daughters betrayed him by remaining loyal to their mothers' people; the third remained loyal to him and was banished when her sisters came to power. Paxson plays historical detective as well as fantasist and does it so well that the book will appeal not only to her staunch readers but also to aficionados of historical fantasy in general. —*Roland Green*

Pohl, Frederik and Williamson, Jack.
The Singers of Time.
Doubleday, $21.95 (0-385-26507-7). 358p.

Earth has been taken over by aliens who resemble 10-foot turtles and have given us their technology in return for raw materials and the abolition of war. Humans who remain interested in science are a despised minority, but they become invaluable to the aliens when their home planet and their one and only fertile female vanish into a wormhole. This is a satisfactory book in every way—infused with warmth and humor, probably the best collaboration yet from a pair of old masters who do not seem to have lost much ground to their advancing years. —*Roland Green*

Reaves, Michael.
Street Magic.
Tor, $18.95 (0-312-85125-1). 320p.

Reaves' latest is a fantasy set in contemporary San Francisco. A human runaway, Danny Thayer, discovers that the city is also a haven for the Scatterlings, runaways from Faerie. Danny turns out to be a changeling from Faerie himself and a key to the Scatterlings' finding a way home. The book breaks no new ground in contemporary fantasy, but Reaves is working his way up toward the high standard of Charles De Lint in characterization, setting, and folkloric scholarship. His book belongs in any contemporary fantasy collection. —*Roland Green*

Rosenberg, Joel.
D'Shai.
Berkley/Ace, paper, $4.95 (0-441-15751-3). 327p.

Rosenberg's latest begins a series set in feudal D'Shai, a land where the nobles know their place and are quick to make sure that everyone else knows theirs. Kami, a wandering (and somewhat inept) acrobat, learns this fact the hard way when he dares to fall in love with a nobleman's daughter. The result is a beating for him and death for his sister. This thoroughly absorbing novel emerges as Rosenberg's most original and possibly best work since *Ties of Blood and Silver*, and this new series as a whole promises to greatly enhance his reputation. —*Roland Green*

Rosenberg, Joel.
The Road to Ehvenor.
Penguin, $19.95 (0-451-45140-6). 432p.

The sixth volume of Rosenberg's popular Guardians of the Flame series is the longest and most ambitious. It also has some claim to being the best. Karl Cullinane is indisputably dead. His work, however, is far from finished. His widow, Africa; his son, Jason; and the dwarf Ahira not only have to fight the Slavers, they have to contend with an intrusion of evil magic from Faerie. What with plenty of action, good world building, and a cast of characters aging and changing in a manner that speaks well for both their creator and the series, *Road* is recommended for most fantasy collections. —*Roland Green*

Scarborough, Elizabeth.
Phantom Banjo.
Bantam/Spectra, paper, $4.99 (0-553-28761-3). 272p.

Scarborough's first volume in the Songkiller Saga trilogy. A cabal of devils discovers that music is one of the few things that the human race can use against them and sets out to wipe music from the face of the earth. They begin with folk music, using as their weapons lawyers (an easy mark for the diabolical) and both natural and induced disasters. This book has just about every virtue one can reasonably expect in a contemporary fantasy tale, including a vivid portrait of the contemporary folk scene and a chilling emotional impact that makes many horror novels look pedestrian. Highly recommended. —*Roland Green*

Sheffield, Charles.
Divergence.
Ballantine/Del Rey, $16.95 (0-345-36039-7). 283p.

Book two of the Heritage Universe series begins where *Summertime* left off. The cast of the first book and several new members (including a computer within a human body) all head for the local gas giant, Gargantua, on the trail of the secret of the long-dead Builders. They find more traces of the Builders than they dreamed of, plus another race long thought to be dead and much less friendly. The result is a cornucopia of fast action, scientific puzzles, vivid images, and technological marvels—the liveliest sort of hard-science sf. Recommended wherever Sheffield or the first Heritage Universe book has found readers. —*Roland Green*

Shepard, Lucius.
The Ends of the Earth.
Arkham House, $24.95 (0-87054-161-7). 484p.

Nebula winner Shepard is emerging as one of the leading lights of literary science fiction. This volume contains 14 stories representative of his recent work, with appropriate illustrations by Jeffrey K. Potter. While Shepard's concern with U.S. involvement in Central America is somewhat obsessive— Will it become another Vietnam?—there's no denying that the author has a superior global vision, deep humanistic concerns, and a command of the English language rare for mainstream or sf writers. Highly recommended, especially for larger collections or those with a strong audience for experimental sf. —*Roland Green*

Silverberg, Robert.
The Face of the Waters.
Bantam, $20 (0-553-07592-6). 368p.

Silverberg offers a vivid demonstration of his gifts for large-scale, panoramic world building. On the planet Hydros, the human settlers are forced out of their precarious home on floating islands by the hostility of the native Hydrans. The humans face a long and perilous journey across the watery face of the planet to the legendary safe place, the Face of the Waters. Hydros is a notably well-done water world, and the book is crammed with incident and action enough to keep readers turning pages. In addition, most of the characters will be familiar to the many Silverberg devotees. —*Roland Green*

Spinrad, Norman.
Russian Spring.
Bantam, $20 (0-553-07586-1). 656p.

Here is a major example of fictional futurism and space exploration advocacy. It is the story of an American engineer who emigrates to an economically revitalized Russia in order to participate in that country's burgeoning space program, marries a Russian woman, and has two children (as well as an identity crisis). Once one has suspended one's disbelief in the premise and ignored minor stylistic quirks rooted in Spinrad's New Wave origins, one recognizes the author's best novel in many years—intelligent, detailed, well constructed, and emotionally compelling. Highly recommended. —*Roland Green*

Stasheff, Christopher.
A Company of Stars.
Ballantine/Del Rey, $19 (0-345-36888-6). 309p.

Stasheff's long-awaited breakthrough into hardcover is the first in a series punningly entitled Starship Troupers. It begins the tale of a traveling stock theatrical company obliged to hastily leave Earth to avoid right-wing religious fanatics. Stasheff has his share of flaws, and parts of the book are yet another artist's grumble against caricatured conservatives. However, he also has a lifelong association with the theater, and his knowledge of and love for it breathe life into the greater part of the book. It's the best work from Stasheff in some time, recommended for nearly any collection. *—Roland Green*

Tarr, Judith.
The Dagger & the Cross: A Novel of the Crusades.
Doubleday, $21.95 (0-385-41181-2). 474p. paper, $10.95 (0-385-41182-0).

The sequel to *Alamut* completes Tarr's five-book cycle, which began with the Hound and the Falcon trilogy. Set against the Battle of Hattin during the Crusades, Tarr's tale depicts Saladin's victory and the fall of Jerusalem. The element of magic still remains (perhaps stronger here than in any other book in the series), as Prince Aidan is finally allowed to marry Morgiana, former assassin and infidel, while two children, Ysabel, Aidan's daughter by a Christian noblewoman, and Akiva, a Jew, begin to realize their special gifts. Church politics, prejudice, and the war get in the way of Aidan and Morgiana's plans, forcing them to fight on opposite sides of the battle. Attempts to save the holy city and reach holy matrimony intertwine. A thoroughly enjoyable read, this historically based novel belongs in the fantasy collections of all public libraries. *—Jill Sidoti*

✓Tepper, Sheri S.
Beauty.
Doubleday, $20 (0-385-41939-2). 432p. paper, $12 (0-385-41940-6).

Tepper, author of *The Gate to Women's Country* and *Grass*, is known for her feminist viewpoint and skill at infusing sf and fantasy with emotional authenticity. Her latest novel is an inventive, sometimes outrageous, shamelessly allegorical, and irresistible retelling of "Sleeping Beauty." Tepper's Beauty is both spunky and sensitive, half-mortal, half-fairy. She has been chosen to preserve all that is good, decent, and, yes—beautiful—in the world by politically correct fairy folk, but she gives them a run for their money. Her favorite prank is to change places with her look-alike, illegitimate half-sister, Beloved, and it is Beloved who falls into the fated century-long sleep, leaving Beauty wide awake and in all kinds of mystifying trouble. For starters, she is kidnapped by a documentary film crew from the twenty-first century who take her back to the future where she is held captive in a claustrophobic hive of humanity on an ugly, over-farmed Earth. Beauty escapes and embarks on a series of fantastic journeys to different times and realms. Each richly evoked locale and complicated predicament is fertile ground for Tepper's outrage over environmental abuse, graphic violence in film and literature, and anti-choice propaganda. The plot swells to embrace a veritable dynasty of fairy tale heroines, including Cinderella and Snow White, as well as a showdown with the Dark Lord and his forces of evil. A good old-fashioned cautionary tale told with contemporary frankness, great zest, and unbridled imagination. —*Donna Seaman*

Vance, Jack.
Ecce and Old Earth.
Tor; dist. by St. Martin's, $21.95 (0-312-85132-4). 436p.

It is a mistake to call the science in this sequel to *Araminta Station* "hard." Although the novel typifies Vance working at a high level, that fact does not necessarily imply strict scientific rigor (the planet Cadwal's flora and fauna are, however, brilliantly conceived). It does mean a story rich in image, incident, memorable characters, and even more, memorable prose. The struggle of the human conservators of Cadwal to prevent exploitation and colonization of their home world will be continued in a third book. Meanwhile, virtually any worthwhile sf collection ought to have both this and *Station*. —*Roland Green*

Vinge, Joan D.
The Summer Queen.
Warner, $21.95 (0-446-51397-0). 688p.

Any novel as successful as Vinge's Hugo-winning *Snow Queen* would be sure these days to generate a sequel, even if one had not been built into the underlying concepts of the original novel. Fortunately, Vinge is up to the challenge. This novel takes 17-year old Moon, the Summer Queen, through the early part of her reign, as she faces learning the secret of the planet's native mers, restoring interstellar communications, and at the same time keeping the planet free of the tyrannical Hegemony. There are some minor negatives here: Moon borders on a wish-fulfillment figure, and the pacing is uncertain in spots. But overall the book is almost as splendid a creation as its predecessor, and it is certain to win readers in nearly any collection. —*Roland Green*

✔**Watson, Ian.**
The Flies of Memory.
Carroll & Graf, $18.95 (0-88184-782-8). 224p.

Beneath an urbane facade, mannered European stylings, and horror-shock trappings lies the choicest of sf splicings, where philosophical musings meet narrative invention and wonder. There's certainly cause to wonder here, what with giant alien flies scampering about, seemingly interested only in studying the planet's treasures—cathedrals, works of art, that sort of thing. "We have come to your planet to *remember* it," the flies explain. Charles, an expert in the language of the body, is selected to interpret what's really going on with these peculiar culture vultures. Like the flies, Charles, too, has had a go at making experience into indelible memory, but he has usually failed. The flies try that much harder, eventually abducting the artifacts, which causes panic and violence. The novel chips away at notions of reality and memory, of things remembered or else simply fancied, or wished for, or forgotten. A quirky and

Science Fiction

playful author, Watson mixes mainstream sf with the dreamscape visions of authors like D. M. Thomas. The result is an appealing tale that applies several coats of high-gloss literary veneer to the usual scenario of earthlings alternately repelled, fascinated, threatened, and instructed by ugly creatures from far away. —*Peter Robertson*

Watson, Ian.
Stalin's Teardrops and Other Stories.
Victor Gollancz; dist. by Trafalgar Square, $23.95 (0-575-04942-1). 270p.

Ian Watson's numerous short stories have never pretended, for the most part, to be other than what they are: literary, experimental, cerebral, and often more sketch than narrative. They are also excellent, as the 12 pieces here indicate. Watson uses historical material well, as in the title story, comfortably mixes narrative and drama (in "The Pharoah and the Mademoiselle"), conjures horror effectively ("The Case of the Glass Slipper"), and even draws imaginatively upon current events ("The Eye of the Ayatollah"). Recommended for collections with an audience for either Watson or experimental sf in general. —*Roland Green*

Woolley, Persia.
Guinevere: The Legend in Autumn.
Poseidon, $20 (0-671-70831-7). 432p.

The final volume of the Guinevere trilogy opens with the queen awaiting dawn, when she is to be burned at the stake. One of the Companions, Gareth, remains with her, and together they recall the wonder and pageantry of Camelot. Like the two previous volumes (*Child of the Northern Spring* and *Queen of the Summer Stars*), Woolley grounds the Arthurian legends firmly in the Dark Ages, surrounding them with enough facts to make the book more historical fiction than fantasy. Although the characters have noble aims, they also have distinctly human proportions and are moved by greed, lust, revenge, and love. Once Mordred sets the wheels in motion, Arthur, Guinevere, and Lancelot can only accept their fates, or "morias," and watch as the kingdom crumbles around them. Woolley stays within the boundaries of the legends, but Guinevere's developing viewpoint gives them a freshness. A totally satisfying conclusion to an inspired trilogy. —*Candace Smith*

Wrede, Patricia C.
Mairelon the Magician.
Tor, $17.95 (0-312-85041-7). 288p.

Wrede here returns to the same magical alternate-world Regency England featured in her enchanting *Sorcery and Cecelia* (written with Caroline Steverner). In this novel, a female street waif is taken up by a magician who appropriates her skills for thievery, and the two find themselves launched on an adventurous, at times perilous, quest across England. Readers looking for the effervescent quality of the earlier book will not find it here. Nevertheless, Wrede's general craftsmanship is high, and the book can be highly recommended. —*Roland Green*

AUTHOR INDEX

Author Index

Author Index

Author Index

Author Index

Author Index

449

TITLE INDEX

Title Index

Title Index